- Does the task have experimental realism?
- Should you hide measurement tasks using unobtrusive techniques?
- Do you need a placebo for the control group?
- Should you disguise conditions with deception or conduct a field experiment?

Considering ethical issues

- Are there physical risks to participants?
- Are there psychological risks to participants?
- Can you eliminate or minimize risks?
- Can you justify risks in terms of the scientific value of results?
- Are you obtaining informed consent?
- Are you providing debriefing and care for participants afterwards?
- Did you submit the planned procedure to the IRB for review?

Considering participant variables

- Do the characteristics of participants limit generalizability?
- Is the sample size (N) sufficient to represent the population?
- Does the volunteer bias or participant sophistication influence the results?
- Are participant variables correlated with your variables?
- Will fluctuating participant variables within conditions reduce reliability and the relationship's strength?
- Will fluctuating participant variables between conditions reduce internal validity and the relationship's strength?

Considering a between-subjects design

- Will random assignment control important participant variables?
- Will balancing control important participant variables?
- Will matching control important participant variables?
- Will pretesting create major problems?
- Will limiting the population restrict generalizability?
- Will controls increase error variance that weakens the relationship?

Considering a within-subjects design

- Must many participant variables be controlled?
- Are subject history, maturation, and mortality a problem?
- Do stimuli and other aspects fit a repeated-measures design?
- Will nonsymmetrical carry-over effects occur?
- Is randomization or partial or complete counterbalancing of order of conditions needed?

RESEARCH METHODS IN PSYCHOLOGY

Third Edition

GARY W. HEIMAN

Buffalo State College

HOUGHTON MIFFLIN COMPANY   **Boston**   **New York**

To my wife, Karen, for the "good stuff inside"

Editor in Chief: Kathi Prancan
Senior Sponsoring Editor: Kerry Baruth
Development Editor: Marianne Stepanian
Senior Project Editor: Tracy Patruno
Senior Manufacturing Coordinator: Marie Barnes
Marketing Manager: Katherine Greig

Cover image: photographer/Stone by Getty Images

Printed in the U.S.A.

Library of Congress Control Number: 2001091592

ISBN: 0-618-17028-6

123456789-DOC-05 04 03 02 01

Brief Contents

PART 4

Putting It All Together

APPENDIXES

Contents

4

Creating a Reliable and Valid Experiment   94

5

Risk, Deception, and the Ethics of Research   129

6

Controlling Participant Variables Using Between-Subjects and Within-Subjects Designs   157

PART 2

The Statistical Analysis of Experiments

7

Applying Descriptive and Inferential Statistics to Simple Experiments   192

8

Designing and Analyzing Multifactor Experiments   225

PART 3

Beyond the Typical Laboratory Experiment

9

Correlational Research and Questionnaire Construction   266

PART 4

Putting It All Together

12

A Review: Examples of Designing and Evaluating Research   366

Appendixes

Appendix A

Reporting Research Using APA Format   401

Appendix B

Sample APA-Style Research Report   433

Appendix C

Statistical Procedures 445

Appendix D

Statistical Tables 475

Preface

I wrote the first edition of this book because I could not find a methods book whose style and organization satisfied the demands of the course. My goal was to write a book that allowed students to (1) understand the terminology, logic, and procedures used in research; (2) integrate statistical procedures with research methods; (3) develop critical thinking skills regarding research; and (4) learn to design and conduct research and write APA-style reports. I have attempted to create a textbook that recognizes students' initial weaknesses in all of these areas but that eventually brings students up to the level of understanding that most instructors seek.

I also tried to create a textbook that would meet the needs of instructors who teach this material in different ways. In particular, the discussion of APA format (updated for the 3rd edition) occurs in an appendix and was designed to be discussed at virtually any time during the course. Likewise, the chapters dealing with statistical issues (Chapters 7 and 8) can be discussed at any time or be omitted, without affecting the other chapters. And finally, the order in which chapters can be presented is reasonably flexible, because when an important concept from a previous chapter is mentioned, it is also reviewed, so that every chapter can effectively stand alone.

PEDAGOGICAL APPROACH

Rather than present a laundry list of the components and characteristics of various research approaches, I have attempted to teach methods (and statistical applications) in an integrated, cohesive manner. My approach is to place students in the role of researchers, focusing on the specific decisions they make. I believe this teaches students both the critical-thinking skills and the concepts necessary for designing research. Within this framework, the book presents concepts, procedures, and evaluation of research in an organized manner; provides an integrated review and discussion of statistics with methods; reviews terminology and concepts frequently, especially as they are reintroduced in new settings; and fosters understanding through application to specific examples.

By rehearsing new terms and concepts as they reappear throughout the book, I have tried to anticipate and alleviate students' confusion, recognizing that an introductory methods course is in part a language course and that achieving literacy requires practice. When introducing a general technique, I also cite several examples so that students gain an appreciation of the variety and scope of the technique. I then present the material in more depth using one or two detailed example studies. Throughout, I have sought simple examples that are easy to understand, avoiding unnecessarily sophisticated studies that might obscure the illustrative purpose of the example. Also, I have selected interesting examples— spanning the last 30 years of psychology—that convey the elegance and challenge of research and that students can easily replicate in class projects.

Teaching critical thinking is not easy. Often textbook discussions end abruptly, just prior to answering the question "So what?" I have tried to include the "so what" by pointing out the logical ramifications behind each issue and by providing critical analysis. To this end, several themes recur throughout the text. Reliability and validity appear repeatedly as the basis for making decisions among various design options. The importance of the interaction between statistics and design recurs in discussions of demonstrating relationships and maximizing statistical power. Basic issues such as confounding, demand characteristics, and counterbalancing are also repeatedly addressed. My intent is that students understand that the nature of the research question and the goals of the researcher dictate the design, but that every design has strengths and weaknesses, which in turn dictate the interpretation of the results.

ORGANIZATION OF THE TEXT

Overall, this text uses a "top-down" approach that stresses context and the interrelatedness of topics. Unlike many textbooks, the text focuses on laboratory experiments first and other types of designs later. This is because once students understand a controlled laboratory study, they can more easily understand the strengths and weaknesses of other types of designs. Further, discussing experiments early in the course leaves more time in the semester for students to practice designing and reporting them in lab exercises.

To give students a background for thinking scientifically and to enable them to begin conducting lab exercises, Part I presents the conceptual, design, and ethical issues in conducting experiments. The goal is to provide a general context for all research designs. Chapter 1 is a simplified introduction to the philosophy of science, presenting the goals of research, the basics of the scientific method, and the logic of research. To avoid overwhelming students, I've used simple, everyday examples of behavior here. The new Chapter 2 then presents the basics of creating and testing a hypothesis (including searching the literature), centered around demonstrating and interpreting a relationship. Experimental versus descriptive approaches are also discussed. The new Chapter 3 then discusses the flaws in research and introduces the concepts of reliability and construct, content, internal and external validity. These are linked to the common threats to reliability and validity, and the basic techniques for controlling them. I took great care to keep these chapters from reading like a disjointed list of definitions. Rather, I show how each concept affects our confidence in a study's conclusions. Chapter 4 introduces the major common techniques used to ensure reliability and validity. Essentially, this chapter answers the question: "How do you conduct a psychological experiment?" Chapter 5 then discusses the ethics of research and the APA guidelines. Rather than presenting ethics as a dry set of prescriptions, however, the chapter explores the realistic dilemmas that researchers face when they encounter potentially risky procedures and when they use deception and unobtrusive measures to deal with demand characteristics. Chapter 6 then covers how to deal with participant variables. The pros and cons of techniques for controlling variables in between-subject and within-subject designs are presented, and a complete discussion of counterbalancing is provided. Throughout these and earlier chapters, students examine the ways their design decisions affect the data through the issue of designing a powerful study. The discussion is simplified, however, by presenting the individual scores in idealized examples of strong versus weak relationships, instead of using more obtuse summary statistics.

Part II presents more advanced design issues and the statistical analysis of experiments. Chapter 7 reviews common descriptive and inferential statistics and shows how they are used to interpret simple experiments. This chapter was written without assuming that students perfectly recall their previous statistics course, but without talking down to them either. Chapter 8 expands the discussion to multifactor designs and includes common advanced statistical procedures. These chapters emphasize understanding the practical uses of statistics in the research process without clouding the issue with statistical theories or formulas. Further, all statistical discussions go beyond the mere numbers, covering the psychological interpretation of each study in terms of behaviors and variables. (Computational formulas and critical values for the most common procedures are presented in Appendixes C and D.)

With this background in laboratory experiments, students are ready to learn about and evaluate other types of designs presented in Part III. These chapters provide a straightforward presentation while integrating previous relevant design, ethical, and statistical issues. Chapter 9 presents correlational designs, including questionnaire development and a brief discussion of advanced correlational statistics. Chapter 10 discusses field experiments and single-subject designs. Chapter 11 presents quasi-experiments, survey techniques, and observational and descriptive methods.

The final chapter, Chapter 12, is a unique review chapter designed to help students apply and integrate issues covered throughout the course. The first part of the chapter provides a detailed review of the questions and issues addressed in previous chapters. Then, the discussion takes students through an analysis of several research studies from start to finish, focusing on designing, evaluating, and interpreting each project. The discussion is set up as a question-and-answer exercise. The problem is first presented, and then students are asked how they would go about studying it. The solution the cited researchers took is then presented, and given this, students are asked subsequent questions about how to proceed. Questions include how to perform the literature search, and the research cited is intentionally older to provide more practice at this. Follow-up studies and additional potential designs are also discussed. The chapter contains four involved discussions of experimental and descriptive examples, and then five briefer discussions of research that students might pursue. This material may serve as an end-of-course capstone chapter, or, because it includes most of the designs discussed in the text, specific examples may be used in conjunction with earlier chapters.

Appendix A, "Reporting Research Using APA Format," provides a comprehensive look at how to read and write a research report using APA format. It is designed for use at any point in the course, and the appendix is presented as a complete chapter, with learning objectives, *Chapter Summary*, *Key Terms,* and *Review* and *Application Questions*. A complete example manuscript is featured in Appendix B, describing a simple yet engaging two-sample experiment.

SPECIAL FEATURES

A full set of learning tools provides extensive pedagogical support in every chapter.

- Each chapter begins with a *Getting Started* section that lists the learning objectives for the chapter and identifies relevant concepts from previous chapters for students to review.

- Important points are emphasized throughout the text by *Remember* statements, which are summary reminders set off from the text.

- Key terms are highlighted in bold type, and formal definitions are accompanied by numerous mnemonics and analogies to promote retention and understanding. A *Key Terms* list appears at the end of each chapter, and a complete glossary appears at the end of the text.

- Summary reference tables and *Checklists* that build across chapters integrate topics and help students select from various design options.

- At the end of each chapter, a *Putting It All Together* section provides advice, cautions, and ways to integrate material from different chapters.

- Each *Chapter Summary* provides a substantive review of the material, not merely a list of the topics covered.

- Approximately 25 study questions are provided at the end of each chapter. These include *Review Questions* and *Application Questions* to help students study the concepts and to learn to use them. More involved *Discussion Questions* (including challenging ethical questions) are also provided for use in class. Answers to Review Questions and suggestions for Discussion Questions are provided in the instructor's resource manual and at the Houghton Mifflin website.

New to the Third Edition

The entire text was updated and revised to ensure clear and crisp explanations of each concept and to produce the best pedagogical devices. In particular:

- To better relate the general philosophy of science issues presented in Chapter 1 to practical research, the previous Chapter 2 was divided into two chapters.

- The new Chapter 2 provides a general overview of the research process, beginning with searching the literature, then developing the hypothesis, examining a relationship, and then translating the findings back to the original hypothetical constructs. The chapter ends with how to demonstrate relationships using experiments versus descriptive/correlational studies.

- The new Chapter 3 covers reliability and various types of validity and shows how to control threats to reliability and validity.

- Chapter 3 also contains an expanded explanation of confounding and a better discussion of how to critically evaluate a study.

- Chapter 4 now includes an introduction to *power* that had appeared over several chapters. Also, it includes an example of instructions for participants for an experiment.

- Chapter 5 contains expanded sections on debriefing and IRBs and an example informed consent form.

- Chapters 6, 7, 8, and 9 were revised to make the statistical issues more comprehensible.

- Chapter 10 includes a revised discussion of field experiments.

- Chapter 11 contains more information on data collection in naturalistic observation.

- The review Chapter 12 contains an expanded review of the issues addressed in previous chapters and new questions about performing a literature search for each study.

- The appendix dealing with APA format was updated for the newest, fifth edition of the *APA Publication Manual*.

- Key terms are now italicized when reviewed in *Remember* statements or in later chapters.

- The final *Putting It All Together* sections of the first six chapters were reworked and now include checklists for the major points discussed. These checklists grow to form the combined, master checklist presented inside the front cover of the text.

- The study questions at the end of each chapter were reworked and expanded, now with some 25 questions per chapter. The questions are organized as *Review Questions* (which test definitions and basic knowledge), *Application Questions* (which require using information from the chapter in a real-world context), and *Discussion Questions* (which provide issues that work well as in-class exercises).

- The answers to the end-of-chapter questions can now be found both in the *Instructor's Resource Manual* and at the Houghton Mifflin website *(www.college.hmco.com)*. The website is password protected so that instructors can assign the questions as graded homework assignments. Otherwise, the password is available to instructors simply by calling a Houghton Mifflin sales representative.

SUPPLEMENTS

The accompanying *Instructor's Resource Manual and Test Bank* includes suggestions for classroom activities and discussions and multiple-choice and short-answer test items. The test questions are also available on disk in a program that allows instructors to add or edit questions and generate exams. In addition, a student manual called *Using SPSS for Windows,* by Charles Stangor of the University of Maryland, and a set of accompanying datasets are available for shrinkwrapping with the text. You can also visit the Houghton Mifflin College Psychology Website for additional teaching and learning activities that support this course.

ACKNOWLEDGMENTS

Many people contributed to the production of this text. At Houghton Mifflin Company, I want to thank all those who saw the project through to completion, including Kerry Baruth, Marianne Stepanian, Tracy Patruno, and Merrill Peterson.

I am also grateful to the following reviewers, who provided invaluable feedback that helped shape this edition:

K. D. Biondolillo, Arkansas State University

Susan D. Lima, University of Wisconsin – Milwaukee

Blaine F. Peden, University of Wisconsin – Eau Claire

William E. Roweton, Chadron State College

Beth M. Schwartz-Kenny, Randolph-Macon Woman's College

Aurora Torress, University of Alabama – Huntsville

—Gary W. Heiman

1 ///////

INTRODUCTION TO PSYCHOLOGICAL RESEARCH

OK, so now you're taking a course in research methods. Because you are a student of psychology and psychology is a science, you are in some sense training to be a scientist. Regardless of whether you intend to become an active researcher, if you want to understand, use, and evaluate psychological information, you must understand the methods used in psychological research. This book will teach you those methods.

Research methods are the most enjoyable—and the easiest to learn—when you are actively involved, so this text places you in the role of a researcher. As a researcher, you will learn the goals of science and how scientists operate. You will learn how to phrase questions scientifically, how to design and conduct scientific research, and how to interpret and communicate your results. Along the way, you will also learn about the imperfections and limitations of scientific research. Ultimately, you will not only understand the research of others but also be able to conduct and correctly interpret research on your own.

This course aims to discipline your mind so that you can answer questions scientifically. Toward this end, you must deal with three major concerns. First, being a researcher involves a combination of thinking logically, being creative, and, more than anything else, applying a critical eye to all phases of your research. Second, although knowing the rules of science is important, learning to *apply* those rules in the contexts of different research problems is vital. Third, research has its own language. Psychologists use very specific terms—with very specific meanings—that you must learn. You must strive for a degree of precision that you seldom experience in your day-to-day life, so that you can accurately and concisely communicate the procedures and findings of a study. Practice using the special vocabulary of research at every opportunity.

Introduction to the Scientific Method

GETTING STARTED

As you read this chapter, your goals are to learn:

- The assumptions and attitudes of scientists.
- The goals of science.
- The difference between basic and applied research.
- The criteria for scientific hypotheses and for acceptable evidence for testing them.
- Why literal and conceptual replication are necessary.

Psychology is usually defined as the scientific study of the behavior of humans and nonhumans. In this chapter, we examine how the "science" gets into the science of psychology. The discussion is general, with few of the details of research, because the purpose here is to see the broad perspective that researchers take. Essentially, it is an introduction to what's called the *philosophy of science*. Once you understand this philosophy, the details discussed in later chapters will make much more sense.

Because the behavior of living organisms is part of the natural world, psychologists study "nature," just as biologists, physicists, and other scientists do. At the heart of all sciences is the scientific method.

THE SCIENTIFIC METHOD

If you are at all curious about behavior, you are well on your way toward becoming a researcher. All sciences are based on curiosity about nature, and psychology is based on curiosity about behavior. Your curiosity is important, because it is the basis for deciding what you want to learn and how to go about learning it.

REMEMBER Every decision a researcher makes depends first and foremost on the question the researcher is asking.

But being curious is not enough. Creating, conducting, and interpreting research require mental discipline, because nature is very secretive and not easily understood. On the one hand, psychological research is fun because it is a challenge to devise ways to unlock the mysteries of behavior. But, on the other hand, caution is needed at every step because it is easy to draw *incorrect* conclusions about a behavior. This is a critical problem because psychology is used by society in ways that have a serious impact on people. For example, at one time, people with a criminal history were thought to have "defective" personalities, which were "remedied" by the removal of portions of their brains. Unfortunately for those undergoing the surgery, this approach was just plain wrong! Thus, because the knowledge produced by research can drastically influence the lives of others, psychology's goal is to be perfectly accurate.

To meet this goal, we must be very concerned about avoiding the pitfalls that occur when studying nature, so that what we *think* is true really *is* true. In other words, our *research methods* (the name of this book) are of critical importance. Therefore, psychological research is based on the "scientific method." This is a rather broad term, but essentially, the **scientific method** is a set of rules consisting of certain assumptions, attitudes, goals, and procedures for creating and answering questions about nature.

Why do we use the scientific method? There are many ways to acquire knowledge, but some are better than others. We might base our study of behavior on our intuitions and personal experiences, or make logical deductions, or use common sense, or defer to authority figures. But! Science (and scientists) do not trust intuitions or personal experience because everyone has different feelings about and experiences of the world. (Whose should we believe?) We do not trust logic because nature does not always conform to our logic. We cannot rely on common sense because it is often contradictory. (Which is true: "Absence makes the heart grow fonder" or "Out of sight, out of mind"?) And we cannot rely on what the so-called experts say because there is no reason to believe that they correctly understand how nature works either. The problem with all of these sources of knowledge is that they ultimately rely on opinions or beliefs that may be created by someone who is biased or wrong (or downright crazy). After all, merely because someone says that something is true, that does not make it true.

Psychology relies on the scientific method because it is the best approach for eliminating bias and opinion, for reaching a consensus about how a behavior truly operates, and for correcting errors. It does this by requiring that whenever someone makes a statement about behavior, we ask that person, "How do you *know* that?" We do not mean "believe," "feel," or "think"; we mean *know*, with certainty! In science—just as in a court of law—it is the *evidence* supporting a statement that is most important. The scientific method provides the most convincing evidence, because instead of relying on opinions or intuitions, it is based on the actual events themselves as they occur in nature. Then, because an event is available for all of us to see, we all have the same basis for describing and explaining it. Thus, in psychology, the scientific method is specifically geared toward learning about an organism's behavior by *observing* that behavior, while minimizing the influences of bias or opinion.

The remainder of this chapter examines the components of the scientific method as they apply to the study of behavior. To start with, the following sections look at how scientists approach the task of science.

The Assumptions of Science

What first distinguishes scientists from nonscientists is the philosophy about nature that scientists adopt. At first glance, any aspect of nature, especially human behavior, seems to be overwhelmingly complex, verging on the chaotic. Scientists have the audacity to try to understand such a complicated topic because they do not consider nature to be chaotic. Instead, scientists make certain assumptions about nature that allow them to approach it as a regulated and consistent system. These assumptions are that nature is *lawful, deterministic*, and *understandable*.

By saying that nature is **lawful**, we mean that every event can be understood as a sequence of natural causes and effects. We assume that behavior is lawful, because if it isn't (and instead is random), then we could never understand it. Thus, in the same way that the "law of gravity" governs the behavior of planets or the "laws of aerodynamics" govern the behavior of airplanes, psychologists assume that there are laws of nature that govern the behavior of living organisms. Although some natural laws do not apply to all species (for example, laws dealing with nest building among birds do not apply to humans), a specific law does apply to all members of a group. Thus, when psychologists study the mating behavior of penguins, or the development of language in people, they are studying laws of nature.

Recognize that most psychologists would think it too grandiose to claim that any single study directly examines a law of nature. As you'll see, any study will have a very narrow focus, and researchers are frequently confronted with contradictory findings and opposing explanations. Thus, a considerable amount of research is required to reach a consensus about even a small aspect of a behavior, and so a conclusive description of any law requires an extremely slow and complicated process. We do assume, however, that eventually all of the diverse findings will be integrated so that we can truly understand each law of nature.

Viewing behavior as lawful leads to a second, related assumption: We assume that behavior is "determined." **Determinism** means that behavior is solely influenced by natural causes and does not depend on choice or "free will." If instead we assumed that organisms freely decide their behavior, then behavior truly would be chaotic, because the only explanation for every behavior would be "because he or she wanted to." Therefore, we reject the idea that free will plays a role. After all, you cannot walk off a cliff and "will" yourself not to fall, because the law of gravity forces you to fall. Anyone else in the same situation will also fall because that is how gravity operates. Likewise, we assume that you cannot freely choose to exhibit a particular personality or to behave in a particular way in a given situation. The laws of behavior force you to have certain attributes and to behave in a certain way in a certain situation. Anyone else in the same situation will be similarly influenced, because that's how the laws of behavior operate. Thus, in a sense, determinism views all living organisms as machinelike: When a specific situation is present, organisms behave in a predictable, lawful way.

Note that determinism is not the same as *predestination*. Predestination suggests that our actions follow some universal plan that is already laid out for us. Determinism, however, means that there are identifiable, natural causes for every behavior. Thus, there is no grand scheme governing your life so that at noon on Tuesday you'll walk off a cliff. If you do walk off a cliff, however, it's because specific natural causes make you do this—causes operating in a lawful manner so that anyone else similarly exposed to them would also walk off the cliff.

The third assumption is that the laws of nature are **understandable**. Regardless of how complicated nature may appear or how confused we currently are about some aspect of nature, we expect to understand it eventually (or there is no point in studying it). Thus, any scientific statement must logically and rationally fit with the known facts, so that it can be understood. Part of an explanation can never be that we must accept a mystery or an unresolvable contradiction. If two statements contradict each other at present, it must be logically possible to resolve the debate eventually so that only one statement applies.

***

REMEMBER   To be studied scientifically, any behavior must be assumed to be *lawful*, *determined*, and *understandable*.

Notice that the above assumptions exclude certain topics from being studied scientifically. For example, miracles cannot be studied scientifically because, by definition, miracles do not obey the laws of nature. Likewise, because of determinism, we cannot study free will. (We can study people's *perceptions* of miracles or free will, because their perceptions are behaviors that fit our assumptions about nature.) Further, because nature is assumed to be understandable, any topic that requires faith cannot be studied scientifically. Faith is the acceptance of a statement without questions or needing proof. But in science it is *always* appropriate to question and to ask for proof. Thus, for example, according to the Judeo-Christian tradition, God created the universe in six days. Some people refer to the study of this idea as "creationism science." There can be no *science* of creationism, however, because creationism requires belief in God, but science does not allow for such a requirement. Likewise, although scientists are entitled to the same religions and beliefs as anyone else, these beliefs cannot play a part when producing and evaluating scientific evidence. After all, if science did allow statements of faith, whose faith would we use . . . yours or mine?

The Attitudes of Scientists

To help prevent their biases and beliefs from creeping into their conclusions, scientists explicitly adopt certain attitudes toward the process of learning about nature. Therefore, as a scientist, you should be *uncertain, open-minded, skeptical, cautious,* and *ethical.*

The starting point is to recognize that the purpose of science is to learn about nature, admitting that no one already knows everything about how nature operates. There is always some degree of *uncertainty.* For psychologists, this means that no one knows precisely what a particular behavior entails, what the factors are that influence it, or what the one correct way to study it is. All other steps in scientific research stem from this simple admission.

If no one knows for certain how nature operates, then any explanation or description of it might be correct. Therefore, you should be *open-minded*, leaving your biases and preconceptions behind. An explanation may offend your sensibilities or contradict your beliefs, but that is no reason to dismiss it. You must look in all directions, at all possible explanations, when trying to understand a behavior.

At the same time, you should be *skeptical*: Never automatically accept the truth of any scientific description. Because no one already knows how nature works, any description of a behavior might also be *incorrect* (no one is perfect, not even psychologists). After all, the history of science is littered with descriptions that at first appeared accurate but later turned out to misrepresent nature. (The earth is not flat!) Therefore, you must skeptically and critically evaluate the evidence produced by any study: Using logic and your knowledge of psychology, always question whether the factors proposed as important might actually be irrelevant (or at least not the whole story) and whether the factors proposed as irrelevant might actually be important. To aid in this process, researchers share their research through professional publications, meetings, and so on. Then, eventually, psychology will identify and rectify any mistakes, to arrive at the best, most accurate information.

If we assume that critical analysis will eventually produce an error-free understanding of nature, then we must also recognize that we are currently in the process of discovering which parts of our information are incorrect. Therefore, you must be *cautious* when dealing with scientific findings. Any scientific con-

TABLE 1.1 How the Attitudes of Researchers Influence Their Approach to Psychological Findings

Attitude	Approach
Uncertain	No one already knows how a behavior operates.
Open-minded	Any approach or statement may be correct.
Skeptical	Any approach or statement may contain error.
Cautious	Any conclusion is not a "fact."
Ethical	Research should not harm others.

clusion implicitly contains the qualifying statement "given our present knowledge and abilities." Never treat the results of a single study as a "fact" in the usual sense. Instead, phrase your conclusions using words such as *possibly* or *suggests*—in essence saying, "It *appears* that the behavior *might* operate in such-and-such a way." Remember that a research finding is merely a piece of evidence that provides some degree of confidence in a description about nature. But, it may actually misrepresent nature.

Finally, there is one other attitude that scientists adopt: you must behave *ethically* when conducting research. In Chapter 5 we'll discuss the specifics of **research ethics**, but the basic principle is that neither researchers nor their research should cause harm to others.

Table 1.1 will help you to remember these attitudes by relating each one to the approach that scientists take. Whenever you conduct research or encounter that of others, be sure that these attitudes are present.

REMEMBER Scientists are *uncertain, open-minded, skeptical, cautious,* and *ethical.*

As scientists, psychologists are led by their assumptions to continually evaluate their own research and the research of others. Evaluating a study means evaluating the evidence the study provides. As with the rules of evidence in a court of law, science has rules governing what evidence is admissible and how it must be gathered.

The Criteria for Scientific Evidence

When people think of scientific research, they usually think of "experiments." Although psychologists often perform experiments, they also conduct other types of research. In fact, there is an infinite number of different ways to "design" a study. The **design** of a study is the specific manner in which the study is set up and conducted. First, the design must identify the specific people or animals to study. (Note that, historically, published research has referred to these individuals as **subjects**. As discussed in Appendix A, however, beginning with research published after 1994, these individuals are now called **participants**.) In addition, a design includes the specific situation or sequence of situations under which participants are studied, the way their behavior is examined, and the components of the situation and behavior that are considered.

As an example of a behavior we might study, let's discuss the tendency of people to "channel surf"—to grab the television's remote control and change the channel whenever a commercial appears. (If this seems too mundane a behavior to be "psychological," stay tuned . . . .) In designing a study of this behavior, remember that we seek the most convincing evidence for answering the question "How do you know that?" In science, convincing evidence is *empirical, objective, systematic,* and *controlled.*

First, scientific evidence must be **empirical**—meaning learned by *observation.* Psychologists study everything that an individual does, feels, thinks, wants, or remembers, from the microlevel of neurological functioning to the macrolevel of complex, lifelong behaviors. Yet ultimately, all evidence is collected and all debates are resolved through observable, public behaviors. Thus, to understand channel changing, we should *observe* channel changing. Because anyone else can observe this behavior in the same way, everyone shares the same basis for determining how it operates.

Second, several people can observe the same event and still have different impressions of it. Therefore, science requires **objectivity**. This means that, ideally, a researcher's personal biases, attitudes, or subjective impressions do not influence the observations or conclusions. Although people can't be perfectly objective, scientists strive for this by obtaining *measurements* that are as empirical, as objective, and as precise as possible. Through objective measurement of a behavior we obtain a *score* for each participant. The scores then comprise the study's **data**. For example, counting the number of times someone changes channels during a specified time period results in objective, precise data. Or, in other studies, we might use equipment that times someone's responses or measures his or her physiological reactions, we might interview participants or have them perform mental or physical tests, we might observe people surreptitiously, and so on. Regardless, we always try to be as objective as possible, so that the data reflect what participants actually do in a given situation and not our personal interpretations of what they do.

In addition, nature is very complex. Consequently, the research situation must be simplified so that we are not confused by all that is going on. Therefore, evidence is gathered systematically. Being **systematic** means that observations are obtained in a methodical, step-by-step fashion. For example, say we think that boring commercials cause channel changing. After we've objectively measured "boring," we would then objectively measure the channel changing that occurs with very boring commercials, with less boring commercials, and again with interesting commercials. If we also think that the number of people in the room influences channel changing, we would observe a person's responses to the preceding commercials first when alone, then when another person is present, then when two other people are present, and so on. By being systematic, we determine the role of each factor and combination of factors as they apply to a behavior.

TABLE 1.2 How the Criteria for Scientific Research Translate into the Rules for Designing Research

Criteria	Rule
Empirical	All information is based on observation.
Objective	Observations must be free from bias.
Systematic	Observations are made in a step-by-step fashion.
Controlled	Potentially confusing factors are eliminated.

Finally, evidence must be obtained under controlled conditions. **Control** is another way to simplify the situation by eliminating any extraneous factors that might influence a behavior and thus create confusion. For example, while observing whether more boring commercials produce more channel changing, we would try to control how boring the television program is, so that this factor would not influence channel changing. Likewise, we'd control the situation by having participants watch television only, so that other distractions don't influence their channel changing. In short, with control we attempt to create a clearly defined situation in which to observe only the specific behavior and the relevant factors that interest us.

Table 1.2 will help you remember the above criteria by relating them to the rules we have for designing research. The more that a study deviates from these rules, the more its results are likely to misrepresent nature, and so the less convincing they are.

> **REMEMBER** Acceptable scientific evidence is obtained through *empirical*, *objective*, *systematic*, and *controlled* research.

As you will see, many different research designs are possible that meet the preceding criteria. Which design you should use depends first on the type of question being asked—the specific goal of the study.

THE GOALS OF PSYCHOLOGICAL RESEARCH

Overall, the goal of psychology is to understand behavior. But what does "understand" mean? Science defines understanding an event in terms of the four simultaneous and equally important goals of being able to *describe*, *explain*, *predict*, and *control* the event.

Obviously, psychologists want to know what behaviors do and do not occur in nature, so the first goal is to **describe** each behavior and the conditions under which it occurs. To describe channel changing, we would specify how frequently channels are changed, whether they are changed during all commercials, whether they are changed at all times of the day, and so on. We could also describe channel changing from various perspectives, in terms of the hand movements necessary to operate the remote, or the cognitive decision making involved, or the neurological activity occurring in the brain.

Mere description of a behavior, however, is not enough to completely understand it: We also need to know *why* the behavior occurs. Therefore, another goal is to **explain** behaviors in terms of their specific causes. Thus, we want to explain what aspect of a commercial, either present or absent, causes channel changing and why. Also, we want to identify the factors—the channel changer's personality, the type of program, the presence of other people in the room—that cause more or less channel changing and why. And again, there are various perspectives we can take, such as neurological, cognitive, motivational, or environmental causes.

Note that in explaining a behavior, it is important to avoid pseudo-explanations. A **pseudo-explanation** is circular, giving as the reason for an event another name for that event. For example, a pseudo-explanation of channel changing is that it is caused by the motivation to see what is on other channels—really just another way of saying that people change channels because they want to change channels. The key to avoiding a pseudo-explanation is to provide an *independent* verification of the supposed cause. If, for example, we could discover a gene that motivates people to change channels, then we would be confident that we were talking about two different things—a cause (the gene) and an effect (changing channels)—and not merely renaming one thing.

A third aspect of understanding a behavior is to know when it will occur or what will bring it about, so an additional goal of psychology is to **predict** behaviors. Thus, we want to be able to accurately predict when channel changing will and will not occur, the amount or degree of the behavior to expect from a particular person, or when and how the behavior will change as a person's physiological, cognitive, social, or environmental conditions change. In addition, the accuracy with which a behavior can be predicted is an indication of how well we have explained it. If we say that a behavior has a particular cause but the presence of the cause does not allow us to accurately predict the behavior, then the explanation is wrong, or at least incomplete.

Finally, if we truly understand a behavior, we should be able to create the situation in which it occurs. Therefore, the fourth goal is to **control** behavior. Thus, in studying channel changing, we want to know how to alter the situation to produce, increase, decrease, or eliminate the behavior. And note that being able to control events is another test of an explanation. If a cause of a behavior is identified, then *manipulating* that cause—turning it on and off or providing more or less of it—should produce changes in the behavior. If it does not, the explanation is again either wrong or incomplete.

Table 1.3 will help you to remember the above goals by relating them to the types of activities psychologists pursue when conducting research. Any psychological study will entail one or more of these activities.

TABLE 1.3 How the Goals of Science Translate into the Activities of Psychologists

Goal	Activity
Describe	Learn what a behavior entails and the situations in which it occurs.
Explain	Learn the causes that determine when and why a behavior occurs.
Predict	Learn to identify the factors needed to predict when a behavior will occur.
Control	Learn to manipulate the factors needed to produce or modify or eliminate a behavior.

REMEMBER To completely understand a behavior, researchers strive to *describe, explain, predict,* and *control* it.

Meeting the Goals of Science

Now you can see how the science of psychology proceeds. As shown in Figure 1.1 below, it is through the combination of our attitudes and the requirements of research that we expect to understand behavior. That is, psychologists learn about a behavior by obtaining empirical, objective, systematic, and controlled observations that allow them to describe, explain, predict, and control the behavior. Each finding is rigorously evaluated in a cautious, skeptical, and open-minded manner, so that an accurate understanding of the laws of behavior can be developed.

You may think that this approach is massive overkill when studying a behavior as mundane as channel changing. Is it really necessary to be that fussy? Well, yes, if we want to *fully* understand the behavior. Granted, it would be easier to see why we should be so fussy if, for example, we were studying something like airplane pilots who turn off their planes' engines in midflight. There is an urgency to this behavior, so that understanding it in such great detail would not be overkill (pardon the pun). But recognize that channel changing is not so mundane

FIGURE 1.1 How a Scientist's Attitudes Plus the Criteria for Acceptable Evidence Lead to Meeting the Goals of Science

Attitudes of scientists		Criteria for research		Accurate understanding
Uncertain Open-minded Skeptical Cautious Ethical	+	Empirical Objective Systematic Controlled	=	Describe Explain Predict Control

This behavior involves major psychological processes such as decision making, information processing, communication, neural-pathways control, motivation, and social processes. Thus, an in-depth study of channel changing is worthwhile because, for example, by studying the decision making involved in channel changing, we can learn about decision-making processes in general. Further, another reason for a detailed study of channel changing is that research often leads to *serendipitous* findings: In the process of studying one aspect of nature, we may accidentally discover another aspect, unrelated to the original research. (In studying channel changing, we might stumble onto a cure for boredom.) Thus, because we never know where an investigation will lead, we take the study of every behavior very seriously and do the best, most thorough job we can.

Applied and Basic Research

Studying the errors an airplane pilot makes involves a greater urgency because this behavior represents a real-life problem. Such research is called applied research. **Applied research** is conducted for the purpose of solving an existing, real-life problem. For example, the companies that pay for television commercials might conduct applied research into channel changing during their commercials so that they can eliminate the resulting problem of wasted advertising money.

On the other hand, **basic research** is conducted simply for the knowledge it produces. Thus, we might study channel changing simply because it is interesting and adds to our understanding of behavior in general. Although people often have a hard time understanding why we conduct basic research, it is justified first and foremost because science seeks to understand *all* aspects of nature. Also, basic and applied research often overlap. For example, basic research into channel changing might provide information that advertising agencies can apply to solve their problem (and applied research designed to eliminate channel changing will also add to our basic understanding of behavior). A third justification of basic research is that past basic research might someday be valuable in a future applied setting. Say that we learn that channel changing and turning off airplane engines in midflight share some common factor (perhaps both are caused by boredom). At that point, our basic research into channel changing would be very useful for the applied problem of preventing airplane crashes. And, finally, a justification for basic research is that it often results in serendipitous applied findings. For example, some of the most common medicinal drugs have been discovered totally by accident during the course of basic research.

In sum, the terms *basic* and *applied* are general, describing a study only in terms of its obvious, stated purposes. In reality, we never know the ultimate purpose that research will serve (which is another reason for employing very rigorous methods).

———————

REMEMBER   The primary purpose of *basic research* is to obtain knowledge; the primary purpose of *applied research* is to solve an existing problem.

The Role of a Single Study

Regardless of whether we conduct applied or basic research, *completely* describing, explaining, predicting, and controlling a behavior are the *ultimate* goals of research. But, because of the extreme complexity of behaviors, no single study can fully meet this goal. Consider the variety of perspectives we can take when studying channel changing and the many factors that might influence it. Because we cannot study everything at once, we must simplify nature by examining one factor and taking one perspective at a time. Thus, one study will describe certain aspects of a behavior, another will examine an explanation, another will investigate ways to predict the behavior, and still others will focus on controlling it. Any single study is therefore a momentary "snapshot" of one small portion of a behavior. As a result of this piecemeal approach, the science of psychology—and publications describing it—may appear to be disjointed and unfocused, going off in many directions at once. Yet, as these individual pieces of information gradually combine, we eventually do come to understand all aspects of a behavior.

———————

REMEMBER   Any study represents a very limited and simplified view of the complexity found in nature and contributes minutely to the goals of describing, explaining, predicting, and controlling a behavior.

Every decision a researcher makes depends first and foremost on whether the primary goal is to describe, explain, predict, or control a behavior. Therefore, the first step in any study is to formulate the specific question you wish to answer. That question is called the hypothesis.

SCIENTIFIC HYPOTHESES

To begin our study, you might ask the question, "What causes channel changing?" However, this is actually a very ambiguous question, with no hint as to the type of "snapshot" needed to answer it. Do you mean "what" in terms of the cognitive, physiological, or environmental causes? And which aspect of the cognitive, physiological, or environmental causes are you talking about? Such an ambiguous question cannot be directly answered by a study. After all, at some point you must go out and actually collect some data, so sooner or later you need to know precisely which behavior to examine and how to examine it. Therefore, you must translate any general question into a specific hypothesis that directs the research.

Creating Hypotheses

A **hypothesis** is a formally stated expectation about how a behavior operates. It is, in essence, a tentative guess about a behavior that usually relates the behavior to some other behavior or influence. Rather than asking a question beginning with "why" or "what," a hypothesis is phrased as a declarative statement or description. Then we test the hypothesis: We conduct an empirical, controlled, systematic study that provides data that help us determine if the statement is correct or not.

There are two general types of hypotheses. To meet the goal of explaining and controlling the causes of behavior, we create a **causal hypothesis**: This tentatively identifies a particular cause for, or influence on, a behavior. For example, we might hypothesize that "channel changing is caused by the boring content of commercials." (Implicitly, we recognize that there may be many other influences on channel changing, but for now, this is the one we'd study.)

On the other hand, to meet the goal of describing and predicting behavior, we create a **descriptive hypothesis**: This tentatively describes a behavior in terms of its characteristics or the situation in which it occurs, and allows us to predict when it occurs. For example, we might hypothesize that "channel changing occurs more frequently when someone is watching television alone than when other people are present." Notice that even though the number of people present might partially cause channel changing, we have not stated this. A descriptive hypothesis does *not* attempt to identify the causes of a behavior. In fact, sometimes it states simply that certain behaviors occur and can be measured, giving a general direction to our observations. For example, we might hypothesize that "channel changers have certain personality characteristics" and then set out to discover and describe them.

REMEMBER   A *causal hypothesis* proposes a particular cause of a behavior; a *descriptive hypothesis* proposes particular characteristics of a behavior or provides a goal for observations.

It is extremely important to state explicitly whether a study is examining the causes of a behavior, because this is a critical factor in determining the design of the study. Before designing the study, however, you must be sure the hypothesis reflects our assumptions about the lawfulness and understandability of nature. If it does not, then the hypothesis is not scientific, and the evidence that supports it is not scientifically admissible. Therefore, there are specific rules for creating scientific hypotheses.

The Criteria for Scientific Hypotheses

Regardless of whether we have a causal or descriptive hypothesis, any hypothesis should have five attributes: It should be *testable, falsifiable, precise, rational*, and *parsimonious*.

A hypothesis must first be testable and falsifiable. **Testable** means that it is possible to devise a test of a hypothesis. **Falsifiable** means that the test can potentially show that the hypothesis is incorrect. Our previous channel-changing hypotheses are testable and falsifiable because we can devise a study to test them, and we might find evidence indicating they are incorrect. It is possible, however, to create hypotheses that are not testable or falsifiable. Consider the hypothesis "When people die, they see a bright light." This is not a testable hypothesis because it's not possible to study people's experiences after death—they're dead! (Studying people who are declared dead and then revived is a poor substitute because they are not truly dead.) Because it is not testable, the hypothesis is also not falsifiable. Or, consider Sigmund Freud's hypothesis that the "id" leads people to express aggression directly as well as indirectly through superficially nonaggressive behaviors. Although this hypothesis is testable through observation, it cannot be shown to be false: If we observe aggression, it's because of the id. If we don't observe aggression, it's still because of the id, expressing aggression through nonaggressive behavior. Given the circular logic here, this hypothesis cannot tell us anything about the id (even Freud wasn't perfect). When a hypothesis is not testable or falsifiable, it is impossible to determine its accuracy. Instead, we must take the hypothesis on faith, which is a nonscientific approach.

A hypothesis must also add to knowledge about the laws of nature in a meaningful and understandable way, so a hypothesis must be precise and rational. A **precise** hypothesis contains terms that are clearly defined. The use of ambiguous terms opens the hypothesis to interpretation and opinion, making it less clearly testable and falsifiable. A **rational** hypothesis logically fits what is already known about the laws of behavior. For example, our hypothesis about boring commercials causing channel changing fits with what we already know about behavior and, if shown to be correct, will mesh easily with existing knowledge. In contrast, consider the claim that some people exhibit extrasensory perception (ESP), the ability to send and receive mental messages. Any hypothesis about this supposed ability is not rational, because it contradicts existing knowledge about the brain and physical energy that has already been developed in psychology, biology, and physics.

Finally, a hypothesis must be parsimonious. A **parsimonious** hypothesis is one that is as simple as possible. The assumption that nature is lawful implies that many diverse events can be accounted for by an economical combination of relatively few laws. If we propose new laws for every situation, we are merely renaming nature without explaining it. Therefore, the rule of parsimony says that we begin with a relatively simple hypothesis that applies to a broad category of behaviors. Then, only if the simple explanation fails to account for an aspect of the behavior, are we justified in proposing a more complex explanation. Thus, any hypothesis about ESP would not be parsimonious, because it would require proposing all sorts of new brain components and new energy waves, just to make it a viable hypothesis. To be parsimonious, however, there would first need to be scientific evidence for ESP that could not be explained using brain mechanisms and energy forms that are already established by previous research. Only then

TABLE 1.4 How the Criteria for a Hypothesis Translate into a Question about Your Hypothesis

Criteria	Question about the hypothesis
Testable	Can a test be designed for it?
Falsifiable	Can it be possibly proved false?
Precise	Are its terms clearly defined?
Rational	Does it fit with the known information?
Parsimonious	Does it involve the simplest possible approach?

would it be acceptable to propose the existence of new brain components and new energy waves.

Table 1.4 will help you remember the criteria for acceptable hypotheses by relating each one to the question you should ask about a hypothesis. The more that a hypothesis deviates from these criteria, the less confidence we have in any conclusions about it.

> **REMEMBER**   Scientific hypotheses must be *testable*, *falsifiable*, *precise*, *rational*, and *parsimonious*.

Sources of Hypotheses

How do you come up with a hypothesis? One obvious source for generating a hypothesis is a researcher's own opinions, observations, or experiences. It is perfectly acceptable to base a hypothesis on such sources, as long as you then conduct an empirical, objective study to provide evidence for the hypothesis. A second source is existing research: When reading the results of a study that tested one hypothesis, you'll usually see the basis for several additional hypotheses. For example, if we find that channel changing increases when someone is alone, we would then want to determine why, identify the factors that modify this influence, and so on. A third source of a hypothesis, as we'll see, is the retesting of a hypothesis previously tested by another researcher.

Theories are another source of hypotheses. A **theory** is an integrated set of statements that defines, explains, organizes, and interrelates knowledge about many behaviors. Theoreticians may develop a theory beginning with certain ideas and concepts for which there is little scientific evidence. The theory then provides a direction for the evidence researchers will seek. Or theoreticians may develop a theory after substantial evidence has been collected, providing a way to organize diverse findings. Either way, a theory is a framework of abstract concepts that helps to explain and describe a broad range of behaviors in a parsimonious way. For example, "Freudian theory" attempted to explain and relate a vast array of normal and abnormal behaviors using the abstract concepts of id, ego, and superego. Likewise, the most common psychological terms are actually theoretical concepts, such as learning, memory, intelligence, creativity, personality, and schizophrenia. These are not real things; you cannot place your personality on a table. Rather, they are abstract general descriptions that help you to organize and understand categories of behaviors.

Theories serve two major functions. First, they help to *organize* empirical findings. Additional research can then be tied to the theory, providing a framework for developing the "big picture" regarding a behavior. Thus, for the sake of rational and parsimonious hypotheses, especially when research begins with your personal opinions or experiences, you need to relate any behavior being researched to theoretical concepts. Then if you find evidence that supports the hypothesis, your explanation is likely to mesh with existing knowledge in an understandable way. For example, we might tie our ideas about boring commercials to existing concepts of "information processing" and "motivation" to explain channel changing, and then design a study using these concepts.

The other, simultaneous function that theories serve is to *guide* research. To test or add to a theory, researchers derive a specific hypothesis, test it in a research study, and then apply the study's outcome to the theoretical concepts, either adding to or correcting the theory. Then, from the modified theory, researchers develop additional hypotheses, which, after testing, are used to further modify the theory. (*Note*: A study cannot test a theory; it can test only a hypothesis derived from a theory. Be careful when using the word *theory*.)

REMEMBER   A *theory* is an organized body of research that describes and explains a wide array of behaviors.

A final, related source of hypotheses is a model. A **model** is a general description that, by analogy, explains the process underlying particular behaviors. Whereas a theory tends to be very abstract and broad in scope, a model tends to be more specific and concrete. For example, consider a model airplane: It provides a solid way to discuss and understand how the components of an airplane operate. Contrast this with the theory of aerodynamics that explains the general principles of flight. Likewise, in psychology, a theory accounts for broad, abstract components of behaviors, while a model provides a more concrete analogy for discussing and understanding the specific behaviors. A psychological model usually involves a flow chart or diagram. For example, Figure 1.2 shows the Information Processing Model of human memory. Each box represents a different type of memory system that produces different kinds of behaviors, and the arrows represent the flow of information from one system to the next. Although no one believes the brain contains little boxes labeled short-term and long-term memory, they are useful for deriving specific hypotheses about how and when information remains in temporary or more permanent memory. Researchers then test these hypotheses and use the results to modify the model, in the same way that theories are modified.

FIGURE 1.2   The Information Processing Model of Memory

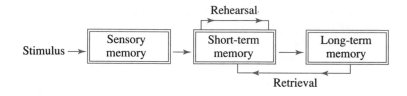

REMEMBER   A *model* is a description that, through analogy, explains related behaviors.

Testing Hypotheses through Research

The "model" in Figure 1.3 summarizes how hypotheses are tested and how the results are incorporated into scientific knowledge. The first step is to create an acceptable hypothesis using theoretical concepts, models, or your own observations about behavior, so that we can better describe, explain, predict, and control a behavior.

The second step is to design a study that tests the hypothesis. Just how you do that, of course, is the topic of this book. Suffice it to say that there are many designs to choose from, depending on whether the major goal of the study is to describe, explain, predict, or control the behavior. Regardless of the design, we attempt to obtain objective, systematic, and controlled measurement of the intended behavior, so that we clearly and confidently test the hypothesis.

The third step is to derive our predictions. Whereas a hypothesis is a general statement about how a behavior operates, a **prediction** is a specific statement about how we will see the behavior manifested in the research situation, describing the specific results that we expect in our study. We test the accuracy of a hypothesis using the logic that, if the hypothesis is correct, then participants should behave in a certain way, resulting in certain data: The behavior should occur in such a way that participants' scores will be high or low, or will change in a predictable manner. For example, if we hypothesized that boring commercials cause channel changing, we'd predict that as more boring commercials occur, participants' scores will reflect more frequent, more rapid, or more motivated channel changing.

With a prediction in hand, the fourth step is to conduct the study and collect the data. Here, *statistical procedures* come into play. There are various types of statistics to use, depending on the specific design of a study. Regardless, essentially statistics are used to make sense out of data so that we can see whether the scores form the predicted pattern. Thus, if we are testing whether more frequent channel changing occurs with more boring commercials, we'll use statistical procedures to determine if this pattern occurs in the data.

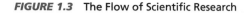

FIGURE 1.3   The Flow of Scientific Research

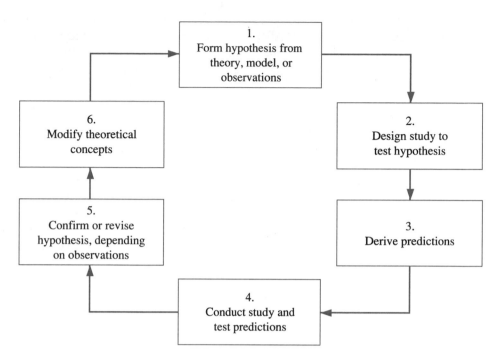

Based on the data, we next work back to our hypothesis. If the data fit the prediction, there is evidence to support the original hypothesis. If they do not, there is not support for the hypothesis.

Finally from the conclusions about the hypothesis, we work back to the theoretical concepts or model from step 1, either adding to or correcting the description. Future research then uses the modified theory or model, testing additional hypotheses that are used to further modify the description, and the cycle begins again. It is through this continual cycle that the science of psychology collates, organizes, and resolves the diverse "snapshots" of behaviors that individual studies provide, so that we can eventually understand the broader laws of nature.

THE FLAWS IN SCIENTIFIC RESEARCH

Recall that it's easy to make mistakes when studying nature because nature is complex and mysterious, and we don't already know how it works. Although the rules we've examined may seem sufficient to eliminate bias and error, they do not guarantee this. There are many opportunities for researchers to make errors. Therefore, we must be skeptical, remembering that what we know—or *think* we know—depends on (1) the evidence presented and (2) how it is interpreted.

First, let's consider the evidence.

The Flaws in the Evidence

An ideal study would produce perfectly accurate measurement of the exact behavior we seek to describe, with only the relevant factors coming into play. However, *no study is ideal*. Rather, four general aspects of a study can reduce our confidence in the data and thus in the conclusions of the study.

First, some behaviors cannot be studied in a completely empirical, objective, systematic, and controlled manner. For example, it's impossible to directly observe "thinking." Instead, we must observe some other behavior—such as the errors in logic that people make—from which to draw inferences about thinking. However, the greater the inferential leap from the observed to the unseen behavior, the less confidence we have in a conclusion. Also, there is no "yardstick" for objectively measuring some behaviors (such as aggressiveness or love). Instead, we must employ more subjective procedures that may include bias and error. Finally, researchers cannot always observe a behavior in a systematic and controlled fashion. For example, in studying the attitudes of women toward childbearing, we cannot separate the fact that participants have female personalities from the fact that they have female bodies. Therefore, it's impossible to be sure whether it's a woman's personality or her physiology (or both) that influences her attitudes. Because similar limitations are found in every study, we are never completely confident that we *know* what the measurements reflect about the behavior or which factors were truly operating.

Second, the decisions made when designing a study can also reduce confidence in the findings. For example, if we study channel changing as it occurs in someone's living room, we cannot control such distractions as whether the phone rings in the middle of a commercial and thus prevents channel changing. But if we study channel changing in a controlled "laboratory" setting, we create an artificial and thus biased picture of the behavior: People do not normally watch television in a laboratory! Likewise, the particular participants in a study, the way a behavior is measured, and the way factors are controlled might all bias the results.

Third, often there are technical limitations that produce misleading information. For example, in the late 1800s, psychologists studied "phrenology," the idea that various personality traits are reflected by the size of bumps on the skull. Considering current techniques for studying personality and brain physiology, however, phrenology now seems silly. Always consider the possible limitations in our current technical abilities.

And finally, the results of one study can never tell the whole story. Because a single study is a "snapshot," it necessarily provides a biased perspective, considering certain factors and ignoring others (some of which we don't even know about). Depending on what is ignored, the study may seriously misrepresent nature. This is illustrated by the fable about several blind men trying to describe an elephant (Shah, 1970). One, touching the animal's trunk, describes the elephant as like a snake. Another, touching the ear, says the elephant is like a fan. Another, touching the leg, describes the elephant as resembling a tree. And so on.

In studying a behavior, researchers are like the blind men, trying to describe the entire elephant from one limited perspective. For example, say our study supports the hypothesis that channel changing is caused by boring commercials. If we do not consider the television program during which the commercials appear, however, then a different study might indicate that channel changing is caused by boring programs. The problem is that either study alone does not give the complete picture if channel changing is actually caused by a combination of boring commercials and a boring program. Remember, being skeptical means not falling for the obvious explanation provided. Always consider whether your attention has been misdirected by the limited perspective of a study.

Thus, depending on the behavior being studied, the researcher's decisions, technical limitations, and the perspective taken, individual studies can vary greatly in the extent to which they provide "good" data that accurately reflect the behavior and situation as they occur in nature. The bottom line here is that not all research is created equal! Therefore, you must critically evaluate any study to determine the extent that it might misrepresent nature. The most important factor to consider is the design of the study. As you will see again and again, the design and interpretation of a study are completely interrelated: Whether the design is flawed determines whether the data is flawed, which determines whether the conclusions of the study are flawed. So, whether you're evaluating your study or one performed by someone else, always consider if there are flaws in the design that suggest reasons for doubting the study's conclusions.

> **REMEMBER** A study's design determines the "snapshot" of a behavior it produces and thus ultimately the evidence for a particular hypothesis.

Even when a study contains a minimum of flaws, you still cannot have as much confidence in the conclusions as you might think. This is because of the intrinsic difficulty in "proving" that a hypothesis is true.

The Flaws in Testing Hypotheses

You've seen that in science we learn about nature by testing hypotheses: If the data fit the hypothesis, we believe that it describes how nature operates. If the data do not fit the hypothesis, then we conclude that it does not describe how nature operates. As simple as this process appears, however, there are potential flaws in it. To see this, look at the deck of cards shown in Figure 1.4. The card on the top of the pile shows a "4." Say our hypothesis is "If there is an even number on one side of any card, there is always a vowel on the other side."[1] The way to test this hypothesis is to turn over the card showing the "4" and see if we find a vowel.

---

[1]From the four-card problem in Wason (1968).

FIGURE 1.4   Testing a Hypothesis

Shown here is a deck of cards used to test the hypothesis "If there is an even number on one side of any card, there is a vowel on the other side."

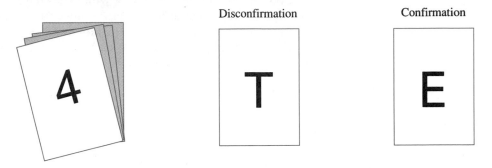

First, say we find the consonant "T." Then the hypothesis has been *disconfirmed*, so we are confident it is false. Note, however, that although we have disproved the hypothesis as stated, it may contain some element of truth. Maybe the rule does apply, but only if the even number is greater than 4.

Instead, say we turn over the card and "E" is there. A "4" with an "E" *confirms* the hypothesis that even numbers are paired with vowels. But does this prove that the hypothesis is true for the deck? Absolutely not! Some other rule may be operating, and though the card we observed is produced by it, the card also, *coincidentally*, fits our original hypothesis. For example, our observation also fits the *rival* or *competing* hypothesis "When there is any kind of number on one side, there is any kind of letter on the other side." Our observation supports both the original hypothesis and the rival hypothesis. Therefore, we do not *know* for sure which hypothesis is true, so we have not proven our hypothesis.

You might claim that if we examined more cards and they also confirm our hypothesis, we would prove it to be true. However, for as many cards as we examine, seeing a vowel and an even number will confirm both of the above hypotheses, so we can never know which is true. Only if we can disconfirm and thus eliminate one hypothesis can we be confident that the other is true. Thus, you must fight the urge to seek only confirming evidence. *The best evidence comes from disconfirming rival hypotheses while simultaneously confirming your own hypothesis.*

Even then, confirming the hypothesis is not the same as proving it. Confirming a hypothesis is actually a failure to "disprove" it. We may fail to do this for one of two reasons: (1) It is the correct hypothesis, or (2) it is an incorrect hypothesis, but our observations coincidentally fit it. We can never "prove" that our original hypothesis is correct, because for as many cards as are drawn, we can always argue that one more card might be the one to disprove it.

Although this is a serious objection when we've examined only a few cards, it becomes less convincing as we observe more cards. After enough tries we can argue that if a disproving card were out there, we would have found it. If we continually fail to disconfirm the hypothesis, we come to believe that we have eliminated the coincidence argument and that the hypothesis is not disprovable—that it is correct. Thus, the best we can expect is that if we repeatedly find cards that confirm our hypothesis while disconfirming competing hypotheses, we become *confident* that our hypothesis is true. Eventually, with enough cards, we will come to accept the truth of the hypothesis, even though, technically, we can never "prove" it.

The same rationale applies to our channel-changing study. Say that we find that people change channels more frequently with more boring commercials. We haven't proven that the boring content of commercials causes channel changing. It may be, for example, that unknown to us, our boring commercials coincidentally contain less visual stimulation. The correct hypothesis may be that participants change channels to obtain more visual stimulation, and do so *regardless* of how boring a commercial is. The hypothesis about boredom could be totally wrong, but we've simply observed results that *coincidentally* confirm it because of the nature of the true explanation. Given this possibility, we cannot be sure whether the amount of boredom or the amount of visual stimulation in a commercial actually causes channel changing. Only by performing additional experiments in which we confirm our original hypothesis and disconfirm the visual stimulation hypothesis (and any other competing hypotheses) can we confidently conclude that boring commercials cause channel changing.

Testing hypotheses in real research is even more difficult, because some data may confirm a hypothesis, while other data may disconfirm it. Therefore, we must critically evaluate the evidence and the design that produced it. For example, do you accept the hypothesis that dreams predict the future? If you do, it's probably because you've occasionally dreamt of events that later occurred. But consider the quality and quantity of this evidence. First, such a hypothesis is suspect because it's neither rational nor parsimonious. (How in the world could your dreams know what the future holds?) Second, your belief that you accurately recall dreams and that they match up with real events lacks objectivity and is thus also suspect. Third, you are relying on confirmation: Your observation is merely consistent with the hypothesis that dreams predict the future. But weigh this weak evidence against the amount of disconfirmation that is available. How many times have your dreams *failed* to come true? On balance, the preponderance of evidence heavily disconfirms the hypothesis that dreams predict the future. It makes much more sense to say that those few confirming instances are nothing more than coincidence: Some event occurred after you had coincidentally dreamt about it.

Likewise, our confidence in any scientific hypothesis is based on the quantity and quality of evidence that confirms *and* disconfirms it. Do we accept the hypothesis that "positive reinforcement" facilitates learning? Yes, there is a tremendous body of convincing evidence that confirms this hypothesis, while there is little disconfirming evidence. Do we accept the hypothesis that UFOs exist? Most scientists are not convinced because we have not seen enough confirming, scientifically acceptable evidence, and also because the observations can be explained by rival hypotheses. (Reports in supermarket tabloids never concern themselves with these criteria.) Of course, some people feel that there is sufficient evidence to believe in UFOs. As in all scientific debates, additional evidence must be gathered so that, eventually, we'll all be convinced one way or the other.

And remember, any statement must be precise so that it accurately reflects the current evidence. Above, I said that we are not convinced that UFOs exist; I did not say that UFOs *don't* exist. Being both open-minded and cautious means that when one hypothesis has not been confirmed sufficiently to accept with confidence, our conclusion must be that the jury is still out, not that the opposite of the hypothesis is true.

REMEMBER   If we *confirm* a hypothesis, we are merely more confident that it is true than we were before testing it, so the more often we confirm it, the greater our confidence in it.

Using Replication to Build Confidence in Psychological Findings

Researchers ultimately develop confidence in a hypothesis by repeatedly confirming the hypothesis while disconfirming competing hypotheses. This final component of the scientific method is called replication. **Replication** is the process of repeatedly conducting studies that test and confirm a hypothesis so that we develop confidence in its truth. The logic behind replication is that because nature is lawful, it is also consistent. Over many studies, therefore, the correct hypotheses will be consistently supported, while the erroneous, coincidental ones will not.

Researchers perform two types of replication. In a **literal replication**, the researcher tries to duplicate precisely the specific design and results of a previous study. This approach, also called *direct* or *exact* replication, is used because there are always chance factors at work—the particular participants, the unique environment of the study, and so on—that may mislead us. But chance factors that appear in one study are unlikely to appear consistently in others. Therefore, literal replication demonstrates that the original results are not likely to be due to chance factors. If different researchers can repeatedly obtain the same evidence in similar situations, we are more confident that the hypothesis is accurate.

On the other hand, in a **conceptual replication**, the researcher provides additional confirmation of a hypothesis, but does so while measuring the behavior in a different way, examining different types of participants, or using a different design. Conceptual or *indirect* replication provides greater confidence in the general applicability of the hypothesis while testing and disconfirming competing hypotheses. Thus, for example, conceptual replications of our channel-changing study might involve observing children watching Saturday-morning cartoons and adults watching late-night shows, or include various commercials for toys, automobiles, and so on. Then, by combining the findings from these different studies, researchers can determine how the behavior generally operates and which factors influence it.

Note that there is a name for how conceptual replications build confidence in a particular explanation. **Converging operations** are two or more procedures that together eliminate competing hypotheses and bolster our conclusions about a particular behavior. By comparing studies that employ different procedures—different "operations"—we can eliminate some hypotheses and obtain different perspectives that "converge" to provide an accurate picture of a behavior. Thus, we might define boring commercials in terms of their content in one study and in terms of their visual stimulation in another. Then these different lines of research converge on what the term *boring* means in this situation, and whether it is the content, the visual stimulation, or both that causes channel changing.

Thus, scientists use replication to build confidence in their "facts" in the same way that lawyers build a legal case. Literal replication is analogous to repeatedly questioning the same witnesses to make sure they keep their stories straight. Conceptual replication is akin to finding a number of witnesses who, from different vantage points, all report the same event. With enough consistent evidence from both sources, we eventually come to believe that we have discovered a law of nature.

The need for replication often frustrates society because it thinks science should quickly provide a solution to every problem. For example, a newspaper story may report the discovery of a new drug for treating cancer, but sadly, the researcher notes that it could be many years before the drug is available to the public. This reflects the recognition that consistent, convincing evidence of the effectiveness of the drug can be obtained only through time-consuming replication. After all, we accept the "law" of gravity because it always works, in every situation, from every perspective. The same logic must be used when making any other scientific claim as well.

REMEMBER   Science relies on *literal* and *conceptual replication* to build confidence in conclusions.

PUTTING IT ALL TOGETHER

We've seen that, because of the importance of scientific findings, we take the job of "scientist" pretty seriously. Therefore, to have confidence in our conclusions, we've created rules for science called the scientific method. These rules form the background for any study, so we'll use them to begin creating a checklist to follow when designing a study. As shown in Checklist 1.1, we begin by focusing on creating our hypothesis. First, we limit the hypothesis to those behaviors that can be scientifically studied, and we identify the general purpose of the study. We also consider whether the hypothesis can be examined in a way that will provide useful information about it. Further, we define the nature of acceptable evidence for testing the hypothesis. These decisions then set the stage for obtaining data and drawing conclusions that we can have confidence in. In the remainder of this text, we'll simply fill in the many details involved in conducting acceptable research (and we'll add to this checklist).

CHECKLIST 1.1 Questions to consider when designing research

Creating the Hypothesis
- Is the behavior lawful, determined, and understandable?
- Is the hypothesis testable, falsifiable, precise, rational, and parsimonious?
- Is the design empirical, objective, systematic, and controlled?
- Is the hypothesis causal or descriptive?

It should be clear, however, that even when we adhere to all of the rules, a study never provides unquestionable "proof." First, we can never be completely confident that the data reflect the precise behavior we wish to measure, in the precise situation we wish to observe. Further, even with good, convincing data that confirm a hypothesis, the hypothesis may still be incorrect. For that matter, even when a hypothesis is disconfirmed, it may still contain some elements of truth.

Given these problems, you may be wondering why we even bother to conduct research. Well, the issues we've discussed are reasons for being skeptical about any single research finding, not for being negative about the research process. Instead of being paralyzed by such limitations, you should view dealing with them as a challenge. Simply recognize that testing a hypothesis involves translating a general statement about a behavior into a concrete measurable situation, and then translating the measurements back into conclusions about the general behavior. There is always room for error in the translation.

Do not automatically accept or dismiss any single study. On the one hand, researchers try to design the best study they can, providing the clearest evidence for answering the question at hand. Thus, even with flaws, a study usually tells us something about a behavior. On the other hand, what seems to describe a behavior correctly from one perspective may be incorrect when viewed from a different perspective. Look for that different perspective. And always keep in mind that a single study will not tell us everything about a behavior. A complete understanding can be gained only by replication, as we repeatedly obtain numerous and varied "snapshots" of the behavior.

CHAPTER SUMMARY

1. The *scientific method* includes certain assumptions, attitudes, goals, and procedures for creating and answering questions about nature.

2. The assumptions of psychology are that behaviors are *lawful, determined,* and *understandable.*

3. Scientists are *uncertain, open-minded, skeptical, cautious,* and *ethical.*

4. The *design* of a study is the specific manner in which the study is conducted. It should provide for *empirical, objective, systematic,* and *controlled* observations of a behavior. "Control" refers to eliminating factors that might influence the behavior or our observations of it.

5. The goals of psychological research are to *describe, explain, predict,* and *control* behavior.

6. A *pseudo-explanation* is circular, explaining the causes of an event by merely renaming the event. Pseudo-explanations are avoided by obtaining independent verification of a supposed cause.

7. The primary purpose of *basic research* is to obtain knowledge. The primary purpose of *applied research* is to solve an existing problem.

8. A *hypothesis* is a formally stated expectation about how a behavior operates. A *causal hypothesis* postulates a particular causal influence on a behavior. A *descriptive hypothesis* postulates particular characteristics or aspects of the behavior.

9. Scientific hypotheses must be *testable, falsifiable, precise, rational,* and *parsimonious.*

10. A *theory* is a logically organized set of statements that defines, explains, organizes, and interrelates knowledge about many behaviors.

11. A *model* is a description that, by analogy, explains the process underlying common behaviors.

12. A *prediction* is a statement about the data that are expected in a specific study if the hypothesis is correct.

13. When the results of a study *confirm* a hypothesis, this does not prove that the hypothesis is true. *Disconfirming* a hypothesis provides the greatest confidence in a conclusion about the hypothesis.

14. *Replication* is the process of repeatedly conducting studies to build confidence in a hypothesis. *Literal replication* is the precise duplication of a previous study. *Conceptual replication* repeats the test of a hypothesis but uses a different design.

15. *Converging operations* are two or more procedures that together eliminate rival hypotheses about a behavior.

KEY TERMS   (with page references)

applied research 12	model 17
basic research 12	objectivity 8
causal hypothesis 14	parsimonious 15
conceptual replication 24	participants 8
control 9, 10	precise 15
converging operations 25	predict 10
data 8	prediction 18
describe 9	pseudo-explanation 10
descriptive hypothesis 14	rational 15
design 7	replication 24
determinism 5	research ethics 7
empirical 8	scientific method 3
explain 10	subjects 7
falsifiable 15	systematic 8
hypothesis 14	testable 15
lawfulness 4	theory 16
literal replication 24	understandable 5

REVIEW QUESTIONS

1. What is the scientific method?

2. Why is the scientific method the best approach for learning about a behavior?

3. What three assumptions do scientists make about nature?

4. (a) What attitudes characterize scientists? (b) Why are they necessary?

5. (a) What are the four goals of research? (b) What are the four criteria for scientific evidence, and what does each term mean?

6. (a) What is the difference between a theory and a model? (b) How do theories and models simplify nature for us? (c) What are the two general uses of a theory?

7. What are the five criteria for a scientific hypothesis, and what does each term mean?

8. What is the difference between a causal hypothesis and a descriptive hypothesis?

9. What is the difference between a hypothesis and a prediction?

10. Why must we critically evaluate the design of any study?

11. Why does disconfirmation provide greater confidence than confirmation?

12. What is replication, and why does science rely on it?

13. What is the difference between literal replication and conceptual replication?

APPLICATION QUESTIONS

14. On a television talk show, a panelist says that listening to popular music causes the listener to become a devil worshiper, a homicidal maniac, or a suicide victim. What questions would you ask the panelist before voting to ban this kind of music?

15. You've read some research in a developmental psychology text that contradicts what you've observed about your younger brother. Whose claim should you believe, yours or the researcher's? Why?

16. A theorist claims that men become homosexual when, as they are growing up, their mother either (1) tried to control them or (2) did not try to control them. Scientifically speaking, what is wrong with this hypothesis?

17. The government has announced a large monetary grant awarded to a scientist to study the sex life of a nearly extinct butterfly. A commentator claims that such research is a waste of money. Why do you agree or disagree?

18. A researcher explains that the reason people can remember smells is because they have a memory for smells. What is wrong with this explanation?

19. Some researchers who accept the existence of extrasensory perception argue that the reason others have not found convincing evidence for it is that they do not believe such mental powers exist. What rule of science is violated by this argument?

20. An old tale states that if you dream you are falling off a cliff, you must wake up prior to dreaming that you hit the ground, or you will actually die. (a) Why couldn't you devise a test that confirms this hypothesis? (b) What is the way to test this hypothesis? (c) Even if you collect the appropriate dream information, what problems remain?

21. I conduct a study "to test the theory that adequate amounts of sleep are necessary for emotional balance." What error is in this statement?

22. If a study violates the rules of the scientific method, why is our confidence in its conclusions decreased?

DISCUSSION QUESTIONS

23. (a) Is astrology a science? List the reasons why or why not. (b) Explain the problems involved in "proving" that statements from astrology are true.

24. Some students argue that they learn better while listening to the radio when studying. (a) What descriptive and causal hypotheses might you create about this behavior? (b) What predictions do these hypotheses lead to? (c) How would you obtain empirical and objective observations of the behavior? (d) Why would the study need to be replicated?

25. Some people argue that, along with the theory of evolution, high-school students should also be taught the "Science of Creationism"—the Judeo-Christian belief that God originally created the humans and animals we see today. (a) Why is it a contradiction in terms to call creationism a science? (b) Some people argue that the theory of evolution is only a "theory," and therefore has no basis in fact. What don't they know about theories?

26. Some people argue that the U.S. Food and Drug Administration should not require extensive replication studies before allowing the use of drugs for treating AIDS, so that the drugs can be made available sooner. Identify the two sides of the ethical dilemma here. (*Hint*: The drug might work, or it might not.)

2

An Overview of Creating and Testing Hypotheses

GETTING STARTED

To understand this chapter, recall the following:

- We create either a descriptive or a causal hypothesis about a behavior.
- Then we conduct a study that measures the behavior of participants.
- Depending on whether the data support our predictions, we have evidence that either confirms or disconfirms the hypothesis.

Your goals in this chapter are to learn:

- How to conduct a "literature search" using the different components of the psychological literature.
- How to translate a hypothetical construct into a variable and then an operational definition.
- What a relationship is and what is meant by the "strength" of a relationship.
- How the strength of a relationship is used to determine the impact that a variable has on a behavior.
- How a relationship in a sample of scores is used to draw inferences about the behavior of a population.
- What the difference between experimental and descriptive research is.

- What true experiments, quasi-experiments, and correlational designs are.
- What the independent variable, conditions, and dependent variable are in an experiment.

As you know, in research we translate a general hypothesis about a behavior into objective measurements and then translate the measurements back into conclusions about the behavior. This chapter looks more closely at this translation process: First, we will see how to formulate a hypothesis and then how to find relevant previous research reported in the psychological literature. Next, we'll define the individuals to study and specify the terms in our hypothesis, so that we can actually go out and measure participants' scores. We'll also discuss the general approach to examining a "relationship" in the data to test a hypothesis. Finally, we'll introduce the two major types of research designs we might create.

BEGINNING THE DESIGN: ASKING THE QUESTION

It's pointless to design a study by simply grabbing some behavior out of the blue to examine; you'll end up with an answer in search of a question. Instead, research proceeds well only if you first clearly determine the question being asked and then design a study to answer it. Therefore, the starting point of any study is to form a specific hypothesis about a specific behavior. The hypothesis may stem from questions raised by previous research, from your own observations of a behavior, from theories or models, or as an attempt at a literal or conceptual replication of a previous study. However, developing a hypothesis is not an instantaneous thing. There are several aspects to it, and it will take some effort before you are finished.

The behavior that you choose to study is determined first by the topic you find interesting—developmental psychologists find children interesting, animal psychologists think animals are nifty, or neuropsychologists are intrigued by the brain's physiology. Thus, to become a researcher, begin by choosing an aspect of behavior that interests you. For example, say that in a cognitive psychology course, we encounter the idea that information is better remembered when we "rehearse" it (by repeating it, thinking about it in various ways, or creating associations with other information.)

The next step is to "play psychologist." Psychologists "wonder" about behavior, and this leads to the questions and goals discussed in the previous chapter. Thus, wondering about memory might lead to a *causal hypothesis* if we ask what it is that rehearsal causes to happen so that memory is better or worse, whether one way of rehearsing causes better memory than another way, or how the memory mechanisms work so that rehearsal influences them. We'd have a *descriptive hypothesis* if we wonder who exhibits differences in memory or at what age they start, how memory changes as we grow older, or whether memory is different for different cultures or genders. Further, while the above imply *basic research* questions, we'd have a more *applied* question if, for example, we reframed our questions about memory in terms of an educational setting, leading to the idea that the more you study, the more you learn.

Obviously, to examine any of these issues, we must, *in some way*, examine people to see if and when their memory is actually different. The problem, however, is that we have been so general: Everything hinges on "in some way." Therefore, the process of creating a hypothesis involves continuously refining and specifying all aspects of the behavior, participants, and situation that we will observe. However, also remember that the hypothesis must be acceptable in terms of the rules of science discussed in the previous chapter: that it is testable and falsifiable, that it fits with previous research and theory in a parsimonious and rational manner, that it is ethical, that it doesn't involve faith, and that it is approached in an empirical and objective fashion.

For help in whittling down a behavior to study, finding different perspectives for it, complying with the rules of science, and fitting a hypothesis into previous research, remember that a study is never invented in a vacuum. Instead, a critically important first step is to examine the psychological research literature.

THE RESEARCH LITERATURE

Published reports of past research are the ultimate source for learning about a psychological topic. The **research literature** contains research results, terminology, definitions, hypotheses, and theories regarding virtually any behavior. You'll also find numerous ideas for interesting studies as well as proven techniques and procedures that you can incorporate into your study. In short, you cannot design an acceptable study without being familiar with the relevant research literature.

However, the term "research literature" refers to published reports found in *professional-level* books and journals. It does not refer to books and newspapers found in the supermarket or bookstores, or to popular magazines such as *Time* or *Newsweek*. At best, these contain synopses of research articles that are likely to omit important details. Therefore, go to the professional books and journals written for psychologists. Recognize, however, that although books provide useful background, because of the time required to create them, even new books will be several years behind the latest developments. Therefore, focus on journals for the most current developments in a topic, because they are published once or more a year.

Not all professional journals, however, are of the same quality. In some, the primary requirement for publishing an article is that the author(s) pay the publication costs. These journals have less stringent requirements for quality research.

Other journals are "refereed," meaning that each article undergoes "peer review" by several psychologists who are knowledgeable about the topic being studied. To gauge the quality of a journal, check the section that describes its editorial policies. Also, look for journals published by professional organizations of psychologists such as the American Psychological Association, the American Psychological Society, or the Psychonomic Society. One function of these organizations is to disseminate quality research. However, although such journals tend to report convincing research, you still should approach each study with a critical eye.

Searching the Literature

To find past research that is relevant to a topic, we must "search" the literature. To search the literature, you need at least a general topic in mind. Most journals are organized around a subarea of psychology (e.g., social, cognitive, abnormal) identified by the journal's title (e.g., *Cognitive Psychology* or the *Journal of Personality and Social Psychology*). If you have only a vague idea of a behavior to study, perusing a journal will suggest more specific ideas to explore. If you have a specific behavior in mind, however, you can consult reference sources that search the literature in an organized manner. Either way, remember that, eventually, the goal of a study is to understand a behavior. This goal should be your focus when searching the literature. Start by trying to find *all* published research that *might* relate to the topic. Then whittle it down to those that actually do.

Listed below are several tools that greatly facilitate a literature search.

Psychological Abstracts   *Psychological Abstracts* is a monthly publication that describes studies recently published in other psychology journals. Its index is organized using the terminology commonly used by psychologists. Therefore, try to select specific terms you think would be used in the titles of relevant articles. For our research about memory and learning, to exclude animal research we'd look in the *Abstracts* under such headings as *human* cognition or *human* memory. Then, we'd examine such subheadings as *short-term memory* or *long-term memory*, and then look specifically for *rehearsal* and other terms related to it. If we're interested in memory as it relates to studying, we could look under *education* for such terms as *study techniques*. If we're interested in differences between groups, we might look under *gender differences* or *cross-cultural differences*. Often you have to play detective, so look for many ways to describe a topic. Also, pay close attention to the terminology that other researchers use: For example, in cognitive research, "rehearsal" is used with verbal or written information, but "practice" is used with physical activity.

For each article in the index, a corresponding "abstract" or synopsis of it is provided. By reading the abstract, we determine whether to go to the journal where the article was originally published to read the entire report.

The *Abstracts* also provides a separate author index. When we find relevant articles, we can look under the authors' names to see if they have published other related articles.

Computerized Literature Searches   Many college libraries provide a user-friendly computer program that searches the literature for you. These programs have a large database covering years of research literature. You simply enter the relevant terms, and the computer provides abstracts and the references for studies filed under those terms. In fact, the computer will call up many unrelated references for a general term, so cross-reference your terms to ensure a more selective search. For example, merely entering "memory" as a search term will produce hundreds of irrelevant studies for us. But, for example, entering "memory" and "rehearsal" will produce a smaller set of articles that are more likely to relate to our topic.

Often some form of a "thesaurus" of psychological terms is available in the computer program (and your library may have a hardbound copy as well). Here you will find suggestions for search terms to use in the computer program (and in *Psychological Abstracts*).

Bibliographies of Research Articles   When you find a relevant article, its bibliography will contain references to other relevant studies. By reading these articles, and then reading the references in them, you can work backward in time and learn about research that came *before* the original study. Sometimes there will also be references to psychological conventions and meetings at which researchers orally presented their research. For a copy of a presentation, contact the first author cited in the reference. (For assistance, the American Psychological Association provides a directory of its members' addresses.)

Social Science Citation Index   When you find a relevant article that is several years old, search for more recent articles that came *after* that article by using the *Social Science Citation Index*. This publication identifies a research article by authors and date, and then lists other articles published in a given year that have cited it. Thus, for example, say we find an important article that was published in 1995. We would look up this article in the *Index* for the years 2001, 2000, 1999, and so on. Listed there will be articles published in those years that cite the 1995 article. Presumably, these later studies also deal with the topic we're interested in.

Review Articles   A **review article** surveys and summarizes a large body of published theoretical and empirical literature dealing with a particular topic. Such articles provide a useful overview as well as references to many specific studies. The title of a review article usually contains the word *review*. Some books and journals specialize in review articles (such as *Psychological Bulletin* and *Annual Review of Psychology*).

References on Testing Materials   Often a study will use a paper-and-pencil test to measure such things as intelligence, personality, creativity, or attitudes. Instead of creating your own test and being uncertain of its effectiveness, look for acceptable tests that already exist. To find them, consult reference books that describe common psychological tests. Such books usually have titles indicating that they describe tests (such as *The Mental Measurements Yearbook* or *Measures of Personality* and *Social Psychological Attitudes*).

A computerized search is also useful for finding articles that have employed such tests. To be efficient, cross-reference the name of the attribute to be measured with the term *assessment*. For example, if you wish to measure depression, using the terms *depression* and *assessment* will limit the search to studies that involve the measurement of depression.

Interplay Between the Literature and Decision Making

Using any of the above sources will be difficult as long as you have only a general idea of the study. Therefore, while searching the literature, you also start to whittle down the hypothesis (doing the things we'll discuss in the next sections). Based on the literature, you begin making decisions, and then, with a better idea of the study, you go back and examine more specific, relevant literature. Then, being more knowledgeable, you make more refined decisions, and so on. In this way, the design of the study will emerge.

REMEMBER   Search the literature early and often when designing a study.

As you'll see, all final design decisions are ultimately made simultaneously, because one decision impacts on all others. However, a useful starting point is to identify the relevant population and sample.

IDENTIFYING THE POPULATION AND SAMPLE

By saying that more rehearsal leads to better memory and learning, we have essentially hypothesized a component of a law of nature. Any law applies to a specific group, which is called the **population**. Part of designing a study is to specifically define the target population. Are we talking about young children, college students, senior citizens, or all of the above? Does the hypothesis apply to all cultures, socioeconomic classes, intelligence levels, and personality types? Typically, we strive for the broadest population possible, so say that in studying memory, we define our population as college-aged men and women. Notice that now we also know the specific participants we will observe (and we are most concerned with reading the literature dealing with such individuals).

A population is usually considered to be infinitely large (but it need not be). To examine the behaviors of an infinitely large population would take forever, so instead, we study a sample. A **sample** is a relatively small subset of a population that is selected to represent, or stand in for, the population. It is the sample or samples of participants that are measured in a study, and the scores from the sample(s) constitute the data.

The logic behind samples and populations is this: We assume that the participants in a sample are basically interchangeable with any other participants we might obtain from the population. Therefore, any sample should produce scores similar to those of any and all others in the population. In other words, we assume the sample will be representative of the population. In a **representative sample**, the characteristics of the participants—and thus their behaviors—accurately reflect the characteristics and behaviors of individuals in the population. Thus, a representative sample of college students will contain the same proportion of good and poor, motivated and unmotivated, and male and female students as in the population.

The basic technique for attempting to produce a representative sample is simple random sampling. **Simple random sampling** is the selection of participants in an unbiased manner so that all members of the population have an equal chance of being selected. Any technique that is similar to placing the names of everyone in the population into a large hat and then blindly selecting participants is random sampling. Thus, there are books that contain tables of random numbers: We can close our eyes, select some numbers, and then select those participants having the same identification numbers. Or, we might program a computer to randomly select in this way.

An alternative approach is **systematic random sampling**. Here we select every nth person from a list of the population. That is, after randomly choosing a starting point in the list, we might select every third or every tenth name in the list. However, be careful that everyone has an equal chance of being selected. If potential participants are listed by age, for example, we might fill our sample with younger people before we get to any older ones down the list.

REMEMBER *Simple random sampling* is selecting participants so that all members of the population have an equal chance of being selected. *Systematic random sampling* is selecting every nth person from the population in an unbiased fashion.

Random selection *should* allow the diverse characteristics of individuals in the population to occur to the same degree in our sample so that it is representative. (Chapter 10 discusses additional sampling techniques that may be needed to ensure this.) Then, the behavior observed in the sample should match the behavior of the population. Likewise, because we obtain data by measuring a behavior, a representative sample provides scores that are a good example of the scores we would find if we could measure the entire population. Ultimately, our conclusions based on a representative sample will accurately apply to the population, so we will meet the goal of understanding a law of behavior as it applies to everyone.

Note, however, that random sampling implies that we have a list of the population and that everyone on the list is available to us. In actual practice, researchers can seldom identify—let alone contact—all members of the population. Instead, we randomly select from the segment of the population that is available, and so, there are always some members of the population who have no chance of being selected. Thus, in reality, a truly random sample is an ideal that is seldom attained.

Therefore, any sample can be *unrepresentative* to some degree because we miss some individuals having important characteristics that are found in the population. This creates a serious problem: The sample that we observe may *misrepresent* the population and thus *mislead* us about how a behavior actually operates. For example, for our memory study, say that we decide to "randomly" sample the population of college students by selecting students at your school. This will impact the study because, at best, we'll obtain only students who are typical of your school, excluding those attending a college different from yours. And, at worse, simply by the luck of the draw we might even miss some types of students that are commonly found at your school. It's possible, for example, that we might select only males. Then our sample may mislead us about the population of college men and women, because our observations are heavily biased by men while totally missing women.

This is a very serious potential problem and one reason that we must be very cautious and skeptical about the results of any single study. We will examine potential solutions to it in several later discussions. For now, to proceed with our memory research, once we have identified the population to be studied, completing the design involves first deciding what behavior to observe and how to measure it.

DEFINING THE TERMINOLOGY IN THE HYPOTHESIS

Once you have a general idea for a study, the key to designing it is to translate the hypothesis into very specific terms and definitions. With a very specific hypothesis, it will become obvious how to conduct the study.

REMEMBER   The design of a study becomes obvious when the hypothesis is very specific.

The following sections describe how to whittle down a hypothesis. Throughout each step, continue to play psychologist, always wondering about what the behavior entails, the various ways that it occurs, the various situations in which it occurs, and the factors that can influence it.

Typically, we go through three levels of specifying the components of a hypothesis: from *hypothetical constructs* to *variables* to *operational definitions*.

Identifying the Hypothetical Constructs

Usually, when we think about a behavior, we think in general terms. "Memory," for example, applies to many situations. It can refer to retrieving a word just heard or to recalling an event from the distant past; it is knowing the definition of a word, being able to ride a bicycle, or mentally picturing a map of your college campus. Thus, "memory" actually refers to a conglomeration of different behaviors, which seem to share certain properties and causes. Likewise, most of the terms in psychology are actually broad conglomerates, such as intelligence, thinking, personality, or motivation.

Such terms have an important name. "Memory" is not a real thing—if we open your brain, we will not find a hunk that is your memory. Rather, memory is a *hypothetical* thing that we have *constructed* as a convenient way of combining many behaviors under one umbrella term. Such terms are called hypothetical constructs. A **hypothetical construct** is an abstract concept used in a particular theoretical manner to relate different behaviors according to their underlying features or causes. It is used to describe, organize, summarize, and communicate our *interpretations* of behaviors. Thus, we describe the differences in people's mental capabilities using the construct of "intelligence." Or, we summarize an individual's traits and characteristics as his or her "personality." And, in our study, "memory" refers to the storage and retrieval of information. Further, there can be subparts to constructs, such as "short-term" versus "long-term" memory or "visual" versus "verbal" memory. Likewise, "rehearsal" refers to the mental activities of repeating and, in some sense, "strengthening" the memory "trace."

REMEMBER   A *hypothetical construct* is an abstract term used to summarize and describe behaviors that share certain attributes.

It is important to recognize the hypothetical constructs involved in a study, because the way to ensure that a hypothesis is rational and parsimonious is to incorporate accepted hypothetical concepts. That's because when we talk about understanding a behavior, we are really talking about understanding the constructs that describe the behavior.

We study constructs, however, by observing components of the physical world that we think reflect them. But because constructs are intentionally general, they can be examined from many perspectives. Therefore, in designing a study, you must define each hypothetical construct in terms of a specific measurable event that reflects the construct. You accomplish this using variables.

Identifying the Component Variables of a Construct

The way we learn about a hypothetical construct is by measuring a variable that reflects the construct. A **variable** is any measurable aspect of a behavior or influence on a behavior that may change. Measuring a variable is what produces the scores and data of a study. Thus, a variable can reflect a participant's physical action, mental reaction, or physiological response. Or, a variable can reflect an influence on a behavior, such as a characteristic of the participants, of the situation, or of a stimulus to which participants respond. A few of the variables found in psychological research include your age, gender, and personality type; how anxious, angry, or aggressive you are; and how hard you will work at a task or how accurately you recall a situation.

When selecting the variables for a study, first, consider the many variables that may reflect a construct. Then, select the specific variables to examine. However, not all variables are created equal, and which you should use in a specific study depends on a number of important considerations (discussed in later chapters.) Essentially, though, a variable should be a good example of the hypothetical construct as it is conceptualized, it should allow for objective and precise measurement as much as possible, and it must be compatible with other aspects of the study's design.

REMEMBER   We examine an aspect of a hypothetical construct by selecting a specific *variable* to measure.

Variables fall into one of two general categories. If a score indicates the amount of a variable that is present, it is a "quantitative" variable. A person's height, for example, is a quantitative variable. Some variables, however, cannot be measured in amounts. Instead, a score *classifies* an individual on the basis of some characteristic. Such variables are called "qualitative" variables. A person's gender, for example, is a qualitative variable.

Thus, for our study, we must decide whether to measure "memory" by measuring how accurately the material is retained, how long participants must study in order to have perfect retention, or some other indication of retention. Is the material to be learned a list of words, a list of pictures, or written paragraphs? Also, we must define "rehearsal": Is it rote rehearsal, the number of verbal or visual associations one creates, or some other measure of mental activity?

By selecting one variable to measure rehearsal and one variable to reflect memory, we have a much more specific hypothesis. Thus, instead of saying that "rehearsal improves memory," let's say that we translate this into "the more times that participants rote rehearse a list of words, the better their retention of the list." This is better, but we are still being too general.

Creating Operational Definitions

For any variable you select, there will be a variety of ways to measure it. Ultimately, you must specifically define each variable, and the way to do that is through its operational definition. An **operational definition** defines a variable by the specific operations used to measure it. Operational definitions are very important because they eliminate ambiguity. For example, although you and I may disagree about exactly what the construct of intelligence means, I might operationally define it as a score on the XYZ intelligence test. Now, at least, there is no debate about what I had my participants do, how I've measured their intelligence, and what you'd need to do to replicate my study. This is far clearer than simply stating, "I determined each person's intelligence."

Essentially, each variable we select is our operational definition of the underlying construct (e.g., "we've defined 'memory' as participants' retention of a list"). Then, we must operationally define each variable (how will we measure "retention of a list"?). Give considerable thought to each operational definition because they are major potential flaws in a study and can produce all kinds of controversy among researchers. (For example, I would be in big trouble if most researchers did not accept that the XYZ test measures intelligence.) Therefore, first generate a list of potential approaches, and then select the best one. For help, consult the research literature for definitions that have been used successfully in previous research.

In the example, "retention of a list" must be operationally defined in terms of whether to have participants recall the material or recognize it. If recalling it, must it be recalled in the same order as it was presented or in any order? Likewise, will participants be free to rehearse at their own pace for a set period of time, or will we determine the number of times they rehearse? Will they rehearse silently or out loud? And so on.

Note that in Chapter 1 we saw how replications improve confidence in a finding through *converging operations*, the process of using different procedures that together eliminate competing hypotheses. These different "operations" result from using different "operational" definitions. For example, if we measure retention by measuring both recall and recognition, we should "converge" on the general construct of memory with a more well-rounded and more accurate perspective than if we used either definition alone.

Thus, the process of designing a study involves translating the hypothetical constructs into variables, and then translating the variables into the specific operations used to measure them. It is through this process that researchers whittle away at the complexity of a behavior to produce a "snapshot" of it that meets the scientific goals of obtaining empirical, objective, systematic, and controlled observations. Likewise, designing the remainder of a study essentially involves operationally defining all other aspects of the situation in which we examine the behavior. Thus, how will participants recall a list (in writing or orally)? Will we measure performance as the number of errors or the number correct? Where will the study take place (in a classroom, the library, or at our "laboratory")? And so on. Think of it this way: To conduct the study, eventually we must go out and enlist some specific participants, put them in a specific situation, tell them exactly how to perform a specific task or ask them specific questions, and then produce some specific measurements to use as their scores. Operational definitions indicate exactly how we will do this.

TABLE 2.1   The Steps in Defining a Research Concept

Step	Definition
1. Hypothetical construct	General theoretical term that summarizes common behaviors or processes
2. Variable	Measurable component of a construct
3. Operational definition	Definition of a variable in terms of the method used to measure it

REMEMBER   Create an *operational definition* for each variable by defining it in terms of how it is measured.

So that you remember the preceding terminology, Table 2.1 summarizes the steps in defining a concept in psychological research.

Defining the variables in a study produces a very specific situation in which to observe a behavior and a specific hypothesis about the behavior. Then, we are ready to actually test the hypothesis.

TESTING A HYPOTHESIS BY DEMONSTRATING A RELATIONSHIP

Notice that by operationally defining our constructs and variables, we have translated a general hypothesis into a specific *prediction* about the scores that we will observe in our study: If we're correct about how nature ties those mental activities we call "rehearsal" to those mental activities we call "memory," then the more that participants rehearse a list of words, the better their recall of the list should be. To determine if we're correct, all we must do is go out and observe some participants who rehearse for different amounts, and see if their recall changes as predicted. We should see that when one person rehearses more than another, that person also performs better when recalling the list. But, when two people rehearse the list equally, they should produce the same recall scores. In other words, the test of a prediction is to look for a *relationship* in the data.

Understanding What a Relationship Is

A **relationship** occurs when a change in one variable is accompanied by a consistent change in another variable. Because we measure scores, a mathematical relationship is a *pattern* in which specific scores on one variable are paired with certain scores on the other variable, so that as the scores on one variable increase or decrease, scores on the other variable tend to also change in a consistent manner.

TABLE 2.2 Scores Showing a Relationship
Between the Variables of Number of Rehearsals
and Number of Items Recalled

Participant	Number of rehearsals	Number recalled
1	1	6
2	1	6
3	2	8
4	2	8
5	3	10
6	3	10
7	4	12
8	4	12

For example, say that we ask some participants to study a list of 15 words. Then, we measure the number of words in the list that they correctly recall, and also ask them how many times they rehearsed the list. Say that we obtain the data shown in Table 2.2. Each row in the table is for one participant. Look at how a particular rehearsal score is paired with a particular recall score: The two people who had 1 rehearsal had recall scores of 6; those who had rehearsal scores of 2 had recall scores of 8, and so on. These data form a relationship, because as participants' rehearsals increase, their number correctly recalled also increases in a consistent fashion. Further, when rehearsal scores do *not* change, their corresponding recall scores also do not change (e.g., *everyone* who rehearsed once had a recall score of 6.) Thus, a relationship reflects an *association* between the variables: Here, low recall scores are associated with low rehearsal scores, and high recall scores are associated with high rehearsal scores. Similarly, another name for a relationship is a *correlation*, and so in these data, rehearsal scores and recall scores are *correlated*.

REMEMBER In a *relationship*, as participants' scores on one variable change, their corresponding scores on another variable change in a consistent fashion.

As in Table 2.2, a simple relationship may fit the pattern "the more you *X* the more you *Y*." (We'll cover this in detail in Chapter 7, but you may already know that such a relationship is called a "positive linear relationship" or a "positive correlation.") However, a relationship may also fit the pattern "the more you *X*, the *less* you *Y*." For example, say we had measured the number of times a list was rehearsed and the number of errors that participants made when recalling it. We might find the relationship shown in Table 2.3. Here, higher rehearsal scores are associated with *lower* error scores. (As we'll see, this illustrates a "negative linear relationship" or a "negative correlation.")

TABLE 2.3 Scores Showing a Relationship Between Number of Rehearsals and Number of Errors in Recall

Participant	Number of rehearsals	Number of errors
1	1	12
2	1	12
3	2	11
4	2	11
5	3	9
6	3	9
7	4	6
8	5	4

Relationships can also form more complicated patterns where, for example, more X at first leads to more Y, but beyond a certain point, even more X leads to *less Y*. For example, at first, the more you exercise, the better you feel. Beyond a certain point, however, more exercise leads to feeling less well, as pain and exhaustion set in.

Although the above examples involve quantitative variables, relationships may also involve qualitative variables. For example, typically men are taller than women. If you think of male and female as "scores" on the qualitative variable of gender, then this is a relationship: As gender scores change (going from male to female), height scores tend to decrease in a consistent fashion.

On the other hand, when no relationship is present, there is no discernible pattern. Instead, essentially the same batch of Y scores shows up with each X score. For example, say that we obtained the data shown in Table 2.4. Here, no particu-

TABLE 2.4 Scores Showing No Relationship Between Number of Rehearsals and Number of Errors in Recall

Participant	Number of rehearsals	Number of errors
1	1	5
2	1	10
3	2	5
4	2	12
5	3	4
6	3	10
7	4	5
8	4	10

lar error score is associated with a particular rehearsal score, and error scores do not consistently change as rehearsal scores increase.

Strength of a Relationship

Previously, Tables 2.2 and 2.3 showed *perfectly* consistent relationships: Everyone having a particular rehearsal score had the same recall score. In the real world, however, such perfect consistency does not occur. Nonetheless, a relationship can be present, even if the association between scores is not perfectly consistent. There can be some *degree* of consistency so that as the scores on one variable change, the scores on the other variable *tend* to change in a consistent fashion. The extent to which a relationship is consistent is called its strength: The **strength of a relationship** is the extent to which there tends to be one value of Y consistently associated with one and only one value of X. It is the *degree of association* between the variables.

For example, Table 2.5 shows two relationships that differ in their strength: The data on the left show a rather inconsistent or "weak" relationship, because there is barely a pattern of fewer errors occurring with more rehearsal: Not every increase in rehearsal scores is matched with the same decrease in errors, often the same error score appears with different rehearsal scores, and often very different error scores occur with the same rehearsal score. However, the data on the right-hand side of Table 2.5 show a more consistent, "stronger" relationship: There is only one or close to one error score found at a particular rehearsal score, and the same error scores do not occur with different rehearsal scores. In other words, there tends to be one batch of similar recall scores at one rehearsal score, and a different batch of similar recall scores at the next rehearsal score. We'll discuss strength again in later chapters, but for now, a stronger relationship is closer to

TABLE 2.5 Examples of a Weaker Relationship and a Stronger Relationship Between Rehearsal and Recall

Weaker relationship		*Stronger relationship*	
Number of rehearsals	*Number of errors*	*Number of rehearsals*	*Number of errors*
1	12	1	12
1	6	1	12
2	11	2	9
2	8	2	8
3	10	3	7
3	6	3	6
4	8	4	5
4	6	4	4

the kind of perfect pairing shown back in Tables 2.2 and 2.3; a weaker one is closer to a pattern of no relationship, as in Table 2.4.

> **REMEMBER**   A relationship is *stronger* the more that one or close to one *Y* score is paired with each *X* score.

There are two reasons that a relationship is not perfectly consistent. First, there may be external, extraneous influences operating on the participants. For example, perhaps a sudden, distracting noise occurred while one participant rehearsed the list three times, but not when another participant rehearsed three times. Because of this, their rehearsals are not equally effective, resulting in different recall. The more that this happens for more participants, the more often we'll see different recall scores paired with the same rehearsal score, resulting in a weaker relationship. If the noise never occurred, however, then when participants rehearsed the same amount, they'd be more likely to produce the same recall scores, producing a stronger relationship. (A major aspect of research methods, beginning in the next chapter, is learning how to eliminate—*control*—such external influences.)

The other reason for weaker relationships is individual differences. The term **individual differences** refers to the fact that no two individuals are identical and that differences in genetic makeup, experience, intelligence, personality, and many other variables all influence behavior in a given situation. Because of individual differences, a particular law of nature operates in *more or less* the same way for all members of a population. Thus, for example, our participants will exhibit individual differences in terms of their basic memory ability, causing them to have different recall scores, *even when they rehearse to the same extent*. The more that participants differ in memory ability, the more their recall scores will differ at the same rehearsal score, so that we'll see a less consistent, weaker relationship. Conversely, if everyone at a given rehearsal score has the same memory ability, they should recall the list to the same degree. Then, recall scores will change only when rehearsal changes, producing a stronger relationship. (Later, you'll also learn ways of controlling individual differences.)

> **REMEMBER**   Individual differences and changes in external influences produce a weaker relationship.

Mathematically, the scores from two variables can form a relationship of any strength, from perfectly consistent to no association, in which case there is no relationship. Real research, however, never produces a perfectly consistent relationship because we can never perfectly control external influences and individual differences. Instead, we see relationships that are consistent only to some degree. Therefore, it is never enough merely to say that we have observed a relationship—we must also consider the strength of the relationship.

We'll discuss relationships more in later chapters. For now, it is important to understand why, as the next section shows, a relationship in the data provides evidence that a law of nature is at work.

INTERPRETING A RELATIONSHIP

In case it hasn't been obvious: *The goal of most research is to demonstrate and then examine the predicted relationship*. This is because if Y is influenced by or otherwise related to X by a law of nature, then *different* amounts or categories of Y will occur when *different* amounts or categories of X occur. Therefore, we translate our general hypothesis about a law of nature into a specific predicted relationship between scores. If we then demonstrate the predicted relationship (confirming the prediction), we have obtained empirical evidence that confirms our hypothesis. By confirming our hypothesis, we have evidence that the laws of nature do operate in the way we think they do.

Thus, we first examine the relationship between the scores in the sample. However, remember we must always be cautious and skeptical. Therefore, the data in the previous relationships *apparently* confirm that memory does operate as we've proposed; *apparently*, as more rehearsal occurs, better recall scores also occur. (In the next chapter, we discuss all of the reasons that we might be misinterpreting these scores.)

With real data, however, we do not merely eyeball the scores as we have done here. Researchers are invariably confronted with a mind-boggling array of different numbers that may have a relationship hidden in it. Therefore, at this point, we employ statistical procedures to bring order to the chaos. We first apply various procedures that are used to describe and summarize the sample data. (As we'll see in Chapter 7, such procedures are called "descriptive statistics.") Using them, we answer such questions as: Is the predicted relationship present? Do the Y scores increase or decrease as X increases? What is the typical or average Y score that is paired with each X score? How strong is the relationship? And so on.

Considering the strength of the relationship is especially important, because it suggests the role that our variables play versus the impact that other external influences or individual differences have. Remember that individual differences and outside influences weaken a relationship. Therefore, the stronger the relationship, the *less* of a role these factors must be playing. For example, if we found a perfectly consistent relationship between amount of rehearsal and recall scores, then we could argue that rehearsal is the *only* variable that determines good or poor memory: The only time we see a difference in recall scores is when rehearsal scores change, so recall must depend *entirely* on the amount of rehearsal. Individual differences (such as memory ability) and extraneous influences (perhaps random noises in the room) are probably not operating here. This is because, for example, it is likely that two people with different memory abilities would end up rehearsing to the same degree. But, if they still produce the same recall score, then, literally, differences in memory ability do not make a difference in recall scores. Likewise, the stronger the relationship, the more we assume that all other such factors are not operating.

Conversely, a weaker relationship would mean that these factors *are* playing a role, so amount of rehearsal is a less important variable when it comes to memory. This is because we assume that nature is *lawful* so that *everything* has a cause. So, if two people rehearse to the same extent but get different recall scores, *something* must be causing this difference. Therefore, it must be that other factors (such as differences in memory ability or random noises) are operating. The weaker the relationship (the more that people differ when they rehearse to the same degree), the less important their rehearsal apparently is, and the greater the importance of these other factors.

By observing and understanding the predicted sample relationship as above, we *begin* to have evidence that supports our hypothesis. After all, we have observed one instance, at least, (our sample) where nature seems to operate as we have proposed. However, our interpretation does not stop there. Using the sample data, we seek to *infer* that the observed relationship would also be found for everyone in the population, if we could measure them. But remember, a sample might not be *representative*. Therefore, again we use statistical procedures, essentially deciding whether to believe that the sample is representative so that we would find a similar relationship in the population. (We'll see in Chapter 7 that such procedures are called "inferential statistics.") If we can argue that our sample data reflects the relationship that the population would produce, we can argue that everyone in the population would behave in this way. "Everyone in the population" constitutes a part of nature. Therefore, by concluding that this relationship holds for the population, we are describing a law of nature: For everyone, the laws of nature operate such that higher rehearsal scores are associated with better recall scores.

By claiming that our observations provide evidence for the general case, we are generalizing. To **generalize** means to apply conclusions to other individuals or situations. When interpreting research, we generalize in two ways. First, as above, we generalize the relationship between the *variables* in the *sample* to a relationship between the *variables* in the *population*. Second, we then generalize the relationship between the *variables* to the relationship between the *hypothetical constructs* we originally set out to study. That is, we translate the scores back into the behaviors and events they reflect and then argue that a similar relationship would be found with other variables and operational definitions. Thus, we want to conclude that as scores on *any* variable reflecting rehearsal increase, scores on any variable reflecting better memory will also increase. If we can make this claim, we have come full circle, confirming the original hypothesis that nature lawfully operates in such a way that when more of the process we call rehearsal occurs, more of the reaction we call memory also occurs.

REMEMBER   The focus of research is to examine and then generalize relationships.

SUMMARY OF THE FLOW OF A STUDY

Now you can see how it all comes together. A typical research study involves translating from the general to the specific and then back to the general again, as illustrated by the diagram in Figure 2.1.

Begin with broad hypothetical constructs regarding a behavior. Then, search the literature to be sure the hypothesis is acceptable and to obtain ideas for the best design to use. Then, narrow the scope by identifying the applicable population and specify the hypothesis as a relationship between variables. Next, whittle down the situation to a very specific one by creating operational definitions of the variables, and then predict the relationship between the scores that you seek. Then, select a "random sample" from the population, and develop the method for measuring participants. After obtaining the scores, identify and examine the relationship between the scores in the sample. If you find the relationship between the scores in the sample, begin widening the scope by deciding whether

FIGURE 2.1   The Steps in a Typical Research Study

The flow of a study is from a general hypothesis to the specifics of the study, and then back to the general hypothesis.

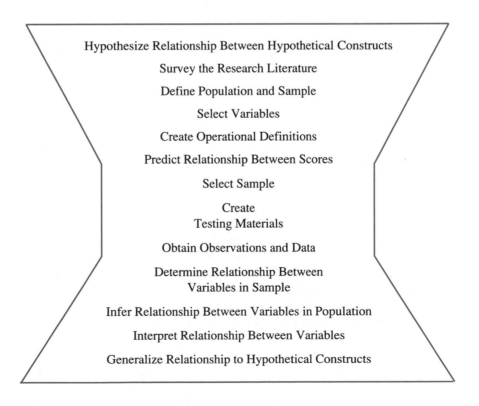

Hypothesize Relationship Between Hypothetical Constructs

Survey the Research Literature

Define Population and Sample

Select Variables

Create Operational Definitions

Predict Relationship Between Scores

Select Sample

Create
Testing Materials

Obtain Observations and Data

Determine Relationship Between
Variables in Sample

Infer Relationship Between Variables in Population

Interpret Relationship Between Variables

Generalize Relationship to Hypothetical Constructs

the relationship is likely to be found in the population. If so, infer that the variables are related in this way for everyone in the population. Then, interpret this relationship, describing how the scores are related and what the consistency of the relationship indicates about nature in general. Finally, on the basis of this inference, generalize to the relationship in nature involving the hypothetical constructs that you began with.

Note that this flow from the general to the specific and back to the general is mirrored in the organization that psychologists use when publishing research reports in the psychological literature. This organization was created by the American Psychological Association or APA, the national association of psychologists in the United States, and is known as "APA style" or "APA format." (This format is presented in Appendix A in detail.) A published report will basically follow the above discussion, although the sequence may not be so obvious. The trick to reading the literature is to look for what the author is saying about each of the above steps.

When reading the literature, you will come across a variety of research designs because there are many ways to demonstrate a relationship. However, research can be broken into two major types: *experiments* and *descriptive studies*.

EXPERIMENTAL RESEARCH METHODS

Recall that a causal hypothesis proposes the causes of a behavior. To test such a hypothesis, we usually employ *experimental methods*. The logic of an experiment is this: If my hypothesis is correct, then if I *do* this or that to participants, I should see an influence or change in their behaviors. Therefore, in an **experiment**, the researcher actively changes or *manipulates* one variable and measures the participants' resulting behavior by measuring another variable. Then, we look to see if the manipulation changed the behavior so that the predicted relationship is produced.

Although usually an experiment implies a laboratory setting, this need not be the case. (And, though the term *laboratory* might conjure up images of elaborate equipment and mad scientists, a laboratory is simply a location in which the researcher can conduct a study while controlling the situation.) Instead, the hallmark of experimental methods is that researchers manipulate certain aspects of a situation. Essentially, they try to *make* a relationship occur by changing one variable and then seeing if scores on the other variable change in a consistent fashion.

Here's an extremely simple example: If, originally, we had proposed that more rehearsal *causes* better retention, we could manipulate the amount that participants rehearse a list of words to see if it does change their recall. For example, to compare rehearsing a list 1, 2, or 3 times, we might randomly select three samples of participants. We'd have one sample rehearse the list once and then recall it; we'd have another sample rehearse the list twice and then recall it, and so on.

If we understand how nature operates, we should see that higher recall scores occur with greater amounts of rehearsal.

There are names for the components of any experiment, and you will use them daily.

The Independent Variable

An **independent variable** is a variable that is directly changed or manipulated by the experimenter. Implicitly, it is the variable that we think causes a change in behavior. Above, we manipulate rehearsal because we think it influences recall, so amount of rehearsal is the independent variable. You can remember the independent variable as the variable that the experimenter manipulates *independent* of what the participant wishes: Some of our participants will rehearse 3 times whether they want to or not. (An independent variable is also called a **factor**.)

Following the same procedures discussed earlier in this chapter, we select an independent variable because it is relevant to our hypothetical construct. Then we create an operational definition of the variable, stating how we will measure and manipulate it. An independent variable can be *quantitative* (manipulating the *amount* of the variable that is present), or an independent variable can be *qualitative* (manipulating a *quality* or *attribute* of the situation). For example, if in a different study, we compare the performance of students who rehearse the list in the library to those who study it in a classroom, we are manipulating a quality of the room.

Although there is an unlimited variety of independent variables, common approaches to manipulating them include changing a physical aspect of stimuli (e.g., changing the color or brightness of geometric shapes or the loudness or pitch of tones that people must recognize) or changing the meaning of stimuli (e.g., manipulating whether words to be remembered have similar meanings or have a positive or negative emotional connotation). Sometimes researchers manipulate the environment (e.g., changing the color of the walls in a room where participants study, altering the furniture arrangement in an office, or varying the number of people present when someone gives a speech). Or, we change the attributes of the stimuli or task (e.g., providing different instructions or varying the rewards or punishments given); or, we alter the social setting in which participants are placed.

***

REMEMBER   A researcher changes the *independent variable* to produce a corresponding change in participants' behavior and thus demonstrate a relationship.

Conditions of the Independent Variable

An independent variable is the *overall* variable we manipulate that may have many different amounts or categories in it. A **condition** is a specific amount or category of the independent variable that the researcher selects to create the situation under which the participants are observed. Thus, although our independent variable of amount of rehearsal could be any amount, our conditions were 1, 2, or 3 rehearsals. Likewise, if we compare testing in a classroom to that in a library room, the independent variable is type of room, and the conditions are "classroom" and "library." (A condition is also known as a **level** or a **treatment**.)

> **REMEMBER**   The independent variable is the entire causal variable of interest. Conditions are the specific amounts or categories of the variable under which participants are tested.

The other variable we examine in an experiment is called the *dependent variable*.

The Dependent Variable

The **dependent variable** reflects some aspect of participants' behavior. You can identify the dependent variable as the one in which scores are presumably caused or influenced by the independent variable, so scores on the dependent variable *depend* on the conditions of the independent variable. We've proposed that recall depends on amount of rehearsal, so recall scores are our dependent variable. (The dependent variable is also called the **dependent measure**.)

As with everything else, you must operationally define any dependent variable. Most of the time, the dependent variable *quantifies* a behavior: It measures the amount or degree of a behavior—how strongly it is exhibited, or its frequency of occurrence. At other times, the variable *qualifies* the behavior, distinguishing one behavior from another in terms of a quality or characteristic. For example, if we look at the causes of different personalities, personality type is the dependent variable, even though instead of measuring more or less personality, we would just identify different ones.

Essentially, the dependent variable measures participants' responses to the particular situation created by a condition. Some of the dependent variables you'll find in the literature include those that measure physical actions, perceptual and sensory responses, or internal physiological reactions. They may also measure how well or how often a behavior is performed. Other measures include asking participants to describe the feelings, beliefs, or attitudes that a situation elicits, or to indicate their social reactions to, or judgments about, others.

> **REMEMBER**   The *dependent variable* measures participants' behavior under a condition of the independent variable.

Thus, after conducting an experiment, we hope to see a relationship such that changing the independent variable results in a corresponding change in the dependent variable. A useful way to diagram an experiment is shown in Table 2.6. Each column represents a condition under which some participants are tested (here, after either 1, 2, or 3 rehearsals of the list). Each score in a column is a participant's score on the dependent variable when tested under this condition. (Here, scores reflect the number of items correctly recalled from the list.)

To see whether there's a relationship, think of the condition under which participants are tested as their "score" on the independent variable. Then look to see if, as the conditions of the independent variable change, scores on the dependent variable change in a consistent fashion. Looking at Table 2.6, we see the predicted relationship: Low recall scores occur with a rehearsal score of 1, medium recall scores are associated with 2 rehearsals, and higher recall scores occur with 3 rehearsals. Thus, there is a relationship in an experiment when one batch of similar recall scores occurs in one condition, but a different batch of similar scores occurs in another condition, and so on. If we find a relationship, then, as always, we generalize from the relationship between the variables in the sample to the broader relationship between the hypothetical constructs in the population.

REMEMBER   In experiments, we look for a relationship such that as we change the conditions of the independent variable, participants' scores on the dependent variable change in a consistent fashion.

True versus Quasi-Experiments

Although all experiments have the above components, there are two major types of independent variables and, therefore, two types of experiments. On the one

TABLE 2.6 Diagram of an Experiment Involving the Independent Variable of Number of Rehearsals of a List and the Dependent Variable of Number of Items Correctly Recalled from the List

Each column contains participants' scores measured under one condition of the independent variable.

Independent variable: number of rehearsals

	Condition 1: *1 rehearsal*	*Condition 2:* *2 rehearsals*	*Condition 3:* *3 rehearsals*
Dependent variable: number of items correctly recalled →	6	9	11
	7	10	11
	5	8	12
	6	9	13
	7	9	10
	6	10	12

hand, in a **true experiment** there is a **true independent variable**. Here, the experimenter manipulates the variable by doing something *to* participants. You can recognize a true independent variable because participants can be randomly assigned to any condition. **Random assignment** means that the condition of the independent variable a participant experiences is determined by random chance. Random assignment is a second step that occurs after we use random sampling to select the individuals for a study. For example, we might write the names of the rehearsal conditions (1, 2, or 3) on slips of paper and, when a participant we've randomly selected arrives for the study, we would select a slip to randomly assign him or her to one of the conditions.

Although a true independent variable is something that a researcher exposes participants to, there are many behavior-influencing variables that we cannot manipulate in this way, such as age, race, background, or personality. Such variables are called **quasi-independent variables**, and studies that employ them are called **quasi-experiments**. A quasi-independent variable is *not* something that the experimenter does to participants, and so they cannot be randomly assigned to conditions. Instead, participants are assigned to a particular condition because they *already* qualify for that condition based upon some *inherent* characteristic. For example, say in a different study we hypothesize that growing older causes higher recall scores. We can't randomly select participants and *make* some of them 20 years old and others 40 years old. Instead, we would randomly select one sample of 20-year-olds and one sample of 40-year-olds. Similarly, if we wanted to examine whether a qualitative variable such as gender was related to recall, we would select a sample of females and a sample of males.

REMEMBER   A *true experiment* with a *true independent variable* allows *random assignment* of participants to any condition. A *quasi-experiment* with a *quasi-independent variable* involves an inherent characteristic of participants that does not allow random assignment.

Note that with both a true or quasi-independent variable, the experimenter always determines a participant's "score" on the independent variable. Thus, students who rehearsed once have a score of 1 on our rehearsal variable, or people in the 20-year-olds sample have a score of 20 on our age variable. Thus, both a true and a quasi-experiment have the same purpose: to demonstrate a relationship in which as the conditions of the independent variable change, participants' scores on the dependent variable also change in a consistent fashion. As we'll see in the next chapter, however, there are some major differences in each type of design.

Table 2.7 will help you to remember the previous terminology used to describe experiments.

TABLE 2.7 Summary of Terminology Used in Experiments

Term	Definition
Independent variable	The variable manipulated to cause a change in a behavior
Condition	A specific amount or category of the independent variable that participants experience
Dependent variable	The variable measuring the behavior being changed
True independent variable	Produces conditions to which participants can be randomly assigned
Quasi-independent variable	Produces conditions to which participants cannot be randomly assigned
Random assignment	Using random chance to determine which condition a participant will experience

DESCRIPTIVE RESEARCH METHODS

In addition to testing causal hypotheses, recall that we may also create a descriptive hypothesis that describes a behavior without identifying its causes. Researchers test such hypotheses using *descriptive* or *nonexperimental methods*. In a **descriptive design**, we simply observe behaviors or relationships. In particular, we do *not* manipulate or change any of the variables of interest. The logic behind descriptive methods is that if my hypothesis is correct, then I should observe the predicted characteristics of the behavior, participants, or situation. To test such hypotheses, we may interview participants, have them complete questionnaires, directly measure their behavior, or examine their history. We may study only one subject or conduct a survey of many people. Or, we may surreptitiously watch people or animals in their natural habitat.

The most common descriptive method is a correlational design. In a **correlational design,** we measure participants' scores on at least two variables (which, as usual, we operationally define) and then determine whether the scores form the predicted relationship. For example, we'd have a correlational study if we left it up to participants how many times they rehearsed a list, and simply asked them how many times they rehearsed, measured their recall of the list, and then looked for a relationship between the two variables. Or, in a different study, we would have a correlational design if we measured participants' career choices and their personality type, asking, "Is career choice related to personality type?" Notice, here we have no independent or dependent variable, and we simply look to see if Y scores consistently change as the X scores change.

> **REMEMBER**   In a *correlational design*, the researcher passively measures both variables, asking whether a relationship can be *found*. But in an *experiment*, the researcher actively changes one variable and measures the other, asking whether a relationship can be *produced*.

A correlational design may test a hypothesis that specific variables are related, or it may be to discover which variables are related. In doing so, researchers often look for a relationship between scores on two tests or questionnaires (e.g., determining whether higher IQ scores occur with higher creativity test scores). We can also "correlate" test scores with some measure of physical or mental performance (e.g., relating personality type to problem-solving ability). Or, we might relate a participant's record to his or her performance (e.g., relating school-attendance records to measures of subsequent job success). As always, if we find a relationship, we then generalize from the specific variables we observe to a more general description in terms of hypothetical constructs and broad behaviors.

Correlational studies are often especially useful for meeting the goal of *predicting* behaviors. This is because by not actively manipulating variables or otherwise tinkering with the situation, we may observe more natural behaviors. Then, once we've established a relationship through a study, we can use an individual's score on one variable to predict their score (and corresponding behavior) on the other variable. For example, after our research we'll know the typical recall score that occurs with a particular rehearsal amount. Using this relationship, we would predict this recall score for other people when they rehearse a particular amount.

Not all descriptive designs, however, are correlational designs. Sometimes the hypothesis is simply that certain behaviors or situations operate in a certain way. Then we merely observe participants on one or more variables, without predicting that they form a relationship. Thus, say that we wanted to examine different ways of rehearsing information, so we asked the more applied question of how people study for a college exam. We might then surreptitiously observe people while they study, simply to describe this behavior. Or, we might distribute a survey regarding various variables that we think constitute studying to then describe what studying is, develop theoretical constructs, or derive additional hypotheses for a later study.

> **REMEMBER**   *Descriptive designs* are used to demonstrate a relationship, predict behaviors, and describe a behavior or participant.

PUTTING IT ALL TOGETHER

We will discuss descriptive and experimental designs in detail in later chapters. For now, think of them as part of your overall mental checklist of the issues to consider when designing a study. Thus, after checking that you meet the rules of science from the previous chapter, then, as shown in Checklist 2.1, perform the steps from this chapter: Begin by searching the literature, identifying the population and considering selection of the sample. Next, translate the hypothetical constructs into variables and then translate the variables into operational definitions. Then decide whether you have a descriptive or causal hypothesis, and so design a descriptive study or an experiment. For the latter, identify whether it is a true or quasi-experiment. Then apply the overall logic of research to generalize the results. Remember that usually the goal is to observe a relationship, first in the sample, and then to infer that a similar relationship would be found if we could study everyone in the population. Because scores reflect behaviors and events, by describing the scores that would be found in the population, we are actually describing the behavior of everyone of interest in a particular situation. Describing the behavior of everyone in a particular situation *is* describing how a law of nature operates.

CHECKLIST 2.1 **Questions to consider when designing research**

Overview of the Study
- Have you searched the relevant literature?
- What population is involved, and how will you select participants?
- What hypothetical constructs are involved?
- What variables reflect the constructs?
- What is the operational definition of the variables of the study?
- Should you conduct an experiment or a descriptive design?
- Is the experiment a true or quasi-experiment?
- Will the results generalize back to the hypothetical constructs?

CHAPTER SUMMARY

1. The *research literature* contains research results, terminology, definitions, hypotheses, and theories.

2. The *Psychological Abstracts*, the *Social Science Citation Index*, *computerized literature searches*, and *review articles* are major tools for searching the literature.

3. A *population* is the group of all individuals to which a hypothesis applies. A *sample* is a subset of the population that is actually studied.

4. *Simple random sampling* is selecting participants so that all members of the population have an equal chance of being selected. *Systematic random sampling* is selecting every *n*th individual from a list of the population.

5. The goal of random sampling is to produce a *representative sample* in which participants have the same characteristics and scores as the population. By chance, however, a sample may be *unrepresentative*.

6. A *hypothetical construct* is an abstract concept used in a particular theoretical manner to relate different behaviors according to their underlying features or causes.

7. A hypothetical construct is studied by measuring a *variable*, which is any measurable aspect of a behavior or influence on behavior that may change.

8. An *operational definition* defines a construct or variable in terms of the operations used to measure it.

9. Most studies focus on demonstrating a *relationship*, a pattern in which, as the scores on one variable change, scores on another variable also change in a consistent fashion.

10. The *strength* of a relationship is the degree of consistent association between the scores on the two variables.

11. The term *individual differences* refers to the fact that no two individuals are identical.

12. The strength of a relationship is decreased by fluctuating external influences, and by individual differences between participants. Therefore, the strength of a relationship is used to gauge the importance of our variables on the behavior versus the impact of these other factors.

13. We *generalize* the results of a study, first by using the relationship between the variables in a sample to infer the relationship between the variables that would be found in the population. Second, based on this relationship, we make inferences about the hypothetical constructs.

14. Causal hypotheses are tested using *experiments*, in which the researcher demonstrates a relationship by manipulating the *independent variable* and then measuring participants' scores on the *dependent variable*.

15. Each specific amount or category of the independent variable is a *condition*.

16. In a *true experiment*, with a *true independent variable*, participants can be randomly assigned to any condition. *Random assignment* means that the condition a participant experiences is determined in a random manner.

17. In a *quasi-experiment*, with a *quasi-independent variable*, participants cannot be randomly assigned to any condition because they already belong to a particular condition based upon some inherent characteristic.

18. Descriptive hypotheses are tested using *descriptive designs*, in which no variables are manipulated. Instead, variables are simply measured as they occur. In a *correlational study*, two or more variables are measured to determine whether the predicted relationship occurs.

KEY TERMS   (with page references)

condition 51	quasi-independent variable 54
correlational design 55	random assignment 54
dependent measure 52	relationship 42
dependent variable 52	representative sample 37
descriptive design 55	research literature 33
experiment 50	review article 35
factor 51	sample 37
generalize 48	simple random sampling 37
hypothetical construct 39	*Social Science Citation Index* 35
independent variable 51	strength of a relationship 45
individual differences 46	systematic random sampling 37
level 52	treatment 52
operational definition 41	true experiment 54
population 36	true independent variable 54
Psychological Abstracts 34	variable 40
quasi-experiment 54	

REVIEW QUESTIONS

1. Why is it necessary to conduct a literature search when beginning a study?

2. (a) What information does *Psychological Abstracts* contain? (b) What information does the *Social Science Citation Index* provide? (c) What is a "review article"?

3. How would you go about finding literature that investigates the connection between violence in television shows and heightened aggressiveness in adolescents?

4. In question 3, you find a useful article that was published in 1997. (a) How can you use this article to find related articles that occurred prior to it? (b) How can you find related articles that were published after 1997?

5. You wish to measure the aggressiveness of a sample of adolescents. Other than creating the test, what two approaches can you take to find an acceptable test of aggressiveness?

6. (a) What is a representative sample, and how do they occur? (b) What is an unrepresentative sample, and how do they occur?

7. What is the difference between simple random sampling and systematic random sampling?

8. (a) What does the term *hypothetical construct* mean? (b) How do hypothetical constructs simplify nature? (c) Why does incorporating hypothetical constructs help you create scientifically acceptable hypotheses?

9. (a) What is the difference between a hypothetical construct and a variable? (b) What is the difference between a variable and an operational definition. (c) Why are operational definitions important?

10. (a) How can you recognize when a relationship exists between two variables? (b) What is the difference between a strong relationship and a weak relationship?

11. How do we use the scores in a sample relationship to test a hypothesis about hypothetical constructs?

12. (a) What is the difference between descriptive and experimental research? (b) What is the primary consideration for selecting one approach over the other?

13. (a) What is the difference between the independent variable and the conditions of the independent variable? (b) What is the dependent variable?

14. (a) What is the difference between a true independent variable and a quasi-independent variable? (b) What is random assignment?

15. (a) What is the difference between a correlational study and other descriptive research methods? (b) What is the difference between an experiment and a correlational study?

APPLICATION QUESTIONS

16. In study A, a researcher gives groups of participants various amounts of alcohol and then observes any decrease in their ability to walk. In study B, a researcher notes the various amounts of alcohol that people drink at a party, and then observes any decrease in their ability to walk. What is the name for each type of design? Why?

17. In each of the following, identify the independent variable, the conditions, and the dependent variable: (a) Studying whether scores on a final exam are influenced by whether background music is played softly, is played loudly, or is absent. (b) Comparing freshmen, sophomores, juniors, and seniors with respect to how much fun they have while attending college. (c) Comparing whether being first-born, second-born, or third-born is related to intelligence. (d) Studying whether length of daily exposure to a sun lamp (15 minutes versus 60 minutes) accounts for differences in self-reported depression. (e) Investigating whether being in a room with blue walls, green walls, red walls, or beige walls influences aggressive behavior in a group of adolescents.

18. In question 17, which are true experiments and which are quasi-experiments?

19. For the following data sets, which sample or samples have a relationship present?

Sample A		Sample B		Sample C		Sample D	
X	Y	X	Y	X	Y	X	Y
1	1	20	40	13	20	92	71
1	1	20	42	13	19	93	77
1	1	22	40	13	18	93	77
2	2	22	41	13	17	95	79
2	2	23	40	13	15	96	74
3	3	24	40	13	14	97	71
3	3	24	42	13	13	98	69

20. In which sample in question 19 is there the strongest relationship? How do you know?

21. In studying memory processes, to represent the population of college students, you select a random sample of psychology majors. (a) Why are you likely to have an unrepresentative sample? (b) Even if you select from all college students, why might you still obtain an unrepresentative sample?

22. We find a weak relationship between an independent and dependent variable. (a) Explain how individual differences between participants in the same condition could weaken the relationship. (b) Explain how fluctuating external influences could weaken the relationship. (c) Why does a weak relationship suggest that the independent variable does not play a major role in the dependent behavior? (d) Why would a very strong relationship suggest that the independent variable does have a major role?

23. A student proposes studying the differences between men and women in their ability to recall a list, and wants to conduct a true experiment. Why is this a problem?

DISCUSSION QUESTIONS

24. In question 17 on page 60, assume that we find only a moderately strong relationship each time. For each experiment, identify an external influence and an individual difference that might be weakening the relationship.

25. In the past, nurses wore hats as part of their uniforms. A nurse claims that then patients followed her instructions better than they do now without the hat. (a) What hypothetical constructs might this situation reflect? (b) Translate the hypothetical constructs into variables, and operationally define them. (c) Outline an experiment for studying this situation in the laboratory. (d) Outline a correlational design for studying this in a natural hospital setting.

26. Perform a literature search on the issue described in discussion question 25 above.

27. Perform a search of recent literature on aggressiveness in adolescents as it relates to violence on television.

28. Create a descriptive hypothesis about a behavior and describe how you would test it.

29. Create a causal hypothesis about a behavior and describe how you would test it.

3

Evaluating A Study: Is It Reliable and Valid?

GETTING STARTED

To understand this chapter, recall the following:

- From Chapter 1, recall how a potential rival hypothesis can weaken a conclusion.
- From Chapter 2, understand the flow of a study, what a relationship is, and how experimental and descriptive designs differ.

Your goals in this chapter are to learn:

- The strategy for critically evaluating a study.
- What is meant by reliability and the various types of validity.
- How participant, environmental, researcher, and measurement variables threaten reliability and validity.
- How to control threats to reliability and validity.
- What a confounding variable is and how it interferes with conclusions about causality.
- What the difficulties are in showing causality and proving a hypothesis.
- How experimental and descriptive designs differ in terms of reliability and validity.

Recall that a rule of science is that for any study conducted by ourselves or someone else, we critically evaluate it in a cautious and skeptical manner. In this chapter, we first discuss how to go about evaluating a study and what flaws to look for. Then we'll introduce the terms that researchers use to communicate common flaws (centered on the terms "reliability" and "validity"). Once you understand the basics, we'll then see the particular flaws that are common in experiments or descriptive designs, and how they impact on the interpretation of each.

IDENTIFYING POTENTIAL FLAWS WHEN DESIGNING A STUDY

In Chapter 2, we saw what is *apparently* a pretty straightforward process: From our hypothesis we predict and then examine a relationship between variables, and then use the relationship to draw conclusions about the hypothesis. You may be wondering why then, in Chapter 1, I made such a big deal of the potential flaws in research and the need for skeptical and critical evaluation of every research finding. Well, although *overall* research is straightforward, it is in the specifics of a study that all sorts of errors can creep in. This is because nature is very complex, so that any research situation can be loaded with all sorts of unwanted influences. The reason that research is not such a simple process is that such influences in a study are a flaw that may mislead us about a behavior and thus cause us to draw an incorrect conclusion about a hypothesis.

Because we could measure these extraneous influences, we'll call them variables. An **extraneous variable** is an aspect of a study that can influence the results, but is not a variable we wish to examine. The previous chapter actually introduced the two general sources of extraneous variables—individual differences among the participants and external influences that operate on them. There we saw that fluctuations in variables from these sources may reduce the strength of a relationship. In fact, as we'll see, these variables can be operating to such an extent that we can not even make sense out of the relationship. Therefore, *the* issue in designing research is to identify and control extraneous variables.

REMEMBER   The key to designing good research is to control *extraneous variables.*

To see how the influence of extraneous variables creeps in, let's design a study. Say that while in the student lounge, you observe that your friends are more successful at meeting members of the opposite sex than you are (aren't they always?). You believe this is because they are better-looking than you (aren't they always!). You decide to investigate this topic and so, of course, you go to the literature. However, not much has been written about dating at your school! But, if you think about it, you've observed part of the general behavior that psychologists call "first impressions." Sure enough, there is a large literature in social psychology dealing with the hypothetical constructs of first impressions and attractiveness, showing that greater attractiveness does lead to more positive first impressions (e.g., Eagly, Ashmore, MaKijani & Longo, 1991). Although this finding holds for *both* genders, let's first examine the descriptive hypothesis that females form more positive first impressions of males who are more physically attractive. (If this hypothesis offends you because it suggests people are shallow and insensitive, remember that scientists must be open-minded and accept nature as it is, warts and all.)

Your first step in testing this hypothesis should be to take a moment and think about the behavior.

Considering the Context of the Behavior

Recall that when designing a study, you should "play psychologist." This means that you should consider the overall context or situation in which the behavior occurs. Then, using your knowledge of psychology and some common sense, try to identify all of the factors that might influence the behavior and your study of it. This will not only provide numerous ideas for the specific study, but it will also allow you to foresee potential problems. So, what's involved when a woman forms a first impression and judges a man as attractive?

First, what might a female consider when determining a man's attractiveness? She probably considers his face, but also the color and style of his hair, his height and weight, his posture, his body's shape, his style of dress, his cleanliness, and so on. She might also consider his behavior: Is he silent or talkative, what does he say and how does he say it, is he friendly or condescending? Does he exhibit nervous tics or irritating mannerisms? Does he make eye contact? Does he smile? Does he make physical contact, and how? (Is his handshake firm or mushy?)

The personal characteristics of the woman can also influence her perceptions. Her height and weight determine whether she judges a male as tall or short, heavy or thin. Also, is she different from him in age, style of dress, educational level, culture, or language? Is she actively seeking to meet men, or is she happily married? Further, how does she form a first impression? It may involve judging him to be intelligent, creative, sexy, likable, interesting, decisive, or some combination of these qualities. How long after she meets him is she beyond first impressions and getting to know him?

We should also consider the environment for the meeting. Is she interviewing him for a job, or is the meeting social? Is the meeting in a crowded room or an empty one? Does it occur at a shopping mall, a party, or a funeral? Is the place noisy or quiet, dark or well-lit? Remember, too, that we must somehow observe her behavior. Doing so may make her nervous and interfere with her "normal" reactions. Does the gender of the researcher make her more or less self-conscious? How will we measure her impressions? Will she answer questions honestly?

The above is only a partial list of the many questions to consider when studying how a female forms a first impression and judges a male's attractiveness. Each question refers to an aspect of the situation that can potentially influence a woman's perceptions, so on the one hand, these are the things to consider when deciding on the exact study to conduct. On the other hand, as we'll see, if we ignore any of them, they can turn out to be extraneous variables that ultimately mislead us.

Notice, however, that these questions center around four general components found in any study. The *researcher* observes the *participants* in a specific *environment* and applies a *measurement procedure*. When designing a study, always consider the variables related to each component.

1. **Participant variables:** The personal characteristics and experiences of participants that may influence their responses.
2. **Researcher variables:** The behaviors and characteristics of the researcher that may influence the reactions of participants.
3. **Environmental variables:** The aspects of the environment that can influence scores.
4. **Measurement variables:** The aspects of the stimuli presented or the measurement procedure employed that may influence scores.

It is by dealing with these variables that we reduce a complex situation into a controlled and understandable one. Therefore, much of designing a study involves deciding how to deal with these variables.

Refining the Design

Let's first identify the population (and the sample). Physical appearance is probably irrelevant to blind people or children when forming first impressions, so let's limit the population to adult, sighted females who are citizens of this country. We must locate a random sample of such women, and given your initial observations at the lounge, we'll sample from among the women attending your college. In fact, we'll go to the most common source for participants—the current introductory psychology course.

To actually test our hypothesis, we must observe our participants when they first meet a man, to see if they do form more positive impressions when they feel he is more attractive. How do we do this? The answer is to operationally define our constructs in terms of specific variables, and then to operationally define each variable in terms of how we will measure it.

From the literature search, it appears that a good way to determine a male's physical attractiveness is to measure the variable of his "facial attractiveness." There are many ways to operationally define facial attractiveness: we might rate it ourselves or have a panel of judges rate it. Instead, let's directly ask female participants how attractive a man is. Say that we also decide that an important component of a first impression is how much he is initially "liked" by the woman. We might measure the variable of "likability" by determining whether a female agrees that he meets some definition of likability, or by recording the number of times she uses "like" when describing him. Instead, let's simply ask her how much she likes him.

Finally, we must devise a way to quantify exactly how much a woman likes the man and how attractive she finds him. From the literature, we see that a common method is to have participants complete a rating of the man. Therefore, to keep things (very) simple, we'll have participants complete these two questions:

How much do you like this person?

1   2   3   4   5   6

DISLIKE   LIKE

How attractive is this person's face?

1   2   3   4   5   6

UNATTRACTIVE   ATTRACTIVE

Now we have our prediction: At an initial meeting between a male and our participants, women who produce higher attractiveness ratings for a man should also produce higher likability scores for him. Completing the design involves defining the individual components of "an initial meeting between a male and our participants." Say we define "participants" as 20 females from an introductory psychology class. We define the "meeting" as a social, one-on-one introduction, and "initial" as lasting about 2 minutes. And we define "meeting males" as bringing each woman to a student lounge and introducing her to each of 10 of our male friends—we'll call each man a *model*. After each meeting, a participant will rate the model's likability and attractiveness, answering our questions using pencil and paper.

You may think that this design is finished. However, it's not a good design, because we have not completely thought it through.

CRITICALLY EVALUATING A STUDY

Say that we conducted the likability study and some of the data is in Table 3.1. For simplicity, the likability scores are separated into two groups based on whether a model was less attractive (rated a 3 or below) or more attractive (rated a 4 or above). Sure enough, higher likability scores were given to the more attractive models. It looks like a woman's first impression of a man is related to his physical attractiveness.

But, recall that the goal is to *know* how a behavior operates. However, in any study, the only thing we "know" is that each participant obtained a particular score—a number—at a particular time. You can stare at these numbers all day long, but you won't *know* what they actually reflect: We don't *know* that participants are really—and only—reacting to the variables we want them to, so we *don't* know what a score really measures, and so we *don't* know what the relationship really reflects. That's why we must always critically evaluate a study. Critically evaluating a study means answering the question, "How confident are you that the scores actually reflect the hypothetical constructs, variables, and behaviors you think they reflect, and that the observed relationship actually reflects the relationship you think it reflects?"

TABLE 3.1 Some Data from the Likability Study

	Less attractive models	More attractive models
Likability scores ⟶	2	5
	1	6
	2	6
	1	5
	3	4
	3	6
	3	5

REMEMBER   Critically evaluating a study means questioning whether the scores and relationship reflect what we think they do.

The *only* way to be confident of what the data reflect is to consider the design of the study, to see if we can detect potential flaws that might produce misleading scores. The fewer flaws, the more confidence we can have that the scores *do* measure what they are supposed to measure. In the likability study, we took many components for granted, so there are many potential flaws that reduce our confidence that the data reflect what we think they do. These flaws can again be grouped in terms of those four types of variables—participant, environment, researcher, and measurement. Here are just some of the things that could go wrong:

Participant variables

- Some females barely speak English. Their answers to the questions are partially a test of their language skills.
- Some participants are extremely nearsighted (but don't wear glasses). They can barely see the model and, instead, guess at his attractiveness.
- Some participants already know the models. Our measurements do not reflect an *initial* anything.

Environmental variables

- The lounge is usually lit by sunlight, but when clouds pass by, some participants meet the models in a darkened room. Everyone looks more attractive in the dark.
- Sometimes the lounge is hot, sometimes it's noisy, and sometimes other people are wandering through it. Therefore, some participants don't pay much attention to the model.

Researcher variables

- The researcher is a female who introduces the more attractive models in a more positive manner. Or, the researcher is a male who's jealous of the attractive males and gives negative introductions for them. Either way, likability scores reflect the tone of the introduction.
- An introduction of a model sometimes lasts only 30 seconds and sometimes lasts over 2 minutes, so we don't always measure the same kind of first impression.

Measurement variables

- The truth is that "facial attractiveness" and "likability" cannot be accurately measured by this procedure.
- Some females cannot decide between a "4" and a "5" on the rating scales, and mentally flip a coin when responding.
- Some models wear a more pleasant aftershave, have more muscular bodies, and dress better than others, and some talk warmly to the females while others talk only of car engines and beer blasts. Some models will be rated as more attractive, but *not* because of their faces.
- Two females are inadvertently given a pencil with a broken point and think that their reaction to this is what is actually being studied. They focus not on attractiveness or likability but on where the hidden camera might be.

Although such problems may strike you as unlikely, they can and do occur. For example, May and Hamilton (1980) found that something as mundane as the type of background music being played influenced how females rated a male's attractiveness. Therefore, because we are skeptical and open-minded, we always consider whether such things might be occurring in a study, in which case the scores do not really reflect what we think they do. Thus, go back and look again at Table 3.1: Because we don't *know* that the above potential flaws were *not* occurring, we cannot be *sure* that these scores show that some men *really* were perceived as having more attractive faces, and that, *only because of this*, these men also *really* were perceived as more likable. On the other hand, if the above flaws could not possibly occur, then we would have greater confidence that we are really observing the relationship between attractiveness and likability.

REMEMBER The more potential flaws that we find in a design, the less confidence we have that the data reflect what we think they do.

There are two general strategies for critically evaluating a study: First, look for potential problems in the operational definitions being used. There are many ways to define a construct or variable, and each might produce a misleading picture of the behavior. For example, maybe the likability question in no way taps into a woman's "first impression," so this approach is just plain wrong. Or, perhaps it also inadvertently measures other attitudes.

Second, look for extraneous variables that may be fluctuating. This boils down to looking at those four components—the researcher, participants, environment, and measurement task—for any inconsistent aspect of the study that might raise or lower scores. For example, the extraneous variables of a researcher's rudeness and the participant's nearsightedness may flaw the attractiveness scores, and the environment's temperature and participants' difficulty with English may flaw likability scores.

Look for such variables by again "playing psychologist," considering the context of the behavior and the research situation. And, as we did above, consider anything that could go wrong with the original, planned study. The more that such variables are operating, the more that the scores and relationship do not reflect what we think they do.

Look for extraneous variables that fluctuate in either of two ways. Sometimes a variable changes **unsystematically**, changing with no consistent pattern. If, for example, the lounge is sometimes dark and sometimes light in a random pattern, then lounge lighting changes unsystematically. On the other hand, an extraneous variable may also change **systematically**, either increasing or decreasing in a way that forms a consistent pattern. For example, if the researcher becomes more polite when introducing later models, then politeness changed systematically.

REMEMBER   The flaws that decrease confidence in a study come from inappropriate operational definitions and from *systematic* and *unsystematic extraneous variables.*

Understand that systematic and unsystematic extraneous variables influence a study in two ways. First, as above, they lead to errors when interpreting and generalizing the study, because the variables that we think are operating are not those that are really operating. Above, we think we are seeing the relationship between attractiveness and likability, but really it might involve the influences of lounge lighting and how polite an introduction was.

Second, before you even get to the interpretation, extraneous variables can influence the scores and thus the mathematical relationship produced. Recall that our first concern is producing a consistent relationship in the sample data. But, as we saw in the previous chapter, fluctuations in extraneous variables can reduce a relationship's strength. For example, if the lighting in the lounge fluctuates unsystematically, then we may see different attractiveness scores for men having the same likability score, so that there is a less consistent pairing of a particular attractiveness score with a particular likability score. In fact, the scores could be so inconsistent that no relationship is observed. If the lighting is constant, however, a more consistent relationship might occur.

Likewise, a systematic extraneous variable might raise or lower scores in a consistent way so that the sample relationship is different than it would be if the variable were not operating. For example, the researcher might—out of pity—

give especially nice introductions for the less attractive models, and more abrupt introductions for the attractive models. This could raise likability scores for the less attractive models while lowering scores for the attractive ones. Then the data will show that as attractiveness goes up, likability goes *down*, even though normally in nature the reverse might be true.

> **REMEMBER**   Extraneous variables can produce misleading scores and a misleading relationship, as well as a misleading interpretation of how nature operates.

So, the process of interpreting a relationship and testing a hypothesis is *not* so straightforward after all. The ultimate question is always whether the data actually reflect what we think they do. Because of the complexity of this question, however, researchers have special terminology for communicating different aspects of it. These aspects fall under two general concerns, called *reliability* and *validity*.

UNDERSTANDING RELIABILITY

One component of asking whether the data actually reflect what we think they do is asking whether the data are reliable. **Reliability** is the degree to which the same event or behavior produces the same score each time it is measured. With reliability we ask, "Regardless of what the scores actually measure, do they at least measure it consistently, without introducing random error, so that measuring an event produces the same score whenever we measure it?" In other words, a reliable measurement is repeatable and stable over time. Reliability is necessary because a law of nature is consistent and stable over time, so a measurement reflecting the law should also be consistent and stable. For example, we assume a female's liking of a particular male will not change rapidly. If she likes him now, she should like him to the same degree five minutes from now. If her two ratings for him differ, however, then we have some measurement error: Either the first, the second, or both scores contain error in measuring her behavior.

The problem with *unreliable* scores is that they reflect random error instead of what they are supposed to reflect. Then, we obtain different scores each time we measure the same behavior, leading to different conclusions each time, so that we don't know which conclusion is correct. Thus, unreliable data are "untrustworthy" in the sense that they reflect error and lead to inconsistent conclusions. Therefore, how reliable the data are influences our confidence in a study.

To obtain reliable data, the goal is to design a study in which the research situation is as consistent as possible. Anything that adds sloppiness or random errors when measuring a variable—whether an independent, a dependent, or other variable—threatens reliability. Often reliability is reduced by unsystematic extraneous variables, so again consider those four components of a study, and ask,

"Might a particular score be different if we measured it again in the same situation?" Thus, we have an unreliable measurement of the duration of a meeting if our stopwatch is inaccurate. Or, we have unreliable scores if, because of their eyesight or their indecision, females guess when rating a model's attractiveness.

REMEMBER   *Reliability* is the degree to which measurements are consistent and do not contain error.

(*Note*: Although previously, we used the term *consistency* when referring to the strength of a relationship, a reliable relationship is *not* the same as a strong relationship. A reliable relationship is one that—whether strong or weak—is found repeatedly every time a particular situation is examined. That is, there is not random error being measured, so the particular relationship that we observe is stable over time.)

UNDERSTANDING VALIDITY

The other concern when asking what the data actually reflect is in terms of whether the data accurately reflect the constructs, variables, and relationships we think they do. Any time researchers question whether they are drawing the correct inferences from results, they are concerned with validity. **Validity** is the extent to which a procedure measures what it is intended to measure. When a procedure lacks validity, it is "untrustworthy" because it reflects the "wrong" aspects of a situation to some degree, so we cannot trust our conclusions about the situation.

As you'll see below, researchers break the issue of validity into several subparts, depending on the particular inference being drawn.

Content and Construct Validity

First, we are concerned with whether a score actually reflects what we think it does, in terms of the variable and in terms of the hypothetical construct we wish to measure. For each type of inference, we have a corresponding type of validity.

Content validity is the degree to which measurements actually reflect the *variable* of interest. Here, we question whether a procedure actually and only measures all dimensions of the behavior we seek: Are we tapping the appropriate "contents" of the target behavior? Thus, when females are supposedly rating facial attractiveness, we ask, "Are their scores actually and only measuring the facial attractiveness of the model?"

A procedure lacks content validity, first, if it lacks reliability. For example, if participants are guessing somewhat when rating a model's attractiveness, then a score partly reflects his attractiveness and partly reflects guessing. Second, content validity is decreased if any systematic or unsystematic extraneous variable is also measured by a score. Thus, we lose content validity in measuring attractiveness when participants barely speak English, because their scores partially reflect their language ability. Likewise, content validity is decreased if a woman's rating partially reflects her response to a model's behavior or style of dress. By reflecting these other variables, such scores can mislead us about the variable of facial attractiveness. In essence, we don't know what we're talking about when it comes to facial attractiveness, because we have not measured facial attractiveness alone.

On the other hand, **construct validity** is the extent to which a measurement reflects the *hypothetical construct* of interest. Here, we question whether the variable we are measuring actually reflects the construct as it is conceptualized from a particular theoretical viewpoint. If a procedure lacks construct validity, then any inferences drawn about the broad underlying psychological processes will be wrong.

A classic question of construct validity occurs with intelligence tests, which measure such variables as a person's vocabulary or problem-solving ability. While content validity is the question of whether we really measure these variables, construct validity is the broader question of whether these variables really measure "intelligence." Perhaps some other variables more accurately reflect this construct. Likewise, some females might argue that they are not so shallow as to judge a man's attractiveness based on his facial appearance. They are essentially theorizing about what should constitute the construct of attractiveness and its relationship to first impressions. For them, our study lacks construct validity because it examines the "wrong" variable of facial attractiveness and thus will lead to an incorrect interpretation of the behavior.

> **REMEMBER** *Content validity* refers to whether we actually and only measure the intended variable. *Construct validity* refers to whether the variable actually and only reflects the intended hypothetical construct.

In addition to considering the content and construct validity of any *single* variable, we are also concerned with the validity of our conclusions about the *relationship* between the variables. Because we can consider the relationship either in terms of the sample data or when generalizing, we have two types of validity here—*internal* and *external validity*.

Internal Validity and Confounding Variables

Internal validity is the degree to which the mathematical relationship we observe between the *scores* actually and only reflects the relationship between the *variables* of interest. Thus, we have internal validity if the X and Y scores reflect only the relationship between the intended X and Y variables, so that we draw the correct inferences about what was going on *in* ("internal" to) the study. Internal validity is reduced, however, if the *apparent* relationship between the *X* and *Y* scores actually reflects *another* relationship involving *other* variables. Thus, when a relationship lacks internal validity, it is "untrustworthy" in the sense that it does not reflect the relationship that we think it does. This is important because if we don't know what the sample relationship reflects, then we cannot draw correct inferences about the relationship in nature.

REMEMBER *Internal validity* is the extent to which the apparent relationship in the data actually reflects the intended relationship between our variables.

Don't confuse content and construct validity with internal validity. If, for example, our questions do accurately measure a model's likability and attractiveness, then we have content and construct validity. But, if in addition, some other variable is operating that influences the relationship, then we lose internal validity because the real relationship involves this other variable, so we are not actually and only seeing the relationship between likability and attractiveness.

We have a special name for the presence of such extraneous variables that reduce internal validity. A **confounding variable** is an extraneous variable that systematically changes at the same time that our variables of interest change. Then we cannot tell which variables are actually operating, and so we are confused or "confounded." For example, say that coincidentally our more attractive models were also better dressed, while the less attractive models were poorly dressed. Then, we would say that "style of dress is a confounding variable" or that "attractiveness and manner of dress are confounded." This confounding is illustrated in Table 3.2.

TABLE 3.2 Diagram of a Confounded Relationship

Intended variable ⟶	Less attractive models	More attractive models
Confounding variable ⟶	Poorly dressed	Well dressed
Likability scores ⟶	2	5
	1	6
	2	6
	1	5
	3	4
	3	6

In the left-hand column are likability scores for the less attractive models and in the right-hand column are likability scores for the more attractive models. We have the predicted relationship here, because those we are *calling* the more attractive models did receive higher likability scores. The problem is that because of the confounding variable of style of dress, the less attractive models can also be described as poorly dressed, and the attractive models as well dressed. Therefore, we don't know which variable is the correct label. Maybe facial attractiveness was irrelevant in this situation. Maybe we should be calling the groups "poorly dressed" and "well-dressed" because this was the variable that is actually related to likability.

Thus, we have reduced internal validity, because the possible relationship between style of dress and likability reduces our confidence that we are really seeing the relationship between likability and attractiveness. And if we are unsure what the relationship shows, then we cannot say that we've confirmed our hypothesis.

REMEMBER If an extraneous variable changes simultaneously with a variable of interest, then the variables are *confounded*.

Confoundings are important in science because they are at the heart of the difficulty of "proving" a hypothesis that we discussed in Chapter 1. Essentially, a possible confounding produces a rival hypothesis—the hypothesis that the confounding variable is reflected in our relationship. Thus, the above data support our hypothesis that "greater attractiveness is related to greater likability," *and* they support the rival hypothesis that "better dress is related to greater likability." The data cannot help us to select between these hypotheses, and because the results confirm them both, we are stuck: we cannot, in any way, "prove" our hypothesis that attractiveness and likability are related.

Confoundings and their rival hypotheses are most important when we are testing causal hypotheses. If we had proposed that attractiveness *causes* likability, then a potential confounding by style of dress would seriously weaken our conclusions and defeat the whole purpose of the study. Or, say that the researcher gave some models a more positive introduction, making them seem *both* more attractive and more likable. Then, internal validity is reduced because the "real" relationship is between the confounding variable of how positive an introduction was and the combination of how attractive/likable a model is.

Confounding variables can arise from any source. There's a confounding if a male researcher introduces the unattractive models and a female researcher introduces the attractive ones. Also, confoundings occur if, with more attractive models, there are systematic changes in the temperature or noise level of the lounge, or in how interested participants are in meeting men. Or, say that in a different study we examine the influence of background music on a model's likability, comparing a song that has lyrics with another that does not. Confoundings are present if one song is louder than the other, or if one is more familiar than the other. In every case, we will not be able to determine which variable is the one that produced differences in likability scores.

REMEMBER   The internal validity of a study depends on the likelihood of confounding variables.

Drawing Externally Valid Inferences about the Relationship

Recall that after we conclude what was going on *in* a study, we then *generalize* the conclusions beyond the study to everyone in the population. But, are we correct in this conclusion? **External validity** is the degree to which the results accurately generalize to other individuals and other situations. Thus, external validity is the question of whether the study provides a good example of the relationship that occurs in situations "external" to our study.

External validity is threatened by any extraneous variable that makes observations unique or atypical, so that they are unrepresentative of the relationship generally found in nature. For example, our female participants are all from the same college, so the sample represents the type of women who attend that college. And by testing only *college* women, our results may not apply to women who don't go to college. Likewise, the way we operationally define the variables and our procedure might result in scores or a relationship that would not be found in other settings. If a similar relationship cannot be found with other participants in other settings, then we have a biased and misleading perspective: We will incorrectly describe the relationship between likability and facial attractiveness—as well as incorrectly describing the relationship between the constructs of first impressions and physical attractiveness.

REMEMBER   *External validity* is the degree to which we can draw the correct inferences when generalizing beyond a study.

Several subparts to external validity arise, depending on the researcher's perspective when generalizing. Two important subparts are *ecological validity* and temporal validity.

Ecological Validity   **Ecological validity** is the extent to which research can be generalized to common behaviors and natural situations. A design that lacks ecological validity focuses on what participants *can do* in a study instead of what they *usually* do in everyday life. This issue is most important in highly controlled laboratory experiments. For example, for years researchers studied "paired-associate learning," in which participants learned pairs of nonsense syllables (e.g., learning that BIM goes with YOB). But learning nonsense syllables is not a real-life behavior, and so such research lacks ecological validity: We cannot be confident that it accurately generalizes to natural learning processes.

Researchers often lose ecological validity in their quest for internal validity, developing a rather unusual measurement task in order to control and simplify the behavior. (Paired-associate learning allows for much more controlled observations than, say, classroom learning.) However, where possible, a balance between internal and ecological validity is best. The challenge is to maintain control while having participants perform tasks that bear some resemblance to those found in the real world.

> **REMEMBER** *Ecological validity* is the extent to which the situation and behaviors in a study are found in the natural environment.

Temporal Validity   Another aspect of external validity is **temporal validity,** the extent to which results generalize to other time periods. Temporal validity has two applications. First, any study incorporates certain time frames, such as our measuring likability after a two-minute meeting. Temporal validity is the extent to which the observed relationship generalizes to other time frames (e.g., to a one- or five-minute meeting.)

Second, a study is conducted in a particular month and year. Temporal validity is also the extent to which a study generalizes to other months or years. This is important because people often make the mistake of thinking that research conducted several years ago must be out of date. However, such research often *does* have temporal validity, so do not automatically dismiss "old" research. In particular, such basic behaviors as memory or emotion are not greatly influenced by societal changes over time, so previous findings regarding them tend to apply today. However, research into behaviors that are influenced by societal changes (e.g., social trends, fads, or attitudes) may generalize less well.

> **REMEMBER** *Temporal validity* is the extent to which generalizations are accurate across other time periods.

The preceding issues of reliability and validity are *the* issues in designing and critiquing research. They are summarized for you in Table 3.3. (You need to know these terms.)

DEALING WITH VALIDITY AND RELIABILITY WHEN DESIGNING A STUDY

The preceding discussion boils down to this: The key to creating a "good" study is to select the appropriate operational definitions and to limit systematic and unsystematic extraneous variables. Then it is "good" in the sense that we are more confident that we know what the data actually reflect. Poor definitions and the presence of extraneous variables reduce our confidence: we are less confident that the results are *reliable* (are error free), have *content* and *construct validity*

TABLE 3.3 A Researcher's Terminology for Questioning the Different Aspects of a Study

Question	Research term
Do the scores contain random error?	Reliability
Do the scores reflect the variable?	Content validity
Does the variable reflect the hypothetical construct?	Construct validity
Does the relationship reflect the variables we think it reflects?	Internal validity
Does the relationship generalize beyond the study?	External validity
Do the results generalize to natural behaviors and situations?	Ecological validity
Do the results generalize to other time periods?	Temporal validity

(actually measure the variables and constructs we intend), have *internal validity* (reflect the intended relationship) and have *external validity* (describe the relationship found in nature).

The above describes how to "critically evaluate" all research, whether it is conducted by you or by someone else. If you are conducting the study, however, then the time to consider these issues is *before* you actually collect the data. The design and interpretation of a study are completely interwoven, because after the data are collected, there is no way to solve such problems, and the presence of confoundings or other threats to reliability and validity just make it impossible to interpret the study. Therefore, the goal is to identify and prevent potential confoundings and other important flaws when designing the study.

For help, first rely on the psychological literature to find operational definitions that are reliable and have the various types of validity. Remember that we always build upon replications. In particular, *literal replications* (studies that duplicate a previous study) suggest that a particular technique is reliable and internally valid. *Conceptual replications* (studies that employ somewhat different procedures) suggest that the approach is externally valid. Alternatively, you can devise your own procedures, but then their reliability and validity will be unknown. Therefore, you must explicitly demonstrate that the procedure is reliable and valid. (Some techniques for demonstrating this are discussed in Chapter 9.) Whenever possible, however, it is best (and easiest) to adopt procedures that are commonly accepted in the literature.

In addition, you'll make arbitrary decisions about how to test a hypothesis, so that in some ways, every study is unique, with its own particular threats to reliability and validity. As we've seen, such threats stem from uncontrolled extraneous variables, so the first step is to identify potentially important extraneous variables. For any serious threats to reliability and validity we identify, we then prevent their influence by *controlling* them.

Controlling Extraneous Variables

There are many techniques for controlling extraneous variables (and it will take several more chapters to describe them all). But, the basic approach for controlling extraneous variables is either to *eliminate* them, to keep them *constant*, or to *balance* their influence.

Many problems can be solved by *eliminating extraneous variables*. For example, in the likability study, we could improve reliability and content validity by eliminating distracting noises by moving to a lounge where they do not occur. We could also refuse to admit intruders who might distract participants. Further, we could ensure the models are all unknown to participants by obtaining them from a different school, and we could avoid the use of broken pencils.

If we cannot eliminate an extraneous variable, we may keep it *constant* for all participants. For example, to improve reliability, and to eliminate potential confoundings, we should keep the temperature and illumination in the lounge at constant, normal levels. Likewise, we should keep the researcher's behavior constant, precisely defining how all participants are treated. Also, we could redefine our participants, selecting only females who speak English well and have corrected vision. And, we can select models with the same body type and manner of dress, and provide them with a "script" of what to say and how to behave.

Sometimes an extraneous variable cannot be eliminated (for example, we cannot eliminate the variable of a researcher's gender). Likewise, keeping the variable constant may not be feasible, because if it is present in one particular way, it creates a rather unique situation, reducing external validity (e.g., employing only a male researcher or only a female researcher might influence participants in a particular way, and this would reduce generalizability). In such cases, we intentionally change the variable in a systematic fashion so that we *balance* its biasing influence. For example, we could balance the researcher's gender as shown in Table 3.4. We would have a male researcher introduce half of the less attractive and half of the more attractive models, while a female researcher would introduce the remaining models. Any bias due to a researcher's gender is eliminated, because any influence of the male researcher is present to the same degree as that of the female researcher. Further, another benefit is that we demonstrate a more generalizable relationship, because it applies to when both male and female researchers are present.

Likewise, if we thought the time of day participants were tested might have an influence, we'd balance those tested early in the day with those tested later. Or, if we thought a particular lounge could influence first impressions, we'd balance testing some participants in each of several different lounges. (We'll see more about balancing variables in the next chapter.)

REMEMBER   To control extraneous variables, we *eliminate* them, keep them *constant*, or *balance* their influence.

TABLE 3.4 Diagram of Likability Study Where Researcher's Gender Is Balanced

	Less attractive models	More attractive models
Likability scores with male experimenter	2 2 3 1	5 5 6 6
Likability scores with female experimenter	2 1 1 3	4 6 5 4

Deciding on the Controls to Use

Ideally, we seek the best possible study, so on the one hand, we always try to correct any flaws that we easily can. But, on the other hand, all research will suffer some problems of reliability and validity. The best that we can do is to minimize the *major* threats to reliability and validity, so that we are as confident in a conclusion as possible. We cannot control every threat, because there are often trade-offs, so that improving one aspect of a study negatively impacts another aspect (e.g., the most reliable procedure may be less construct valid). In particular, those procedures that increase internal validity tend to decrease external validity, and vice versa.

Therefore, there is no set of rules to follow when dealing with an issue of reliability and validity: It depends on your particular research hypothesis and how you examine the behavior. In fact, you may simply accept a threat to reliability or to a certain type of validity because the threat is not all that important to your study. Then, however, recognize the limitations produced by the threat and refrain from drawing inferences that are invalid because of them.

The threats to reliability and validity that will be present are determined primarily by the type of hypothesis you are testing and by whether you conduct a descriptive study or an experiment.

ISSUES OF VALIDITY AND RELIABILITY IN DESCRIPTIVE STUDIES

Recall that in descriptive designs, we simply observe a behavior or situation. Most commonly, this involves a *correlational* design, in which we measure scores on two variables to see if they form the predicted relationship (as in our likability study). What characterizes descriptive research is that the researcher does not tinker with the situation much, so that it tends to be a natural, realistic situation. In fact, such studies are often conducted outside of the laboratory, as "field research," where few variables are controlled and a wide variety of natural behaviors are likely. This is both an advantage and a drawback.

The advantage is that descriptive studies tend to have high external validity: They tend to be repeatable with other participants and settings, so they generalize well to the real world. For example, even with the controls we've discussed, the likability study has much in common with the way people meet in the real world. Therefore, our results should generalize to such meetings.

It is because of their high external validity that descriptive methods are best for testing descriptive hypotheses. Here, the goal is to describe behaviors as they normally occur and to predict their occurrence in natural settings. Therefore, we use the methods that produce observations of more natural behaviors.

The disadvantage of descriptive studies is that they tend to involve less control. In our likability study, for example, we saw that uncontrolled variables in the student lounge reduce the reliability, content validity, and construct validity of the measurements. Most important, the major disadvantage of descriptive designs is that they tend to have very weak internal validity. That is, with so many uncontrolled extraneous variables, there are many potential and likely confounding variables. Thus, for example, in our likability study, we identified so many potential confounding variables that we have little confidence that the relationship that we observe *actually and only* reflects the relationship between attractiveness and likability.

REMEMBER   Descriptive approaches tend to have greater external validity but less internal validity than experiments.

It is because of their weak internal validity that descriptive approaches cannot be used to make valid inferences about the causes of a behavior.

Problems in Inferring the Causes of a Behavior

Recall that experimental methods are used to test causal hypotheses. It's not that we can't test causal hypotheses using descriptive procedures, it's just that they provide minimal confidence in our conclusions. This is because merely showing a relationship between X and Y does not automatically mean that changes in X *cause* changes in Y. One variable can be related to another variable without causing it to change: A person's weight is related to his or her height, but greater weight does not cause greater height. The key to inferring a causal relationship lies in the *manner* in which the relationship is demonstrated. Two components are needed.

First, it is necessary to produce the correct temporal sequence: To say that X causes Y, we must show that X occurs *before* Y. Descriptive methods are poor for identifying the causes of behavior, however, because they do not establish positively which variable occurs first. In the likability study, we cannot say that greater attractiveness causes greater likability, because we are unsure of the order in which these reactions occur. Perhaps, females first perceived a model as more attractive and this then caused greater likability. Or, perhaps, females first decided they liked the model, and this then caused him to be rated as more attractive.

The second requirement for demonstrating a behavior's cause is to be sure that no extraneous variable could actually be the cause—in other words, that there are no confounding variables present. We have so little confidence in our conclusions about causality from descriptive studies because they are so likely to contain all sorts of confoundings. As we have seen, for example, we would have little confidence that we have shown that attractiveness *causes* likability.

Thus, with descriptive designs, we only *describe* the relationship between the variables, without inferring that one causes the other. Changes in X might cause changes in Y, but it's also possible that (1) changes in Y cause changes in X, or (2) some other, third variable causes both X and Y to change. (This latter idea is often called "the third variable problem.") Therefore, all we can say with confidence is that there is a relationship, or association, between the scores on the two variables. We can make no claim, *one way or the other*, regarding what causes the scores to change.

> **REMEMBER** In descriptive designs, we are unsure that changes in X cause changes in Y because we cannot be sure that X changes first or that it is the only variable that could cause Y to change.

The way to demonstrate a relationship so that we have greater confidence about the causes of a behavior is to conduct an experiment.

ISSUES OF VALIDITY AND RELIABILITY IN EXPERIMENTS

Causal hypotheses are tested by conducting experiments, because in this design we *do* tinker with the situation: We systematically manipulate or change the independent variable, and then measure participants on the dependent variable. Usually, by controlling and measuring these variables, we also control other, extraneous variables as well (by balancing, eliminating, or keeping them constant). Then we have a better idea of the influences that are actually operating in the situation. As usual, however, this control has both its advantages and its drawbacks.

To see this, here are some controls we could employ to create a likability *experiment*. We might have a panel of judges rate different models' facial attractiveness prior to the study, and then create conditions of the independent variable of attractiveness by selecting one model consistently rated as low to create a "low attractiveness" condition, one rated as medium to create a "medium attractiveness" condition, and so on. We could control extraneous participant variables by selecting English-speaking females with corrected eyesight. To eliminate extraneous variables stemming from a model's behavior, dress, or body type, we could show participants a photograph of each model's face. To give all models the same personality characteristics, all participants would read the same paragraph describing the model. Finally, we could conduct the study in a controlled laboratory, keeping the environment constant, keeping the researcher's behavior constant, and balancing the researcher's gender in each condition. As the conditions change so that the model's attractiveness increases, his likability score should also increase. Now, however, we have a much clearer idea of what the scores and the relationship reflect, because by controlling these variables, we will have potentially more reliable and valid measurements.

In particular, the advantage of experiments is that they tend to have greater internal validity: With greater control, we eliminate potential confoundings, so we have greater confidence that the apparent relationship between our variables actually shows that changing the independent variable *caused* the dependent variable to change. Thus, above, we have greater confidence that our relationship involves only facial attractiveness and likability. Because participants don't experience a model's behavior or dress, it makes no sense to argue that differences in likability were caused by these variables. Because the environment and the researcher are more consistent, it is also unlikely that these variables influenced the ratings. And so on.

On the other hand, the disadvantage of experiments is that they may have reduced external validity. In all designs, there is usually a trade-off between internal and external validity, because more controls produce a more unusual and unnatural situation that does not generalize well. For example, we've created a rather strange situation in our likability experiment, because women do not normally meet men and form first impressions based solely on a photograph! Therefore, we may have reduced external validity, with the results generalizing poorly to other individuals and settings. Thus, with experimental methods, we tend to have greater internal validity for understanding a particular relationship, but at the cost of getting results that may be atypical of, and thus less generalizable to, other settings.

REMEMBER   Experiments tend to have greater internal validity but less external validity than descriptive methods.

Although experiments are better than descriptive studies for demonstrating causality, they are not perfect.

The Limits to Showing Causality in Experiments

Experiments are usually preferred when testing causal hypotheses because (1) they provide greater control of extraneous, potentially confounding, variables, and (2) often we are more confident that the independent variable occurred first, followed by the dependent behavior. However, experiments are not infallible, and they do not provide "proof" of a hypothesis. Remember that we have confidence in a study only if we cannot *see* any confounding variables that might be operating. But, we can never be certain we've eliminated all potential confounding variables, because we do not *know* what all of these variables are (e.g., we don't know the *complete* list of things that influence a man's likability). Thus, because we can never know if some unknown confounding variable is causing the behavior, we can never "prove" that changes in our independent variable alone caused the dependent variable to change. Instead, being skeptical and cautious, we recognize that we've eliminated only *some* of the extraneous variables that are possible, and that we may have missed an important one. (Also, measurements are never perfectly valid and reliable.)

Compared to a descriptive study, then, an experiment merely tends to provide better evidence that allows us to *argue* for a certain proposed cause. But a single experiment does not provide "proof." Proof can come only as researchers perform many replications. Each time, exactly the same set of extraneous, potentially confounding variables are unlikely to be present, so that after enough studies, we can eliminate them as potential causes. Then we come to believe that the relationship reflects what we think it does, and so we are confident that the independent variable is a cause of the behavior.

REMEMBER   The potential presence of an unknown confounding variable means that one study is never "proof" of a hypothesis.

Not all experiments are equally strong in internal validity or equally weak in external validity. Two aspects of an experiment that influence its validity are whether it is a quasi-experiment, and whether it is a field experiment.

Internal Validity in True versus Quasi-Experiments

Recall that with a true independent variable, participants can be randomly assigned to any condition, but with a quasi-independent variable, this is not the case. Random assignment is important because it is a way of "balancing" and thus controlling extraneous participant variables. Quasi-experiments, by not allowing for random assignment, are likely to be confounded by participant variables.

For example, say we conduct a quasi-experiment to determine whether a model's likability changes as a function of a female's age, comparing the conditions of 18- or 22-year-old women. We cannot randomly assign females to be a particular age, so we must select participants for each condition who are already that age. However, we may then end up with two groups who also differ in terms of all sorts of other participant variables. For example, older women have probably had a greater amount of dating experience. Thus, we might have the study shown in Table 3.5, in which the quasi-independent variable of age is confounded by the extraneous variable of dating experience. Further, the women in these groups might also differ in terms of their year in college, their maturity, their preferences in men, and so on. Differences in any of these variables might actually be causing the differences in likability scores. Therefore, we have little confidence that age is actually the causal variable. In other words, the absence of random assignment severely reduces internal validity.

Note that the lack of random assignment also limits the internal validity of descriptive designs. For example, when we measured likability and attractiveness in the lounge, those women who found certain models less attractive might coincidentally have been younger or shorter, or have had less dating experience. These variables might have then determined likability here as well.

On the other hand, the likability experiment in the laboratory that we proposed is an example of a true independent variable: Here, we can randomly assign each participant to see the photo in either the low, medium, or high attractiveness condition. Then we would be confident that the above confoundings do not occur, because by luck, we should obtain various types of females in each condition, so that differences in participant variables should balance out. That is, we'd expect each condition to contain some women who are experienced daters and some not, some older and some younger, some taller and some shorter, some freshmen and some seniors, and so on. Overall, each condition should contain a balanced mix of the same types of subjects as the other conditions. Therefore, we have greater confidence that the independent variable is not confounded by extraneous participant variables.

REMEMBER Random assignment to conditions balances participant variables, so true independent variables provide greater internal validity than quasi-independent variables.

TABLE 3.5 Diagram of Quasi-Experiment Showing a Confounding of the Independent Variable of Age with Amount of Dating Experience

	Condition 1	Condition 2
Independent variable	18-year-olds	22-year-olds
Confounding variable	Little dating experience	Much dating experience
Likability scores	X X X X X	X X X X X

Thus, a well-designed true experiment provides the most confidence that we have demonstrated a causal relationship because true experiments are inherently set up to provide the two things needed to infer causality. First, we know which variable comes first because participants have not already experienced the independent variable, so we have them experience a condition *and then* measure the dependent behavior. Second, we minimize the possibility that an extraneous variable is the cause because random assignment balances extraneous participant variables, reducing their potential as confoundings, and other controls eliminate other extraneous variables. Then, *hopefully* the only variable that systematically changes will be the independent variable, so that it must be causing the dependent scores to change.

On the other hand, in a quasi-experiment we cannot perform random assignment, so we are much less confident we have shown the causes of a behavior. This is because, without random assignment, not only are we likely to have many confoundings present, but sometimes, we cannot even be sure of the temporal sequence of our variables. For example, say that in a different study we create the two conditions of left- or right-handed participants, and then measure the dependent variable of their intelligence. It might appear that differences in handedness cause differences in intelligence. However, we don't know exactly when hand preference or intelligence is first determined in a child, so it is also possible that intelligence occurs first and then causes a particular handedness.

REMEMBER   True experiments have substantially greater internal validity for identifying the causes of a behavior than quasi-experiments.

We also influence internal and external validity by creating either a laboratory or field experiment.

Issues of Validity and Reliability in Laboratory versus Field Experiments

Experiments conducted in a "laboratory" typically yield the greatest control, because we select participants who come to our controlled environment, to be tested under situations that we determine. However, laboratory experiments may have reduced external validity because a laboratory setting is not a slice of real life. The situation is artificial, participants know they are being tested, and a researcher is present who is "studying" them. Also, participants may be unrepresentative because we can study only individuals who will come to our laboratory. Therefore, the results may generalize poorly to other individuals and settings.

To increase external validity, we may leave the laboratory and conduct a field experiment. A **field experiment** is a true or quasi-experiment conducted in a natural setting. Field experiments are common in social psychology, industrial psychology, and other areas when it is appropriate to study a behavior as it occurs in the real world. The setting may be a factory, a school, a shopping mall, a street corner, or any place the behavior occurs. One common approach is to disguise the fact that an experiment is being conducted and secretly study the public so that we can generalize to the typical person. The other approach is to study an existing group—such as a group of police, teachers, or medical personnel—because only they experience certain situations or exhibit particular behaviors.

A field experiment is still an experiment, so we try to randomly select and assign participants to conditions, systematically manipulate the conditions of the independent variable, control extraneous variables, and measure the dependent variable in a valid and reliable manner. Then, because the experiment is conducted in a more natural setting, we should have greater external validity when generalizing the results. On the other hand, in the field we tend to have less control of all extraneous variables. We therefore usually have the trade-off in which—you guessed it—we lose internal validity. Thus, the result is that we have increased confidence that a natural behavior operates in a particular way but less confidence that there is not some hidden extraneous variable at work. (We'll discuss field research in detail in Chapter 10.)

> **REMEMBER**   *Field experiments* tend to have greater external validity but less internal validity than laboratory experiments.

SELECTING A DESIGN

Researchers use the terms *descriptive* and *experimental* as a shorthand way of communicating the overall approach of a design. These terms distinguish the extent to which variables are controlled and, often, the degree to which observations are reliable and have certain types of validity. However, in creating a specific design, you have wide latitude in applying controls and mixing experimental and descriptive methods. In general, there are three major factors that determine the overall approach to select.

First and foremost, the method selected depends on the question being answered. Use correlational and other descriptive designs when testing descriptive hypotheses. True experiments are best for testing a causal hypothesis, because they provide the greatest control over potentially confounding variables. Sometimes, however, you do not have a choice. For example, we cannot *make* people be Republican or Democrat, have a certain personality, be alcoholic, be the victim of sexual abuse, or have a criminal record. Although these variables may influence behavior, they cannot be true independent variables to which we expose participants. Thus, regardless of the nature of the hypothesis, we are sometimes forced to accept weaker evidence. We may have to study alcoholics using a quasi-experiment, in which the conditions are formed by people who already exhibit different degrees of alcoholism. We might be forced to merely describe the relationship between sexual abuse and other variables by asking questions of abuse victims using a correlational design. And we may have to examine records in order to study criminals. Based on such studies, we might propose the causes of behaviors, but without conducting true experiments, we recognize that the evidence only *suggests* possible causes.

Second, how you conduct a study using a particular method is determined by your concerns with reliability and validity. In particular, you must decide whether the primary issue is internal or external validity. On the one hand, we can study a highly controlled situation that is easier to understand, but it might also be a rather atypical situation that does not generalize well. On the other hand, with fewer controls, we can study a situation that is more natural and realistic, so that the results generalize better, but we might also experience greater confusion about what specifically influenced the behavior *in* the study. Fortunately, the choice is not completely all-or-nothing. If we added controls to the original likability study in the lounge, we would have a more internally valid correlational design. If we went further and introduced models representing conditions of low, medium, and high attractiveness, we would have a less controlled but more externally valid field experiment.

For "basic" research in which we seek the underlying causes of behavior or test hypotheses derived from theories, we are usually concerned with internal validity and thus lean toward highly controlled laboratory experiments. These procedures help to develop our understanding of basic processes, even though they may create a unique or artificial situation that is less externally valid. Conversely, for "applied" research or when we seek to determine whether theoretical explanations are supported in the real world, we lean toward less controlled field experiments or toward descriptive designs that are less artificial and thus have greater external validity.

The third consideration is to be ethical and practical. We must not harm participants, either physically or emotionally, and we must respect their rights. (Another reason not to make people alcoholic.) In deference to such ethical requirements, we always accept reduced reliability and validity. We also must be practical and realistic, accepting that we cannot devise a perfectly reliable and valid study. For example, many studies have tested participants drawn from college Introductory Psychology courses, because they are easily accessible. Such selection is not random, however, because people are not randomly selected for college, and students are not randomly assigned to Introductory Psychology. This may reduce external validity, because such subjects primarily represent the population of Introductory Psychology students and may not represent any broader population. But unless there is a compelling reason to select a different type of participant, we are practical and use these students.

PUTTING IT ALL TOGETHER

Designing a study is a problem-solving task. The problem is to produce the best and clearest evidence you can for testing a particular hypothesis. Solve the problem by designing the study in such a way that it shows the relationship between the variables, minimizes confusion produced by extraneous variables and untrustworthy measurements, and generalizes appropriately. For help, consult Checklist 3.1, which shows the important aspects of a study to consider that we've discussed.

CHECKLIST 3.1 **Questions to consider when designing research**

- What important extraneous variables are likely in this situation?
- Is a descriptive design or a field/laboratory experiment needed?
- Is it a true or quasi-experiment?
- Have important variables been controlled?
- Is the measurement of variables reliable?
- Do the scores have content and construct validity?
- Does the relationship have internal validity, or are confoundings present?
- Does the relationship have external, ecological, and temporal validity?
- How much confidence do you have in your conclusions?

As we've seen, the key to designing a good, convincing study is to anticipate potential threats to reliability and validity and to build in controls that eliminate them. Therefore, keep these points in mind. (1) State the hypothesis clearly, asking one question about one specific behavior. (2) Be a psychologist, using your knowledge of behavior to identify potential flaws in the design. (3) Rely on the research literature, using solutions that others have already developed. And (4) assume that "Murphy's Law" always applies: Anything that *can* go wrong *will* go wrong. Design your study accordingly.

At the same time, recognize that you cannot control every aspect of a situation. Therefore, deal with the *serious* threats to validity and reliability. You can never create the perfect study, so every decision must necessarily be "the lesser of two evils." Any study ultimately involves two major concerns. First, try to eliminate flaws that can be dealt with practically. Second, consider any remaining flaws when interpreting the results. Leave everything else for the next study.

CHAPTER SUMMARY

1. *Extraneous variables* are variables that can influence the results, but are not variables we intend to study. They can be *participant*, *environmental*, *measurement*, or *researcher variables*, and they can be *systematic* or *unsystematic*.

2. Extraneous variables are a problem because they can (1) influence scores and alter the sample relationship, and (2) lead to errors when interpreting the study, because they are operating in addition to the variables we think are operating.

3. *Reliability* is the degree to which the same event or behavior produces the same score each time it is measured, so that a measurement is consistent and repeatable.

4. *Content validity* is the degree to which a measurement reflects the variable of interest.

5. *Construct validity* is the degree to which a measurement reflects the hypothetical construct of interest.

6. *Internal validity* is the degree to which the relationship found in a study reflects only the relationship between the variables of interest.

7. When an extraneous variable changes systematically with a variable of interest, then the extraneous variable is a *confounding* variable.

8. *External validity* is the degree to which the relationship found in a study generalizes to other individuals and situations.

9. *Ecological validity* is the extent to which a study's results generalize to natural settings and natural behaviors. *Temporal validity* is the extent to which results generalize to other time frames.

10. Extraneous variables are controlled by *eliminating them*, *keeping them constant*, or *balancing their influence*.

11. To demonstrate that changes in variable *X cause* changes in variable *Y*, a study must show that *X* occurs first and is the only variable that could be causing the change.

12. *Descriptive methods* are best for testing a descriptive hypothesis because they tend to have greater external validity. However, they may also have less internal validity.

13. *Experimental methods* are best for testing a causal hypothesis because they tend to have greater internal validity. However, they may also have less external validity.

14. In a *true experiment*, randomly assigning participants to conditions helps to balance out participant variables between the conditions and thus prevent confounding.

15. In a *quasi-experiment*, participants cannot be randomly assigned to conditions, and thus participant variables may confound the independent variable.

16. A *field experiment* is an experiment conducted in a natural setting. Field research tends to have greater external validity, but reduced internal validity.

KEY TERMS   (with page references)

confounding variable 74
construct validity 73
content validity 72
ecological validity 76
environmental variables 66
external validity 76
extraneous variable 64
field experiment 86
internal validity 73

measurement variables 66
participant variables 66
reliability 71
researcher variables 66
systematic variable 70
temporal validity 77
unsystematic variable 70
validity 72

REVIEW QUESTIONS

(Answers for odd-numbered questions and problems are provided in Appendix D.)

1. What is the general question to ask about the data when evaluating any study?

2. What are the two strategies to follow when critically evaluating a study?

3. (a) What is an extraneous variable? (b) What is the difference between a systematic and unsystematic extraneous variable? (c) How do extraneous variables influence the sample relationship? (d) How do they influence our interpretation of nature?

4. (a) In general, what does the term *validity* mean? (b) Why must scientists be concerned about drawing valid inferences?

5. Define the following: (a) content validity, (b) construct validity, (c) internal validity, (d) external validity.

6. (a) What does reliability mean? (b) Why is reliability a necessary part of science? (c) How does unreliability weaken the relationship in the sample data?

7. How do you control an extraneous variable by (a) eliminating it? (b) keeping it constant? (c) balancing it?

8. What do we mean by the term *confounding variable*?

9. (a) What question about a study is raised by the term *ecological validity*? (b) What are two ways the term *temporal validity* is applied?

10. How does randomly assigning participants to conditions prevent confounding from participant variables?

11. (a) Why does increasing internal validity tend to decrease external validity? (b) Why does increasing external validity tend to decrease internal validity?

12. (a) What are the advantages and disadvantages of descriptive research methods? (b) How do they influence a researcher's conclusions?

13. (a) What are the advantages and disadvantages of experimental methods? (b) How do they influence a researcher's conclusions?

14. (a) What are field experiments? (b) What is their major advantage? (c) What is their major potential weakness?

15. (a) What is the difference between a true independent variable and a quasi-independent variable? (b) What is the problem with using the latter to draw causal inferences?

APPLICATION QUESTIONS

16. After taking a test, you hear the following complaints. Each is actually about whether the test is reliable or valid. Identify the specific issue raised by each. (a) "The test is unfair because it does not reflect my knowledge of the material." (b) "The questions were 'tricky' and required that I be good at solving riddles." (c) "My essay makes the same points as my friend's, but I got a lower grade." (d) "Based on my grade and how I studied in this course, I believe I know how well I'll do in other courses." (e) "I doubt that what caused students to perform poorly or well on the test was how much they studied."

17. While testing the less attractive models in the likability study, you are in a nasty mood. Coincidentally, while testing the more attractive models, you are in a good mood. (a) What do we call the variable of your mood? (b) What two techniques could you use to deal with this variable?

18. You study participants' memory for a story, comparing the recall of those who read it silently to that of others who read it out loud. (a) Will you have greater external validity if you test only males or only females, or if you test both genders? (b) Draw a diagram to show how you would balance participants' gender.

19. To test the hypothesis that drinking red wine daily prevents heart disease, we select elderly people who have consumed either zero, one, or two glasses of red wine daily during their lives and determine the health of their hearts. (a) What type of design is this? (b) What term do we use to refer to the amount of wine a person drinks? (c) What do we call the amounts we examine? (d) What do we call the healthiness of participants' hearts? (e) How confident can we be when concluding that drinking more wine reduces heart disease? Why?

20. How would you conduct the above study using a correlational design?

21. Red wine contains an acid that causes headaches, so people who drink more red wine probably take more aspirin. Taking aspirin may prevent

heart disease. (a) In the study in question 19, what term do we use to refer to the aspirin that people take? (b) What problem of validity pertains to this situation, and how does it affect our conclusions?

22. In the study in question 19, describe how you would control the variable of aspirin by (a) eliminating it, (b) keeping it constant, and (c) balancing it.

23. When conducting a study, a researcher wears a white "lab coat" and carries a clipboard and stopwatch. How might these details influence the internal and external validity of the study?

24. We hypothesize that a person's frequency of changing sexual partners is related to how much the person fears sexually transmitted diseases. How should we study this relationship, and what inherent research flaws must we accept?

DISCUSSION QUESTIONS

25. Consider the hypothesis that greater exposure to violence from television or movies results in more aggressive behavior. (a) For ethical reasons, what might be the best design for determining whether this relationship exists? (b) What is the trade-off involved in being ethical?

26. A researcher reads numerous traffic accident reports and finds that red-colored automobiles are involved in the most traffic accidents. He concludes that certain colors cause more accidents. (a) What type of research method was used? (b) Are the researcher's inferences correct? Why? (c) What specific confounding variables might be operating? (*Hint*: Think participant variables.) (d) What design is needed to more convincingly support his inference? Describe this study.

27. You test the effectiveness of motivational training by providing it to half of your college's football team. The remaining members receive no training. The dependent variable is the coach's evaluation of each player. (a) What type of design is this? (b) What is the advantage to testing the football team, instead of testing introductory psychology students? (c) What specific flaws occur as a result of your design?

28. Create a descriptive hypothesis and describe how to test it using a correlational design. (a) Identify at least two important extraneous variables that might be operating. (b) How would these variables impact on the reliability and/or validity of your study? (c) How could you control these variables?

29. Create a causal hypothesis and describe how to test it in an experiment. (a) Is it a true or quasi-experiment? (b) Identify at least two important extraneous variables that might be operating. (c) How would these variables impact on the reliability and/or validity of your study? (d) How could you control these variables?

Creating a Reliable and Valid Experiment

GETTING STARTED

To understand this chapter, recall the following:

- What a relationship is and what its "strength" is.
- What an independent variable (factor) is and what the conditions (levels) of an independent variable are.
- What a dependent variable is.
- What extraneous variables are and how they threaten reliability and validity.

Your goals in this chapter are to learn:

- How to select the conditions of a factor, how control groups are used, and what a strong manipulation is.
- How to design scoring criteria, create a sensitive dependent variable, and observe reliable behaviors.
- What order effects are and how to deal with them.
- How to maintain consistency in a study.
- How a powerful design is created and what error variance is.

This chapter presents the specific techniques used in designing a reliable and valid study. For now, we'll focus on *true experiments*, because they provide the greatest opportunity to control extraneous variables. Similar techniques, however, are used when conducting quasi-experiments and descriptive research.

As you know, we begin a design by creating an acceptable scientific hypothesis, identifying the relevant population, and considering the sample we'll select. In conjunction with this, there are essentially three steps to designing an experiment: operationally defining the independent variable, defining the dependent variable, and designing the remainder of the testing situation to control extraneous variables. In the following sections, we'll discuss each of these steps separately, although in real research, they must all be considered simultaneously.

SELECTING THE INDEPENDENT VARIABLE

Once you have developed a hypothesis about a behavior's cause, you then select and define the independent variable. The specifics of the "treatments" you choose, however, depend on the specific behavior, variables, and participants being studied. As you'll see repeatedly, design decisions are always made in response to the questions "What is it you wish to study?" and then "What aspects must you control?"

In the literature you'll find various ways of manipulating an independent variable to choose from.

Approaches to Manipulating an Independent Variable

Researchers often manipulate a factor by presenting participants with different *stimuli* or changing the characteristics of a stimulus. Thus, we might present stimuli that differ along some physical dimension and then measure participants' detection or recognition of the stimuli. Or we might measure the attitudes of children after playing with different types of toys or adults after being exposed to words having different meanings or connotations. We can study the causes of aggression and such by showing participants videos that depict different behaviors and then measuring participants' subsequent aggression or other reactions.

The independent variable may also be the context in which a stimulus is presented, while the stimulus itself is kept constant. For example, we might present various amounts of background noise, change the arrangement of furniture, or vary the number of people present while measuring participants' performance of a task. We might examine how people develop attitudes by presenting a point of view using different types of arguments or speakers. We can study learning processes by presenting different rewards or punishments and measuring participants' rate of learning. Or we can examine participants' memory or thought processes under conditions of different moods that are created by exposure to different words or stories, or even through different levels of hypnosis.

Instead, a factor can consist of the instructions or information given to partici pants in each condition. We might tell different participants that they are involved in different social situations or levels of competition. We can study participants' recall for an event by varying the type and amount of information conveyed in questions about the event. We might tell participants different types of information about another person or event to see how they then react to the person. Or we might expose participants to situations that conflict with an attitude they advocate or have them fail at a task, to study how they resolve conflicts or attribute blame.

To manipulate a social setting, researchers often employ **confederates,** who are people enlisted by a researcher to act as other participants or "accidental" passersby, creating a particular social situation to which the "real" participants then respond. For example, we create various types of games involving a participant and a confederate to study the participants' cooperativeness, aggressiveness, or competitiveness. Or, researchers have had confederates claim to have health problems, be lost, or need money, and then measured participants' helpfulness depending on the characteristics of the confederate or situation. Similarly, we can increase peer pressure in a situation by varying the number of confederates present.

Sometimes researchers manipulate internal, physiological processes. Here, the conditions might involve giving participants different amounts of alcohol or other drugs, manipulating the amount of food, water, or sleep participants get, or varying the levels of sensory stimulation they receive. Using animal subjects, researchers employ surgical techniques to create different conditions in which parts of the brain are altered and then measure the differences produced in the animals' motivation, emotion, or memory.

Often researchers manipulate a variable because they believe it changes an internal psychological state called an intervening variable. An **intervening variable** is influenced by the independent variable, which in turn influences the dependent variable. It "intervenes" or comes between the independent and dependent variable. For example, we might hypothesize that being frustrated makes people angry, and that greater anger then leads to more aggressive behavior. Here, we would manipulate the independent variable of frustration—for example, by preventing participants from obtaining a desired reward. This should change the intervening variable of anger, which should then influence participants' scores on the dependent variable of aggressiveness.

Recognize that psychologists distinguish between two general types of internal psychological states. A **state characteristic** is a temporary, changeable attribute that is influenced by situational factors. For example, you have a certain "state anxiety," the level of anxiety you experience depending on the situation you are in. (Suddenly realizing you have an exam will raise your state anxiety.) Conversely, a **trait characteristic** is stable over time and not easily influenced by situational factors. (Think "personality traits" here.) For example, self-esteem is generally defined as a trait characteristic because it is relatively unaffected by the situation you're in. Some attributes have both state and trait components:

A person has a momentary state anxiety as well as a general trait anxiety. Other attributes, such as self-esteem, are considered to have only a trait component. The distinction between state and trait is important, because only state characteristics are studied in true experiments: We can manipulate the situation to alter temporary states, such as state anxiety, but not rather permanent traits, such as self-esteem.

REMEMBER   *State characteristics* are transient and can be experimentally manipulated. *Trait characteristics* are rather permanent and cannot be easily manipulated.

Selecting a Valid and Reliable Manipulation

Recall that we always want to build in validity and reliability, and in experiments, this begins when selecting the independent variable.

First, consider whether the variable has *construct validity*: Does it allow valid inferences about the underlying construct as we conceptualize it? For example, are we truly increasing the "social pressure" a person experiences by increasing the number of confederates in a room? If a variable lacks construct validity, then any inferences we draw about underlying psychological processes will be in error.

Likewise, we are concerned with *content validity*: Does the procedure allow accurate inferences about the variable of interest? If, for example, the objective is to create videos containing different amounts of violence, then we must completely measure *this* aspect of the films. But if we select different videos based on their humorous content or their plots, then we are not dealing with only the violent content.

Of paramount importance is *internal validity*: We want to show that changing the independent variable causes changes in the dependent variable, so we must be sure to eliminate the potential influence of *confounding* variables that might actually be a cause. Thus, we want to be sure that whether a participant helps a confederate does not depend on the confederate's looks, mannerisms, and so on. Or, if we show participants videos depicting violence, we want to be sure their responses are to the film and not to the social situation created by the presence of an experimenter.

In addition, we also seek *external validity*: Can we confidently generalize the results to other individuals and situations? The independent variable should not create situations that are so atypical that they generalize to a very limited type of participant or situation. Also, look for *ecological* and *temporal validity*.

Don't forget that the procedure also should be reliable. Recall that reliability is defined as consistently measuring a variable, without error. By consistently measuring the independent variable, we can then consistently manipulate it. The goal is that all participants in one condition should receive exactly the same amount or category of the variable, and when we change to another condition, everyone there should receive exactly the same new amount. Thus, if we are comparing the influence of violence in videos, the low-violence film should be consistently perceived as "low" by all participants, and the high-violence one should be consistently "high" for everyone. If there is inconsistency in a manipulation, then we are not always presenting the condition we think we are, and our conclusions will be based on the wrong amounts of the independent variable.

And finally, the situation created by the independent variable must be *ethical*. As we'll see in the next chapter, researchers do not have the right to callously harm others in the name of science.

Questions of reliability and validity are ultimately resolved by theoretical discussion, replications, and research showing that a procedure is reliable or valid because it produces the same results as other accepted procedures. Therefore, as usual, the research literature is the first and best source for finding reliable and valid ways of creating independent variables.

An Example Study

As an example of an experiment we might conduct, say that we are interested in the influence of the physical environment on behavior, and in the literature we find studies that examine the influence of different temperatures. In particular is the hypothesis that people become more aggressive as room temperature increases. It might be fun to test this hypothesis: We'll place participants in a laboratory room under a particular temperature level, and then measure the dependent variable of their aggression. People need to be aggressive toward something, so we'll measure how aggressively they feel toward the experimenter. But! Being psychologists, we recognize that in most normal social settings, participants will tend not to act very aggressively. To make participants more inclined to respond aggressively in our study, we'll have the experimenter provoke participants by being a little rude and nasty to them (as in Bell, 1980).

SELECTING THE CONDITIONS OF THE INDEPENDENT VARIABLE

Assuming you've selected a valid and reliable independent variable, the next step is to select the specific conditions to expose participants to. There are two decisions about the conditions to simultaneously consider: the number of conditions to present and the amount of the variable in each.

First, decide on the *number* of levels of the independent variable to include. You can examine virtually any number of conditions, but you need at least two to show a relationship: to show that aggressiveness increases with higher temperatures, we must show that aggression scores increase when changing from one temperature to at least one other temperature. Beyond that, the number of levels to include depends on the specific hypothesis being tested (and on a small statistical issue we'll discuss later). At the same time, remember that the purpose of research is to learn about nature, and the more conditions you include, the more you learn. In fact, once you've gone to the trouble of creating a procedure, contacting participants, and so on, it's not much more work to test another condition or two.

The other decision is to select the specific amount or category of the independent variable that each condition will present. The particular levels to choose also depend first on the hypothesis. We're investigating the influence of "hot" temperatures, so we don't want conditions where it's cold. Of course, we don't want to kill anybody either, so we'll avoid extremely high temperatures. So we might compare the influence of some temperatures between, say, 70 and 90 degrees Fahrenheit.

An important consideration when selecting the amounts for the conditions is whether to include a *control group*.

Control Groups

Sometimes we create a condition under which we measure participants on the dependent variable after presenting zero amount of the independent variable. A **control group** is a group that receives zero amount of the independent variable or otherwise does not receive any treatment. Groups that receive a nonzero amount of the independent variable or otherwise *do* experience the treatment are called **experimental groups**. A control group shows how individuals behave without the treatment, providing a "baseline" or starting point for evaluating the influence of the variable in the experimental groups. For example, say that in a different experiment we have students study for various amounts of time and then measure their performance on a later exam. The control group would be students who spend zero time studying for the exam. Their exam scores then provide a starting point for determining, literally, whether other amounts of studying in the experimental groups are better than nothing.

A control group is not always essential to a design—whether to include one depends on the question being asked. Control groups are especially useful, however, for eliminating rival hypotheses about what causes dependent scores to change. For example, say that in a memory study, we present a loud background noise to people while they read a story, and find that they poorly remember the story. It appears that the noise interferes with memory, but only if we assume that participants would *otherwise* retain the story well. But, perhaps the story is intrinsically difficult to recall. To eliminate this rival hypothesis, we would compare the noise condition to a control condition—an identical condition but with no noise. If retention is poor in both conditions, we could conclude that this was due to the story and that the presence of noise literally does not make a difference. But if retention is lower with noise, then we'd have support for the hypothesis that noise lowers retention.

Sometimes it's not possible to administer zero amount of an independent variable, and then the control group is tested under a "normal" or "neutral" condition. For example, for our temperature study, there must always be *some* temperature present, so using a 70-degree condition would actually be the control condition of normal room temperature. Or, if we are presenting cheerful or sad statements to alter participants' mood, the control condition might involve emotionally neutral statements.

And sometimes the equivalent of a control condition involves comparing participants' performance to the result we would expect if they were guessing. For example, to study "psychic abilities," researchers "send" participants a telepathic message about a card drawn from a deck of playing cards. The number of cards someone correctly selects is then compared to the number we'd expect if the person were merely guessing. (As it turns out, "psychics" do not perform above a chance level [e.g., Hanssel, 1980].)

REMEMBER   *Control conditions* provide a clearer indication of the influence of a manipulation and of the causes of participants' responses.

Creating a Powerful Design Through the Independent Variable

There is an important principle underlying many of the design decisions researchers make that we'll now introduce. As you know, we cannot claim to have demonstrated anything about a behavior unless we find a relationship in the sample data. Therefore, at every step of the design, we are concerned about whether we will see a relationship in the scores. We can do nothing if the predicted relationship does not exist in nature. However, the real shame is if there is the relationship in nature, but because of some mistake on our part, we fail to produce it in our sample and therefore miss that the relationship exists. To prevent this, in research terminology, we try to create a "powerful" study.

First, understand what a powerful study is. "Power" is actually a statistical term, so a precise definition is in Chapter 7, where we review statistics. For now, a **powerful design** is one that, when the predicted relationship exists in nature, is more likely to produce a clear and convincing sample relationship. That is, we try to design a study that will convincingly show the predicted relationship. Then, we are unlikely to miss that the relationship exists in nature, so we are unlikely to *erroneously* conclude that our hypothesis is wrong. If we still do not find the sample relationship, then we can be confident that we didn't miss it, but rather that it does not exist and so the hypothesis really *is* wrong.

Conversely, designs that are not powerful are less likely to show a relationship in the data. The problem is that if we fail to find the relationship in such a study, we are unsure if it is because the variables are not related, or if we simply missed seeing the real relationship. Therefore, anytime we end up failing to support our hypothesis, we worry whether we had a sufficiently powerful design: Were we likely to have shown the relationship if, in fact, it exists in nature?

REMEMBER   With a *powerful design*, we are more confident that, if the predicted relationship exists, we will see it in our sample data.

But, you say, how can we be fooled into missing a relationship when it exists? To see how, let's look at an unconvincing sample relationship. Say that in the temperature study, higher scores indicate greater aggressiveness. Then say that, as we increase room temperature, participants' aggression scores barely increase in a consistent fashion, as in Table 4.1. This is an unconvincing relationship because it is so "weak" or inconsistent. The inconsistency occurs because of two aspects of the data. First, in a consistent relationship, one or close to one score on the dependent variable tends to appear in one condition, and a different dependent score tends to show up in a different condition. In Table 4.1, however, rather different aggression scores are occurring *within* each temperature condition (within each column in the table).

Notice that we have two important terms for describing this inconsistency in scores. First, when there are more frequent and/or larger differences among scores, the scores are described as more *variable*, or as showing greater **variability**. Second, as we'll review in Chapter 7, a way to measure variability is to compute the statistic called *variance*. Specifically, the variability in scores that decreases the strength of a relationship is called **error variance**. Thus, greater *variability* among scores within each condition, or in other words, larger *error variance* results in a weaker relationship.

REMEMBER *Variability* refers to differences among scores. Greater variability within each condition—called *error variance*—reduces the strength of a relationship.

The second aspect of the data in Table 4.1 that weakens the relationship is that the scores from the different conditions overlap, so there is not much change in aggression scores *between* the conditions. Overall, as we increase temperature (traveling from left to right in the table), largely the same batch of scores show up in each condition. Thus, changing temperature *literally* does not make much of a difference in participants' aggressiveness.

As we'll see later, we should compute *descriptive statistics* to more precisely summarize the data and relationship. The starting point in most experiments

TABLE 4.1 Example of an Unconvincing Relationship between Room Temperature and Aggression Scores

	Conditions of room temperature		
	Low temperature	*Medium temperature*	*High temperature*
Aggression scores →	5	7	6
	6	4	4
	2	5	6
	7	6	8
	$\overline{X} = 5.0$	$\overline{X} = 5.5$	$\overline{X} = 6.0$

is to compute the average or *mean* of the scores in each condition (each column). As shown in Table 4.1, the symbol for a sample mean is $\overline{X}$, and the means here are 5.0, 5.5, and 6.0 for the three levels, respectively. These means also suggest a weak relationship, because increasing temperature did not, *on average*, produce much of a difference in aggression.

With such data, we—and our statistical procedures—could easily conclude that there really is no relationship here. This is because, even when our hypothesis is wrong, we do not expect everyone to get *exactly* the same aggression score. Instead, individual differences and fluctuating extraneous variables will always produce some differences in scores, but they signify nothing. Thus, these data are of the sort we'd expect if there were *not* a relationship between our variables, so we are likely to conclude that our hypothesis is wrong. If, however, the variables *are* related in nature as we proposed, then we will be *erroneously* concluding that there is not the predicted relationship and that our hypothesis is wrong.

On the other hand, say we had obtained the more consistent, "stronger" relationship shown in Table 4.2. This is stronger because, first, there is less error variance, so there tends to be one or *close* to one score in one condition, and a different, one score in another condition. Second, there tend to be large differences in scores *between* the conditions. The result is that the scores in each condition do not overlap with the scores in other conditions, so that we see one batch of similar aggression scores in one condition, and a very different batch of similar scores in the next. Likewise, the means of the scores in each column suggest a stronger relationship, because quite literally, increasing temperature *did*, on average, produce a substantial difference in aggression. When a sample relationship looks like this, we—and our statistical procedures—are unlikely to conclude that the predicted relationship is not present. Such a distinct pattern is unlikely to occur simply through *random* individual differences and extraneous variables, so instead, these data seem to convincingly show a relationship. And, if our variables are related in nature as we proposed, then with such data, we are likely to *correctly* conclude that there is the predicted relationship and that our hypothesis is confirmed.

TABLE 4.2   Example of a Convincing Relationship between Room Temperature and Aggression Scores

Conditions of room temperature

	Low temperature	Medium temperature	High temperature
Aggression scores ⟶	5	24	46
	4	23	45
	3	22	44
	4	23	45
	$\overline{X} = 4$	$\overline{X} = 23$	$\overline{X} = 45$

Thus, assuming that room temperature and aggression are related in nature, we would prefer to obtain the stronger relationship in Table 4.2, because then we will not miss that the relationship really exists. A design that is more likely to accomplish this is a more powerful design. Therefore, designing a powerful study boils down to trying to *decrease* the variability among scores *within* each condition, and to *increase* the differences among scores *between* conditions.

REMEMBER   To design a powerful study, minimize error variance and maximize the differences in scores between conditions.

Three aspects of building a powerful study are related to designing the independent variable. The first is to create a *strong manipulation*.

A Strong Manipulation   As we've just seen, large differences in scores *between* the conditions help to produce a convincing relationship. We assume that changing the conditions of the independent variable causes differences in the scores, so we select conditions that will potentially produce large differences. A **strong manipulation** involves conditions that are likely to produce large differences in scores between the conditions. It will "strongly" influence participants' behavior and produce large, obvious differences in their scores between the conditions. And, if there are large differences in the scores between conditions, then there will also be large differences between the means from the conditions. You can create strong manipulations in two ways.

First, select amounts or categories of the independent variable that are substantially different from one another. For example, using temperatures of 70, 80, and 90 degrees Fahrenheit seems to be a reasonably strong manipulation of room temperature: If higher temperatures do influence aggressiveness, adding 10 degrees in each condition should show this. Conversely, comparing temperatures of 70, 71, and 72 degrees Fahrenheit would not be a strong manipulation: Even if temperature does influence aggression, we might not detect a change in behavior with such subtle temperature changes. Likewise, in a different study, say we are presenting happy or sad words to alter participants' mood. For a strong manipulation, the happy words should be *very* happy and the sad ones should be *very* sad.

The second aspect of a strong manipulation is to have participants experience a condition sufficiently for it to dramatically influence their behavior. For example, a strong manipulation would also have participants experience the temperature for a long enough period of time (say 20 minutes) so that we dramatically alter their aggressiveness. Being in the room for only a minute or two would hardly be expected to "strongly" influence anything. Or, if we're presenting happy or sad words to influence participants' mood, a strong manipulation would be to present *many* happy words or *many* sad ones. Or, say we are studying how different speaking styles influence the persuasiveness of a message. Rather than presenting a short message with only one example of the style, we'd present a longer message with many aspects conveying that style.

> **REMEMBER**   With a *strong manipulation,* changing the conditions is
> likely to produce large differences in dependent scores.

Another way to ensure a strong manipulation is to prevent *diffusion of treatment.*

Diffusion of Treatment   A **diffusion of treatment** occurs when participants in one condition are aware of the treatment given in other conditions. People who have already participated in a condition may tell future participants about their experience, or while participating in the study, some may "figure out" what we're doing. Either way, when participants are aware of the various treatments, the influence of a particular condition can be reduced or eliminated. Thus, if participants are aware that we're manipulating room temperature, they may not react normally to any temperature condition they're in. And, not only will the strength of a treatment be reduced, but internal validity will be threatened as well: Instead of being influenced only by a condition, participants will be influenced by information they have about the nature of the study.

Our first line of defense against diffusion of treatment is to explain to participants why they should not tell other potential participants about the study. However, the more interesting, creative, or bizarre our treatments, the more people will want to talk about them. Therefore, another strategy is to try to complete the study in a brief period, to minimize the time during which people discuss it. Or, we can test participants from different locations so that they have little contact with one another. And finally, as you'll see, we can also disguise a treatment.

> **REMEMBER**   *Diffusion of treatment* occurs when participants are
> aware of a treatment so that it has less impact.

One other aspect to having a powerful independent variable is to reliably manipulate it.

A Reliable Independent Variable   We saw that reliably manipulating the independent variable is important so that we know what really occurs in each condition (when we think its 70 degrees in a room, it should *be* 70 degrees). In addition, however, an unreliable manipulation decreases the power of a design. For example, say that temperature does influence aggressiveness as we predict. Then, anytime the temperature fluctuates even slightly for people who are in the same condition, we will see differences in their aggression scores. With more variability in scores *within* each condition—more *error variance*—we will see a weaker relationship, or perhaps no relationship at all. Conversely, reliably manipulating the independent variable helps to minimize error variance, so that we are more likely to see the predicted relationship when it exists.

REMEMBER   The more that the independent variable fluctuates *within* each condition, the more inconsistent the relationship is likely to be.

Manipulation Checks

So far, we've been *planning* the conditions of an independent variable that *should* influence participants as predicted. We can, however, also check that the manipulation *does* have its intended effect. A **manipulation check** is a measurement, in addition to the dependent variable, that determines whether the conditions had their intended effect. Usually this check is made after participants have been measured on the dependent variable (otherwise it might provide cues that create diffusion of treatment). Then we might ask participants to answer questions about their experience in a condition, have them complete a task that reflects its influence, or measure their physiological responses to it. So, if the goal was to test people in a hot room, we check that they thought it really was hot. Or, if the intent was to make participants happy, we check that they really were happy. Such procedures are especially important for checking on an intervening variable. Thus, if we thought that higher room temperature produced greater aggressiveness by way of the intervening variable of producing greater anger, we could also directly measure each participant's anger. Such checks increase our confidence that the independent variable worked as intended, which in turn increases internal validity for explaining why dependent scores changed as they did.

REMEMBER   A *manipulation check* is a measurement for confirming that the independent variable had its intended effect.

For help remembering the issues when designing the independent variable, consult Checklist 4.1.

CHECKLIST 4.1 **Questions to consider when designing an independent variable**

- Will the variable provide content and construct validity?
- Will the operational definition prevent confounding?
- Will the conditions generalize well?
- Is a control group appropriate?
- Is the manipulation strong and reliable, without diffusion of treatment?
- Is a manipulation check needed?

SELECTING THE DEPENDENT VARIABLE

Along with designing the conditions of the independent variable, we must also develop an operational definition of the dependent variable. As with everything, which dependent variable to select and how to measure it depend on the hypothesis and behavior we're investigating, our participants, and the perspective we are taking. Most dependent variables, however, employ one of the following approaches.

Approaches to Measuring the Dependent Variable

Often the dependent variable involves direct observation and measurement of the behavior under study. For example, we measure eating behavior by measuring the quantity of food that participants eat, or if studying helping behavior, we measure whether participants help or not. At other times, the behavior we observe is an indirect measure of an unseen, internal process. For example, researchers take physiological measurements of respiration and heart rate to make inferences about a person's anxiety or stress level. Or, the number of associations between words that participants provide is used as a measure of their creativity. In studying social processes, we might infer a person's response to peer pressure by measuring the amount of time needed to complete a task or the number of mistakes made while doing it.

A common indirect measure is **reaction time**, the amount of time a participant takes to respond to a stimulus. After presenting stimuli that differ along a physical or mental dimension, we use differences in reaction time to infer the underlying cognitive or emotional processes involved.

Researchers also examine participants' judgments about events or other people. Such judgments are often measured using a **forced-choice procedure**, in which participants must select from the possible choices we provide (e.g., a multiple-choice test). The simplest of these is a **yes-no task**. Researchers in perception, for example, might manipulate characteristics of a visual illusion and have participants indicate whether they still perceive the illusion. Note that any recognition judgment about a stimulus actually reflects two components: a basic ability to detect the stimulus and a bias toward making a particular response. (For example, are we cautious or liberal when saying yes?) Researchers use a statistical procedure called "signal detection analysis" to separate these two components. (Many introductory perception texts discuss this procedure.)

Sometimes, instead of an all-or-none choice, researchers obtain more refined judgments. For example, in studying how people perceive the passage of time, we might ask them to indicate the duration of an interval in seconds, or to draw a line to indicate its duration. In other situations we may use a **sorting task**, in which participants indicate their judgments by sorting stimuli into different groups to show the categories they are using to organize them.

Another approach is to directly ask participants to describe their feelings or thoughts, providing what are called **self-reports**. Often self-reports involve completing a rating scale called a **Likert-type question**. Here, a statement is presented, and participants rate their response to it, typically using a scale between "strongly agree" and "strongly disagree." (We used Likert questions in the previous chapter when measuring a female's judgment of a male's attractiveness and likability.) Similar rating scales can be used to measure such things as participants' attitudes, their perceptions, or their confidence in a response. In other forms of self-reports, participants may provide a running commentary of their mental activities or keep a diary.

Selecting a Valid and Reliable Dependent Variable

You should critically evaluate the operational definition of the dependent variable using the same criteria we previously applied to the independent variable. First, does the dependent variable provide *construct validity*, reflecting the hypothetical construct as we conceptualize it? In particular, state characteristics are transient attributes that we can change by manipulating an independent variable. Trait characteristics, however, are rather immune to momentary events, so it is usually pointless to have them as dependent variables. The dependent variable should also provide *content validity*, such that we actually and only measure the variable of interest. A score should not depend on a person's abilities and experiences unrelated to the behavior we are studying. Further, we also seek *internal validity*, such that changes in scores reflect the influence of the independent variable but do not reflect changes in extraneous variables. And we seek *external validity*, such that the observed relationship generalizes to other individuals and settings. This especially includes ecological validity, so that we measure a participant's real-world behaviors that generalize to real-world psychological processes. We are also concerned that measurements of the dependent variable be *reliable*, so that the scores do not reflect random error. And, as always, the dependent variable should be *ethical*. As we'll discuss in the next chapter, our measurements should not intrude on participants' rights or cause them undue stress.

On the other hand, any dependent variable will have some weakness in terms of reliability and validity. When directly observing a behavior, for example, we may observe an unreliable example of the behavior. (By watching people eat, we might cause them to eat less than usual.) Self-reports can be unreliable and invalid because people may not know or care to divulge their true feelings. Asking participants to sort words into categories might reduce content validity because the sorting process could partially be a test of vocabulary, or asking people to indicate a response by drawing may partially be a test of their drawing ability. We also must be careful when making inferences about any internal construct. (If participants fail to recall a stimulus, is it because they initially "stored" it poorly or because they cannot "locate" it in memory?) Likewise, with physiological measurements, we do not always know which psychological response is being reflected. (For example, anger and fear produce very similar physiological reactions.)

Recall that one strategy for bolstering a conclusion is to use *converging operations*—different approaches that "converge" on the same behavior. We can employ this strategy by testing the same participants on multiple dependent variables within a single study. If the same conclusion about a treatment or behavior is reached from each measure, we have greater confidence that we are not being misled by any one of them. For example, say we obtain physiological measurements and self-reports of participants' emotional state. If they report greater anxiety when also physiologically more anxious, we have greater confidence in the validity of either variable. Measuring participants on more than one dependent variable is also very cost-effective, yielding considerably more information for the effort involved in a study. On the other hand, it's not always necessary or even a good idea to employ multiple measures. A single variable—especially if it is an accepted measure—can be satisfactory. Using just one variable is particularly beneficial because then we don't overload participants with many confusing tasks or make their participation too tedious.

DESIGNING THE DEPENDENT VARIABLE

Assuming you've selected a construct- and content-valid dependent variable, you must determine exactly how you'll use it to produce participants' scores. The primary concern at this point is to develop a reliable procedure, so that any time participants exhibit a particular behavior, they are consistently assigned the same particular score. The way to accomplish this is first through the scoring criteria. **Scoring criteria** define the system for assigning different scores to different responses. These criteria determine when a response is correct or not, what constitutes the beginning and end of a response, how to distinguish one response from another, and all of the other decisions necessary for consistently assigning a particular score to a particular response. Then we'll "know" what participants did or did not do to receive a certain score, and that any one else who received that score did the same things.

You need scoring criteria even for apparently straightforward variables. For example, say we test participants' memory by presenting them a list of words, and then counting the words correctly recalled. Is it a correct response if someone writes "bare" but the list contained "bear"? What if for "mother" people recall "mom"? What if they recall the correct words but in a different order than in the list? Likewise, in the temperature study, we might obtain *self-reports* asking participants to describe their feelings toward the experimenter. But then we must decide what scores are to be assigned when participants say, for example, "She's not very nice" versus "I hate him." Asking participants multiple-choice questions might seem more straightforward, but we still must decide what aggression score to assign for each choice.

Scoring criteria will be even more elaborate when a behavior is more difficult to quantify, as when measuring creativity, sexism, or motivation, because here you must evaluate a participant's behavior subjectively. For example, in the temperature study, instead of asking participants questions, we might surreptitiously observe them while interacting with the experimenter (perhaps watching them through a one-way mirror). We would assign each participant an aggression score based on our judgments of how aggressively he or she behaved. Then, we might define an aggression score as the number of aggressive acts exhibited toward the researcher. But what is an aggressive act? The strategy is always to minimize inconsistency and bias by minimizing the *interpretation* you must give to a behavior. Instead, look for observable, concrete behaviors that have a distinct beginning and end. Thus, we could define aggressive acts in terms of such observable behaviors as yelling, hitting, slamming things on the desk, and so on.

You must also define how to assign scores when such behaviors occur. Does each word a participant yells count as one aggressive act, or is each uninterrupted string of words one aggressive act? Does a nasty look receive the same score as a punch? And so on. Or, if you are observing whether someone smiles in response to a stimulus, how shortly after the stimulus must a smile occur to be considered a response to that stimulus? How long must a smile last for it to be counted?

Recognize that participants *never* behave in an ideal way. Therefore, try to anticipate every possible variation on the expected response, so if it happens, you know how to score it. For help, refer to the literature to find acceptable scoring criteria. Beyond this, your decisions are usually arbitrary: Simply define one way to score each behavior so that you eliminate inconsistency, sloppiness, and error.

REMEMBER   Precise *scoring criteria* that focus on observable behaviors are necessary for measuring a behavior reliably.

When designing the scoring criteria and other aspects of the dependent variable, remember that we want to create a powerful design. A major contributor to this is to create a sensitive measure.

Creating a Sensitive Measure

The goal of an experiment is to observe different behaviors as the conditions change. Therefore, the measurement procedure must *discriminate* or distinguish between behaviors, giving a different score each time a behavior is even slightly different. Only when two individuals exhibit the identical behavior should they receive the same score. In other words, we seek a sensitive measure. A **sensitive dependent measure** produces different scores for small differences in behavior. This lets us detect even a small influence that a manipulation produces.

Sensitivity is increased through observing responses that can differ subtly, and by precisely measuring those differences. For example, a 5-point rating scale is more sensitive for measuring aggression than a yes-no question. This is because if we can indicate only "yes" when someone is either somewhat aggressive or very aggressive, then we will miss such differences. But, using a "Likert scale," we might assign a "3" to somewhat aggressive people and a "5" to very aggressive people. Now these subtle differences in aggression will be reflected in the data. Using a physiological measurement might be even more sensitive.

As the above illustrates, to produce a sensitive measure, always try to measure a *quantitative* variable that reflects the amount or degree of a behavior. Not only does this provide more precise information about the behavior, it also produces a more powerful study. For example, even if the temperature conditions produce only subtle differences in the behavior, with a sensitive measure we are likely to see differences in the scores *between* conditions. On the other hand, it is less desirable to use a *qualitative* variable that merely categorizes a behavior (such as yes-no), because it will miss small differences in the behavior. This reduces the "power" of the study because we are less likely to see much difference in scores between the conditions.

REMEMBER   Create a *sensitive* dependent variable by precisely measuring subtle differences in behavior.

Part of creating a sensitive measure is to avoid restricting the range.

Avoiding a Restricted Range of Scores

So that we can distinguish subtle differences in participants' behavior, it should be possible for them to obtain any of a wide range of scores. If the design artificially limits participants to only a few possible scores, then we have a restricted range. **Restriction of range** occurs when the range of possible scores on a variable is limited. For example, people can exhibit great differences in aggressiveness, so our procedure should allow scores that also reflect these differences. But say we restrict the range, so that participants can score only one of three different scores. This reduces sensitivity because we can detect only three levels of aggression, and it reduces our power because everyone will score close to or at the same score, so there cannot be large differences in scores between the conditions.

To avoid a restricted range, first consider the scores you will assign. If in the temperature study, participants can obtain an aggression score of only 1, 2, or 3, the range is restricted. But if they can score anywhere between 0 and 100, the range is not restricted. Second, look for aspects of the testing situation that, *practically speaking*, limit the behaviors or scores that might occur.

One such aspect is when the task is too easy or otherwise biased so that all scores are likely to be near the highest possible score. In that case, the data will show **ceiling effects**: The lowest potential scores—from the worst-scoring participants—are very high, so scores cannot differ much because would-be higher-scoring individuals cannot get much higher (everyone's scores are "hitting the ceiling"). For example, if in the temperature study we accept almost any action as being aggressive, then not-so-aggressive people will have a high score. Then the range is restricted, because other people who get seriously aggressive cannot score higher, and we will fail to detect differences in aggressive behavior.

The range is also restricted if the task is too hard or otherwise biased toward producing low scores. Here, the data will show **floor effects**: The highest potential scores—from the best-scoring participants—are very low, so scores cannot differ much because would-be lower-scoring individuals cannot get much lower (everyone's scores are "hitting the floor"). For example, most laboratory subjects will not physically assault a researcher, so it's unreasonable to make a high aggression score depend on such extreme actions: Realistically, no one will obtain high scores, and everyone will have low scores. Then, truly nonaggressive participants cannot score lower than more aggressive ones, and, again, we will fail to discriminate between behaviors.

Thus, a sensitive procedure is, in part, one that avoids ceiling and floor effects. To achieve this, the typical participant should start with scores in the middle between very low and very high scores. But it should also be realistically possible to obtain higher or lower scores as the conditions of the independent variable change.

REMEMBER   A *restricted range* occurs when the range of possible scores is limited.

Observing Reliable Behaviors

So far we've discussed unreliability in terms of inconsistency and error when we measure a behavior. However, unreliability can also come from inconsistency in the *behavior* itself. If a participant's behavior is an atypical, unrepresentative response to a condition, then it and the resulting score will be misleading. Instead, we want participants' scores in a condition to accurately reflect their typical behavior in this situation.

There are two strategies for increasing the reliability of the behaviors we observe: *practice trials* and *multiple trials*.

Practice Trials   A participant's behavior—and score—can be unrepresentative because he or she has not "warmed up" on the measurement task. When this is a possibility, we provide **practice trials**: We test participants as in the real study, but we then ignore these trials when analyzing the results. (A "trial" is one complete measurement or observation.) Practice trials are especially useful when studying physical reactions, as in a reaction-time task. Or, if the task is complicated or involves elaborate equipment, practice trials ensure that participants understand the task. In addition, practice trials allow people to get used to being observed, so they are behaving more naturally when providing the real data.

Multiple Trials   A major component of reliability is the number of real trials a participant performs in a condition. A score that is based on only one trial can reflect all sorts of extraneous factors: A participant might be momentarily distracted or might guess, the trial might be especially easy or difficult, or some other aspect of the situation might make the trial peculiar. In such a case, the response and score are not representative of a participant's typical response and score.

To avoid the bias from one unique trial, we observe each participant several times in a condition, observing **multiple trials**. Again we are using the strategy of *balancing* extraneous variables. We assume that differences in a participant's motivation or attention on different trials balance out, that easy trials balance with hard ones, and so on. We then compute each participant's total score or an average (mean) score based on all trials in a condition. When interpreting these summary scores, we are more confident that they reliably reflect the typical response, because we have balanced out the random fluctuations found in individual trials. Also, we have a more powerful design, because by glossing over the unique aspects of individual trials, the scores *within* each condition are more likely to be similar, producing a stronger relationship.

Thus, in the temperature study, we might be inclined to simply ask participants the one question: "How aggressive do you feel toward the researcher?" But, they might not interpret "aggressive" as we intend, they might not recognize their feelings as aggression, or they might not wish to divulge this negative emotion. To overcome such problems, we should instead ask participants several questions that, from different perspectives and using different wording, address participants' positive and negative feelings. Then, by scoring and combining responses to all questions, we produce one score that should accurately reflect a participant's level of aggressiveness toward the experimenter. Likewise, if we're studying memory by testing recall of a list of words, we present several lists per condition, so that we balance out differences in the familiarity, pronounceability, or memorability of any one list. Or, if measuring reaction time to a stimulus, we present many trials per condition to balance out differences in any single stimulus, and to balance momentary lapses that result in being very fast on some trials and asleep at the switch on others.

There is no magic number of trials to observe per condition, although to prevent confounding, all conditions should have the same number of trials. Observe more trials when a trial is more easily influenced by extraneous variables and likely to be unreliable. For example, reaction time is usually measured in milliseconds, so responses—and scores—can be easily influenced by extraneous influences. Therefore, we usually measure many trials per condition (in the range of 40 to 200) to produce a reliable estimate of a participant's typical reaction time. On the other hand, if a behavior is less influenced by momentary, extraneous variables, only one or a few trials are necessary. Also, consider the influence that multiple trials will have on participants and their performance. People can perform many reaction-time trials quickly and easily; they cannot, however, perform great elaborate tasks for hours on end without becoming unduly fatigued or stressed. (If many trials are necessary and mental or physical fatigue is a problem, break up the testing over several days.) Also, multiple trials are not possible if we are surprising participants with a particular stimulus or instructions. (You can surprise someone only once!) As with everything in research, weigh the pros and cons of each choice (and check the literature to see what others have done).

REMEMBER   Provide *practice trials* and test *multiple trials* to increase the reliability of the data.

Although multiple trials add reliability, they also create the problem of *order effects*.

The Problem of Order Effects

Multiple trials introduce a new extraneous variable called order effects. **Order effects** are any influence on performance of a particular trial that arises from its position in the sequence of trials. Two common subtypes of order effects are *practice effects* and *carry-over effects*.

Practice effects are the influence on performance that arises from practicing a task. Even after practice trials, participants may perform initial trials poorly because they are still not warmed up. After more trials, performance can improve because participants become quicker or more accurate. With even more trials, however, performance may decrease again because participants become fatigued or bored.

Carry-over effects are the influence that a particular trial has on performance of subsequent trials. Carry-over effects arise from simply experiencing a trial. For example, if one trial happens to be very frustrating, this feeling may "carry over," lowering performance on subsequent trials. A trial might also be especially boring, easy, or anxiety-provoking, all of which can influence responses to later trials.

A special type of carry-over effect is a **response set,** a bias toward responding in a particular way because of previous responses made. Essentially, responding becomes more of a habit than a natural reaction to a stimulus. Thus, you have a response set when completing a multiple-choice exam if, after the first few questions, you superstitiously believe the correct answer is always choice 4. You might also develop response sets from strategies that have proven successful. For example, unscramble each of the following words:

> ookb
>
> reet
>
> oatc
>
> oabt

You can solve the first three words quickly because of the response set that says to place the final letter first. If you stumbled on the fourth word, however, it's because this strategy no longer worked.

The problem with practice and carry-over effects is that a response is unique because of *where* in the sequence it occurs. Above, your solution of each word is faster or slower than it would be if the word were in a different location in the list. Therefore, participants' overall performance is tied to the particular order used, and so the summary scores are an unreliable indication of the typical response, especially when compared to other orders.

REMEMBER *Order effects* result from *practice*, from *carry-over* of the experience of a trial, and from *response sets*.

Counterbalancing Order Effects

To solve the problem of order effects, we again use the strategy of balancing. Here, we balance the effect of any single order by including different orders. Balancing order effects is called counterbalancing. **Counterbalancing** is systematically changing the order of trials for different participants in a *balanced* way to *counter* the biasing influence of any one order. For example, say that in a temperature study comparing 70 versus 90 degrees, we measure how aggressive participants feel toward the experimenter by having them answer 10 different questions. If we number the questions 1 through 10, a simple counterbalancing scheme is to present the questions to half of the participants in each condition in the order 1 through 10, and to the remaining participants in the order 10 through 1. This design is shown in Table 4.3. Each X represents a participant's summary score for the 10 questions, such as his or her mean aggressiveness score. We then ignore the order in which participants completed the questions and look at *all* aggression scores found in each condition (each column). To summarize these scores, we usually compute the mean of the scores in each condition, computing the mean of all summary scores in each column. (That's right: We compute the average of participants' individual average scores.) Higher scores in the 90-degree condition will support the hypothesis that increasing temperature increases aggressiveness. Further, we are confident that the results are not biased by the particular order in which questions were answered, because there is not one particular order present. To be even more confident that the order of trials was not biasing the results, we could test additional participants using other orders. (Several variations of this technique are discussed in Chapter 6.)

REMEMBER When measuring multiple trials, it is appropriate to *counterbalance* the order of trials.

Note that some researchers use the term *counterbalancing* when balancing *any* extraneous variable, in addition to the variable of order. Thus, if a male experimenter tests half the participants in each condition and a female tests the remainder, we have counterbalanced for experimenter gender. If half the participants in each condition are male and half are female, we have counterbalanced participants' gender.

Judging a Behavior and Inter-rater Reliability

So far we've discussed measuring rather concrete, obvious behaviors. Special problems arise, however, when (in experimental or descriptive designs) a score is based on a researcher's subjective judgment about a participant's behavior. For example, in the temperature study, instead of using a questionnaire, we might secretly observe and rate participants' aggressive actions toward the experimenter. Not only will the scoring criteria be rather elaborate, but then we must apply them reliably. The problem is, we—the experimenters—know that participants are "supposed" to be more aggressive with hotter temperatures, and try as we might, we cannot prevent this expectation from biasing how we'll rate their behaviors in the different conditions. Therefore, we will not produce objective, reliable, and valid judgments.

TABLE 4.3 Diagram of Temperature Experiment with the Order of Trials within Each Condition Counterbalanced

Each X represents a participant's summary score from 10 questions.

Independent variable of temperature

	70-degree condition	*90-degree condition*
Participant's scores obtained with order 1–10	X X X X	X X X X
Participant's scores obtained with order 10–1	X X X X	X X X X
	$\overline{X}$	$\overline{X}$

To solve this problem, we enlist the aid of **raters** to judge participants' behavior. These are people who are usually kept in the dark—"blind"—to our hypothesis and the specific conditions they are viewing, and who are trained to use our scoring criteria. Such raters provide us with much greater confidence in subjective scores. For example, in research into whether chimpanzees can learn American Sign Language, one test is whether a chimp can correctly name objects. The problem is that the researcher might cue the chimp as to the correct sign to use, or erroneously give the chimp credit for a sign because it was "close enough" to the desired sign. To eliminate these biases, one researcher shows the object, and another "rater," who cannot see the object, observes and records the chimp's sign. Raters are also common in studies that involve subjectively scoring such behaviors as creativity or nonverbal communication.

Of course, *one* rater might not reliably score a given behavior. At times the rater might miss or forget part of a participant's action. Or, over the course of a study, the rater might become more attuned and sensitive, or become fatigued and less motivated. Also, one rater might judge a behavior differently than would another. (What you consider a neutral facial expression, I might consider an aggressive glare.) Any rater can introduce such errors, and we cannot eliminate them.

As usual, when we cannot eliminate an extraneous influence, we try to balance it out. The approach with raters is to employ **multiple raters**, having more than one rater judge each participant's behavior. Then we combine the ratings from the different judges, usually computing the mean rating given to each participant. This mean should balance out the biases of each individual rater, giving us a more reliable measure of each participant's behavior. Further, multiple raters form a sample of observers from which we can infer that any observer would judge the behavior in roughly the same way, so we can generalize the results with greater confidence.

To be convinced that the raters are consistent, it is important to determine their inter-rater reliability. **Inter-rater reliability** is the extent to which raters agree on the scores they assign. We can determine inter-rater reliability by computing the percentage of agreements between raters—for example, the percentage of times that raters agreed on the sign a chimp produced. (Better than 90% agreement is usually considered reliable.) Or, as discussed in Chapter 9, we may "correlate" the scores from two raters. In the temperature study, for example, we'd hope to find that low aggression scores assigned to a participant by one rater are consistently matched by low scores assigned by the other, but when high scores are given by one, they are also given by the other.

REMEMBER When designing the dependent variable, consider *multiple raters* and *inter-rater reliability*.

For help remembering the issues when designing the dependent variable, consult Checklist 4.2.

CHECKLIST 4.2 **Questions to consider when designing the dependent variable**

- Does the variable provide content and construct validity?
- Will the variable be confounded?
- Will the variable provide external validity?
- Do dependent scores reflect common, real-life behavior?
- Are scoring criteria complete and sensitive to differences in behavior?
- Is range unrestricted, with no ceiling/floor effects?
- Are practice trials needed?
- Are multiple trials needed?
- Are order effects counterbalanced?
- Are raters with high inter-rater reliability needed?

CONTROLLING EXTRANEOUS VARIABLES

Throughout this chapter, there have been two recurring themes: We seek reliability and validity, and we seek a powerful design that is likely to produce a strong relationship. In fact, both of these goals are achieved by controlling the situation so that we produce minimum differences in scores *within* each condition while producing large differences in scores *between* conditions. We've seen that to some extent this depends on how we design the independent and dependent variables. Beyond that, however, the key is to control extraneous variables that might fluctuate within or between conditions.

Variables that fluctuate *within* a condition can reduce reliability by introducing error, or they reduce content and construct validity because we are not measuring the events and behavior we think we are. At the same time, they also reduce the power of a design, because participants respond differently to their individual situations, producing more variability in scores within each condition.

Extraneous variables that fluctuate *between* conditions are potential confoundings, reducing internal validity for concluding that changing the independent variable caused dependent scores to change. And, if we are unsure what the scores and relationship reflect, we have little external validity for generalizing the results. At the same time, fluctuations between conditions may lessen power, because their influence can reduce or eliminate the differences in scores between conditions that we might otherwise see.

Therefore, after designing the independent and dependent variables, the final step is to identify any uncontrolled extraneous variables. Look for them by considering those four components of a study—the researcher, participants, environment, and measurement task. For each, the goal is to prevent extraneous variables from fluctuating *within* and *between* the conditions. You can view all fluctuating extraneous variables as essentially resulting in inconsistency, so the basic strategy is to build in consistency. Thus, everyone in the temperature study should be dressed the same way, seated the same distance from the heater, acclimated to the temperature to the same extent and for the same length of time, treated the same by the experimenter, perform the same task while sitting in the room, and so on. If everything is the same for all participants except for the conditions of the independent variable, then we are more likely to see the predicted relationship, and we will have greater confidence that we "know" what the scores and relationship reflect.

REMEMBER   The key to designing a convincing experiment is to build in consistency within and between conditions.

Although every study will necessitate its own controls, there are several general techniques for creating consistency.

Instructions to Participants

Always provide **instructions** that clearly explain what the task is and how participants should approach it: Describe the sequence of events, identify the stimuli participants should attend to, and explain how to respond. The goal is to have all participants perform the same intended task, without introducing extraneous stimuli or behaviors that make the task different for different participants.

Creating effective yet consistent instructions requires considerable effort because if you must stop during testing of a participant to further explain the task or correct a behavior, then *your* actions become an inconsistency. Therefore, instructions should be clear for the least sophisticated participants, avoiding psychological jargon and unfamiliar words. They should anticipate participants' questions. (Should people guess when responding? Should they hurry?) Instructions should also prohibit unwanted behaviors. (Participants should not look around, fidget, or talk, so they don't miss crucial aspects of the task.) And the same instructions should be presented to everyone. (When manipulating a variable through instructions, change only the necessary parts and avoid a confounding by keeping constant all other aspects.) Never "ad lib" instructions, because you can't reproduce them reliably. Instead, read from a prepared script. (If you tell participants to read written instructions, you can't be sure they'll do so.) To reliably present the instructions, speak in an easily reproduced, neutral voice, or, better yet, play a tape recording of them.

There is nothing like thinking about the instructions to make you finalize a design. For example, in the temperature study, we need to give participants a reason to sit in a hot room for a while. One approach is to have them perform some bogus task, like completing a questionnaire. We also need to measure participants' aggressiveness. Something that fits with the questionnaire is to include in it questions that measure their aggression toward the experimenter. So that this all makes sense to participants, the questionnaire could ask about their attitudes and feelings toward various types of people, finishing up with their attitudes towards the experimenter.

Recall that to provoke participants into feeling aggressive, our experimenter will be a little rude and nasty. For consistency, we need to precisely plan when and how this will occur. We might tell participants that there is a time limit for completing each page of the questionnaire. Then using a stopwatch, at specified times while participants are on specified pages of the questionnaire, we'll say "stop." At these times, the experimenter has an opportunity to interact rudely with the participants.

The usual sequence for beginning a study is this: We bring participants into the laboratory, introduce ourselves, and seat them where appropriate. Everything is prepared, so for example, we would have our questionnaire (turned face down) on a desk for participants, complete with a sharpened pencil. We then give them a brief description of the study and formally obtain their consent to participate in the study. (This "informed consent" is discussed in the next chapter.) Then, we present the complete instructions. Figure 4.1 shows an example of the instructions we might use in our temperature study.

Notice that a good way to organize instructions is in terms of the temporal sequence: what happens first, what's next, and so on. Also include even the obvious things, because they won't be obvious to a novice participant, and you may forget to mention them sometimes, introducing confounds. Further, notice how the instructions anticipate undesirable actions or questions by participants: Our instructions mention the booklet, so some participants might immediately try to turn it over while we're still giving the instructions. Or, during the task, participants might be inclined to finish the word or sentence they're working on at the time we say "stop," so we tell them how to handle this. In addition, note how the

FIGURE 4.1   Example of Instructions for the Temperature Study

---

Please adjust your chair so that you can comfortably write on the booklet in front of you, which I'll tell you to turn over in a moment. The booklet contains questions about your attitudes toward different people and personalities. When I instruct you to begin, please turn over the booklet and using the pencil provided, begin completing the questions, starting with the first question at the top of the first page. Please answer all questions, in order, as honestly and as accurately as you can. Some of the questions are multiple choice, in which case please check only one choice. If two choices seem to apply, pick the one that applies most often. Other questions require a short answer of one or two words. Please print the words, neatly and legibly, and try to spell them correctly.

For reasons that I will explain later, there is a time limit for you to complete each page of questions. Therefore, when I say stop, please stop writing immediately, even if you are in the middle of a word. Then, when I say begin, please turn to the next page of the questionnaire, and complete those questions, beginning with the question at the top of the page. Please, no talking once we begin. Do you have any questions? Ok, then, Ready, Begin.

---

instructions can help our scoring criteria: By explicitly telling participants how to respond, it will be easier for us to reliably and validly score the data later. And finally, always ask participants if they have any questions. You should be able to answer their questions either by rereading part of the instructions, or by telling them you'll answer the question after the study. If not, then they are asking legitimate procedural questions you haven't anticipated, so rewrite your instructions. (As we'll discuss in the next chapter, after the study we'll let participants in on our little deception.)

Using Automation

The way we present stimuli, obtain responses, and assign and record scores during the measurement task can be additional sources of inconsistency. The way to control extraneous variables here is through **automation**: using electronic or mechanical devices to present stimuli and to measure and record responses. Electronic timers, slide projectors, video and audio recorders, and computers ensure controlled and reliable stimulus presentations. Automating the data collection ensures that the scoring system is consistently and accurately applied and provides for more reliable and sensitive measurement. Automation also eliminates experimenter errors and inconsistency that could result because (1) the experimenter is so busy directing the study that parts of a behavior are missed and (2) the experimenter has expectations about how the study should turn out and thus inadvertently influences participants or records scores accordingly.

With automation, however, you must guard against the problem of instrumentation effects. **Instrumentation effects** are changes in the measurement materials that occur because of use, making the measurements less reliable. This occurs when, over the course of a study, slides, films, and videotapes become scratched and blurred, paper materials get mutilated, or equipment and timers become less accurate. Part of the "instrumentation" is also the experimenter, who could become more experienced, more bored, or more crazed as time passes, and who then inadvertently changes the procedure. Because of changes in the material or procedure, the measurements obtained later in a study can be different from those obtained early on, making the experiment unreliable overall.

To minimize instrumentation effects, always keep equipment in order and make copies of materials so that all participants are shown pristine stimuli. Also, keep the experimenter's behavior constant. Finally, test some participants from each condition during the early, middle, and late stages of the study, so that potential instrumentation effects are balanced in all conditions and thus cannot confound the study.

Testing Participants in Groups

An important issue to consider is whether to test participants individually or in groups. Group testing is most common when the task requires written responses, such as on a questionnaire. The advantages of group testing are: (1) data collection is more efficient and (2) if you can test everyone in a particular condition at once, then all participants will experience the same consistent condition. The disadvantage is that participants may make noise, block one another's view, or otherwise distract one another so that extraneous variables are introduced. Therefore, you need to control participants carefully when testing in groups. Usually, you can do this through particularly explicit instructions. However, also consider the particular behaviors being studied, because participants may be reluctant to display them in front of others. In our temperature study, for example, participants are less likely to be overtly aggressive when others are present. Thus, the wisdom of group testing depends on how susceptible participants will be to the influence of others.

Pilot Studies

To be sure that they have developed a reliable and valid procedure, researchers often conduct a pilot study. A **pilot study** is a miniature version of a study that tests a procedure prior to the actual study. (*Note*: A pilot study is different from a manipulation check: Pilot studies occur *before* a study; manipulation checks occur *during* the study.) Using participants similar to those in the actual study, pilot studies determine such matters as whether the instructions are clear, whether the task can be done in the time allotted, and whether you have developed a workable, sensitive, and reliable scoring procedure. Pilot studies also allow you to train raters and to confirm that they have high inter-rater reliability. And, they allow you to work out any bugs in the equipment or procedure so that the actual study runs smoothly and consistently.

We can also ask pilot subjects questions that will help us develop our scoring procedures or stimuli. For the temperature study, we could ask pilot subjects to indicate how much aggressiveness various words or statements reflect, so that we would know what aggression scores to assign them when used by participants to describe the experimenter. Or, in a different study, say that our independent variable involves showing participants videos that contain different amounts of violence. Our personal judgment is of little help in determining the amount of violence in each because we might be particularly sensitive or insensitive to violence. Therefore, we would show the videos to pilot subjects and have them rate the amount of violence each contains.

For any problems identified, we alter the stimuli, task, or instructions and conduct more pilot studies until we have the desired situation in each condition.

REMEMBER   To maintain consistency, create clear *instructions*, use *automation* but limit *instrumentation effects*, consider *group testing*, and conduct *pilot studies*.

Eliminating Participants from the Data

Even with all of these precautions, research never runs as smoothly as planned (Murphy's Law always applies!). Some participants will behave strangely (I've had them go to sleep!), others may be downright uncooperative, some might be too "dim" to grasp the instructions, or others may be biased because they've learned the details of the study from a previous participant. A fire drill may occur while you are testing someone, or your equipment can blow a fuse.

In such situations, participants are not experiencing the study that you designed: They are not being exposed to the independent variable reliably, they are not responding as directed, or they are being influenced by extraneous variables. Therefore, you can exclude their scores from the data. Be *very* sure that these participants do not belong in the study, and do not exclude them just because their scores do not confirm the prediction. (That's rigging the results and committing fraud: You might as well make up the data.) When in doubt, therefore, include a participant's data. But, if scores are obtained in a clearly inappropriate situation, you can exclude them. Then, test additional participants to fill in for them. (Any study that produces many excluded participants, however, is a problem, because it contains a consistent hidden factor that is selecting a biased sample and thus may reduce external validity.)

PUTTING IT ALL TOGETHER

Now, you are a little more familiar with how to design a good study (actually, you're a lot more familiar). Because the issues are largely the same, you also understand how to approach descriptive designs. In *any* research, we examine the operational definitions, create clear instructions, consider automation and multiple trials, watch out for order effects, or use multiple raters with high interrater reliability. On the other hand, don't develop a false sense of security about the "proof" that such controls provide. We are still only collecting evidence, and the techniques we've discussed are necessary simply for producing "good" convincing evidence.

You may think that producing good evidence requires remembering an overwhelming number of details. (As a friend once remarked, "First you have to think about *everything*!") However, instead of approaching these issues as a long list to memorize, view them as a way to think about the research setting: You're creating a complete social and physical environment in which to observe participants, and you must take charge of all aspects of this environment. If instead you prefer a list, Checklist 4.3 presents the issues we've discussed. (And the complete checklist we're creating is presented inside the front cover.)

CHECKLIST 4.3 **Questions to consider when designing an experiment**

Designing the independent variable

- Will the variable provide content, construct, and external validity?
- Will the operational definition prevent confounding?
- Is a control group appropriate?
- Is the manipulation strong, reliable, and without diffusion of treatment?
- Is a manipulation check needed?

Designing the dependent variable

- Does the variable provide content, construct, and external validity?
- Are the measurements reliable and without confoundings?
- Are scoring criteria complete and sensitive to differences in behavior?
- Is the range unrestricted, with no ceiling/floor effects?
- Are practice trials needed?
- Are multiple trials needed and are order effects counterbalanced?
- Are raters with high inter-rater reliability needed?

Creating consistent procedures

- Are instructions clear and complete?
- Can automation be used without instrumentation effects?
- Is group or individual testing best?
- Is a pilot study needed?

CHAPTER SUMMARY

1. *Confederates* are people enlisted by a researcher to create a particular social situation for participants.
2. An *intervening variable* is an internal characteristic that is influenced by the independent variable, which in turn influences the dependent variable.
3. A *state characteristic* is a transient attribute that can be experimentally manipulated. A *trait characteristic* is a more permanent attribute that is not easily manipulated.
4. A *control group* is measured on the dependent variable but receives zero amount of the independent variable, or otherwise does not receive the treatment. An *experimental group* receives a nonzero amount of the independent variable.

5. A *powerful design* is one that, when the predicted relationship exists in nature, is more likely to produce a clear and convincing sample relationship.

6. *Variability* refers to differences among scores, and *error variance* is the variability within each condition that weakens a relationship.

7. A *strong manipulation* involves conditions that potentially produce large differences in dependent scores between the conditions. *Diffusion of treatment* occurs when participants in one condition are aware of the treatment given in other conditions.

8. A *manipulation check* is a measurement, in addition to the dependent variable, used to confirm that the independent variable had its intended effect.

9. The dependent variable may involve *forced-choice* procedures (including *yes-no* and *sorting tasks*) and *self-reports* (including *Likert-type* rating questions).

10. *Scoring criteria* define the system for assigning dependent scores to participants' responses. The system should provide for a *sensitive* measure that produces different scores for small differences in behavior.

11. *Restriction of range* occurs when the range of possible scores on a variable is limited. *Ceiling effects* restrict the range because all scores tend to be very high, so scores cannot get much higher. *Floor effects* restrict the range because all scores tend to be very low, so scores cannot get much lower.

12. Reliability is improved with *practice trials* and by observing each participant on *multiple trials* within each condition.

13. *Order effects* are the influence on a particular trial that arises from its position in the sequence of trials. *Practice effects* are the influence that comes from practicing a task. *Carry-over effects* are the influence that experiencing a trial has on subsequent trials. A *response set* is a bias toward responding in a particular way because of previous responses made.

14. *Counterbalancing* controls for order effects by presenting different orders of trials within each condition.

15. When scores are based on subjective evaluation of a participant's behavior, use *multiple raters*. They should have high *inter-rater reliability*, the extent to which raters agree in the scores they assign.

16. The key to designing a convincing experiment is to build in *consistency*, both *within* and *between* conditions.

17. Consider *automation* for presenting stimuli and measuring scores. *Instrumentation effects* produce unreliable measurements because of changes in equipment and materials that occur through use. *Instructions*, *group testing*, and *pilot studies* also determine the consistency of a procedure.

KEY TERMS (with page references)

automation 120
carry-over effects 113
ceiling effects 110
confederates 96
control group 99
counterbalancing 114
diffusion of treatment 104
error variance 101
experimental group 99
floor effects 111
forced-choice procedure 106
instructions 118
instrumentation effects 120
inter-rater reliability 116
intervening variable 96
Likert-type question 107
manipulation check 105
multiple raters 116
multiple trials 112

order effects 113
pilot study 121
powerful design 100
practice effects 113
practice trials 111
raters 116
reaction time 106
response set 113
restriction of range 110
scoring criteria 108
self-reports 107
sensitive dependent measure 109
sorting task 106
state characteristic 96
strong manipulation 103
trait characteristic 96
variability 101
yes-no task 106

REVIEW QUESTIONS

1. What does it mean to use (a) a "forced-choice" procedure? (b) "Likert-type" questions? (c) a "sorting task"?

2. (a) What does the term *self-reports* mean? (b) What is the major disadvantage of this procedure?

3. (a) What is a powerful design? (b) Why is creating a powerful design important?

4. (a) What is variability? (b) What is error variance?

5. (a) What is a strong manipulation? (b) Why do we seek strong manipulations? (c) What are the two approaches to creating a strong manipulation?

6. (a) What is a control group? (b) What is an experimental group? (c) Why do we employ control groups?

7. (a) What is meant by reliable manipulation of the independent variable? (b) What effect does an unreliable manipulation have?

8. (a) What is a manipulation check? (b) What is the difference between a pilot study and a manipulation check?

9. (a) Why do we give participants practice trials? (b) Why are multiple trials generally better than a single observation? (c) What problem arises with multiple trials?

10. (a) What are practice effects? (b) What are carry-over effects? (c) What is a response set?

11. What is counterbalancing?

12. What is a sensitive measurement procedure?

13. (a) In terms of fluctuating extraneous variables, what is the key concern when developing a testing procedure? (b) How do fluctuating extraneous variables increase error variance? (c) Why does increased error variance reduce power?

14. What are the pros and cons of testing participants in groups?

15. (a) What do we mean by automation? (b) Why can automation be good for a study? (c) Why can automation be bad for a study?

APPLICATION QUESTIONS

16. To study nonverbal communication, our conditions involve presenting a picture of a person making different kinds of faces (smiling, frowning, smirking). We ask participants to indicate the person's emotional state as either happy or sad. (a) What flaws are built into dependent scores? (b) How can you improve this procedure?

17. In question 16, participants answer happy and sad about the same number of times, regardless of the face they see. Why would it be important to have designed a powerful study here?

18. (a) What aspects of how we manipulate an independent variable can produce error variance? (b) What aspects of how we measure the dependent variable can produce error variance?

19. To study how practice influences physical ability, you manipulate three conditions of the amount of practice that participants have while playing basketball and then measure the number of baskets they make out of 50 tries. Your participants are all physical education majors. (a) What flaw is built into these scores? (b) How can you improve this procedure?

20. In question 19, (a) to make the task challenging, you have participants stand at the far end of the basketball court when testing their basket-shooting. What flaw is present in this procedure? (b) Instead, you have participants stand almost directly underneath the basket. What flaw is present now?

21. In a study of memory, you read aloud one list of either similar or dissimilar words and then measure participants' memory for the list. (a) What problems might occur because you read the lists? (b) How can you eliminate them? (c) What problem might now arise over the course of testing many people?

22. In question 21, you ask participants to write down the list of words. (a) To score recall reliably, what decisions should you make? (b) How could you ensure you did not score the responses in a biased fashion? (c) What aspect of reliability must you then check?

23. In question 21, (a) what problem affects the reliability of the memory *behavior* you are observing? (b) What preliminary task can you add to improve reliability? (c) How can you expand your observations of each participant to improve reliability? (d) What problem have you created? (e) Precisely describe how you would deal with the problem.

24. (a) In question 21, what would constitute a strong manipulation? (b) How could you perform a manipulation check? (c) What questions would a pilot study answer?

25. Your independent variable is to deliver different speeches to participants to make them more or less sexist. Then, you examine whether they help a confederate of the opposite sex. (a) What can you do to check that your speeches actually altered sexism? (b) If the speeches had little or no effect, what design principle would be your goal when rewriting them? (c) What would be your approach for accomplishing this? (d) What would you do to be sure you had created effective speeches before conducting the study again?

26. You create different conditions by playing different types of music to participants. After a while, you suddenly pull out and shoot a (blank) pistol. You then measure participants' anxiety level to determine whether different types of music cause people to remain more or less calm in the face of startling stimuli. (a) What threat to internal validity might arise as you test more and more people? (b) How would you counteract it?

DISCUSSION QUESTIONS

27. Your conditions consist of three types of instructions on how to be logical. The dependent variable is participants' ability to solve three logic problems. (a) What threats to reliability and validity are present in this dependent measure? (b) How would you deal with them?

28. You compare the number of typing errors that people produce when copying material onto a computer when using either a black-and-white or color monitor. (a) What potential sources of inconsistency in and between conditions might arise? (b) How would you control such variables?

29. You conduct the temperature study discussed in this chapter, comparing the levels of 70, 80, and 90 degrees Fahrenheit. You'll ask participants 10 questions about their aggressiveness toward the researcher. Diagram how you'll counterbalance order effects, as well as participants' gender in each condition.

30. Create a set of instructions for participants in the following studies, adding any details to the design as needed. (a) The study in application question 16, above. (b)The study in application question 21, above.

31. You wish to study how hard participants will work for food depending on how hungry they are. (a) Create an operational definition for manipulating the independent variable and diagram your design. (b) Evaluate your definition in terms of reliability, as well as construct, content, internal, and external validity.

5

Risk, Deception, and the Ethics of Research

GETTING STARTED

To understand this chapter, recall the following:

- From Chapter 2, recall the differences between laboratory and field experiments.
- From Chapter 4, recall the components of an experiment and how to design them.
- Also from Chapter 4, recall what we mean by a powerful design, error variance, a strong manipulation, a sensitive measure, a restricted range, and floor/ceiling effects. Also, recall what automation and diffusion of treatment are.

Your goals in this chapter are to learn:

- What demand characteristics are and how to prevent them from threatening a study.
- What research ethics are and how to design and conduct an ethical study.
- What animal research involves and the ethical issues in animal research.

We've seen that researchers *do* things to participants that sometimes aren't the nicest experiences: we manipulate—or some would say "rig"—the situations under which participants are observed, we control participants' behavior, or we observe their personal activities that people would rather keep to themselves. Yet, researchers are a part of society, subject to the same ethical responsibilities as anyone else. Therefore, part of designing a study involves considering whether you've crossed the line. In this chapter, we discuss the ethical issues that arise in human and animal research and how to handle them.

Before we get to ethics, however, we'll first discuss one more important potential flaw to deal with when designing a study, because how we deal with it has a major impact on the ethics of a study. The flaw is called demand characteristics.

DEMAND CHARACTERISTICS

Imagine you are a participant in an "experiment" taking place in a "laboratory." A "psychologist" with lab coat and clipboard puts a plate of cookies in front of you and says, "Normal people crave cookies at this time of day, so eat if you want." I bet you'll eat one. On the other hand, imagine the psychologist says, "Only people who have no self-control eat at this time, but eat if you want." I'll bet you don't. In any situation, the social and physical surroundings provide cues that essentially "demand" that we behave in a certain way. In research, these cues are called demand characteristics. A **demand characteristic** is an extraneous cue that guides or biases a participant's behavior. Participants rely on demand characteristics to answer such questions as "What's really going on here?" "What am I supposed to do?" and "How will my response be interpreted?" Demand characteristics arise despite the instructions we provide and participants don't necessarily respond to them intentionally or even consciously.

To understand demand characteristics, consider this interesting study by Strack, Martin, and Stepper (1988). They hypothesized that the facial muscles used for smiling provide neurological feedback that actually improves mood. (In other words, being happy makes you smile, but then smiling makes you even happier.) To test the hypothesis, they measured the dependent variable of mood after participants had held a pen in their mouths, either using their teeth (which mimics smiling) or using their puckered lips (which does not mimic smiling). Imagine that you are in this study, sitting in a room with a pen sticking out of your mouth, with *a psychologist!* watching you. What would you be thinking and feeling, and how would that influence what you said and did? Would you really react naturally? If the answer is no, then it's because of the demand characteristics. Demand characteristics can be grouped using those four components of any study (the participants, environment, measurement task, and experimenter), and there are common ones that we have names for.

First, participants bring with them certain attitudes that influence their behavior. Research procedures are mysterious, and rumor has it that psychologists do strange things to people and study only intelligence, sexual deviance, and crazy people. Therefore, participants tend to be on guard: They are sensitive to being "studied" and may alter their behavior accordingly. This is the demand characteristic called reactivity. **Reactivity** is the bias in responses that occurs because participants are aware that they are being observed. Participants know they're under the gun, and they "react" to the mere presence of an experimenter who is observing and possibly "analyzing" their behavior. Therefore, some participants may do and say what they think they are "supposed" to, or others may act to hide their true behaviors. The end result of reactivity, however, is that participants respond very differently than if they did not know they were being observed.

In the smile study, because of reactivity, some participants might laugh and act happy simply because they think it's expected. Others who feel happy could act sad so that they don't divulge their inner feelings. Still others might become very self-conscious, nervous, or giddy so that their response is not what they'd normally do, or they make more errors than they normally would. In fact, such reactivity can even be physiological: For example, when measuring blood pressure, the mere act of attaching the measuring cuff to people raises their blood pressure.

Participants also respond to another demand characteristic called **social desirability**. This occurs when people provide the socially acceptable response. Essentially, participants "edit" their responses so that they aren't embarrassed or so they won't appear strange or abnormal. Thus, in the smile study, some participants might act happy, not so much because they *are* happy, but because they think it's the normal response. Others may want to act happy but inhibit this because they're afraid they'll be perceived as weird.

The environment in which a study takes place also produces demand characteristics that cause participants to react unnaturally. Often participants use such things as random noises, changes in lighting, or a broken pencil point as cues for erroneously concluding what is being studied and how they should respond. This is especially true in fancy laboratories with one-way mirrors and complex equipment that can play on someone's fears. (Once, when using a bank of electronic timers, I had to convince participants that they would not be electrocuted by having them look under their chairs to see that there were no wires!)

The measurement procedure also communicates demand characteristics that participants use to modify their responses. For example, in studies of mental imagery, participants must envision a previously presented map, and the time they take to mentally travel between different locations on the map is measured. Participants take longer when the locations on the map are more distant. However, this result might occur not because it reflects how participants travel along mental maps, but because participants know that longer distances "should" take longer, so they oblige. Or, in a different situation, participants might interpret an opinion survey as really being a personality test. Then, instead of honestly answering the questions, they respond in ways they think will project their ideal personality.

Finally, the experimenter is an important source of demand characteristics. Researchers usually dress and behave rather formally to inspire serious cooperation from participants. But, this formality can inhibit participants' normal reactions. On the other hand, if we act and dress too informally, we may encourage inattentiveness and sloppy performance. Further, people are very sensitive to **experimenter expectancies,** which are cues the experimenter provides about the responses that participants should give in a particular condition. These cues occur because the researcher knows the predictions of the study and may inadvertently communicate them. Then, the ultimate self-fulfilling prophecy is produced. In the smile study, for example, we expect people to be happier when mimicking a smile. Subtle actions on our part can register on participants, and, sure enough, they'll respond with the predicted mood.

As these examples illustrate, demand characteristics cause people to play a role, being good (or not so good) participants who perform on cue. The problem is that they are responding to these cues, instead of to our variables. Then, reactions such as reactivity or social desirability may *restrict the range* of scores, reducing the *sensitivity* and *power* in the study. If we're measuring aggressiveness, for example, all participants might stifle their aggression so they don't look bad. This will produce low scores for all conditions, producing *floor effects.* If we're measuring "niceness," we're likely to see ceiling effects. In addition, we lose *internal validity* because it is the cues that cause a particular response, instead of the independent variable. Thus, if people act happy when smiling because they think it's expected, then it will appear that our manipulation influences their behavior when it really has no effect. Or, the cues can cause participants to behave contrary to our prediction: If they force themselves to act sad when using their smile muscles, it will appear that our manipulation does not influence their behavior as we predict, when otherwise it would. We also lose *reliability,* because scores are different from what they would be if such cues were not present. And because not all participants react to the same cues in the same way, scores will be more *variable* and inconsistent. Finally, we lose *external validity* because the results will not generalize to other situations where such demand characteristics are not present.

REMEMBER   *Demand characteristics* are cues that bias participants, resulting in responses that are not valid, reliable reactions to our variables.

Fortunately, we have several techniques for controlling demand characteristics.

General Controls for Demand Characteristics

Our first line of defense against demand characteristics is to provide participants with as few cues as possible. If they have no cues, their only recourse is to act naturally. Thus, instructions to participants should not divulge the specific purpose, manipulation, or predictions of a study. (And note: Any time we keep participants in the dark regarding the specifics about a condition they receive, we are using a **single-blind procedure**.) In addition, instructions should not include extraneous, distracting information (such as placing an unnecessary time limit on a task). Also, hide threatening equipment and avoid threatening actions or extraneous comments by the experimenter.

It is especially important to limit the cues from the experimenter. A prime reason for using *automation* is that equipment will not communicate experimenter expectations. When a potentially biasing experimenter must be present, however, we create a double blind. In a **double-blind procedure**, both the participants and the researcher who interacts with them are unaware of the specific condition being presented. The original researcher trains others to actually conduct the study, but they do not know the conditions or predictions—they are "blind" to them. Such procedures are especially common when testing the effect of a drug or other medical treatment. If the researcher knows when a particular drug is being administered, his or her expectations about it may be communicated to patients. These expectations *alone* can produce the expected physical reaction. If the experimenter is blind to such information, however, no expectations can be communicated.

Our second defense against demand characteristics is to make those cues that must be present as neutral as possible. Thus, the researcher tries to be rather bland, being neither overly friendly nor unfriendly. In the instructions, we try to neutralize participants' fears and suspicions by presenting the task without implying that it is difficult or easy and without indicating what the "normal" or expected response is. Further, we encourage participants to respond naturally and honestly, and tell them that they should not be upset if they make errors, and that we are not using the data for any sinister purpose. Thus, for example, when conducting a memory study, we might tell participants that we are simply studying memory processes, that we expect errors to occur, and that regardless of their performance, it will not reflect on their personality or intelligence. Also, we try to provide a response format that participants are comfortable with: We have children act out responses using toys, or we give college students a paper-and-pencil test. And, we try to select a researcher with whom participants will be comfortable (in terms of gender, age, and so on). This is especially important when responses are likely to be influenced by reactivity and social desirability (for example, in a study of sexual fantasies), because participants' willingness to risk making mistakes or to honestly divulge personal information depends on the characteristics of who is observing them. (You behave very differently in a locker room than when meeting a date's parents!)

We can also try to make a situation feel more neutral by making participants more comfortable by allowing them to "habituate" to it. With **habituation**, we familiarize participants with a procedure before beginning actual data collection. For example, one reason to have participants perform practice trials is so the researcher's presence becomes a "habit" and is no longer disruptive. Or, when testing children, we play with them and get to know them before testing begins. We also allow participants to habituate to any equipment being used: If we are videotaping responses, we allow participants to become comfortable with being recorded before the study begins.

Our final defense against demand characteristics is to have participants ignore them by creating experimental realism. **Experimental realism** is the extent to which the measurement task engages participants. The goal is to create a task that people find so engrossing that they "forget" about demand characteristics. Thus, in the smile study, if participants forget about the pen in their mouth, the results will be less influenced by their feeling awkward about it. Experimental realism does not mean, however, that the task is like real life, so experimental realism is different from *ecological validity*. With experimental realism, the task may be very strange and unreal, but because they're involved in it, participants' responses are actual, honest responses to it.

> **REMEMBER**   *Single-* and *double-blind* procedures, *habituation*, and *experimental realism* help to reduce demand characteristics.

Demand characteristics are *always* a potential problem, whether in an experiment or a descriptive study. Therefore, the above strategies are a basic component of all types of designs. However, sometimes a study is likely to produce very strong demand characteristics despite these efforts. In such cases, we have two additional techniques to use: *unobtrusive measures* and *deception*.

Using Unobtrusive Measures and Deception

When the procedure for measuring the dependent variable will strongly encourage reactivity and social desirability, researchers sometimes employ unobtrusive measures. With an **unobtrusive measure**, we measure participants' behavior without making them aware that the measurement is being made. Thus, an unobtrusive measurement of aggressiveness might involve observing participants through a one-way mirror. Other unobtrusive measures may include the use of hidden cameras and recorders. Or, we may observe telltale evidence left by participants (for example, to measure how far people sit from one another, we could measure the distance separating their chairs after they've left the room). In each case, participants cannot be overly influenced by demand characteristics if they are unaware that the measurement is being made.

Sometimes an unobtrusive measure is used in conjunction with deception. **Deception** involves creating an artificial situation or "cover story" that disguises a study. Participants are then unaware of the manipulation or the behavior being studied, so they do not feel pressured to respond in a certain way. For example, in the smile study, if the researcher simply said, "Here, hold this pen in your lips," participants would probably feel very self-conscious and behave unnaturally. The original researchers eliminated such problems by telling participants that the study investigated how physically impaired people use their mouths to do tasks that others do by hand. Then, while holding the pen in either their lips or teeth, participants used the pen for various tasks, including marking various stimuli. Among the stimuli were several cartoons, and participants' rating of how humorous they found the cartoons was the dependent variable for measuring their mood. Thus, what might have been a bizarre task was transformed into a rational, engaging task in which participants were less self-conscious and responded in a more natural way.

Likewise, Schachter, Goldman, and Gordon (1968) sought to measure how much food people would eat under different conditions. But blatantly watching people as they eat is likely to make them highly reactive. Therefore, the researchers told participants that they were in a taste study in which they were to rate the taste of different crackers, and that they should eat as many crackers as necessary. The real dependent variable was the number of crackers eaten.

Conversely, we can sometimes use demand characteristics to our advantage, disguising a task by incorporating elaborate scientific-looking procedures. For example, Duclos et al. (1989) manipulated the posture that people adopted in order to determine how posture influences mood. So that the participants would maintain a posture without being overly conscious or suspicious of it, fake electrodes for measuring "brain activity" were attached to them, and they were told that their posture was important for accurate measurements.

(*Note*: the term **distractor task** is a common name for any task used to "distract" participants' attention away from demand characteristics. So above, eating crackers or measuring brain activity were distractor tasks.)

A special type of deception is often used in conjunction with a *control condition* (a condition that receives zero amount of the independent variable). Because only the experimental group receives the treatment, only it experiences the associated demand characteristics. Therefore, we have a confounding: The experimental group behaves differently from the control group either because of the treatment or because of the accompanying demand characteristics. For example, let's say we give an experimental group a drink of alcohol while a control group receives nothing. Any impairment the experimental group exhibits may be due to the alcohol, or it may arise because giving people alcohol implies that we expect them to act drunkenly, so they do. To keep such demand characteristics constant, control groups are given a placebo. A **placebo** provides the demand characteristics of a treatment. Thus, we would give the above control group something that smells and tastes like alcohol but that is not alcohol. Then we communicate to both groups the same demand characteristics for acting drunkenly, so any differences in their behavior are due to the real alcohol given to the experimental group. Similarly, when testing other drugs, we give placebo "sugar" pills or injections to the control group so that all participants experience the same procedure and form the same expectations. And in studies that require the experimental group to perform an involved task prior to making a response, we have the control group perform a similar, placebo task to eliminate differences between the groups in terms of motivation or fatigue.

> **REMEMBER**   A *placebo* is anything given to control groups so that
> they experience the same demand characteristics as experimental
> groups.

Note that placebos and deceptions have another positive effect because they help to reduce *diffusion of treatment*. They make it more difficult for participants to identify a control versus an experimental condition, or to identify a particular treatment. If participants can't readily identify the treatments, they can't tell others, or be influenced themselves.

On the other hand, deception is not always necessary or wise (as with everything in research, you must balance the pros and cons). For example, in the previous chapter, we discussed manipulating a room's temperature. Research has shown that, we should not try to hide this by, say, remarking that the room's thermostat is broken. Participants will often guess that the study deals with temperature anyway (Bell & Baron, 1976). Catching the researcher in a lie will worsen the demand characteristics, because then participants *know* they should be on guard.

Concealing the Experiment

When we are especially concerned about reactivity and social desirability, the final approach is to conceal the entire experiment. Many studies, for example, have been performed while participants sit in a waiting room, supposedly waiting to be taken into the experiment. For example, researchers have studied helping behavior using confederates who indicate they need help by dropping their books or asking for money. Doing this in a formal laboratory with the experimenter watching might communicate that helping behavior was being studied and that the expected behavior was to help. Instead, the confederate indicates the need for help while in a "waiting room" with the participant, and then the person's response is unobtrusively observed.

The most extreme way to conceal an experiment is to move out of the laboratory and conduct a *field experiment*. Recall that here we unobtrusively conduct the experiment by observing people in shopping malls, student unions, and so on. One reason that field experiments have greater external validity is that they can disguise the fact that an experiment is being conducted. So, for example, to study helping behavior in even less suspicious settings, researchers have had confederates drop things, solicit money, or ask for directions while stopping random individuals (who become the participants) in shopping malls or on the street. At the same time, researchers have surreptitiously manipulated independent variables by, for example, having confederates dress differently at different times or by having the participants "find" different amounts of money to alter their mood. Such field studies overcome the reactivity or social desirability that occurs with laboratory experiments because reactivity, experimenter cues, and so on are minimized, and the situation tends to have high experimental realism. Likewise, recall that descriptive studies are often conducted in the field and typically have greater external validity. This is mainly due to the fact that the researcher plays a much less active and obvious role, the environment is more natural, and there is greater realism, so there are usually fewer demand characteristics present that bias participants away from behaving naturally.

REMEMBER   Reduce demand characteristics by minimizing cues through *unobtrusive measures*, *deception*, and *field experiments*.

For help remembering the questions to ask when dealing with demand characteristics in a study, consult Checklist 5.1.

So, as we've seen, it is often because of demand characteristics that psychological research becomes most devious and creative. In fact, researchers can probably manipulate virtually any independent variable, get participants to do just about anything, and have them divulge their most private and personal feelings. This raises the important question, however, of whether researchers *should* do such things.

CHECKLIST 5.1 **Questions to consider when identifying and preventing demand characteristics**

Will demand characteristics be present?

- Will the participants show reactivity to being observed?
- Will the participants give socially desirable responses?
- Will the environment bias the participants' responses?
- Will the experimenter's characteristics or expectancies influence scores?

Choices for preventing demand characteristics

- Are participants "blind" to the procedure?
- Are all cues as neutral as possible?
- Should participants "habituate" to being observed?
- Should automation be used?
- Should you use single- or double-blind procedures?
- Does the task have experimental realism?
- Should you hide measurement tasks using unobtrusive techniques?
- Is a placebo needed for the control group?
- Should you disguise the study with deception or a field experiment?

RESEARCH ETHICS

As a researcher, you face a dilemma: On the one hand, you need a well-controlled, informative study, even if this means being deceptive, eliciting responses that participants want to keep private, or doing things that cause them discomfort. We justify these actions on the grounds that sound scientific knowledge is needed to benefit humanity. On the other hand, you should treat participants properly because they have basic rights to privacy, to respect, and to safety. Therefore, the issue of **research ethics** can be summed up as the concern for balancing a researcher's right to study a behavior with the right of participants to be protected from abuse.

The Cooperativeness of Participants

Why do people allow themselves to be abused by a researcher? First, researchers are often viewed as authority figures and, people tend to think that all authority figures, are benevolent and honest. Second, people assume that research is valuable for society, so they believe their participation is important. The result is that participants respect the goals of research and trust the researcher, so they are open to abuse.

An example of how motivated participants are was demonstrated in a classic study by Orne (1962), who tried to give participants a task they would refuse. He gave each person 2,000 sheets of paper, each of which contained 224 addition problems. No justification for the task was given, and participants were merely told that the researcher would return "sometime." Five and one-half hours later, the participants were still working, but the experimenter gave up! In the next attempt, participants were told that, after completing each sheet, they should tear it up into a minimum of 32 pieces and then continue with the next sheet. Participants performed this task for *several hours* until, again, the experimenter gave up. The subjects later reported that they viewed this task as an important psychological endurance test.

As the above illustrates, an overriding demand characteristic in any study is for participants to be cooperative. In fact, people cooperate even to their own detriment. The classic example of this is Milgram (1963). He convinced participants that they were assisting him to train a "learner" confederate to learn verbal stimuli. Each time the learner made an error, the participant pressed a switch that he or she believed administered an increasingly larger electrical shock to the learner. Despite protests from the learner (who could be heard but not seen, and who eventually emitted *deathly* silence), and despite the fact that the electrical switches were labeled "DANGER: SEVERE SHOCK," a *majority* of participants delivered what they believed was as much as 450 volts of electricity! (This is several *times* as much voltage as in the electrical outlets in your home!)

Milgram applied no coercion other than to tell participants to continue, using only the authority that they had implicitly given him. Yet they complied, even though they believed they were harming another person, and in many cases became *very* emotionally and physically distressed themselves. Further, these were not young, impressionable freshman college students, but adults of various ages and backgrounds.

Milgram was soundly criticized for his tactics, but the above and other "classic" studies in the 1960s and 1970s began to alert and alarm many psychologists that the rights of participants were not always being respected. In fact, a number of studies suggest that a researcher can probably get participants to put up with almost any mental or physical discomfort, and they are reluctant to protest or to protect themselves. However, the profession of psychology gradually came to officially recognize that merely because people volunteer for a study does not mean that we have the right to take advantage of them. In essence, there is an implicit contract between participants and researchers. Their side of the contract is to help in the study and to trust us. Our side of the contract is to not abuse their trust. Being ethical means living up to our part of the bargain.

REMEMBER   Conducting *ethical* research means protecting participants from abuse.

The APA Principles of Ethical Conduct

To assist researchers when dealing with ethical issues, the American Psychological Association (APA) adopted the Ethical Principles of Psychologists and Code of Conduct (1992). These principles govern the full range of a psychologist's activities. In particular, they deal with the care of human and nonhuman research participants and apply to any type of study (not just experiments). For now, we'll discuss human participants. These principles can be summarized as follows.

Identify Potential Risks   The first ethical consideration is to identify any potential **physical risk** in the study: Is there anything that could physically endanger participants? Are you manipulating a potentially dangerous independent variable? Could measuring the dependent variable be harmful? Is all equipment working properly and safely, and will presenting stimuli cause pain or physical damage? Are you adhering to all accepted procedures when injecting drugs, drawing blood, and the like? So, in the smile study, people are not going to want to put someone else's pen in their mouth, so we should sterilize the pen before each use, or buy a box of identical pens and use a new (sterilized) pen each time.

Second, identify any potential **psychological risks**: Will participants experience undue anxiety, depression, or other unpleasant feelings because you are invading their privacy, producing negative emotions, or lowering their self-confidence? Distress can occur directly as the result of a manipulation, as when we intentionally cause people to become sad or depressed. Distress may also result indirectly. For example, you might think Milgram's study was not so bad because no one actually got hurt. But, if Milgram had not disconnected the electrical wires, the participants would have killed—murdered—the learner! Think about how they felt when *that* dawned on them.

When identifying potential risks, consider not only the procedure but also the participants. Having healthy teenagers perform strenuous exercise might not be risky, but it is risky for the elderly or for people with heart conditions. Likewise, films containing sex, violence, and mayhem are standard fare for some adult moviegoers, but they may be upsetting for others, or for children. So, in the smile study, the obvious emotional risk is the embarrassment that looking silly with a pen in one's mouth might cause. However, also consider the discomfort we might cause people who wear braces on their teeth, wear dentures, or are missing their front teeth, and select participants accordingly. (Recall that *pilot studies* are for resolving questions about a procedure, and this includes ethical questions. Thus, if we are unsure how uncomfortable participants will be, we can have pilot subjects go through the procedure and ask them.)

Dealing with deception is a particularly difficult issue. On the one hand, Christensen (1988) found that among people who had participated in deceptive and nondeceptive experiments, those in the deceptive studies enjoyed the experience more, became better educated about psychological research, and did not mind being deceived. On the other hand, this does not mean you can freely deceive participants on a whim. Deception could be harmful because, when participants learn of it, they may feel foolish, depressed, or angry. Therefore, the APA guidelines explicitly require that deception be used *only* when it is a necessary component of a design. Thus, first consider whether deception is truly necessary for producing the desired study. (It is doubtful, for example, that Milgram could have elicited such extreme obedience without using deception.) Second, consider the amount of deception involved. The greater the deception—the bigger the lie—the more objectionable it is. Finally, and most important, consider how severe the impact of deception will be on participants. The extreme emotional turmoil resulting from Milgram's deception is a serious ethical concern. This is very different, for example, from the minor reactions we'd expect in our smile study, so the deception here is much less objectionable.

Protect Participants from Physical and Psychological Harm   Once the potential risks have been identified, try to eliminate or at least minimize them. Simply put, although we recognize the necessity of certain techniques, we should also try to be nice to participants. So, if participants will be stressed or embarrassed, can we alter the design to eliminate these feelings and still get at the intended behaviors? In particular, recall that we seek a *strong manipulation* of the independent variable by giving participants a substantial exposure to very different conditions. Balance this goal with the ethical goal of minimizing the negative impact of the treatments: Can we "tone down" the manipulation so that it affects participants but still is not too extreme? Thus, if we want to make one group more depressed than another, we don't need to make the group suicidal! In fact, will the study work if, instead, we make one group happier than another? We can also minimize risks by screening out high-risk individuals. If the study involves exercise, for example, screen out people with a heart condition. If we're manipulating depression, screen out people who are already clinically depressed.

One important rule is to minimize participants' anxiety by keeping all information about them confidential. We report results only in group form, and participants are never identified in publications or discussed in casual conversations. (Often, we assign participants numbers instead of recording their names, so they remain anonymous.)

Justify Remaining Risks   For any risks to participants that you cannot eliminate, you must fairly and honestly decide whether they are justified by the study's scientific worth. The knowledge to be gained from a study must convincingly justify the risk to participants. Thus, ask yourself such things as: Will the study demonstrate something new and important? Is exposing participants to the risky independent variable really informative? Will the highly stressful or invasive dependent variable tell you that much more than a more mundane, safe one? Is determining causality important enough to justify manipulating the variable as an independent variable, or could you forego causality and use a descriptive/correlational study with people who have already experienced the variable in the real world? Throughout, recognize that as the potential for physical or psychological risk increases, you must have a corresponding increase in the scientific worth of the study. If not, don't conduct the study.

REMEMBER   The primary ethical concern in any study is to minimize potential physical or psychological harm to participants and to ensure that any remaining risk is justified.

All in all, the risks in the smile study seem pretty minimal, although participants might feel self-conscious. We can try to minimize these feelings first in our instructions, reassuring them that everyone may feel like that (misery does like company). Further, it will probably help to put participants at ease if, as part of the instructions, the experimenter also puts a pen in his/her mouth. Otherwise, the risks seem small, and the knowledge about emotion that we'll obtain seems to justify them.

However, we also must inform participants of the risks.

Obtain Informed Consent   Out of respect for participants' right to control what happens to them, you should inform them about the study *prior* to their participation and then let them decide whether they wish to participate. That is, you should obtain **informed consent**. The APA's Ethical Principles state that informed consent is required unless there is minimal risk, such as when we merely observe anonymous people in a field setting. But always obtain informed consent when conducting laboratory experiments. The usual procedure is to provide participants with a written description that contains four components.

First, describe the purpose and procedures of the study. Sometimes you must withhold specific details to prevent diffusion of treatment and to reduce demand characteristics, but usually you can provide general information without biasing the participants. Tell them as much as you can. Tell them the tasks they'll perform, the amount of time that is required, and any other information that you (who knows all of the details) would want before making a decision about whether to participate in the study. In addition, participants have the right to know what you'll do with their data, and you should tell them if their individual performance will be kept confidential (this information will also reduce reactivity).

Second, explicitly warn participants of any physical or psychological risks associated with the procedure. Even if you cannot divulge all aspects of a procedure, you must warn participants of the negative consequences of it. (For example, Milgram should have at least warned his subjects that they might learn some unpleasant things about themselves.)

Third, inform participants that they are free to discontinue their participation at any time during the study, and to remove any responses or data already given, *without penalty*. Volunteering for a study produces such strong demand characteristics to be cooperative that this option *does not* occur to people. Be sure that withdrawing is a realistic option, without any hidden coercion because participants are enrolled in a class or have a job where the study is being conducted.

Finally, obtain participants' signatures as their explicit consent to participate. In the case of minors and others who are not capable of making this decision, obtain consent from their parents or guardians.

Informed consent is usually dealt with prior to giving participants the instructions. Thus, after greeting and seating participants, provide a brief description of the study and the above details about risk, confidentiality, being free to leave, and so on. Then, explain the informed consent procedure and give each participant the consent form to read and sign. (Use no coercion or pressure of any kind here.)

Figure 5.1 shows an example consent form we might use for the smile study. Notice, this is essentially a contract, so it is formal and direct. Begin by identifying yourself (and your supervising professor). Then cover each point, being as truthful as possible. For example, we are up front about the pen-in-mouth routine, and it is true that participants will be asked to pretend they are physically impaired. Conversely, we are building our cover story, and the fact that we have a devious reason for this pretending is not relevant. Likewise, do not give other details of the study unless participants need them to make an informed decision (e.g., don't include the hypothesis). Further, don't minimize any risks, but don't heighten demand characteristics by being overly negative, either. For example, we tell participants that they might feel self-conscious, but without such fanfare that we communicate they are *supposed* to feel self-conscious. Finally, after giving participants a chance to read and ask any questions about the form, have participants sign and complete it. Then we have a record, and we can contact them in the future if need be.

We provide participants with all of the unspoken details during the debriefing.

FIGURE 5.1 Example of an Informed Consent Form for the Smile Study

---

I, [filled in by participant], voluntarily agree to participate in the psychological research being conducted by [name of student researcher] under the supervision of [name of student researcher's professor].

I understand that my participation will require approximately 30 minutes. I will be asked to pretend that my arms and hands are physically disabled, and I will be given a sterilized pen to hold in my mouth. I will then use the pen to perform simple tasks involving drawing and answering questions. I understand that, although I may feel somewhat self-conscious, there is no other known or suspected physical or psychological harm associated with the tasks I will perform.

I understand that all of my answers will be held in strict confidence, that the results will be reported in group form only, and that at no time will my name be reported.

I understand that I am free to withdraw from this study at any time without penalty, to remove any data that I have contributed, and to still receive full credit for my participation.

I understand that at the conclusion of the study, I will be given complete information about the study.

Name (print) _____

Signature _____

Date _____

Phone number _____

Debriefing and Taking Care of Participants after the Study   After testing a participant, provide him or her with a debriefing. In a **debriefing**, we inform participants of all aspects of the study, and remove any negative consequences of the procedure. Thus, here we inform participants about the hypotheses and variables being studied, how we manipulated things, our expected results, and any other reasonable information that participants desire.

The debriefing is also an opportunity to talk with participants, so often the first thing we do is to check for problems (before we bias participants with too much information). For example, we ask questions as a *manipulation check* to see if the conditions had the desired effect. We can check for *demand characteristics* by asking participants what they thought was really going on. And to check for *diffusion of treatment*, we ask if they knew any details of the study. If there is a problem, we can always eliminate a participant's data afterwards. But, be gentle when asking such questions, because *social desirability* operates here, too, with participants being afraid they'll ruin the study, so they may not be forthcoming. After such checks, then describe the study.

In particular, fully disclose any deception and explain why it was necessary. A useful way to structure a debriefing is in terms of *dehoaxing* and *desensitizing* (Holmes, 1976a, 1976b). *Dehoaxing* is informing participants about deception so they understand the true nature of the experiment. *Desensitizing* is making participants feel comfortable with their performance and responses. So, for example, we would dehoax the smile study by telling participants of the hypotheses and the reasons we had them pretend to be disabled. We would desensitize them by indicating that they were fooled because of our deception, and not because of any mental defect on their part, and that others react the same way. Also, we would convey that it is normal regardless if holding the pen did or did not do anything to their emotions. The goal is to inform participants while also making them feel as good about themselves as they did before they entered the study.

Besides providing information, the debriefing should also involve whatever other steps are needed to remove any adverse physical or emotional reactions in participants that may have been created. Thus, if we tested the effects of alcohol, we care for participants until they are sober. If we created anxiety or depression, we try to reverse these feelings, explaining why we think they are normal reactions to our manipulation. If follow-up counseling or check-ups even might be needed, we provide qualified, professional help. Finally, we give participants a means of contacting us later in case unforeseen problems arise. (Researchers often give participants a written summary of the study that contains the researcher's address.)

REMEMBER   Always obtain *informed consent*, *debrief* participants, and *care* for them after the study.

Ethical procedures are not always clear cut, so after we think we have dealt with them appropriately, we are required to double-check with others.

Human Subjects Review Committees   The APA's Ethical Principles (as well as federal and state regulations) require that educational and research institutions maintain an oversight committee, usually called the **Human Subjects Review Committee** (also called the *Institutional Review Board* or *IRB*.) The committee consists of individuals from many disciplines beyond psychology, so that a broad perspective is represented. The committee's job is to review every study conducted at the institution that involves human participants, to ensure that they are treated ethically and appropriately. Researchers must obtain approval from their IRB *before* conducting *any* type of research, be it an experiment or a descriptive study. And yes, projects conducted by students must also be approved.

REMEMBER   The *Human Subjects Review Committee* must approve every study dealing with human participants.

Regardless of whether you're conducting an experiment or a descriptive study, you should approach the above ethical issues in the same manner. To help you remember them all, they're listed in Checklist 5.2.

CHECKLIST 5.2 **Ethical questions to consider when designing a study**

- Are there physical risks to participants?
- Are there psychological risks to participants?
- Can you eliminate or minimize risks?
- Can you justify risks in terms of the scientific value of results?
- Are you obtaining informed consent?
- Are you providing debriefing and care for participants afterwards?
- Did you submit the planned procedure to the IRB for review?

The Ethics of Unobtrusive Measures and Field Research

Ethical issues get particularly complicated with unobtrusive and deceptive procedures, especially in terms of informed consent. In a laboratory setting participants are aware that they will be observed even if they cannot see the observer, so using one-way mirrors and other unobtrusive measures is usually acceptable. Likewise, in a waiting-room situation, participants have given tacit agreement to be observed by showing up for the study. But, if a procedure might embarrass, victimize, or otherwise harm a person, then explicit *prior* informed consent is needed.

When people *know* they are participating in a field study, we deal with informed consent and debriefing as described previously. However, the most difficult ethical situation arises with unobtrusive or hidden field research. After all, it involves the ultimate deception, because participants are not even aware a study is being conducted! As a result, they have not formally volunteered, nor have they been given a chance to provide informed consent. The problem is that, without informed consent, we are essentially spying on people.

The classic example of this dilemma is a study by Middlemist, Knowles, and Matter (1976). They wanted to study the "personal space" that people use to separate themselves from others in social settings. Their goal was to eliminate demand characteristics while measuring whether invading one's personal space created physical tension. Their solution was to observe males as they visited the urinal in a public restroom! They invaded personal space by having a confederate use the adjacent urinal, and the measure of a participant's resulting tension was the amount of time he took to urinate. To be unobtrusive, a researcher hid in one of the stalls and used a *periscope* to observe each participant, timing the interval between when he unzipped and when he rezipped!

Although this was a field experiment, the ethical issue here is with the secret observation of participants, which also may occur in descriptive/correlational studies. We might justify this study by claiming that it is "scientific research" for the "good of humanity." But, some would argue, this is no different from when a government agency or the police spy on citizens, claiming that it helps catch criminals. After all, spying is spying, and it is wrong to invade people's privacy and violate their rights, regardless of whether it is for scientific advancement or for rooting out evil.

Others argue that a public behavior is just that—public—and so it's open to anyone's observation. Thus, a male who uses a public restroom has tacitly agreed to be observed by other males. If a male wishes to keep his urinal behavior private, he should not use a public restroom. From this perspective, some researchers claim that it is unethical for scientists *not* to conduct unobtrusive field research, because they would miss potentially valuable information.

There is no easy resolution to this debate. You might suggest that we obtain informed consent after the study, but by then the person's rights are already violated (and telling people afterwards might be more upsetting than not informing them at all). Instead, we resolve the issue for each specific study by weighing the violation of a person's rights against the potential scientific information to be gained. Therefore, first decide just how "public" participants consider a behavior to be. Are you invading their expected privacy? How strenuously would they object if you asked their permission? How upset would they be if they found out about your spying after the fact? (If you are unsure of the answers, conduct a pilot study in which you ask people these questions.)

Then, weigh the invasion of privacy against the potential scientific benefits. For example, Koocher (1977) argued that the above urinal study needlessly invaded participants' privacy because it replicated findings already demonstrated by other, less questionable techniques. (But see the reply of Middlemist, Knowles, & Matter [1977].) Also, consider whether the procedure really needs to be conducted as an unobtrusive field study. Do the benefits outweigh the resulting ethical problems and reduced control that would not be problems in straightforward laboratory research? And finally, remember that the APA's Ethical Principles state that (1) deception must be necessary and (2) informed consent is required unless the risk to participants is minimal. The more the behavior being studied is an innocuous, mundane public behavior, and the greater the necessity for an unobtrusive field study, the more the study can be justified ethically.

Also, be especially sensitive to the issue of risk in field *experiments*, because they allow us to manipulate all sorts of real-life situations. However, we are *not* free to abuse the unsuspecting public in the name of "science." (You don't have the right to yell "Fire!" in a crowded theater just to see what happens!) In a laboratory setting, informed consent and a lack of realism are protection for participants: Because they have volunteered to experience our artificial situation, it has less of a real impact on them. In field experiments, however, this is not the case. Our deceptions and pranks can cause people to become really frightened, really angry, or really dangerous! Therefore, researchers have an even greater responsibility to respect and protect participants. In short, there are limits to our right to conduct field studies that impose on others. And, as usual, after resolving the ethical issues for ourselves, we obtain approval from our Human Subjects Review Committee.

REMEMBER Be particularly sensitive to the ethics of unobtrusive field research.

Role Playing and Simulations

One possible solution when a laboratory or field procedure is just too risky is to have people simulate being in the experiment through **role playing**: Participants pretend they are in a particular situation, and we either observe their behavior or have them describe how they would behave. Because the situation is not real, physical or psychological harm is unlikely. However, caution must still be exercised. For example, Haney, Banks, and Zimbardo (1973) created a notorious prison simulation that turned sinister: College men pretending to be guards or prisoners exhibited the worst, most dangerous behaviors associated with a real prison.

Role playing is found infrequently in the research literature, because it has very limited validity and reliability. First, demand characteristics can run rampant: Participants may alter their reactions or descriptions to conform to perceived expectations or to keep their real behaviors private. (Would people simulating the Milgram study actually admit that they'd electrocute someone?) Second, people often cannot accurately predict how they would respond. For example, in studies of personal space, participants have given verbal descriptions, manipulated dolls, or drawn lines on paper to indicate how far they would stand from someone else. Yet such predictions seldom match the person's actual behavior when observed under real conditions (Hayduk, 1983).

RESEARCH INVOLVING ANIMALS

So far, we've discussed the ethical issues regarding human participants. Psychological research, however, is not limited to the study of humans, and we face similar ethical concerns with animal participants. First, however, let's consider why we even study animals.

In part, psychologists study animals simply because they demonstrate interesting behaviors that we want to understand. Researchers also study the behavior of a species to compare it with other species, such as when we compare the cognitive capabilities of animals with those of humans.

Further, sometimes researchers study animals as the first step in testing a *model* about a behavior that can then be generalized to all species, including humans. For example, much of what we know about basic brain functioning is based on animal research. A common design is to surgically alter an area of the brain and then determine how a behavior differs relative to unaltered animals. For example, researchers have learned a great deal about how the hypothalamus is involved in eating behavior by surgically damaging different parts of the hypothalamus in white rats. Likewise, researchers using nonsurgical techniques have found much of what we know about genetics by breeding rats and mice. And it was animal research that led to many developments in learning and conditioning: Ivan Pavlov's principles of classical conditioning were developed using dogs, and B. F. Skinner's work on operant conditioning involved rats and pigeons.

Though some people are incensed by the comparisons, animal research often has substantial external validity, generalizing well to many aspects of human behavior, such as education, clinical therapy, and the workplace. Humans are animals, too, and some laws of nature apply to all animals in the same ways. For example, a hypothalamus is a hypothalamus, and the model of how a rat's hypothalamus influences eating behavior has generalized well to humans. Likewise, animal research is often the first step in the development of a new drug or physical treatment. When the treatment works with animals, it often works with humans.

Controls Used with Animal Research

Many animal studies are true experiments conducted in a laboratory: We obtain a random sample of animals (sometimes trapped in the wild but usually purchased from commercial suppliers), randomly assign them to conditions, and apply all of the controls we've discussed for reliably and validly manipulating the independent variable. For internal validity, we keep constant the extraneous variables that might produce a confounding, so we maintain the cages and environment consistently for all animals, test them in the same manner, and so on. Similarly, for a valid and reliable dependent variable, we define scoring criteria, provide practice trials, observe multiple trials, and counterbalance order effects.

Believe it or not, experimenter expectancies and demand characteristics can be a problem even in animal studies. A researcher can inadvertently make errors in measuring or recording scores that are biased toward confirming a hypothesis. And a researcher's expectations can produce subtle differences in the way that animals are handled and tested, biasing their behavior so that they confirm the hypothesis. These problems occur even when dealing with something as simple as a rat, but they are especially serious when dealing with higher species. In particular, the experimenter must avoid the famous problem of "Clever Hans" (Pfungst, 1911). Hans was a horse that apparently could perform addition! If asked for the sum of 2 plus 2, Hans pawed the ground 4 times; if asked 3 plus 3, he pawed 6 times. It turned out, however, that Hans mysteriously lost his mathematical ability if he was blindfolded. Apparently Hans produced correct answers by watching his owner. At the point when the correct sum was reached, the owner showed a relaxed look and Hans stopped pawing the ground.

To minimize such biases, researchers handle all animals in the same way, automate where possible, and use multiple raters and double-blind procedures when subjectively scoring responses. Further, control groups are given appropriate placebos and are handled and tested in the same ways as experimental groups. For example, when testing a drug or surgical procedure, control animals are injected with a placebo or undergo the anesthesia and surgery without receiving the actual treatment. As a result, they experience the same trauma that experimental animals experience.

REMEMBER We control extraneous variables in research involving animals in the same ways as in research involving humans.

The Ethics of Animal Research

Scientists and the general public continue to debate the ethics of laboratory experiments involving animals. It is true that such research often exposes animals to unpleasant and harmful manipulations, such as surgical procedures, electric shocks, food or water deprivation, exposure to toxins, and other aversive conditions. Further, the way to conduct a manipulation check of a surgical procedure is to perform an autopsy. And, even with nonsurgical procedures, animals may be physically or psychologically altered by the treatments, so they usually cannot be studied again and are destroyed.

On the one hand, some animal rights advocates say that animal experiments are unethical because they violate the rights of animals to live free and unharmed. They argue that even though humans have the *ability* to exploit other animals, we do not have the *right* to do so. Some even make the radical argument that animal studies do not even provide useful information, so there is no justification for what is seen as animal abuse. From these perspectives, the only ethical way to study animals is through descriptive studies conducted in natural settings.

On the other hand, animal researchers argue that most experiments are justified by the knowledge they produce: It is just plain wrong to say that animal research has been uninformative. Animal research has most definitely added substantially to the well-being of humans (and other animals) in important ways. Animal research has been the basis for virtually all modern drugs and surgical techniques, for the identification of numerous toxins and carcinogens, and for many psychological principles. From this perspective, it would be *un*ethical if researchers did *not* conduct animal research to benefit society. Thus, they argue, researchers have the right—and the responsibility—to pursue any useful scientific information.

This issue boils down to whether you think the goal of benefitting humans takes precedence over the rights of other animals. If you think it does, then animal research is justified, because there is no other way to obtain the data. It would be more unethical to perform surgical or medical procedures on humans: Often we cannot undo surgical alterations, and when first testing a drug, we may have no idea of the harmful side effects that can occur. Likewise, we cannot control the breeding practices of humans in order to study genetics, nor can we administer to humans the aversive conditions that have led to important discoveries with animals.

In addition, there are scientific and practical reasons for conducting animal laboratory studies. Descriptive research limits the variables and controls we can employ, so this approach is an inadequate substitute. Also, laboratory research with animals can be conducted quickly and efficiently: Animals are easily obtained and housed, their environment can be controlled and manipulated easily, and, for genetic studies, they have a short gestation period.

Regardless of where your personal feelings fall in this debate, it is wrong to think of animal research as involving the mindless torture of abused animals. As with all people, some researchers may be unethical and misbehave. But, for the vast majority of researchers, laboratory animals are valued participants in whom we invest much time, energy, and expense. It is in the researchers' interest to treat them well, because abused animals make poor subjects for a reliable and valid study. Further, the APA's Ethical Principles (1992) provide guidelines for the treatment of research animals, and there are federal, state, and local regulations for the housing and care of animals as well. Because of such rules, animals are well cared for, undergo surgery in sterile settings with anesthesia, and are disposed of in a humane manner.

Finally, the APA's guidelines require that we evaluate animal research in the same way we do human research. First, the harm caused to an animal must be minimized. Thus, we prefer designs that provide positive events as opposed to aversive events, we prefer mildly aversive events to drastic ones, and we prefer temporary external manipulations to permanent surgical ones. Second, we are not frivolous in the treatment of animals, so every aspect of a procedure must be necessary. As usual, the key is whether the procedure is justified by the scientific information that will be learned. Finally, every research institution must have an institutional review board that ensures the ethical treatment of animal subjects.

REMEMBER   Acceptable animal research minimizes the harm done to subjects and must be justified as scientifically important.

SCIENTIFIC FRAUD

There is one more aspect of ethics to consider. Unfortunately, one reason that scientists must always be skeptical about research findings is that other scientists are sometimes guilty of **scientific fraud**: They may report data from a study inaccurately, they may publish data when no research was conducted, or they may be guilty of *plagiarism*, passing off the ideas and conclusions of others as their own. Often their motivation is to provide further support for their previous conclusions: They needed a replication that failed to materialize, so they "faked" the data. At other times, they are responding to professional pressures to be productive researchers.

An example of the problems caused by fraud is that of Sir Cyril Burt, the first British psychologist to be knighted. Burt studied the inheritability of intelligence during the 1930s, concluding that intelligence is genetically determined. This view then became so pervasive that it influenced the educational system in Great Britain. From the genetic perspective, it made sense to limit education to those who had the innate intelligence to benefit from it. Therefore, based on an intelligence test, children would either go on to high school and college, or end up virtually relegated to the coal mines. However, using Burt's research to justify such a program turned out to be a mistake, because Dorfman (1978) convincingly showed that Burt had faked his results (but there is some debate here; see Joynson, 1989).

Science tries to prevent fraud in two ways. First, most published research reports have undergone **peer review**: Prior to publication, a report is sent to several psychologists who are knowledgeable about the research topic. They review the study, checking that conclusions make sense, appropriate procedures are followed, ideas are not plagiarized, and so on. Such peer review not only helps to ensure that the research meets high standards, it also helps to prevent fraudulent research from making it into the research literature. Second, science prevents fraud through replication: Fraudulent conclusions that do make it into the literature will not be replicated. Then, even though not identified as fraudulent, these conclusions will be dropped from the accepted literature.

Regardless, though, it is unethical to perpetrate any form of scientific fraud. This includes falsifying results, as well as keeping secret a result that contradicts one's views. In particular, because you are a beginning research report writer, be very careful to avoid plagiarism. (As discussed in Appendix A, always reference the source for any idea that you get from others.) Fraud not only violates every rule of science, but it also causes enormous harm: Given the extent to which researchers share and integrate research findings, a fraudulent finding can undermine many areas of psychological knowledge. There is no justification for research fraud.

PUTTING IT ALL TOGETHER

Don't underestimate the influence that demand characteristics—especially reactivity and social desirability—can have on the results of a study. Therefore, play psychologist: Use what you know about human nature, defense mechanisms, anxiety, and the like to anticipate demand characteristics. Also, place yourself in the role of a participant and imagine how you would respond. Then, pretend you're someone just the opposite of yourself and imagine how you'd respond. If people are likely to be biased—or downright dishonest—in their responding, then alter the situation.

Also, research ethics are not some stuffy topic to merely give lip-service to. Unethical practices are unacceptable to the community of scientists, and, practically speaking, you'll never get them past an Institutional Review Board: For a clearly risky procedure, there usually is no convincing scientific justification. Besides, as you've seen, one study never definitively "proves" a hypothesis, so conducting an unethical or dangerous study is just not worth it.

To help you remember about demand characteristics and the ethical issues, we've discussed, consult Checklist 5.3.

CHECKLIST 5.3 **Questions to consider about demand characteristics and ethics**

Will demand characteristics be present?

- Will the participants show reactivity to being observed?
- Will the participants give socially desirable responses?
- Will the environment bias participants' responses?
- Will the experimenter's characteristics or expectancies influence scores?
- Do you keep cues as neutral as possible?
- Should you "habituate" participants to being observed?
- Should you use automation?
- Should you use single- or double-blind procedures?
- Does the task have experimental realism?
- Should you hide measurement tasks using unobtrusive techniques?
- Do you need a placebo for the control group?
- Should you disguise the study with deception or a field experiment?

Considering ethical issues

- Are there physical risks to participants?
- Are there psychological risks to participants?
- Can you eliminate or minimize risks?
- Can you justify risks in terms of the scientific value of results?
- Are you obtaining informed consent?
- Are you providing debriefing and care for participants afterwards?
- Did you submit the planned procedure to the IRB for review?

CHAPTER SUMMARY

1. *Demand characteristics* are extraneous cues that guide or bias a participant's behavior.

2. *Reactivity* is the demand characteristic occurring because participants are aware that they are being observed.

3. *Social desirability* is the demand characteristic occurring because participants want to behave in a socially acceptable manner.

4. *Experimenter expectancies* is the demand characteristic from cues the researcher provides about the responses participants should give.

5. Reduce demand characteristics by minimizing and neutralizing cues that could bias participants.

6. *Habituation* familiarizes participants with a procedure before actual data collection begins.

7. With *experimental realism*, participants are engaged by the task and thus are less concerned with demand characteristics. A *distractor task* directs participants' attention away from demand characteristics.

8. An *unobtrusive measurement* is one in which participants' are unaware that they are being measured. *Deception* involves creating an artificial situation that disguises a study.

9. A *placebo* provides the demand characteristics of a treatment.

10. In a *single-blind* procedure, participants are unaware of the nature of the treatment. In a *double-blind* procedure, the researcher who tests participants and the participants are unaware of the nature of the treatment.

11. *Research ethics* deal with balancing the right of a researcher to study a behavior with the right of participants to be protected from abuse.

12. The *APA's Ethical Principles of Psychologists and Code of Conduct* require that animal and human participants be protected from physical or psychological harm and that potential harm is scientifically justified.

13. Research with humans must receive prior approval from the appropriate *Human Subjects Review Committee*. Animal research is reviewed by the appropriate animal *IRB*.

14. Researchers obtain *informed consent* and *debrief* participants.

15. In *role playing*, participants pretend they are in a particular situation.

16. Animal research is conducted to study animals and to test models that can be generalized to humans. This research requires the same controls, including dealing with demand characteristics, as those found in research with humans.

17. Ethical research with animals minimizes the risk to them and is scientifically justified.

18. Science prevents fraud through replication and *peer review*.

KEY TERMS   (with page references)

APA's Ethical Principles 139
debriefing 143
deception 134
demand characteristic 130
distractor task 135
double-blind procedure 133
experimental realism 134
experimenter expectancies 132
habituation 133
Human Subjects Review
  Committee 145
informed consent 141

peer review 151
physical risk 139
placebo 135
psychological risk 139
reactivity 131
research ethics 138
role playing 147
scientific fraud 150
single-blind procedure 133
social desirability 131
unobtrusive measure 134

REVIEW QUESTIONS

1. (a) What do we mean by demand characteristics? (b) In terms of reliability, internal validity, and external validity, how do demand characteristics harm a study?

2. (a) What is experimental realism, and why do we seek it? (b) How is experimental realism different from ecological validity?

3. (a) What are unobtrusive measures? (b) What is deception? (c) Why do researchers use unobtrusive measures or deception?

4. What is meant by research ethics?

5. What are the three major issues about risks you must resolve to *design* an ethical study?

6. What are the two major ethical steps you must include when *conducting* a study?

7. (a) Why is informed consent needed? (b) What four components must you include when obtaining informed consent?

8. (a) What is role playing? (b) What is the advantage of this approach? (c) What is the disadvantage of this approach?

9. (a) What is a debriefing? (b) What is the general sequence of events in a study, from when participants arrive to when they leave?

10. In terms of demand characteristics, (a) why could automation be good for a study? (b) Why could it be bad?

11. (a) In terms of demand characteristics, what potential confounding occurs between a control group and an experimental group? (b) How do you eliminate this confounding?

12. (a) What particular ethical issue occurs in unobtrusive field research? (b) According to the APA's Ethical Principles, when don't you need to obtain informed consent?

APPLICATION QUESTIONS

13. In study 1, the researcher is intentionally either friendly or unfriendly, predicting that being friendly will induce greater levels of cooperation from participants. In study 2, the researcher reads either a list of similar or a list of dissimilar words and then measures participants' memory for the list. (a) How might the researcher bias the outcome of each study? (b) How can this bias be eliminated in each study?

14. You wish to test the proposal that women become more sexually aroused by erotic films depending on whether the plot has a weak or strong theme of love and romance. After showing participants one type of film, you measure the dependent variable using a questionnaire about their arousal. (a) What demand characteristics are a problem? (b) How would you reduce these demand characteristics? (c) What ethical problems might arise with this study?

15. In question 14, instead of a questionnaire, you decide to personally interview each participant. (a) What technique for controlling demand characteristics should you use? (b) What researcher variables should you control?

16. (a) What are two major criticisms of laboratory animal research? (b) How would you answer these criticisms?

17. When conducting a study, a researcher wears a white lab coat and carries a clipboard and stopwatch. How might these details influence the internal and external validity of the study?

18. Consider the hypothesis that greater exposure to violence on television results in more aggressive behavior. (a) For ethical reasons, what might be the best design for determining whether this relationship exists? (b) What is the trade-off in being ethical?

19. Your experiment tests whether studying for more time results in higher test grades. You select participants from your research methods class and have them study for either 0, 1, 2, or 3 hours before they take their regular course exam on Chapters 4 and 5 in this book. Ethically speaking, what's wrong with this design?

20. You deliver different speeches to make participants more or less sexist. Then you measure their sexist attitudes using a questionnaire titled "Survey of Sexist Attitudes." (a) What demand characteristics are likely, and how will they influence participants' responses? (b) Why is it that your manipulation could appear to work even though it does not really alter participants' views? (c) Why could your manipulation appear not to have worked although it really did alter their views? (d) How can you alter and add to the questionnaire to reduce demand characteristics? (*Hint*: how can you *distract* participants?)

21. In question 20, you instead measure participants' sexism by observing whether they help a confederate of the opposite sex. (a) What demand characteristics might mislead you here? (b) How would you attempt to avoid this problem?

22. In the smile study in this chapter, should participants be tested individually or in small groups? Why?

DISCUSSION QUESTIONS

23. Say that you conduct a study in which you play one of several types of music to people, and then suddenly pull out and shoot a (blank) pistol. You measure participants' anxiety level to determine whether different types of music cause people to remain more or less calm in the face of startling stimuli. (a) How might demand characteristics influence your data? (b) What specific information must you include when obtaining informed consent? (c) What risks are present in this study? (d) To minimize risks, what aspects of the participants you select should be considered? (e) What should your debriefing include? (f) What major flaw will occur in this study as you continue to conduct it? (g) Should you conduct this study? Why?

24. You have discovered a new drug treatment for a serious mental illness that you wish to test. What conflicting ethical and design principles do you face when considering whether to include a control condition?

25. You want to unobtrusively observe children at a day-care center, judging how aggressively they behave when playing with dolls after watching an adult behave aggressively. (a) What problems do you foresee arising from demand characteristics? (b) How would you deal with these biases? (c) Why is this design a problem ethically? (d) Explain how you would meet each of the APA guidelines in this study.

26. For the study in question 14, each film lasts 25 minutes and is in black and white. The questionnaire consists of 20 Likert-type statements in which the scale for each is between 1 (strongly agree) and 5 (strongly disagree.) Write the instructions you would give to participants, create an informed consent form, and determine what you would say during the debriefing.

6

Controlling Participant Variables Using Between-Subjects and Within-Subjects Designs

GETTING STARTED

To understand this chapter, recall the following:

- From Chapter 3, recall what reliability and internal and external validity are.
- From Chapter 4, recall why we use multiple trials and what order effects are.
- Also from Chapter 4, recall what the restriction of range is, what a powerful design is, what variability and error variance are, and why a powerful design is important.

Your goals in this chapter are to learn:

- How participant variables influence external validity.
- How participant variables influence reliability and internal validity.
- What constitutes a between-subjects design and how to control participant variables in this design.

- What constitutes a within-subjects design and how to control participant variables in this design.
- The difference between matched-groups and repeated-measures designs.
- What randomization, partial counterbalancing, and complete counterbalancing are.

So far, we've taken the participants in a study pretty much for granted. Yet participants are thinking, feeling, and behaving organisms who can drastically influence a measurement procedure. Therefore, an important aspect of designing a study is to consider the characteristics of the participants. In this chapter, we discuss how to recognize participant variables that can influence our results, examine techniques for controlling such variables, and consider the impact that such controls then have on the interpretation of a study.

We'll focus on experiments, but these issues also apply to descriptive studies.

PARTICIPANT VARIABLES AND INDIVIDUAL DIFFERENCES

Recall that participant variables are the personal characteristics that make one individual different from the next. Further, recall that the term *individual differences* is used to communicate these differences. When discussing participant variables, we really mean any variable that makes one individual different from another.

Because no two individuals are identical, no two individuals will behave identically when in the same situation. Thus, physically, participants differ in gender, age, metabolism, hormones, musculature, coordination, height, and weight. Because their physical machinery is not identical, their physical reactions are not identical. Cognitively, they differ in style, strategies, intelligence, and memory, so they do not all process a stimulus identically. They also differ in terms of personal histories and experiences, social and economic standing, and so on. As a result, some are more familiar with a task than others, they are influenced by their moods in different ways, and they have different motivations. Socially, their attitudes and personalities differ, so some will be more reactive, more competitive, or more attentive.

Depending on the situation, a participant variable can be an independent variable, a dependent variable, or an extraneous variable. For now, we'll discuss how extraneous participant variables can influence a study. This begins with external validity.

HOW PARTICIPANT VARIABLES INFLUENCE EXTERNAL VALIDITY

Remember that part of designing a study is to identify the population that our hypothesis applies to. Then, after the study, part of having *external validity* means that the results accurately generalize to this population. Participant variables are important to external validity because they describe the characteristics of the individuals in the population. Therefore, we use participant variables to describe the population we'll generalize to, and at the same time, this defines the participants we'll actually test in our study.

Thus, part of creating a study is to essentially create an *operational definition* of the participants in terms of the participant variables we will use to select them. This is called our selection criteria. **Selection criteria** define participants in terms of the characteristics we require for them to participate in the study. Thus, by deciding the gender, age, educational level, and physical requirements of participants, we are creating the selection criteria. These criteria then also define the population that the sample represents.

Defining the participants depends first on the constructs and hypothesis being investigated. When studying the behavior of children, for instance, the sample and population should be composed of children of a specified age. Recognize, however, that a population is not a fixed entity defined by one variable. Members of a population will still differ along many variables: The population of children, for example, contains males and females from different cultures and backgrounds, with different abilities, and so on. How well results generalize to the population depends on how much the sample has in common with the population in terms of *all* of the participant variables that can influence responses. If individuals having a particular characteristic are excluded, we may end up with a biased and unrepresentative example of the target population, thus creating a biased picture of how all members of that population behave. Therefore, the selection criteria should produce a sample that is similar to the target population along *all* relevant participant variables so that the sample is essentially a miniature version of the population.

> **REMEMBER** The *selection criteria* for the sample should reflect the important characteristics of the population being studied.

Limitations on the Representativeness of a Sample

Recall that we randomly select participants so that all individuals in the population have the same chances of being selected. As discussed in Chapter 2, we may use *simple random sampling* (similar to drawing names from a hat) or *systematic random sampling* (selecting every *n*th name from a list). By selecting participants in an unbiased and unselective manner, we allow the diverse characteristics of the population to occur in the sample as often, and to the same degree, as they occur in the population. As a whole, therefore, the individuals in the study should be representative of the population.

However, two de facto limitations will always be present to prevent some members of the population from being selected. First, the entire population may not be identifiable. For example, if you peruse the research on alcoholism and its treatment, you'll find that it is largely limited to males. Historically, female alcoholics have been unwilling to identify themselves, so they have been unavailable as research subjects. Second, we are unable to contact all identifiable members of the population. Usually, the sample is limited to those people living near us. If, for example, we then solicit participants using the telephone directory, the population is further limited, excluding the rich and famous with unlisted numbers, as well as poor people who have no phone. Many experiments are even more limited, because the samples are composed of students at only the researcher's university, and then often restricted to those enrolled in only psychology courses.

Because of such limitations, we usually cannot obtain a truly random sample from the population. Instead, selection is random only in the sense that we give every individual in the *available* portion of the population an equal opportunity to volunteer for the study. Often we then test all volunteers who meet the selection criteria, or we use simple or systematic random sampling to select from those who constitute the volunteer pool.

By excluding some members of the population, it is possible to overrepresent some participant variables and fail to represent others, so that the sample is unrepresentative of the population. For example, because of its admission standards and cost, a particular college will attract a certain type of student. Then, whether external validity is reduced depends upon the behavior under study. For example, behaviors such as memory or other cognitive processes, may not generalize well to the adult population as a whole, because college students are better educated and smarter than adults in general. Therefore, for some behaviors you may need to broaden the population. Milgram's infamous electric-shock study did not rely on college students, because, given their age and position, they might have been especially responsive to authority figures. Instead, the general adult population was sampled. On the other hand, college students are conveniently available, and findings about many of their basic behaviors do generalize well to the larger population.

Thus, always consider the population you wish to generalize to, and determine whether any limitations in the sample will seriously reduce the validity of your conclusions. If so, take the necessary steps to obtain a more representative sample. (Chapter 10 examines techniques for contacting a wider range of participants.)

Sample Size and Representativeness

Working within the available population, we then seek to adequately represent it. An important aspect of this process is deciding on N: The symbol N stands for the number of participants in a study, and n stands for the number of participants observed in a condition (adding all of the ns equals N). To maximize external validity, the general rule is "the more the merrier": The larger a sample, the more of the population that is observed, so it is more likely that the sample will include all relevant types of participants. Therefore, we are more likely to obtain an accurate, representative sample. Conversely, with only a few participants, we are more likely to obtain a sample having rather atypical characteristics, so that it is not representative of the population.

"The more the merrier" does not mean that we test hundreds of participants per condition. The range of N in laboratory experiments is often between 50 and 100, with ns in the range of 15 to 30. The results of such studies are replicated with considerable frequency. Thus, with Ns in this range, one random sample is roughly comparable to another, and the findings they produce *are* externally valid. Of course, if more participants can easily be tested, they further increase external validity.

You are not required to have the same number of participants—"equal ns"—in all conditions of an experiment. However, remember that you want to generalize the results of each condition and seek the same level of confidence in each. Therefore, avoid having only a few participants in a particular condition. Instead, there should be close to the same number of participants per condition and therefore an adequate, comparable representation of the population in each. (*Note*: Statistical procedures are most accurate, and often *much* easier to perform, with equal ns.)

Limitations on the Representativeness of Volunteers

Even with a large N from a broad population, the representativeness of a sample still can be limited because only some individuals will end up in the study. Then external validity suffers because of the peculiar characteristics of these participants.

First, external validity is limited because of the volunteer bias. The **volunteer bias** is the bias that arises because a sample contains only those individuals who are willing to participate in the study. There are considerable differences between people who volunteer for a study and those who do not (Rosenthal & Rosnow, 1975). Among other things, volunteers tend to have a higher social status and intelligence, to exhibit a greater need for approval, and to be less authoritarian and conforming. Also, participants who find the research topic interesting or personally relevant are more likely to volunteer, as are those who expect to be positively evaluated.

Second, those who complete a study often are biased because they are not naive about psychological research. **Subject sophistication** is a bias that occurs when participants are knowledgeable about research. People may have participated in previous experiments, or they may have studied research methods or the psychological topic under investigation. Participants also gain experience and knowledge about our manipulations over the course of their participation.

Because of this knowledge, they may be more or less susceptible to reactivity and other demand characteristics, or they may be aware of our deceptions or predictions and more prone to diffusion of treatment. Then, their behavior is different from the general, unsophisticated population. (And note that subject sophistication applies even to animal participants that, through experience, become more relaxed or anxious during testing, learn how to perform a task better, and so on.)

> **REMEMBER**   A biased sample can occur because of *volunteer bias* and *subject sophistication.*

Although these threats to external validity are not entirely controllable, you can try to limit them. Try to make the mechanics of volunteering and participating in the study easy for all potential participants. And initially solicit a wide range of both sophisticated and unsophisticated subjects. As usual, also consider a study's possible flaws when interpreting it. Thus, during debriefing, you can question participants about their sophistication or their reasons for volunteering to determine how biased the sample is.

HOW PARTICIPANT VARIABLES INFLUENCE A RELATIONSHIP

Once you have identified the sample's characteristics needed to maximize external validity, then consider any additional participant variables that could influence your results. To see how this is done in an example study, consider the hypothesis that "people can recall an event better when they are hypnotized." The simplest way to test this is to compare two samples of participants, comparing those who have been hypnotized to those who have not. One approach would be to show all participants a videotape of an event, like a supposed robbery. One condition of the independent variable will be the hypnotized group, who will then answer, let's say, 30 questions about the robbery. The other, *control* condition will answer the questions without benefit of hypnosis. (For ethical safeguards, we use a trained hypnotist, obtain informed consent, ensure that hypnosis has little risk, debrief participants, and obtain approval from our IRB.) This design (with an unrealistically small N) is shown in Table 6.1. Each score is a participant's recall score—the total number of questions correctly answered. The data shown are the ideal kinds of scores we would hope to see, demonstrating a relationship in which, as the amount of hypnosis increases, recall scores also tend to increase. Likewise, we can summarize the scores in each condition by computing the mean ($\overline{X}$) of the scores in each column. Comparing these should show that, "on average," scores increase with increased hypnosis.

To allow a clear interpretation of the variables and behaviors under study, we apply all of the controls discussed previously for designing a "good" study.

Recall that the key to *reliability* and *validity*, as well as to a *powerful* design, is controlling extraneous variables that might fluctuate *between* and *within* con-

TABLE 6.1 Diagram of Hypnosis Study

The independent variable is degree of hypnosis and the dependent variable is recall.

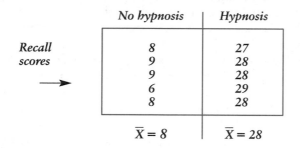

	No hypnosis	Hypnosis
Recall scores →	8	27
	9	28
	9	28
	6	29
	8	28
	$\overline{X} = 8$	$\overline{X} = 28$

ditions. In addition to environmental, researcher, and measurement variables, we are especially concerned about extraneous participant variables. Because all individuals in a population differ somewhat, we are always likely to select participants who differ in ways that can influence the results.

First, if participants selected for the *same* condition differ from each other, they might respond differently to the same stimuli. For example, people who differ in their general memory ability will recall our robbery differently, even when in the same hypnosis condition. This reduces the reliability and validity of our measurement of the influence of hypnosis on their memory for the robbery. It also produces *variability* (differences) in scores within each condition, producing a weaker, less convincing relationship.

Second, if participants differ *between* conditions, we have a *confounding*. For example, say that we are unaware that, simply because of the luck of random assignment, people with a good memory are all assigned to one of our conditions, while people with a poor memory all fall into the other. Then, on the one hand, we could be fooled into thinking hypnosis improves memory even if it does not: If people with a good memory are all in the hypnosis group, their inherently better memory will make it appear that the presence of hypnosis produced better memory. On the other hand, we might be fooled into thinking that hypnosis does not work when it does: If, by luck, the experimental group contains people with a poor memory, and the control group contains those with a good memory. Then, the benefit of hypnosis coupled with a poor memory might produce scores similar to those of people receiving no hypnosis but having a good memory. Then no overall differences in recall scores will be found between the conditions. Or, hypnosis might add so little that those with a better memory in the control condition produce higher recall scores than those with a poor memory who are under hypnosis. Then, we'll see data showing that hypnosis actually worsens memory.

REMEMBER Extraneous participant variables create problems when participants differ *between* or *within* conditions.

Ideally, therefore, we seek to control any participant variables so that every aspect of participants that might influence scores is the same, both within and between conditions. The first step is to identify potentially important participant variables that need controlling. To do so, look for any characteristic of an individual that is substantially correlated with—related to—the independent or dependent variables. First, look for differences among participants that might influence the impact of the independent variable. In the hypnosis study, for example, people differ in how easily they are hypnotized, how long they will remain "under," and so on. If our participants differ along these variables, then not everyone in the hypnosis condition will experience the same hypnosis, producing inconsistent differences in recall between the conditions. Or, say we're studying the effects of alcohol. Because of differences in weight, metabolism, or tolerance, people will be more or less affected by a particular amount of alcohol, producing an inconsistent effect of each condition of the independent variable.

Second, look for differences among participants that might influence responses on the dependent variable. For example, a person's inherent motivation to succeed is another possible influence on his or her recall of the robbery. Or, if we have participants read a description of the robbery, a person's vocabulary and reading skills are correlated with, and thus might influence, his or her comprehension of the description, in turn influencing retention of it. These variables will produce differences in recall scores between or within conditions, although they will have nothing to do with the effect of hypnosis.

Generally, when the stimulus is rather concrete and elicits a physical response, look for participant variables that influence physical responses. These can be physiological, such as participants' height or degree of coordination, or psychological, such as their cognitive abilities or motivation. For stimuli and responses that involve social behaviors or attitudes, look for variables that influence social processes, such as personality or cultural differences. As usual, the research literature is helpful in identifying important participant variables to control: Research specifically related to your study will indicate variables that others believed needed controlling, and general research investigating individual differences will indicate variables that can influence the behavior you're studying.

REMEMBER   A participant variable that will influence the impact of the independent variable or performance on the dependent variable is a variable to control.

Thus, in summary, we've seen that we consider participant variables from two perspectives: how they influence external validity, and how they influence the relationship and conclusions in our data. For help in remembering the particulars here, consult Checklist 6.1.

Once you've identified the important participant variables, then you control them. The remainder of this chapter discusses various techniques for controlling participant variables. Which techniques we use depend first on which of the two

CHECKLIST 6.1 **Questions to consider when controlling participant variables**

- Do the characteristics of participants limit generalizability?
- Is the sample size (N) sufficient to represent the population?
- Does the volunteer bias or subject sophistication influence the results?
- Are extraneous participant variables strongly correlated with the independent or dependent variable?
- Will fluctuating participant variables within conditions reduce reliability and the relationship's strength?
- Will fluctuating participant variables between conditions reduce internal validity and the relationship's strength?

types of designs for dealing with participant variables we choose: You can create either a *between-subjects design* or a *within-subjects design*.

CONTROLLING PARTICIPANT VARIABLES IN A BETWEEN-SUBJECTS DESIGN

In a **between-subjects design**, a different group of participants is randomly selected for each condition of an independent variable. You can recognize this type of design because participants are tested under only one level of the independent variable. We simply select one random sample for one condition, and a different, separate sample for the other condition(s).

A between-subjects design is appropriate when it's appropriate to compare one group of participants in one condition to an entirely different batch of participants in another condition. (As opposed to testing the same batch of participants under all conditions.) For example, in the hypnosis study, we might not want participants to have practice by seeing the videotape and answering the memory questions in more than one condition. If this is an important consideration, we'd select different, "fresh" participants for each condition, creating a between-subjects design.

For a between-subjects design to be appropriate, however, it must also provide acceptable control over extraneous participant variables. With a between-subjects design, our first line of defense for controlling participant variables is **random assignment**.

Random Assignment

In a between-subjects design involving a true independent variable, we randomly assign participants to each condition. This controls participant variables by randomly mixing them, so that differences in a variable are balanced out in each condition. For example, by randomly assigning people to our hypnosis conditions, some who have a good memory and some who do not should end up in each condition. Overall, differences in recall scores between the conditions should not be due to differences in the memory ability of the respective participants, so this potential confounding should be eliminated.

Be careful, however, to assign participants in a truly random way, avoiding any hidden variable that determines their assignment. For example, we wouldn't assign students who sit in the front of a class to one condition and those sitting in the back to the other. Where a student sits is not random, so we might confound the conditions with various personal characteristics. Similarly, do not assign to the same condition all people who first volunteer for a study. Those who participate early in a study might be more prompt, compulsive, or ambitious than later subjects. Instead, randomly assign participants to different conditions as they arrive, so that such characteristics are spread out between conditions.

Pros and Cons of Random Assignment   Given how frequently research findings can be replicated, random assignment—and random selection—are powerful tools for producing balanced, representative samples in each condition. This is especially heartening because often we cannot identify the important participant variables to be controlled. With random assignment, we don't need to know the variables that are being controlled, because whatever they are in the population, they are likely to occur in a balanced way in each condition.

There are, however, three potential problems with random assignment. First, random assignment is not guaranteed to balance participant variables within each condition. For example, by chance we might still have people in one hypnosis condition who all have a much better memory than those in the other. Second, random assignment works less well with small samples, so if ns are small, we are likely to have groups that differ along important participant variables. Third, when random assignment does balance out a variable effectively, the variable then fluctuates *within* each condition. Remember that the reason we control a variable is because we think that more or less of it makes a *difference* in scores. Therefore, random assignment intentionally changes such variables within each condition, producing potentially larger differences in scores within each condition—larger *error variance*. This produces a weaker, less powerful relationship. For example, random assignment should produce participants in the *same* hypnosis condition who have different memory abilities. This may then cause them to produce different recall scores, so that we end up with a weaker, less consistent relationship.

Because of these potential problems, researchers sometimes take control of individual participant variables. One approach is to actively balance a variable.

Balancing Participant Variables

We do not leave the balancing of a critical participant variable to random chance because the possibility of a serious confounding is too great. Instead, we control the variable by systematically balancing or "counterbalancing" its influence within each condition.

To balance a participant variable, we first make the variable part of the *selection criteria*. For obvious physical or personal characteristics (gender and age), we merely solicit participants who meet the criteria. For less obvious characteristics, we **pretest** participants: Prior to conducting the study, we measure potential participants on the variable to be controlled. For example, we might measure a physical attribute (strength), a cognitive skill (reading ability), or a personality trait (anxiety level). Recognize that conducting a pretest is no different from measuring participants on a dependent variable, so we need a valid and reliable measurement technique that takes into account such issues as *scoring criteria, sensitivity, demand characteristics, order effects,* and so on.

Using the pretest information, we create a separate subject "pool" for each aspect of the variable we wish to balance. For example, in the hypnosis study, we could control participants' gender by creating a pool of males and a pool of females. To control for memory ability, we could identify those males and those females who have good and poor memory using an appropriate pretest. Then we would assign participants so that each pool is represented in each condition in a balanced way. For example, we could randomly select and randomly assign participants so that 25% of those assigned to each condition are from the male good-memory pool, 25% are from the female good-memory pool, and so on. This design is shown in Table 6.2. The Xs in each row represent participants' recall scores. To determine the effect of the conditions of hypnosis, we ignore gender and memory ability and average all scores vertically in a condition (a column). Then the scores in each condition should be equally influenced by differences in memory ability and gender, so that any differences between conditions cannot be confounded by these variables. (All other design issues still apply, so we could also counterbalance the order in which participants complete the 30 questions, and so on.)

TABLE 6.2 Diagram of the Hypnosis Experiment Showing Balancing of Gender and Memory Ability

Each row represents people having the same gender and memory ability.

Participant pool	No hypnosis	Hypnosis
Male, good memory	XXX	XXX
Female, good memory	XXX	XXX
Male, poor memory	XXX	XXX
Female, poor memory	XXX	XXX
	$\overline{X}$	$\overline{X}$

This procedure introduces an important new term: Above, when we ignore the gender and memory ability of participants and obtain an overall mean score in each column, we "collapse" across these participant variables. **Collapsing** across a variable means that we combine scores from the different amounts or categories of that variable. Thus, if we used a male experimenter with half the participants in each condition and a female experimenter with the other half, we would "collapse across experimenter gender" by combining the scores of people tested by both experimenters, computing one overall mean for each condition. Likewise, when we test participants on multiple trials in a condition, we average the scores from the trials together, so we "collapse across trials."

REMEMBER *Collapsing* across a variable means that we combine the scores from the different levels of the variable.

Pros and Cons of Balancing   The benefit of balancing is that if we find the predicted relationship, then, because we've balanced the participant variable, we can be sure that it was not a confounding, so we have greater internal validity. We also have greater external validity because we demonstrate the relationship even with the different levels of the variable present. Above, we are sure gender and memory ability do not confound the results, and we demonstrate a more general relationship because different genders and memory abilities are present.

The drawback to balancing is that we might not find the predicted relationship. As with random assignment, counterbalancing involves changing a variable *within* conditions, so there may be greater variability in the scores within each condition. Above, by including the scores of males and females who have good and poor memories, we are likely to see larger variability in recall scores within a condition than if we tested only males or only people with a good memory. Thus, counterbalancing can produce relatively large error variance, so we obtain a less consistent relationship and have less power.

Also, if you think about it long enough, you can identify many variables to counterbalance in any study. The drawback is that extensive balancing schemes greatly complicate the design of a study. Further, because different participants must be tested with each level of a balanced variable, this can dramatically increase the number of individuals required in each condition. And finally, a pretest can alert participants to the variables under study or to the purpose and predictions of the research. This knowledge can lead to *diffusion of treatment*, or it can communicate *demand characteristics* that participants respond to during the experiment proper. (To avoid such problems, some form of *deception* in the pretest may be necessary.)

REMEMBER   Balancing a participant variable ensures that it cannot confound the results, but it may result in increased error variance, and pretesting may communicate demand characteristics.

With random assignment and counterbalancing, our *hope* is that, overall, the group tested in one condition is comparable to the group in the other condition. The problem, however, is that this balancing act simply may not work, and then the independent variable is confounded by a participant variable. Therefore, we can more directly ensure that the individuals in one condition are comparable to those in the other conditions by using a *matched-groups design*.

Matched-Groups Designs

In a **matched-groups design,** each participant in one condition "matches" a participant in the other conditions on one or more participant variable. For example, to control the participant variable of memory ability, we could create two samples containing participants who have "matching" memory abilities.

To create matched samples, first identify pairs of participants who have the same score on the variable to be controlled (using a pretest if necessary). Then, randomly assign each member of the pair to one condition. Thus, we would identify matching pairs of people who have the same memory ability and assign one member of each pair to a condition. If we select two people who have a very good memory, we'll randomly assign one person to the hypnosis condition and the other person to the control condition. Likewise, someone with a terrible memory in one condition is matched with someone having a terrible memory in the other condition, and so on.

We can also match participants on more than one variable. For example, we might want to create matching samples in terms of gender as well as memory ability. This would produce the design shown in Table 6.3. Each row contains the scores of a matched pair of participants: The first pair consists of two males,

TABLE 6.3 Diagram of the Hypnosis Experiment

Each row represents two people who are matched on gender and memory. Xs represent each person's recall score.

	No hypnosis	Hypnosis
Pair 1: Male, good memory	X	X
Pair 2: Female, good memory	X	X
Pair 3: Male, poor memory	X	X
Pair 4: Female, poor memory	X	X
	$\overline{X}$	$\overline{X}$

both with a good memory. The second pair is two females, both with a good memory, and so on. Think of a row as representing a very small experiment with one participant per condition. Any difference in the scores between the conditions cannot be due to differences in participants' memory ability or gender, because these variables are constant. Then, because having one participant per condition is not a reliable approach, we replicate this study with other pairs.

Participants can be matched using any relevant variable, such as weight, age, physical ability, or the school they attend. We can also rely on natural pairs to match participants. For example, roommates or husband-and-wife teams are already matched in terms of having the same housing arrangements. Another common approach is to test identical twins, assigning one twin to each condition. Because genetic influences are equated, any differences in a behavior between the groups must be due to environmental causes. Likewise, in animal research, pairs are created from litter mates to match them on variables related to their experiences.

If it is difficult to find participants who have identical scores on the matching variable, we rank-order participants and create pairs using adjacent ranked scores. Thus, above, the two males whose memory ability ranks them as first and second in our subject pool would form one pair; the two with the next best memory would form the next pair, and so on.

REMEMBER   In a *matched-groups design*, each participant in one condition matches a participant in every other condition in terms of one or more extraneous variables.

Pros and Cons of Matched Groups   The advantage to matching is that it ensures that in every condition there is a participant with virtually the same score on the variable(s) we wish to control. Then these variables are constant across the conditions, eliminating these potential confoundings. By controlling memory ability and gender in the hypnosis experiment, for example, we have greater internal validity for inferring that differences between the conditions are due to our treatment.

There are, however, limitations to a matched-groups design. Again, we have the problem that pretesting may create diffusion of treatment or communicate demand characteristics. Also, we are again intentionally changing the levels of an extraneous variable within each condition, so we might increase the variability of scores within each condition and produce a less powerful relationship. (But as you'll see in Chapter 7, the statistical analysis for matched groups reduces this problem.) Finally, there is the practical problem that, to find matching participants, we might have to pretest many individuals and/or settle for a very small N. This is especially so with a design that involves several conditions of the independent variable, in which matching triplets or larger numbers can be very difficult if not impossible.

> **REMEMBER** A matched-groups design ensures that the conditions are comparable on the matching variable, but matching can increase error variance, and it can be impractical.

Limiting the Population

An alternative to counterbalancing or matching a participant variable is to limit the population based on that variable, so that we keep the variable constant. Then the variable cannot influence the results. For example, if we expect males and females to differ greatly in how hypnosis influences their memory, we might limit the population to males only or to females only.

We limit the population through selection criteria. We pretest participants to identify those who meet the criteria and are approximately the same on the participant variable. For example, we might create a pool of males who all have a good memory. Then, from this pool, we would randomly select and assign participants to our conditions.

Pros and Cons of Limiting the Population There are two advantages to selecting participants from a more limited population. First, this increases internal validity by eliminating a potential confounding that might occur with random assignment: By testing only males, for example, we need not be concerned about whether gender is balanced in each condition. Second, this increases power by reducing the error variance: The more similar the participants, the less variable the scores are likely to be within each condition. Above, differences in scores within a condition that might occur between males and females will not occur when all participants are males.

There are also two drawbacks to limiting the population. First, if we become too selective, we can overly *restrict the range* of scores. For example, by limiting the study to just men with a good memory, we might see little or no difference in recall scores between the hypnosis conditions. Second, because we are more selective in choosing participants, they represent a more limited population, and so external validity is reduced. Thus, if we test only males, we will have no basis for generalizing to females.

> **REMEMBER** Limiting the population eliminates potential confounding by a participant variable and reduces variability within conditions, but at the possible cost of restricted range and reduced external validity.

Deciding How to Deal with Participant Variables in a Between-Subjects Design

Random assignment, counterbalancing, matching, and limiting the population are not mutually exclusive procedures. We could, for example, limit the population to only one gender and then balance or match memory ability. And, regardless of the extent to which we counterbalance and limit the population, we still rely on random selection and random assignment to balance any other participant variables within and between conditions.

When deciding on the specific procedure(s) to use for controlling a variable, there are two considerations. First, how influential is the variable? The more likely it is to influence the results, the more that it must be actively controlled. Never leave the control of a highly influential variable to random assignment: Either counterbalance it, match it, or limit the population to keep it constant.

Second, weigh the goal of finding a convincing, powerful relationship with the goal of making internally and externally valid inferences about the relationship. On the one hand, the more variables that you actively balance, the more that things are changing within a condition, and so the greater the variability in scores will be. On the other hand, keeping a variable constant by limiting the population reduces potential variability, but at the cost of reduced external validity because a more limited type of participant is being tested.

Recognize that the same problems arise when controlling *any* environmental, researcher, or measurement variable as well. For example, we could balance experimenter gender, employing a male experimenter with half of the people in each hypnosis condition and a female experimenter with the other half. This would produce greater generalizability, because we demonstrate the relationship with both types of experimenter. But, we would balance this variable because we expect that the presence of a male or female experimenter *makes a difference* in participants' scores. Therefore, counterbalancing with both genders will produce greater variability in scores within the conditions. If only a male or only a female experimenter is present throughout, however, we will see less variability, but we will also demonstrate the relationship in a more limited situation.

REMEMBER   When deciding to control *any* extraneous variable, consider its threat to reliability and internal validity versus whether the control will substantially increase error variance or limit external validity.

There is no easy solution to this predicament. You should strive for a happy medium, but, if pushed, researchers generally opt for increased power and internal validity, even at the risk of producing a unique situation that limits external validity. Therefore, counterbalance those variables that must be present and that are *likely* to confound the independent variable or that *seriously* bias dependent scores. Control other, more minor variables by keeping them constant.

You can see all of the questions to consider when designing a between-subjects study in Checklist 6.2. If the answers to these questions are such that you cannot solve the problem of controlling participant variables, you might instead use a *within-subjects design*.

CHECKLIST 6.2 **Questions to consider when selecting a between-subjects design**

- Will random assignment control important participant variables?
- Will balancing control important participant variables?
- Will matching control important participant variables?
- Will pretesting create major problems?
- Will limiting the population restrict generalizability?
- Will controls add error variance that weakens the relationship?

CONTROLLING PARTICIPANT VARIABLES IN A WITHIN-SUBJECTS DESIGN

On the one hand, a problem with the preceding methods is that we may not even know which participant variables we should control in a particular study. Also, often when we need to control participant variables, there are *many* to control, and it's almost impossible to counterbalance or match numerous variables. On the other hand, however, the more variables we can equate participants on, the more we eliminate potential confounding. In fact, the ideal would be to have participants who are identical in every respect. The way to have identical participants is to test the *same* individual in each condition. Therefore, when matching or counterbalancing is unworkable but the study calls for tightly controlling participant variables, we employ a within-subjects design. Another name for a within-subjects design is repeated measures. In a **within-subjects** or **repeated-measures design**, we repeatedly measure the same participants under all conditions of an independent variable.

Notice that repeated measures are different from multiple trials. With multiple trials we repeatedly observe a participant *within* a condition to reliably measure responses to that condition. With repeated measures, regardless of the number of trials per condition, we observe the same participants under *all* conditions to control participant variables.

For example, in the hypnosis study, consider all of the cognitive, motivational, physiological, and experiential differences between participants that might influence their memory. The same old problem of a possible confounding exists: Just because of the luck of the draw, the people in one condition might be more influenced by any or all of these attributes so that differences in recall that we think result from hypnosis are really due to these attributes. However, we do not understand these attributes sufficiently to know which are the most important to control, and even if we did, counterbalancing them all in a between-subjects design would be unworkable, limiting the population would severely limit generalizability, and finding participants who match on so many variables would be impossible. Therefore, the solution is a repeated-measures design: We'd show one group of participants two videotapes of two different robberies—once when participants are hypnotized and once when not—and for each condition we'd have them complete a series of questions about the robbery.

The layout for this design is shown in Table 6.4. Each row represents the summary recall score from one participant tested under both conditions, so although we have one sample of participants, we have two samples of scores. Again, think of a row as representing an experiment with one participant in both conditions. Any difference in recall cannot be due to participant variables, because they are all constant. Then, for greater reliability, we replicate this study with other participants.

All of the usual design requirements apply. Repeated measures don't control for differences among participants *within* a particular condition, so we rely on random assignment or counterbalancing to control individual differences here. Thus, for example, as in Table 6.4, we control participants' gender within each condition by counterbalancing it, testing an equal number of males and females. Further, we still have the problem of order effects from the particular order in which participants complete the recall questions within a condition. Therefore, we might control order effects by testing each half of the participants under one of two orders (indicated in Table 6.4 as order1 and order2).

Collapsing vertically in each column, the mean score summarizes the recall scores per condition. These scores should not be biased by participants' gender or by the order in which they completed the questions because no one gender or order is present. And, because the same people are being observed, any differences in scores between the conditions cannot be due to differences in participants' memory abilities, attentiveness, and so on, because such variables are represented equally in both conditions.

TABLE 6.4   Diagram of Repeated-Measures Design of Hypnosis Experiment

Each row represents the scores of one person tested under both conditions.
Each X represents a person's total recall score for the trials in that condition.

	No hypnosis	Hypnosis
Participant 1 (male, order1)	X	X
Participant 2 (male, order2)	X	X
Participant 3 (female, order1)	X	X
Participant 4 (female, order2)	X	X
	$\overline{X}$	$\overline{X}$

REMEMBER A *repeated-measures* design matches participants along all participant variables by testing each participant under all conditions of an independent variable.

Note that a special type of repeated-measures design is used when participants are measured before and after some event or treatment. In a **pretest–posttest design,** participants are measured on the dependent variable before they experience the condition of the independent variable, and then again after they receive the treatment. Thus, for example, to test whether meditation reduces physical stress, we might measure the same person's blood pressure before and after a period of meditation. Or, to determine the effectiveness of a new weight-loss diet, we would measure each person's weight before and after a period of dieting.

Pros and Cons of Repeated Measures

The strength of repeated measures is that they should eliminate potential confounding from virtually all participant variables: Differences between the conditions should not be due to differences produced by these variables because each participant, with the same characteristics, is in every condition.

On the other hand, repeated measures have several drawbacks. First, although this design keeps most participant variables constant, *individuals change even from moment to moment*, and these changes can influence the results. For example, participants eventually become aware of all our conditions. Therefore, participants may identify what they think is the purpose and hypothesis of the study, producing *diffusion of treatment* or creating *demand characteristics* that lead to unnatural behavior.

Also, because we must test the various conditions in a sequence, scores will be influenced by several factors that occur due to the passage of time. **Subject history** refers to the fact that participants continue to have a life and experience things that can change them and influence their responses. Similarly, scores are influenced by **subject maturation**: As someone grows older and more mature, he or she changes in ways that influence responses. Thus, *subject history* refers to changes due to participants' external experiences, whereas *maturation* refers to changes due to their internal development and growth. Both, however, can reduce internal validity: A response to one condition measured now and a response to another condition measured later might be confounded by changes in a participant because of history and maturation.

Another drawback to repeated measures is that they can produce substantial "subject mortality." This doesn't mean that participants literally die (usually). Rather, **subject mortality** is the loss of subjects because their participation dies out before the study is completed. Also known as "subject attrition," this can occur in a between-subjects design or anytime that participants refuse to continue their testing in a condition. It is most common when repeated testing requires a considerable amount of time per participant, so that, to reduce fatigue and overload, we spread out testing over several days. Then, people show up for the initial session but do not return for later ones.

The problem is, mortality effects are not random: People who continue to participate may find the study more interesting, perform better at the task, be more committed to helping science, or be more desperate for college credit or money. Then, the results are biased: First, we may lose internal validity. For example, in testing a new diet, the people who give up on dieting are likely to disappear. Those who stay may be so motivated that *any* diet would work well. Then, what is apparently the influence of our diet is actually due to a characteristic of the participants.

Second, we may lose external validity. Subject mortality results in our testing only a certain type of participant, and so we lose external validity for generalizing to the broader target population.

To counter subject mortality, try to conduct repeated measures (and multiple trials) within a short time span. Also, attempt to make the mechanics of participating in the study easy, with a task that is interesting, so that its completion does not require extremely dedicated volunteers. And, pay attention to the degree of subject mortality that occurs, so that you can gauge how biased the sample is.

REMEMBER   The results of a repeated-measures design can be biased by *diffusion of treatment, subject history, subject maturation,* and *subject mortality*.

Finally, a major problem with repeated measures is that they produce a new kind of order effects. As we've seen, order effects are the influence of performing a series of trials. These effects include (1) *practice effects*—getting better at the task over trials; (2) *fatigue effects*—getting worse at the task over trials; (3) *carryover effects*—the experience of any one trial that influences scores on subsequent trials; and (4) *response sets*—developing a habitual response for subsequent trials. Although previously we discussed order effects as they occur over multiple trials *within* a particular condition, the new problems with repeated measures is that these same effects also occur *between* conditions. After all, from a participant's perspective, changing from one condition to another largely involves an additional sequence of trials—more of the same, as it were. Thus, in the hypnosis study, by the time participants get to the second condition they could be tired and inattentive, or they might be very good at identifying the details of a robbery, or they may be very reactive to having the experimenter around. If the second condition were performed first, however, these influences might not be present.

Further, order effects interact with the previous problems of subject maturation, history, and mortality. If a particular condition were performed at a different point in the sequence, perhaps maturation and history would not have changed participants so much. Or, perhaps subject mortality would have selected a different type of participant who performs differently if other, less boring conditions were performed first.

Thus, we never know whether performance in one condition is higher or lower than in another condition just because of when in the sequence the conditions were performed. We cannot prevent order effects, but we can attempt to balance their influence.

CONTROLLING ORDER EFFECTS IN A REPEATED-MEASURES DESIGN

To control order effects in a repeated-measures design with two conditions, we counterbalance the order in which participants perform the conditions: Half the participants perform condition 1 followed by condition 2, and the remaining participants perform condition 2 followed by condition 1. Thus, in the hypnosis study, half the participants would be tested first with the control condition, and half would start with the experimental condition, as shown in Table 6.5. All other design requirements still apply, so within each order (1) the participants' gender is counterbalanced and (2) because we're testing multiple trials, we control their order effects by testing different participants under different orders of the questions (indicated as order1 and order2). When we examine all scores in a condition—collapsing in a column—the mean recall score within each group will not be influenced by participants' gender or by the order in which they completed the

TABLE 6.5   Diagram of Hypnosis Experiment Showing Counterbalancing of Order of Conditions

The top half of the diagram shows participants tested with one order, and the bottom half shows those tested in the reverse order.

		No hypnosis	Hypnosis
Participants tested in control condition first	Participant 1 (male, order1)	X	X
	Participant 2 (male, order2)	X	X
	Participant 3 (female, order1)	X	X
	Participant 4 (female, order2)	X	X
Participants tested in experimental condition first	Participant 5 (male, order1)	X	X
	Participant 6 (male, order2)	X	X
	Participant 7 (female, order1)	X	X
	Participant 8 (female, order2)	X	X
		$\overline{X}$	$\overline{X}$

questions. And, because the same people are being observed, virtually all participant variables should be constant between conditions. And finally, any difference between the two conditions is not due to the particular order in which the conditions were performed, because both possible orders are present.

With only two conditions, the above counterbalancing scheme is quite adequate. For more than two conditions, however, there are several common techniques for controlling order effects. To see them, say that we expand the hypnosis study by adding a third condition, comparing the influence on memory from a no hypnosis, a mild hypnosis, and a deep hypnosis condition. For each condition, we'd still present participants a videotape of a robbery and then have them complete 30 recall questions. We're still using repeated measures, but with more than two conditions we deal with order effects using either *complete counterbalancing*, *partial counterbalancing*, or *randomization*.

Complete Counterbalancing of Conditions

Complete counterbalancing is the balancing of order effects by testing different participants using *all* possible orders. For example, let's call the three conditions of the expanded hypnosis study, A, B, and C. Three conditions produce six possible orders:

ABC   ACB   BCA   BAC   CAB   CBA

Notice two things about these orders. First, each condition appears in every position within the sequence: A appears twice as the first condition, twice as the second condition, and twice as the third condition (likewise for B and C). Second, every possible sequence is included: For the sequence beginning with A, the two possible orders ABC and ACB are included, and so on. Thus, complete counterbalancing balances both a condition's position in the sequence and the order of the conditions coming before and after it. Applying this technique to the hypnosis study, we have the diagram shown in Table 6.6. For one-third of the participants, condition A is first, so performance under this condition might be biased because of its location in the sequence. However, condition B also occurs first for one-third of the participants, as does condition C, so these conditions are equally biased. Likewise, each condition occurs second at times, and third at times.

Note that, although not shown in the table, we would still balance other variables of concern: We'd balance gender by testing both males and females and we'd balance the order of the recall questions. The only novelty here is that we do this balancing *within each order of conditions*. For example, for participants tested using the ABC order of conditions, half would be male and half female, and some of each would answer the questions using order 1–30, with the remainder using order 30–1. The same would be true for each of the other orders of conditions.

When we examine all scores in a condition—in a column—they will not be biased by participants' gender or by the order in which they completed the questions. And, there should be no confoundings between conditions: (1) by partic-

TABLE 6.6 Diagram of Completely Counterbalanced Expanded Hypnosis Experiment

Each row represents participants tested under a particular sequence of the three conditions. Each X represents a person's total recall score.

Orders	A No hypnosis	B Mild hypnosis	C Deep hypnosis
Participants tested using ABC	XXX	XXX	XXX
Participants tested using ACB	XXX	XXX	XXX
Participants tested using BCA	XXX	XXX	XXX
Participants tested using BAC	XXX	XXX	XXX
Participants tested using CAB	XXX	XXX	XXX
Participants tested using CBA	XXX	XXX	XXX
	$\overline{X}$	$\overline{X}$	$\overline{X}$

ipant variables, (2) by unique order effects from performing the three conditions in a particular order, and (3) by history, maturation, or mortality effects.

(*Note*: The term *complete counterbalancing* also applies when counterbalancing the order of multiple trials *within* a condition. If above, for example, all possible orders of the 30 questions were given in each condition, then we'd have completely counterbalanced the order of trials.)

The advantage of complete counterbalancing is that all possible orders are present, so no bias due to any one order is possible. However, as you may have noticed, the major drawback to complete counterbalancing is that it creates a *very* complex design, especially if you are also counterbalancing other variables. Further, you will need many more participants so that you can test some under each order. Such problems suggest that we might be going overboard by completely counterbalancing order effects. After all, the goal is simply to ensure that the results are not confounded or unduly influenced by one particular order. Therefore, instead, we sometimes only *partially counterbalance*.

Partial Counterbalancing of Conditions

Partial counterbalancing is the balancing of order effects by using only *some* of the possible orders. For example, with three conditions, it is common to use the following three orders of conditions:

ABC   BCA   CAB

As here, typically a partial counterbalancing scheme systematically changes the position of each condition in the sequence, but does not change the conditions coming before or after the condition. (The procedure for creating this type of counterbalancing scheme is sometimes called a "Latin square design.") Applying this scheme to the hypnosis study, we have the diagram shown in Table 6.7.

This is much simpler! And that's the advantage of partial counterbalancing. Sometimes the goal is only to prevent confounding from one particular order, so all we need to do is include some other orders.

The disadvantage of this technique, however, is that it balances only practice effects or other biases that occur because of *where* in the sequence a condition occurs (whether first, second, or third). Partial counterbalancing does not balance out carry-over effects or response sets that result from having performed a particular previous condition. In Table 6.7, for example, B follows A, and C follows B in two-thirds of the sequences, but C never immediately follows A. The problem is that maybe the carry-over from B–A would have been balanced by C–A. Yet we don't include C–A, so the bias of B–A remains.

Therefore, when such carry-over effects are likely to occur between conditions, we instead include all orders, and use complete counterbalancing.

> **REMEMBER**   *Partial counterbalancing* presents some of the possible orders of conditions to control practice effects. *Complete counterbalancing* includes all possible orders to control practice and carry-over effects.

The term *partial counterbalancing* also applies to multiple trials within each condition. If in the design, half the participants per row answered the questions in one order, and the remaining participants per row answered them in the reverse order, we'd have partial counterbalancing of the order of trials.

A third approach to controlling order effects is *randomization*.

TABLE 6.7 Diagram of Partially Counterbalanced Expanded Hypnosis Experiment

Each row represents those participants tested under a particular sequence of the three conditions.

Orders	A No hypnosis	B Mild hypnosis	C Deep hypnosis
Participants tested using ABC	XXX	XXX	XXX
Participants tested using BCA	XXX	XXX	XXX
Participants tested using CAB	XXX	XXX	XXX
	$\overline{X}$	$\overline{X}$	$\overline{X}$

Randomizing the Order of Conditions

Randomization is the balancing of order effects by randomly creating different orders under which different participants are tested. In the hypnosis study, we could randomize the order of conditions by randomly creating a sequence for each participant (e.g., writing the three conditions on slips of paper and randomly drawing a sequence for each participant). Likewise, we could randomize the order of trials within a condition by essentially shuffling the 30 questions in a condition for each participant.

Randomization is especially useful when there is not much difference between the conditions, because then we can simultaneously randomize both the order of trials and the order of conditions. For example, say that in a different study, we measure participants' reaction time to recognize whether individually presented words occurred in a previously read paragraph. We compare conditions involving either 1, 2, or 3 syllables. To randomize, we might arbitrarily decide to create groups of 15 trials, and in each, randomly select and mix 5 trials from each condition. When we unscramble the responses, each condition will have been performed at the beginning, middle, and end of the sequence, and each particular trial will have been sometimes performed early in the sequence and sometimes performed later in the sequence.

On the other hand, we do not usually intermix conditions when each condition requires us to stop and change the instructions or procedure. Instead, to prevent confusion, participants complete all trials in one condition before going on to the next condition. This method is known as "blocking" trials (all similar trials are performed in one "block"). Then, we control order by having different participants perform the conditions in different orders.

Randomization works best when there are many conditions or trials, and the goal is simply to include some different orders, in an *un*systematic way. It is not so useful when there are only a few conditions, because we might, by chance, fail to produce balancing orders. For example, in the hypnosis study, by chance we might get many orders with A–B, but few with B–A, and with only three conditions, this could be a critical omission. Therefore, partial or complete counterbalancing is usually employed when there are only a few conditions, so that order effects can be directly and systematically controlled.

REMEMBER In a repeated-measures study, use *complete counterbalancing*, *partial counterbalancing*, or *randomization* to control effects due to the order of conditions.

CHOOSING A DESIGN

There is much to consider when deciding whether to use a between-subjects or within-subjects design. A repeated-measures design is preferred when participants' responses are likely to be strongly influenced by individual differences in cognitive strategies, physical abilities, or experiences. Essentially, this design is used when it makes sense to compare a person or an animal in one condition to the same person or animal in the other conditions. Thus, studies involving memory and learning are usually conducted in this way, as are studies that examine a sequence—such as when studying the effects of practice or maturation. (As always, reading the research literature will help you to make this decision.) Further, we select such designs because, repeated measures (and matched groups) are analyzed in a way that results in a more powerful design than a comparable between-subjects design.

Other design considerations, however, may prevent you from using repeated measures: First, consider whether a particular condition might produce rather permanent changes in behavior so that one order of conditions has unique carry-over effects. If so, we have **nonsymmetrical carry-over effects**, which occur when the carry-over effects from one order of conditions do not balance out those of another order. Such effects occur whenever performing task A and then task B is not the same as performing task B and then task A. For example, we would not want to test the same participants in more than one condition if each involved some sort of surprise. Likewise, once you have taught participants something in one condition, you cannot "unteach" them in a subsequent condition. Or, as often found in animal research, a condition may involve some surgical technique that cannot be undone. In such situations, counterbalancing will not effectively balance out the bias produced by a particular order of conditions. Instead, use a between-subjects design, because no carry-over effects are possible.

Second, do not underestimate the influence of subject history, maturation, and mortality. These can be more detrimental to a study than the lessened control that occurs in a between-subjects design. Third, a repeated-measures design often requires more stimuli and other testing material than a between-subjects design. This is because we usually don't want participants to have practice with exactly the same stimuli, so we create additional, similar stimuli for each condition. A between-subjects design requires only one set of stimuli because participants see them only once. Thus, in the between-subjects version of the hypnosis study, you'd need only one videotape of a robbery with 30 recall questions to show to all conditions. In the within-subjects version with three levels of hypnosis, you'd need three different videotaped robberies. Yet the tapes would have to be very comparable in terms of the details and events in the story as well as in the lighting, sound, and mechanics of taping. You'd also need a different set of 30 questions for each robbery, yet with all being comparable in terms of wording, reading level, degree of memory difficulty, and so on. Any differences in the tapes, story details, or questions could be a confounding. Although you might be able to create comparable materials (that's why we have pilot studies), you want to be sure that this is possible and that such effort is really necessary before you select such a design.

Finally, consider the advantages of repeated measures versus the disadvantages of counterbalancing. Remember that controlling *any* variable through counterbalancing changes the variable *within* the conditions and thus tends to produce greater variability among scores within the conditions. Repeated-measures designs almost always require extensive counterbalancing, and, including the influence of many changing variables tends to increase error variance and reduce our power to show a clear and convincing relationship.

The key to selecting a design depends on the number and importance of participant variables that must be controlled. If numerous uncontrolled participant variables could seriously reduce reliability and validity, then a repeated-measures design is preferred despite the difficulties it presents. If there are only a few crucial participant variables, however, a repeated-measures design can create more problems than it solves, and so a better choice may be to identify the most serious variable and control it by matching participants on that variable in a matched-groups design. Or, you can still obtain valid and reliable results from a between-subjects design, especially if you balance important participant variables or limit the population.

REMEMBER Between-subjects designs are preferred if there are *nonsymmetrical carry-over effects*, if the task does not allow repeated testing, or if extensive counterbalancing is unwise.

Whether to use a between-subjects design, matching, or repeated measures is a *major* aspect of designing any study, so to help you remember the pros and cons of each, consult Table 6.8.

PUTTING IT ALL TOGETHER

When you start to counterbalance many variables, the design of a study can become very complex. But you don't have to control *everything*. Although you want data from a well-controlled experiment, you must actually get the data! Don't try to control so many variables that you can't conduct the study. Instead, control those variables that seriously confound the results or severely reduce reliability. Keep in mind that when you institute a control to eliminate one problem, you often produce other problems. Therefore, you are never going to produce the perfect study, so produce the best study you can within practical limits.

Dealing with participant variables is a major aspect of designing a study. To review all of the questions about them that you should consider, consult Checklist 6.3. The good news is that participant variables is the final major aspect of designing a true experiment that we'll discuss, and so you now know all of the basics. To review the entire list of questions we've asked when designing an experiment, consult the checklist on the inside front cover of this book.

TABLE 6.8 Pros and Cons of the Methods for Controlling Participant Variables

Method	Pros	Cons
Random assignment	1. Produces balanced representative samples	1. May not balance important variables 2. Works poorly with small ns 3. May increase error variance
Balancing a variable	1. Prevents confounding by the variable	1. May increase error variance 2. Complicates design and inflates N 3. Pretest may bias participants
Matching groups	1. Keeps matched variable constant between conditions	1. Finding matching participants is difficult 2. May increase error variance 3. Pretest may bias participants
Limiting population	1. Eliminates fluctuating variables 2. Reduces error variance	1. May restrict range of dependent scores 2. Reduces external validity
Repeated measures	1. Eliminates confounding from all participant variables 2. Requires small N 3. Design is statistically more powerful	1. Allows diffusion of treatment 2. Confounding by subject history and maturation 3. Subject mortality reduces external validity 4. Order effects require balancing that reduces power 5. Increases stimulus requirements 6. Incompatible with nonsymmetrical carry-over effects

CHAPTER SUMMARY

1. Participant variables are personal characteristics that distinguish one subject from another, resulting in individual differences in how each responds to the same situation.

2. Selection criteria are the characteristics of participants that we require for allowing them to participate in a study.

3. A *pretest* is used to identify participants who meet the selection criteria.

4. External validity depends on the sample size (N), on whether participants are drawn from a limited population, and on whether participants differ from nonparticipants because of participant variables, including the *volunteer bias* and *subject sophistication*.

CHECKLIST 6.3 **Questions to consider when dealing with participant variables**

Considering participant variables

- Do the characteristics of participants limit generalizability?
- Is the sample size (N) sufficient to represent the population?
- Does the volunteer bias or subject sophistication influence the results?
- Are extraneous participant variables strongly correlated with the independent or dependent variable?
- Will fluctuating participant variables within conditions reduce reliability and the relationship's strength?
- Will fluctuating participant variables between conditions reduce internal validity and the relationship's strength?

Considering a between-subjects design

- Will random assignment control important participant variables?
- Will balancing control important participant variables?
- Will matching control important participant variables?
- Will pretesting create major problems?
- Will limiting the population restrict generalizability?
- Will controls increase error variance that weakens the relationship?

Considering a within-subjects design

- Must many participant variables be controlled?
- Are subject history, maturation, and mortality a problem?
- Do stimuli and other aspects fit a repeated-measures design?
- Will nonsymmetrical carry-over effects occur?
- Is randomization or partial or complete counterbalancing of order of conditions needed?

5. The *volunteer bias* refers to differences between the individuals who participate in a study and those who do not. *Subject sophistication* is the bias that results because participants are knowledgeable about research.

6. Participant variables correlated with the influence of the independent variable or with performance on the dependent variable should be controlled because they reduce reliability and internal validity. They also increase error variance and thus reduce the strength of the relationship.

7. In a *between-subjects design*, a different group of participants is randomly selected for each condition of an independent variable.

8. In a between-subjects design, participant variables are controlled by balancing them through *random assignment*, by *balancing* them, by keeping them constant through *limiting the population*, and by *matching participants*.

9. *Collapsing* across a variable means that we combine the scores from the different levels of the variable.

10. Random assignment can control for many unknown participant variables, but it may not evenly balance them, and if it does, it increases error variance.

11. Balancing a variable prevents it from confounding the results and increases external validity, but at the cost of increased complexity, a larger N, and increased error variance.

12. Limiting the population prevents confounding and minimizes error variance, but at the cost of reduced external validity.

13. In a *matched-groups design*, each participant in one condition is matched with a participant in every other condition along an extraneous variable. This controls the variable between conditions, but pretesting creates problems and matching is not always workable.

14. In a *within-subjects* or *repeated-measures* design, each participant is measured under all conditions of an independent variable.

15. A repeated-measures design that involves measuring participants before and after some event is called a *pretest–posttest design*.

16. Repeated measures are especially prone to confounding by *subject history*, *subject maturation*, *subject mortality*, and *order effects*.

17. *Subject history* refers to the fact that participants continue to have experiences that can change them and influence their responses.

18. *Subject maturation* refers to the fact that, as an individual grows older and more mature, he or she changes in ways that influence responses.

19. *Subject mortality* refers to the loss of participants because their participation dies out before the study is completed.

20. With *complete counterbalancing*, different participants are tested with different orders so that all possible orders of conditions or trials are present. With *partial counterbalancing*, participants are tested using only some of the possible orders of conditions or trials. With *randomization*, different participants are tested using different random orders of conditions or trials.

21. *Nonsymmetrical carry-over effects* occur when the carry-over effects from one order of conditions do not balance out those of another order.

KEY TERMS   (with page references)

N 160
n 161
between-subjects design 165
collapsing 168
complete counterbalancing 178
matched-groups design 169
nonsymmetrical carry-over effects 182
partial counterbalancing 179
pretest 167
pretest–posttest design 175

randomization 181
repeated-measures design 173
selection criteria 159
subject history 175
subject maturation 175
subject mortality 175
subject sophistication 161
volunteer bias 161
within-subjects design 173

REVIEW QUESTIONS

1. What is meant by the term *selection criteria*?

2. (a) How can participant variables influence external validity? (b) How can they influence internal validity? (c) How can they influence reliability?

3. What is meant by (a) volunteer bias? (b) subject mortality? (c) subject sophistication? (d) How does each bias your results?

4. (a) What do *N* and *n* symbolize? (b) Why is a larger *N* important for external validity? (c) What range of *n* is usually adequate?

5. How do you identify participant variables that might confound a study?

6. (a) How does random assignment to conditions control participant variables? (b) When is balancing participant variables more appropriate than random assignment? Why?

7. What problems arise with pretesting?

8. (a) What does it mean to collapse across a variable? (b) What is error variance, and how does it affect a study?

9. (a) What positive impact does counterbalancing participant variables have on a study? (b) What negative impact does it have?

10. (a) What positive impact does limiting the population have on a study? (b) What negative impact does it have?

11. (a) How is a between-subjects design created? (b) How do you control participant variables here? (c) Why would you choose this design?

12. (a) How is a matched-groups design created? (b) How does it control participant variables? (c) Why would you choose this design?

13. (a) How is a within-subjects design created? (b) How does it control participant variables? (c) What is the other name for this design? (d) Why would you choose this design?

14. (a) What problems are created by repeated measures in terms of changes in participants? (b) What problems are created by repeated measures in terms of the measurement task? (c) What problem is created in terms of order effects?

15. (a) What are the three ways to control order effects? (b) How do complete counterbalancing, partial counterbalancing, and randomization differ? (c) What is the major advantage and disadvantage of each?

16. (a) How does matching or counterbalancing participant variables increase internal and external validity? (b) What is the major difficulty in using matching when there are several conditions of the independent variable? (c) What is the major difficulty in using repeated measures when there are several conditions of the independent variable?

APPLICATION QUESTIONS

17. You conduct a study involving the members of your research methods class. (a) What limitations on external validity might this produce? (b) Why might this limitation not arise?

18. A study measures participants' helpfulness in aiding a confederate to study for a psychology exam. In each condition, participants must help for five consecutive days. (a) What problem is likely to develop over the course of testing participants? (b) Why might the remaining participants bias the results?

19. Someone proposes that a person's tendency to become "absorbed" in a fantasy situation is an important variable to control in the hypnosis study discussed in this chapter. (a) How would you determine whether this proposal is correct? (b) If necessary, what are three ways to control this variable? (c) What is the best way, and why?

20. Identify the type of design being used in the following. (a) When studying the effects of a new memory-enhancing drug on Alzheimer's patients, testing a group of patients before and after administration of the drug. (b) When studying the effects of alcohol on motor coordination, comparing one group of people given a moderate dose of alcohol with another group given no alcohol. (c) When studying whether males and females are persuaded differently by a female speaker. (d) The study in (c), but with the added requirement that for each male of a particular age there is a female of the same age. (e) When studying how the amount of body fat changes in a group of athletes, measuring it weekly over a two-month training program.

21. You conduct a repeated-measure design, comparing a condition in which you train people to improve their memory with a control condition. What problem is produced here that counterbalancing the order of conditions will not solve?

22. A student proposed comparing the conditions of "male" and "female" in a repeated-measures design. (a) Why or why not is this an acceptable approach? (b) What control techniques can be applied instead?

DISCUSSION QUESTIONS

23. You conduct a repeated-measures study of the effects of three different types of motivational messages. Participants listen to one message every day for two weeks, then they complete a 20-question test of well-being. Then, the next day they begin listening to the next message, and so on. (a) Specify your scheme for dealing with order effects. (b) What three problems will arise with your participants during the study that might confound the results? (c) What problem is likely to be created by any one message that makes repeated measures a problem? (d) What ethical problems are present here?

24. Instead, you decide to conduct the study in question 23 as a between-subjects design. (a) Describe this design. (b) How does it eliminate the problems in 23(b) and 23(c)? (c) What new problems does it create?

25. For the studies in questions 23 and 24, (a) what participant variables are important for you to control? (b) Which of these would you control by limiting the population, and how would you do it? (c) Which of these would you control by balancing, and how would you do it? (d) What positive or negative impact will each approach have?

26. During the preceding studies, one participant was out sick for one week. (a) What should you do about this person's data, and why? (b) What new selection criterion should you add? (c) What impact might this criterion have on the strength of the observed relationship? (d) How does this criterion affect external validity?

THE STATISTICAL ANALYSIS OF EXPERIMENTS

Now that you understand how to design experiments, we'll discuss how to analyze them. In the upcoming chapter, we'll review the descriptive and inferential statistical procedures used in simple experiments involving one independent variable. Then in Chapter 8 we'll look at how to analyze experiments that involve more than one independent variable.

7

Applying Descriptive and Inferential Statistics to Simple Experiments

GETTING STARTED

To understand this chapter, recall the following:

- From Chapter 2, recall what a relationship is, and how we generalize the sample relationship to the population.
- From Chapter 4, recall what scoring criteria and a sensitive measure are.
- From Chapter 6, recall what a powerful design is, what error variance is, what collapsing is, and what between- and within-subjects designs are.

Your goals in this chapter are to learn:

- What the "type" and "strength" of a relationship are.
- What the four scales of measurement are.
- How an experiment is summarized using the means of the conditions.
- How the standard deviation and variance summarize the strength of a relationship.
- How to interpret and graph the results of an experiment.
- The logic of inferential statistics and the errors they produce.

Once you've collected the data, the next step is to examine and interpret the observed relationship and that's where statistical procedures come in. This chapter presents a simple review of statistics to show you how they are used in the process of conducting research, focusing on how to analyze the results of experiments. We analyze all experiments using the same procedures, whether a laboratory or field experiment, and whether a true or quasi-experiment. First we'll examine the procedures for summarizing the sample relationship, and then we'll review the methods for drawing inferences about the relationship in the population.

SELECTING THE STATISTICAL PROCEDURES

There are two major types of statistical procedures that are applied to any set of data: First, **descriptive statistics** are for summarizing and describing the important characteristics of data. These procedures tell us whether a relationship is present and, if so, what the particular characteristics of the relationship in each condition are. (Don't confuse descriptive *research* with descriptive *statistics*. Descriptive research refers to designs that describe *behaviors*. Descriptive statistics are used to describe *data* from any type of design, whether it be experimental or descriptive.) Second, we want to generalize this sample relationship, describing the relationship we'd expect to find if we could observe everyone in the population. **Inferential statistics** are for deciding if a sample relationship represents a relationship found in the population. Then these procedures also help us to describe the characteristics of the relationship in the population.

> **REMEMBER** Always apply the appropriate *descriptive* and *inferential* procedures to a study.

There are many ways to describe and summarize a relationship, so part of designing a study is to identify the appropriate statistical procedures to use. Do this, however, when first *designing* the study, because otherwise it's possible to complete a study that cannot be analyzed. Further, some statistical procedures are better than others, and whether you can use the best procedure depends on other decisions you make.

Which statistical procedures to use depends on two major issues. The first is the type of design you have: Experiments are analyzed using certain statistics, and descriptive studies are analyzed using others. Second, the procedure to use depends on the way that you measure a behavior and obtain the scores on the *dependent* variable. That is, it depends on an aspect of your *scoring criteria*. You can measure scores using one of four **scales of measurement**: nominal, ordinal, interval, and ratio.

With a **nominal scale,** each score identifies membership in a particular category—for example, if you assign a "1" to identify people as "Republican" and a

"2" to identify them as "Democrat." The numbers on football jerseys, the letters representing blood type, whether someone passes or fails a test, and a person's gender are examples of nominal scales.

With an **ordinal scale**, the scores indicate rank order relative to other participants: A score of 1 means the most or least of the variable, a 2 means the second most or least, and so on. The letter grade you get in a college course and military rank are other examples of ordinal scales.

With an **interval scale**, the scores reflect an actual amount of a variable, but zero does not truly mean zero amount, so negative scores are possible. For example, temperature is usually measured on an interval scale. "Zero degrees" does not mean that zero amount of heat is present, only that the temperature is less than 1 degree and more than -1 degree. Likewise, interval scales are involved when measuring participants' over- and underestimates of the weight of an object, or the balance in their checking accounts.

With a **ratio scale**, the scores reflect an actual amount, but zero means zero amount, so negative scores are not possible. Measuring the number of errors participants make on a test, the number of calories they consume in a day, or the amount of money in their pockets involves ratio scales.

For help in remembering the different scales of measurement, consult Table 7.1.

Impact of a Particular Scale of Measurement

There are three important reasons to pay attention to the scale of measurement used to measure the dependent variable. First, different scales provide different degrees of precision and *sensitivity*. Recall that a sensitive measure is one that distinguishes subtle differences in behavior. Nominal scores only grossly discrim-

TABLE 7.1 Summary of Types of Measurement Scales

Each column describes the characteristics of the scale.

	Type of measurement scale			
	Nominal	*Ordinal*	*Interval*	*Ratio*
What does the scale indicate?	Quality	Relative quantity	Quantity	Quantity
Is there a true zero?	No	No	No	Yes
How might the scale be used in research?	To identify males and females as 1 and 2	To judge who is 1st, 2nd, etc., in aggressiveness	To convey over- and under-estimates	To measure the number of correct answers on a test

inate between participants, because they essentially categorize based on a yes/no decision. Ordinal scales are somewhat more sensitive, but they still lack precision. (In a race, for example, we cannot tell whether those in first place are only slightly ahead or miles ahead of those in second.) However, interval or ratio scales—especially when involving fractional scores—are most sensitive because they can reflect very small differences in behaviors.

The second reason to pay attention to your scale of measurement is that only certain descriptive procedures (certain formulas) can be used with certain types of scores. It makes no sense, for example, to compute a football team's average jersey number, or the average position of all runners in a race.

Third, the scale of measurement determines which inferential procedure is appropriate. As you'll see, some inferential procedures are used with interval or ratio scores, others with ordinal scores, and still others with nominal scores.

> **REMEMBER** The statistical procedures to apply and the sensitivity of scores depend on the *scale of measurement* used to measure the dependent variable.

Psychological research usually involves interval or ratio scores, and in the following sections, we'll discuss the most common procedures used with such data. First, though, let's review the characteristics of the relationship that we ultimately describe.

The Characteristics of a Relationship

As a very simple example, let's say we conduct an experiment to investigate that old rumor that the more you study, the better you perform on a test. We'll manipulate the independent variable of amount of time participants study a set of material in a controlled laboratory, using the conditions of studying for either 1, 3, or 5 hours. Then we'll measure the dependent variable of participants' performance on a college-like multiple-choice test. We could conduct either a between- or within-subjects design, and regardless, all of the usual issues of producing reliable, valid, and consistent results apply. With the data in hand, we'll look for the relationship in which increased test grades are associated with increased study time.

Recall that any relationship, whether in an experiment or a descriptive study, forms the same pattern: As the scores on variable X change, the scores on variable Y change in a consistent fashion. But how do we decide which variable to call X or Y? In any study, the researcher implicitly asks, "For a given score or amount of one variable, what scores occur on the other variable?" The "given" variable is always then called the X variable, and the "other" variable is always called the Y variable. In the example, we're asking, "For a given amount of study time, what test grades occur?" So study time is X, and test grades is Y. In fact, an experiment always asks, "For a given level of the independent variable, what scores occur on the dependent variable?" Therefore, the independent variable is always the X variable, and the dependent variable is always the Y variable. (A participant's "score" on the independent variable is the condition under which he or she is tested. Notice that this means that when we graph the results of an experiment, the independent variable is *always* placed on the X axis, and the dependent variable is *always* placed on the Y axis.

Also, note that there is a special language for describing a relationship. We use the general format "Y scores change **as a function of** changes in X." Our experiment examines changes in test grades as a function of changes in hours spent studying. In fact, because the independent variable is always X, experiments always look for a change in scores on the dependent variable as a function of changes in the independent variable.

> **REMEMBER** The independent variable is graphed on the X axis, and the dependent variable on the Y axis. We look for changes in the dependent variable *as a function of* changes in the independent variable.

To summarize a relationship, there are two aspects to examine. First, the **type of relationship** is the overall direction in which the Y scores change as the X scores increase. One type of relationship is a linear relationship. In a **linear relationship**, as the X scores increase, the Y scores change in only one direction, continuously increasing or continuously decreasing in a straight-line pattern. For example, say that we obtain scores such as those in Figure 7.1. First, look at the scores. These are linear relationships, because in both the Y scores change in one direction. However, there are two subtypes of a linear relationship. Data Set A shows a **positive linear relationship**, in which as the independent variable (X) increases, the dependent (Y) scores increase. On the other hand, Data Set B shows a **negative linear relationship**, in which as the independent variable (X) increases, the dependent (Y) scores decrease.

The second aspect of a relationship to examine is its strength. Recall that the **strength of the relationship** is how consistently the Y scores change as the X variable increases. Coincidentally, in Figure 7.1, both relationships are perfectly consistent and thus have maximum strength: All participants with the same study-time score have the same test score, and when study time changes, test scores all change in a perfectly consistent way.

> **REMEMBER** The important characteristics of a relationship to understand are its *type* (direction) and its *strength* (consistency).

You can also see these characteristics in the graphs in Figure 7.1. Hours studied are plotted on the X axis, and test scores are plotted on the Y axis. Each "dot" on the graph is a "data point," representing a participant's X–Y pair. (Such a graph is called a *scatterplot*.) Data Set A shows a positive linear relationship

FIGURE 7.1 Data Producing Perfect Positive and Negative Linear Relationships

The data are test scores after studying for either 1, 3, or 5 hours.

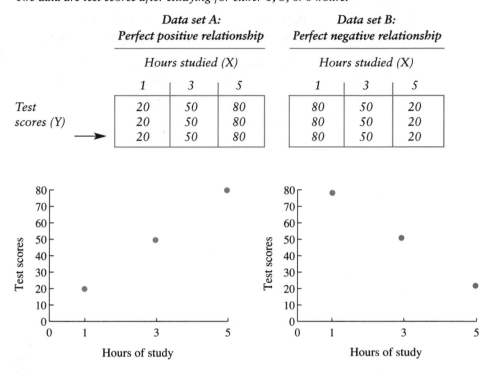

because the pattern indicates that as the level of study time increases, test scores also increase. Data Set B shows a negative linear relationship, indicating that as study time increases, test scores decrease. Each scatterplot also shows a perfectly consistent relationship, because there is only one data point above each X, indicating that all participants in a particular condition received the same test score. All of the data points fall on a straight line, so these are perfect *linear* relationships.

Perfect relationships, however, do not occur in real research, and most relationships have an intermediate strength: One value of Y *tends* to be paired with a value of X, and as X changes, the value of Y *tends* to change in a consistent fashion. Figure 7.2 presents examples of intermediate-strength relationships. (*Note:* The pattern here is idealized; real data never form such symmetrical patterns!) These data show *variability* in the Y scores, or *error variance*, because the test scores at a particular study time differ from one another. It is the variability in Y scores at each X that works against the strength of a relationship. Instead of consistently seeing one test score at one level of study time, we see (1) different test scores paired with one level of study time, and/or (2) the same test score paired with different amounts of study time. Thus, in the tables in Figure 7.2, Data Set A forms the stronger relationship because there are smaller differences and/or

FIGURE 7.2   Data Producing Intermediate-Strength Relationships

The data are test scores after studying for either 1, 3, or 5 hours.

Data set A: Strong positive relationship			Data set B: Weak positive relationship		
Hours studied			Hours studied		
1	3	5	1	3	5
10	40	70	10	30	50
20	50	70	30	50	70
20	50	80	50	70	90

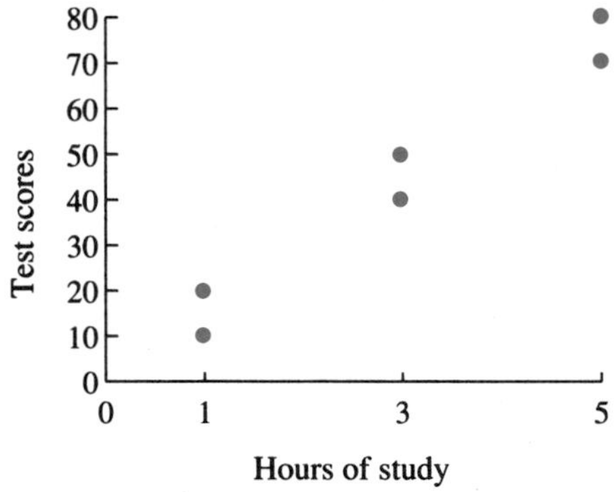

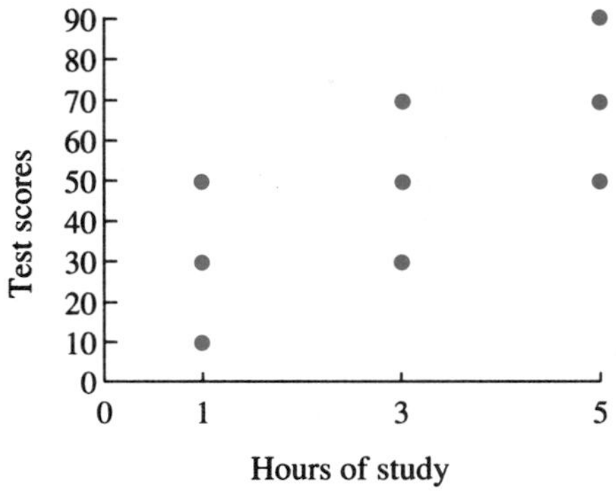

less frequent differences among the scores within each condition. Conversely, Set B shows greater variability in scores within each condition, and thus a weaker relationship. These patterns can also be seen in the scatterplots. In Graph A, different test scores are associated with each study time, so several data points appear above each X. However, the data points are not vertically spread out much, indicating relatively small error variance and a strong relationship. Conversely, Graph B shows a weaker relationship, because the greater vertical spread among the data points above each X shows greater variability in Y scores.

At the other extreme, Figure 7.3 shows data that form zero relationship. This pattern is as far from a relationship as you can get. There is not one or even close to one test score associated with one study time, nor is there a trend toward changing Y scores as X changes. Instead, the same batch of Y scores tends to show up at every value of X.

On the other hand, we do not always have a linear relationship. In a **nonlinear relationship**, as the X variable increases, the pattern of changing Y scores does not fit one straight line. Figure 7.4 shows two examples of nonlinear relationships. (Again, such symmetrical patterns are the ideal, not the norm.) In Graph A, as the X scores increase, at first the Y scores also increase, but beyond a certain X, the Y scores change direction and tend to decrease. Coincidentally, these

FIGURE 7.3 Data Producing No Relationship

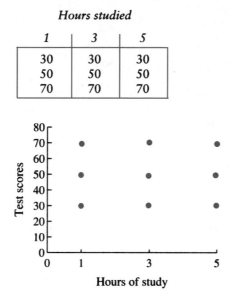

Hours studied

1	3	5
30	30	30
50	50	50
70	70	70

data show a relatively strong relationship, because there is relatively little variability in Y scores at each X. In Graph B, as X scores increase, at first Y scores tend to increase sharply, but beyond a certain X they change their direction, tending to increase only slightly. Coincidentally, these data show a weaker relationship, because there is larger variability in Y scores at each X.

Other nonlinear relationships might follow any pattern that repeatedly changes direction. Regardless, the strength of the relationship is always how

FIGURE 7.4 Scatterplots Showing Nonlinear Relationships

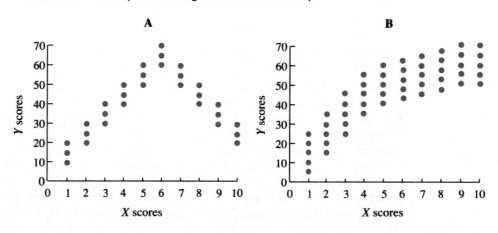

consistently one or close to one value of Y is associated with one particular value of X.

APPLYING DESCRIPTIVE STATISTICS TO EXPERIMENTS

So far, we've simply *looked* at a table or graph to see how the individual scores change from one condition to the next. However, we need more precise ways of describing a relationship than merely "eyeballing" it. Therefore, the first step is always to compute descriptive statistics to summarize the scores *within* each condition. We begin by describing central tendency and variability.

Describing Central Tendency

To summarize the different dependent scores in each condition, we seek one score that can be viewed as the "typical" score, or the score "around" which everyone more or less scored. To find this summary score, we compute a **measure of central tendency**. There are three common measures of central tendency. (1) The **mean** score, symbolized by $\overline{X}$, is the average of a group of scores. It is used with normally distributed interval or ratio scores. (2) The **median** is the 50th percentile, meaning that 50% of the scores are at or below this score. It is computed with interval or ratio scores that are not normally distributed, or with ordinal scores. (3) The **mode** is the most frequently occurring score. It is used with nominal scores. Each of these is used to indicate where the *center* of a group of scores *tends* to be located, so they indicate the score "around" which everyone in the condition tend to score. (Calculations can be found in Appendix C.1.)

> **REMEMBER**   A *measure of central tendency* is the typical score around which everyone in the condition scored. Which measure to compute depends on the scale of the dependent variable.

Usually, psychological research involves normally distributed interval or ratio scores, so usually we compute the mean. For example, say we obtained the data in Table 7.2. First we see that the individual scores tend to increase with increased study time. To summarize this, we compute the mean test score for each condition: The 1-hour condition produced scores "around" the mean score of 20, the 3-hour condition produced a different distribution of scores around 25, and the 5-hour condition produced still another distribution around 31.67. Because the means are changing, the test scores that produced them must also be changing. Therefore, *a relationship is present whenever there are differences between the means of the conditions*. Further, the way the mean scores change as the conditions change indicates the type of relationship present. Here, because the means tend to *increase* as study time increases, the individual test scores also tend to increase as study time increases. (Likewise, had we computed the median or mode for each condition, the way that they differ would also indicate the way

TABLE 7.2 Test Scores as a Function of Hours Studied

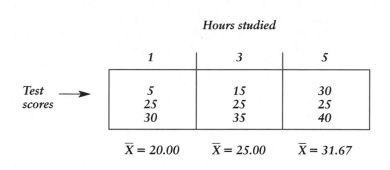

	Hours studied		
	1	3	5
Test scores	5	15	30
	25	25	25
	30	35	40
	$\overline{X} = 20.00$	$\overline{X} = 25.00$	$\overline{X} = 31.67$

that the scores that produce them differ, and so would indicate the relationship that is present.) Conversely, if the means (or medians or modes) remain the same for all conditions, this would indicate that essentially the same batch of scores is present in each condition, and thus that no relationship is present.

Not all of the means must differ, however, for a relationship to be present. For example, we might find that only the means in the 1-hour and 3-hour levels are different. This is still a relationship because, at least *sometimes*, as the conditions change, the dependent scores also tend to change.

> **REMEMBER** When the mean scores for the conditions differ, then the individual dependent scores are changing with the conditions, so a relationship is present.

Graphing the Results of an Experiment

Instead of plotting the individual data points, published research usually presents the results of an experiment using a **line graph**. Create a line graph when the levels of the *independent variable* are measured using an interval or a ratio scale of measurement. The hours someone studies is a ratio scale, so the previous data are plotted as the line graph on the left in Figure 7.5. The X axis is labeled with our conditions, and the Y axis is labeled as the mean dependent score. Then each data point is the mean score for a condition, and adjacent data points are connected with *straight* lines. (If the median or mode is appropriate, then it is plotted as the Y variable.) The data points are connected with straight lines, because we assume that the relationship continues in a straight line between the points shown on the X axis. Thus, we would assume that the mean of a 4-hour condition would fall on the line that connects the means for the 3- and 5-hour conditions.

> **REMEMBER** Draw a *line graph* when the independent variable reflects an interval or ratio variable.

The way to interpret a line graph is to envision the scores that would produce each mean. As shown on the right in Figure 7.5, we envision the individual data points of participants as around (above and below) the mean's data point. Then, the different vertical location of each *set* of data points indicates a different batch of *Y* scores at each *X*, so a relationship is present. Further, as shown here, a line graph that generally slopes upward indicates a largely positive linear relationship. If the line slopes downward, it indicates a negative linear relationship, and if the line fluctuates up and down, it indicates a nonlinear relationship. Conversely, if the line graph is horizontal (flat), it indicates the same mean is occurring in every condition and thus the same batch of scores are in every condition, so no relationship is present.

Experiments are not always summarized using line graphs. If the *independent* variable reflects a *nominal* or an *ordinal* scale of measurement, we create a **bar graph** in which the height of each bar reflects a data point, and the bars do not touch. For example, say that in a different study, we compared the mean test performance of students majoring in either physics, psychology, or English. Such *categories* might produce the data in Figure 7.6. This shows a relationship because the tops of the bars do not form a horizontal line, so there are different means and thus different scores in each condition. However, the bars communicate that the relationship does *not* continue between the groups, because, for example, there is not a particular major that goes between psychology and English. Therefore, if we inserted the new category of sociology between psychology and English, we could not assume that the mean for sociology majors would fall on a line running between the means for psychology and English majors.

REMEMBER   The measurement scale of the dependent scores determines which measure of central tendency to calculate, and the scale of the independent variable determines the type of graph to create.

FIGURE 7.5   Line Graph Showing (A) the Relationship between Mean Test Scores and Hours of Study, and (B) the Data Points We Envision around Each Mean

Data points are the means from the conditions.

Data points are the scores from the conditions.

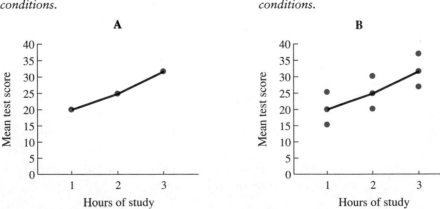

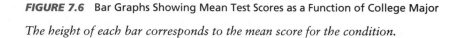

FIGURE 7.6   Bar Graphs Showing Mean Test Scores as a Function of College Major

The height of each bar corresponds to the mean score for the condition.

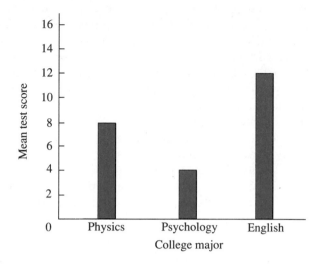

Finally, notice that you must have at least three conditions—and three data points on a graph—to see a *nonlinear relationship*. With just two conditions, one group's mean can be only higher or lower than the other group's, so the data can depict only a linear relationship, even if the relationship in nature is nonlinear. Therefore, when designing a study, be sure to consider the number of conditions of the independent variable that you must include in order to show the type of relationship you are predicting. When practical, research typically involves at least three conditions, in case the relationship is nonlinear. The maximum tends to be six to eight conditions, which is more than adequate for describing most relationships.

Describing Variability

To see the strength of a relationship in an experiment, we often compute statistics that reflect the variability of the dependent scores in each condition. **Measures of variability** are numbers that summarize the extent to which scores in a distribution differ. When the mean is the appropriate measure of central tendency, the appropriate measures of variability are: (1) the **sample variance,** which is the average squared difference between each dependent score and the mean, and (2) the **sample standard deviation,** which is the square root of the sample variance. (Calculations can be found in Appendix C.2.) The standard deviation can be most directly interpreted as indicating roughly the "average" amount that the scores in the condition deviate from the mean of the condition.

The larger the standard deviation and variance, the more the scores in a condition differ from the mean, and thus the greater the inconsistency in the scores in that condition. Thus, we can gauge the amount of this *error variance* in a relationship by looking at the pattern of variances or standard deviations across all conditions. The original scores (back in Table 7.2) produce the means and standard deviations shown in Table 7.3. The 1-hour condition produced scores around the mean of 20, but individual scores differ above or below this by an "average" of about 10.8. The 3-hour condition produced scores around 25, but here scores differ by about *plus or minus* 8.16. And in the 5-hour condition, scores differ from the mean of 31.67 by about 6.24. Are these large amounts? Well, back in Table 7.2 the lowest score in the experiment was 5 and the highest was 40, so overall the scores differ by as much as 35 points. Therefore, this relationship is *relatively* consistent, because the scores in each condition differ by about only 6 to 10 points. (If each standard deviation equaled zero, we would find one *Y* score in each condition and have a perfectly consistent relationship.)

As you'll see in Chapter 8, we compute a statistic (called the "effect size") to obtain a less subjective description of the strength of a relationship.

REMEMBER   We usually summarize the relationship in an experiment by computing the *mean* and *standard deviation* in each condition and by plotting a line or bar graph.

Interpreting the Relationship to Test a Hypothesis

The next step in any analysis would be to perform the appropriate inferential procedure. If the data pass this test, then the preceding descriptive statistics are the basis for testing the hypothesis of the study and for interpreting the results. For example, look again at the results in Table 7.3 and note the type of relationship. We originally predicted that test grades would increase as study time increased. Because the means form a largely positive linear relationship, these data confirm our hypothesis. A negative or very nonlinear relationship would contradict our prediction and disconfirm the hypothesis. In a different study, the hypothesis might lead us to predict only some kind of relationship, and then a positive, negative, or nonlinear relationship would confirm the hypothesis.

TABLE 7.3   Mean and Standard Deviation of Test Scores in Each Condition of Study Time

	Hours studied		
	1	3	5
Mean	20.00	25.00	31.67
standard deviation	10.80	8.16	6.24

We also note the *strength* of the relationship. Recall that the inconsistency in a relationship suggests the extent to which *other* variables influence the behavior, and that there are two sources of such variables. First, there could be *unsystematic external variables* operating on participants. For example, within a study-time condition, perhaps sometimes the laboratory was noisy or the experimenter was distracting, so studying was less effective for some participants than for others. This would produce differences among test scores within a condition, even though everyone there had studied the same amount. Second, different scores result from *individual differences* among participants. People in our study will exhibit differences in intelligence, aptitude, and motivation that can cause them to score differently on the test, even when they study the same amount.

Thus, the extent to which test scores are consistently related to study time suggests the extent to which test grades are "caused" by study time alone. A very strong relationship will suggest that amount of study time has a major, controlling effect on test scores: It seems to be *the* variable that determines someone's score, with other variables having only a minor influence on test grades. Conversely, a weak relationship will suggest that, in addition to study time, there are other factors that substantially influence test grades.

Following this line of reasoning, we begin to interpret our results "psychologically," explaining how we think these variables operate in terms of the theoretical explanations, models, and constructs about learning and memory that initially led us to conduct this study.

REMEMBER Support for a hypothesis is in the *type* of relationship found, and the *strength* indicates the degree to which the independent variable influences the dependent behavior.

We cannot, however, *confidently* draw any conclusion until we've performed the appropriate inferential procedures.

APPLYING INFERENTIAL STATISTICAL PROCEDURES

Ultimately, we want to generalize the sample relationship to everyone in nature—to everyone in the population. However, we can never be certain how the population would behave, because there is no guarantee that the sample accurately represents the population. How *representative* a sample is depends on the luck of the draw of the participants and their scores that are selected. Just by chance, our data might contain too many high scores or too many low scores relative to the population, so that a sample is *un*representative to some degree. In statistical terms, we then have sampling error. **Sampling error** results when the characteristics of the sample data are different from the population they represent. Because of the luck of the draw, the *sample* is in *error* in representing the population.

REMEMBER *Sampling error* results from the luck of which scores are obtained, so that the sample is different from the population it represents.

There is always the possibility of sampling error, and so *sampling error is the reason researchers perform inferential statistics*. We would like to say that if we measured the entire population under each condition, we would find different scores—and means—in each condition just as in our sample data. BUT! Maybe we're being mislead by sampling error. Maybe this relationship is *not* present in the population. Maybe if we tested everyone in the population under our conditions, we'd find the same scores (and the same means) each time.

For example, pretend there is not really a relationship between studying and test scores out there in nature. And, assume we could see the scores for everyone in the population under our different levels of study time, producing Figure 7.7. Imagine that the three circles on the graph enclose the scores that, simply by chance, we happened to obtain in each condition of our experiment. Because of chance—sampling error—the scores in our samples tend to increase with amount of study time, even though this is not the case for everyone in the population. Likewise, our sample means tend to increase, even though the *same* mean would be found for each condition in the population.

Thus, even when we find a relationship in the sample, it may not represent a real relationship that occurs in nature. Instead, the data may *coincidentally* form a relationship by chance. Therefore, before we can generalize any relationship we observe, we must first decide whether the relationship in the sample is "believable," representing a relationship that actually exists in nature. To do so, we apply inferential statistics.

FIGURE 7.7 Hypothetical Population Scatterplot

This scatterplot shows a sample relationship (in the circles) even though no such relationship exists in the population.

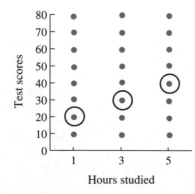

The Logic of Inferential Statistics

In statistical terminology, we sum up the preceding issue using two hypotheses. On the one hand, the predicted relationship might not exist in the population: The **null hypothesis** implies that, because of sampling error, the sample data poorly represent the *absence* of the predicted relationship in the population. On the other hand, the sample data might represent the real relationship found in the population: The **alternative hypothesis** implies that the sample data reflect the presence of the predicted relationship in the population. (*Note*: We're not talking about whether the data are reliable or valid. We're saying that whatever the scores measure, they at least form a relationship.)

We can never know whether a relationship really exists. We can, however, determine the probability of obtaining a particular sample relationship by chance when there is not a relationship. The logic of all inferential statistics is this: Say we obtain a very weak, barely consistent sample relationship. The null hypothesis says this pattern is due to chance, and in reality the sample poorly represents no relationship. This hypothesis makes sense, because the odds are high that a few scores might pair up by chance to form a sample relationship even when no real relationship exists. Therefore, we "retain" the null hypothesis.

However, with a stronger relationship, the null hypothesis becomes less convincing. Say we obtain a perfectly consistent relationship. Again, the null hypothesis says that this pattern is due to sampling error. However, the probability is incredibly small that, *by luck*, we would select scores that match up perfectly when there is no relationship in nature. Such a low probability is taken as evidence that disconfirms the null hypothesis. Because such a sample relationship is *too unlikely* to be produced by sampling error, we "reject" the null hypothesis. Then, the only explanation left is the alternative hypothesis that the data represent a real relationship.

REMEMBER We *reject the null hypothesis* when it is too unlikely that we'd obtain our data if a real relationship does not exist in nature.

Selecting an Inferential Procedure

How we determine the probability of obtaining a particular relationship by chance depends on the characteristics of the design (the scale of measurement used, the way the relationship is summarized, how many groups are involved, and so on). Therefore, you must select the appropriate inferential procedure to use. So far we've examined the influence of manipulating *one* independent variable, discussing **one-way designs**. Then, consider the scale of measurement used to measure the *dependent variable*. Usually, you'll have interval or ratio scores that form "normal distributions" in the population. (If you are unsure about the distribution of your scores, check the literature to see what others say.) Then **parametric inferential procedures** are used with normally distributed, interval, or ratio scores. On the other hand, **nonparametric inferential procedures** are used with interval or ratio scores that are not normally distributed, or with nominal or ordinal scores.

Parametric Procedures: The *t*-test and ANOVA   The most common parametric procedures for a one-way design are the two-sample *t*-test and the analysis of variance.

The **two-sample *t*-test** is performed when we examine only two conditions of one independent variable. We could use the *t*-test, for example, if we compared only the effects of 1 hour versus 3 hours of study time. However, you calculate *t* in one of two ways, depending on how you select your participants. When you use either a repeated-measures design or a matched-groups design, perform the **dependent samples *t*-test**. When you select a random sample for each condition without repeated measures or matching, perform the **independent samples *t*-test**.

When you test three or more conditions of one independent variable, perform the **one-way analysis of variance (ANOVA)**, computing an *F*. (When there are only two conditions, you can use either the *t*-test or ANOVA.) Thus, the original study-time experiment examined studying for 1, 3, or 5 hours, so here we'd perform ANOVA. However, there are again two sets of formulas, depending on whether you have a between- or within-subjects design. But here's a confusing tidbit: Statistically, *between* and *within* are defined differently than they were before. In the research terminology of Chapter 6, matched groups produce a between-subjects design and repeated measures produce a within-subjects design. However, perform the **within-subjects ANOVA** when you have either a repeated-measures *or* matched-groups design (Cohen, 2001). Perform the **between-subjects ANOVA** when you don't use matching or repeated measures.

For either a between- or within-subjects design, the logic is the same. First, we *collapse* across all counterbalanced variables to compute the mean of each condition. As you've seen, different means in different conditions indicate a relationship, and the bigger the differences, the more convincing the relationship. Then, we compute a statistic—*t* or *F*—that summarizes the sample relationship by comparing the difference in scores *between* conditions relative to the error variance *within* conditions. If *t* or *F* is large enough, then we conclude that the scores (and means) differ so much between conditions that we have a believable relationship.

Nonparametric Procedures: Ranked Scores and Chi Squares   Sometimes you'll have scores that are measured using a nominal or ordinal scale of measurement, and then you should compute a nonparametric inferential statistic. As with the *t*-test or ANOVA, these procedures also produce a statistic that summarizes the sample relationship.

We obtain ordinal scores in a study for one of two reasons. Sometimes participants are directly measured using ranked scores (such as when "raters" rank-order participants on some characteristic). At other times we initially measure the dependent variable using interval or ratio scores, but because they are not normally distributed, or otherwise violate the rules of parametric procedures, we transform them into ranks: The highest original score is ranked 1, the next highest is ranked 2, and so on.

The logic using ranked scores is similar to that of previous studies. For example, say we ranked the test scores of eight students after they studied for 1 or 3 hours, giving the highest test grade a rank of 1, the second highest score a 2, and so on. Now look at the pattern the ranks form, as shown below:

Hours studied

1	3
3	1
6	2
7	4
8	5

There is apparently a relationship here, because participants tend to have higher test scores—obtaining lower ranks—when they study longer. It looks like a relationship, but maybe the lower ranks occurred in the 3-hour condition simply by luck. With ranked scores, when testing two conditions without matching or repeated measures, compute the **Mann-Whitney test**. If you test more than two conditions, perform the **Kruskal-Wallis test**. If you test two conditions but use matching or repeated measures, compute the **Wilcoxon test**. And if you test more than two conditions using this design, compute the **Friedman test**. In each, depending on the obtained statistic, we may conclude that we have a believable relationship.

Finally, sometimes the dependent variable involves categorizing participants using a nominal scale. There is no common inferential procedure for a matched-groups or repeated-measures design. However, if you don't use matching or repeated measures and you have one independent variable, then compute the **one-way chi square**. For example, say that we categorized all those who failed the exam in terms of whether they studied for 1, 3, or 5 hours, and found the following number of failing participants in each category:

Hours studied

1	2	5
12	5	2

It looks like there's a relationship here, because the frequency of category membership—how often participants fail—changes depending on the number of hours studied. (With no relationship, we'd see about the same number of participants in each condition.) But, maybe we have these frequencies just because of sampling error. Therefore, we compute the chi square, (symbolized as χ^2), and if it is large enough, we conclude that we have a believable relationship.

The formulas for parametric and nonparametric procedures, and instructions for using them, are presented in Appendix C. To help you select a procedure, the previous discussion is summarized in Table 7.4.

INTERPRETING SIGNIFICANT RESULTS

In each of the previous procedures, we decide whether to reject the null hypothesis (that there is no relationship) by comparing the obtained statistic we compute to the appropriate "critical value." (For details, see the specific procedure in Appendix C.) If we reject the null hypothesis, we then accept the alternative hypothesis and conclude that there really is a relationship. We communicate this decision by stating that the results are significant. A **significant** sample relationship is too unlikely to occur by chance, so we assume that it represents the real, predicted relationship found in the population. You'll also read research that finds "significant differences," meaning that the differences between the means of the conditions are too large to explain as merely sampling error, so they must represent real differences that occur in the population. Either way, "significant" indicates that we conclude that we have a believable sample relationship and so we then go on to interpret and generalize it accordingly.

TABLE 7.4 Parametric Procedures and Their Nonparametric Counterparts Used in Experiments with One Independent Variable

Between-subjects analysis (no matching or repeated measures)

Number of conditions	Parametric scores (Interval or Ratio)	Nonparametric scores	
		Ordinal	Nominal
Two	Independent samples *t*-test	Mann-Whitney test	Chi square
Three or more	Between-subjects ANOVA	Kruskal-Wallis test	Chi square

Within-subjects analysis (matched groups or repeated measures)

Number of conditions	Parametric scores (Interval or Ratio)	Nonparametric scores	
		Ordinal	Nominal
Two	Dependent samples *t*-test	Wilcoxon test	None
Three or more	Within-subjects ANOVA	Friedman test	None

_____

REMEMBER In every study, you must determine whether or not the sample relationship is *significant*.

Comparing the Conditions in ANOVA

You are not finished with inferential procedures when you obtain a significant F in any ANOVA that involves more than two levels of the factor. A significant F indicates only that two or more conditions differ significantly, but it does not indicate *which* conditions differ significantly. Therefore, the next step is to perform **post hoc comparisons**. Theses compare all possible pairs of conditions to determine which ones differ significantly from each other. In the literature, you'll encounter several post hoc tests (each named after their developers), such as the Scheffé test, the Newman-Keuls test, or the Duncan test. The major difference between them is in how likely they are to produce significant results versus producing errors. An in-between procedure is the Tukey *HSD* test. (This and analogous methods for nonparametric procedures are shown in Appendix C.)

Performing these procedures is similar to performing a *t*-test on each pair of means from the factor. Thus, in the study-time experiment, we'll end up comparing the means of the 1- and 3-hour conditions, the means of the 1- and 5-hour conditions, and the means of the 3- and 5-hour conditions. This will identify where, among the three levels of study time, significant (believable) differences in test scores occur. Then, we will infer that the "real" relationship involves only those conditions that differ significantly, and we will discuss only these differences when generalizing the results.

Instead of computing F and then performing post hoc tests, researchers sometimes take a different approach and perform planned comparisons. **Planned comparisons** compare only some conditions in an experiment. In the study-time experiment, for example, a hypothesis might lead us to compare the 1-hour condition to every other condition, but without comparing the 3-hour to the 5-hour condition. Planned comparisons are also called "a priori comparisons." (In these procedures, F need not be computed.)

_____

REMEMBER Perform either *post hoc comparisons* or *planned comparisons* to determine which levels in a factor differ significantly.

Estimating the Population Mean

If the results of the study-time experiment are significant, then we'll use the mean in each level to estimate the mean we'd find if we studied the entire population. (A population mean is called mu, symbolized as μ.) For example, if our sample mean of 20 in the 1-hour condition differs significantly from the other means, we'd estimate that after testing the population under this condition, the population's μ would be "around" 20. However, our participants in that condition probably do not *perfectly* represent the population, so we probably have some sampling error in this estimate. To factor in sampling error, we compute a confidence interval. A **confidence interval** describes a range of μs, any one of which the sample mean is likely to represent. You can see this in the following diagram:

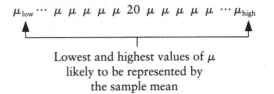

$$\mu_{low} \cdots \; \mu \; \mu \; \mu \; \mu \; \mu \; 20 \; \mu \; \mu \; \mu \; \mu \; \mu \; \cdots \mu_{high}$$

Lowest and highest values of μ
likely to be represented by
the sample mean

Computing the confidence interval involves computing the lowest and highest value of μ that the sample mean is likely to represent. In the example, this gives us a range of values around 20. Then, even if our sample mean contains sampling error, we conclude that μ is probably within this range. (Computations are shown in Appendix C.7.)

Restrictions on Interpreting Significant Results

Based on a significant sample relationship (and post hoc tests and confidence intervals), we can begin to describe the relationship we'd expect to find if we could study everyone in the population. On the one hand, this means we are confident that we know how nature works in this situation. On the other hand, remember that researchers are always cautious in their conclusions. When making inferences about a significant relationship, bear in mind two restrictions.

First, a significant result does not "prove" that the relationship exists in the population. All we have "proved" is that chance—sampling error—would be unlikely to produce our data if a relationship does not exist in the population. But unlikely does not mean impossible. It is still possible that the relationship does not exist in the population and simply by the luck of the draw we obtained data that give the appearance of a relationship. Thus, whenever results are significant, it's possible that we've made a Type I error. A **Type I error** occurs when we reject the null hypothesis, but it is the correct hypothesis. In other words, we say the data reflect a real relationship—and the independent variable works—when in fact they do not.

Thus, sometimes (though we never know when) the null hypothesis is really true. In that case, rejecting null is a Type I error (and retaining it is the correct decision). However, in setting up an inferential test, we set **alpha** (symbolized by α) which is the probability that we will make a Type I error. Psychologists have agreed that alpha can be no greater than .05, so that the probability that we'll reject a true null hypothesis is always less than .05. Thus, on the one hand, it is unlikely that we've made a Type I error, but on the other hand, it's still possible.

The second restriction is that the term *significant* indicates only that the *numbers* in the data are unlikely to occur if the sample represents a population of *numbers* in which the relationship does not exist. It does not mean that these numbers accurately reflect our variables, or that the behaviors and constructs are related in the way that we've hypothesized. Therefore, as usual, you must evaluate the study in terms of reliability and the various types of validity we've discussed to be sure that you are not being misled by flaws in the design. Only if you've performed a well-designed study can you be confident that the relationship between the scores reflects the relationship between the *variables* that you think are present. If so, you'll be confident both that you're not being misled by flaws in the design, and that you're not being misled by sampling error. Then, you can confidently interpret the relationship "psychologically" in terms of the variables and constructs you set out to study.

> **REMEMBER**   Significant results may *not* represent a real relationship in the population or reflect the relationship between the variables that you think they do.

INTERPRETING NONSIGNIFICANT RESULTS

Sometimes our obtained statistic indicates that our results are *not* too unlikely to occur through sampling error. Therefore, we do not reject the null hypothesis, we *retain* it. We describe such results as **nonsignificant**.

However, nonsignificant results do not "prove" that the predicted relationship does not exist in the population (and we have not proved that the independent variable doesn't work as predicted). We have simply found that chance could reasonably produce data such as ours when a real relationship does not exist. But, just because chance *could* do this does not mean that it *did*. For example, let's say we obtain a very weak, nonsignificant relationship when comparing the influence of different study times. There are three possible reasons why this might happen. (1) Maybe we're correct and there is no real relationship here, and the sample relationship occurred because of sampling error. (2) Maybe there *is* this relationship in the population, and the sample perfectly represents it, but being so weak, we—and our statistics—misinterpret it as reflecting no relationship. (3) Maybe there is a very strong relationship in nature, but, because of sampling error, we have a very unrepresentative sample that produced this weak example of it.

With nonsignificant results, we have merely failed to reject the null hypothesis, so both it and the alternative hypothesis are still viable proposals: Literally, we cannot decide whether the relationship exists in the population or not. Therefore, we do not say anything about the relationship: We do not perform any additional statistical procedures to describe the relationship, we do not conclude whether it confirms or disconfirms our original hypothesis, and we do not even begin to interpret it psychologically.

> **REMEMBER**   *Nonsignificant* results provide no convincing evidence—one way or the other—as to whether a "real" relationship exists.

Because it's possible that a particular relationship exists in the population even though our results are nonsignificant, it is possible that we are making an error whenever we retain the null hypothesis. A **Type II error** occurs when we retain the null hypothesis when it is false and the alternative is the correct hypothesis. (The probability of a Type II error is called beta, symbolized as β). Thus, sometimes (we never know when) the null hypothesis is really false. Retaining the null is a Type II error (and rejecting it is the correct decision). Here, we conclude that there is no evidence for the relationship in nature (no evidence that our manipulation works) when in fact the relationship exists (and the manipulation does work!).

COMPARING TYPE I AND TYPE II ERRORS

Type I errors and Type II errors are mutually exclusive: If there's a possibility you've made one type of error, then there is no chance of making the other type. This is because whether you're making a Type I or Type II error is determined by the true state of affairs in nature: Is the null hypothesis true (there is *not* the relationship in nature), or is the null hypothesis false (there *is* the relationship.) You can't be in a situation where, *simultaneously*, there is and is not the relationship, so you can't simultaneously be at risk of making both errors. Also, if you don't make one type of error, you are *not* automatically making the other, because sometimes you'll make the *correct* decision.

To understand these errors, look at it this way: The type of error you can *potentially* make is determined by the situation—what nature "says" about whether there is or is not the relationship. Then, whether you make the error depends on whether you agree or disagree with nature. Thus, there are actually four possible outcomes in any study. Look at Table 7.5. As in the upper row of the table, sometimes the null hypothesis really is true: Then, if we reject null, we make a Type I error. We don't know if this has happened, but its probability equals alpha. If we retain the null hypothesis, we avoid a Type I error and make the correct decision (and the probability of this is 1 − alpha.) But, as in the lower row of the table, sometimes the null hypothesis is really false: Then, if we retain it, we make a Type II error (with a probability equal to beta). If we do reject the null hypothesis, we avoid a Type II error and make the correct decision (and the probability of this is 1 − beta).

In any experiment, the results of your inferential procedure will place you in one of the columns of Table 7.5. If you reject the null hypothesis, then either you worry that you've made a Type I error, or you've made the correct decision and avoided a Type II error. If you retain the null hypothesis, then either you worry that you've made a Type II error, or you've made the correct decision and avoided a Type I error.

Statistical procedures are designed to minimize the probability of Type I errors, because the most serious error is to conclude that an independent variable works when really it does not: Basing scientific "facts" on chance relationships that do

TABLE 7.5 Possible Results of Rejecting or Retaining the Null Hypothesis

		Our decision	
		Reject null	Retain null
The truth about nature	Type I situation: *Null is true* *(no relationship exists)*	We make a Type I error $(p = \alpha)$	We are correct, avoiding a Type I error $(p = 1 - \alpha)$
	Type II situation: *Null is false* *(a relationship exists)*	We are correct avoiding a Type II error $(p = 1 - \beta)$	We make a Type II error $(p = \beta)$

not exist in nature can cause untold damage. (That's why we make alpha so small.) On the other hand, Type II errors are also important. To learn about nature, we must avoid making Type II errors and conclude that an independent variable works when it really does. For that, we need power.

STATISTICAL POWER AND RESEARCH DESIGN

A researcher's goal is to avoid Type II errors, so that we identify real relationships and thus learn something about nature. This ability has a special name: **Power** is the probability that we will reject the null hypothesis on those occasions when null is actually false, correctly concluding that the sample data reflect a real relationship. In other words, power is the probability that we will not make a Type II error.

Power is important because, after all, why bother to conduct a study if you're unlikely to reject the null hypothesis even when the predicted relationship really *does* exist? Therefore, whether you have sufficient power is crucial whenever you have nonsignificant results. Because you do not conclude that there is the predicted relationship, the question is "Did I just miss a relationship that really exists in nature?" Therefore, the idea is that, in case we are dealing with a real relationship, we do everything we can to ensure that we—and our statistics—will not miss it. If we still end up retaining the null hypothesis, we know it's not for lack of trying. With power, we're confident that if there were a relationship out there, we would have found it. Therefore, we are confident in our decision about the null hypothesis, and in statistical lingo, we're confident we've avoided making a Type II error. (There are statistical procedures for calculating the power of a study; see Cohen, 1988, or other statistics books.)

However, you cannot add power after a study is completed. Instead, the goal is to *design* a powerful study. As we've seen in previous chapters, a powerful design is one that is likely to produce a convincing relationship that we are un-likely to miss.

Now you can understand the logic behind this: We are talking about those times when the null hypothesis is false and there *is* a relationship in nature. On those occasions, we "should" reject the null hypothesis, so our results "should" be significant. Therefore, maximizing power essentially means that we maximize the probability that results will be significant. As you've seen, an inferential pro-cedure uses the strength of a relationship to determine how likely the relationship is to occur by chance. On those times when the null hypothesis is false, it is better to have a stronger sample relationship because then, instead of missing a real relationship by concluding that it is due to chance, we make the correct decision, concluding that the results are significant. There are two general approaches for maximizing the power in a study.

First, as we've seen in previous chapters, a powerful design is one that is likely to result in a strong, convincing sample relationship. To obtain this, we seek large differences in scores—and means—*between* the conditions by using a *strong manipulation* and obtaining *sensitive measurements*. We also minimize error variance *within* conditions by building in controls that eliminate the influence of extraneous variables from the participants, experimenter, environment, or mea-surement task that create inconsistency in scores.

An additional, new component of a powerful design involves N, the number of participants that you test. *The greater the* N, *the more powerful the design.* The size of N is important, because a relationship of a given strength is more "believ-able" if it's based on more observations. For example, while two participants might be likely to produce a relationship by chance when there is no real rela-tionship present, 200 are not. This logic is built into significance testing because the larger the N, the more likely that a particular obtained statistic will be signifi-cant. (*Note*: We are discussing relatively small samples. Generally, an N of 30 is needed for minimal power, and increasing N up to 121 increases power substan-tially. However, an N of 500 is not much more powerful than an N of, say, 450.)

REMEMBER   The stronger the sample relationship and the larger the N, the more *powerful* the study.

The second approach to maximizing power is to use powerful inferential sta-tistics. First, because of their theoretical foundations, parametric procedures are more powerful than nonparametric procedures: That is, data that are analyzed using a parametric test are more likely to be significant than if the same data are analyzed using a nonparametric procedure. Therefore, try to design any study so that you can use parametric procedures.

With designs testing only two conditions, power is also determined by whether you perform a one-tailed or two-tailed test. A **one-tailed test** is performed when you predict which mean will be larger, predicting whether the relationship is pos-itive or negative. A **two-tailed test** is performed when you do not predict which mean will be larger and so you will be satisfied with either type of relationship. (Analyses with three or more conditions always use a two-tailed test.) A one-tailed test is more powerful than a two-tailed test. However, if the sample relationship turns out to be the opposite of what you've predicted, then the relationship is not significant. Therefore, if you are not sure of the prediction, use the safer two-tailed test, because you can find a significant relationship regardless of its type and still draw inferences from the study.

> **REMEMBER** The *power* of a design is increased by using parametric procedures and one-tailed tests.

PUTTING IT ALL TOGETHER

Inferential statistics are a necessary component of research. However, remember that finding a significant result is not the end of a study, but rather the beginning: Once there, you've only concluded that you are seeing a believable relationship. Then you play psychologist, interpreting and explaining the relationship. To do so, look at your measures of central tendency (usually the means) and variability, to see what happened to the dependent scores as you changed conditions, and how consistently it happened. "Interpret" the relationship by describing what the increasing or decreasing scores indicate about how the behavior is changing. "Explain" the relationship by speculating how the independent variable might cause someone's behavior to change this way, and consider the strength of the relationship to gauge the impact of your factor versus other, extraneous factors. The goal is to try to make sense out of what the data seem to be telling you about how the behavior operates in this situation. Recognize, however, that you are often making an educated guess. This is OK, because ultimately we find out who's correct through replication, so speculate away.

CHAPTER SUMMARY

1. Experiments investigate changes in the dependent variable *as a function of* changes in the independent variable.

2. *Descriptive statistics* summarize and describe the important characteristics of a sample of data. *Inferential statistics* are procedures for deciding whether a sample relationship represents a relationship that exists in the population.

3. A *nominal scale* reflects the category a participant falls in; an *ordinal scale* reflects a participant's rank order; an *interval scale* measures an amount, and negative scores are possible; and a *ratio scale* measures an amount, but negative scores are not possible.

4. *Parametric* inferential statistics are used with normally distributed interval or ratio scores. *Nonparametric* statistics are used with nonnormal interval/ratio scores, or with nominal or ordinal scores.

5. To describe a relationship, determine (a) the *type* of relationship—the direction in which the Y scores change as the X scores change, and (b) the *strength* of the relationship—the extent to which one value of Y is consistently associated with one value of X.

6. In a *positive linear relationship*, as the X scores increase, the Y scores tend to increase. In a *negative linear relationship*, as the X scores increase, the Y scores tend to decrease. In a *nonlinear relationship*, as the X scores increase, the Y scores alter their direction of change. When no relationship is present, the distribution of Y scores at one X is virtually the same as at other Xs.

7. *Measures of central tendency* indicate the score around which the distribution tends to be centered. The common measures are the *mean*, the *median*, and the *mode*. Which measure to compute depends on the scale used to measure the dependent variable.

8. In graphing the results of an experiment, the independent variable is plotted on the X axis and the dependent variable on the Y axis. A *line graph* is created when the independent variable is measured using a ratio or interval scale. A *bar graph* is created when the independent variable is measured using a nominal or ordinal scale.

9. *Measures of variability* describe how much the scores differ from one another. The common measures of variability are the *variance* and the *standard deviation*.

10. The *strength* of a relationship in an experiment indicates the degree to which changes in dependent scores are caused by changing the levels of the independent variable.

11. The *null hypothesis* implies that the sample poorly represents the absence of the predicted relationship in the population. The *alternative hypothesis* implies that the sample data reflect the presence of the predicted relationship in the population.

12. A *one-way design* has only one independent variable. The *two-sample* t-test is the appropriate parametric inferential procedure when there are only two conditions and the *analysis of variance (ANOVA)* is appropriate when there are two or more levels. Use the *dependent samples* t-test or the *within-subjects ANOVA* with matching or repeated measures. Otherwise, use the *independent samples* t-test or the *between-subjects ANOVA*.

13. With ranked data (without matching or repeated measures), compute the *Mann-Whitney test* with two conditions and the *Kruskal-Wallace test* with more than two conditions. With matching or repeated measures, use the *Wilcoxon test* with two conditions and the *Friedman test* with more than

two conditions. Use the *one-way chi square* with nominal data and two or more conditions.

14. *Alpha* (α) is the probability of making a Type I error.

15. In a *one-tailed inferential* test, only a positive linear relationship or only a negative one is predicted. In a *two-tailed test*, either a positive or a negative relationship is predicted.

16. *Significant* indicates that the sample relationship is too unlikely to occur if the predicted relationship does not exist in the population. *Nonsignificant* results provide no convincing evidence, one way or the other, about the predicted relationship.

17. In ANOVA, *post hoc tests* compare all possible pairs of conditions to determine which ones differ significantly. *Planned comparisons* are performed to compare only some pairs of conditions.

18. A *confidence interval* describes a range of values of the population mean (μ), any one of which the sample mean is likely to represent.

19. A *Type I error* is rejecting the null hypothesis when it is true. A *Type II error* is retaining the null hypothesis when it is false.

20. Power is the probability of rejecting the null hypothesis when it is false. Power is increased by maximizing the differences in scores between conditions, minimizing the error variance, and increasing *N*. Also, parametric statistics are more powerful than nonparametric statistics, and one-tailed tests are more powerful than two-tailed tests.

KEY TERMS   (with page references)

REVIEW QUESTIONS

1. What two major characteristics of a study determine the type of statistical procedures you should use?

2. When do you perform parametric or nonparametric procedures?

3. (a) What is the difference between a positive and a negative linear relationship? (b) What is the difference between a linear and a nonlinear relationship?

4. Summarize the steps involved in describing and interpreting the results of an experiment.

5. (a) What is the mode? (b) What is the median? (c) What is the mean? (d) With what type of data is the mean appropriate?

6. How does the size of a measure of variability communicate (a) the size of the differences among the scores and (b) how consistently the participants scored?

7. (a) What is sampling error? (b) Why does the possibility of sampling error present a problem to researchers when inferring that a relationship exists in nature?

8. (a) What does the null hypothesis communicate? (b) What does the alternative hypothesis communicate?

9. (a) When do you use a one-tailed or a two-tailed test? (b) What is the advantage and disadvantage of each?

10. What does the term "significant results" convey?

11. (a) Why is it important to create a powerful design? (b) What four things can you do to increase power when designing a study? (c) What two statistical aspects should you consider to increase power?

APPLICATION QUESTIONS

12. In the following chart, identify the measurement scale of each variable.

Variable	Scale
Gender	_____
Academic Major	_____
Time	_____
Restaurant Rankings	_____
Speed (miles per hour)	_____
Position in Line	_____
Change in Weight	_____

13. For each of the following, identify the independent and dependent variable, indicate the scale of measurement being used with each variable, and describe how you would graph the results. (a) You examine whether amount of graffiti changes as a function of a males' versus a females' restroom. (b) You study the relationship between students' choice to sit toward the front, middle, or back of a classroom and their grade in the class. (c) You conduct a study of memory for pictures as a function of participants' mood, ranging from very sad to very happy.

14. Consider the results of the following experiments. (Scores are normally distributed ratio scores.)

Experiment 1

Condition 1	Condition 2	Condition 3
12	30	45
11	33	48
14	36	49
10	35	44

Experiment 2

Condition 1	Condition 2	Condition 3
18	8	3
13	11	9
9	6	5

(a) What should you do to summarize these experiments? (b) Which experiment produced the stronger relationship? (c) In each experiment, what does the amount of error variance tell you about the impact of the independent variable?

15. Consider the following graph of data from a study comparing the test scores of participants after various amounts of study time.

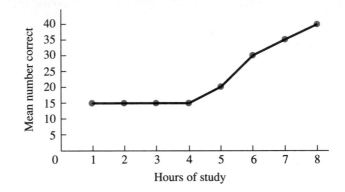

(a) Interpret specifically the relationship. (b) Give a title to the graph, using "as a function of." (c) If you participated in this study and had studied for 5 hours, estimate your test score. (d) If we tested all the people in the world after 5 hours of study, what test score for them would you expect? (e) What symbol stands for your prediction in part (d)? (f) What statistical issue arises in your conclusion in part (d)? (g) What issue of validity arises in part (d)?

16. In an experiment, a researcher observes that participants' interest in a lecture increases as a function of whether they are paid $1, $5, or $25 to listen to it. What statistical procedures must be performed before we can accept that each amount of money causes a difference in interest level?

17. A television commercial claims that "ultra-bleach" toothpaste significantly reduces tooth decay compared with other brands. What does this statement imply about (a) the type of research method used and (b) the statistical procedures performed and their outcome?

18. Say that the researcher in question 17 used an alpha equal to .25. What problems are raised by this alpha level?

19. A researcher hypothesizes that males and females are the same when it comes to intelligence, predicting a nonsignificant difference. Why is this hypothesis impossible to test statistically?

20. Researcher A finds a significant negative relationship between increasing stress level and participants' ability to concentrate. Researcher B replicates this study but finds a nonsignificant relationship. Identify the statistical error that each researcher might have made.

21. We measure the emotional responses of people after exposure to different amounts of sunlight. The resulting line graph slants downward. What does this tell you about (a) the means for the conditions, (b) the raw scores for each condition, and (c) the relationship between emotionality and sunlight?

22. In a one-way design with two levels: (a) How do we know whether to perform a parametric or nonparametric procedure? (b) What two general types of parametric procedures might we use? (c) What two types of *t*-test do we choose from? (d) What two types of ANOVA do we choose from? (e) In parts (c) and (d), what aspect of the design indicates which type to choose?

23. A between-subjects, one-way ANOVA with five levels produces a significant *F*. (a) Describe this design. (b) What does the significant *F* indicate? (c) What inferential procedure is needed now? (d) What descriptive statistics are needed now, and what would you look for?

24. What statistical procedure is needed for each of the following? (a) Comparing random samples of men and women using their number-correct scores on a statistics exam. (b) Comparing rankings of the football teams from a sample of eastern colleges to a sample of western colleges. (c) Comparing the number of left- and right-handed people who we describe as creative. (d) Comparing the mean language scores of the same sample of children when they are 1, 2, 3, and 4 years old. (e) Comparing the normally distributed "neatness scores" for men to those of their wives.

DISCUSSION QUESTIONS

25. We test whether attending a private or public high school influences performance on a test of social skills, and find significant results. (a) What is the probability that we made a Type I error, and what would the error be in terms of the independent and dependent variables? (b) What is the probability that we made a Type II error, and what would the error be in terms of the variables? Say we find nonsignificant results. (c) What is the probability that we made a Type I error, and what would the error be in terms of the independent and dependent variables? (d) What is the symbol for the probability that we made a Type II error, and what would the error be in terms of the variables?

26. If we conduct the study-time experiment discussed in this chapter using a between-subjects design, random selection and random assignment should result in a mix of different participants for each condition. (a) How might this mix adversely affect the power of the study? (b) Should this be a within-subjects design instead? (c) Describe completely how you would study whether test grades increase as a function of increased study time.

27. A researcher obtains large error variance when studying children's ability to remember a passage they read as a function of the number of hours they have previously watched television. (a) What does this statement indicate

about the scores in each condition? (b) What might cause such variability?
(c) What impact will such variability have on the statistical results?
(d) What impact will it have on the conceptual interpretation of the
variable of television watching?

28. Immediately prior to an exam, we ask students the number of hours they
studied. We then conduct an experiment by randomly selecting a group of
10 participants who had studied for 1 hour and a group of 10 who had
studied for 2 hours. The mean exam scores for the two groups were 35 and
50, respectively. An independent samples t-test yielded an obtained
$t = +1.70$. (a) For alpha = .05, what conclusion do you draw from this
study? (b) What statistical flaw should concern you, and how would you
fix it? (c) If t had equaled $+2.70$, what conclusion would you draw? (d) In
part (c), what additional information about the data would you seek? (e)
How confident are you in your conclusions in part (c), and why? (*Hint*:
Remember to consider the type of experiment this is.)

Designing and Analyzing Multifactor Experiments

Believe it or not, so far we have discussed *simple* experiments. They are simple because they involve manipulating only one independent variable and performing only basic statistics. In actual practice, however, psychologists often manipulate more than one independent variable. Using other terminology, an independent variable is a factor, so manipulating more than one independent variable produces a **multifactor experiment**.

To introduce you to multifactor experiments, this chapter first discusses between- and within-subjects experiments containing two factors. Our emphasis will be on experiments that are analyzed using the ANOVA, but we will focus on how to *interpret* such results and not on their formulas. (The way to perform complex analyses is to use computer programs, such as the very versatile SPSS.) After discussing two factor designs, we'll discuss the logic of designs involving more than two factors—and a few other advanced topics—so that if you encounter them in the literature, you'll understand their basics.

THE REASON FOR MULTIFACTOR STUDIES

Why should we study two (or more) factors in one experiment? After all, we could perform separate studies, each testing the influence of one factor. The answer is that a multifactor design has three advantages over a single-factor design. First, in most natural settings there are many variables present that combine to influence a behavior. By manipulating more than one independent variable in the same experiment, we can examine the influence that each factor by itself has on a behavior, as well as the influence that combining these factors has on the behavior. As you'll see, when a combination of independent variables produces an effect, we have an *interaction*. The primary reason for conducting multifactor studies is to study the interaction between independent variables.

A second advantage of multifactor designs is that once you have created a design for studying one independent variable, often only a minimum of effort is required to study additional factors. Thus, multifactor studies can be an efficient and cost-effective way of determining the effects of—and interactions among—several independent variables at once.

Finally, multifactor experiments are often produced when you set out to study only one factor but then *counterbalance* an important extraneous variable. As you'll see, instead of collapsing across and ignoring such a variable as we've done previously, we can treat it as an additional factor and examine its influence on dependent scores as well.

THE TWO-WAY BETWEEN-SUBJECTS ANOVA

Recall that when you manipulate one independent variable, you have a *one-way design*. Not surprisingly, in a **two-way design** we simultaneously manipulate two independent variables. The logic in a two-way design is the same as that for a one-way design: For each variable, we formulate hypotheses and make predictions regarding the effect of the manipulation on the dependent variable. Here's an example from real research. As part of a multifactor design, Berkowitz (1987) examined the hypothesis that the more positive a participant's mood, the more that person will help others. Berkowitz induced either a positive, negative, or neutral mood in participants by having them read 50 mood-influencing statements. Then participants were asked to help in scoring data sheets from another, fictitious experiment. The number of columns of data scored within a 5-minute period was the dependent measure of helping. The design of this factor is shown in Table 8.1.

All of the principles we've discussed for designing the independent and dependent variable and controlling extraneous variables also apply to a multifactor design: Berkowitz limited the population to females, devised a plausible request for help that minimized reactivity and other demand characteristics, kept the experimenter's behavior constant, and developed constant scoring criteria. Because the amount of help that a person provides is a ratio scale, computing the mean helping score in each condition is appropriate. Thus, averaging vertically in each column in Table 8.1 yields the mean for each mood level, showing how helping scores change as a function of improving mood. To be sure that any relationship we see here is not due to sampling error, we'll perform an ANOVA. But matching participants seems unnecessary, and repeated measures of the same participants under all three moods might produce uncontrollable carry-over effects. Therefore, in statistical terms, this is a between-subjects factor.

Another of Berkowitz's hypotheses about helping behavior was that heightened self-awareness—or self-consciousness—increases helpfulness. To manipulate self-awareness, some participants saw their reflection in a mirror throughout the experiment while others did not. This portion of the design can be envisioned as shown in Table 8.2. The only novelty here is that each *row* identifies a different level of awareness. Again we apply the necessary controls: Demand characteristics are reduced by explaining that the mirror is part of another study being conducted in this lab (and that we can't move it), and, in the no-mirror condi-

TABLE 8.1 Diagram of the Factor of Mood

Each column represents a mood level, each X represents a participant's helping score, and each $\overline{X}$ represents the mean helping score in that condition.

Mood factor

Negative	*Neutral*	*Positive*
X	*X*	*X*
X	*X*	*X*
X	*X*	*X*
X	*X*	*X*
$\overline{X}$	$\overline{X}$	$\overline{X}$

TABLE 8.2   Diagram of the Factor of Self-Awareness

Each row represents a level of self-awareness, each X represents a participant's helping score, and each $\overline{X}$ represents the mean helping score in that condition.

Self-awareness factor

| High self-awareness (mirror) | X X X X X X X X X | $\overline{X}$ |
| Low self-awareness (mirror) | X X X X X X X X X | $\overline{X}$ |

tion, the mirror is present but turned away from participants. Averaging horizontally across the scores in each row yields the mean helping score for each level of self-awareness. This factor also involves no matching or repeated measures, so it, too, is a between-subjects factor.

To create a two-way design, we manipulate *both* mood and self-awareness. The diagram of this design is shown in Table 8.3. Note that the columns still represent the levels of mood, and the rows still represent the levels of self-awareness. Each small square in the diagram is called a cell. A **cell** is produced by combining a level of one factor with a level of the other. For example, the upper left cell in Table 8.3 contains the scores of people who received the combination of high self-awareness and negative mood. Their mean helping score, the *cell mean*, is 2.0.

Researchers have a code for communicating the layout of a multifactor design. The design in Table 8.3 has one factor with three levels and one factor with two levels, so it is called a "three by two" design, written as "3 × 2" (or as a "2 × 3"). The number of digits indicates the number of factors in the study, and each digit indicates the number of levels in that factor. Thus, if we had two factors, each with two levels, we'd have a 2 × 2 design. You can have any number of levels in either factor. Also, because we combine all levels of one factor with all levels of the other, it is a **complete factorial design** or simply a **factorial design**. If for some reason we did not include all cells (e.g., omitting testing the positive mood–low self-awareness cell) we would have an *incomplete* factorial design. Incomplete factorial designs require special statistical procedures.

REMEMBER   In a *complete factorial design*, the *cells* are produced by combining each level of one factor with every level of the other factor.

All of the controls we discussed still apply in the two-way design. The major difference in multifactor designs lies in the way we analyze and interpret the results. As always, the goal is to determine whether a significant relationship

TABLE 8.3 Two-Way Design for Studying the Factors of Type of Mood and Level of Self-Awareness

The means shown here are similar to those found in Berkowitz (1987), Experiment 2.

		Negative	Neutral	Positive	
		Mood factor			
Awareness factor	*High*	$\overline{X} = 2.0$	$\overline{X} = 8.9$	$\overline{X} = 16.8$	$\overline{X} = 9.2$
	Low	$\overline{X} = 2.4$	$\overline{X} = 9.6$	$\overline{X} = 9.5$	$\overline{X} = 7.2$
		$\overline{X} = 2.2$	$\overline{X} = 9.3$	$\overline{X} = 13.2$	

exists between the independent and dependent variables. Usually, the dependent variable is measured with interval or ratio scores that form normal distributions so the data meet the rules for the two-way analysis of variance. As with the one-way ANOVA, however, there are different formulas depending on how you select and assign participants to the levels of each factor. If, as in the example, you have simply randomly assigned participants to every cell with no matching or repeated measures, then perform the **two-way between-subjects ANOVA**. As you'll see, the two-way ANOVA essentially creates a series of one-way ANOVAs. First, we examine the relationship produced by each individual independent variable.

Main Effects

When we examine the effect of an individual independent variable, we examine its main effect. The **main effect** of a factor is the influence that changing it has on the dependent scores, ignoring any other factors in the study. In our helping study, for example, we will determine the main effects on participants' helping behavior produced by (1) changing the levels of their mood and (2) changing the levels of their self-awareness.

To find the main effect of mood, we examine the scores as if they were from the one-way design shown in Table 8.4. That is, we *collapse* vertically across the different self-awareness conditions, ignoring the levels of self-awareness, just as we've collapsed across counterbalanced variables in prior chapters. To compute the mean score in a column, you can either average all participants' scores in that column or average together the cell means in that column. The means obtained in the columns are the *main effect means* for that factor. Thus, the main effect means are 2.2 for negative mood, 9.3 for neutral mood, and 13.2 for positive mood.

These means appear to show a relationship between mood and helping: As we change mood level, the means change, so the scores that produced the mean in

TABLE 8.4   Diagram of the Main Effect of Mood

In each column are the two cell means from the original diagram in Table 8.3.

Mood factor

	Negative	Neutral	Positive
Collapsing over self-awareness factor	2.0	8.9	16.8
	2.4	9.6	9.5
	$\overline{X} = 2.2$	$\overline{X} = 9.3$	$\overline{X} = 13.2$

each condition are also changing. Thus, we would say "there appears to be a *main effect* of mood," because mood, by itself has an effect (an influence) on helping scores.

REMEMBER   A *main effect* is the relationship produced by changing the conditions of one independent variable that results in different *main effect means.*

However, we also have the usual problem: Maybe there is no "real" relationship here, and instead the means form a relationship because of sampling error and the luck of the draw of who was tested. As usual, this is the null hypothesis, and we test it in the two-way ANOVA by computing a "main effect F" based on the means from the column factor. If the F is significant, then changing a person's mood by itself produces significant differences in helping scores.

Remember, however, that a significant F indicates only that, somewhere in the factor, at least two of the levels differ significantly. Therefore, as in Chapter 7, you perform post hoc comparisons whenever the F is significant and the factor has more than two levels. Often computer programs do not perform post hoc comparisons easily. Instead, perform the Tukey HSD procedure presented in Appendix C.5. This formula is appropriate for *both* a one-way ANOVA and the *main effects* in a multifactor design. Therefore, we would perform this test on the above main effect means of 2.2, 9.3, and 13.2, to determine which ones differ significantly. Then, as usual, we consider the means, and the type and strength of relationship they form to describe and explain "psychologically" how changing mood level influences helping behavior.

Once you have analyzed the main effect of one factor, then analyze the main effect of the next. To find the main effect of self-awareness, we examine the one-way design shown in Table 8.5. Here, we collapse *horizontally*, ignoring whether participants had a negative, neutral, or positive mood, to obtain the overall mean helping score in each row. To compute each mean, again either

TABLE 8.5 Diagram of the Main Effect of Self-Awareness

In each row are the cell means from the original diagram in Table 8.3.

		Negative	Neutral	Positive	
Self-awareness factor	High	2.0	8.9	16.8	$\overline{X} = 9.2$
	Low	2.4	9.6	9.5	$\overline{X} = 7.2$

Collapsing over mood factor →

average all scores in the row or average the cell means in the row. Then, you have the main effect means for high self-awareness (9.2) and low self-awareness (7.2).

Because there are differences among the main effect means, there appears to be a main effect of self-awareness. Again, however, we are faced with the null hypothesis that this, too, is not a real relationship. Therefore, we compute a second main effect F to test the differences between the means of the rows. If it is significant, then at least two of the row main effect means differ significantly. In this design, the factor contains only two levels, so the significant difference must be between low and high self-awareness. If there are more than two levels, post hoc comparisons are again performed to determine which means differ significantly. Once you know which conditions are part of a "real" relationship, you then examine and interpret the relationship as we've done previously.

Graphing the Main Effects   To adequately interpret your results, as well as to present them in a written report, you can produce graphs to show each main effect. Usually, this is done when (a) the main effect is significant, and (b) the pattern in the relationship is sufficiently complex that we benefit from seeing a graph. Assuming that the above main effects met these criteria, then we would produce the graphs shown in Figure 8.1. As usual, the independent variable is plotted on the X axis and the dependent variable on the Y axis. Each data point is a corresponding main effect mean. Because each independent variable reflects interval or ratio scales, we create a *line graph* for each.

After examining the main effects for each variable, the final step is to examine the interaction effect.

Interaction Effects

When we examine the **interaction effect**, we examine the influence that combining the levels from the different factors has on dependent scores. In the helping study, for example, we examine how a particular mood level combined with a particular self-awareness level influences scores, compared with the influence

FIGURE 8.1 Graphs of the Main Effects of Mood and Self-Awareness

Graph A shows the main effect of mood, and Graph B shows the main effect of self-awareness.

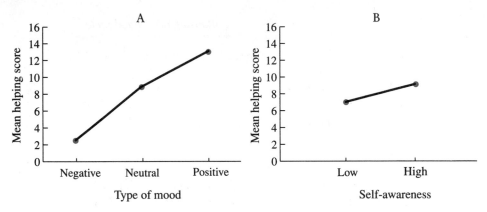

when other levels of mood or awareness are present. The interaction of two factors is called a "two-way interaction." It is identified using the number of levels in each factor. Here, one factor has three levels and one has two, so we have a "three by two" ("3 × 2") interaction.

To examine a two-way interaction, we do not collapse across or ignore either of the original factors. Instead, we treat each *cell* in the study as a level of the interaction factor. You can think of this factor as the original six cell means arranged in the one-way design shown in Table 8.6. The relationship in an interaction is complex because it involves three variables that are changing: two independent variables and the dependent variable. *To interpret an interaction, look at the relationship between one factor and the dependent scores, and see if that relationship changes as the levels of the other factor change.* Thus, in the left portion of Table 8.6, under low self-awareness, changing mood from negative to neutral increases helping scores, but changing mood from neutral to positive then slightly decreases them. (This is a nonlinear relationship.) However, this relationship is not found on the right; under high self-awareness, mean helping scores consistently increase as mood improves (forming a positive linear relationship.)

Thus, a **two-way interaction effect** is present when the influence of changing one factor is not consistent for each level of the other factor: The effect of improving mood under high self-awareness is not the same as that under low self-awareness. In other words, any conclusion we make about the effect of changing the levels of one factor *depends on* which level of the other factor we're talking about: Whether we should conclude that improving participants' mood increases their helping behavior in a linear fashion depends on whether we're talking about participants having high or low self-awareness. Or, from the opposite perspective, whether we should conclude that helping is greater with high or low self-awareness depends on which mood level we're talking about.

> **REMEMBER** A *two-way interaction* indicates that the relationship between one factor and the dependent scores depends on which level of the other factor is present.

Conversely, an interaction would *not* be present if the pattern of cell means produced by changing mood for high self-awareness is the same as that for low self-awareness. When there is no interaction present, (1) the effect of changing one factor is the *same* for all levels of the other factor, and (2) the influence of changing the levels of one factor does *not* depend on which level of the other variable is present.

Of course, once again we have that problem: Although these means *appear* to show an interaction, this might be due to sampling error while there is not a "real" interaction in nature. Therefore, we calculate another, separate F for the interaction. If the interaction F is significant, then somewhere among the cell means there are significant differences. As we'll see in a moment, you'd next perform post hoc tests to determine specifically which cell means differ significantly. Then, as usual, you examine the means that differ significantly, describe the type and strength of the relationships present, and interpret them "psychologically."

But first, recognize that an interaction can be a beast to interpret. Therefore, always graph the interaction.

Graphing the Interaction An interaction is graphed on a *single* graph. As usual, label the Y axis as the mean of the dependent variable. Label the X axis with the levels of one factor (usually placing the factor with the most levels here). Usually, you'll create a line graph. Then, show the second factor by drawing a

TABLE 8.6 Interaction of Type of Mood and Self-Awareness Level

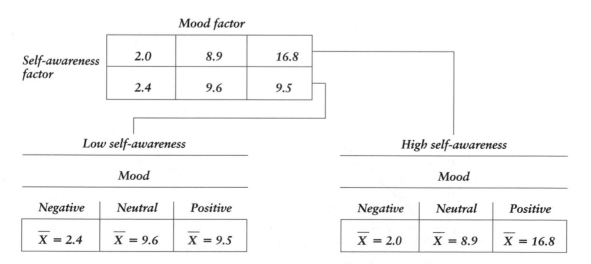

separate line for each of its levels. Thus, for our helping study, as in Figure 8.2, we label the X axis with the three mood levels. Then, we connect the data points from the three cell means for high self-awareness with one line and those from the three cell means for low self-awareness with a different line. (A legend or key is always included in such graphs to define the different lines.) To read the graph, look at one line at a time. For low self-awareness (the dashed line), there is the nonlinear relationship in which helping scores first increase but then level off as mood improves. However, for high self-awareness (the solid line), there is a different—linear—relationship in which helping scores continuously increase as mood improves. Therefore, this graph shows that an interaction effect is present.

Note that there is one more way to recognize when an interaction effect is apparently present. An interaction can produce an infinite variety of different graphs, but an interaction will always produce lines that are *not parallel*. Remember that each line summarizes the relationship between X (the factor) and Y (dependent scores). A line that is shaped or oriented differently depicts a different relationship between X and Y. Thus, when the lines from an interaction are not parallel, we have a different relationship between X and Y depending on which level of the other factor we examine.

For example, let's say our study had produced one of the graphs in Figure 8.3. On the left, changing mood level has an opposite effect depending on the self-awareness condition. On the right, the slopes of the lines are different, indicating that improving mood with high self-awareness more dramatically increases help-

FIGURE 8.2 Graph of an Interaction, Showing Mean Helping Scores as a Function of Mood and Self-Awareness Level

The six means being plotted in the graph are the cell means shown in the small matrix below.

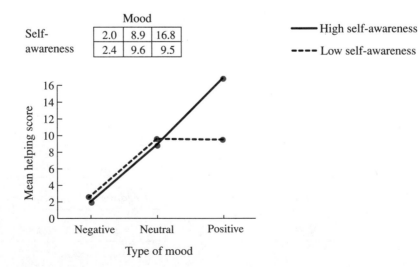

FIGURE 8.3 Two Graphs Showing that an Interaction Is Present

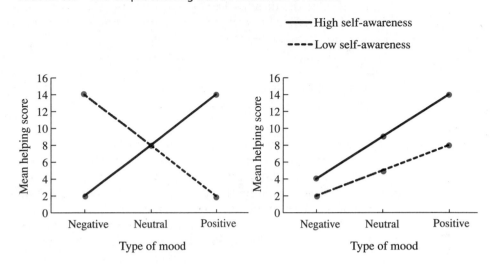

ing scores than does improving mood with low self-awareness. On the other hand, when *no* interaction exists, the lines are parallel. Say that our data produced one of the graphs in Figure 8.4. In both, the lines indicate that as mood level changes, the scores change in the same way *regardless of* level of self-awareness. Thus, neither graph shows an interaction. (The difference in the height of the two lines in each graph simply shows the main effect of self-awareness: On the left, the low awareness groups consistently scored higher, while on the right they consistently scored lower.)

FIGURE 8.4 Two Graphs Showing No Interaction

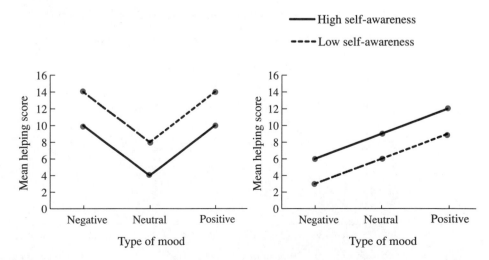

Think of a significant interaction F as indicating that somewhere in the graph, the lines deviate significantly from parallel. A nonsignificant F indicates that any deviance from parallel is likely to be due to sampling error in representing parallel lines—no interaction—in the population.

REMEMBER   When an interaction *is* present, the lines on the graph are *not* parallel.

Visualizing the Main Effects from the Interaction Graph   When reading a research article, you are often expected to visualize the main effects from a graph of the interaction. Because cell means are averaged together to obtain main effect means, you should envision the data points for the main effect of a factor as the average of the appropriate data points in the interaction graph.

To see how this is done, assume that we obtained the interaction data at the left of Figure 8.5. On the graph, the asterisks show where the overall mean for each level of mood is located after mentally collapsing vertically across high and low self-awareness (averaging the two data points in each circle). Then, as on the right, if we plotted these envisioned data points, they'd show the main effect of mood. Likewise, on the left in Figure 8.6, the asterisks show where the overall mean for each level of self-awareness is located after collapsing across mood (mentally averaging the three data points in each circle). Then, as on the right, if we plotted these envisioned data points on a separate graph (with the X axis labeled for low and high self-awareness) they would show the main effect of self-awareness.

Of course, we don't believe the graph of an interaction unless its F is significant. Even then, not all of the means may differ significantly. Therefore, you must investigate a significant interaction further.

FIGURE 8.5   Main Effect of Mood Seen in the Graph of an Interaction

The dots are cell means and the asterisks are visualized main effect means.

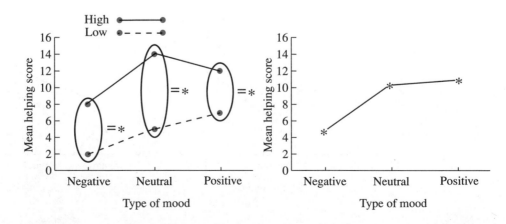

FIGURE 8.6 Main Effect of Self-Awareness Seen in the Graph of an Interaction

The dots are cell means and the asterisks are visualized main effect means.

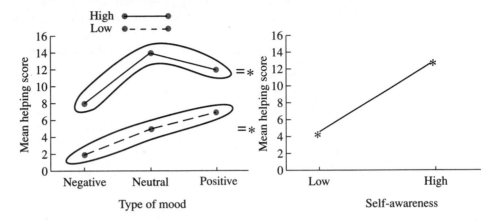

Post Hoc Comparisons in the Interaction When the interaction is significant, the most common approach is to then examine all cell means in the interaction by performing post hoc comparisons. A simple procedure for this is again the Tukey HSD. However, the procedure described in Appendix C.5 for comparing the means of an interaction is slightly different than that for comparing the means of a main effect.

REMEMBER Appendix C shows *different versions* of the Tukey HSD test for main effects and interaction effects.

Further, note that we do *not* compare every cell mean to every other cell mean. In Table 8.7, we would not compare the cell mean for negative mood–high self-awareness to the mean for neutral mood–low self-awareness, because doing so would create a *confounded comparison*: The cells differ along more than one

TABLE 8.7 Cell Means as a Function of Type of Mood and Level of Self-Awareness

The connected cells illustrate a confounded comparison.

		Mood factor		
		Negative	*Neutral*	*Positive*
Self-awareness factor	*High*	$\overline{X} = 2.0$	$\overline{X} = 8.9$	$\overline{X} = 16.8$
	Low	$\overline{X} = 2.4$	$\overline{X} = 9.6$	$\overline{X} = 9.5$

factor, so we cannot identify which factor produced the difference in scores (the change in mood or the change in awareness?). Thus, in the diagram of a study, do not compare cells that are diagonally positioned. Instead, perform only **unconfounded comparisons**—comparing cell means that differ along only one factor. Therefore, compare all possible pairs of cell means that are in the *same row*, and compare all possible pairs of cell means that are in the *same column*.

Simple Main Effects   A different way to examine an interaction is through simple main effects. A **simple main effect** is the effect of one independent variable at one level of a second independent variable. Essentially, we examine the overall relationship within any row or any column in the diagram of the study. For example, we might examine the simple main effect of changing mood under the high self-awareness condition, looking only at these cell means from the original interaction:

	Negative	*Neutral*	*Positive*
High self-awareness	$\overline{X} = 2.0$	$\overline{X} = 8.9$	$\overline{X} = 16.8$

The simple main effect is analyzed as a one-way ANOVA on these cell means, but with somewhat different computations. (See, for example, Hinkle, Wiersma & Jurs, 1998.) If this F is significant, it indicates that in the high self-awareness condition, changing mood produces a significant relationship, and that significant differences occur somewhere among these three means. This information is helpful if, for example, there is not a significant simple main effect for mood in the low self-awareness condition. Then, we'd know that the interaction reflects a relationship for high self-awareness and no relationship for low self-awareness.

> **REMEMBER**   In the interaction, *post hoc tests* compare all pairs of cell means within every row and column, and a *simple main effect* involves a one-way ANOVA performed on a row or column of cell means.

Interpreting the Two-Way Experiment

In a multifactor ANOVA, whether any one F is significant is not influenced by whether the other Fs are significant. Also, in the post hoc comparisons on the main effects and interaction, any combination of significant differences between means is possible. So that you can see the results of your various comparisons, Table 8.8 shows a way to identify the significant differences that we might find in the helping study. Outside the diagram, main effect means that differ significantly

TABLE 8.8 Summary of Significant Differences in the Helping Study

Each line connects two means that differ significantly.

Mood factor

		Negative	Neutral	Positive	
Self-awareness factor	*High self-awareness*	$\overline{X} = 2.0$	$\overline{X} = 8.9$	$\overline{X} = 16.8$	$\overline{X} = 9.2$
	Low self-awareness	$\overline{X} = 2.4$	$\overline{X} = 9.6$	$\overline{X} = 9.5$	$\overline{X} = 7.2$
		$\overline{X} = 2.2$	$\overline{X} = 9.3$	$\overline{X} = 13.2$	

are connected by a line. Inside the diagram, interaction cell means that differ significantly are connected by a line.

We interpret main effects in a two-way study the same way we would in a one-way design. Thus, from Table 8.8, we would *like* to conclude that, overall, the main effect for awareness indicates that people with high self-awareness help more than those with low awareness (comparing the means of 9.2 and 7.2). Likewise, we would like to claim that overall, the main effect of each improvement in mood is to produce higher scores (comparing 2.2 to 9.3 to 13.2).

The problem is that main effect means are based on an average of the cell means of the interaction. But, when we examine these cell means, the significant interaction *contradicts* the overall influence of the main effects. Literally, the effect of a factor *depends* on the other factor and vice versa. Thus, looking at the cell means, high self-awareness does not always produce significantly higher scores than low self-awareness: Instead, it does so only in the positive mood condition. Likewise, improving mood does not always increase scores: With high self-awareness it does, but there is no significant difference between neutral and positive mood in the low self-awareness condition.

Because an interaction indicates that the effect of one factor depends on the level of the other, you usually *cannot* make an overall, general conclusion about any main effects when the interaction is significant. Instead, the interpretation of the study is based on the significant differences between the cell means of the interaction. In the helping study, therefore, we would not pay attention to the main effects of mood or awareness level. Rather, our interpretation would center on explaining why, regardless of self-awareness level, negative mood produced less helping than neutral mood, but positive mood increased helping only when participants also experienced high self-awareness. We might propose, for example, that whether they are self-aware or not, a negative mood is sufficiently aversive to make people unwilling to help. For a positive mood to increase helpfulness, people must also have a high level of self-awareness so that they attend to their mood.

Usually, only when the interaction is not significant can we base the interpretation of a study on the significant main effects.

> **REMEMBER** The two-way ANOVA produces an F for each main effect and for the interaction. When the interaction is significant, we usually cannot draw a general conclusion about each main effect's influence.

USING COUNTERBALANCED VARIABLES TO PRODUCE TWO-WAY DESIGNS

As another example of a two-way design, recall that whenever an extraneous variable might seriously confound an independent variable or otherwise influence the results, you often control it through counterbalancing. In such cases, you can *analyze* the study as a two-way design, even though you originally set out to test only one independent variable. For example, say that in a different study, we compare the influence of participants' positive or negative mood on how helpful they perceive another person to be. In each condition, participants read some mood-inducing statements. Then they read descriptions of several fictitious people and rate each one's perceived helpfulness. We might counterbalance for participants' gender, with half of the people in each condition male and half female. Or, we might control order effects by changing the order in which the fictitious individuals are described and rated. These designs are shown in Table 8.9.

Analyzing these studies as two-way designs provides much more information than if, as in previous chapters, we ignored—*collapsed*—gender or order and created a one-way design. In addition to obtaining an F for the influence of mood, we will also obtain an F for gender, to see whether males and females differ on this task. Or, we'll obtain an F for order of trials, to see whether one order produced a difference in scores relative to the other. We can also examine the interaction between these variables and mood. If the interaction is significant, then we will discover that the influence that the mood manipulation has depends on a person's gender or on the order in which trials are performed.

A further advantage of treating these designs as two-way designs involves error variance. Recall that counterbalancing can add error variance: Combining males and females produces greater differences in scores *within* each column than does testing only one gender. By treating gender as a separate factor, however, the ANOVA removes this component of the error variance. This reduces the error

TABLE 8.9 Two-Way Designs Produced by Counterbalancing Either Gender or Order of Trials

	Mood factor Positive	Negative			*Mood factor* Positive	Negative	
Males	$\overline{X}$	$\overline{X}$	$\overline{X}$	Order 1	$\overline{X}$	$\overline{X}$	$\overline{X}$
Females	$\overline{X}$	$\overline{X}$	$\overline{X}$	Order 2	$\overline{X}$	$\overline{X}$	$\overline{X}$
	$\overline{X}$	$\overline{X}$			$\overline{X}$	$\overline{X}$	

variance that is present when the mood factor is analyzed, so there should be a stronger relationship between mood and dependent scores that is more likely to be significant.

Thus, always consider whether to analyze any single-factor study as a multi-factor design involving counterbalanced variables. You will obtain considerably more information from a study that, regardless, you are going to conduct in the same way. Likewise, remember that your goal as a researcher is not only to demonstrate a relationship but to understand it. Therefore, after you've performed your primary analyses, explore the data. You might group scores along any potentially relevant variable to create additional factors to analyze. For example, did the time of day participants were tested produce differences? Does their age relate to their performance? The more precisely you examine the data, the more precisely you'll be able to describe the variables that influence a behavior and to explain how it operates.

THE TWO-WAY WITHIN-SUBJECTS ANOVA

If you (1) repeatedly measure the same group of participants in all conditions of two independent variables, (2) match participants in all cells, or (3) have matched groups on one variable and repeated measures on the other, then the parametric procedure to use is the **two-way within-subjects ANOVA**. Although the calculations for this procedure are different from those for the between-subjects ANOVA, its logic and interpretation are identical.

Here's another example from real research. An issue in cognitive psychology is how different aspects of a stimulus can interfere with successful processing of the stimulus. The classic example of this is the "Stroop interference task" (Stroop, 1935), which examined participants' reaction time to report the color of the ink that a word is printed in when the word is the name of some other color. For example, you'd see the word yellow printed in green ink. A variation of this approach involves numbers (as in Flowers, Warner, & Polansky, 1979). To see how this works, below, how many number are in a row:

2 2 2

three three

Say that we replicate this study presenting one row of numbers at a time. In one factor, interference is created because the number present is incongruent with the number of numbers present (e.g., 2 2 2), or interference is not created because the number present is congruent with the number of numbers present (e.g., 2 2). In a second factor, we use digits (e.g., 2 2 2) versus words (e.g., two two two). The dependent variable is a person's reaction time to report the number of numbers present in a row. You can envision this 2×2 factorial design as shown in Table 8.10.

To control the many relevant extraneous participant variables, we test the same participants in all conditions, so this is a 2×2 repeated-measures design. (We could have any number of levels in either factor.) Then, we apply the usual controls, such as creating comparable stimuli for each condition, testing multiple trials per condition, and counterbalancing order effects that are due to the order of trials per condition and to the order of conditions.

We collapse across the different orders, computing each participant's mean reaction time (in seconds) in each of the four cells (as in Table 8.10). Then, collapsing vertically across the conditions of whether words or digits were presented, we examine the main effect for the factor of type of pairing: Apparently,

TABLE 8.10 2×2 Repeated-Measures Design for the Factors of Digit–Word and Congruent–Incongruent Pairings

Each X represents a participant's mean reaction time. Cell means are taken from Flowers et al. (1979), Table 1.

		Type of pairing		
		Congruent (2 2)	Incongruent (2 2 2)	
Type of number	Digit	X X $\overline{X} = .493$ X X	X X $\overline{X} = .543$ X X	$\overline{X} = .518$
	Word	X X $\overline{X} = .505$ X X	X X $\overline{X} = .542$ X X	$\overline{X} = .524$
		$\overline{X} = .499$	$\overline{X} = .542$	

incongruent pairings produced interference, resulting in a slower mean reaction time (.542) than with congruent pairings (.499). Next, collapsing horizontally across type of pairing, we examine the main effect for the type of number presented: Apparently, mean reaction time for digits (.518) was faster than for words (.524). Finally, we examine the interaction, comparing the four cell means: When congruent numbers producing no interference were presented, participants responded to digits more quickly than to words (.493 vs. .505, respectively). But when incongruent numbers producing interference were presented, there was virtually no difference in reaction time between digits and words (.543 vs. .542, respectively).

However, each of these apparent influences on reaction time might really be mere sampling error. Therefore, we compute an *F* for each main effect and an *F* for the interaction, and perform post hoc comparisons for any significant effects that have more than two levels. (The formulas for the Tukey HSD in Appendix C.5 are appropriate for a within-subjects design, too.) Then, we explain psychologically why the difference between digits and words disappears when the incongruent, interfering stimuli are present. If the interaction is not significant, we focus on any significant main effects: Why, overall, did participants respond more quickly to digits than to words, and why did using incongruent words or digits both produce interference?

REMEMBER   A *two-way within-subjects ANOVA* is used when two independent variables both involve matched groups or repeated measures.

THE TWO-WAY MIXED ANOVA

Recall that a problem in creating a matched-groups design is that it can be difficult to find sufficient numbers of matching participants. A problem when using repeated measures is that they create order and carry-over effects (including nonsymmetrical ones), so that we may have an unworkable counterbalancing scheme. These problems are multiplied in a two-way design. Therefore, we may prefer to create a within-subjects factor only when it critically requires control of participant variables, and to test the other variable as a between-subjects factor. When a design involves a "mix" of one within-subjects factor and one between-subjects factor, it is called a **two-way mixed design.**

One common mixed design arises when you begin with one factor that is set up as a *pretest-posttest design*. Recall that here the same participants are tested before and after presenting the treatment. Let's take another example from real research, this one involving "subliminal perception." Such research typically entails presenting a stimulus that is visible only very briefly—say, for about 5 milliseconds. (It takes about 150 milliseconds to blink.) The hypothesis is that the stimulus can in some way be processed, even though people do not consciously recognize that it was even present.

Before we proceed, let's look at the research regarding subliminal perception. There is *no* accepted evidence that brief messages hidden in advertisements make you buy a product, or that hidden messages in music turn you into a devil-worshiping psychopath! These misconceptions can be traced to a *rumor* about a study from the 1950s (relayed in McConnell, Cutler & McNeil, 1958). The subliminal messages "Buy popcorn" and "Drink Coca-Cola" were supposedly inserted in a film being shown at a theater, and then sales at the theater's refreshment stand supposedly increased dramatically. However, the duration of each message was supposedly only 1/3000 of a second (an impossible speed for a 1950s movie projector), no control group was used, and no distinction was made between refreshments bought during the movie and those bought before the movie started! Further, these results were never reported in *any* journal, and there are no published replications of this or similar claims under controlled conditions. (To understand how such misconceptions become part of the folklore, consider two possible explanations: [1] the public's fear of brainwashing and other such mysteries, and [2] self-proclaimed "experts" who say that subliminal messages are effective, and who will *sell* you information to "prove" it.)

There is, however, well-controlled, experimental evidence that a subliminal stimulus can register. For example, in social research, flashing words that describe honesty or meanness produce a corresponding bias in participants' later description of a confederate (Erdley & D'Agostino, 1988). Or, in clinical research, flashing soothing types of subliminal messages appears to have a positive influence (Silverman & Weinberger, 1985).

Let's consider a study conducted by Silverman, Ross, Adler, and Lustig (1978). They tested males' ability at dart-throwing before and after presentation of the subliminal message "Beating Dad is OK." The message was hypothesized to reduce residual guilt developed from childhood feelings of competition with father figures. A *poor* way to design this study is shown in Table 8.11. If the mean dart scores are significantly higher after the message, we'd *like* to conclude

TABLE 8.11   Diagram of a Poorly Designed One-Way Dart-Throwing Experiment

Xs *represent each subject's dart score.*

Before message	After message
X	X
X	X
X	X
X	X
$\overline{X}$	$\overline{X}$

that the message improved performance. But! There is something very wrong with this design in terms of potential confoundings. Here's a hint: Remember *maturation, history, reactivity,* and *practice effects*? Perhaps the after-message scores improved because of changes in these variables. That is, maybe the men acclimated to being tested, their brains matured and developed better eye-hand coordination, or they got better at dart throwing because of the practice provided by the before-message condition. For any of these reasons, participants might be better at darts after the message, but not because of the message.

To eliminate these rival hypotheses, we need a *control group* that does everything the experimental group does, but, instead of seeing the message "Beating Dad is OK," sees a *placebo* message that does not alleviate guilt. Adding a control group creates a between-subjects factor, with some individuals tested with the experimental message and others tested with the control message. This gives us the much better, two-way mixed design shown in Table 8.12.

If a parametric procedure is appropriate, we compute the *two-way mixed design ANOVA* (the design need not be a 2×2). This uses the same logic as in previous examples. Therefore, we'll compute and test an F for the column factor (comparing the Before–After means), an F for the row means (comparing the influence of the "Dad" vs. the control message), and an F for the interaction, comparing the four cell means. Then, for any effects with more than two levels, we again perform post hoc tests. (You can use the formulas for the Tukey HSD in Appendix C.5 for a mixed design as well.)

The main effects, however, are not likely to indicate anything interesting. By collapsing vertically the main effect means of Before-message and After-message include both the experimental and control messages. Therefore, any

TABLE 8.12 Diagram of the Two-Way, Mixed-Design Dart-Throwing Experiment

Each *X represents a participant's dart-throwing scores.*

difference between these two means will show only that scores change between the two testings. But, we won't know whether such differences are due to the experimental message or to maturation and practice effects. Likewise, collapsing horizontally gives the main effect means for the two types of messages. However, if the "Dad" message produces a higher mean than the control message, we won't know whether this occurred because the Before scores were higher or because the After scores were higher.

The specific test of the hypothesis that the "Dad" message increases performance comes when comparing the four cell means in the interaction. Ideally, we would predict a significant interaction that produces the graph shown in Figure 8.7. This shows an interaction (the lines are not parallel), and ideally the post hoc comparisons will confirm the following: (1) that there is no difference in the Before scores for the two groups, suggesting that the study is not contaminated by initial differences in dart-throwing skills between the two groups of men; (2) that there is no change in scores from Before to After for the control group, indicating that maturation, acclimation to testing, practice, and so on did not produce a Before–After difference in the control group, suggesting that they also did not produce the Before–After difference in the experimental group; and (3) the After scores of men receiving the "Dad" message are significantly higher than the After scores of those receiving the control message. This combination of findings would convincingly support the hypothesis that the "Dad" message does improve dart-throwing. (As this example illustrates, with a little thought you can predict and understand interaction effects, so, regardless of the type of design, don't think solely in terms of main effects.)

You have a mixed design whenever you set out to investigate two independent variables, one of which is best tested as a within-subjects factor while the other is

FIGURE 8.7 Ideal Interaction between Pretest versus Posttest and Control versus Experimental Cells

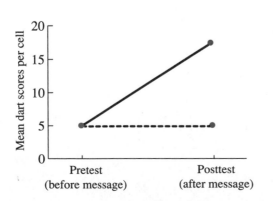

best tested as a between-subjects factor. Thus, in a different study, you might originally seek to investigate only one within-subjects factor, but end up also examining the effects of a counterbalanced between-subjects variable. Or, you might start with a between-subjects variable but then also analyze the repeated-measures factor of multiple trials, so that you can examine practice effects.

REMEMBER   A *two-way mixed design* consists of one within-subjects factor and one between-subjects factor.

THE THREE-WAY DESIGN

The beauty of ANOVA is that it can be applied to experiments with as many factors as you wish, regardless of whether the design is all between-subjects, all within-subjects, or mixed. You may add more independent variables or analyze more counterbalanced control factors.

For example, say that we add the variable of participants' gender (male vs. female) to the previous two-way dart study. With three factors, we have a **three-way design,** which with two levels of each factor is a $2 \times 2 \times 2$ design. Say that we obtained the data for this *mixed* design shown in Table 8.13. The previous 2×2 design for males is on the left. On the right, that design is replicated, but with females. If the data fit the criteria of a parametric procedure, then a three-way mixed-design ANOVA is appropriate.

Main Effects

Because there are three independent variables, the ANOVA produces a separate F for three main effects. As usual, to find a main effect for one factor, we collapse

TABLE 8.13 Diagram of a Three-Way Design for the Factors of Before and After Message, Type of Message, and Participant Gender

Each mean is the mean dart score of participants in that cell.

	Males		Females	
	Before message	After message	Before message	After message
"Dad" message	$\overline{X} = 10$	$\overline{X} = 20$	$\overline{X} = 8$	$\overline{X} = 12$
Control message	$\overline{X} = 10$	$\overline{X} = 10$	$\overline{X} = 8$	$\overline{X} = 10$

across the other factors. Thus, to find the main effect of gender, we average all of the males' scores together (for the box on the left, $\overline{X} = 12.5$) and all of the females' scores together (in the box on the right, $\overline{X} = 9.5$). Apparently, males were better at throwing darts than females. To find the main effect of Before message versus After message, we average together the columns containing Before scores, regardless of gender ($\overline{X} = 9.0$), and the columns containing After scores ($\overline{X} = 13.0$). Apparently, participants scored higher on the posttest than on the pretest. Finally, the main effect of type of message is the average of the scores in the rows of the "Dad" message ($\overline{X} = 12.5$) and in the rows of the control message ($\overline{X} = 9.5$). Apparently, people who saw the "Dad" message scored higher than those who saw the control message.

Two-Way Interactions

A design with three factors produces *three* two-way interactions, and each has a separate *F*. Each interaction is produced by collapsing across *one* factor. Collapsing across gender produces the interaction of Before–After and Dad–Control messages, shown here:

	Before	*After*
"Dad"	$\overline{X} = 9$	$\overline{X} = 16$
Control	$\overline{X} = 9$	$\overline{X} = 10$

Each cell mean is based on both males' and females' scores. Note that the difference between the Dad and control messages is greater in the After-message condition. (To put it another way, the difference between Before message and After message *depends* on the type of message.) Apparently, therefore, there is an interaction effect between these two factors.

To produce the other two-way interactions, we collapse across the third factor as shown here:

Gender and type of message interaction	*Male*	*Female*
"Dad"	$\overline{X} = 15$	$\overline{X} = 10$
Control	$\overline{X} = 10$	$\overline{X} = 9$

Gender and before–after interaction	*Male*	*Female*
Before	$\overline{X} = 10$	$\overline{X} = 8$
After	$\overline{X} = 15$	$\overline{X} = 11$

On the left, collapsing across Before–After produces the interaction between Gender and Type of Message. Note that the difference between the "Dad" and control messages is greater for males than it is for females. (To put it another way, the difference between males and females depends on which message they receive.) Thus, there is an apparent interaction effect here.

On the right, collapsing across Type of Message produces the interaction between Gender and Before–After. Here, males show a greater increase from Before to After than do females. (In other words, the difference between males and females depends on whether we examine the Before scores or the After scores.) Thus, we apparently have a two-way interaction effect here, too.

The Three-Way Interaction

Finally, we do not collapse across any factor, computing an F for the three-way interaction: This is the effect of simultaneously changing the levels of all three factors. We saw that in a two-way interaction, the effect of one variable changes depending on the level of the second factor we examine. In a **three-way interaction effect,** the two-way interaction between any two variables changes depending on which level of the third factor we examine. (Conversely, if the three-way interaction is not significant, then we have basically the same two-way interaction regardless of the level of the third factor we examine.) The only way to understand a three-way interaction is to graph it. Graphing the original cell means from Table 8.13 produces the three-way interaction in Figure 8.8. Notice

FIGURE 8.8   Graphs Showing How the Two-Way Interaction between Pretest and Posttest and "Dad"–Control Message Changes as a Function of Participant Gender

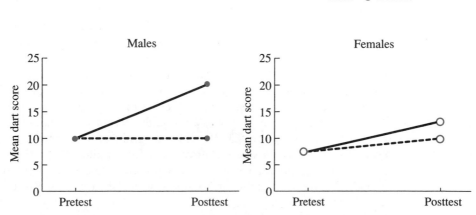

that the pattern in each graph (the form of the "<") changes depending on whether participants are male or female. For males, there is a dramatic change from pretest to posttest scores with the "Dad" message, but the control males show no change. For females, there is a different two-way interaction: There is slight improvement in dart-throwing following the control message, suggesting that the control females benefited from practice at throwing darts. Following the "Dad" message, experimental females showed a slight, additional improvement beyond the practice effects of the control females. Thus, the "Dad" message had a minimal positive influence on females, so maybe they aren't intensely guilty about competing with their fathers to begin with. There is dramatic improvement after the "Dad" message among males, however, so maybe males do feel guilty about this competition, and thus the message reduces an otherwise serious restriction on their performance.

> **REMEMBER**   A *three-way interaction effect* occurs when the interaction between two factors changes depending on which level of the third factor is present.

In a published report (using the APA format discussed in Appendix A), a three-way interaction is always plotted on *one* set of *X–Y* axes. Thus, the four line graphs in Figure 8.8 would be plotted on one graph. We identify the different conditions by using different styles of lines. As shown in the legend in Figure 8.8, for example, we can use solid lines for experimental groups and dashed lines for controls, combined with solid dots for males and open dots for females. Thus, ●————● connects the means of the Male–Experimental group, ○————○ connects the means of the Female–Experimental group, ●--------● connects those of the Male–Control group, and ○--------○ connects those of the Female–Control group.

Of course, we would not believe any of the previous interpretations unless the main effects and interactions were significant, and for each we'd perform post hoc comparisons to determine which specific means differ significantly. (And yes, you can use the Tukey HSD here, too.) Then, as usual, we interpret the results by first focusing on significant interactions, because they contradict main effects. A significant three-way interaction, however, contradicts any two-way interactions: Above we saw that the two-way interaction between Dad–Control and Before–After *depends on* whether it involves males or females. Therefore, the interpretation of a three-way design focuses on the significant three-way interaction. Thus, based on Figure 8.8, we would attempt to explain the psychological reasons behind why the "Dad" message produced a dramatic improvement in scores for males but a small improvement for females. If the three-way interaction is not significant, we focus on significant two-way interactions. If these interactions are not significant, we focus on significant main effects.

THE TWO-WAY CHI SQUARE

Recall that there are times when we do not measure the *amount* of a variable but, rather, we count whether someone falls into one or another *category* of a variable. In Chapter 7 we used the one-way chi square to determine whether the frequency of category membership differed significantly along one variable. With two such variables, we compute the **two-way chi square**, again calculating χ^2. For example, we might categorize people in terms of their gender and political party, counting the frequency of male Republicans, female Republicans, and so on. Or, say that back in our mood-and-helping study, we conduct a manipulation check and categorize those participants who report having a negative or a positive mood after testing. Then, we count the number of people who helped as a function of type of mood. A requirement of chi square, however, is that the responses of *all* participants in the sample be included, so we must count both the frequency of participants who helped *and* of those who did not. Let's say we obtain the data shown in Table 8.14. Here, we have a 2×2 design in which we categorize participants along two variables: whether they were in a positive or negative mood and whether they were helpful or not. (Other designs might be a 2×3, a 4×3, etc.)

Although this looks like a two-way ANOVA, the two-way chi square examines only the *interaction* of the two variables. That is, we determine whether the frequencies in the categories of one variable *depend* on which category of the other variable we examine. (The two-way chi-square is also called the "test of independence.") Here, we will determine whether the frequency of helping or not helping is independent of participants' mood. Essentially, we ask whether a relationship exists between the two variables. When the variables are independent, there is no relationship between category membership on one variable and category membership on the other variable. In Table 8.14, however, the two variables appear somewhat related or dependent: Saying "No" is more often associated with being in a negative mood, and saying "Yes" is more often associated with being in a positive mood.

The null hypothesis is that the variables are "really" independent in the population, and that any appearance of a relationship is due to sampling error. If the

TABLE 8.14 Frequency of Participants Who Helped or Did Not Help as a Function of Their Reported Mood

		Mood	
		Negative	Positive
Helping	Yes	5	18
	No	20	2

obtained χ^2 is significant (calculations in Appendix C.10), we conclude that the variables are dependent. Thus, we would conclude that the frequency of helping or not helping depends on a person's mood. We would then examine the type and strength of the relationship and, using this information, attempt to explain "psychologically" why those participants in a positive mood were more likely to help.

REMEMBER   A significant *two-way chi square* indicates that category membership along one variable is dependent on or related to category membership along the other variable.

DESCRIBING EFFECT SIZE

Our discussions have treated all independent variables as being of equal importance. In nature, however, some variables are more important than others. Therefore, a critical question in any experiment is "How important is this independent variable?" In answering this question, do not confuse importance with significance. "Significant" indicates only that the data reflect a "real" relationship and not a chance pattern of scores produced by sampling error. To be important, a variable must first produce a significant relationship. But, a significant relationship is not necessarily important.

In experiments, we determine a variable's importance by measuring its effect size. **Effect size** is an indication of how dramatically an independent variable influences a dependent variable. Presumably, manipulating the independent variable "causes" participants' scores—and behavior—to change. The effect size indicates the extent to which the manipulation causes this change.

One crude measure of effect size is the difference between the means of the conditions. Say that after manipulating three levels of mood, we obtain the helping scores shown here:

	Mood level	
Negative	*Neutral*	*Positive*
0	5	12
4	13	19
8	18	29
$\overline{X} = 4$	$\overline{X} = 12$	$\overline{X} = 20$

The difference between these means averages out to 8 points. Because this seems to be a relatively large difference in helping scores, we can argue that mood has a relatively large *effect* on a person's helping behavior.

The problem, however, is that we have no way of knowing whether a difference of 8 points is really a large difference in nature, so we must be very subjective when evaluating it. Further, an important variable need *not* produce large differences in the behavior. Rather, a scientifically important variable will *consistently* influence the behavior in question. Recall that the degree of consistency or inconsistency in a relationship indicates the extent to which variables other than our factor influence dependent scores. Therefore, when describing an independent variable's effect size, we usually compute how *consistently* the variable influences the behavior. The generic name for this computation is *the proportion of variance accounted for*.

Understanding the Proportion of Variance Accounted For

To evaluate the importance of a relationship, we examine the data from two perspectives. First, we examine the scores as if there were no independent variable—as if we had simply measured the entire sample of participants on the dependent variable. Then, we determine how much information is gained if we do not ignore the independent variable. We do this by looking at the variance. In an experiment, the term *proportion of variance accounted for* is a shortened version of *the proportion of total variance in the dependent scores that is accounted for by the relationship with the independent variable*. The total variance in dependent scores is simply a measure of how much all of the scores in the study differ from one another when we ignore the independent variable. For example, let's say we compare the helping scores of people in the conditions of positive or negative mood. We obtain the scores shown below.

Finding the total variance in dependent scores		*Finding the systematic variance in dependent scores*	
		Negative	Positive
4	8	4	8
4	8	4	8
4	8	4	8
Overall $\overline{X} = 6$		$\overline{X} = 4$	$\overline{X} = 8$

On the left, we ignore the levels of the independent variable and simply compute the total variance in the scores—how much the six scores differ from the overall mean of the study. On the right, we do not ignore the independent variable, grouping scores in their respective conditions. Look what happens: All of the differences in scores occur *between* the conditions with no differences in scores *within* a condition. In other words, there is no error variance. Rather, all of the differences between scores form systematic variance. **Systematic variance** refers to that portion of the differences among the scores that is associated with changes in the independent variable. It is the changes in scores that occur with—are related to—changing the conditions.

Because this is a perfectly consistent relationship, all of the total variance is systematic variance. Thus, the mood factor accounts for 100% of the variance. Or, as a proportion, it accounts for 1.0 of the total variance in helping scores. In an experiment, the **proportion of variance accounted for** is the proportion of total variance in dependent scores that is systematic variance. In other words, it is the proportion of total variance in scores that is associated with or related to changes in the independent variable.

We "account" for the variance in helping scores in that we know when and why different scores occur. Participants will have a score of 4 when their mood is negative. They will have a *different* score of 8 when their mood is positive. Thus, the effect size of the mood manipulation is 1.0: It produces or accounts for *all* of the observed differences in helping behavior.

A perfectly consistent relationship does not normally occur, so we usually won't account for 100% of the variance. For example, we might obtain the following helping scores:

Total variance in dependent scores		Systematic variance owing to mood	
		Negative	Positive
2	6	2	6
4	8	4	8
6	10	6	10
Overall $\overline{X}$ = 6		$\overline{X}$ = 4	$\overline{X}$ = 8
Total variance = 6.67		Error variance = 2.67	

Again, on the left, we ignore the independent variable and obtain the total variance, the amount that all scores differ from the mean of the experiment. Say that we calculate this variance as 6.67. On the right, when we do not ignore the independent variable, we see that although there is a relationship, there is also some error variance. With negative mood, scores are around the mean of 4, but some are above and some are below. With positive mood, scores are around 8. Essentially, we compute the error variance by determining the amount the scores in each condition differ from the mean of the condition and then average across the different conditions. Here, the error variance is 2.67.

Of all the differences between the scores in a study, to some extent the differences are associated with changing the independent variable, and to some extent they are not. In other words, the total variance is the sum of the systematic variance plus the error variance. Thus, out of a total variance of 6.67, about 2.67 is error variance, and the remainder is systematic variance. Whether 2.67 represents a large amount is difficult to judge, so to make this number easier to interpret, we transform it into a proportion of the total: 2.67 divided by 6.67 equals .40. In this study, 40% of the total variance in scores is error variance. This means that 60% of the total variance is not error variance, so it must be systematic variance. Thus, the effect size of the independent variable is .60: Of all the differences in the study, 60% of them are associated with and presumably caused by changing the independent variable.

One other way to interpret the proportion of variance accounted for is in terms of how well the relationship allows us to predict each participant's score—and behavior. When ignoring the independent variable, we would predict each participant's score as the overall mean score, and be in error—be "off"—by whatever amount the actual scores differ from the mean. The differences between the actual scores and the overall mean comprise the total variance, so using the overall mean of 6, we are off by an "average" of 6.67. However, when we consider the conditions of the independent variable, our best estimate of participants' scores is the mean of their condition. By predicting that people will score around 4 when in a negative mood and around 8 when in a positive mood, we are closer to their actual scores than if we predicted a score of 6 for them. How much closer? Using the mean of each condition, our predictions are off by only an average of 2.67, compared with being off by 6.67 when we ignore the relationship. In other words, our errors when using this relationship are 40% of what they are when we ignore the relationship, so using the relationship improves predictions by 60%: We are, on average, 60% closer—60% more accurate—when we use the means of the conditions to predict scores than when we use the overall mean of all scores. Thus, by using the relationship between helping and mood, we are 60% more accurate in predicting, explaining, and understanding the differences in helping scores than if we do not consider this relationship.

REMEMBER   The *proportion of variance accounted for* is the proportional improvement in predictions that is achieved when we use a relationship to predict scores, compared with if we did not use the relationship.

In actual research, the effect size of a particular factor is usually in the neighborhood of .15 to .30. In plain English, the proportion of variance accounted for tells us how much better off we are by knowing about and using a relationship than if we had never heard of it. Therefore, we can use the proportion of variance accounted for to evaluate the importance of different independent variables. Say that variable A accounts for .10 of the variance in a particular behavior, while variable B accounts for .20 of the variance. Variable B is twice as important for understanding the behavior as variable A: We are twice as accurate in knowing when and why participants will exhibit a particular score and behavior under the conditions of B than we are by knowing their condition under A. Essentially, by studying variable B, we are 20% better at understanding the behavior than if we had not studied this variable. By studying variable A, we are only 10% better off than if we had not bothered. (Recognize, however, that effect size indicates importance in a statistical sense, not in a practical sense: A variable that accounts for only 3% of *deaths* is, practically speaking, very important. Scientifically, though, it does not advance our knowledge greatly.)

Any time you obtain a *significant* effect of an independent variable in an experiment, you should determine its effect size. (With a nonsignificant result, you cannot believe that a "real" relationship even exists, so a nonsignificant effect always accounts for zero proportion of the variance.) The proportion of variance accounted for is *the* way to determine whether a relationship is scientifically important or merely much ado about nothing. In fact, the American Psychological Association (1994) now wants all published research to include a measure of effect size. Effect size has not always been reported in the literature, and huge, elaborate experiments have been performed to study what are actually very minor variables. By computing effect size, you determine the importance of your variables.

REMEMBER The *effect size* of an independent variable indicates how dramatically it influences dependent scores and, thus, how important it is for understanding the dependent behavior.

Computing the Proportion of Variance Accounted For

Mathematically, comparing the total variance to the error variance to compute the proportion of variance accounted for as we did earlier can be accomplished by simply computing an appropriate *correlation coefficient* and then *squaring* it. (Recall that a correlation coefficient is a statistic that summarizes the strength of a relationship, and as you saw above, the weaker a relationship, the smaller the proportion of variance accounted for.) As usual, however, there are different formulas to use, depending on your scale of measurement and the nature of your design.

1. **The Point-biserial Correlation Coefficient** When you have two conditions of the independent variable and perform a *t*-test, compute the squared **point-biserial correlation coefficient**. Symbolized as r^2_{pb}, this statistic describes the effect size of two conditions of the independent variable on an interval or ratio dependent variable (calculations in Appendix C.6).

2. **Eta Squared** When you perform any of the single- or multifactor ANOVAs that we have discussed, determine the proportion of variance accounted for by each significant main effect or interaction by computing **eta squared**, symbolized as η^2 (calculations in Appendix C.6). There are also nonparametric versions of η^2 for use with ranked scores (also in

Appendix C). In multifactor designs, use the size of each η^2 to determine the emphasis to give to a factor when interpreting the study. The larger the η^2, the more important the main effect or interaction was in influencing scores in the experiment, so the more central it should be in your interpretation. Note that the one exception to the rule of always focusing on the significant interaction is when it has a very small effect size. Recall that an interaction contradicts the general pattern shown in a main effect. However, if the interaction has a very small effect size, then it only slightly and inconsistently contradicts the main effect. In this case, focus your interpretation on any more substantial significant main effects instead.

3. **The Phi and Contingency Coefficients**   There is no measure of effect size for a one-way chi square. For the two-way chi square, describe effect size by computing either of the following (shown in Appendix C.10). When dealing with a 2×2 design, compute the squared **phi coefficient**. When dealing with a two-way design that is *not* a 2×2 (e.g., a 3×2, a 3×3, etc.), compute the squared **contingency coefficient**. Each indicates how much you can account for or predict the frequency of category membership on one variable by considering category membership on the other variable. In the study described back in Table 8.14, for example, we would see the degree to which the frequency of helping behavior is determined by participants' mood.

A WORD ABOUT MULTIVARIATE STATISTICS AND META-ANALYSIS

In the literature, you'll encounter two types of research approaches that expand on the designs we have discussed. The first approach is called "multivariate statistics."

Everything we've discussed has involved *one* dependent variable, and so our statistics are called **univariate statistics**. Researchers can, however, measure participants on two or more dependent variables in *one* experiment. For example, in our mood study, we might have measured helping behavior as well as participants' attitudes toward the experimenter. Statistics for multiple dependent variables are called **multivariate statistics**. These include the multivariate *t*-test and the multivariate analysis of variance (MANOVA). Although these are very complex procedures, the basic logic still holds: If the results are significant, the observed relationships are unlikely to be the result of sampling error. Given these significant results, the researcher then examines the influence of each independent variable on each dependent variable, using the *t*-tests or ANOVAs we've discussed.

The other new approach is "meta-analysis." Recall that, ultimately, our confidence in the external validity of research is developed through studies that literally and conceptually *replicate* a finding. Rather than subjectively evaluating the extent to which several studies support a particular hypothesis, however, researchers perform a meta-analysis. **Meta-analysis** is a statistical procedure for combining, testing, and describing the results from different studies. For example, Carlson, Marcus-Newhall, and Miller (1990) performed a meta-analysis of some 22 published studies that investigated the influence of cues for aggression (e.g., weapons) on participants' aggressive behavior. With meta-analysis, researchers generally take one of two approaches: Either they determine whether the experiments taken together consistently show a significant effect of a particular variable, or they estimate the effect size of a variable based on all of the studies.

On the one hand, a meta-analysis provides objective methods for generalizing a variable's effect, and because the results are based on many participants tested under varying procedures, we have a high degree of confidence in the conclusions. On the other hand, a meta-analysis glosses over many differences in operational definitions, controls, measurement procedures, and other aspects of the studies. Therefore, although a meta-analysis adds to our understanding of a behavior, we must necessarily speak in *very* general terms.

PUTTING IT ALL TOGETHER

There is no limit to the number of factors you can test in an ANOVA. You can study four independent variables and perform a four-way ANOVA, or you can create a five-way design, and so on. There are, however, practical limits to such designs. The number of participants needed becomes quite large, and the counterbalancing scheme or stimulus requirements become extremely complex. Although with effort these problems can be solved, researchers are also limited by their ability to *interpret* such studies. If you conduct a "simple" four-way study—a ($2 \times 2 \times 2 \times 2$) design—the ANOVA provides separate Fs for four main effects, six two-way interactions, four three-way interactions, and one monster four-way interaction (there would be eight lines on its graph). If this sounds very complicated, it's because it *is* very complicated. Three-way interactions are difficult to interpret, and interactions with more than three factors are practically impossible to interpret.

Remember that a major concern of science is to simplify the complexity found in nature. Duplicating this complexity in a study is counterproductive. Therefore, unless you have a good reason for including many factors in one experiment, it is best to examine only two or, at most, three factors at a time. Then, conduct additional experiments to investigate the influence of other variables. In each, you can perform a literal replication of portions of your previous studies, thus greatly increasing their internal and external validity. And, although you will not learn of the simultaneous interactions of many variables, you will understand what you do learn.

CHAPTER SUMMARY

1. In a *multifactor experiment*, the researcher examines several independent variables and their interactions. In a *complete factorial design*, all levels of one factor are combined with all levels of the other factor.

2. In a *two-way between-subjects ANOVA*, there is no matching or repeated measures of participants in conditions of either of the two independent variables. In a *two-way within-subjects ANOVA*, matched groups or the same repeatedly measured participants are tested in all conditions of two independent variables. In a *two-way mixed design*, one within-subjects and one between-subjects factor is examined.

3. In any two-way ANOVA, an *F* is computed for the *main effect* of each factor and for the *interaction*.

4. A *main effect* of a factor is the effect that changing the levels of that factor has on dependent scores, while collapsing across—ignoring—all other factors in the study.

5. An *interaction effect* is the influence that the combination of levels from the factors has on the dependent scores. In a *two-way interaction*, the relationship between one factor and the dependent scores is different for and depends on each level of the other factor. When the cell means of a significant interaction are graphed, the lines are not parallel.

6. A *simple main effect* is the effect of one factor at one level of a second factor within the interaction. Post hoc comparisons in an interaction should involve only *unconfounded comparisons*—comparisons of cell means that differ along only one factor.

7. Because an interaction contradicts the overall pattern suggested by the main effects, the interpretation of a study usually focuses on the significant interaction.

8. A *three-way design* produces three main effects, three two-way interactions, and a three-way interaction. In a *three-way interaction*, the two-way interaction between two factors changes as the levels of the third factor change.

9. The *two-way chi square procedure* is used when counting the frequency with which participants fall into the categories of two variables. If χ^2 is significant, the frequency of participants in the different categories of one variable depends on their category membership along the other variable.

10. For any significant main effect or interaction, the *effect size* indicates how dramatically the variable influences the dependent scores.

11. The *total variance* in dependent scores indicates how much all of the scores in the study differ, and it equals the error variance plus the systematic variance. *Systematic variance* refers to the differences in scores that occur with, or are associated with, changes in the conditions.

12. Calculating effect size as the *proportion of variance accounted for* indicates the proportion of total variance in dependent scores that is systematic variance. It reflects the proportional improvement in predictions that is achieved when we use a relationship to predict scores, compared with if we do not use the relationship.

13. The effect size is calculated as (1) the *squared point-biserial correlation coefficient* when performing a *t*-test, or (2) *eta squared* for each significant factor or interaction effect when performing ANOVA.

14. The effect size in a significant 2 × 2 chi square is the *squared phi coefficient*. With a two-way design that is not a 2 × 2, effect size is the *squared contingency coefficient*.

15. *Multivariate statistics* are inferential statistical procedures for a study involving more than one dependent variable.

16. *Meta-analysis* involves statistical procedures for combining, testing, and describing the results from different studies.

KEY TERMS   (with page references)

cell 228	simple main effect 237
complete factorial design 228	systematic variance 253
contingency coefficient 257	three-way design 247
effect size 252	three-way interaction effect 249
eta squared 256	two-way between-subjects ANOVA
factorial design 228	229
interaction effect 231	two-way chi square 251
main effect 229	two-way design 226
meta-analysis 258	two-way interaction effect 232
multifactor experiment 226	two-way mixed design 243
multivariate statistics 257	two-way within-subjects ANOVA
phi coefficient 257	241
point-biserial correlation coefficient 256	unconfounded comparisons 238
proportion of variance accounted for 254	univariate statistics 257

REVIEW QUESTIONS

1. (a) What are the reasons for conducting multifactor designs? (b) What is a complete factorial design?

2. A student hears about a 2 × 3 design and concludes that six factors were examined. Is this correct? Why or why not?

3. What is the difference between a two-way within-subjects ANOVA and (a) a two-way between-subjects ANOVA? (b) a two-way mixed ANOVA?

4. Identify the *F*s that are computed in (a) a two-way ANOVA involving factors *A* and *B*. (b) A three-way design with the factors A, B, C? (c) What does a three-way interaction effect indicate?

5. (a) What is the difference between a main effect mean and a cell mean? (b) What does it mean to collapse across a factor?

6. (a) A significant main effect indicates what about an independent variable? (b) A significant interaction effect indicates what about an independent variable? (c) Why do we usually base the interpretation of a two-way design on the interaction when it is significant?

7. In a 3 × 4 ANOVA, all effects are significant. What other statistical procedures are appropriate?

8. (a) When is it appropriate to compute the *effect size* in ANOVA? (b) What does the effect size tell you?

9. (a) What is the difference between systematic variance and error variance? (b) What does the total variance refer to? (c) In terms of the concepts in parts (a) and (b), what does "the proportion of variance accounted for" refer to?

10. Why does "the proportion of variance accounted for" indicate how important an independent variable is?

11. What statistic indicates the proportion of variance accounted for in (a) the *t*-test? (b) an ANOVA? (c) the chi square?

APPLICATION QUESTIONS

12. A researcher studies participants' frustration levels when solving problems both as a function of the difficulty of the problem and as a function of whether they are math or logic problems. She finds that logic problems produce more frustration than math problems, that greater difficulty leads to greater frustration, and that more difficult logic problems produce greater frustration than more difficult math problems. In the ANOVA performed for this study, what effects are significant?

13. In question 12, say the researcher instead found that math and logic problems lead to the same frustration levels, that frustration consistently increases with greater difficulty, and that this is true for both math and logic problems. In the ANOVA performed for this study, what effects are significant?

14. To study the volunteer bias, you advertise your experiment first as a memory study and again later as an attitude study. For each, you pass around a sign-up sheet in some psychology courses and then count the number of volunteers who actually show up for the experiment. (a) What statistical procedure should you use? (b) What factor (or factors) do you examine?

15. A researcher examines performance on an eye–hand coordination task as a function of three levels of reward and three levels of practice, obtaining the following cell means:

Reward

		Low	*Medium*	*High*
	Low	4	10	7
Practice	*Medium*	5	5	14
	High	15	15	15

(a) What are the main effect means for reward, and what do they indicate about this factor? (b) What are the main effect means for practice, and what do they indicate?

16. (a) In question 15, is an interaction effect likely? (b) How would you perform unconfounded post hoc comparisons of the cell means? (c) What would be confounded comparisons?

17. (a) In question 15, why does the interaction contradict your conclusions about the effect of reward? (b) Why does the interaction contradict your conclusions about practice?

18. (a) What is a simple main effect? (b) In question 15, what will the simple main effects of reward (at each practice level) apparently indicate?

19. In question 15, the researcher reports that the effect size of reward is .14, that the effect size of practice is .31, and that the interaction accounts for .01 of the variance. What does each value indicate about the influence of these effects?

20. In a research report, you read that the researcher used (a) a meta-analysis, (b) a multivariate statistic, or (c) a univariate statistic. Based on this information, what do you know about each study?

21. The following are the cell means of three experiments. For each experiment, compute the main effect means and indicate whether there appears to be an effect of A, B, or A × B.

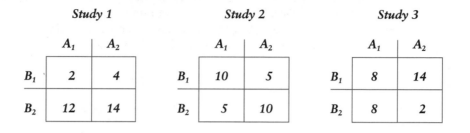

	Study 1			Study 2			Study 3	
	A_1	A_2		A_1	A_2		A_1	A_2
B_1	2	4	B_1	10	5	B_1	8	14
B_2	12	14	B_2	5	10	B_2	8	2

22. In question 21, if you graph the cell means (labeling the X axis with factor A), what pattern will you see for each interaction?

23. In an experiment, you measure the popularity of two brands of soft drinks (factor A), and for each brand you test males and females (factor B). The following table shows the main effect and cell means from the study:

Factor A: Brand

		Brand X	Brand Y	
Factor B: Gender	Male	14	23	18.5
	Female	25	12	18.5
		19.5	17.5	

(a) Describe the graph of the interaction means with factor A on the X axis. (b) Does there appear to be an interaction effect? Why? (c) Why will a significant interaction prohibit you from making conclusions about the main effects?

DISCUSSION QUESTIONS

24. Create a graph of the interaction in the reaction-time study shown in Table 8.10, placing "type of number" on the X axis.

25. In a study, factor A has 3 levels and factor B has 4 levels. In each cell, the n—the number of participants or scores—is 5. What is the n that occurs in each mean when examining (a) the main effect means of A? (b) the main effect means of B? (c) the interaction means?

26. Design a two-way study, diagram it, and place mean scores in each cell that appear to produce the predicted main effects and interactions.

27. In a between-subjects design, you investigate participants' hypnotic suggestibility as a function of whether they meditate before being tested and whether they were shown a film containing a low, medium, or high amount of fantasy. For the following data, perform all appropriate statistical analyses and determine what you should conclude about this study.

Amount of fantasy

		Low	Medium	High
	Meditation	5	7	9
		6	5	8
		2	6	10
		2	9	10
		5	5	10
Amount of meditation	No meditation	10	2	5
		10	5	6
		9	4	5
		10	3	7
		10	2	6

28. When designing a two- or three-way repeated-measures study with many trials and conditions, (a) what potential biases and confoundings owing to participants might be especially prominent? (b) What ethical concern arises regarding the demands you place on participants?

3 /////////

BEYOND THE TYPICAL LABORATORY EXPERIMENT

It's time to shift mental gears. Our previous discussions have focused on true laboratory experiments involving groups of human participants. Such studies are common in psychological research because they usually produce the greatest internal validity for arguing that a particular variable causes people's behavior to change. However, the goal is always to design the best study so that we can most clearly and confidently answer the question at hand. Therefore, psychologists often choose an alternative to the typical laboratory design. In some cases, the reason may be that the laboratory setting creates an artificial setting and the observed behavior is too unnatural. At other times, the variables cannot be manipulated or measured in a way that conforms to an experiment. And sometimes the hypothesis being tested and the goals of the research require a different approach. In these situations, other designs—or a combination of designs—are better suited for answering the research question. In the following chapters, we examine these other designs.

Correlational Research and Questionnaire Construction

Recall that researchers do not test only experimental or causal hypotheses but also descriptive hypotheses. The most common descriptive approach in psychological research is the **correlational design**. Here, we test the hypothesis that a relationship between the variables is present. The term *correlation* is synonymous with *relationship*, so in using a correlational design, we set out to describe the relationship—examine the correlation—between variables.

In this chapter, we will first discuss the logic of correlational designs and contrast them with experimental designs. Then, we'll review basic correlational statistics and discuss a number of ways they are used. Finally, we'll cover two major tools that are commonly used for gathering data in correlational designs: interviews and questionnaires.

THE DIFFERENCE BETWEEN TRUE EXPERIMENTS AND CORRELATIONAL STUDIES

Although both experimental and correlational designs are for demonstrating a relationship, they differ in *how* the researcher goes about it. To illustrate, consider a research hypothesis from industrial-organizational psychology: Supposedly "job satisfaction," the degree to which workers find their jobs satisfying, is related to their wages. In a true experiment, we might attempt to demonstrate this by manipulating the independent variable of amount of pay that participants receive while performing a laboratory task. For example, we could randomly assign people to various pay levels and have them perform a "job" of assembling "widgets" out of toy building blocks. Then, after an interval, we'd obtain participants' answers to a series of questions that measure their job satisfaction. Our research hypothesis implies the question, "For a given pay rate, what is a person's job satisfaction?" Recall that the "given" variable is always graphed as the X variable, and that we examine "Y scores as a function of X." Therefore, we place the independent variable of pay rate on the X axis and the dependent variable of job satisfaction on the Y axis. For now, we'll create a *scatterplot* of the individual data points that we might obtain, as shown in graph A of Figure 9.1. (As usual, I've created unrealistically symmetrical scatterplots so that you can easily see the pattern.)

The important thing to recognize here is that, by randomly assigning participants to a pay condition, we, the *researchers*, determine each person's X score: we decide whether their "score" will be \$3, \$6, or \$9. Then, we show that, for an *assigned* X, people tend to produce a certain Y score. On the other hand, the distinguishing aspect of a correlational design is that we do not manipulate the X variable, so we do not determine participants' X scores by assigning them to an amount of the variable. Rather, the X scores reflect an amount or category of a variable that the individual has *already* experienced. Thus, to conduct this study using a correlational design, we might randomly select some people who are already employed at jobs and then measure their hourly pay and their job satisfaction. As shown in graph B of Figure 9.1, we examine the same relationship as in the experiment: We again ask the question "For a given pay rate, what is a person's job satisfaction?"—so pay rate is still the X variable. But! Here, we show that for a *reported* X score of pay rate, people tend to produce a certain Y score of job satisfaction. Thus, the defining feature of a correlational design is that the participants are *not* randomly assigned to the levels of the X variable as with a true independent variable. Instead, the researcher is a more passive observer, merely looking for a relationship between the variables.

REMEMBER   In a *correlational design*, a participant's score on the X variable is an amount or category of the variable that the participant *already* demonstrates or has experienced.

Any of the approaches to measuring variables in experiments can also be used in correlational designs. A common approach is to measure participants' scores using different tests and then to correlate their scores (e.g., relating participants' intelligence test scores with their creativity test scores). Sometimes questions measuring several variables are included in one test (e.g., the *Minnesota Multiphasic Personality Inventory* or *MMPI* measures numerous variables), and then the researcher correlates scores from each variable. Researchers also examine the relationship between test scores and a physical or physiological attribute (e.g., relating participants' self-esteem scores to their gender). Or, we might obtain data from records, such as when examining police shooting incidents or the attendance records of factory workers. These may be "official" records, or we can have participants create the record themselves by keeping a diary to record certain behaviors. We can also examine environmental events (e.g., correlating daily temperature changes with the frequency of violence or depression). We may

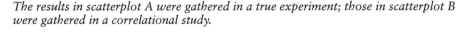

FIGURE 9.1   Job-Satisfaction Scores as a Function of Pay Rate

The results in scatterplot A were gathered in a true experiment; those in scatterplot B were gathered in a correlational study.

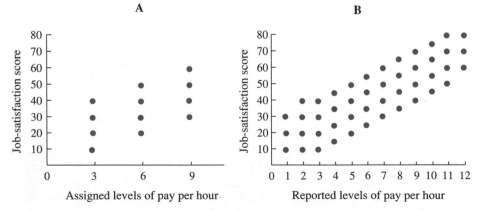

also measure one or the other variable in a laboratory procedure, such as correlating reaction times with intelligence or personality scores.

Interpreting Correlational Designs

Our confidence in the conclusions drawn from a correlational design is influenced by the same concerns we saw previously with experiments. Thus, the procedures for measuring each variable should have *construct* and *content validity*. They should be *reliable* and provide *sensitive* measurements that can detect subtle differences in behavior. Extraneous influences such as *demand characteristics*, *response sets*, and the *volunteer bias* should be eliminated. And, as always, we seek consistency throughout by considering the four components of any study—the participants, environment, researcher, and measurement task.

However, recall that, compared to true experiments, correlational designs have two flaws that severely reduce internal validity for concluding that differences in the X variable *cause* differences in Y scores. The first flaw is that we do not randomly assign participants to a score on the X variable. Therefore, we do not control participant variables by randomizing and thus balancing them. Because of this, differences between participants on the X variable are very likely to be confounded by differences in extraneous variables. For example, in our job-satisfaction study, workers who differ in their existing pay rates might also differ in job type, length of employment, or education level. Because the variable of pay rate is confounded with these variables, we cannot say that it is pay that *causes* job satisfaction.

The second flaw in correlational designs is that often we cannot be certain that X occurred before Y. Yet to conclude that X causes Y, we must *know* that X occurred first. For example, we cannot know for sure that a worker's low pay rate occurred first, which then caused low job satisfaction. Perhaps for some reason participants were first dissatisfied with their job and, because of resulting poor motivation and performance, they then received low pay. Or, perhaps a third variable was operating first: Perhaps some workers suffered discrimination, and this caused both low pay and low job satisfaction.

Thus, the relationship found in a correlational design might mean that changes in X cause changes in Y, that changes in Y might cause changes in X, or that some third variable might change both the X and Y scores. Therefore, a single correlational study is, at most, interpreted as *suggesting* that changes in X cause changes in Y. It is for this reason that correlational designs are best for testing a descriptive hypothesis that a relationship exists between the variables.

REMEMBER   *Causal relationships are not inferred* from a correlational study, because (1) the absence of random assignment allows for potential confoundings and (2) the order of occurrence of the variables is unknown.

Reasons for Using the Correlational Approach

Though we must accept the limited evidence for causality found in a correlational design, it is still a legitimate research method. In fact, a correlational design may be preferable for four reasons.

First, because of ethical and practical considerations, some relationships cannot be studied using a true experimental design. For example, physical and sexual abuse, accidents, crime, and recreational drug use are important psychological variables. Ethically, however, we cannot study such variables by assigning people to experience them in a true experiment. Likewise, many variables simply cannot be manipulated, such as a person's career, race, gender, personality traits, or mental and physical illness. On the other hand, such variables and behaviors do occur in the real world, so we *can* study them through correlational methods. In fact, although any *single* correlational study provides poor evidence of causality, through literal and conceptual replication, together with experimental studies of relevant constructs, we can even eventually develop some confidence that we have identified the causes involved with such variables.

Second, correlational procedures are useful for discovering new relationships. For example, we might measure workers on numerous variables that we suspect are related to job satisfaction (their work history, training level, motivation, pay, and so on) and then discover which variables produce relationships. Such research is useful not only for describing behavior but also for identifying relationships that might be causal that we can then investigate using experimental designs.

Third, a laboratory experiment creates a rather artificial situation and involves only participants who will come to us. An advantage of the correlational approach is that often it can be conducted outside of the laboratory, where, potentially we have greater *ecological* and *external validity*. For example, measuring the pay and job satisfaction of employed workers is a more valid way to study this relationship than studying laboratory subjects who make widgets.

Finally, recall that part of understanding a behavior is being able to predict when it will occur. The relationship found in a correlational study may be better for predicting behaviors than that found in an experiment, because part of the greater external validity of a correlational design is that it usually provides a broader description of the relationship. Typically, an experiment involves a limited set of conditions (X scores) with gaps between them. For example, back in graph A of Figure 9.1, our experiment studied only the three pay rates of $3, $6, and $9 dollars per hour. Therefore, we have no data for predicting satisfaction levels for, say, a $5 or $7 rate. In a correlational study, however, we are likely to obtain a wider variety of X scores to relate to Y, thus possibly improving predictions. Look at graph B of Figure 9.1. Here, actual workers reported pay rates between $3 and $12 per hour, so we have data for predicting job satisfaction scores throughout a much wider range of pay.

Because of this wider range, a correlational design is often preferred in *applied research* were we create a **selection test**. If, for example, people take a test when applying for a job, they are taking a selection test. The logic is that previous correlational research might have shown that people who score higher on the test also tend to be better workers. Therefore, only those job applicants who perform above a certain score on the test will be hired, because we predict that they will also be better workers. Similar selection tests are being used when people take college entrance exams for predicting their future college performance, or when clinical patients take diagnostic tests for identifying people who are at risk of developing emotional problems.

> **REMEMBER** Correlational designs are useful for *discovering relationships*, they *solve ethical and practical problems*, and they may provide *better validity and accuracy in predictions*.

ANALYZING DATA WITH CORRELATIONAL STATISTICS

Usually, data from correlational research is analyzed by first computing a correlation coefficient. A **correlation coefficient** is a statistic—a number calculated using the pairs of X and Y scores in the sample data—that summarizes the type and strength of the relationship that is present. However, computing a correlation coefficient does *not* create a correlational *design*. A correlational design occurs whenever you do not randomly assign participants to the levels of the variable, *regardless* of how the data are analyzed. You can compute correlations within experimental designs, and you can apply ANOVAs or *t*-tests to correlational designs. Generally, the rule is this: On the one hand, ANOVA, *t*-tests, and similar procedures are the primary analysis when the X variable consists of a few different levels or X scores. Then, we examine the mean Y score per condition and look at how the means change as a function of changes in X. On the other hand, correlational statistics are the primary method of analysis when the X variable consists of a wide range of scores. Usually, we don't compute the mean of Y for each X here, because we'd end up with an unwieldy number of different means that would be difficult to compare. For example, using an ANOVA to compare the mean job-satisfaction score for each of 20 different pay rates would be overwhelming. Instead, we use the correlation coefficient to summarize the *entire* relationship formed by all of the data at once. This is the major advantage of a correlation coefficient: It takes a very complex relationship involving a wide range of scores and simplifies it into one easily interpreted statistic.

> **REMEMBER** The advantage of a *correlation coefficient* is that it summarizes a relationship with one number.

As with other statistics, the specific correlation coefficient to compute depends on the nature of the X and Y scores we measure. Most psychological research typically involves the **Pearson correlation coefficient**, which is the parametric procedure used to describe the *linear* relationship between normally distributed interval or ratio scores (calculations are given in Appendix C.8). Symbolized by r, this statistic is technically the "Pearson Product Moment Correlation Coefficient." Also, a common nonparametric procedure is the **Spearman correlation coefficient**. This coefficient is employed when both variables are measured using an ordinal scale, showing participants' rank order (calculations given in Appendix C.9). Other types of coefficients are used with other types of data, but, regardless, we interpret every coefficient in the same way.

To see how the correlation coefficient communicates the type and strength of a relationship between variables, let's correlate workers' job satisfaction scores with their corresponding pay rates, as shown in Figure 9.2. These are both normally distributed ratio scales, so we compute the Pearson r. Summarizing the data in this way is usually the starting point for most correlational research, because a straight-line relationship is the simplest, most common type. An r will have a value between -1.0 and $+1.0$. A positive coefficient indicates a positive linear relationship (as in scatterplot A of Figure 9.2.) A negative value indicates a negative linear relationship (as in scatterplot B). The absolute value of the coefficient communicates the strength of the relationship. A value of ± 1.0 indicates a perfectly consistent relationship in which *one* value of Y is associated with only one value of X so that all data points fall on a straight line. A coefficient less than ± 1.0 indicates the degree to which the data approximate a perfect linear relationship. The way to interpret an r less than ± 1 is to compare it to 1: The closer the r is to 1, then the closer we are to having one value of Y at each X, and the more the scatterplot forms a straight line. For example, Figure 9.3 shows two intermediate-strength relationships. As the coefficient approaches 0, it indicates a less consistent linear relationship, with greater variability in Y scores at each value of X. Note that the components of a relationship in a correlation are analogous to those in an experiment, so the variability in Y scores at each X is again the *error variance*. In Figure 9.3, scatterplot A shows greater error variance and

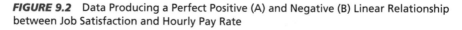

FIGURE 9.2 Data Producing a Perfect Positive (A) and Negative (B) Linear Relationship between Job Satisfaction and Hourly Pay Rate

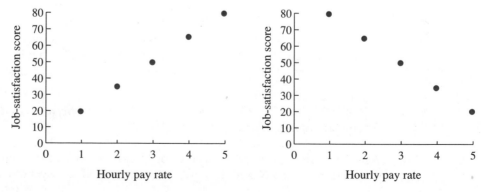

FIGURE 9.3 Two Scatterplots Showing Intermediate-Strength Relationships Between Job-Satisfaction Scores and Hourly Pay Rate

Data in A produce a smaller r *than the data in B.*

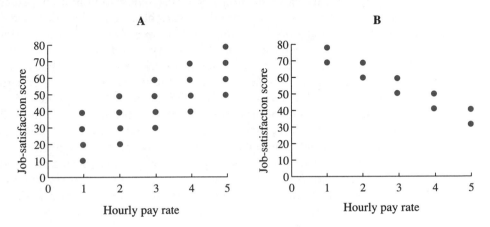

thus a less consistent relationship, which produces a lower correlation coefficient than in scatterplot B.

As a frame of reference, a relationship in psychological research is considered reasonably strong when it produces an *r* in the neighborhood of ±.40. Any behavior is extremely complex and influenced by many variables, so any *single* variable will not show that strong of a relationship with the behavior. Therefore, for example, an *r* of +.60 is downright impressive.

At the opposite extreme, Figure 9.4 shows data that do not form a relationship, and so *r* equals zero. This pattern is as far as you can get from a straight line, and *r* = 0 is as far as you can get from ±1.

Of course, merely calculating the correlation coefficient is not enough. As with experiments, it might be that the relationship in the sample data is the result of

FIGURE 9.4 Data Producing No Relationship Between Hourly Pay Rate and Job Satisfaction

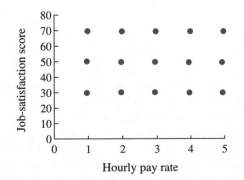

random chance—a coincidental pairing of *X–Y* scores so that by luck we happen to see a linear pattern. For example, it's possible that in nature, job satisfaction and pay rate are *not* really related, but by luck, the workers we selected at each pay rate produced satisfaction scores that tend to fall in a line, creating the illusion of a relationship between these variables. If so, then the *r* we've calculated reflects nothing more than sampling error, poorly representing a population correlation of 0. Therefore, you must always determine whether any correlation coefficient you've computed is significant (as described in Appendix C.8).

If the correlation coefficient is significant, we're confident that the relationship is not a chance occurrence and so it is "believable." Then, we interpret the study by examining the value of the correlation coefficient. Say, for example, that job satisfaction and pay rates produce a significant *r* of +.50. First, we know that there is a positive linear relationship here. Originally, we predicted a positive relationship, so this *r* confirms the hypothesis. (Recall that in statistics, such a prediction involves a *one-tailed test*.) A negative *r* would contradict and thus disconfirm the hypothesis. In a different study, we might predict merely some kind of relationship, either positive or negative (and use a *two-tailed test*). Then, either a positive or negative value of *r* would confirm the hypothesis.

Further, an *r* of +.50 indicates a strong, consistent relationship. As usual, the inconsistency in a relationship suggests the extent to which other variables are operating. An *r* of +.90, for example, would indicate extreme consistency, suggesting that only a few, rather unimportant variables are related to job satisfaction in addition to hourly pay. Conversely, an *r* of +.09 would indicate great inconsistency, suggesting there are other important variables related to job satisfaction that we have not considered. Following this line of reasoning, we interpret the results "psychologically," considering what the consistency and inconsistency in the relationship indicate about job satisfaction and hourly pay rate, and how they relate to the theoretical explanations, models, and constructs that we began with. However, this is a descriptive, correlational design, so do not infer causality.

For help in understanding the relationship, we perform additional statistical procedures, starting with linear regression.

Linear Regression

Perform linear regression only when the Pearson *r* is significant. **Linear regression** is the procedure for predicting participants' scores on one variable based on the linear relationship with their scores on another variable. Thus, once we know there is a significant, believable relationship between pay and job satisfaction, we can then predict a worker's job satisfaction by knowing his or her pay rate. Simultaneously, the linear regression procedure allows us to describe the straight line that summarizes a scatterplot, capturing the linear relationship in the data.

Perform regression procedures by using the sample data to calculate the **linear regression equation** (shown in Appendix C.8). This equation allows you to graph the straight line that summarizes the scatterplot, called the **linear regression line**. To draw the line, perform the following steps: (1) select some values of *X* and, using the regression equation, calculate the corresponding values of *Y*; (2) plot these *X*–*Y* data points; and (3) connect the data points with a straight line. For example, an idealized scatterplot and its corresponding regression line are shown in Figure 9.5. The regression line fits the scatterplot so that the distance some *Y* scores are above the line equals the distance other *Y* scores are below the line. Thus, the line summarizes the scatterplot by, on average, passing through the center of the *Y* scores at each *X*. Think of the regression line as reflecting the linear relationship hidden in the data. Because the actual *Y* scores fall above and below the line, the data more or less form this straight line. But there's no system for drawing a more or less straight line. Instead, the regression line is what a perfect version of the linear relationship hidden in the data would look like.

To read the regression line, travel vertically from any *X* until you intercept the regression line and then travel horizontally until you intercept the *Y* axis. The value of *Y* that you find is called "*Y* prime," symbolized as *Y*′. Each *Y*′ is a summary of the *Y* scores at *X* based on the linear relationship in the data. Because there is balance of the *Y* scores above and below the line, the value of *Y*′ at an *X* is *more* or *less* the *Y* score that everyone at that *X* obtained. Therefore, *Y*′ is our best prediction of any individual's *Y* score at that *X*. **Y prime** is the predicted value of *Y* for anyone who scores at a particular value of *X*. By entering the value of any *X* into the regression equation, we can calculate the corresponding *Y*′ score. In Figure 9.5, for example, we predict a *Y*′ of 30 for an *X* of $1. The *Y* scores are evenly spread out *around* (above and below) each value of *Y*′. So, considering the entire linear relationship, participants with an *X* of $1 scored *around* a *Y* of 30, so 30 is our best prediction and summary for any other person scoring an *X* of $1.

REMEMBER The *linear regression equation* summarizes the linear relationship in a sample of data, producing the *linear regression line*. From this, we use the relationship to predict the *Y* score—*Y*′—at any *X*.

FIGURE 9.5 Idealized Scatterplot Showing a Linear Regression Line

The arrow indicates Y′ for X = 1.

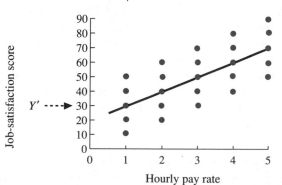

It is by using the regression procedure that we create *selection tests*. First, we measure a sample on both the X and Y variables to determine the regression equation. Then, after testing new individuals on the X variable, we enter their X scores into the regression equation and calculate their values of Y'. If a person's predicted Y' score meets our "criterion," he or she is selected for the job, and so on. Thus, for example, students must take the Scholastic Aptitude Test (SAT) to be admitted to some colleges, because researchers have already established that SAT scores are somewhat positively correlated with subsequent college grades. Therefore, by applying regression techniques to the SAT scores (X scores) of would-be college students, we predict their future college performance (their Y' score). If the predicted grades are too low, the student is not admitted to the college. (Because of this procedure, in correlational designs the X variable is also called the *predictor variable* and the Y variable is also called the *criterion variable*.)

Errors in Prediction and the Variance Accounted For

It is not enough to say that a relationship can be used to predict scores. We should know the amount of error to expect in such predictions so that we know how much credence to give them. To estimate the amount of error we'll have when predicting unknown scores, we examine how well we can predict the known scores in a sample. That is, we'll pretend we don't know the Y scores in the sample, predict them using the regression equation, and then compare the predicted Y' scores to the actual Y scores. The predictions for some participants will be close to their actual Y scores, while predictions for others may contain more error. Therefore, to summarize the error across the entire relationship, we compute *something like* the "average error" in the predictions.

To understand this, we'll start with those people paid $1 an hour, who we predict have a satisfaction score of 30. Our **error in prediction** is the difference between the score we predict for someone—Y'—and the score actually obtained—the Y score. Thus, if some of the workers paid $1 actually score 40, our prediction error is $40 - 30$ or $+10$. If they score 20, the error is $20 - 30$ or -10. And so on. To summarize the entire relationship, we determine the errors we'd have at the other pay rates and then average them together to find one number for the whole sample. These calculations (shown in Appendix C.8) produce the statistic called the standard error of the estimate. The **standard error of the estimate** communicates the amount that the actual Y scores in a sample differ from their corresponding predicted Y' scores. Essentially, it is interpreted as something like the "average error in prediction" when we use linear regression to predict Y scores. Thus, say that our standard error of the estimate equals 2.0. We interpret this as indicating that "on average" each predicted Y' differs from a participant's actual Y score by about 2 points.

REMEMBER   The *standard error of the estimate* describes the "average" prediction error when using the linear regression procedure.

Notice that the size of r gives a hint about your prediction errors. The larger the r, the closer the Y scores are to the regression line, so the smaller the difference between each Y' we predict for participants and the Y scores they actually obtain. When r is ± 1, everyone at an X has the same Y score that falls *on* the regression line, and so there is zero difference—no error—between the predicted and actual Y scores, and the standard error of the estimate equals 0. Conversely, as r approaches 0, the Y scores are more spread out above and below the regression line at each X, so there will be larger differences between the Y' and the actual Y scores at that X.

It is difficult to determine whether being off by an average of, say, 2 points is a lot, so it's still difficult to evaluate the prediction errors occurring with this relationship. Instead, a less subjective way is to determine the **proportion of variance accounted for**. In Chapter 8, you saw that this is the proportion of the total variance in Y scores that we can predict or account for by knowing the condition under which a participant was tested. Because a condition of the independent variable is simply a special type of X score, the proportion of variance accounted for is *always* the proportion of the total variance in Y scores that is accounted for by knowing participants' X scores. In other words, the proportion of variance accounted for is the proportion of total variance in Y that is *systematic variance*—the extent to which differences in Y occur with changes in X.

To calculate the proportion of variance accounted for when using linear regression, we again determine the improvement in predictions we have when we use the relationship to predict scores, as compared to when we do not use the relationship. For example, let's say that we obtained the job-satisfaction scores shown in Figure 9.6. On the left are the scores we obtained, and all of the differences between them constitute the total variance. Without utilizing the relationship with pay rate, we cannot predict any of these differences. On the right is the regression line for this study. To the extent that satisfaction scores increase with pay, some differences in satisfaction scores are now predictable. To this extent, the scores exhibit systematic variance. At the same time, to some extent, the Y scores do not follow this trend, so they also exhibit error variance. Therefore, a predicted Y' score gets us only in the neighborhood of the actual Y scores: For example, in this relationship, we know that people tend to score *around* 30 when paid $1 and around 40 when paid $2, but we don't know precisely when they score 10, 20, 30, or 40. Thus, compared to when we don't utilize the relationship, using a person's pay rate improves our accuracy in predicting job satisfaction by some proportion.

Mathematically, it turns out that the proportion of variance accounted for in a correlational design equals the **squared correlation coefficient**. Thus, after a Pearson r has been computed (and is significant), the r^2 indicates the proportion of total variance in Y scores that is systematically associated with changing X scores. Essentially, r^2 communicates the proportional improvement in predicting Y scores that occurs when we calculate the regression equation and use it to predict Y scores, compared with when we do not use this procedure. Thus, if the r in the job-satisfaction study is $+.50$, then the variable of pay rate accounts for $.5^2$ or $.25$ of the variance in satisfaction scores: We are, on average, 25% more accurate at predicting—and

FIGURE 9.6   Proportion of Variance Accounted for in a Job-Satisfaction Study

Differences between scores on the left constitute the total variance. By correlating the scores with pay rates on the right, we identify both systematic and error variance.

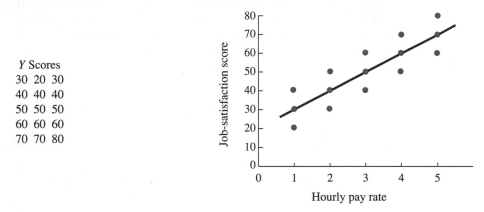

Y Scores
30 20 30
40 40 40
50 50 50
60 60 60
70 70 80

understanding—differences in satisfaction if we consider a person's pay rate than if we don't consider this variable. (Likewise, squaring other types of correlation coefficients provides the same kind of information about the relationship found in those situations.)

In a correlational design, r^2 is *not* called a measure of effect size: To say that X has an "effect" would imply causality. Instead, r^2 is called the **coefficient of determination**. However, as with effect size, we compare different relationships by comparing their values of r^2 to determine which is the most useful, scientifically important relationship. Thus, for pay rate and job satisfaction, r^2 is .25. But say that the correlation between years on the job and satisfaction is $r = +.23$, so r^2 is about .05. Because .25 is five times .05, the relationship involving pay is five times more useful than that involving years on the job: pay rate is five times as useful for predicting scores and, thus, five times more important for understanding differences in job satisfaction. (All of the measures of proportion of variance accounted for that we've discussed are for describing sample data. They are *very* rough estimates of how useful the relationship is if applied to the population.)

REMEMBER   The *squared correlation coefficient* indicates the proportion of variance in Y that is accounted for by the relationship with X, so it indicates how useful and important the relationship is.

Maximizing the Power of the Correlation Coefficient

Remember *power*? It's the probability of not missing a relationship that really exists. Power is also important with correlation coefficients. If a coefficient is not significant, we don't know whether it describes a "real" relationship, so we do not perform linear regression or compute r^2, and we cannot draw any conclusion about how the variables or underlying constructs are related. At such times, however, it would be a shame if we were missing the real relationship. Therefore, to ensure that we won't miss a relationship, we create correlational designs that maximize power.

Remember, the discussion of power is confined to those times when the null hypothesis is false, so to avoid an error, we should conclude that r is significant. Therefore, we maximize power with a design that will produce a strong relationship and thus a large coefficient that is likely to be significant. To illustrate, say that the graphs in Figure 9.7 depict the results of two studies investigating the relationship between hourly pay and job satisfaction. Study A produces a pattern that forms a narrow ellipse that will produce a large correlation coefficient that is likely to be significant. Study B, however, produces a relatively wide, circular pattern that will produce a smaller coefficient that is less likely to be significant. Study B has two problems that produced this pattern of scores.

First, study B reflects greater variability in Y scores at each X, producing a weaker relationship and thus a smaller correlation coefficient. Thus, to increase power, we seek to control any extraneous variables that might produce error variance. Further, we seek a precise and sensitive measurement of each variable. If, for example, we round off the pay rates to whole-dollar amounts, then we may be forcing different job satisfaction scores to occur at the same pay score, artificially increasing error variance.

Second, study B suffers from *restriction of range*, because it involved a limited range of pay scores. Because the scatterplot is not very elliptical, it doesn't look like much of a relationship, and that is exactly what the small r indicates. But, this small coefficient is *misleading*, and we are likely to be missing what would actually be a stronger relationship if the range were not restricted: Had study B included pay scores below $3 and above $5, even with the same variability in Y scores, the overall pattern would be more elliptical, producing a larger coefficient that is more likely to be significant. Thus, if study A reflects the real relationship out in nature, results such as those in study B lack power because we are likely to obtain a nonsignificant result that causes us to miss the relationship. (We can

FIGURE 9.7 Scatterplots from Two Studies of the Relationship Between Hourly Pay Rate and Job Satisfaction

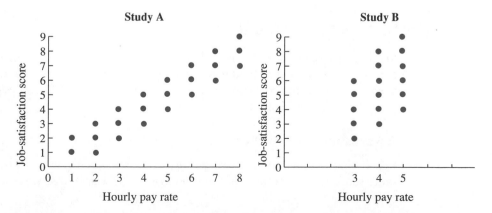

place either variable on the X axis, so restricting the range of either will produce a truncated, circular scatterplot and an artificially low correlation coefficient.)

Often, restriction of range in a correlational study results from the way we select participants. For example, in our study, we should avoid selecting only workers who have the same job because they will all receive very close to the same pay. Similarly, if we're correlating students' overall college grade-point average with their later job success, our selection criteria should not be limited to honor students or to students taking a particular course: Such selectivity could produce *ceiling* or *floor* effects, or otherwise restrict the range of grade-point averages.

In addition, there are three general principles for increasing the power of correlational designs. First, increasing the size of N increases power. Correlational designs often provide less control of extraneous variables which increase error variance and weaken the relationship. Therefore, researchers often compensate by using larger Ns than those found in experiments, often in the range of several hundred participants. Second, recall that *parametric* statistical procedures are more powerful than *nonparametric* procedures, so when possible, we prefer to measure scores using an interval or ratio scale that meets the requirements of the parametric Pearson correlation coefficient. And third, remember that the Pearson r describes the extent to which the data form a *linear* relationship. We compute r when we predict a linear relationship, or when we wish to determine the degree to which a linear relationship is present. However, if the data form a distinctly nonlinear pattern, they will not fit a straight line very well, and the coefficient may not be significant. Then, we lose power because we conclude that there is no relationship when, in fact, a consistent and significant *nonlinear* relationship exists. Therefore, to maximize power, compute the coefficient that is appropriate for the type of relationship in the data.

REMEMBER   Maximize the *power* of the correlation coefficient by minimizing error variance, avoiding restricted range, testing a large N, and computing parametric, linear statistics when appropriate.

ADDITIONAL USES OF CORRELATION

In addition to describing the overall results of a study, computing a correlation coefficient is the statistical technique for demonstrating the *reliability* and the *validity* of a new measurement procedure in any experimental or correlational design.

Ascertaining Reliability

Recall that a measurement procedure is reliable when participants receive the same score for the same particular behavior. There are three ways a correlation coefficient is used to show reliability: It is used to show *inter-rater reliability*, *test–retest reliability*, and *split-half reliability*.

First, recall that often a measurement involves judging or rating a participant's behavior, and for reliability we use *multiple raters*. To demonstrate that the behavior is judged reliably, we need to show high *inter-rater reliability*, which means that we have highly consistent ratings. For example, say that we are studying creativity and have two judges rate how creative participants are when "doodling." If the judges are reliable, then we should see a large positive correlation between their ratings: We should find that low creativity scores assigned to a participant by one rater are consistently matched by the other, while high scores given by one are also given by the other.

Second, a similar approach is used to show the reliability of a testing procedure that does not involve raters. **Test–retest reliability** indicates that participants tend to obtain the same score when tested at different times. For example, if a college exam has test–retest reliability, a student who produces a low score now should also produce a low score tomorrow, and a student scoring high now should also score high tomorrow. In other words, test–retest reliability is evident when there is a high, positive correlation between the scores obtained from the two testings.

Test–retest reliability reflects the reliability of a participant's total score on a test from one testing *session* to another. The third approach is to determine whether the *trials* within one testing session are reliable. **Split-half reliability** indicates that participants' scores on some trials consistently match their scores on other trials. Typically, we first split a test in half by comparing the odd-numbered trials to the even-numbered trials. (This balances order effects due to fatigue or practice.) Next, we compute a summary score—such as a mean or the total number correct—for each participant on each half of the test. Then, we correlate the summary scores. For example, if the questions on a college exam have split-half reliability, then students scoring low on the odd questions should also score low on the even questions, and so on. Likewise, we might determine the split-half reliability of a series of reaction-time trials by correlating the times from even- and odd-numbered trials.

REMEMBER *Test–retest reliability* is the correlation between repeated testings, and *split-half reliability* is the correlation between different trials within one test.

For any of the above, a coefficient of $+.80$ or higher is usually required for the procedure to be considered reliable.

Ascertaining Validity

Recall that the issue of validity is whether a procedure actually measures what it is intended to measure. Believe it or not, one approach to demonstrating validity is simply a researcher's judgment that the procedure looks valid. **Face validity** is the extent to which a measurement procedure appears to measure what it's intended to measure. Thus, if we judge that on its "face" a procedure looks reasonable, we have one, very limited way of arguing that the procedure is valid. For example, an intelligence test has face validity if it appears to measure intelligence.

> **REMEMBER**   *Face validity* means that a procedure is valid because it *looks* valid.

To produce more objective evidence of validity, however, we use correlational procedures. One approach is to determine the convergent validity of a procedure. **Convergent validity** is the extent to which the scores obtained from one procedure are positively correlated with scores obtained from another procedure that is already accepted as valid. For example, say that we develop a new test for measuring job satisfaction. Then, we give the same people both our test and another, accepted test. If our test is valid, then when workers are satisfied, they should score high on both our and the old accepted test. When they are dissatisfied, they should score low on both tests. Therefore, there should be a strong, positive correlation between the scores from the two tests. If so, we can argue that both procedures "converge" on and measure job satisfaction.

On the other hand, **discriminant validity** is the extent to which the scores obtained from one procedure are *not* correlated with scores from another procedure that measures other variables or constructs. Thus, our job satisfaction test is valid if it does not correlate with accepted measures of personality or motivation. In this case, we would argue that the procedure "discriminates" between what it is and is not intended to measure.

> **REMEMBER**   With *convergent validity*, a procedure correlates with another procedure that is valid. With *discriminant validity*, a procedure does not correlate with other, unintended measures.

Even though two *procedures* correlate with each other, this does not necessarily mean that they reflect the intended *behaviors*. After all, it might be that neither our new test nor the old accepted test actually measures job satisfaction. Therefore, another approach for demonstrating validity is to correlate the scores from a procedure with an observable behavior. **Criterion validity** is the extent to which a procedure can distinguish between participants on the basis of some behavior. There are two subtypes of criterion validity.

Concurrent validity is the extent to which a procedure correlates with an individual's *present* behavior. For example, say that our definition of job satisfaction includes that it is negatively related to absenteeism. Concurrent validity would be demonstrated if people who scored high on the satisfaction test were seldom absent, while those scoring low were frequently absent. Then, we'd think the test is valid, because test scores correlate with an actual behavior in exactly the way they should if the test does measure what it's supposed to measure.

On the other hand, **predictive validity** is the extent to which a procedure correlates with an individual's *future* behavior. For example, say we used our satisfaction test to predict participants' future absenteeism. The test has predictive validity if, when we later examine their absentee rates, workers' actual rates are positively correlated with their predicted rates.

> ───────
> **REMEMBER** *Criterion validity* is the extent to which a procedure relates to a specific behavior, either distinguishing the behavior concurrently or predicting future behavior.

Not surprisingly, predictive validity is of paramount importance when creating selection tests: After all, we use these tests to predict someone's future performance. What is surprising is that a measurement can lack construct, content, and even face validity but still have predictive (and concurrent) validity. Essentially, in such cases, the procedure does distinguish an individual's behavior, but we don't understand why. For example, we might find that the number of cups of coffee a worker drinks daily is an accurate predictor of—is positively correlated with—job satisfaction. Even if we haven't a clue as to why this relationship occurs, coffee consumption still has predictive validity.

To help you remember the names of the various approaches to demonstrating reliability and validity, consult Table 9.1.

TABLE 9.1 Summary of Methods for Ascertaining Reliability and Validity

Reliability

Inter-rater	Ratings from two raters are positively correlated.
Test–retest	Participants' test and retest scores are positively correlated.
Split-half	Participants' scores from half of the trials correlate positively with their scores from the other half of the trials.

Validity

Face	Procedure appears valid.
Convergent	Procedure correlates with other accepted measures.
Discriminant	Procedure does not correlate with other unintended measures.
Criterion	
Concurrent	Procedure correlates with a present behavior.
Predictive	Procedure correlates with a future behavior.

CONDUCTING RESEARCH USING INTERVIEWS AND QUESTIONNAIRES

A common method of gathering data in descriptive or correlational research is to ask people questions using interviews and questionnaires. (The preceding procedures for ascertaining validity and reliability are especially common in the development of such questions.) However, such *self-reports* are often used in experiments to measure the dependent variable and as a manipulation check.

When developing an interview or questionnaire, your first step should be to search the psychological literature for existing questionnaires and tests. The advantage of using existing procedures is that their reliability and validity have already been established. Detailed descriptions of various psychological tests can be found in research reports, as well as in specific reference books (e.g., Robinson, Shaver, & Wrightsman, 1991).

On the other hand, creating your own questions involves a lot of work, and then *you* must demonstrate their reliability and validity. As you'll see below, when developing questions, you'll first have a number of decisions to make. As an example, say that we set out to create a procedure for measuring job satisfaction.

The first step is to consider the type of questions to ask.

Using Closed-Ended versus Open-Ended Questions

In a **closed-ended question,** the researcher provides the alternatives from which the participant selects. Multiple-choice, true–false, yes–no, and rating-scale questions are all closed-ended questions. Some closed-ended questions that might reflect job satisfaction are:

(a) At work, my favorite activity is
1. Working with my hands.
2. Solving mental problems.
3. Supervising others.
4. Completing paperwork.

(b) At work I become angry
1. Never.
2. Once in a while.
3. Frequently
4. Most of the time.

(c) Check all the words that describe your co-workers:
__ Stimulating
__ Stupid
__ Helpful
__ Boring

(d) On most days, do you look forward to going to work?
1. Yes
2. No

Closed-ended questions are also called "objective" questions, and that is their overwhelming strength: A response can be assigned a score objectively and reliably, with a minimum of subjective interpretation or error on the researcher's part. For example, in question (a) above, when participants select choice 1, we can assign them a score of 1 on that question, reliably assigning the same score to all people who prefer working with their hands.

The disadvantage of closed-ended questions is that they yield limited information. First, they measure only the variable(s) we've selected. In question (b), we asked about anger at work, but participants might feel that happiness is the more relevant emotion. Second, participants can select only from the choices provided, even if they would like to give a different response. In question (c), perhaps a worker considered co-workers to be "intelligent," a response that is not available. For these reasons, closed-ended questions are used when reliability is a major concern but we are not interested in discovering new variables that might be relevant.

Conversely, in an **open-ended question**, the participant determines both the alternatives to choose from and the response. Any question equivalent to an essay question, whether written or oral, is open-ended. Thus, we might ask the open-ended questions "Describe your favorite activities at work" and "How often do you become angry at work?" Open-ended questions can also be projective. In a **projective test** the participant describes or interprets an ambiguous stimulus. This approach is used when participants might not be conscious of their feelings, or when social desirability is likely to prevent them from explicitly revealing them. Instead, people will "project" their feelings into the ambiguous situation. Two classic examples of projective tests are the *Rorschach test*, in which participants interpret ambiguous inkblots, and the *Thematic Apperception Test*, in which they interpret ambiguous pictures.

The advantages of open-ended questions are the opposite of those of closed-ended questions. Open-ended questions allow for a wide range of responses, so researchers may discover new relevant variables. Further, participants can respond in their own words, so they are not limited to just the one perspective or phrasing that is present in a closed-ended question. On the other hand, the disadvantage of open-ended questions is that scoring each response requires subjective interpretation by the researcher, so scores may not be reliable. Two people who should be given the same score because their behaviors are the same might obtain different scores because of differences in the wording of their responses. (How would you score the responses "The paperwork is easy" versus "The paperwork is very easy"?) Also, the scoring of open-ended questions is highly susceptible to experimenter biases and expectations.

As usual, we counteract problems of subjective scoring by using double blinds and multiple scorers who demonstrate high inter-rater reliability. The crucial component, however, is the scoring criteria. One way to score open-ended questions is the technique called content analysis. In **content analysis**, we score a participant's written or spoken answer by counting specified types of responses. We can assign a score based on the number of times a certain word, a certain feeling, or a particular perspective occurs. For example, a worker's score might simply reflect the number of positive references made to paperwork, regardless of whether the word *very* occurs. (See Krippendorf, 1980, for further information on content analysis.)

Even with strict scoring criteria, open-ended questions tend to provide less reliable and objective data, so they are used when reliability is not a major concern. In particular, open-ended questions are used when we are beginning to study a previously unexplored behavior so that we can identify potentially relevant variables, or when we are studying a behavior for which each participant's response is likely to be unique.

Of course, we can employ both open-ended and closed-ended questions in the same questionnaire. This mix has the advantage of providing both reliable questions that are narrow in scope and less reliable questions that are wider-ranging.

Using Interviews versus Questionnaires

You must also decide whether to use an interviewer to ask the questions or to provide participants with a written questionnaire to complete. One advantage of interviewers is that they ensure that participants complete the questions as instructed. In addition, an interviewer can react to the information provided by a participant, either requesting clarifying information or exploring new topics that arise. The drawback to interviewers, however, is that they can heighten the demand characteristics of *reactivity* and *social desirability*, or they may inadvertently communicate *experimenter expectancies* about the desired response.

Just the opposite is true of questionnaires: The interaction between the researcher and participant is minimal, so there is less risk of transmitting experimenter expectations, or of producing reactivity, and social desirability. (Completing a questionnaire anonymously can be much less threatening than talking to another person.) Questionnaires also provide more efficient data collection, because many people can be tested at one time. The disadvantages of questionnaires, however, are that participants might not complete them as instructed, and the information obtained is limited to the inflexible questions presented.

The role of an interviewer is not all-or-nothing. At one extreme is the structured interview. In a **structured interview**, participants are asked specific, predetermined questions in a controlled manner. The most structured interview is when the interviewer simply reads closed-ended questions to participants and records their responses. Questions are read in a neutral manner with no comments or hints, and a participant's extraneous comments are handled by merely repeating the question. (This approach is common in telephone surveys or when testing young children.) A less structured interview may involve asking open-ended questions, but the interviewer follows a script to ensure that all participants are treated in a consistent fashion. (This approach is common with intelligence tests.)

At the opposite extreme is an **unstructured interview** in which the researcher has a general idea of the open-ended questions that will be asked, but there is freedom of discussion and interaction between participant and interviewer. Such interviews are common when a researcher begins studying a behavior or is developing a complete description of an individual, such as during a clinical diagnosis. The lack of structure allows us to explore a wide range of issues, but the trade-off is reduced reliability, and the interviewer might lead participants into saying things they do not mean.

REMEMBER *Interviews* are preferred when the researcher must react to a participant's responses, but *questionnaires* are more reliable and less susceptible to demand characteristics.

Constructing Questions

The principles for creating questions in interviews and questionnaires are largely the same. Any question constitutes a *trial* in which what we ask is a stimulus and a participant's answer is his or her response. Therefore, we exercise the same concerns when designing a question that we did when presenting an independent variable and measuring a dependent variable.

First, recognize that participants must interpret the meaning of a question and that we must interpret the meaning of their response. For valid inferences, first minimize the extent to which participants must decide what it is you are asking. For example, the question "Are you satisfied with your job?" is a problem because most workers will not know what *we* mean by job satisfaction. Instead, we should ask participants to report specific behaviors. If job satisfaction is related to being paid enough, we should ask workers whether they are paid enough. Then *we* translate their responses back into our variables and constructs. Therefore, the elements of a question should have construct validity (reflecting the hypothetical construct as it's defined) as well as content validity (so that the question and the response actually and only reflect the variable or behavior you seek to measure). In addition, each question should have face validity, temporal validity, ecological validity, concurrent validity, and predictive validity.

Second, design questions that are *sensitive* to the subtle differences that exist between people. A question should *discriminate* or differentiate between participants on the variable being measured. After all, we assume there are differences between people on the variable because, otherwise, why bother to measure it? Therefore, design sensitive and precise questions that people will answer differently, to reflect such differences. Also, design questions that avoid ceiling effects, floor effects, or any other restriction of range in participants' scores. This includes avoiding questions that bias participants toward selecting a response because of reactivity, social desirability, or perceived experimenter expectancies. Realize that this goal may contradict the goal of having face validity. The problem is that the more obvious it is to a researcher that a question measures a particular variable, the more obvious it is to participants, too. Because this can then increase demand characteristics, researchers sometimes sacrifice face validity by disguising questions or by measuring a behavior less directly.

Finally, recall that a score should reflect a participant's "typical" behavior. However, a response to a particular question might be atypical because of the question's unique wording or perspective, or because the participant experiences a momentary distraction or misinterprets the question. As usual, we counter such problems by increasing reliability through *multiple trials*: We create a number of different questions designed to measure the same variable or behavior. By varying the wording and perspective in different questions, we should balance out the unique aspects of any one question. Then, we compute a summary score for each participant, such as a total score or mean score. This provides a more reliable estimate of a person's typical response to such items. Also, computing a summary score from many questions increases sensitivity, because participants' scores will tend to span a wider range, so that we are more likely to distinguish between one individual and another.

REMEMBER   The *goal of question construction* is to reliably and validly discriminate between participants on the variable being studied.

When generating questions, try to create many examples that reflect a variable. Then, select those questions that are best suited to your purposes. Select questions using the following criteria.

Wording the Questions   Phrase questions so that you are confident you know what participants are communicating by their response and so that you can discriminate between different people. To meet these goals, avoid the following types of questions.

First, avoid **double-barreled questions**. These are questions that have more than one component. Consider the question "Should you be given more flexibility and less supervision on your job?" What if a person agrees to one part but not the other? The meaning of any response here will be unclear, so instead, ask two separate questions. *Always phrase a question so that it states just one idea.*

Second, avoid **leading questions**. These are questions that communicate social desirability or experiment expectancies so that there is only one obvious response. Consider the question "Should very bad workers who are always late receive low pay?" This question won't discriminate between participants, because everyone knows what the correct answer "should be." *Always phrase questions in a neutral manner, avoiding biased or inflammatory statements.*

Third, avoid **Barnum statements**. These are questions that are so global and vague that everyone would agree with them or select the same response for them. (They are named after P. T. Barnum, who was famous for such statements.) For example, asking "Do you sometimes worry?" or "Have you had difficulty in some college courses?" will elicit the same answer from virtually everyone. This is the problem with horoscopes and palm readings: They are so general that people can always think of personal experiences that seem to fit. *Always phrase a question so that it targets a specific behavior.*

Finally, avoid questions that contain *undefined terms*. For example, asking "Should workers who are always late receive low pay?" will leave you wondering how participants interpret "always" and "low pay." Instead, either define such terms in the question or have participants provide the definition in their response. Thus, you might ask "What pay should a worker receive who is late for work an average of twice a week?" In this version you define "always late" and you allow participants to define "low pay" in their response.

REMEMBER A question should be a *clear, precise, and unbiased statement of a single idea*, to which different participants are likely to respond differently.

Creating the Responses for Closed-Ended Questions The preceding guidelines also apply to the wording of the response alternatives in closed-ended questions. Each alternative should be constructed to maximize your confidence that you know what participants wish to communicate when they select it. Therefore, the choices should be worded in a precise and unbiased manner, should convey one idea each, and should be mutually exclusive.

You must also determine the **response scale**, which is the number and type of choices to provide for each question. Be sure to provide enough choices. For example, we might ask yes–no (or true–false) questions, such as "Do you deserve a raise in pay?" Then, we can assign a score of 1 for "yes" and a 2 for "no" (or any other two numbers). With only two scores, however, we have a *restricted range*, so we cannot finely discriminate between participants: We'll gloss over differences between those who firmly believe a statement is true and those who think it is only sometimes true. Also, if we are scoring a test in terms of right or wrong answers, someone's *apparent* correct response might actually be a lucky guess. To alleviate problems of restricted range, sensitivity, and guessing, increase the number of response choices.

Multiple-choice questions are most appropriate for measuring factual information or discrete responses. For example, we might ask:

Do you deserve a raise in pay?

1. No
2. Yes, a $1 raise
3. Yes, a $2 raise
4. Yes, more than a $2 raise

Four choices allow for more precise discrimination. However, the fourth choice does not distinguish between those who seek a $3 raise and those who seek a $4 or $5 raise. To obtain finer discriminations, we'd provide additional choices.

Use **Likert-type questions** when measuring responses that fall along a continuum. These consist of a declarative statement accompanied by a rating scale. Most often, the scale is "anchored" at each end by the words *agree* and *disagree*. Thus, we might ask:

My hourly salary is sufficient for me.

1   2   3   4   5

STRONGLY   STRONGLY

AGREE   DISAGREE

You can also change the wording of the question to measure other experiences and attitudes, using such anchors as *seldom/frequently* or *like/dislike*.

Notice that creating a Likert-type question involves three decisions. First, consider the wording of the anchors. Above, for example, including the word "strongly" implies extreme feelings. Because of social desirability, participants may be less likely to select the extreme positions of 1 or 5. Labeling the anchors with only *agree/disagree* would imply less extreme feelings, and thus would be more likely to get a wider range of responses. However, we'd also have a less clear definition of what participants were communicating. The way to resolve this issue depends on how threatening a particular question is. Usually, we define the anchors clearly and then attempt to minimize demand characteristics by our wording of the statement being rated.

The second decision is selecting the number of response alternatives. A five-point rating scale discriminates among only five levels of agreement. When greater sensitivity is needed, include more alternatives. (Do not allow participants to place responses between the points on the scale, because such responses cannot be scored reliably.) How large a scale you should select depends on participants' ability to differentiate their feelings. On a scale of 1 to 20, for instance, people probably cannot distinguish between a 16 and a 17. Instead, they are likely to guess between the two, and then your interpretation of what a 16 or 17 indicates is in error. Resolving this issue depends on the particular question, but we usually use scales with 5 to 7 choices.

Finally, note that with 5, 7, or any odd number of choices, there is one neutral "middle of the road" choice. The more threatening an issue, the more likely it is that everyone will play it safe and choose the midpoint. This defeats our primary purpose of discriminating among participants. The solution is to use an even number of choices. With six options, for example, there is no middle ground, so participants must commit one way or the other. In general, use an odd-numbered scale when you assume that people can be legitimately neutral on an issue. Use an even-numbered scale to force participants to take a stand.

Once you have created the basic questions to ask, you can often generate additional, comparable questions to create multiple trials by merely changing the wording and perspective. For example, to measure how interesting workers find their job, we can ask them to answer these two questions:

My job is interesting.

1   2   3   4   5

STRONGLY   STRONGLY

AGREE   DISAGREE

My job is boring.

1	2	3	4	5
STRONGLY			STRONGLY	
AGREE			DISAGREE	

Then we "code" similar responses across related questions so that a particular score always means the same thing. That is, strongly agreeing with "My job is interesting" is equivalent to strongly disagreeing with "My job is boring." Therefore, we can record a response of 5 on the "boring" question as a score of 1, a 4 as a 2, and so on. Then, for both questions, the lower the score, the more interesting the job. Likewise, with multiple-choice questions, we score the choices so that each score reflects the same response (e.g., a 1 is assigned to any choice implying minimum job satisfaction).

Dealing with Order Effects

By presenting participants with a *series* of questions, we once again create the problem of order effects. *Practice effects* occur if participants first find the questions to be novel or they feel great reactivity, but with more questions, they become comfortable, or later, they become *fatigued* or bored. Likewise, *carry-over effects* occur if participants respond in a biased fashion to later questions because of earlier questions. (Have you ever found that the way one question on an exam is worded provides the answer to a later question?) Participants can also develop *response sets*, especially over repeated closed-ended questions. If, for example, initial multiple-choice questions consistently call for choice 1, participants may superstitiously select choice 1 for subsequent questions. Or, if people select the strongly agree option on initial Likert-type questions, they may continue to make this response automatically.

There are several techniques for dealing with order effects:

1. **Provide practice questions**   By providing practice questions prior to presenting the questions of interest, we allow participants to warm up to the question format and to habituate to their content, without contaminating the data.

2. **Use funnel questions**   **Funnel questions** are general questions that lead to more specific questions. Just as a funnel opens large and then narrows, we order questions from the general to the specific. Often an initial open-ended funnel question is followed by more specific, closed-ended questions, creating a block of questions that all pertain to the same issue. This order gets participants thinking about a topic before they can be biased by the specific choices provided in subsequent closed-ended questions. Thus, for example, we might first ask workers to describe their general satisfaction with their pay, and then follow up with specific multiple-choice or Likert-type questions.

3. **Use filter questions**   **Filter questions** are general questions that determine whether participants should answer additional, detailed questions. For example, an interviewer might ask a worker whether he or she has experienced sexual harassment on the job, and if the answer is "no," the interviewer would not ask any additional follow-up questions about harassment. (On a questionnaire, participants would be instructed to skip the follow-up questions.) Thus, we "filter out" those participants who would be needlessly fatigued, annoyed, or biased by answering irrelevant questions. In addition, the follow-up questions can be more clearly phrased, because they are directed at specific participants (here, at only those who have experienced harassment).

4. **Counterbalance order effects**   Balance the effects of one particular order by creating different orders of questions for different participants so that questions that appear early in some questionnaires appear later in others, and vice versa. Across all participants completing the different versions, the total sample will not be biased by one unique order of questions.

5. **Prevent response sets**   To prevent rote responding, vary the question format to try to force participants to read and think about each question. Thus, in multiple-choice questions, randomly vary which choice is correct. In Likert-type questions, present both positive and negative statements to be rated, and vary the scale by mixing agree/disagree with frequently/ infrequently, and so on. You can also intermix multiple-choice with Likert-type questions, but do not change the format from question to question: This will confuse participants and increase their errors. Rather, we generally present a "block" of one type of question, containing, say, 10 questions, before changing to a different format for the next block.

6. **Use alternate forms**   **Alternate forms** are different versions of the same questionnaire given to different participants. Here, we change the order, wording, and perspective of questions so that the questionnaires appear to be different yet they still measure the same variables. Alternate forms are especially necessary when we employ *repeated measures* of the same participants, such as in a *pretest–posttest design*. For example, say we wanted to measure workers' job satisfaction immediately before and after giving them a raise. If we used the identical questionnaire both times, people might duplicate their previous responses on the second testing in order to appear consistent, or they might intentionally change their responses because they think we expect them to. Instead, the alternate forms should hide the similarity of participants' past and present responses so that they answer the second version honestly. (Alternate forms involve different questionnaires, so you demonstrate the validity and reliability of each.)

Creating Catch Trials

Sometimes participants do not follow instructions when completing question-naires and interviews. Some people give no thought to the questions and select answers randomly, just so they can be finished. Others are untruthful, responding solely to demand characteristics. And still others make errors when responding. If possible, we want to identify these people and their inappropriate responses. Therefore, researchers incorporate specific questions to "catch" such participants.

To identify people who might be answering questions randomly, we can include a specific question several times throughout the questionnaire, but reorder the choices. Consider these examples:

When working I prefer to be	When working I prefer to be
1. Left alone.	1. Supervised occasionally.
2. Supervised occasionally.	2. Supervised frequently.
3. Supervised frequently.	3. Left alone.

A person's preference should be the same on both questions. Anyone who fails to be consistent is either responding randomly or recording responses erroneously.

To identify participants who are responding to demand characteristics, we can create questions for which we know the truthful response. Say that when questioning teenagers about their use of recreational drugs, we are concerned that peer pressure may cause some to overstate their experiences. To identify these people, we might ask the following:

I have taken the pill known as a "watermelon"

1. Never.

2. Between 1 and 5 times.

3. Between 5 and 10 times.

4. More than 10 times.

There is no pill known as a watermelon. All participants should select response 1, unless they are untruthful or made an error.

With such questions, we can estimate the frequency with which participants were untruthful or made errors when responding to all questions. Or, we can use such questions to prevent the responses of untrustworthy participants from being included in the data.

Conducting Pilot Studies

Pilot studies are extremely valuable when developing questionnaires and interviews. Instead of having pilot subjects complete the questions, however, you can ask them questions about the questions. Thus, you can check that the questions convey the intended meaning, that the rating scale is appropriate for differentiating their feelings, that the response scale fits the nature and wording of the question, or that there are minimal demand characteristics present. You can also check that, as when we equated the interesting and boring questions, the responses you see as equivalent actually *are* equivalent for participants. (One indication of this would be a strong correlation between responses to any two questions you think are equivalent.) Based on participants' responses, alter any problem questions and conduct additional pilot studies until you have constructed the desired questions.

A pilot study can also be used to determine whether a questionnaire has convergent or discriminant validity compared with other questionnaires, or to determine criterion validity by correlating scores with a present or future behavior. Likewise, you can determine whether alternate forms of a questionnaire have comparable reliability and validity. For example, we can have the same participants complete each separate alternate version in a test–retest procedure, or complete a combined version that we then separate in a split-half procedure. Either way, participants' scores from the two forms should produce a high, positive correlation. In addition, both forms should show high convergent and criterion validity with other measures.

Administering the Questionnaire or Interview

Administering a questionnaire or interview requires the same controls that are found in experiments. You should limit or balance participant variables so that the sample is representative. You should control the environment so that there are no extraneous distractions. You should avoid complicated and tiring questions so that participants do not make errors in responding. You should provide unbiased instructions for completing the questions (even if they seem self-explanatory). And you should keep the behaviors of the researcher neutral and consistent.

To minimize demand characteristics, first be careful when creating a title for a questionnaire. Is a title really necessary? Does it bias participants? (Think how you would respond to a questionnaire titled "Survey of Deviant Sexual Fantasies." What if it were titled "Survey of Common Sexual Fantasies"?) Second, consider whether deception is needed, in the form of "filler" or "distracter" questions. These are not included in the data, but they alter the overall appearance of the questionnaire and disguise its actual purpose. (For example, you might include filler questions about nonsexual fantasies to reduce reactivity to sexually oriented questions, and title the questionnaire "Survey of Common Fantasies.")

Ethical considerations are always important. A questionnaire or interview should not be unduly stressful for participants, and, as with all research, your procedure should be approved by the Human Subjects Review Committee. Participants' responses are always kept confidential, and care should be taken to alleviate their fears about what the questions will divulge about them or what the data will be used for. As always, you must obtain explicit informed consent: The fact that people complete a questionnaire or interview is *not* informed consent, because they might feel coerced in the same way they might during an experiment. After testing, provide a debriefing.

With the data in hand, we apply the usual statistical techniques to summarize the results and make the proper inferences. Again consider the scale of measurement you've used, but otherwise statistics don't care whether the scores are measured by a questionnaire, by an interview, or by any other approach. Thus, for Likert-type questions, you can summarize each participant's responses by computing a mean rating per participant. For a test, you can determine the total

---

Checklist 9.1 Question construction

Should closed- or open-ended questions be used?

- Is reliability or breadth of information most needed?

Should an interview or a questionnaire format be used?

- How strong are demand characteristics?
- Must responding be structured for the participants?
- What breadth of information is needed?

Are questions worded correctly?

- Are double-barreled questions avoided?
- Are leading questions avoided?
- Are Barnum statements avoided?
- Are undefined terms avoided?

What is the response scale?

- Are measurements sensitive to subtle differences?
- Are multiple-choice or Likert-type questions appropriate?
- What description should anchor Likert-type questions?
- How many choices should each scale contain?
- Is an odd or even number of choices needed?

How will questions be administered?

- Are practice questions needed?
- Are funnel or filter questions needed?
- Are demand characteristics a problem?
- Are ethical obligations being met?
- Have order effects, especially response sets, been avoided?
- Are alternate forms needed?
- Are catch trials needed?
- Are clear instructions provided?
- Is a pilot study needed?

number of correct or incorrect responses. For multiple-choice or open-ended questions, you can count the frequency of certain responses. You can then combine individual scores to compute the overall mean or total score to summarize a sample. If you're comparing different samples or changing the conditions of an experiment, you can perform *t*-tests, ANOVA, chi square, and the like to identify significant differences between the groups in terms of how each responds to the questions. Or, you can compute a correlation coefficient to relate a participant's summary score on the questions with a score measured by another questionnaire or by some other procedure. If the questions measure several variables, you can correlate participants' scores on these "subtests." And, when testing different samples or conditions of an experiment, you can compute the correlation for each group and then determine whether the coefficients for the groups differ significantly.

Then, as usual, you interpret the results "psychologically," relating your results back to the constructs and models you began with. However, remember that you are obtaining participant's *self-reports* about their behaviors or feelings, instead of directly observing them. Even with all of the preceding controls, there is always room for skepticism about whether participants' responses actually reflect the variables you're attempting to measure.

To help you remember the various issues when constructing a questionnaire or interview, Checklist 9.1 summarizes the previous sections.

A WORD ABOUT ADVANCED CORRELATIONAL PROCEDURES

Often researchers examine relationships involving more than two variables, and then there are a number of advanced correlation and regression procedures to use. Although these procedures are appropriate regardless of how the variables are measured, they are frequently found in questionnaire and interview research. Four methods that you will find in the literature are *multiple correlation* and *regression*, *discriminant analysis*, *partial correlation*, and *factor analysis*.

Multiple Correlation and Regression

Researchers frequently discover more than one variable that predicts a behavior. For example, let's say that we can predict job satisfaction based on workers' pay rate or that we can predict job satisfaction based on workers' feelings toward their supervisor. If we want the most accurate prediction of job satisfaction, we should simultaneously consider *both* a worker's pay and his or her feelings toward a supervisor. **Multiple correlation** and **multiple regression** are employed when *multiple* predictor (X) variables are used to predict one criterion (Y) variable. These procedures are similar to those discussed earlier. The multiple correlation coefficient, called the multiple R, indicates the strength of the relationship between the multiple predictors and the criterion variable. The multiple regression equation allows us to predict an individual's Y score by simultaneously considering his or her scores on the different variables. And the squared multiple R is the proportion of variance in the Y variable accounted for by using the X variables to predict Y scores.

Discriminant Analysis

A variation of multiple correlation is used when the Y variable reflects *qualitative* differences between participants. This procedure is common in clinical research, for example, when using test scores to categorize people who are schizophrenic versus borderline personality versus paranoid, and so on. **Discriminant analysis** is for categorizing participants along a qualitative Y variable using several quantitative predictor (X) variables. The procedure calculates what are essentially selection criteria or "cutoff" scores. Individuals whose combined scores fall below a cutoff score are categorized in group A of the Y variable (e.g., as borderline personality). Those whose scores are above the cutoff score are classified in group B (e.g., as paranoid). And those with scores beyond a higher cutoff score are categorized in group C (e.g., schizophrenic). By using this technique, researchers determine the best X variables and the best cutoff scores for maximally separating or "discriminating" between individuals so that there is a minimum of overlap or similarity between the groups.

Partial Correlation

Sometimes instead of using multiple predictors, we take the opposite approach: We wish to examine the relationship between one X and Y variable, without including the influence of other X variables. For example, say we wish to examine the relationship between job satisfaction and pay rate. However, this relationship might be tinged by workers' feelings toward their supervisor. Essentially, there might be an *interaction*, such that the relationship between workers' pay and job satisfaction *depends* on their feelings toward their supervisor. The ideal would be to find workers who all feel the same way toward their supervisor, so that, with this variable constant, we can examine just the relationship between job satisfaction and pay rate. Unfortunately, it may be impossible to keep such an extraneous variable constant in the real world. It *is* possible, however, to mathematically keep its influence constant. A **partial correlation** indicates the correlation between two variables while keeping the influence of other variables constant. Essentially, this procedure would remove the influence that workers' feelings toward their supervisor has on their job satisfaction. What would remain are only the differences in job satisfaction that are correlated with pay rate.

Factor Analysis

So far, our approach has been to begin with a specific hypothesized relationship and then to create questions to test whether two or more variables are related. A more exploratory approach, however, is to create a variety of questions that address many aspects of a behavior and then to determine which are correlated. From such relationships, we attempt to identify the common, underlying constructs that they measure. The statistical procedure used in this process is called factor analysis. **Factor analysis** uses the correlations between responses to discover the underlying constructs they reflect.

For example, in a general questionnaire about the workplace, say we find that a question about being absent from work is positively correlated with a question about taking long lunches: People who are frequently absent tend to frequently take long lunches. Both questions appear to tap the same underlying attitude about work—call it the "lack-of-dedication" factor. At the same time, say that these two questions are not correlated with questions about the importance of friendly co-workers or the time spent in casual conversation, but that these latter questions are highly correlated with each other. These questions appear to tap another aspect of the workplace—call this one the "sociability" factor. Likewise, we might find an "ambition" factor, because questions about how hard people work, how much they desire promotion, and how much they seek added responsibility are correlated only with each other. From such results, the factors of dedication, sociability, and ambition become the constructs of interest when we describe workers. Further, these factors might then be related to other behaviors, such as workers' overall job satisfaction.

REMEMBER *Multiple correlation, discriminant analysis, partial correlation,* and *factor analysis* are used to examine relationships involving several variables.

PUTTING IT ALL TOGETHER

This chapter discussed a number of complex issues that arise when creating questionnaires, as well as several fancy statistical procedures that are used in correlational research. Regardless of how elaborate it is, however, remember that a correlational study cannot be used to infer the causal variable in a relationship. Even with all of the controls used in an *experiment*, you must be cautious when inferring causality because there could be a hidden confounding. In a correlational design, there is no random assignment and so there is almost certainly a confounding. Therefore, always be on guard for identifying this approach. In the newspaper, for example, you might read about teenagers who committed suicide after listening to a particular rock and roll album, or about serial killers who were abused as children. These statements actually involve a correlational approach, because the "participants" here were not randomly assigned to the levels of either variable. Therefore, the apparent causal variable is confounded with other potential causes. The apparent cause might be the actual cause (we're open-minded, remember), but such reports do not confirm this.

CHAPTER SUMMARY

1. In a *correlational design*, the researcher measures participants' scores on two or more variables to observe a relationship. Causality cannot be inferred because participants are not randomly assigned to the levels of a variable, and which variable occurred first is unknown.

2. The *Pearson correlation coefficient* is computed when the X and Y scores are normally distributed and measured using an interval or ratio scale. The *Spearman correlation coefficient* is computed when both variables are measured using an ordinal scale.

3. A *linear correlation coefficient* will range between +1 and −1. The sign indicates the type of relationship. The smaller the absolute value of the coefficient, the greater the variability in the Ys at each X, the greater the vertical width of the scatterplot, and the less accurately Y scores can be predicted from X scores.

4. *Linear regression* is used for predicting scores on one variable based on the linear relationship with another variable. The *linear regression equation* is used to predict a Y score, called Y *prime* (Y'), for a particular X. The *linear regression line* summarizes a linear relationship, with the values of Y' falling on the line.

5. The *standard error of the estimate* communicates the "average" amount that the Y scores in a sample differ from the corresponding predicted Y scores. The *squared correlation coefficient*, called the *coefficient of determination*, is the proportion of variance in Y scores that is accounted for by the relationship with X.

6. The size and power of a correlation coefficient is increased by minimizing error variance, avoiding restricted range, testing a large N, and using parametric, linear procedures when appropriate.

7. *Test–retest reliability* indicates that participants tend to obtain the same score when repeatedly tested. *Split-half reliability* indicates that their scores on some trials consistently match their scores on other trials.

8. With *face validity* a procedure appears to be valid. With *convergent validity* a procedure is correlated with other procedures that are accepted as valid. With *discriminant validity* a procedure is not correlated with procedures that measure other things.

9. With *criterion validity* the scores from a procedure correlate with an observable behavior. With *concurrent validity* a procedure correlates with a present behavior. With *predictive validity* a procedure accurately predicts a behavior.

10. The goal of psychological questions is to reliably and validly discriminate between individuals on the variable of interest.

11. With *closed-ended questions* participants select from alternatives provided by the researcher. With *open-ended questions* participants determine the alternatives to choose from.

12. With *projective tests* participants create a description or interpretation of an ambiguous stimulus, thus projecting their hidden feelings or attributes.

13. *Content analysis* is the procedure used to score open-ended questions by looking for specific words or themes.

14. In a *structured interview*, participants are asked specific, predetermined questions. In an *unstructured interview*, the questions are less rigidly predetermined.

15. We should avoid asking (a) *double-barreled questions*, which have more than one component; (b) *leading questions*, which are biased so that there is only one obvious response; (c) *Barnum statements*, which are global truisms to which everyone responds in the same way; and (d) questions containing *undefined terms*.

16. A *response scale* is the number and type of choices provided for each question.

17. *Funnel questions* are general questions that lead to more specific follow-up questions. *Filter questions* are general questions for determining whether more detailed follow-up questions should be asked.

18. *Alternate forms* of a questionnaire contain differently worded questions that measure the same variables. They are especially important when testing in a repeated-measures design.

19. *Multiple regression* and *multiple correlation* predict scores on one Y variable using multiple X variables. *Discriminant analysis* categorizes subjects along a qualitative criterion variable using several predictor variables. *Partial correlation* determines the correlation between two variables while keeping the influence of other variables constant. *Factor analysis* identifies a common underlying construct by determining which questions are correlated.

KEY TERMS   (with page references)

alternate forms   292
Barnum statement   288
closed-ended question   284
coefficient of determination   278
concurrent validity   282
content analysis   285
convergent validity   282
correlation coefficient   271

correlational design   267
criterion validity   282
discriminant analysis   297
discriminant validity   282
double-barreled question   288
error in prediction   276
face validity   282
factor analysis   298

REVIEW QUESTIONS

1. What is the difference between an experiment and a correlational study in terms of (a) the hypothesis being tested? (b) how the researcher collects the data? (c) how the researcher examines the relationship?

2. What are the two reasons you can't conclude that you have demonstrated a causal relationship based on correlational research?

3. (a) How do you decide which variable to call X in a correlation? (b) What other names are given to the X and Y variables?

4. (a) What is the advantage of computing a correlation coefficient? (b) What two characteristics of a linear relationship are described by a correlation coefficient? (c) When do you compute a Pearson correlation coefficient? (d) When do you compute a Spearman coefficient?

5. (a) Why do we perform linear regression? (b) What is Y'? (c) What does the standard error of the estimate indicate?

6. As the value of r approaches ± 1, what does it indicate about (a) the shape of the scatterplot? (b) the variability of the Y scores at each X? (c) the closeness of Y scores to the regression line? (d) the accuracy with which you can predict Y if X is known?

7. (a) Why is the proportion of variance accounted for equal to 1 with a perfect correlation? (b) Why is it zero when there is no relationship? (c) Why don't you compute r^2 when the correlation is not significant?

8. (a) How do you maximize the power of a correlational design? (b) What produces a restricted range? (c) Why should it be avoided? (d) How is it avoided?

9. What is the difference between test–retest reliability and split-half reliability?

10. (a) What is the difference between convergent and discriminant validity? (b) How does criterion validity differ from the types of validity in part (a)? (c) What are the two types of criterion validity, and how is each determined?

11. What are the advantages and disadvantages of open-ended questions? (b) of closed ended questions?

12. What is a Likert-type question? (b) What is the concern when selecting its anchors? (c) What determines whether to have only a few or many alternatives on its response scale? (d) What determines whether to select an odd or even number of alternatives for its response scale?

13. How do order effects arise in a questionnaire? (b) How do you eliminate the influence of order effects?

14. What are alternate forms? (a) What concerns are important when creating them? (c) When are alternate forms especially necessary?

APPLICATION QUESTIONS

15. A researcher uses an unstructured interview to measure how aggressive a sample of children are. (a) What approach should she use to score their responses? (b) How should she ensure that a participant's score is reliable? (c) How should she ensure that those doing the scoring are reliable?

16. A researcher correlates participants' ability to concentrate and their ability to remember, finding $r = +.30$. He also correlates ability to visualize information and memory ability, finding an $r = +.60$. (a) He concludes that the relationship between visualization and memory is twice as consistent, and therefore twice as informative as that between concentration and memory. Why do you agree or disagree? (b) What advanced statistical procedures can the researcher use to improve his predictions about memory ability even more?

17. A researcher finds that variable A accounts for 25% of the variance in variable B. Another researcher finds that variable C accounts for 50% of the variance in variable B. Why, by accounting for greater variance, does variable C produce a relationship that is scientifically more important?

18. A student complains that it is unfair to use scores from the Scholastic Aptitude Test (SAT) to determine college admittance because she might do much better in college than predicted. (a) What statistic(s) will indicate whether her complaint is correct? (b) What concern about the test's validity is she actually addressing?

19. A researcher correlates how loudly students play music when studying and their exam grades. She tests a very large N, obtaining a significant r of $+.10$. She concludes that playing loud music has a dramatic impact on exam grades. What two errors has she made?

20. A researcher uses mathematical ability to predict sense of humor. He measures creativity in terms of how funny a participant finds three puns to be. He tests 10 math majors and finds a small, nonsignificant r. (a) What characteristic of his participants might account for this result? (b) What problem with his criterion variable might account for this result? (c) What other obvious improvement in power can he achieve?

21. In question 20, say that previous research has shown that people with very high or very low math skills tend to find puns humorous, but those with intermediate skills do not. How can this finding account for the very small r?

22. Here are two rating questions from a survey about college. What three problems in each need to be corrected?

   a. I enjoy living in the dorm with my roommate.

Very Strongly Agree		Very Strongly Disagree
1	2	3

   b. People who don't study very much will do poorly.

Frequently				Seldom
1	2	3	4	5

23. Why would a professor prefer to show the split-half reliability of a college exam instead of its test–retest reliability?

24. For each of the following, indicate whether you should use a written questionnaire, a structured interview, or an unstructured interview: (a) when measuring the attitudes of first-graders, (b) when measuring the contents of people's daydreams, (c) when measuring people's attitudes toward researchers.

25. I ask my students to rate their agreement with the following statements. What is wrong with the wording of each statement? (a) The material in this book is sometimes difficult. (b) I like reading this book, but I dislike the statistics. (c) A good student will like this book. (d) With this book I can get an acceptable grade.

26. A friend says that his reactions to inkblots couldn't possibly indicate anything about him. (a) What aspect of the test's validity is he reacting to? (b) Why is the test doing what it is intended to do?

27. On a personality test, the question "Do you prefer cooked carrots or raw carrots?" is asked several times. (a) Why might a researcher include the responses to this question when predicting someone's personality? (b) For what other reason(s) might the researcher ask this question?

28. As you read a research article, what can you determine about the research when you see that (a) multiple correlation and regression procedures were performed? (b) a discriminant analysis was performed? (c) a partial correlation was performed?

29. From a factor analysis of a personality questionnaire, a researcher identifies the factors of sociability, extroversion, and depression as constituting personality. How were these factors identified?

DISCUSSION QUESTIONS

30. You wish to examine how well people do on a test of problem-solving ability as a function of how anxious they are. (a) Why and how would you conduct this as an experiment? (b) Why and how would you conduct this as a correlational design? (c) How would you analyze the relationship in each case?

31. The original research into smoking and lung cancer showed that people who smoked more often also developed lung cancer more often. (a) Tobacco companies deny that this finding is evidence that smoking causes cancer. Are they correct? (b) This finding has been replicated numerous times in human studies, and experiments show that white rats exposed to cigarette smoke develop lung cancer. Are tobacco companies still correct in disputing the original claim?

32. A student complains that a college exam was unfair because it contained some questions that only a few students answered correctly. How would a researcher justify the inclusion of such questions?

33. Research has found that people from certain races score an average of as much as 15 points lower on standard intelligence tests than do people from other races. This finding has been used as evidence that some races are inherently less intelligent than others. (a) What considerations would cause you to qualify such a conclusion? (b) What would you say to those people who dismiss this conclusion as blatant racism? (c) What are the ethical issues involved in disseminating these findings to the public?

34. In a study, you measure how much participants are initially attracted to a person of the opposite sex (X) and how anxious they become during their first meeting with him or her (Y). For the following ratio data:

Participant	X	Y
1	2	8
2	6	14
3	1	5
4	3	8
5	6	10
6	9	15
7	6	8
8	6	8
9	4	7
10	2	6

(a) Summarize this relationship. (b) Is it significant? (c) Compute the linear regression equation. (d) What anxiety score do you predict for a person who produces an attraction score of 9? (e) When using these data, what is the "average" amount of error to expect in the predictions? (f) What is the proportion of variance in Y that is accounted for by X? (g) Why or why not is this a valuable relationship? (h) Is how much people are attracted to others a major cause of how nervous they become during their initial meeting?

10

Field Experiments and Single-Subject Designs

GETTING STARTED

To understand this chapter, recall the following:

- From Chapter 2, recall how random selection and random assignment produce a representative sample and eliminate confounding by participant variables.
- From Chapter 4, recall what we mean by diffusion of treatment and manipulation checks.
- From Chapter 5, recall what demand characteristics are, including reactivity, social desirability, and experimenter expectancies.
- From Chapter 6, recall what the volunteer bias, maturation, history, and carry-over effects are.

Your goals in this chapter are to learn:

- The pros and cons of field experiments.
- The different probability and nonprobability sampling techniques.
- The flaws in field experiments and how to counter them.
- The pros and cons of conducting small N research.
- The different types of single-subject designs.

In addition to correlational studies, psychological research involves other designs that are different from the standard laboratory study. Sometimes an experiment is conducted outside of a laboratory, and sometimes we study only zone participant. In this chapter, we examine these common alternatives: *field experiments* and *single-subject designs*.

FIELD EXPERIMENTS

Throughout this book, you've seen that controlled laboratory experiments provide the greatest *internal validity*: At the conclusion of such experiments, we are confident that we know what occurred within them, so we can confidently conclude that changes in the independent variable "caused" changes in the dependent variable. Yet, although laboratory experiments increase internal validity, they may simultaneously limit *external validity*, which is the extent that findings generalize to other individuals or settings.

The problem is that a laboratory setting is artificial because participants know they are being studied and a researcher is present who does not behave the way people in real life behave. Therefore, the study can suffer from reduced *experimental realism*, because participants cannot forget they are involved in a study and thus cannot be totally engaged by the task. Their behavior can be biased by *demand characteristics* such as *experimenter expectancies* and *reactivity*. The results can lack *ecological validity* because we observe what individuals can do and not necessarily what they typically do. And our participants can be unrepresentative because of the *volunteer bias, mortality effects*, and a *limited population*. The bottom line is that the results of a laboratory experiment can be peculiar, so that the observed relationship is found only in a literal replication of our design with very similar subjects.

Sometimes this is an acceptable state of affairs. When the hypothesis involves basic research into hypothetical constructs and basic behaviors, researchers are usually most concerned with internal validity, and so they conduct a laboratory experiment. When studying mental tasks, for example, we conduct reaction-time experiments under laboratory conditions, because we're concerned with a basic component of cognitive processing rather than with the way in which the mental tasks translate into everyday behaviors.

When we seek greater external validity, however, we leave the laboratory and conduct field research. When we seek to demonstrate a causal relationship, we perform a **field experiment**. There are four advantages to conducting field experiments.

1. We make observations in natural settings, so we generally have a high degree of external and ecological validity.

2. We can take the experiment to the participants, so the sample can be taken from a select target population or from the broadest population.

3. We can observe behavior when individuals are engaged in a real situation, so we have greater experimental realism.

4. We can replicate laboratory studies to ensure the generality of their findings in the real world.

Remember, however, that a field experiment still incorporates the procedures of an experiment. As much as possible, we randomly assign participants to conditions, reliably manipulate the independent variable, control extraneous variables, and measure the dependent variable in a reliable, sensitive, and powerful manner. We analyze the results using *t*-tests, ANOVAs, or nonparametric procedures. If the results are significant, we examine the scores from each condition as well as the differences between them, and we consider the type and strength of the relationship observed. We then attempt to explain the psychological processes reflected by the results. Because we've conducted an experiment, we have internal validity for arguing that manipulating the independent variable caused the dependent scores to change. Because we've conducted a field experiment, however, we also have greater external validity for concluding that the findings apply to common, realistic situations and actually reflect natural behaviors.

REMEMBER   *Field experiments* are conducted to show a causal relationship in a natural setting.

Sampling Techniques

In previous examples of experiments, we relied on the random selection of participants from the available pool, often consisting of college students. Given our emphasis on internal validity, however, we accept that such samples are not truly "random" because they are restricted to only those people we can solicit and bring to the laboratory. This "pseudo-randomness" can then weaken external validity, because we might be observing an unrepresentative sample. An unrepresentative sample is different from the population, leading to inaccurate descriptions of the typical behavior that occurs in the population. When potential unrepresentativeness is especially important, there are additional techniques for creating a more representative sample that we can use. Although these techniques are appropriate for *any* type of experimental, correlational, or descriptive design, they are especially common in field research because there we can take the study to a very select target population.

To identify members of a more select population, researchers often use governmental or commercial mailing lists, or membership lists of social or civic groups. On the one hand, such lists should not include people from outside the target population. A survey of voter attitudes, for example, should include only those people who vote, so we might use a list of people who voted in the last election (although this does not mean they will vote the next time). On the other hand, we should not exclude any important segments of the population—a list of voters from the last election does not include people who are going to vote for the first time. Likewise, a survey about gun control should not include only registered gun owners, but it should not totally exclude them either. Thus, to obtain a representative sample, the goal is to include all of the important subgroups proportionate to their occurrence in the target population.

How we go about obtaining a sample is, in research language, our "sampling technique." There are two general types of sampling techniques: *probability sampling* and *nonprobability sampling*.

Probability Sampling Techniques   In **probability sampling**, every potential subject has an equal likelihood of being asked to participate. By giving everyone an equal chance, we allow each participant characteristic that occurs with a certain frequency in the population to occur with that same frequency in the sample. As you saw in Chapter 2, one form of probability sampling is **simple random sampling**, in which we randomly select participants from a list of the population. Another form is **systematic random sampling**, in which we select every nth person from the population.

Both simple and systematic random sampling rely on chance, so we might *not* contact all of the types of individuals in the population, especially those who constitute a small proportion of it. To ensure that the various subgroups of the population are represented in a study, we might instead use stratified sampling. In **stratified random sampling**, we randomly select individuals from each important subgroup so that their representation in the sample is proportional to their representation in the population. That is, we proportionally represent the important "strata" in the population. For example, if government records reveal that 70% of the target population is male, then 70% of the sample should be male. If the sample N is to be 100, then from the identified males, we randomly select 70 males (and, from elsewhere, 30 females). If a person declines to participate, we select another male to replace him. We can also combine selection criteria: For example, if 5% of the population are females who own guns, we randomly select 5 participants from the pool of female gun owners. The "strata" that are typically included in field research are socioeconomic level, race, and geographic location. Notice, however, that we still rely on random sampling and random assignment *within* a strata, because this balances out any other participant variables that might otherwise bias the results.

Sometimes it is too difficult to identify and then randomly select from among the individuals in a population. In such cases, we might use an alternative sampling technique called cluster sampling. In **cluster sampling**, certain groups, or "clusters," are randomly selected, and then all members of each group are tested. To study homeless people, for example, we might randomly select a few areas in a city where homeless people are found, and then study all the individuals we can locate in each area. Or, to study workers at a large factory, we might select departments randomly and study the workers in each. Because the clusters are randomly selected, there should be no bias in selecting the participants, so the sample should be representative.

> **REMEMBER** *Simple random sampling, systematic sampling, stratified sampling*, and *cluster sampling* are *probability sampling* techniques that provide all individuals in the population an equal chance of being selected.

Nonprobability Sampling Techniques   In **nonprobability sampling,** every member of the population does *not* have an equal opportunity to be selected. Therefore, we may miss certain types of individuals, resulting in a less representative sample.

Nonetheless, a common form of this approach is **convenience sampling,** in which we study participants who are conveniently available. Testing the students sitting in the student union or the people riding a bus involves convenience samples. However, these are not random samples, because only those people who are present at the one place and time of the study have any chance of being selected, and the reason they are present is usually not a random event. Therefore, a convenience sample is representative of a very limited population.

Recognize that, to at least some extent, most "random" samples are also convenience samples: Given a researcher's limitations in terms of travel, time, and cost, there will always be some members of the population who have no chance of being selected. For example, if we conduct a study only in one portion of a factory, the resulting sample is not representative of all factory workers. In particular, the vast majority of psychological research is based on convenience sampling of college-level introductory psychology courses, and so these participants are technically representative of only the population of students who happen to be taking introductory psychology.

Another type of nonprobability sampling that may produce a more representative sample is **quota sampling.** As in stratified sampling, we ensure that the sample has the same percentage—the same "quota"—of each subgroup as in the population. Unlike stratified sampling, however, here we do not randomly sample from each subgroup. Instead, convenience samples are used to fill each quota. For example, say that we want 20 six-year-olds and 20 seven-year-olds in a sample. If we obtain these participants by testing a convenient class of first-graders and a convenient class of second-graders, we are using quota sampling.

Finally, sometimes we want to study a "hidden" population, such as when we study drug addicts or prostitutes. Then, we may use **snowball sampling.** Here, we identify one participant, and from him or her we obtain the names and locations of other potential participants, and from them we identify others, so that the sample tends to build or "snowball." However, such a sample is probably not very representative, because only those people within our network of acquaintances have any chance of being selected, and they may be different from others in the population.

For a summary of the preceding sampling techniques, see Table 10.1. Both probability and nonprobability sampling techniques play a role in the two general types of field experiments: those involving the general public and those involving selected groups.

TABLE 10.1 Summary of Sampling Techniques

Probability sampling

Simple	Randomly select participants from the population.
Systematic	Select every nth individual from a population list.
Stratified	Randomly select from subgroups, proportionate to each group's representation in the population.
Cluster	Randomly select clusters and test all members per cluster.

Nonprobability sampling

Convenience	Select participants who are conveniently available.
Quota	Obtain convenience samples to represent subgroups, proportionate to each group's representation in the population.
Snowball	Locate participants through other participants.

FIELD EXPERIMENTS WITH THE GENERAL PUBLIC

One approach to field experiments is to conduct the study in an unrestricted public area in order to generalize to the "typical citizen." This kind of study is usually conducted in one of two ways: Either the researcher targets certain people and observes their response to a condition of an environmental independent variable, or the researcher (or a confederate) creates a condition by approaching participants and exhibiting a behavior to elicit a response. Such experiments are especially common when studying social behaviors, such as aggression, helpfulness, or attitudes and prejudice. Therefore, we might observe people at a student union, shopping mall, park, library, restaurant, or when merely walking down the street. Confederates might, for example, seek help, try to distribute brochures, drop things, find money, or ask for directions. The manipulation might be the race, gender, or manner of dress of the confederate, whether he or she violates personal space or makes eye contact, whether the confederate is alone or in a group, or whether the environment is noisy or crowded. In each case, we essentially conduct the study we'd like to conduct in the laboratory, except that the demand characteristics associated with a formal laboratory and experimenter would seriously reduce the validity and reliability of the results. In the field, we disguise the fact that an experiment is being conducted by using deception and unobtrusive measures.

Limitations of Studies with the Public   As with any other study, field experiments are not perfect. We still lack construct and content validity if the operational definition of a variable does not measure what we intend. We still may lack ecological validity, because the situation is somewhat contrived. External validity is still limited to situations similar to the ones we study. And, demand characteristics may still be present, because participants are suspicious and uncooperative (thinking "What kind of weirdo is this?"), or because they give socially desirable responses.

Field experiments are also limited in terms of controlling participant variables. Random selection of participants is limited because we are convenience sampling from among those people who are present at the time and location of the experiment. (People in a park or mall might not represent people who are seldom found there.) Convenience sampling can be imposed further, because there are some people against whom the researcher or confederate may be biased, and thus they conveniently avoid them! Also, we continue to rely on volunteers who may be unrepresentative of nonvolunteers: People who stop for the confederate might be very different from those who do not.

In addition, field experiments allow less control of potentially confounding variables that reduce internal validity. We cannot always balance participant variables because random assignment of subjects to conditions is limited. Also, participants' reactions to the confederate may actually be determined by the time of day and where they are going, if they are late, and so on. Further, often there can be no control group: We cannot measure those people who do not stop for the confederate.

Field experiments also allow a less consistent testing situation, because in the real world, it is difficult to consistently manipulate an independent variable. In particular, a confederate's behavior might be inconsistent because he or she must react to a participant's more natural, uncontrolled behavior. (Some people could be gabby, some not.) Also, we have less control over environmental variables, such as the number of other people present, wind and temperature conditions, or horns blowing and other distractions.

This loss of control also reduces the reliability of scores and statistical power. We cannot provide instructions to guide participants, so we may encounter a wide variety of responses. Obtaining multiple trials per person to increase reliability is usually not possible, because a deception works only once, or a passerby will volunteer only if a task is brief. Likewise, repeated-measures designs are usually not possible. Further, we are often able to obtain only gross measurements of a behavior. (We can indicate only whether a person did or did not interact with the confederate, not how much he or she wanted to.) Not only do such measurements reduce precision and sensitivity, but the data must often be in terms of categorizing or rank-ordering participants, so we are limited to using less powerful, nonparametric statistics.

Controls Used with the Public   To defeat the above flaws, we use the usual methods. To improve random selection and generality, for example, researchers use the equivalent of cluster sampling, testing at several locations (e.g., several randomly selected shopping malls) in a counterbalanced way. We also usually use systematic random sampling, selecting every *n*th person who appears and meets our selection criteria. We can also *stratify* the sample—for example, by observing every *n*th female until we have the desired proportion of females in the sample. Systematic and stratified sampling make selection more random and eliminate experimenter biases in selecting participants. And, we balance participant variables, time of day, and other potential confoundings by randomly alternating the treatment condition assigned as each participant is selected.

For consistency, we set criteria for selecting each participant (doing so only when a certain number of people are present, when no major momentary distractions are occurring, etc.). We control for effects due to one confederate by using several confederates, having each test a portion of the participants in each condition, and we attempt to keep the appearance and behavior of all confederates consistent. Finally, we strive for sensitive scoring criteria using quantitative measurements and parametric procedures where possible. For even greater reliability and validity, we can ask participants questions directly as a manipulation check following our unobtrusive observation of them, we can use multiple raters, and we can test a relatively large N.

Even with such controls, however, be especially careful to critically evaluate all field experiments and to temper your conclusions that changing the independent variable "caused" the dependent variable to change. The trade-off of internal validity for external validity means that we do obtain a general idea about the influence of a variable on a behavior in a natural setting, but we lose precision and confidence in the description of exactly how the variable caused the behavior, and how the behavior was exhibited.

Field Experiments with Selected Groups

The other approach to field experiments involves studying a specific group that already exists. Sometimes we are unable to disguise the study, especially when we have to provide instructions and incorporate the same trappings as those in a laboratory experiment. At other times we operate more unobtrusively. Either way, however, there is some existing factor that creates the group we wish to study, and this factor provides greater external validity. Usually, this is the case because we are studying a behavior that occurs only in certain situations or with certain individuals. This type of field experiment is common in the workplace, with researchers studying such diverse groups as airplane pilots, police officers, factory workers, professional sports teams, or nurses. In each case, the participants are of interest because they exhibit specific types of behavior, they operate in a role of authority or have a certain status, or for such mundane reasons as that they normally wear uniforms. Similarly, educational research often involves existing groups of students. Or, researchers may gain access to a select group by studying young children at a day-care center or elderly people at a senior citizen's home. In an interesting twist on this selected-group approach, Gladue and Delaney (1990) investigated whether men and women become more attractive to one another as the closing time of a bar approaches by studying an existing group of patrons at a bar. Using a repeated-measures design, the researchers asked participants to rate the attractiveness of the other patrons on several occasions during the evening. They confirmed that attractiveness increased as time wore on. (Interestingly, the ratings were *not* positively correlated with alcohol consumption, so alcohol could not have caused increased attractiveness!)

Limitations of Studies with Selected Groups   In addition to the usual loss of control that may occur with field experiments, there are several special problems in testing selected groups. First, researchers are often limited to convenience sampling of those groups that they can obtain permission to test. Another problem occurs if we use cluster sampling but assign one intact group to each condition. Then, we are not randomly assigning participants to conditions, so our manipulation is probably confounded: If, for example, a condition contains all workers from the same department, the reason they are in that department—rather than our manipulation—might cause them to behave differently from workers in another condition. Also, the public may not be as obedient or adventurous as the typical college student. Some workers might refuse to try a particular working condition, or parents might object to their children being in a particular condition. The resistance of such participants is not random, so participant selection and assignment to conditions is likewise not random. Also, in a repeated-measures design, we can see substantial subject mortality, further reducing the randomness of our selection.

Another limitation of such studies is that merely by entering an established setting the researcher can alter the situation and make it artificial and contrived. Therefore, we would prefer to use an unobtrusive measure, but this may not be possible. Most nursery schools, for example, do not have a one-way mirror, and the management or union at most companies will not allow us to videotape workers. As an alternative, we can ask a participant's supervisor or teacher to act as the experimenter. But, such people are not trained researchers, so they may greatly bias the results. For example, the data may not be valid or reliable for our purposes if a supervisor assigns scores, because the purpose of a supervisor's rating may be very different from those of a researcher. Also, supervisors' or teachers' expectations can produce a self-fulfilling prophecy. In a classic study, Rosenthal and Jacobson (1966) found that when students were identified as about to "bloom" intellectually, their teacher assigned them higher intellectual development scores, despite the fact that in reality the identified students had been randomly selected and were not about to bloom at anything.

Existing-group designs are especially prone to *diffusion of treatment*, in which people in one condition are aware of the treatment received by people in other conditions. With field experiments, group membership may overlap or change during the course of a study. Shift workers, for example, might change to a different shift and thus be exposed to another condition. Or, people in existing groups might gossip about the experiment: Senior citizens might talk to others who have not been tested, or children in one class might learn of a desirable treatment given to another class. Such information can then lead participants to react to their conditions in a biased, unnatural manner.

Finally, a special kind of demand characteristic sometimes operates among participants who form a cohesive group. It is called the *Hawthorne effect*, and is named after a study of worker productivity held at the Western Electric Company's Hawthorne factory. The researchers (Roethlisberger & Dickson, 1939) manipulated numerous variables that should have decreased productivity, but, regardless, participants continuously *increased* their productivity! Afterwards, participants indicated that because of the special attention they had received, a team spirit had developed that compelled them to be cooperative and to continuously increase their productivity. (There is, however, some controversy over this account: see Bramel & Friend, 1981.) Nonetheless, the term **Hawthorne effect** has come to refer to a change in participants' performance—usually an improvement—that occurs from the novelty of being in a study and having a researcher pay attention to them. Although this effect can be found in any type of study, it is prevalent when participants already form a cohesive group.

Note that the Hawthorne effect is different from reactivity, which is a participant's reaction to being observed or "analyzed." If participants are unnaturally motivated to stick at a boring task because of their enthusiasm for a study, we have the Hawthorne effect. If their performance is then unnatural because of their nervousness about being videotaped, we have reactivity.

REMEMBER   The *Hawthorne effect* is a bias in participants' performance resulting from the apparently special treatment and interest shown by a researcher.

Controls Used with Selected Groups   By now, you're familiar with the methods used to overcome the above limitations. We seek random assignment of participants to conditions, so in a factory study, for example, we would try to ensure that some workers from each department are assigned to each condition. To minimize diffusion of treatment, we ask participants not to talk about the study, and we test all conditions close together in time. We also give all conditions the same appearance by disguising the control condition with a placebo or by using deception. Then, if participants learn about another condition, it will sound the same as their own. We also test participants from different locations in a counterbalanced way, because this not only improves generalizability but also prevents diffusion of treatment (people from different localities are unlikely to contact one another). Further, if supervisors or teachers must serve as researchers, we give them explicit training and use a double-blind procedure. And, finally, to counter demand characteristics such as the Hawthorne effect, we present neutral cues and instruct participants to behave naturally, and not in the way they think the experimenter wants them to.

Ethics and Field Experiments

Don't forget, ethical concerns are always important, and as usual, you must evaluate a field experiment to ensure that participants experience a minimum of psychological and physical stress, and to protect their rights. When conducting a field experiment in which participants are aware of the study, deal with issues of risky variables, deception, unobtrusive measures, debriefing, and informed consent in the usual ways. Of particular concern is avoiding any implicit coercion of participants because they think they must participate in order to be viewed favorably by their boss, teacher, or peers.

Remember that hidden or unobtrusive field experiments have the additional problem of violating participants' right to informed consent, so you must tread lightly. In such cases, the APA's Ethical Standards requires that there be *minimum* physical or psychological risk to the participants. In deciding the risk, remember that you are manipulating real-life variables and measuring real-life reactions. On the one hand, people will react to the situation or to a confederate in a real way (that's why you perform such studies). On the other hand, this real situation could be very frightening or disturbing to participants. Therefore, *you* are responsible for protecting participants from physical or mental distress. (For help with ethical or other design problems, remember that in *pilot studies* you can ask participants their opinions about your manipulation.) Proceed with the design only if there is minimum risk. Otherwise, rethink it to include informed consent. And, as usual, after you think you've resolved the ethical issues, submit the study to your Institutional Review Board.

REMEMBER   Be particularly sensitive to the *ethics* of field experiments.

SMALL *N* RESEARCH AND THE SINGLE-SUBJECT DESIGN

Now we will discuss an entirely different approach to research. So far, we have focused on experiments involving *groups* of people or animals. However, there is an entirely different kind of experiment in which only one participant is studied. A **single-subject design** is a repeated-measures experiment conducted on one participant. Typically, the experiment (with an N of 1) is then replicated on a few more participants, so this research is also known as **small N research**. Before considering the particulars of such designs, let's discuss why we would want to use them.

The Argument for Small *N* Designs

Some researchers argue that there are three unacceptable flaws in experiments involving groups of participants (Sidman, 1960). The first pertains to error variance, the random differences between scores found within each condition. Typically, with group designs, we use random assignment of participants and counterbalancing of extraneous variables. Because we therefore include the influence of fluctuating variables within each condition, the design itself produces much of the error variance. The inconsistency in scores then makes it difficult to see a relationship hidden in the data (so that we must rely on obtuse, inferential statistics). This is especially a problem given how seldom researchers usually report a variable's effect size (the proportion of variance accounted for). Further, researchers then ignore the differences in behavior reflected by error variance and the variables that cause them. We ignore differences in behavior between participants (*intersubject* differences) and different behaviors in the same participant from moment to moment (*intrasubject* differences). Yet these variables are potentially important aspects of the behavior under study.

The second flaw in group designs is that, because of the variability in individual scores, we must compute the mean (or similar measures) in each condition. Yet a mean score can misrepresent the behavior of any and all individuals. (How often does the mean score accurately describe your performance on an exam?) Then, incredibly, after using group means to describe a relationship, we turn around and generalize the findings to individuals! Psychology is supposed to study the laws of behavior as they apply to the individual, but in group designs we never examine a relationship in terms of the individual.

The third flaw in group designs involves the problem of demonstrating a reliable or reproducible effect of the independent variable. Usually, we demonstrate a relationship only once in a particular study, typically testing participants only briefly under a condition. Then, we rely on inferential statistics to conclude that the study is reliable. That is, when results are significant it means that the relationship is unlikely to be due to random chance. Instead, it is likely to be caused by something that makes it reproducible, so a significant relationship is also described as a reliable relationship. We do not, however, have any *empirical* evidence that the relationship is reproducible. Other researchers might replicate the study, but their situation and participants inevitably will differ from ours. And in their replication, researchers also seldom demonstrate empirically that their relationship is reliable.

REMEMBER   *Group designs* ignore the causes of error variance, they rely on mean scores to describe individuals, and they do not empirically show that an effect is reliable.

A single-subject design addresses these problems in the following ways:

1. We control participant variables not by balancing them but by keeping them constant because, with only one participant, there can be no intersubject differences. Then, if we see an inconsistency in the participant's responses, we know that an extraneous variable is responsible, so we attempt to identify and understand it.

2. Our "analysis" of the data is accomplished by visual inspection. That's right, we don't perform statistics when $N = 1$! Instead, we simply look at the data to see if there is a relationship between the independent and dependent variables. We accept that there is an effect only when it is

obvious. And the size of the effect is the obvious amount that the participant's response changes between conditions.

3. To be sure that the effect of the independent variable is reliable, we perform the manipulation repeatedly on the same participant, or we perform a replication of the experiment on additional participants. Each replication is treated as a separate study, however, so we don't gloss over individual differences by combining the results. Ultimately, then, because the relationship is based on individuals, we are studying the psychology of individuals.

The most common type of single-subject design involves a *baseline*.

The Logic of Baseline Designs

If an experiment contains only one participant, then it must be a repeated-measures design. Typically, such studies involve only two levels of the independent variable: a *control condition* with zero amount of the variable present and a *treatment condition* with some nonzero amount of the variable present. The independent variable usually involves a reward, punishment, or other environmental stimulus. The dependent variable usually reflects the participant's quantity of responding, such as the number of responses made or the magnitude of the responses.

Observing the participant under a control condition establishes a baseline and the general name for these designs is a **baseline design**. A **baseline** is the level of performance on the dependent variable when the independent variable is *not* present. It is then compared to performance when the variable *is* present. To establish the baseline, the participant is observed for a substantial period of time with numerous responses. Once the participant has habituated to the procedure so that the baseline is stable, we introduce the experimental or treatment condition and establish the participant's response rate in this situation. If the response rate with the treatment is different from that without the treatment, we have demonstrated an effect of the independent variable.

Baseline designs are most often associated with animal research. Because of the flaws in group studies, baseline designs became the mainstay of B. F. Skinner and others who study instrumental conditioning. (This approach is often referred to as the "experimental analysis of behavior.") In a typical experiment, we might place a rat in a cage containing a lever and then establish the baseline rate of lever-pressing. A particular reward, punishment, or environmental stimulus is then introduced, and then the response rate with the treatment is compared to the baseline rate. The procedure is then replicated on several other animals, with the results from all published as one research report.

Baseline designs are also performed with humans. For example, in applied studies of "behavior modification," researchers establish baselines for anxiety attacks, phobias, psychotic episodes, eating disorders, and other problem behaviors. Then, they introduce rewards, punishments, or other forms of treatment and observe the change in the frequency or magnitude of the behavior. Similar designs are also used in industrial settings to demonstrate the effects of different variables on a worker's productivity, or in educational settings to study factors that improve a child's learning.

The fundamental logic of baseline designs is to compare the baseline response rate to the treatment response rate, but as the following sections show, there are two general approaches we can take.

Reversal Designs

The simplest approach would be to test a participant first when the independent variable is not present, in order to obtain the baseline (call this condition A). Then, we could observe the participant after the variable is present (call this condition B). This simple "AB" design could be used to show that rats, for example, will press a lever more often when they receive food as a reward than in a baseline condition when they receive no food.

If responding is different when the treatment is present, we might conclude that the treatment has an effect. However, then we would be open to the rival hypothesis that some confounding factor actually produced the change in responding. Maybe some confounding environmental stimulus led to the increased lever-pressing. Or, perhaps changes in the rat's ongoing *history* or *maturation* coincidentally caused the increased lever-pressing (or maybe the rat got bored and started pressing to entertain itself).

To demonstrate that the treatment caused the participant's behavior, the strategy is to return the participant to the control condition after the treatment condition is over. If responding "reverses" to the baseline rate, we have evidence that the behavior is controlled by the treatment. This approach is called a reversal design. In a **reversal design**, the researcher repeatedly alternates between the baseline condition and the treatment condition. When we present the baseline phase, the treatment phase, and then the baseline phase again, the design is described as an "ABA reversal design." For even more convincing evidence, we can reintroduce the treatment condition again, employing an ABAB design (or any extended sequence, such as an ABABAB design).

To see the effects of the manipulation, we graph the results, as shown in Figure 10.1. Going from testing under condition A to testing under condition B, we see that the introduction of food leads to increased responding. Then, by removing the reward and returning to condition A, the response "extinguishes," eventually returning to its original baseline rate. Reintroducing the reward reinstates the response rate, and so on. Because it is unlikely that a confounding variable would repeatedly and *simultaneously* change with each of the conditions, we are confident that our treatment caused the behavioral change. Then, replicating this study on a few other participants further reduces the possibility that the behavior was caused by a confounding variable that coincidentally changed with the treatment.

> **REMEMBER** A *reversal design* demonstrates the effect of a variable by repeatedly alternating between testing with and without the treatment condition.

Multiple-Baseline Designs

Recall that any repeated-measures design can introduce the problem of carry-over effects from one condition to the other. If the previous reversal designs are to work, the carry-over effect of the treatment must be reversible. Many treatments, however, involve a permanent, irrevocable change. (This is the most extreme form of *nonsymmetrical carry-over effects*, as discussed in Chapter 6.) For example, once a rat has learned to respond to a stimulus, some learning always remains, and so the animal's responding never returns to the original baseline rate. Further, some clinical treatments are not reversible for ethical reasons. For example, it might be unethical for a researcher to discontinue a treatment that reduces a person's phobic reactions, just for the sake of the research.

If we do not reverse the treatment in such situations, we do not eliminate the possibility that the change in behavior was due to maturation, to history, or to an environmental confounding that occurred coincidentally with the treatment. The solution is to employ a multiple-baseline design. A **multiple-baseline design** reduces the possibility of confounding factors by examining more than one baseline. The logic is that we eliminate potential confoundings by demonstrating that the behavior changes only when the treatment is introduced, regardless of when it is introduced. There are three general variations of the multiple-baseline design.

One approach is to establish **multiple baselines across participants**. Here, we measure a baseline for *several individuals* on the *same* behavior, but we introduce

FIGURE 10.1 Ideal Results from an ABAB Reversal Design

Lever-pressing rate is shown to be a function of the presence or absence of a food reinforcer.

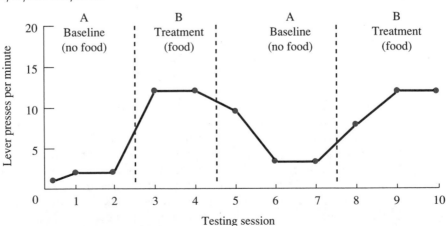

the treatment for each at a different time. For example, the argument that maturation, history, or some other variable might cause a rat to increase lever-pressing relies on the idea that the variable changed at the precise moment that we introduced the treatment. To counter this argument, we might obtain the baselines for several rats, but for each we introduce the food reward at a different point in time. Let's say we obtain the data shown in Figure 10.2. We eliminate the argument that some other variable produced the results because, even though we start the treatment at a different time for each rat, the behavior changes only when the treatment is introduced. An incredible coincidence would be required for a confounding variable to change simultaneously with the different onset of treatment for each rat. (This approach is also used when replicating the previous reversal design with different participants, by varying the time at which the ABA conditions are instituted for each participant.)

A second approach is to collect **multiple baselines across behaviors**. Here we measure a baseline for *several behaviors* from *one* participant and apply the treatment to each behavior at a different time. For example, say that a child is disruptive in school and so we establish baselines for aggressive acts, for temper tantrums, and for attention-seeking behavior. We develop a treatment involving verbal feedback that should reduce all of these behaviors. The treatment is applied first to one behavior, later to the second behavior, and still later to the third. If the incidence of each type of behavior drops only when the treatment is introduced, it is implausible that an extraneous confounding variable coincidentally caused the change in each behavior.

Alternately, we might hypothesize that the treatment will affect only one of the above behaviors. After introducing the treatment, we should find that the target behavior changes but that the other behaviors remain at their baseline rate. If so, we can be confident that it was not changes in some extraneous variable that produced the change, because it should have changed all of the behaviors.

The third approach is to establish **multiple baselines across situations**. Here, we establish baselines for *one* behavior on the *same* participant, but in *different situations*. For example, we might establish a baseline for a child's temper tantrums when at school and also when at home. Then, at different points in time, we apply a treatment phase to eliminate the tantrums. It is unlikely that an extraneous variable that decreases tantrums would coincidentally occur with the treatment at different times, *and* at school and at home.

REMEMBER   A *multiple-baseline design* shows the effect of a variable by demonstrating a change in the target behavior only when the treatment is introduced.

For help in remembering the layout of the different baseline designs, consult Table 10.2.

FIGURE 10.2   Idealized Data from a Multiple-Baseline Design across Participants

Note the different points in time at which a food reward was introduced.

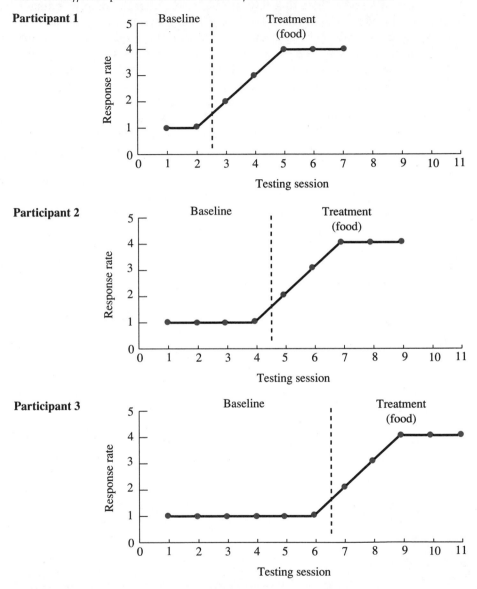

Design Concerns with Baseline Research

In any baseline design, the behavior (and the procedure we use to observe it) must produce a stable or consistent baseline. Therefore, try to operationally define the dependent variable in a way that minimizes variability, and observe the baseline condition for a sufficient period of time so that there are no clear increasing or decreasing trends in responding. Likewise, each treatment condi-

TABLE 10.2 Summary of the Different Baseline Designs Commonly Used in Single-Subject Research

Design	Layout
Reversal Design (ABA)	Alternates between control and treatment conditions
Multiple baseline	Compares influence of treatment with baseline under different situations
Across Participants	Examines treatment effect after different-length baseline for one behavior from different participants
Across Behaviors	Examines treatment effect on different behaviors from one participant
Across Situations	Examines treatment effect on one behavior from one participant in different situations

tion should be observed until the behavior is stable, so that we can clearly compare the effects of the presence and absence of the variable.

As usual, we must be careful to avoid any confounding. In particular, to balance changes due to participants' ongoing history and maturation, each baseline phase should have the same duration as each treatment phase. Also, given that some behaviors are influenced by physiological or seasonal cycles, we prevent confounding by balancing the testing over the entire cycle. Do so either by extending the baseline and treatment phases so that each encompasses the complete cycle or, when replicating with other participants, by testing each at a different point in the cycle.

In multiple-baseline studies involving different behaviors from the same individuals, it is important that the behaviors be independent of one another. If they are not, then an extraneous variable (rather than the treatment) might actually cause one behavior to change, leading to changes in the other related behaviors. Therefore, this design is best for behaviors that are not highly correlated with each other, so that once the treatment is applied to one behavior, the baseline rate of the other behaviors does not change until we introduce the treatment.

Other Approaches to Single-Subject Designs

There are many variations to the single-subject approach. For example, this design can also be used to study several levels of a variable. First, we observe the baseline condition (A), then observe one treatment level (B), then observe a different treatment level (C), and so on. To reverse the effects of each treatment, we insert the control condition between each treatment, producing an ABACADA design.

It's also possible to investigate an interaction effect—the combined effect of two independent variables. However, in a baseline design, we investigate the effect of combining *one* specific level from one variable with *one* specific level of another. For example, we can determine whether there is a particular combined effect of presenting one amount of food with one amount of water as a reinforcer. In addition to control conditions, we test one animal with only food as a reward, then with both food and water, and then with only food again. In testing another animal, we present only water first, then food and water, and then only water. By comparing performance in the food-only and water-only conditions to the control conditions, we see their respective effects. And by comparing performance in the food-plus-water conditions to performance with water-only and food-only, we see whether there is a combined effect that is different from either individual effect. If there is, we have an interaction, a particular influence on responding that occurs with the combination of food and water.

In addition to the baseline designs we've discussed, the term *single-subject design* can also refer to the kinds of repeated-measures experiments described in previous chapters. We test only one participant, but we measure the dependent variable in terms of discrete trials, compute a mean or other summary score per condition, and so on. This approach is common when we study a person with an extraordinary attribute, such as when someone has an exceptional memory, an unusual physiological characteristic, or a unique set of symptoms.

Choosing Between Single-Subject and Group Designs

The major advantage of single-subject designs is that they allow us to examine the relationship using a single individual. Further, sometimes they are necessary because the behavior of interest is found in an extremely small percentage of the population, and a researcher can find only a few individuals to study. Sometimes, too, a design entails so much time and effort per participant that a single or small N is required. And, single-subject designs are useful for initially exploring a behavior, or for studying variables that cause error variance in group studies.

The disadvantages of these designs stem first from the fact that they involve repeated measures. They become less feasible the more that carry-over effects occur. In addition, they are not commonly used for studying an interaction involving several levels of each factor because they create impossibly complex schemes. Finally, any single-subject design is wiped out by mortality effects: Rats may die during a study, and humans require extreme patience and motivation for long-term participation. The solution to such problems is often a between-subjects group design. Such designs also can be conducted more quickly, and they allow for the use of deception and other procedures that often are not feasible with repeated measures.

As usual, selecting a design depends on the hypothesis and variables being studied, as well as on all of the concerns for flaws that we've discussed. Of particular importance is finding a balance between internal and external validity. On

TABLE 10.3 Pros and Cons of a Single-Subjects Design

Pros	Cons
High internal validity	Limited external validity
Eliminates intersubject variance and examines intrasubject variance	Repeated measures influenced by mortality and carry-over effects
Describes relationship for an individual	Biased by characteristics of individual studied
Empirically demonstrates reliability of effect	Not practical for studying interactions

the one hand, the potentially great control of variables in a single-subject design achieves a high degree of internal validity. Therefore, we may prefer a single-subject design when the influence of fluctuating participant variables is of primary concern. On the other hand, a major drawback of single-subject research is its limited external validity. Because results are tied to one or a few unique participants, individual differences can produce results that are very different from those we would find with other participants. (Remember, random sampling does not work well at balancing participant variables with very small samples.) At the same time, the results are tied to a highly controlled and individualized setting, and so generalizability is limited. A group design, however, provides greater confidence that the conclusions generalize to other individuals and settings.

REMEMBER *Single-subject designs* provide substantial internal validity but have limited external validity.

To review the pros and cons of a single-subject design, consult Table 10.3.

PUTTING IT ALL TOGETHER

The typical laboratory experiment involving groups of participants is the most common in psychology because it is practical and efficient, it provides a relatively high degree of internal validity, and it provides some external validity for generalizing to other situations or individuals. Whether you should take this approach, however, depends on your reasons for conducting the study. Switch to field research when you seek increased generalizability to real-world behaviors and other individuals that the generic laboratory study does not provide. Switch to a single-subject design when you seek to eliminate error variance, especially variability due to differences in participants, which group designs incorporate.

The variations on the typical experiment that you've seen in this chapter are a strength of psychological methods, because their inclusion is a form of *converging operations* that allows us to study a behavior using different perspectives and procedures. Ideally, to form a complete body of knowledge, psychology needs both laboratory experiments and field experiments because the reduced internal or external validity of one is made up for by the other. Likewise, we need group studies and single-subject designs because single-subject designs give a specific description of a relationship as it applies to one case, while group designs give a general description of how a relationship tends to operate over numerous cases. So, keep an open mind when designing your research.

CHAPTER SUMMARY

1. A *field experiment* is an experiment conducted in a real-life setting in order to increase external validity.

2. With *probability sampling techniques*, every potential participant has an equal likelihood of being selected. With *simple random sampling*, participants are selected in a random fashion. With *systematic random sampling*, every *n*th individual is selected from the population. With *stratified random sampling*, participants are selected from within each important subgroup in proportion to the population. With *cluster sampling*, specific groups are randomly selected and then all members of each group are observed.

3. With *nonprobability sampling*, every member of the population does not have an equal opportunity to be selected. With *convenience sampling*, participants are those who are conveniently available. With *quota sampling*, the population is proportionately sampled, but convenience samples fill each quota. With *snowball sampling*, potential participants are identified by other participants.

4. Field experiments may lose internal validity because extraneous variables are difficult to control. They may lose reliability because participants' behaviors are unreliable and measurements are imprecise and lack sensitivity.

5. The *Hawthorne effect* is a bias in a person's behavior resulting from the special treatment or interest shown by a researcher.

6. When conducting field experiments, consider the ethics of invading a person's privacy, manipulating variables that can have a real impact, and failing to obtain informed consent.

7. Group designs have been criticized on the grounds that (a) they ignore the variables that cause inter- and intrasubject differences reflected by error variance, (b) they rely on mean scores that are inaccurate for describing an individual, and (c) they do not empirically show that an effect is reliable.

8. A *single-subject* or *small* N *design* involves a complete repeated-measures experiment conducted on each of a few participants. The advantages of this design are that it (a) keeps participant variables constant, (b) provides a clear indication of the effect size of a variable on an individual, and (c) empirically demonstrates the reliability of the effect.

9. A *baseline* is the level of performance on the dependent variable when the independent variable is not present. It is compared to performance when the *treatment* is present.

10. A *reversal design* (such as an ABA design) repeatedly alternates between the baseline condition and the treatment condition.

11. When the influence of a manipulation cannot be reversed, a *multiple-baseline design* is used. Here, a baseline is established either (a) for one behavior from several participants, (b) for several behaviors from one participant, or (c) for one behavior from one participant in several situations.

12. Single-subject designs are appropriate when seeking a detailed description of one individual, when the treatment does not produce large carry-over effects, and when many observations per subject are necessary. Otherwise, a group design is preferable.

KEY TERMS   (with page references)

baseline   318
baseline design   318
cluster sampling   309
convenience sampling   310
field experiment   307
Hawthorne effect   315
multiple-baseline design   320
multiple baselines across behaviors
   321
multiple baselines across participants
   320
multiple baselines across situations
   321

nonprobability sampling   310
probability sampling   309
quota sampling   310
reversal design   319
simple random sampling   309
single-subject design   316
small N research   316
snowball sampling   310
stratified random sampling   309
systematic random sampling   309

REVIEW QUESTIONS

1. (a) What is the difference between a laboratory experiment and a field experiment? (b) What is the difference between correlational field research and a field experiment?

2. In terms of validity, (a) what is the major advantage of field experiments over laboratory experiments? (b) What is the major disadvantage?

3. What are the disadvantages of field experiments in terms of (a) the consistency of your procedures? (b) the reliability of your scoring? (c) power?

4. (a) What are the two major approaches for obtaining participants in field experiments? (b) What are the advantages of each approach? (c) What are the disadvantages of each approach?

5. (a) What are the three ethical problems that can arise from conducting field experiments? (b) What issues guide how you resolve them? (c) Who else do you get involved?

6. What is the *Hawthorne effect* in a study?

7. (a) What is the advantage of probability sampling over nonprobability sampling? (b) What is the advantage of nonprobability sampling?

8. Why does a "random" sample always have limited representativeness?

9. (a) What is the difference between simple and systematic random sampling? (b) What is stratified random sampling? (c) What is cluster sampling?

10. (a) What advantage and disadvantage are associated with convenience sampling? (b) What is quota sampling? (c) What is snowball sampling?

11. (a) What is a reversal design? (b) What is the logic for eliminating confoundings in this design? (c) What is the major factor that prohibits its use?

12. (a) What is a multiple-baseline design involving one behavior from several participants? (b) What is the logic for eliminating confoundings in this design?

13. (a) What is a multiple-baseline design involving several behaviors from one participant? (b) involving one behavior for one participant in several situations?

APPLICATION QUESTIONS

14. You test the effectiveness of motivational training by providing it to half of your college's football team during training camp. The remaining members form the control group, and the dependent variable is the coach's evaluation of each player. (a) Why might diffusion of treatment influence your results? (b) How could the Hawthorne effect influence your results? (c) How could the coach bias your results?

15. In question 14, why would you test the football team instead of conducting a laboratory study of random psychology students?

16. To determine whether attractiveness influences a pledge's acceptability to a sorority, you present participants from one sorority with descriptions of

potential pledges accompanied by photos of unattractive females. Those from another sorority are given the same descriptions along with photos of pledges of medium attractiveness, and so on. (a) What confounding is present in this study? (b) How would you eliminate it?

17. In question 16, (a) why would you choose this design over randomly selecting females from a psychology course? (b) Compared to a laboratory study, what flaws are *not* eliminated by this design?

18. Let's say you conduct a single-subject study of the influence of relaxation training on "state" anxiety (measured on the basis of heart rate). (a) Should this study involve an ABA reversal design or a multiple-baseline design? (b) Describe the specific design to use.

19. (a) In question 18, what are three advantages to using a single-subject design? (b) What are two disadvantages?

20. A researcher claims that participants in an experimental group performed better than those in a control group. A counter proposal is that the results reflect the Hawthorne effect. What does this mean?

DISCUSSION QUESTIONS

21. You wish to examine the influence of wall color on people's mood. (a) How would you conduct this as a laboratory study? (b) as a field experiment on the public? (c) as a field experiment on existing groups? (d) What are the pros and cons of each design?

22. Using the food-plus-water example of a reversal design discussed in this chapter, sketch graphs that would show an interaction.

23. How would you answer people who criticize field experiments as an invasion of people's privacy?

24. (a) What does the fact that research findings are routinely replicated indicate about our samples, even though they are not truly "random" nor "perfectly representative"? (b) What would you say to the criticism that the science of psychology is mainly the study of college students enrolled in Introductory Psychology classes?

25. You have developed a new therapy that helps people to quit smoking. (a) What are the advantages and disadvantages of testing the therapy using a group design (such as in a pretest–posttest design)? (b) What are the advantages and disadvantages of testing the therapy using a small *N* design? (c) Describe the specific baseline design you could use to demonstrate that the therapy helps people to quit smoking. (d) What would you look for in your data to support this hypothesis?

Quasi-Experiments and Descriptive Designs

GETTING STARTED

To understand this chapter, recall the following:

- From Chapter 2, recall why participants are randomly assigned to conditions and the difference between a true and quasi-independent variable.
- Also from Chapter 2, recall the nature and goals of descriptive research.
- From Chapter 4, recall what trait and state characteristics are.
- From Chapter 6, recall what the effects of subject mortality and subject history are.
- From Chapter 8, recall what an interaction is.
- From Chapter 10, recall the definition of a correlational design and its issues of internal and external validity.
- From Chapter 10, recall the different types of sampling techniques.

Your goals in this chapter are to learn:

- The common types of quasi-experimental designs and their pitfalls.
- The different approaches to observational research.
- How field surveys are conducted.
- The ethical issues in descriptive research.

So far we've examined correlational designs and true experiments. But psychological research also uses two other general techniques—*quasi-experiments* and descriptive designs—and this chapter discusses each in detail. We'll also introduce research conducted on a grand scale, called program evaluation. All of these are legitimate research methods, although, as you'll see, they have both strengths and weaknesses. None of these designs is especially complex, but be forewarned: There are a number of variations—each with its own name—so pay attention to the terminology.

UNDERSTANDING QUASI-EXPERIMENTS

Recall that in a *true experiment*, the researcher randomly assigns participants to the conditions of the independent variable, so it is the researcher who determines each individual's "score" on the X variable. Sometimes, however, the nature of the variable is such that participants cannot be randomly assigned to conditions. For example, let's say we think that personality type influences creative ability. We cannot randomly assign people to have a certain personality, so, instead, we would compare the creative abilities of a group of people already having one type of personality to a group having another type, and so on. The layout of this design is shown in Table 11.1. Such a design is a quasi-experiment. As discussed in Chapter 2, the participants in a **quasi-experiment** are assigned to a particular condition because they have already experienced or currently exhibit that condition of the variable. The term *quasi* means "seemingly," so this design has the appearance of a true experiment. But, because we do not truly manipulate the independent variable, a quasi-experiment involves a **quasi-independent variable:**

TABLE 11.1 Diagram of One-Way Quasi-Experiment

Each X *represents a participant's creativity score.*

Personality types

Condition 1	*Condition 2*	*Condition 3*
X	X	X
X	X	X
X	X	X
X	X	X
X	X	X
$\overline{X}$	$\overline{X}$	$\overline{X}$

We lay out the design and compare the scores between conditions as if it is a true experiment, but we only appear to administer the independent variable.

Recognize that, although the preceding design looks like an experiment, any quasi-experiment is actually a correlational design. In both, participants have a score on the X variable because they have already experienced or currently exhibit that level of the variable. Thus, whether we call it an experiment or not, the above design is equivalent to a correlational study in which we approach a number of people, measure their personality and their creativity, and then look at the relationship between their scores.

The name "quasi-experiment," however, communicates two important differences from a correlational design. First, in a correlational design, it is the participants who determine the range of X scores that we examine, and it is usually a fairly wide range. In a quasi-experiment, the researcher chooses a few, specific values of the X variable to examine. Thus, we might identify only three personality types as the conditions of our quasi-independent variable, while in a typical correlational design, participants might demonstrate many more personality types.

The second distinction is that a correlational design usually implies that there is little control of extraneous variables. A quasi-experiment usually implies more control of researcher, environmental, and measurement task variables. Ideally, such controls yield a more reliable and internally valid study.

Thus, a quasi-experiment is essentially a more controlled version of a correlational design. Because it *is* a correlational design, however, a quasi-experiment still has the two limitations on inferring causality of other correlational designs. First, such designs have *reduced internal validity*: Because participants are not randomly assigned to conditions, we do not balance out participant variables between conditions. Therefore, any differences in scores between the conditions might actually be due to a confounding from a participant variable. For example, people differing in personality type might also differ in intelligence, physiology, genetics, or history, any one of which can actually be the cause of differences in their creativity. Second, recall that the cause of a behavior must occur first, but in correlational designs (and in quasi-experiments) we often cannot identify the *true* temporal order in which the variables occur. For example, someone's personality might then cause a certain creativity level to develop, but it's also possible that one's creativity level might then cause a particular personality to develop. Because of these restrictions, a quasi-experiment—even when conducted under highly controlled laboratory conditions—provides little confidence that differences in the independent variable cause differences in the dependent variable.

REMEMBER   A *quasi-experiment* provides little evidence for inferring the cause of a behavior.

Still, a quasi-experiment is a legitimate research approach, and a large portion of psychological research involves this method. Quasi-experiments generally occur in one of three situations: When the independent variable involves a participant variable (e.g., personality type), when it involves an environmental event (e.g., hurricanes or having a particular classroom teacher), and when it involves the passage of time (such as the factor of age). We'll discuss each type separately in the next three sections.

QUASI-INDEPENDENT VARIABLES INVOLVING PARTICIPANT VARIABLES

Researchers are studying a quasi-independent variable whenever they study a participant variable. Such variables include differences in participants' anxiety, depression, self-esteem, attitudes, cognitive or physical characteristics, history and experiences, or socioeconomic classifications. We "manipulate" such variables to the extent that we select the different types of participants to be present in the experiment. Thus, for example, researchers have compared the conditions of male versus female using a host of dependent variables (usually finding gender differences). Likewise, research has examined differences in how left- and right-handers perform various cognitive and artistic tasks. In field research, researchers use quasi-independent variables when they examine factory workers whose jobs differ in level of responsibility, pay rate, and so on. Quasi-independent variables also occur in animal research that compares the behaviors of different species or compares similar animals who differ in innate aggressiveness or dominance. Also, a quasi-independent variable is involved in clinical research any time the conditions compare "normal" to "abnormal" participants.

Creating the Conditions Using a Participant Variable

Identifying the participants for each condition requires first measuring individuals on the quasi-independent variable. Often, a *pretest* is needed, either observing potential participants' overt behavior or administering a questionnaire that measures their characteristics. Often the quasi-independent variable is a rather permanent "trait" characteristic that participants exhibit.

Using the scores from the pretest, we then *operationally define* each condition. For example, let's say we hypothesize a relationship between a person's having low, medium, or high self-esteem and his or her willingness to take risks. From the research literature we can obtain any number of existing self-esteem tests, and one classic measure of risk-taking is the distance at which people stand from the target in a ring-toss game. After administering the self-esteem test to a large pool of people, we'll use their scores to select participants for each condition. Because few people are likely to exhibit an identical level of self-esteem, however, we can define low self-esteem as a test score of between 0 and 10, medium self-esteem as a score between 45 and 55, and high self-esteem as a score between 90 and 100. The design for this study is shown in Table 11.2. Except for the absence of random assignment to conditions, this design is the same as in a true experiment. We face

TABLE 11.2 Diagram of a One-Way Experiment with the Quasi-Independent Variable of Self-Esteem Level

Each X represents a participant's risk-taking score.

Self-esteem level

Low *(0–10)*	*Medium* *(45–55)*	*High* *(90–100)*
X	X	X
X	X	X
X	X	X
X	X	X
X	X	X
$\overline{X}$	$\overline{X}$	$\overline{X}$

all of the usual concerns, such as ethics, standardized procedures, *demand characteristics*, *reliable scoring*, *pilot studies*, and so on. Also, we can combine the factor of self-esteem with other variables in a *factorial* design, employing any combination of true and quasi-independent variables. (You may use a *matched-group* or *pretest–posttest* design, but usually these quasi-independent variables are tested using a *between-subjects* design.)

Recall that a key design issue is to create a *reliable* and *strong* manipulation of the independent variable. How effectively we do this in a quasi-experiment hinges on the selection pretest. (Because this test is itself a measurement procedure, it has the usual design concerns, such as *scoring criteria*, *sensitivity*, *reliability*, and *demand characteristics*.) Then, as always, we seek a valid manipulation of the independent variable, so for example, the above pretest must validly identify differences in self-esteem. Also, we seek a reliable, consistent manipulation, so the self-esteem scores should reliably reflect differences in self-esteem. Finally, we seek to maximize statistical power by creating a strong manipulation. Therefore, first the participants should have *very* distinctly low, medium and high self-esteem scores so that the conditions are very different from one another and therefore likely to produce large differences in risk-taking. Second, we seek to eliminate *error variance* in risk-taking scores *within* each condition. Because we think that differences in self-esteem produce differences in risk-taking, we should narrowly define the range of selection scores for each condition. By selecting very similar people within each condition in terms of self-esteem, we should see consistent scores on risk-taking. Together, these two strategies should produce large, significant differences in risk-taking between the conditions.

If there are not such differences, it may be because of *regression toward the mean*.

The Problem of Regression Toward the Mean

A potential flaw in reliability can occur whenever we seek to identify participants who are relatively extreme on a variable. Recall that any measurement technique can be unreliable to some extent, containing measurement error because of random distractions and flukes. Simply by chance, these influences can conspire in such a way that some participants obtain extreme scores: Some people will be particularly lucky or unlucky at guessing answers, some might be having a particularly good or bad day, or there might be quirks in our procedure that cause some to score especially high or low. Such random, momentary influences will not always be present, however, and they do have a way of averaging out. Therefore, if we measure the same individuals again, their scores will tend to be less extreme, simply by chance. This time, the high scores won't be so high and the lows won't be so low. Instead, all scores will tend to be more toward the middle. Because the mean falls in the middle, another way to say this is that a participant's score will tend to be closer to the mean. This outcome is known as regression toward the mean. **Regression toward the mean** occurs when, because of inconsistent random factors, extreme scores tend to change in the direction of moving closer to the mean.

The problem with regression toward the mean is that with it we do not have a strong manipulation. For example, people identified by the pretest as having very high or very low self-esteem scores are likely to actually exhibit a more average level of self-esteem. Therefore, our three conditions might not actually differ in self-esteem as much as we think. Even if self-esteem does cause risk-taking, with smaller differences between the levels of self-esteem, we may find small, possibly nonsignificant differences in risk-taking.

Also, regression toward the mean threatens internal validity. This is because what appears to be a change in scores due to our treatment may actually be a change in random measurement error. For example, say that in a different study, we test a counseling technique for raising a person's low self-esteem, using a pretest–posttest design. We identify people having very low self-esteem, then apply the treatment, and then measure their self-esteem again. To some extent, the peculiarities that produced very low self-esteem when we tested participants the first time will not be present the second time. Therefore, their second score will tend to be higher (closer to the mean), *regardless* of whether the counseling works or not!

We try to counteract regression toward the mean by using multiple trials from the most reliable selection tests possible. Also, we can include a control group—another group that is measured at the same times as the experimental group but does not experience the treatment. The extent to which the control group's scores change will show the extent of extraneous influences, including that of regression toward the mean.

REMEMBER   *Regression toward the mean* is a change in extreme scores toward less extreme scores that occurs because random influences are not consistently present.

Interpreting the Results

We analyze the results of quasi-experiments using the same procedures used with true experiments. Based on the characteristics of the *dependent* variable, select either parametric or nonparametric procedures. Then, compute the mean (or other summary measure) for each condition and perform the *t*-test, *ANOVA*, and so on to determine if the conditions differ significantly. And, despite the problems of causality, it is again appropriate to compute the *effect size* of any significant quasi-independent variable.

As usual, when we then interpret the results, we are concerned that the observed relationship reflects the variables that we think it does. In particular, therefore, you should still attempt to control extraneous participant variables. You can select participants from a limited population or match them on relevant variables (e.g., we might select only children and match them across the conditions on their ring-tossing ability). You might control other participant variables by balancing them (e.g., by selecting an equal number of males and females for each level of self-esteem). And, of course, we use random sampling: We randomly select participants to pretest, and if enough people meet the criteria for a condition, we randomly select from among them those people we'll actually study. Recognize, however, that such controls do not eliminate the problem that a quasi-independent variable is still likely to be confounded by other extraneous participant variables.

Also, recall that a pretest can add *demand characteristics* because it alerts participants to the variables under study and thus causes them to behave differently than they otherwise would. To counter this, we might use deception to disguise both the pretest and the purpose of the study. Also, recognize that in any correlational study, we can test the variables in the order that is least biasing to participants, capitalizing on the fact that one variable does not truly precede the other anyway. Therefore, we might first measure many people on the dependent variable of risk-taking so that they are not biased, and then give them the selection test to determine who will be placed in each condition when we analyze the data.

As usual, the final step is to explain "psychologically" how and why the independent and dependent variables are related in nature. But, tread softly around the issue of causality. In our example, people who differ in self-esteem probably also differ on many other hidden variables. Therefore, we have little confidence in the conclusion that differences in self-esteem cause differences in risk-taking.

REMEMBER A *quasi-experiment* involving a participant variable may suffer from regression toward the mean, demand characteristics from the selection test, and confounding by participant variables because of no random assignment.

QUASI-INDEPENDENT VARIABLES INVOLVING ENVIRONMENTAL EVENTS: THE TIME-SERIES DESIGN

A second type of quasi-experiment arises when investigating the effect that an uncontrollable environmental event has on behavior. Natural disasters (such as floods, hurricanes, and earthquakes) can dramatically affect an individual's mental health. Governments, schools, and industries institute programs that can influence a person's productivity and satisfaction. And societal events, such as wars, riots, and economic recessions, can alter individuals' expectations and attitudes.

Usually, such variables cannot be studied in the laboratory (how do you create a war?). Instead, researchers study such events using the general quasi-experimental approach known as a time-series design. A **time-series design** is a repeated-measures design in which participants are measured prior to the occurrence of an event and again after it has occurred. Although this sounds like the typical pretest–posttest design, it is a quasi-experiment because participants cannot be randomly assigned to receive the treatment: We cannot randomly select those people who will experience an earthquake or who will have their school adopt a new program. We also have difficulty in creating control groups, and we cannot control the occurrence of the independent variable (in a city hit by a hurricane, not everybody experiences the same ferocity). We therefore have considerably less internal validity for concluding that the independent variable causes the dependent behavior, as well as less external validity for concluding that the same relationship is found with other individuals and settings.

> **REMEMBER**   Do not infer *causality* from a quasi-experiment for *environmental events* because of confounding by participant variables and inadequate control groups.

While there are numerous approaches to time-series designs, the four major types are discussed below. (See Campbell & Stanley, 1963, for the definitive brief text on such designs.)

One-Group Pretest–Posttest Designs

In the **one-group pretest–posttest design,** we obtain a single pretest measure on a group and then, after the event, obtain a single posttest measure of the group. For example, Nolen-Hoeksema and Morrow (1991) examined the mental stress of people before and after an earthquake. Or, Frank and Gilovich (1988) hypothesized that wearing black uniforms leads to more aggressive behavior, so they examined the number of penalty minutes incurred by a professional hockey team before and after it changed to black uniforms.

Note that such designs provide extremely weak internal validity for inferring the causes of a behavioral change. The overwhelming problem is that they lack a control group. For example, without knowing the penalty scores of a control hockey team that is repeatedly measured, we have no idea whether the penalty scores might have changed in the experimental group, even if the uniforms had *not* been changed. To see this, look at the two graphs in Figure 11.1. On the left, the one-group design appears to show that changing uniforms produced an increase in penalties. However, with a control group, we might have obtained the data on the right, which shows that with or without the uniform change, penalty minutes increased. This outcome would suggest that some other, confounding factor simultaneously changed and that it actually produced the increase in penalties: Maybe all teams became more aggressive, or the referees began calling more penalties than they had previously. Or, because the pre- and posttests are separated by a period of time, there is always the possibility that the scores changed because of participants' ongoing *history* and *maturation*: Maybe aggressiveness naturally increases as players become older and more experienced. Maybe the results reflect *mortality effects*, with less aggressive players leaving the team between measurements. Or, if researchers interviewed participants, maybe they introduced a confounding through experimenter expectations or created a *Hawthorne effect* that altered later scores. And, maybe the results reflect *regression toward the mean*: Perhaps at the pretest, players were coincidentally experiencing very low penalty rates, and the increase at the posttest merely reflects natural fluctuations in scores.

Similar problems arise if we study the job satisfaction of workers before and after a major change in a factory's production schedule or if we examine the mental stress of people before and after an earthquake. When a study involves a simple one-group pretest–posttest design, there is no way to eliminate such flaws. Therefore, because the conclusions from such a study are so weak, this design is typically used only when no alternative design is possible.

FIGURE 11.1 Graphs Showing the Potentially Missing Information when a Control Group Is Not Present in a Pretest–Posttest Design

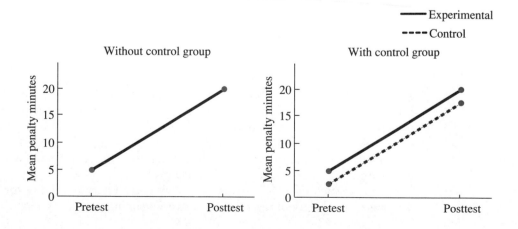

REMEMBER   In the *one-group pretest–posttest design*, the absence of a control group means that we cannot eliminate the possibility that extraneous variables caused the dependent scores to change.

Nonequivalent Control Group Designs

You might think that the solution to the above problems is simply to add a control group. Implicitly, however, we always seek an *equivalent* control group. By *equivalent* we mean that the control group is similar to the experimental group in terms of participant variables and in terms of experiences between the pretest and the posttest. In true experiments, we attempt to obtain an equivalent control group by (1) randomly assigning participants to conditions so that we balance participant variables, and (2) keeping all experiences the same for both groups. Thus, the ideal would be to randomly select half of a team to change uniforms and the other half not to. Or, to select half of a city to experience an earthquake. Then, the experimental and control groups would have similar characteristics and similar experiences between the pretest and posttest. Ideally, the only difference between the groups would be that one group experiences the treatment, so then any differences in their posttest scores could be attributed to it.

The problem is that we cannot create equivalent control groups because, usually, all members of the relevant participant pool automatically experience the treatment. Instead, the best we can do is to create a **nonequivalent control group**—a group that has different characteristics and different experiences during the study. For example, we might observe another hockey team that did not change to black uniforms during the same season we observe our experimental team. This would be nonequivalent, because different teams have players with different styles of play, different coaches, different game strategies, and different experiences during the season. Likewise, if we selected people who live in a different city as the control group for people who experience an earthquake, this, too, would be nonequivalent, because people living in another city might be intrinsically different and have different daily experiences. Nonetheless, a nonequivalent control group is better than nothing.

To analyze such results we should not simply compare the posttest scores of the experimental and control groups. Any difference here is confounded by initial differences between the groups and by differences in experiences during the study. Instead, we examine the *difference* between the pretest and posttest scores in each group. To illustrate, let's say the hockey teams produced the penalty data shown in Figure 11.2. Computing the difference for each group indicates the *relative* change that occurs from pretest to posttest. The experimental team showed an increase in penalty minutes from a mean of 4 to a mean of 10 minutes—a difference of 6. The control team showed an increase from 10 to 12—a difference of only 2. Regardless of the actual number of penalties in each group, the important finding is that, over the same time period, there was a larger increase for the team that changed uniforms.

FIGURE 11.2   Possible Data for a Nonequivalent Control Group Design

These data show penalties for both experimental and control teams over the same pretest and posttest period.

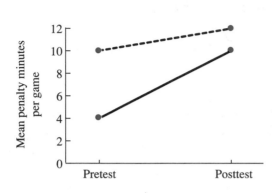

To determine whether this difference is significant, we could first compute a pretest–posttest difference score for each player in the control group and in the experimental group. Then, because this is a between-subjects design involving two independent samples of difference scores, we could perform the independent samples *t*-test, comparing the mean difference score for the control group with that of the experimental group. Alternatively, we could perform a two-way ANOVA on the raw penalty scores and examine the *interaction*. As Figure 11.2 showed, the relationship between pre- and posttest and penalty minutes *depends* on whether we are talking about the control group or the experimental group, so there is apparently a significant interaction effect here. If it is not significant, then the data essentially form the pattern shown in the right-hand graph back in Figure 11.1, where the change in penalty scores does *not* depend on whether a team changed uniforms.

Recognize, however, that a nonequivalent control group design provides only some improvement in internal validity compared to the previous one-group design. The nonequivalent control group helps to eliminate potential confounding, but *only* from factors that are *common* to both groups. In the hockey study, for example, Figure 11.2 suggests that there was no confounding factor common to both teams that produced the increase in penalties. If any maturation, history, or environmental effects common to all hockey players had been operating, then the difference between pretest and posttest would be the same for both teams. Because the experimental group exhibited a larger change, something else was present for only that team which produced the change. However, this "something else" might *not* be the change in uniforms. A nonequivalent groups design does not eliminate the possibility of a unique confounding that occurred only in the experimental group. Thus, it might have been some event specific to only the experimental team that actually brought about the increase in penalties (maybe a new coach was hired who actively promoted more aggressive play).

REMEMBER   A *nonequivalent control group* design eliminates only potential confounding by variables that are common to both the experimental and control groups.

Interrupted Time-Series Designs

Sometimes we do not have access to a control group that is even remotely equivalent. For example, what is the control group for survivors of an airplane crash or for past presidents of the United States? In such cases, we take a different approach by repeatedly testing only the experimental group. In an **interrupted time-series design,** we make observations at several spaced times prior to the occurrence of the independent variable and at several times after it. These other observations tell us whether the same pretest-to-posttest changes occurred at any other times when the independent variable was not present. In fact, this was the approach taken by Frank and Gilovich (1988), who examined the penalty records for 10 years before and 6 years after the hockey team changed to black uniforms. Their results were similar to those shown in Figure 11.3. At the same

FIGURE 11.3   Data for Interrupted Time-Series Design

The yearly penalty records (in z-scores) of the hockey team before and after changing to black uniforms.

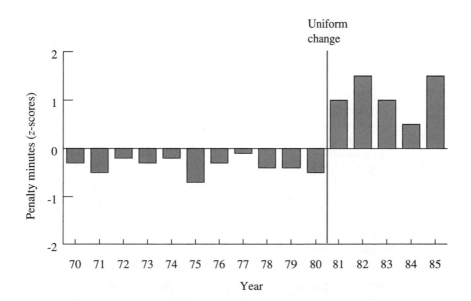

time, the researchers also compared the team to the entire league by transforming the team's yearly total penalty minutes to a "z-score." (Each z-score describes the team's score relative to the average for the league, so that an average score produces a z of zero, a below-average score produces a negative z, and an above-average score produces a positive z.) Figure 11.3 shows that before the uniform change, the team was consistently below the league average in penalties, but after the change, it was consistently above average.

From such a pattern we see two things. First, the many pretest and posttest observations demonstrate the normal random fluctuations in scores from year to year. These are not as large as the change from before to after the uniform change, so the apparent effect of changing uniforms cannot be dismissed as a random fluctuation in penalties. Second, because we see a long-term, stable level of responding before the treatment and a long-term, stable level after the treatment, it is unlikely that history, maturation, or environmental variables produced the observed change. These variables would be expected to operate over the entire 16-year period, producing similar changes at other points in time. Yet, the change occurred *only* when the treatment was introduced. (Advanced statistical procedures are available for determining whether this is a significant change; see Cook and Campbell [1979] and Shadish, Cook, and Campbell, [2002]).

Thus, the interrupted time-series design allows us to confidently conclude that the pretest-to-posttest change in dependent scores did not result from a random fluctuation in scores or from a repeatedly occurring confounding variable. The one weakness in the design is that an extraneous variable might coincidentally change *once* at the same time that the treatment is introduced. For example, hockey teams change players yearly, and perhaps by chance more penalty-prone players were acquired during the same year as the uniform change. However, such an explanation would require a rather exceptional coincidence, considering all of the changes that would occur in the team over a 16-year period. Therefore, we have substantial confidence that the change in behavior is due to the treatment. In fact, Frank and Gilovich (1988) provided additional confidence with a true laboratory experiment that also showed that participants were more aggressive when they wore black clothing. (Notice that by using two, diverse methods, this research is an example of *converging operations*. Also, each study produced the same conclusion and supported the other, providing *convergent validity* for their respective procedures.)

REMEMBER   The numerous pretest and posttest observations of an *interrupted time-series design* reduce, but do not eliminate, the possibility that the treatment is confounded with some other event.

Multiple Time-Series Designs

To further increase confidence in the conclusions from a quasi-experiment, we can combine the interrupted time-series design and the nonequivalent control group design, creating a **multiple time-series design.** Here, we observe an experimental group and a nonequivalent control group, obtaining several spaced pretest scores and several spaced posttest scores for each. Thus, for example, we might examine several years of penalty records both for the team that changed uniforms and for another team that did not, as shown in Figure 11.4. This shows the effect of the treatment in two ways. First, with the experimental group, the change in behavior occurs only *after* the treatment has been introduced, with one stable behavior before and a different stable behavior after the treatment. Second, the change from pretest to posttest scores in the experimental group is larger than that in the control group.

Although there might still be some confounding factor that occurred simultaneously with the treatment, the fact that it does not produce the same results in the control group means that it is specific to the experimental group. Further, throughout all these years, for it to occur only once and simultaneously with the treatment would be an extreme coincidence. Together, therefore, these findings make it very unlikely that a confounding variable produced the change in the experimental group.

REMEMBER   A *multiple time-series design* examines numerous pretest and posttest observations for both an experimental and a nonequivalent control group.

FIGURE 11.4   Data for a Multiple Time-Series Design

The yearly penalty record of a hockey team before and after changing to black uniforms, and of a nonequivalent control team.

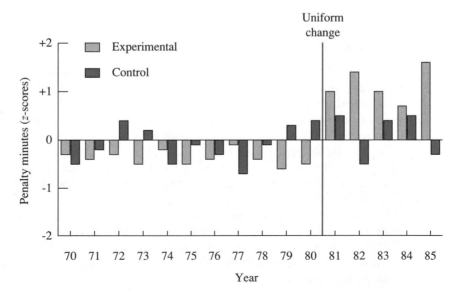

THE QUASI-INDEPENDENT VARIABLE OF THE PASSAGE OF TIME

One more important quasi-independent variable in psychology is the passage of time. The entire field of developmental psychology is built around the variable of age, and how it relates to changes in social, emotional, and cognitive behavior. Researchers also study the passage of time in other settings, as when comparing experienced workers with inexperienced workers. These are quasi-independent variables, because we cannot randomly assign people to be a certain age or to experience only a certain amount of work. Therefore, such studies are like the previous time-series designs, in that we sample participants' behavior at different points, before and after the passage of a certain amount of time. However, they differ from time-series designs in one important way. In the time-series designs, an environmental event was the variable of interest, while the accompanying passage of time between measurements allowed for potential confoundings from maturation, history, and so on. In the present designs, the passage of time—with the accompanying maturation and history—is the variable of interest, while environmental events are potential confoundings. Therefore, we still have the same old problem of inferring causality that results from the lack of random assignment, plus the problem of potential confoundings by environmental variables.

REMEMBER   Do not infer causality from a quasi-experiment involving time, because of confounding by participant and environmental variables.

There are three general approaches to studying the passage of time: *longitudinal designs*, *cross-sectional designs*, and *cohort designs*.

Longitudinal Designs

In a **longitudinal design,** we observe the effect of the passage of time by repeatedly measuring the same group of participants. For example, let's say we want to study vocabulary development in children. To do so, we'll test the same group yearly from ages 4 to 8. As in Table 11.3, such a design is set up and analyzed in the same way as any other repeated-measures experiment. After collapsing vertically, any differences between the mean scores for the conditions will reflect changes in vocabulary as a function of age. (As usual, this factor can be part of a multifactor design, in which other true or quasi-independent variables are examined.)

Researchers also study other periods of time, such as observing participants daily or monthly. In fact, as mentioned in Chapter 10, Gladue and Delaney (1990) technically used a longitudinal design when they repeatedly questioned patrons in a bar to see whether the other patrons appeared more attractive as closing time approached.

TABLE 11.3 Diagram of a One-Way Longitudinal Study Showing Repeated Observations of Each Child at Different Ages

Each X *represents vocabulary score.*

Age (in years)

	4	5	6	7	8
Participant 1	X	X	X	X	X
Participant 2	X	X	X	X	X
Participant 3	X	X	X	X	X
Participant 4	X	X	X	X	X
Participant 5	X	X	X	X	X
	$\overline{X}$	$\overline{X}$	$\overline{X}$	$\overline{X}$	$\overline{X}$

The overriding advantage of a longitudinal study is that, as a repeated-measures design, it keeps participant variables reasonably constant between the conditions. Thus, observing the same children as they age keeps constant such variables as their genetic makeup, their parents, the environments they're raised in, and so on.

There are, however, several disadvantages to longitudinal designs. First, just keeping in touch with participants over a lengthy period can be difficult, so these studies often involve a small N, and the results may be biased by *subject mortality*. Second, the design is repeated measures, and so successive conditions may be confounded by *order effects* (which cannot be counterbalanced). Third, and most important, a longitudinal study is inherently confounded by any extraneous variable that participants experience during the study. For example, an increase in a child's vocabulary between age 4 and 5 might appear to reflect normal development but might actually be due to his learning to read or watching certain television shows. Finally, a longitudinal study may lack *temporal validity*, poorly generalizing to future generations because the society and culture are constantly changing. A study of language development conducted in the 1950s, for example, might not generalize to children today because of such recent innovations as educational television and preschool education.

REMEMBER *Longitudinal designs* are confounded by extraneous events that occur during the course of the study, and they may not generalize over time.

Cross-Sectional Designs

We can also study the passage of time using a **cross-sectional design.** This is a between-subjects quasi-experiment in which different participants are observed at different ages or at different points in a temporal sequence. Thus, for example, we might select a cross section of ages, testing the vocabulary of a group of

4-year-olds, a different group of 5-year-olds, and so on, as shown in Table 11.4. Basically, this is another example of selecting participants for each condition using a participant variable—except that the variable here is based on time. (Again, this factor may be part of a multifactor design, including other true or quasi-independent variables.)

The major advantage of a cross-sectional design is that the study can be conducted rather quickly and easily. The major disadvantage is that the conditions might differ in terms of many confounding variables. For example, our 5-year-old participants will differ from the 4-year-olds in genetic makeup, family environment, and other variables that might cause differences in their vocabulary scores.

REMEMBER   A *cross-sectional design* involves a between-subjects comparison of different age groups that might be confounded by any other variable that also distinguishes the groups.

In fact, a special confounding can occur in cross-sectional studies because of differences in *subject history*. **Cohort effects** occur when age differences are confounded by differences in subject history. The larger the differences in age, the greater the potential for cohort effects. For example, let's say we study memory ability as a function of age by testing people born in the United States in 1930, 1950, and 1970. These groups differ not only in age but also in that each group grew up during a different era. Therefore, their backgrounds differ in terms of health and nutritional care, educational programs, and cultural experiences: One group reached adolescence during World War II, another during the birth of television, and the third when drugs and "disco" were common. Thus, any observed differences in memory ability might actually be due to these differences in history. Further, if each group's unique background influences performance, then the results will generalize poorly to any other generations having different backgrounds.

TABLE 11.4 Diagram of a One-Way Cross-Sectional Study Showing Observations of a Different Group of Children at Each Age

Each X represents vocabulary score.

Age (in years)

4	5	6	7	8
X	X	X	X	X
X	X	X	X	X
X	X	X	X	X
X	X	X	X	X
X	X	X	X	X
$\overline{X}$	$\overline{X}$	$\overline{X}$	$\overline{X}$	$\overline{X}$

> **REMEMBER**   *Cohort effects* are the confounding of age differences with generational history differences.

A more subtle but equally detrimental problem is that a particular testing procedure may not be appropriate for widely divergent age groups. If you test participants' knowledge of common popular culture, for example, older people might be unable to identify the names of current rock-and-roll bands or to understand computer games. But if you test knowledge of political or historical events, older people might perform better, because they lived through the events. Likewise, different age groups will not be equally motivated or equally engaged by a particular procedure. The elderly simply might not want to play at tasks like memorizing word lists or holding a pen in their mouths to make them smile. Take care, therefore, to ensure that differences in the mental and physical abilities, experiences, and motivations of different age groups do not confound the variable of age.

Because of the greater likelihood of potential confoundings, cross-sectional designs are generally considered to be less effective than longitudinal designs. However, especially if you match participants across conditions on relevant variables, such designs do provide an immediate comparison of individuals who differ in age or time-related experiences.

Cohort Designs

We cannot completely prevent cohort effects, but we can identify when they are present by using a cohort design. A **cohort design** is a longitudinal study of several groups, each from a different generation. For example, let's say we repeatedly study the vocabulary development in one "generation" of children beginning when they were 4 years old in 1990 and in another "generation" of children beginning when they were 4 in 1994. As shown in Table 11.5, this design is set up and analyzed in the same way as any other *two-way mixed design* experiment. Collapsing across scores vertically produces the mean score for each age, and differences between the means show the *main effect* of age. This factor provides the longitudinal, developmental information. Also collapsing scores horizontally produces the main-effect mean for each generation. If there is no significant difference between these means, then there is no evidence of differences due to a child's generation. If there is a difference between the two groups, however, then cohort effects are present, and the developmental results are less likely to generalize to other generations. Likewise, the absence of a significant interaction between generation and age would suggest that changes in scores as a function of age are basically similar—parallel—regardless of each generation's history. A significant interaction, however, would indicate that the type of changes with age that we see depends on which generation is examined—in which case, again we have a cohort effect.

TABLE 11.5   Diagram of a Two-Way Cohort Study

Xs represent vocabulary scores.

Repeated measures over age

		4	5	6	7	8	
1990	1	X	X	X	X	X	
Participants	2	X	X	X	X	X	$\overline{X}$
	3	X	X	X	X	X	
	4	X	X	X	X	X	
1994	1	X	X	X	X	X	
Participants	2	X	X	X	X	X	$\overline{X}$
	3	X	X	X	X	X	
	4	X	X	X	X	X	
Age main effect →		$\overline{X}$	$\overline{X}$	$\overline{X}$	$\overline{X}$		

Generation main effect

REMEMBER   A *cohort design* is the longitudinal study of several groups, each from a different generation.

To help you remember the names and procedures of all of the preceding quasi-experimental designs, they are summarized in Table 11.6.

DESCRIPTIVE RESEARCH

The final general research approach for us to discuss is **descriptive research:** studies designed to describe a behavior, the situation it occurs in, or the individuals exhibiting it. You already know that correlational designs—including quasi-experiments—are descriptive procedures used to test a hypothesis that a relationship exists between two (or more) variables. Now, however, we'll discuss other descriptive designs, where the intent is to only observe and describe participants or their behavior, so we do not manipulate or control any variables. In fact, sometimes such studies do not look for a specific hypothesized relationship, so we do not necessarily correlate changing variables. Instead, we describe only one individual or measure only one variable. Because the intent is to describe *natural* behaviors, descriptive research is usually conducted as field research in order to minimize demand characteristics and increase external validity.

REMEMBER   The focus of *descriptive research* is to describe a behavior, the situation in which it occurs, or the individuals who exhibit it.

TABLE 11.6 Summary of Quasi-Experimental Designs

Types of Design	Procedure
Designs involving participant variables	Create conditions on the basis of a participant's characteristic
Time-series designs	
One-group pretest–posttest design	Measure one group once before and once after the event
Nonequivalent control group design	Perform pretest and posttest on both an experimental and a nonequivalent control group
Interrupted time-series design	Obtain repeated measures from one group, both before and after the event
Multiple time-series design	Conduct interrupted time-series design on both an experimental and a control group
Designs involving temporal variables	
Longitudinal design	Obtain repeated measures as a function of age or experience
Cross-sectional design	Use a between-subjects design based on age or experience
Cohort design	Examine repeated-measures factor based on age and between-subjects factor based on generation

On the one hand, the disadvantage of such descriptions is that we examine a behavior without much control, so there is great potential for confoundings, and we might miss hidden influences or misinterpret what we see. Therefore, with descriptive research we can only speculate on the causes of a behavior. On the other hand, there are three advantages to descriptive research:

1. *Descriptions are informative.* For example, we might describe the mating rituals of frogs in the wild or the actions of drivers in a large city, because these are interesting behaviors. For applied research, we might describe consumer attitudes or the behaviors of drug addicts.

2. *Descriptions are the starting point for identifying variables and building hypothetical constructs.* For example, much research in clinical psychology developed from the constructs of Sigmund Freud, even though he only observed and described behaviors. Likewise, descriptions can provide an indirect test of a theory or model. (A researcher might ask, for example, "Are the predictions from a Freudian model confirmed by a description of a schizophrenic?")

3. *Description is sometimes the only way to study a behavior or situation.* Some behaviors are either practically or ethically impossible to produce in an experiment. For example, the only way to learn about the migratory behaviors of whales or the childhood experiences of a serial killer is by observing and describing them.

Thus, descriptive research is a legitimate approach, even though we cannot use it to confidently infer the causes of behavior. In addition to correlational designs, descriptive research falls into the following two general categories: field surveys and observational studies.

Field Surveys

In a **field survey**, people complete a questionnaire or interview in a natural setting so that we can infer the responses we would see if we could poll the population. Field surveys may apply to a narrowly defined population, as when, for example, surveying nurses treating AIDS patients to gauge their burn-out rates (George, Reed, Ballard, Colin, & Fielding, 1993). They are also used to describe the attitudes of the general population, as when, for example, surveying the public's reactions to crime (Harrison & Gfroerer, 1992). Field surveys are also used to describe less common experiences: The Roper Organization (1992) asked a sample if they had ever encountered ghosts and UFOs (more than 30% reported they had!).

All of the considerations about questionnaires discussed previously apply to a field survey: We need *construct* and *content validity*; *reliable* scoring; clear questions with precise, mutually exclusive choices; and consistent behavior from the interviewer. In particular, because we often deal with unsophisticated participants, we have them describe specific *behaviors*. Also, because participants might be busy, we counterbalance the order of questions across different participants and include "catch questions." In this way, we control for and identify response biases that occur when people half-heartedly respond in order to finish the task quickly.

In addition to a good questionnaire, the key to field surveys is to obtain a representative sample—a sample that truly reflects the characteristics and responses found in the population. To improve our chances of doing so, we typically survey a rather large N, often involving hundreds of participants. The survey may be conducted at a particular location, such as a shopping mall or other public place, because we believe members of the target population frequent that place. When we cannot reach a representative sample at one location, we may either mail the survey or conduct it over the telephone.

Mailed versus Telephone Surveys   A mailed survey is most useful when a large sample is needed and/or a lengthy questionnaire is being used—and when the researcher is not in a hurry to get the data. A major problem with mailed surveys, however, is that some people will not bother to complete and mail them back to us (even though we always include a stamped, addressed return envelope). The "return rate" can be very low, with only 10% or 20% of the surveys being returned. In such a case, we could have a sample that is very unrepresentative of the population. Therefore, some researchers use the rule of thumb that to have confidence in a mailed survey, the return rate should be at least 50%.

There are many techniques for improving return rates (see Kanuk & Berenson [1975] for a review). First, include a cover letter that explains the survey's purpose, tells why it is important for participants to complete it, and provides complete information about the researchers and how they can be contacted. Second, make sure that the survey has *face validity*: It should be well organized, neat, and professional, and should look like a serious psychological instrument. Third, both for reliability and to increase return rates, use closed-ended or brief open-ended questions so that it is easy for participants to accurately and rapidly complete the survey. Sometimes researchers include a small reward for participation, or they mail a follow-up letter to remind people to complete the survey. The goal is to convince participants that you are conducting legitimate research and to elicit their interest and cooperation.

Surveys can also be conducted over the telephone (see Lavrakas, 1993). These usually consist of structured interviews, in which the interviewer reads the participant a series of closed-ended questions. With only one interviewer, a telephone survey can be a *very* lengthy enterprise. With many interviewers, however, data collection can be accomplished quickly. For example, telephone surveys are used during election campaigns to get the momentary "pulse" of the voters. Also, telephone surveys may achieve a higher response rate than mailed surveys because people are less likely to refuse when directly asked for help. Conversely, some people might *not* participate because they consider such surveys to be an imposition on their lives. And people may be wary because "psychological surveys" have frequently been used as a cover for obscene phone calls and for fraudulent scams.

Again, the key to enlisting participants is an effective introduction. A professional, straightforward, yet friendly manner adds to your credibility and will engage people. Clearly identify yourself and allow participants to verify who you are (e.g., give them *your* phone number). Describe the survey, the time needed to complete it, its purpose, and the way in which responses will be handled. Keep the length of the questioning brief.

To improve the reliability of a telephone survey, keep each question and the response choices simple: Participants do not have the questions in front of them, so they must rely on their memory. Further, controlling the interviewer's behavior is important, so interviewers should read the questions in an unbiased manner and provide no additional information or hints. To the degree possible, the interviewer should respond to a participant's comments or questions by politely repeating the survey question.

Once you have identified the method for conducting a survey, you must decide how to assemble a representative sample.

Selecting the Sample   As with *any* type of research, surveys can be biased first by how you identify potential participants. On the one hand, we want to avoid including people from outside of the target population. Thus, to contact senior citizens, we might obtain addresses from senior citizen groups. On the other hand, we do not want to exclude any important segments of the population: Some senior citizens do not belong to any group. Thus, the first step is to identify all of the important subgroups in the target population that should be represented in the sample.

A survey can still be biased by how we select the sample. From a mailing list, we might simply contact every person. If this is not feasible, we can use any of the *sampling techniques* discussed in Chapter 10. Thus, when we have a large list of potential participants, *probability sampling*—simple and systematic random sampling—can be very effective. To ensure that the various subgroups of the population are accurately represented, however, surveys often employ *stratified random sampling*. Recall that this is when we identify the important subgroups in the population and then randomly select people from each of them. If we cannot obtain a list of the population, we may use *cluster sampling* and randomly select certain locations or groups to survey. Or, we can use *nonprobability sampling* techniques, such as *convenience sampling, quota sampling,* or *snowball sampling*.

Recognize, however, that any of the above approaches will produce a biased survey if there is any hidden aspect that eliminates certain participants. For example, telephoning at noon on weekdays will find only a certain type of person at home, or calling at dinnertime might be biased against parents who are busy feeding small children. Likewise, when distributing surveys at a public place, remember that the time and place you select, your manner of dress, and your approach to potential participants can all produce a biased sample.

In addition, participants have their own reasons for participating, so surveys are prone to the *volunteer bias*. Those who do not participate might be a certain type (e.g., very busy or very lazy), and those who do participate might be a different type (e.g., very inactive or bored). An especially important bias is how strongly participants feel about the issues being raised in the survey. For example, a mailed survey about abortion in the United States is most likely to be completed by those who very strongly favor abortion or very strongly oppose it. This is the danger with radio and television call-in surveys: The callers are probably a biased sample, consisting of those people who, for some reason, are especially motivated to make the call. Always consider whether you have missed the "silent majority."

REMEMBER In *survey research*, take care to identify the appropriate population and to obtain a *representative sample*.

Analyzing Survey Results   To summarize the results of a survey, use the statistical techniques already discussed. Rely on descriptive statistics, computing summary statistics such as the mean rating for questions, counting the frequency of certain responses, and describing the variability in scores. You might also correlate scores from different questions that measure different variables. As usual, determine whether correlations are significant and use *t*-tests, ANOVA, and chi square to identify significant differences between the groups that you've surveyed.

Because we conduct field surveys to describe the population, we frequently compute a confidence interval. Recall that a confidence interval is a range of values, one of which we would expect to find if we could test the entire population. Thus, for example, if a sample of nurses produces a certain mean rating about dealing with AIDS patients, a confidence interval would provide a range of values within which we expect the average rating of the population of nurses to fall. Likewise, confidence intervals are involved when we report the frequency of a certain response. In this context, however, they are usually called the **margin of error**. If, for example, pollsters report that 45% of a sample support the president's policies, they may also report a margin of error of ±3%. This communicates that if we could poll the entire population, the actual percentage of people who support the president is expected to be within 3 percentage points of 45%, or between 42% and 48%.

Recognize, however, that even with sophisticated sampling techniques and a large *N*, a survey will lack external validity to some degree. Any sample we select is likely to be different from other samples we might have selected. Also, the more we use convenience and other nonprobability sampling techniques, the less representative a sample will be. Finally, because surveys reflect how people feel at the time of the survey, they tend to have little *predictive validity* for describing how people will feel later.

Observational Studies

In a field survey, participants know they are being surveyed, and there is some interaction between them and the researcher, even if only through the mail. A different approach to descriptive research is to use observational techniques. In **observational research,** we observe participants in a less obvious manner. There are three general observational methods.

In **naturalistic observation**, the researcher unobtrusively observes a wide variety of behaviors in a rather unstructured and unsystematic manner. To be unobtrusive, we could use hidden cameras and camouflaged hiding places, or simply blend in with the crowd in a public place. If unobtrusive techniques are not possible, then we first *habituate* participants to our presence. For example, the famous studies performed by Jane Goodall (1986, 1990) involved naturalistic observation of chimpanzees. After they had habituated to her presence, she observed their general lifestyles in the wild. Likewise, Mastrofski and Parks (1990) performed an observational study of police officers in action by riding with the officers on patrol.

More commonly, researchers perform **systematic naturalistic observation.** We are again unobtrusive, but here we identify a particular behavior to observe and are more "systematic" in our observations. For example, Heslin and Boss

(1980) observed the nonverbal interactions of people being met at an airport. This approach is also common in studies of animals in the wild; Boesch-Acherman and Boesch (1993), for example, observed the use of natural tools by wild chimpanzees.

Sometimes the behavior of interest involves private interactions between members of a group that cannot be seen from afar. Then, we perform **participant observation,** in which the researcher is an active member of the group being observed. Usually, the researcher's activities are "disguised" or hidden from participants. In a classic example, Rosenhan (1973) arranged for "normal" people to be admitted to a psychiatric hospital to observe how patients were treated. Less frequently, the participant observer is "undisguised."

REMEMBER   The basic approaches in *observational studies* are *naturalistic observation, systematic observation,* and *participant observation.*

The Pros and Cons of Observational Designs

The overriding advantage of an observational design is that, through unobtrusive observation, we see behaviors in a natural setting that are not influenced by reactivity or other demand characteristics. Therefore, such procedures are useful for identifying potentially important variables, and they provide the ultimate test of models or predictions about a behavior that are derived from laboratory settings. There are, however, several disadvantages.

1. *We do not obtain informed consent.* Especially with participant observation, there is the ethical question of violating a person's expectation of privacy.

2. *Descriptions are highly susceptible to experimenter expectations.* Therefore, we may see only what we expect to see. This is especially a problem with participant observation because the researcher can inadvertently cause participants to behave in the expected way.

3. *Usually, we cannot randomly sample from the population.* Instead, we must rely on convenience samples of individuals we can find.

4. *Usually, we cannot quantify responses.* Instead we have only a verbal description of a behavior. Such *qualitative data* lack precision and accuracy, and are not very sensitive to subtle differences in behavior.

5. *Such designs have little internal validity.* Because of the above problems and uncontrolled extraneous variables, observational designs have little validity for even identifying the presence of a relationship between variables, let alone for identifying causal relationships.

To minimize these problems, researchers include more systematic techniques that build in greater control. For example, we develop scoring criteria using *content analysis* as discussed in Chapter 10. Recall that this involves defining how to assign scores to behaviors by looking for specific movements, speech patterns, facial expressions, and so on. Thus, for example, if we are looking to observe and describe aggressive automobile drivers, then we must specify the actions—and the score we'll give to each—that constitute aggressiveness.

We can also be systematic in terms of *when* observations are made. One approach is to use *time sampling,* in which we break the observation period into intervals and then determine whether the behavior occurs during each interval. And, when dealing with groups, we might observe the entire group all at once, or we might observe only one individual for a certain time, then observe another, and so on.

To facilitate accurate data recording and to minimize the time spent *not* observing, we produce structured scoring sheets so that we can simply check off categories of behaviors. Or we *automate* by tape-recording participants or our verbal descriptions of them for later scoring. To reduce experimenter biases, we use *multiple observers* and *double-blind* procedures. And, finally, to improve external validity, we attempt to obtain more "random" samples, either through systematic random sampling of every *n*th individual or through random selection of clusters.

REMEMBER   *Observational designs* allow descriptions of natural behaviors, but at a cost of reduced reliability and validity.

Additional Sources of Data in Descriptive Approaches

The term *observational research* usually implies that a researcher was physically present to observe participants. In the research literature, however, you'll encounter other procedures that are used to collect data. Whether the researcher's goal is simply to describe individuals or to test a hypothesis about a specific relationship, the three common terms that further identify a design are *archival research*, *ex post facto research*, and *case studies.*

Archival Research   In **archival research,** the source of the data is written records. Typically, these records come from schools, hospitals, government agencies, or police, with researchers focusing on histories of mental illness, academic and professional accomplishments, or criminal behavior. Archival research is also used to describe social trends and events, looking at newspapers, birth certificates, army records, etc. (In an interesting twist, Connors and Alpher [1989] analyzed the alcohol-related themes in country-western songs. They found that in such songs alcohol is usually used for drowning one's sorrows.) (*Note:* As above, archival research often involves descriptive/correlational designs, but such data can also be used to assign individuals to different groups to compare in a quasi-experiment.)

The advantage of archival research is that it allows access to behaviors that would otherwise be unobservable. It also allows us to verify participants' self-reports (e.g., we can compare actual college-grade records to participants' reported grades). However, archival research also presents three disadvantages. First, obtaining access to records can be difficult or impossible. Second, we are obliged to obtain informed consent from the people described in the records, or we have the ethical problem of invading their privacy. And third, the accuracy of the data depends entirely on the people who created the records. Usually, the records are not made with a researcher's question in mind, so they often do not directly address our variables. And, they may contain verbose, open-ended descriptions, requiring much subjective interpretation on our part. We can again attempt to use content analysis, but different record keepers may give such different descriptions that a consistent, reliable approach is not possible. Often, too, there are few controls in place to prevent errors, or to prevent the inclusion of the record keeper's personal biases. Thus, we often have less confidence in archival data than in data derived from direct observations.

Ex Post Facto Research   In **ex post facto research,** an experiment or descriptive study is conducted after the events of interest have occurred (ex post facto means "after the fact"). Usually, this approach involves examining archival records. (Thus, the previous study of hockey team penalties was also ex post facto, because it involved past penalty records.) Less commonly, ex post facto research may involve having participants report a past event (e.g., completing a questionnaire regarding their stress levels before and after an earthquake).

The problem with ex post facto designs is again that we obtain potentially unreliable data. Often we cannot precisely quantify the variables and events that occurred, nor ensure that they reliably occurred for all participants. Likewise, written records are only as accurate as the people keeping them, and participants' self-reports may be biased and error-prone. Also, we usually cannot randomly assign participants to conditions after the fact, so, at best, we have a quasi-experiment and thus cannot infer the cause of any behavior.

Case Studies   A **case study** is an in-depth study of one situation or "case." Usually, the case is a person. However, a case study is different from a single-subject experiment, because here we are not manipulating any independent variables. Some researchers distinguish between a case *study*, implying a prospective, longitudinal approach, and a case *history*, implying a retrospective, archival approach. Either way, such studies are frequently found in clinical research, providing an in-depth description of a particular patient's clinical symptoms and reactions to therapy. Case studies may also involve the normal behavior of an individual, while sometimes the case may involve a specific event or organization (e.g., Anderson [1983] studied the government's decision-making procedures during the "case" of the Cuban missile crisis).

The advantage of case studies is that they provide an in-depth description of an individual or event. The disadvantage is that, because they are essentially longitudinal studies, they are confounded by any extraneous factor that occurs during the period being studied. Further, because they are also archival studies, they may yield data with poor reliability and validity. And, the selection of the participant or case is often a convenience and not random, and with an N of only 1, the external validity of a case study can be poor, probably *not* typifying other cases.

> **REMEMBER** Descriptive procedures may involve *archival research, ex post facto designs,* and *case studies.*

A summary of all of the approaches to descriptive research that we've discussed is presented in Table 11.7.

Ethical Issues in Descriptive Research

The ethical issues in descriptive research are the same as in experiments: To minimize the risks to participants and to justify any remaining risk in terms of the knowledge we gain. Here, the risks arise because being observed by a researcher or completing a survey might be embarrassing, stressful, or unpleasant for participants.

If the participants are aware that a study is being conducted, follow the usual rules. Tell participants that their responses are kept confidential, and alleviate their fears about what the data will divulge about them. Obtain explicit informed consent, even with field surveys. And always provide a debriefing.

The principal ethical dilemma arises with unobtrusive research. From one perspective, observational techniques are another name for spying on people. With disguised participant observation, we are present under false pretenses and

TABLE 11.7 Summary of Terminology Used in Descriptive Research

Field survey	Polling people in the field
Observational research	Observation of participants by
Naturalistic observation	unobtrusive, rather unstructured observations
Systematic observation	unobtrusive but rather structured observations
Participant observation	unobtrusive, systematic observations, with researcher a member of the group being observed
Archival research	Any type of design in which data are collected from formal records
Ex post facto research	Any type of design in which data are collected after events have occurred
Case study	In-depth description of one individual, group, or event

violate a person's expectation of privacy. With archival studies, we might end up examining private records without obtaining the person's consent. Therefore, with any form of unobtrusive field research, we might be violating participants' rights.

As usual, it's your responsibility to weigh the violation of a person's rights—and how private they'll consider a behavior to be—against the potential scientific information that you'll gain. Also, remember that prior informed consent is required unless the physical and mental risk to participants is minimal. And, as usual, descriptive procedures must also be approved by your institution's Human Subjects Review Committee.

A WORD ABOUT PROGRAM EVALUATION

There is one other type of design that you may encounter in the literature, that incorporates a combination of the various procedures we've discussed. It is most common when researchers conduct studies on community human services programs, such as government programs for preventing or treating drug and alcohol abuse or social or educational programs. **Program evaluation** refers to a variety of procedures for developing and evaluating social programs. Think of the social program as essentially *applied research* into social change. We employ the experimental principle that providing some form of treatment to participants—to society—will produce a corresponding change in behavior. Program evaluation is used to set up and evaluate the experiment: It provides feedback to administrators and service providers, as well as providing scientific information about how the program works as a quasi-independent variable.

Although this research encompasses many procedures (see Posavac & Carey, 1989), it usually consists of four basic phases:

1. *Needs assessment.* Before designing a particular program, researchers identify the services that are needed and determine whether potential users of the program will use it.

2. *Program planning.* When designing the program, researchers apply findings from the literature that suggest the best methods to implement for the behavior and situation being addressed.

3. *Program monitoring.* Once the program is implemented, researchers monitor the program to ensure that it provides the intended services and that clients are using them.

4. *Outcome evaluation.* Eventually, researchers determine whether the program is having its intended effect, by using a *time-series design* that compares behaviors before and after the program's implementation.

The data in each of these phases come from such sources as field surveys of the community; archival studies of hospital, school, and police records; and interviews, unobtrusive observations, and case studies of service providers and clients. On the one hand, such procedures suffer from all of the flaws we've discussed, especially because they are quasi-experiments. On the other hand, program evaluation addresses a very real societal need, and so flawed data are better than no data (as long as the flaws are recognized and considered).

> **REMEMBER** *Program evaluation* involves procedures for creating and evaluating social programs.

PUTTING IT ALL TOGETHER

The names of the designs discussed in this chapter communicate different procedures, but they are not always rigidly defined, "either–or" terms. Instead, they can be mixed and matched to suit your particular research question or to identify a characteristic of your study. For example, the hockey penalty study discussed earlier was simultaneously an archival, ex post facto, quasi-experimental, interrupted time-series study of one case. Each of these terms communicates different strengths and weaknesses of the study, so they should cause you to think about the reliability of scores, potential confoundings, and the generality of the conclusions that are drawn.

Perhaps the most important thing to remember about quasi-experiments is that they often look like true experiments, especially when a participant variable is being studied in a laboratory setting. When evaluating your own research or that of others, remember that you won't find a red flag signaling the nature of the design. Therefore, always carefully examine whether the participants are randomly assigned to the conditions of a variable. If not, then the results only *suggest* the causes of the behavior being studied.

CHAPTER SUMMARY

1. In a *quasi-experiment* involving a *quasi-independent variable*, participants cannot be randomly assigned to conditions. Instead, they are assigned to a condition based on some inherent characteristic. Because the independent variable is probably confounded by other participant variables, quasi-experiments have much less internal validity than true experiments.

2. Effective manipulation of a quasi-independent variable involving a participant variable hinges on the selection of participants for each condition who are similar to each other but very different from those in other conditions.

3. *Regression toward the mean* occurs when, because of inconsistent random factors, extreme scores tend to change in the direction of coming closer to the mean.

4. A *time-series design* is a quasi-experimental, repeated-measures design in which a behavior is sampled at different times.

5. A *one-group pretest–posttest* design has no control group.

6. In a *nonequivalent control group design,* the control group and the experimental group have different characteristics and different experiences during the study.

7. In an *interrupted time-series design,* observations are made at several spaced times prior to the treatment and at several times after it.

8. In a *multiple time-series design,* both an experimental group and a nonequivalent control group are observed at several times before the treatment and several times after it.

9. In a *longitudinal design,* participants are repeatedly measured to observe the effect of the passage of time.

10. A *cross-sectional design* is a between-subjects experiment in which participants are observed at different ages or at different points in a temporal sequence.

11. *Cohort effects* occur when differences in age are confounded by differences in subject history.

12. A *cohort design* is a factorial design consisting of a longitudinal study of several groups, each from a different generation.

13. In some *descriptive research,* the goal is to describe a behavior, the situation in which it occurs, or the individual exhibiting it. The three major types of descriptive research are *correlational studies, field surveys,* and *observational studies.*

14. A *field survey* involves having people complete a questionnaire or interview in the field, either in person, by mail, or over the telephone.

15. A confidence interval or the *margin of error* is computed when estimating the population's responses to a field survey.

16. In *naturalistic observation,* the researcher observes participants' behaviors in an unobtrusive and unsystematic manner. In *systematic naturalistic observation*, the researcher unobtrusively observes a behavior in a systematic manner. And in *participant observation,* the researcher is a member of the group being observed.

17. *Ex post facto research* is conducted after a phenomenon has occurred. *Archival research* is conducted using participants' records. A *case study* involves an in-depth description of one individual, organization, or event.

18. *Program evaluation* involves procedures for developing and evaluating social programs.

KEY TERMS   (with page references)

archival research   355
case study   356
cohort design   347
cohort effects   346
cross-sectional design   345
descriptive research   348
ex post facto research   356
field survey   350
interrupted time-series design   341
longitudinal design   344
margin of error   353
multiple time-series design   343
naturalistic observation   353

nonequivalent control group   339
observational research   353
one-group pretest–posttest design   337
participant observation   354
program evaluation   358
quasi-experiment   331
quasi-independent variable   331
regression toward the mean   335
systematic naturalistic observation   353
time-series design   337

REVIEW QUESTIONS

1. (a) What is the difference between a true experiment and a quasi-experiment? (b) In what way are quasi-experiments and correlational designs similar? (c) In what way are they different?

2. (a) What three types of variables are studied as quasi-independent variables? (b) Why can't we confidently infer causality from a quasi-experiment?

3. (a) How do you design a quasi-independent variable in order to study a participant variable? (b) What is the goal when using the scores from a selection pretest to create conditions? (c) What bias might be produced by a pretest?

4. (a) What is a one-group pretest–posttest design? (b) What is missing from this design? (c) What extraneous variables might confound this design?

5. (a) What is a nonequivalent control group design? (b) What potential confounding variables does it eliminate? (c) What potential confounding variables are not eliminated?

6. (a) What is an interrupted time-series design? (b) What potential confounding variables does it eliminate? (c) What potential confoundings does it not eliminate?

7. (a) What is a multiple time-series design? (b) What potential confounding variables does it eliminate? (c) What potential confoundings does it not eliminate?

8. (a) What is a longitudinal design? (b) What is its major advantage? (c) What is its major flaw?

9. (a) What is a cross-sectional design? (b) What is its major strength? (c) What is its major weakness?

10. (a) What are cohort effects? (b) What is a cohort design? (c) What is the advantage of this design? (d) How do you determine whether cohort effects are present?

11. What is the purpose of descriptive research?

12. (a) What is the difference between naturalistic observation, systematic observation, and participant observation? (b) What are the strengths of observational designs? (c) What are their weaknesses?

13. (a) What is archival research? (b) What is ex post facto research? (c) What are the major weaknesses of these designs? (d) Why do researchers use them?

14. (a) What is a case study? (b) What is the strength of this approach? (c) What is its weakness?

15. What is program evaluation?

APPLICATION QUESTIONS

16. (a) When do researchers mail surveys? (b) When do they use telephone surveys? (c) Why is it important to ensure high participation rates in both types of surveys?

17. At the beginning of a gym class, you obtain the highest score on a physical-fitness test. During the semester, however, your scores get worse, while the initially unfit students tend to score higher. You conclude that the gym class helps unfit people but harms the most fit. (a) What rival hypothesis involving random factors might explain these results? (b) How would it cause the changes in scores? (c) How would you test your hypothesis?

18. The results of a survey indicate that 33% of college students are extremely concerned about their future job prospects. The reported margin of error is ±5%. What does this number indicate?

19. A student wants to perform a longitudinal study by measuring yearly the self-esteem scores of a group of students as they pass through their freshman, sophomore, junior, and senior years in college. To control order effects, he wants to counterbalance the order in which participants are tested in these four repeated-measures conditions. What would you tell him?

20. A student measures the happiness of a group of sorority pledges at the beginning of the semester and again at the end of the semester in which they've been admitted to the sorority. She finds that the latter scores are higher and concludes that joining a sorority increases a woman's happiness. (a) What is the name of this design? (b) What major flaw is present?

(c) What rival hypotheses might explain her results? (d) What would you do to improve the study?

21. Why will a quasi-independent variable involving a participant variable usually *not* involve a repeated-measures design?

22. Two politicians are arguing over whether providing free lunches in elementary schools is beneficial to students. (a) If they have data, what research design provided it? (b) What sources would be used to produce the data? (c) What flaws are likely that would weaken the arguments of both politicians?

DISCUSSION QUESTIONS

23. You wish to conduct a field survey to describe the nation's attitudes toward gun control. With a closed-ended questionnaire in hand, (a) How would you identify the population? (b) How would you contact participants and have them complete the questionnaire? (c) How would you select your sample? (d) How would you summarize the data? (e) Evaluate your design.

24. (a) Using the questionnaire in question 23, how would you conduct a quasi-experiment to determine whether people who differ in their attitudes toward gun control (the independent variable) also differ in how frightened they become when confronted by someone carrying a gun? (b) What flaws in manipulating the independent variable should you try to avoid? (c) How will you analyze the study? (d) What ethical problems have you created? (e) Someone claims that people who favor gun control do so because they are afraid of people with guns. What outcome in your study would support this claim and why?

25. You measure the maturity levels of students at four times during the college year (factor A). You compare freshman from 10 years ago with present-day freshman (factor B). (a) What type of variable is factor A? (b) What type of variable is factor B? (c) What type of design have you created?

26. In question 25 you obtain the following cell means. What should you conclude about (a) the presence of cohort effects? (b) how maturity changes during a college student's year?

	Time 1	Time 2	Time 3	Time 4
10 years ago	10	20	30	40
Present day	25	25	25	25

27. In two nonequivalent control group designs, you obtain the following mean stress scores for people before and after an earthquake. (a) What should you conclude about whether the treatment caused the change in scores in the experimental group in Study A? (b) What other hypotheses are plausible? (c) What should you conclude in Study B? (d) What hypotheses are eliminated in Study B? (e) What possible confounding is still possible in Study B?

Study A

	Before	After
Control	60	50
Experimental	30	60

Study B

	Before	After
Control	60	70
Experimental	50	85

4 ////////

PUTTING IT ALL TOGETHER

Believe it or not, you now understand the vast majority of the designs and statistical analyses used in psychological research. Because we always want valid and reliable data, there are actually few differences in the mechanics of designing and conducting most research, and you are familiar with all of the important issues. The trick now is to be able to apply your knowledge. The following chapter provides you with practice at applying design principles by working through several structured scenarios, so that you really can put it all together.

12

A Review: Examples of Designing and Evaluating Research

This chapter is a review of all of the material presented in this book. But, rather than merely repeating everything you've read, the focus is on getting you to apply the design issues we've discussed. Therefore, first we'll review the major questions we've addressed and tickle your memory with the many research terms you've seen. The chapter, then, presents four major research topics that give you practice at making design decisions. For each, you are the researcher, designing the study and dealing with possible follow-up issues. To get the most out of this, don't just passively read along. Instead, actively play this game: Each discussion sets up the research scenario from a somewhat "classic" series of studies. Then, you'll see several questions about beginning the study. Answer the questions at that time as though you are actually conducting this study. In the paragraph following the questions, you'll see the answers (or at least the answers the original researchers chose). From these, we'll develop the study further until we encounter more questions. Answer these, then read on, and so on.

The chapter then ends with brief discussions of five research topics and some example studies. Each discussion provides some ideas for research you might want to pursue, and provides practice at searching the literature.

But first, the review.

SUMMARY OF THE ISSUES WHEN DESIGNING RESEARCH

There are many issues to consider for each aspect of any study, and often the hardest part is just remembering them all. For help at this, first refer to the summaries and checklists inside the front and back covers of this book. Also, there have been a number of summary tables throughout the chapters for you to refer to. In particular, look back at Table 2.1 (on page 42) that depicts the overall flow of a study: It shows how research begins with broad hypothetical constructs that we whittle down into a specific relationship, and then eventually we generalize back to these constructs. Within these steps are the following major questions to ask yourself when designing or evaluating a study.

1. *Purpose of the study?* Is it to test a *causal hypothesis*, to demonstrate a *correlation*, or is it some other *descriptive study*? Does the *hypothesis* conform to the rules of science?

2. *Type of behavior studied?* Does it involve a participant characteristic (*trait* or *state*), opinions and attitudes, or responses to concrete stimuli or to a social interaction?

3. *Type of design?* Is the study a *true experiment* or a *quasi-experiment* (*one-group, times series, etc.*)? Is it *pretest–posttest*? Should it be *single-subject, correlational, observational, archival* or a *survey* (*interview or questionnaire*)? Should it be a *field* or *laboratory* study?

4. *Type of participant and sampling?* What is the *target population*? What *selection criteria* are needed? What *sampling technique* should be used?

Will participants be unrepresentative, including because of the *volunteer bias* or *subject mortality*?

5. *Control of participant variables?* What *confounding* participant variables are present? Should you *balance* participants or *limit the population* in a *between-subjects* design, or create a *within-subjects* design through *matched groups* or *repeated measures*?

6. *How to manipulate variables?* Should you vary the instructions or the stimuli presented? Is a *control group* (with *placebo*) required? Do you need *confederates*? Is the manipulation *strong, reliable,* and *valid*? Do you need a *manipulation check*?

7. *How to measure variables?* Will you measure behaviors overtly or *unobtrusively*? Should you use *self-reports* (with what wording and *response scales*) and do you need *content analysis*? Are *raters* needed and what is their *inter-rater reliability*? Will participants be tested individually? What are the *scoring criteria*, are they *sensitive*, and is there a *restricted range*? Is a *double blind* needed? Have you established the procedure's *split-half* or *test–retest reliability* and its *convergent, discriminant,* or *concurrent validity*?

8. *Materials needed?* What materials and apparatus do you need? Are the *instructions* clear and complete? Are *practice trials* or *habituation* needed? Are stimuli consistent and comparable, or will *instrumentation effects* occur? Are *alternate forms* of a questionnaire needed?

9. *Procedural problems?* Is there *experimental realism*? Are there *order effects, demand characteristics (reactivity, social desirability,* or *experimenter expectations), diffusion of treatment, response sets,* effects of *subject history* and *maturation,* or other biases present? Are *confounding variables* present, and is *partial* or *complete counterbalancing* needed? Should you conduct a *pilot study*?

10. *Ethical problems?* Are you harming participants or violating their rights? Is *deception* justified? Are you obtaining *informed consent*, providing a *debriefing*, and submitting to the *Human Subjects Review Committee*?

11. *Statistical analysis?* What is your N? Have you maximized *power*? Do the scores fit a *parametric* or *nonparametric* procedure? Is a *between-subjects* or a *within-subjects* analysis required?

12. *Validity of conclusions?* Is the *predicted relationship* present, and do the results *confirm* your hypothesis? Have you considered the *strength* of the relationship and *proportion of variance accounted for* to gauge the importance of your variables? Are there *rival hypotheses* that reduce *internal validity*? Have you created a *pseudo-explanation*? Do you have *external, construct, ecological,* and *temporal validity*?

If you understand the italicized terms in the above list, then congratulations, you understand research methods! Refer to this list as you consider each of the following studies.

TOPIC 1: AN EXPERIMENT ON ATTRIBUTION OF AROUSAL

When people become physiologically aroused by one stimulus, their emotional response to other stimuli is heightened. In particular, researchers have proposed that the heightened physiological arousal to a fearful stimulus is "misattributed" (misdiagnosed) as romantic attraction toward a member of the opposite sex. Dutton and Aron (1974) tested this proposal in several studies.

What are the hypothesis and purpose of this study?

What are the variables to be studied, and which design is appropriate?

How would you elicit the dependent behavior?

What sampling would you use, and should you control subject variables?

The *hypothesis* is that greater attraction to a member of the opposite sex occurs when participants experience fear from another source. Because causation is the issue here, a *true experiment* is appropriate. The *independent variable* is amount of fear, a temporary *state* characteristic. The *dependent variable* is the amount of attraction a participant experiences. Although you might perform a field experiment, let's first discuss a laboratory setting, as in Experiment 3 in Dutton and Aron (1974).

The study calls for a *confederate* who will be the object of attraction. Thus, the manipulation is to create conditions of different levels of fear in participants while a confederate is present. The dependent measure is the participants' attraction to the confederate. Because we'd be unlikely to change a person's attraction to the confederate in a repeated-measures design, a *between-subjects* design with a single trial per participant is appropriate.

Participants are tested individually because in a group they might be inhibited and not divulge any attraction. To keep the attractiveness of the confederate constant, one confederate serves for all conditions. Regarding participant variables, Dutton and Aron used a female confederate, thus requiring male participants. They should not know the confederate and ideally should have a minimum of other romantic entanglements (engaged or married people might resist feeling, or at least reporting, any attraction). Participants should be the same age as the confederate, and you might limit or balance race and nationality. Otherwise, there is no unique population here, so a *random sample* from available college students is sufficient.

Now, how should you manipulate participants' fear? You could arrange for an "accident" that raises anxiety or concoct an "experiment" that directly harms participants to make them fearful. But, *ethically*, these tactics are inappropriate, and all you really need to do is threaten them with something fear provoking. But, the threat should be realistic within the context of an experiment, and also allow you to manipulate the amount of fear. You might threaten to hit participants or to embarrass them, for example, but this might cause unintended responses, such as anger or refusal to participate. Instead, Dutton and Aron capitalized on the reputation of psychology experiments by telling participants that they would be electrically shocked as part of the study.

How would you create the conditions to manipulate fear?

How would you confirm that the intended effect occurred?

Dutton and Aron manipulated fear by threatening participants with different levels of shock. The shock was described as either small (low fear condition) or large (high fear condition). To produce a *strong manipulation*, they described the small shock as "a minor tingle which some people actually find pleasant" and the large shock as "quite painful." (You might add a *control group* threatened with no shock.)

A *manipulation check* ensures that the procedure actually influences participants' fear, so at some point we'd actually measure their anxiety level as a function of their assigned shock level.

How would you measure the dependent variable?

Instead of observing participants' behavior and then trying to infer how attracted they were, Dutton and Aron asked participants how sexually attracted they were to the confederate. But rather than asking "Is she attractive?" they achieved greater sensitivity by presenting a 5-point *Likert scale* with the questions "How much would you like to ask her out?" and "How much would you like to kiss her?" Included in the *questionnaire* was a *manipulation check* in the form of the question: "How do you feel about being shocked?" Participants' ratings were on a scale of like/dislike, and the researchers interpreted "greater dislike" as indicating "greater fear." They also included an additional, less threatening measure of arousal by having participants describe an ambiguous picture in a *projective* test. Each description was examined for sexual content using *content analysis* and, for *reliability*, was scored by two scorers.

Considering the reputation of psychology experiments, participants might be very suspicious and show a high degree of *reactivity* and *social desirability*.

How would you ensure experimental realism?

A deceptive cover story is needed so that participants encounter the confederate and are assigned a shock level in a convincing and realistic way. Dutton and Aron introduced the confederate to the participant as a second "participant." Both were ostensibly there for an experiment in which two people would be tested simultaneously, to study the effects of punishment (shock) on learning. The researcher then tossed a coin supposedly to determine which of the two would receive the high or low shock condition (but actually to randomly assign the real participants to their conditions). Then, because it was not necessary to actually administer the shock, participants completed the questionnaire.

How would you address demand characteristics?

To reduce reactivity and social desirability, Dutton and Aron presented the questionnaire under the guise that personality characteristics and feelings between participants can influence this type of learning study. The confederate and participant were taken to separate cubicles while the experimenter "set up the shock equipment." For *face validity*, the questionnaire contained several "filler" questions about the participants, along with the attraction and fear questions and the projective test.

What procedural or ethical problems must be addressed?

Because any subtle differences in the behaviors or demeanor of the confederate might alter her attractiveness, her behavior must be "scripted" so that she acts consistently with all participants. Keeping where she sits constant is also important because participants need to see her and yet not be too near or far away. Keeping her *blind* to the hypothesis is advisable, because she might otherwise emit subtle cues that could *confound* conditions. The experimenter must behave consistently as well. A *pilot study* to practice and debug the procedure is definitely needed.

Ethically, there is a problem if participants feel coerced into participating. Dutton and Aron solved this problem by first telling participants they would be shocked and *then* obtaining informed consent, thus giving them the opportunity to leave before the study continued. Although the researcher lied to participants because they were not actually shocked, the lie would cause them to expect more harm than they experienced—ethically, a much better situation than causing them to expect less harm than they experienced.

Select N, and diagram the study.

What statistical procedures will you perform?

Because of the very controlled setting and the small variability of rating scores, Dutton and Aron had sufficient power to obtain significant results with 20 participants per condition. The study is diagrammed in Table 12.1. Ratings from the "date" and "kiss" questions were averaged together, producing each participant's attraction score. These are *ratio scores* that fit the requirements of a *parametric*

TABLE 12.1   Diagram of the Misattribution Study

Conditions

	Low shock (Low fear)	High shock (High fear)	
Each X represents participant's mean attraction score	X X X X X	X X X X X	$N = 40$
overall mean attraction	$\overline{X} = 2.8$	$\overline{X} = 3.5$	

procedure. Therefore, a *between-subjects (independent samples) t-test* is appropriate. (If you included a control group or other levels, or if you included additional factors, you would perform a *between-subjects ANOVA.*) With higher ratings indicating greater attraction, Dutton and Aron obtained an overall mean attraction rating of 2.8 in the low-fear condition, which differed significantly from the mean rating of 3.5 in the high-fear condition.

Another analysis is also required: The manipulation check must confirm that the shock conditions produced high and low anxiety levels. The rating scores from the question about "disliking the shock" can also be analyzed using the independent samples *t*-test. Dutton and Aron found that the mean dislike rating for the high-shock group was significantly larger than for the low-shock group, suggesting that their manipulation did alter participants' fear levels as intended.

What conclusions can you draw from this study?

What issues of validity need to be addressed?

Significantly higher attraction scores in the high-fear group confirm the hypothesis that attraction is heightened by fear from an extraneous source, so there is support for the idea that participants misattribute their greater fear as being greater attraction to the confederate. Then, we would explain "psychologically" how a person's cognitive and emotional systems might work to produce such an error.

One important concern, however, is whether *demand characteristics* have limited our internal validity for concluding that it was actually fear that caused the attraction. Maybe the participants were dishonest because of reactivity, social desirability, and *experimenter expectancies*. After all, it doesn't take a genius to realize that if a "psychologist" tells you that a shock is very unpleasant, you should then say that you dislike the idea of being shocked! And, just because someone "dislikes" being shocked does not necessarily mean the person is afraid of it. It's possible, therefore, that participants were *not really* more or less fearful in their respective conditions. If so, then we don't know why they were more or less attracted to the confederate. Also, is there *external validity* for concluding that this relationship occurs in other settings? Participating in an experiment is not the usual context in which people become sexually attracted to others. This setting is very contrived, and everything depends on how convincing the confederate and experimenter were.

How would you replicate this study under more natural conditions?

We need a *field experiment* to test this hypothesis in a more naturalistic setting, using a natural fear-arousing stimulus. The idea is to catch participants after experiencing some positive yet fear-arousing event, so any thrill-seeking activity would suffice. For example, you could test at a "bungee cord–jumping" event or at a roller-coaster ride. Dutton and Aron selected a narrow, wobbly, foot-bridge suspended high above a scenic canyon to create the experimental condition of high fear. Nearby was a wide, solid, and sturdy bridge over the canyon, which served as the "control bridge" for the low- (no-) fear condition.

How would you conduct this experiment?

You might strategically place the confederate so that participants walk by her, and then question them to determine their attraction to her. However, participants might not even notice her. Dutton and Aron solved this problem with the following procedure: After a male had crossed the bridge, a female interviewer approached him to answer a questionnaire for a "study" about the effects of scenic attractions on creativity. Among the filler items was a brief projective test, which was later scored for sexual imagery by two trained *raters*. In addition, participants were offered the interviewer's phone number, so they could later call to "discuss the study." Whether participants took the phone number and whether they called were taken as indications of greater attraction to the interviewer. As a control, a male interviewer also tested some males and offered his phone number.

How would you analyze these results?

Dutton and Aron measured three dependent variables here. First, the sexual imagery scores from the projective test produced an *inter-rater* correlation coefficient of $+.87$. Therefore, the imagery scores (a ratio variable) were entered into two between-subjects *t*-tests (one for the female interviewer and one for the male), each comparing the conditions of high and low fear. With the female interviewer, the scary bridge produced significantly greater sexual imagery than did the control bridge. With the male interviewer, no significant difference was found.

Second, the scores for accepting the interviewer's telephone number and third, for actually calling her consist of two yes–no, categorical variables. Dutton and Aron found that 9 out of the 18 high-fear males who took the female interviewer's phone number actually called her. Only 2 out of the 16 low-fear men called. The male interviewer received 2 calls out of the 7 high-fear participants who took his number, and 1 call out of 6 from the low-fear group. To determine whether calling rates for the control and experimental groups differed significantly, Dutton and Aron performed one *chi square procedure* for the female interviewer and one for the male interviewer. They reported significant differences only for the female interviewer.

What procedural and control problems exist in this design?

First, you must confirm that the two bridges actually produce high and low fear, respectively. Because directly asking participants about their fear might have caused suspicion, Dutton and Aron relied on a pilot study in which other, similar males who crossed each bridge answered a questionnaire and confirmed the effect of the bridges.

A second problem is that random sampling was not possible here, because only those males who actually crossed a bridge and who volunteered to complete the questionnaire were tested. (Also, only those of a certain age who were unaccompanied by a female were approached.) Most critical is the fact that the participants themselves decided which bridge to cross. Given that participants were not randomly assigned to the conditions, this is a *quasi-experimental design*. There-fore, in addition to the bridge they crossed, participants might have differed along many other variables. In particular, those who crossed the scary bridge were probably more adventurous and perhaps this made them more likely to call the interviewer and to project more sexual imagery in their stories. In a replica-tion, Dutton and Aron created a more comparable control group by selecting men who had also crossed the scary bridge but who then loitered about until (presumably) the fear had dissipated. They found results similar to those reported above. Nonetheless, it is not appropriate to say that greater fear *caused* the higher attraction scores in this study.

What additional research on this topic would you suggest?

A general question concerns the *construct validity* of whether people actually do misinterpret extraneous arousal as sexual attraction. Do participants really not know that they were scared by the bridge or electric shock? If they can identify the actual source of their arousal, then they are not misattributing it, and some other factor is responsible for heightened sexual attraction. Because of this ques-tion, several alternative explanations for these results have been proposed (see Allen, Kendrick, Linder, & McCall, 1989).

Conceptual replications of misattribution effects are also appropriate. For example, Cohen, Waugh, and Place (1989) observed couples entering and leaving a movie theater and noted that more touching occurred after a scary movie than after a dull one. White and Knight (1984) demonstrated heightened attraction due to misattribution of arousal from physical exercise (running in place). How-ever, misattribution has not always been successfully replicated (e.g., Kendrick, Cialdini, & Linder, 1979). To extend this research, consider that most studies involve male participants. But would the same results occur with female partici-pants and a male confederate? Would they occur with homosexual males or females and a same-sex confederate? Also, studies have been conducted regard-ing the effects of alcohol consumption on sexual arousal (e.g., McCarty, Dia-mond, & Kaye, 1982) and on the dynamics of people meeting in bars, reacting to "opening lines," and so on (e.g., Cunningham, 1989). Both topics would seem relevant to the situation where fear and sexual attraction converge. Further, little evidence is available regarding misattribution of other emotions, such as anger. And, finally, does this process work in reverse, such that increased sexual attrac-tion might be misattributed and result in increased fear?

How would you conduct a literature search for more recent studies?

Start with the search terms "misattribution" or "attribution," and combine them with "fear," "sexual arousal," or "arousal." Also, in recent editions of the *Social Science Citation Index*, look up Dutton and Aron (1974) and any of the articles that were cited in the previous paragraph. For the articles that you find, read the research that they cite (and look them up in the *Citation Index*). Also, search for other articles by Dutton, Aron, and the above authors.

TOPIC 2: AN EXPERIMENT ON TIME PERCEPTION

Have you ever taken a long car trip and noticed that the drive home seemed to take less time than the drive to your destination, even though on the clock both trips took the same amount of time? This experience is an example of the observation that the more a time interval is "filled" with stimuli, the longer it seems to have lasted. As you go toward your destination, the scenery and sights are novel, so that the travel time is mentally "filled" with interesting stimuli. Then, although only 30 minutes might have elapsed, they are overestimated as "feeling like 40." On the return trip, however, you've seen all the sights, so the interval is mentally unfilled. Then, the elapsed 30 minutes feel like 30 or perhaps even 20 minutes.

Based on such observations, Ornstein (1969) hypothesized that people judge the duration of an interval using their memory for the stimuli that occurred during the interval. When the memory is in some sense "larger," the interval is perceived as longer. He therefore set out to show that the more stimuli a person encounters during an interval, the longer the interval is judged to have been.

What are the hypothesis and purpose of this study?

What are the variables to be studied, and which design is appropriate?

How would you elicit the dependent behavior?

What sampling would you use, and should you control participant variables?

This study tests the *hypothesis* that filling an interval with more stimuli causes it to be perceived as longer. Because any extraneous event during an interval helps to "fill" it and thus *confounds* the study, you should conduct a controlled laboratory experiment. You can create a *true experiment* by randomly assigning participants to conditions of the *independent variable*, which is the number of stimuli filling an interval. The *dependent behavior* is participants' estimate of the duration of the interval. Presumably, time perception is similar in all normal humans, so you can *randomly sample* from available college students.

When studying any cognitive process, you are likely to find large individual differences, but you can control them by performing a *repeated-measures design*. In our case, however, once participants know that they will be estimating an interval, they might count or otherwise mentally time it. One solution to this problem is to use repeated measures but also to disguise and deemphasize the time-estimate response. Ornstein, for example, buried the request for a time estimate in a questionnaire that participants completed after each interval. Alternatively, you might use a *between-subjects design* so that in each condition you truly surprise people with a request to estimate the interval. Although this approach is better because it guarantees that participants are not prepared for the time estimate, let's adopt Ornstein's repeated-measures design.

How would you define your conditions and institute needed controls?

The obvious approach is to directly vary the number of stimuli presented to participants during an interval. Ornstein varied the number of tones that they heard. Or, you might vary the number of visual stimuli presented, or change the nature of the task performed during the interval. Let's assume that you use the tones Ornstein used.

You must also define the duration of the interval. Although there is research on the perception of very brief intervals lasting only milliseconds, Ornstein defined an ecologically realistic interval of 9 minutes and 20 seconds. (You wouldn't want an interval as obvious as 60 seconds or 5 minutes, because people would be likely to guess these.) Then, we need to create a *strong manipulation* by filling the interval with a substantially different number of tones in each condition. Ornstein created three conditions, with the tones occurring at the rate of 40, 80, or 120 tones per minute. The duration of the tones was constant regardless of the condition, but the pauses between them was varied so that the tones occurred regularly throughout the interval.

How would you measure the dependent variable?

A person's direct estimate of the interval's duration is needed. Thus, Ornstein asked participants to estimate the duration in minutes and seconds. This score is objective, and participants can easily record their own responses. Alternatively, if you believed that people are unable to translate their subjective impressions of time into these terms reliably, you could ask them to estimate the interval nonverbally by drawing a line to represent its length (Mulligan & Schiffman, 1979).

What testing procedure and what materials are needed?

As long as the *experimenter* does not communicate *expectancies* or create undue pressure and thus *reactivity*, the researcher can be present during testing. For reliability, produce an audio tape recording of the three intervals, using electronic clocks and tone generators to create the stimuli. To eliminate distractions, play the recording over headphones, at a constant volume for all participants. (Be sure to select only people with normal hearing.)

To create a realistic situation and prevent participants from forming hypotheses that might bias their estimates, you need a cover story to "explain" why they are listening to recorded tones. For example, your instructions might say that you're studying the relaxing effect of these stimuli, and that participants are to merely sit quietly during the interval. This also minimizes any extraneous stimulation that might further fill the interval and influence time estimates. Also, this "relaxation therapy" could "require" the removal of any jewelry, so that we prevent participants from looking at their watches during the interval.

For consistency, participants should estimate an interval immediately after being exposed to it, without any distractions between the interval and the estimate. Thus, immediately after the interval, participants could turn over the paper in front of them and answer the questions provided there, including one asking them to estimate the interval's length in minutes and seconds. There could also be other distractor questions regarding their thoughts and relaxation responses. These "other" questions not only add credence to your cover story but also allow you to obtain a manipulation check of whether participants attended to the tones. Afterwards, in your *debriefing*, stress that participants should not tell other potential subjects about the time-estimation task.

What confounding from the three conditions is likely, and how would you deal with it?

A major problem concerns the *order effects* produced by repeated exposure to all three conditions: Whether an interval is *relatively* filled might depend on which intervals were previously heard. Likewise, listening to over 9 minutes of tones is a long, boring task, so fatigue effects are likely. Therefore, we could *partially counterbalance* the order of conditions. Calling the conditions A, B, and C, we would test a third of the participants under each order of ABC, BCA, or CAB.

What is the prediction of the study and the N to be tested?

Diagram the study and determine the statistical procedures to be performed.

The prediction is that intervals containing more tones will be estimated as lasting longer. Because of possibly large error variance due to obtaining estimates in minutes and seconds, a relatively large N is needed, so approximately 50 people per condition will probably provide sufficient *power*.

Time-estimate scores are ratio scores that meet the requirements of a *parametric* procedure. This study has three levels of one within-subjects factor, so perform a *one-way within-subjects ANOVA* of the design shown in Table 12.2. If the F is significant, perform *post hoc comparisons* to determine which means dif-

TABLE 12.2   Diagram of the Time Perception Experiment

The means are from Ornstein (1969), Table 3, p. 56. Each row of Xs represents the time estimates from the same participant.

Conditions of number of tones in the interval

40	80	120
X	X	X
X	X	X
X	X	X
X	X	X
X	X	X
$\overline{X} = 6.42$	$\overline{X} = 7.99$	$\overline{X} = 9.00$

fer significantly. Ornstein found that the interval with 120 tones per minute was significantly longer than that with 80, and that both of these were longer than that with 40 tones per minute. Unfortunately, he did not report *eta squared* to indicate the *effect size* of his manipulation, so we do not know how consistently the number of tones influenced time estimates.

The preceding analysis indicates whether *subjective* impressions of an interval increase as it becomes more filled, but they still might not have any resemblance to the actual duration of the interval. To see a participant's estimate in relation to the interval's actual duration, we can subtract the actual duration of the interval from each estimate. A positive difference indicates that a person overestimated the duration, saying that it seems longer than it actually was. A negative difference indicates a person underestimated the duration, saying that it seems shorter than it actually was. Then, an analysis of these differences will indicate the effect that filling an interval has on participants' *errors* when estimating time.

What conclusions can you draw from this study?

What are the limitations on your conclusions?

Unless unknown confoundings are present, the above finding confirms the hypothesis that a greater number of stimuli in an interval causes the interval to be perceived as longer. Therefore, now we would play "psychologist" and speculate about how the cognitive system works so that it produces such a result.

A limitation, however, is that such tone-filled intervals are never encountered in the real world, so you have limited *external validity*. You also have reduced *generalizability*, because your ultimate purpose is to understand the general perception of the passage of *any* time interval.

How could you increase the generalizability of this finding in another study?

The obvious starting point is to include time intervals of other, different lengths. Thus, you could add a second factor that manipulates the length of the interval and at a minimum, compare the condition containing the above interval (to replicate Ornstein's study) and another condition containing a different size interval. You might include the interval of 4 minutes 40 seconds, which is one-half the size of Ornstein's (or you could add intervals of any size that make sense).

How would you analyze this design, and what will it indicate?

Because you now have the two factors of number of tones per minute and the length of the interval, a *two-way ANOVA* is appropriate. However, do not analyze participants' actual estimates. If their estimates bear any resemblance to reality, then the two interval sizes would automatically produce significant differences in estimates. To equate the different lengths of the intervals, again subtract the actual duration from participants' estimates and look at their estimation errors. For example, say you obtain the mean difference scores shown in Table 12.3. Here, the average error in estimates in each *cell* is positive, so participants consistently overestimated all intervals. The *main effect* of increasing the number of tones (comparing the column means) still tests the original hypothesis that filling the interval with more stimuli increases its perceived duration: With more tones, overestimates increase, indicating that the interval is perceived as increasingly longer than it actually was. The *main effect* of duration (comparing the row means) indicates that, overall, the two intervals produced differences in estimation error. Of most interest will be whether there is a significant *interaction*.

> **Graph this interaction, labeling the *X* axis as the condition of number of tones per minute.**

> **How will a significant or nonsignificant interaction be interpreted?**

The interaction is graphed in Figure 12.1. A *significant interaction* indicates that the way that estimates change with more filled intervals *depends* on the duration of the interval. Note that this conclusion would limit generalizability of your hypothesis, because you would find that it applies differently depending on the interval's length. A *nonsignificant interaction*, however, would suggest that the influence of increasing the number of tones is similar—*parallel*—for both short and long intervals.

So far the results seem to support the hypothesis that people judge an interval as longer when they have a "larger" memory for the contents of the interval. However, there are at least two additional explanations to consider. First, the greater number of tones per minute also creates an interval containing more *complex* stimuli. Perhaps a person's time perception is actually determined by the degree of complexity of the event that fills an interval.

> **How might you manipulate the complexity of the stimuli during an interval, and what variable must you keep constant?**

For a given interval size, the variable to keep constant is the *number* of stimuli presented during the interval. Then, vary the complexity of the stimuli presented.

TABLE 12.3 Example of Mean Differences between the Actual Interval and Participants' Estimates in a 3 × 2 Design for the Factors of Number of Tones and Interval Duration

Number of tones per minute

		40	80	120	
Duration of interval	*4 min 40 sec*	$\overline{X} = +.33$	$\overline{X} = +1.50$	$\overline{X} = +2.00$	$\overline{X} = +1.28$
	9 min 20 sec	$\overline{X} = +.50$	$\overline{X} = +1.70$	$\overline{X} = +2.80$	$\overline{X} = +1.67$
		$\overline{X} = +.44$	$\overline{X} = +1.60$	$\overline{X} = +2.40$	

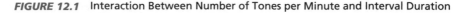

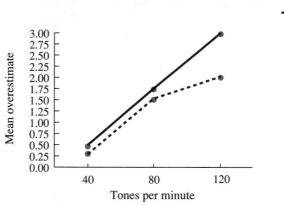

FIGURE 12.1   Interaction Between Number of Tones per Minute and Interval Duration

In fact, Ornstein conducted a second study in which participants viewed drawings of geometric shapes that varied in their complexity. You might also vary the complexity of the participant's response to a stimulus, as in Brown (1985), who had people physically trace patterns that varied in complexity. These studies showed that increased complexity did increase the perceived duration of the interval.

The second explanation to consider is that either a larger number of stimuli or a more complex stimulation might produce a less organized memory for the contents of the interval. Stimuli that are simple to understand are organized in our memory; stimuli that are complex are not. Thus, any time we organize the stimuli in memory, the interval may seem shorter, while with less organization it may seem longer.

How would you manipulate the meaningfulness of stimuli occurring in an interval?

There are a number of ways you might give more or less meaning to a stimulus. Mulligan and Schiffman (1979) presented participants cartoons either with or without a disambiguating caption that made the cartoon more meaningful. (These cartoons—called "droodles"—are discussed in a very different type of study in Appendix B.) Participants viewed a droodle for a fixed period, either with or without a caption, and then estimated the viewing interval. Estimates were shorter when a caption was provided, presumably because it allowed better organization of the components of the cartoon in memory.

To further study this phenomenon, cognitive psychologists have many ways of producing differences in retention, complexity, and organization. Using them, you can determine how altering the stimuli or mental task influences time perception.

Also, the preceding research involves retrospective judgments, in which people learn they will be making the estimate only *after* the interval has ended. However, a paradox occurs when people are aware that they will estimate the interval before it starts (making a "prospective" estimate). Here, the amount of stimulation in the interval has the opposite effect: the more an interval is filled, the *shorter* the interval is judged to be (Hicks, Miller, & Kinsbourne, 1976; but see Brown, 1985). In this context, "time flies when you're having fun" because the fun mentally fills the interval, so time passes quickly. Conversely, "a watched pot never boils" because little is happening, so the interval is mentally unfilled and time drags by. In fact, Cahoon and Edmonds (1980) had participants watch a pot of water come to a boil. They found that the more that participants concentrated on waiting for the water to boil, the longer the interval was judged to be. One possible explanation for this paradox is that when making a prospective time estimate, people do not rely on the amount of stimulation experienced during the interval. Instead, they rely directly on their experience of time. Time estimates become shorter when more stimuli are encountered because greater stimulation directs their attention away from their experience of time. To test whether less attention to time makes it pass rapidly, you can take any established procedure for consuming more or less of a person's attention and incorporate it into a study in which participants estimate an interval's duration.

How would you conduct a literature search for more recent studies?

Start with the search terms "time perception" or "time estimation." Sometimes, this effect has also been called the "filled interval illusion." Depending on your perspective, combine these terms with "prospective" or "retrospective." Also, in recent editions of the *Social Science Citation Index*, look up Ornstein (1969) and any of the articles that were cited in the above paragraph. For any articles that you find, read the research that they cite (and look them up in the *Citation Index*). Also, search for other articles by Ornstein and the above authors.

TOPIC 3: A DESCRIPTIVE STUDY OF FEAR OF SUCCESS IN FEMALES

Every once in a while, psychological research produces an incorrect conclusion in a spectacular fashion. Here's an example. Some people argue that the most insidious effect of racism and sexism is that the victims of such biases are conditioned by society to behave in certain ways that match the stereotype. For example, Horner (1972) proposed that women who avoid striving for success in school or at work may be motivated by "fear of success," or FOS. Supposedly, women might be conditioned to avoid success because they fear the negative consequences associated with it. In particular, they anticipated being perceived as "unfeminine" and socially undesirable if they are successful. On the other hand, Horner proposed that men generally exhibit less FOS because, for them, there are fewer negative consequences associated with success. Horner conducted a study to demonstrate that men and women exhibit different levels of FOS.

What are the hypothesis and purpose of this study?

What are the variables to be studied, and which design is appropriate?

What sampling would you use, and should you control participant variables?

This study is for demonstrating the existence of FOS. Because it would be premature to test variables that cause FOS, you should turn to a *correlational, descriptive* study. The basic proposal is that men and women exhibit different levels of FOS, so at most the design is a quasi-experiment, with the *quasi-independent variable* of males versus females. The *dependent behavior* is FOS, presumably a relatively stable *trait* characteristic. The study does not require a specific field setting, so a laboratory provides the best control. Presumably, FOS is found throughout the general population, so you can select participants randomly from available college students. Note that the quasi-independent variable of gender is a *between-subjects factor*, which is probably confounded by many other participant variables, including race, age, college experience, and so on. To control these variables, you might either *limit the population* to a more homogeneous group or produce *matched pairs* of males and females.

How would you measure the dependent variable?

The key is to operationally define and then measure behaviors that are *construct-valid*—that actually do reflect FOS. You might design a situation to cause participants to strive for success, but if they don't, you cannot be sure that this result reflects FOS. But, you can measure participants' motives more directly using their self-reports from *interviews* or *questionnaires*. *Closed-ended questions*, however, would be unworkable here, because (1) this is exploratory research, so you don't necessarily know the appropriate questions to ask; (2) people might be unaware of their FOS; and (3) demand characteristics may prevent them from giving honest responses. To avoid such problems, Horner employed a *projective test* to infer high or low FOS. Females completed a story that began "After first-term finals, Anne finds herself at the head of her medical school class." Males completed a corresponding story about "John."

What procedure, instructions, and materials are needed?

To ensure *reliability*, participants completed the story in writing. To focus them on the success of the characters, Horner asked participants to comment on Anne's or John's reactions to their grades, other people's reactions, and their past and future lives. Because only one story was completed per participant, *order effects* were not a problem.

By *counterbalancing* the gender of the researcher within each group, you could control for experimenter-produced *demand characteristics*. (A *double-blind* procedure would probably not be necessary if you can minimize the interaction between participants and researcher.) Also, note that participants can be tested in groups. To minimize *reactivity* to divulging personal information, you might frame the experiment as a creativity test, an English composition test, or a test of knowledge about social interactions. The materials you would use consist of a sheet of paper with the appropriate description of John or Anne typed across the top. (By providing more sheets, you imply that participants can or should write more.)

The design is *ethically* acceptable because you're testing knowing volunteers, and *informed consent* can provide straightforward information about the task and situation. However, the *hypothesis* should not be conveyed until *debriefing*.

How would you determine each participant's score and ensure a powerful design?

The major problem with a projective, *open-ended question* concerns reliable scoring. Horner performed a *content analysis*, operationally defining FOS to be present when a person described Anne or John as having negative feelings or negative experiences as a result of achieving high grades. Horner found, for example, that Anne was described as the stereotypical lonely, unattractive "egghead" who was disliked (and even beaten up by classmates when the grades were published!). Multiple scorers (*raters*) are appropriate here, and you should check for high *inter-rater reliability*. A relatively large N is warranted because of potentially high variability in responses and scoring. With so simple a task, you could easily test upwards of 50 people per condition.

You might think that, after scoring the stories, you could assign each participant a score reflecting the number of FOS images in his or her story. However, you do not know that a greater number of FOS images in a story indicates a greater degree of FOS. (Some participants might simply write a more detailed story.) Horner solved this problem by viewing FOS as an all-or-none characteristic. She categorized each participant's story as either exhibiting or not exhibiting FOS and then determined whether more females exhibited FOS than males.

What statistical analysis should you perform?

This is a *between-subjects design* with *nonparametric, nominal,* or *categorical* data, so performing a chi square procedure is appropriate. Technically, you should compute the *two-way chi square* to determine whether the frequency of FOS and non-FOS is independent of participants' gender. This design and the results of Horner's study are shown in Table 12.4. Here, a significant result indi-

TABLE 12.4 Diagram of Two-Way Design and Results of Horner (1972)

	Males (*John Story*)	*Females* (*Anne Story*)
FOS imagery	10%	65%
Non-FOS imagery	90%	35%

cates whether the frequency that people produced an FOS story *depends* on whether they are male or female. Horner reported that females produced a significantly greater number of FOS stories, although, unfortunately, she did not indicate the *strength* of this relationship.

What conclusions can you draw, and are they valid?

Because this is a *quasi-experiment*, you cannot confidently conclude that gender causes the differences in FOS imagery. Rather, you can only speculate on how FOS develops in males and females and how it operates to influence behavior. It is reasonable to expect that other people in similar settings would produce similar results, so there is some external validity for this relationship. But, you won't know whether FOS actually operates in the real world, whether it actually motivates people, or what its components are, so *ecological*, *construct*, and *external validity* are limited. (Then again, this is just the first study.)

However, even your tentative conclusions hinge on whether there are any *confoundings* between the two gender conditions. Look carefully again, at Table 12.4.

What is the major confounding between the Male–Female conditions?

The difference in FOS scores between the conditions might be due to the gender of participants as Horner proposed. But! It might be due to the gender of the *character* in each story: That is, the gender of John and Anne is confounded with the participants' gender. To test this hypothesis, Monahan, Kuhn, and Shaver (1974) had both males and females complete stories about both John and Anne. They found that women *and* men showed greater FOS when describing Anne! Thus, there is something about completing the Anne story that produces greater FOS imagery. What is it about Anne's success in medical school that causes both males and females to imagine her as having negative feelings and experiences because of that success?

What bias is built into the stimuli?

The bias is that Anne is in *medical* school, stereotypically a "male" situation. Thus, Horner's study was also confounded because the two conditions differ in terms of whether the gender of the character fits the stereotype of the school. This conclusion was confirmed by Cherry and Deaux (1978), who had males and females describe John and Anne as being either at the head of their *medical*-school class or at the head of their *nursing*-school class. In the medical-school setting, 60% of the Anne stories indicated FOS, compared with only 30% of the John stories. But in the nursing-school setting, the shoe was on the other foot: 64% of the John stories but only 30% of the Anne stories indicated FOS. Further, both men and women provided more negative descriptions of John in nursing school and of Anne in medical school.

What do these results indicate about the construct of FOS?

If FOS exists, Horner did not measure it. Essentially, her study lacked *construct validity*: Participants never actually stated that they feared success, and, instead of reflecting some intrinsic motivation, their negative descriptions depended entirely on the context of the story. Apparently, we are all aware of stereotypes and tend to predict unpleasant consequences for someone who violates a stereotype. In particular, when describing people who are successful at something that is uncommon for their gender, we expect the social consequences of that success to be negative.

Recall that research explanations are supposed to be *parsimonious*; that is, they should not be complicated by unnecessary constructs. Because the preceding study (and similar research) has not demonstrated that FOS is necessary for explaining behavior, the construct has largely been discarded.

What suggestions do you have for further research?

To retain the construct of FOS, you would have to measure it in an objective, valid, and unconfounded manner. For example, you might develop a *closed-ended questionnaire* to measure FOS and also seek to identify a concrete behavior that reflects avoiding success in real life. Then, you could show both *concurrent* and *predictive* validity by determining the correlation between questionnaire scores and actual avoidance of success. Also, because very young children would not be expected to have learned the negative consequences of violating sex-role stereotypes, you might eliminate the bias in Horner's study by testing young children for FOS (assuming young children develop FOS). And finally, because society and sex-stereotypes presumably have changed since the early 1970s, a replication of the above FOS studies could determine whether there is a generational or *cohort effect* between Horner's participants and those of today.

TOPIC 4: AN EXPERIMENTAL AND CORRELATIONAL STUDY OF CREATIVITY

Creativity is often examined in terms of problem solving. In this context, being creative is defined as making new, uncommon associations between ideas to solve a problem. Isen, Daubman, and Nowicki (1987) suggested that one variable that influences creative problem solving is mood or "affect." When experiencing positive affect, people may organize information into broader, more all-inclusive categories, so that they combine highly divergent information. Because of this new organization, they can see unusual connections or novel associations, thus facilitating problem solving.

What are the hypothesis and purpose of this study?

What are the variables to be studied, and which design is appropriate?

What procedure and subjects would you use?

The study is to show that more positive affect *causes* greater creativity, so a laboratory experiment involving college students is appropriate. Any manipulation that influences a person's *state* characteristic of mood is appropriate. For example, you could present different mood-inducing words or vary the amount of reward that participants receive. In a series of studies, Isen et al. employed several such procedures. In particular, in one study they showed either a five-minute comedy film (consisting of television "bloopers"), a neutral control film (about the normal curve!), or a negative film (a documentary on World War II Nazi concentration camps). Accordingly, the *independent variable* is the type of film being shown. (Technically, a participant's mood is an *intervening variable*, which, presumably, is influenced by the type of film viewed.) Because of potential *carry-over effects*, the films should be presented as a *between-subjects factor*.

The *dependent variable* is a participant's score on creative problem solving. Isen et al. presented a number of "brain-teaser" problems to measure creative problem solving, including the Remote Associates Test (Mednick, Mednick, & Mednick, 1964). Here, each test question contains three words for which there is one "remote" association. The questions are presented in a *questionnaire*, and participants fill in the word that provides the association. For example, given the stimuli *mower*, *atomic*, and *foreign*, the correct answer is power.

How would you ensure that the manipulation worked?

How would you ensure reliable measurement of creativity?

A *manipulation check* is necessary to be sure that the films had the desired effect. Isen et al. accomplished this check by telling participants that the film they would see was being pretested for another experiment. After the film was over, they were asked to rate the pleasantness of several unfamiliar, neutral words. Neutral words should have been rated as unpleasant if participants were in a negative mood, or rated as pleasant if they were in a positive mood. Participants were also asked to rate statements describing how the film made them feel. Participants confirmed that the films produced the intended differences in mood. Following these tasks, the Remote Associates Test was performed under the cover story that norms were being established for another study.

To *reliably* measure creativity, participants completed 21 Remote Associates questions. To control the difficulty of the questions, the researchers used *pilot* data to select 7 easy, 7 medium, and 7 difficult items. A participant's score was the total number of questions correctly answered. Further, to reliably demonstrate the relationship, approximately 50 participants should be tested, and you could *counterbalance* participant gender.

Diagram this study, and select the statistical procedures you should use.

The study is diagrammed as shown in Table 12.5, and the *one-way, between-subjects ANOVA* is appropriate. If the *F* is significant, *post hoc comparisons* and *eta squared* are computed. Based on Isen et al., the number of items correctly solved should be significantly higher when participants experience the positive-mood

TABLE 12.5 Diagram of Affect and Creativity Experiment

Conditions of mood

	Negative	Neutral	Positive
Each X is a participant's creativity score	X X X X X	X X X X X	X X X X X
	$\overline{X}$	$\overline{X}$	$\overline{X}$

condition than when they experience the neutral condition. Negative mood did not, however, produce a significant difference in problem solving compared to the neutral condition.

To obtain greater information from this design, you could analyze an additional, hidden factor that the researchers *collapsed* across.

What additional factor can be analyzed and what design will this produce?

The additional factor to be analyzed is the difficulty of the Remote Associates items. Instead of computing an overall total-correct score per subject, you can examine the number correct for each participant when answering the easy, medium, or difficult questions, respectively. In doing so, you create a *two-way mixed design*. You still have the between-subjects factor containing the three levels of mood, but you also have the *repeated-measures* factor consisting of easy, medium, or difficult questions.

Diagram this design.

What statistical procedure should be used and what will it show?

The three levels of mood and the three levels of difficulty produce the 3×3 mixed design shown in Table 12.6. Each column is a level of mood, and each row is a level of difficulty.

To analyze this, perform the *two-way mixed ANOVA*. From this, you will see the *main effect* of the mood conditions as well as the main effect of the difficulty of problems. Most interestingly, you will see the *interaction* between difficulty and mood. This interaction will indicate whether the relationship between a person's mood and his or her creative problem solving *depends* on how difficult the problems are. Notably, when Isen et al. performed a similar study, they found that, regardless of mood level, the difficult questions were so difficult they tended to produce a *floor effect*, while the easy items were so easy they tended to produce a *ceiling effect*. Therefore, the interaction of mood and difficulty was not significant.

Although Isen et al. found that positive mood conditions produced higher creativity scores, there is reason to question whether participants truly experienced the different moods. Consider the order in which they performed the various tasks described previously: Participants saw a film, then answered questions as a manipulation check to determine their mood, and then they performed the Remote Associates (creativity) Test.

What demand characteristics might have biased this study?

Imagine you are a subject who watches a film that is obviously lighthearted or obviously depressing. Then, you are asked to rate the pleasantness of words or, worse, to describe how the film made you feel. Wouldn't you suspect that the film was *supposed* to produce a positive or negative mood? Thus, this procedure may have communicated *experimenter expectancies* about the mood that participants were supposed to indicate, and they simply complied. If this were the case, then we do not know the cause of the differences in creativity, because we cannot be sure that the intended differences in mood even existed.

To solve this problem, we might present the manipulation check after the creativity test, but having a difficult or easy time in performing the creativity test might change participants' mood from what it was at the beginning of the test. Likewise, we might use different stimuli, but any manipulation that is strong enough to influence mood may also communicate experimenter expectancies. Thus, a better design might be to describe the relationship between mood and creativity, but without actively manipulating mood, so that *demand characteristics* are avoided.

TABLE 12.6 Diagram of the 3 × 3 Mixed Design Combining the Between-Subjects Factor of Mood with the Within-Subjects Factor of Difficulty of Questions

Each X represents a participant's score on the subset of Remote Associates questions.

		Mood level			
		Negative	Neutral	Positive	
	Easy	X X X	X X X	X X X	$\overline{X}$
Difficulty level	*Medium*	X X X	X X X	X X X	$\overline{X}$
	Difficult	X X X	X X X	X X X	$\overline{X}$
		$\overline{X}$	$\overline{X}$	$\overline{X}$	

A further problem is that the manipulation check showed that the *average* mood score differed between the conditions, but there was undoubtedly *variability* in the moods of individuals within each condition. Therefore, this procedure is not a very precise or *sensitive* way of examining how an individual's mood relates to his or her creativity.

Given these criticisms, when designing an extension of this research, you might seek a *description* of the relationship between participants' specific mood level and their creativity, but without actively manipulating mood.

What design might you use to study this relationship?

What are the hypothesis and purpose of this study?

How would you define and measure the variables?

The obvious choice is a *correlational* study: After measuring participants' existing mood when they enter the study, you might correlate these scores with their scores on a subsequent creativity test. The *hypothesis* is that mood and creativity are related. The purpose is to show that the relationship exists, but you are no longer trying to show that a positive mood *causes* greater creativity.

To make this a more literal replication of the Isen et al. procedure, you might again operationally define creativity as performance on the Remote Associates Test. To measure mood, you could use *Likert-type* questions, again having participants rate the pleasantness of uncommon, emotionally neutral words. Your *operational definition* is that the higher the pleasantness ratings of the words, the more positive a person's mood.

How would you conduct a literature search to find testing materials like those used in this study?

Start with the search terms "mood" or "affect" and "creativity" and combine them with "measurement" or "assessment." Also, look for references to the "Remote Associates Test." And, in recent editions of the *Social Science Citation Index*, look up the Isen et al. (1987) study. For any articles that you find, read the research that they cite (and look them up in the *Index* too.) Also, search for other articles by Isen et al. and by the above authors. In any relevant articles you find, see how the authors measured these variables. (For a complete list of the neutral words for participants to rate, you might need to write to an author.) Further, check your library for reference books that contain established psychological tests that measure mood or creativity.

How would you design the response scale for rating the pleasantness of the neutral words?

Because rating a neutral word as *very* pleasant or unpleasant might seem unnatural to participants, the rating scale can be anchored with only *pleasant* and *unpleasant*. Likewise, because it is difficult to make fine discriminations in the pleasantness of a word, it is appropriate to provide only a 5-point scale. Also, an odd number of points allows participants a middle or neutral rating, which in this context is appropriate. In your instructions, however, stress that participants should consider all points on the scale.

A *pilot study* is called for here to determine whether the words are really neutral, whether their pleasantness can be rated, and whether the scale is appropriate. You would ask pilot subjects to rate each word on these dimensions and then include only those words in the mood test that are consistently judged to meet these criteria.

How would you construct the mood questionnaire?

To reflect a person's mood reliably, you would want to get a sufficient number of words rated—say, 24 words total. To cancel out any potential *response biases*, you can counterbalance the placement of *pleasant* and *unpleasant* at the left end of the scale for half of the words and at the right end for the other half.

You might intermix the mood questions with the Remote Associates Test and present them as one questionnaire, but this arrangement could be very confusing for participants. A better approach is to keep the two procedures separate, with individual printed instructions for each.

How would you administer the mood and creativity tests?

There are two reasons that you might have all participants complete the mood questionnaire *before* completing the Remote Associates Test. First, you would avoid any possible influence that the Remote Associates Test might have on a mood. Second, although your emphasis is definitely *not* on causality, you can strengthen such an inference by having what you believe is the causal variable be the one that occurs first.

What participants will you select, and how will you sample?

It is most important to test people who differ greatly in their moods and in their abilities to solve the Remote Associates Test. That is, you want to avoid a *restricted range* on either variable—observing a wide range of different scores on each. This will provide more information and increase your *power*. A target N of around 100 subjects would probably be sufficient.

The hypothesized relationship applies to the general population, so you can *randomly* select college students. Doing so also gives you the advantage of collecting data in a quiet, controlled laboratory setting. If you had reason to believe that college students would produce a restricted range of scores, however, you might instead conduct a *field study* in several randomly selected public locations or in a mailed survey, using *systematic* or *stratified random sampling* techniques.

How would you analyze the data?

First, you must determine each participant's score on each test. For the Remote Associates Test, total the number of correct answers. For the mood test, code all questions so that a higher rating always indicates that the word is rated as more pleasant, implying a more positive mood. Then, each participant's mood score can be either the total or the *mean* of the ratings that he or she selected.

Both of these variables reflect *ratio scales*, and implicitly you have assumed a *linear relationship* here, so compute the *Pearson correlation coefficient* using each participant's pair of scores. Next, determine whether the coefficient is significant. Your prediction is that there will be a positive correlation between mood and creativity, with higher pleasantness ratings associated with higher creativity scores. Because you predict a specific relationship, perform a *one-tailed test* of significance.

If r is significant, you can compute the *linear regression equation*, and then graph the *regression line* to summarize this relationship. You essentially hypothesized that participants' mood predicts their creativity, so word ratings would be the *predictor* (X) variable and Remote Associates scores the *criterion* (Y) variable. Also, compute the *standard error of the estimate* to determine the "average" amount that participants' actual creativity scores differ from their predicted creativity scores when based on their mood score and the regression equation. You would also compute r^2 to describe the *proportion of variance in creativity scores that is accounted for* by the relationship with mood. The larger this statistic, the more important mood is for understanding differences in creativity.

What are the important issues of validity in this study?

The first issue is *content validity*. You want to be sure that pleasantness ratings actually and only reflect the pleasantness that participants attribute to the words. Any flaws in the rating task, or any words that participants have experienced in a way that biases them, will mean that you are not measuring pleasantness as intended. Likewise, the Remote Associates Test must measure a person's ability to make remote associations. If, for example, participants don't know a word's definition, then they will give an incorrect answer for that question because of a variable having nothing to do with making associations.

Your other major concern is *construct validity*. You have defined creativity as participants' ability to perform the Remote Associates Test, reflecting their ability to make uncommon associations. But creativity could be more than that. Also, people who are creative and ingenious might see a unique association that the Remote Associates Test does not anticipate, so it would be scored as incorrect. Likewise, the word-pleasantness ratings might reflect a person's mood, but then again they might not. It's possible to be in a very poor mood and still think a word has a pleasant ring to it (*aardvark* springs to mind). Also, there are many aspects to a person's mood (anger, elation, sadness), and you cannot know which, if any, are reflected by these ratings.

For these reasons, you might select any number of published, objective (*closed-ended*) mood tests from the literature. An established mood test is usually supported by considerable research showing its validity. Further, such tests often contain subscales, each of which measures a certain component of mood: The items in one scale would measure the factor of "depression," those in another "anxiety," and so on. In fact, if you had used such a test in the preceding study, you could use a participant's score from each subscale as one measure of mood, which you could then correlate with creativity. (In this case, using "*multiple correlation* and *multiple regression*" as well as "*partial correlation*" would be appropriate.)

These concerns about validity apply to the original Isen et al. studies, too. The advantages of your correlational study are that it conceptually replicates their laboratory study while reducing their demand characteristics. And, especially if yours was conducted as a field study, it would add to the *external validity* and *generalizability* of the relationship between mood and creativity.

Finally, in designing this correlational study, you assumed that performing the Remote Associates Test first might influence participants' subsequent mood scores. As an additional research question, you could actually test whether word-pleasantness ratings are changed by the Remote Associates Test.

What type of design should you use? Describe it.

How would you create the stimuli?

You could create a *pretest–posttest* design, with participants performing a word-pleasantness rating test once before the Remote Associates Test and then once after. To prevent participants from merely reproducing earlier ratings, you would create *alternate forms*, providing two different sets of words to be rated. You would need to demonstrate high *test–retest reliability* between the two sets and also to *counterbalance* their use, using each set as the pretest or posttest for one-half of the participants. Then, you would examine the difference between the *mean* pleasantness ratings before and after the Remote Associates Test.

However, if you merely test a group of people before and after the Remote Associates Test, you will encounter the problems of a *one-group pretest–posttest* design, having no idea why pleasantness ratings might change between the two testings. After all, you are measuring mood as a *state characteristic* that, by definition, changes from moment to moment. Therefore, you should also test a *control group*, measuring their mood twice, with the interval between testing the same as for the experimental group, but without the Remote Associates Test. (This design would be essentially the same as that of the mixed design involving dart throwing discussed in Chapter 8.) You would analyze the pleasantness ratings using a 2×2 *mixed-design ANOVA* for the between-subjects factor of experimental-control group and the repeated-measures factor of pre- and posttest. If the *interaction* is *significant*, then differences in the pre- and posttest mood scores depend on, and are thus influenced by, whether or not participants perform the intervening Remote Associates Test.

ADDITIONAL RESEARCH TOPICS

In the research literature, you will find studies that deal with almost every behavior imaginable. What follows are some common and not so common research topics that you can rather easily study.

Belief in Astrology

Astrological horoscopes and personality descriptions contain *Barnum statements* such as "You are generally a happy person, although you sometimes become angry." A person's reactions to such descriptions tells us not only about the popularity of astrology but also about general belief systems. For example, Glick, Gottesman, and Jolton (1989) studied "believers" and "skeptics" to determine how they deal with positive and negative descriptions in horoscopes. They proposed that both types of people would be impressed with the accuracy of positive descriptions (e.g., "You are intelligent"), presumably because such descriptions affirm positive self-perceptions. But, they suggested, only believers would accept negative descriptions (e.g., "You are indecisive") because their faith in astrology overrides their self-perceptions. In addition, the researchers tested whether a description not attributed to astrology would be accepted as more accurate, and whether experiencing positive or negative descriptions would alter a person's belief in astrology.

What type of design would you use to study these factors?

Testing any of these factors involves first the quasi-independent variable of conditions of participants who are astrology believers versus those who are skeptics. Additional factors then include whether they receive favorable versus unfavorable personality descriptions, and/or whether or not descriptions are attributed to astrology. The dependent variable would be participants' rating of the accuracy of the descriptions. In their study, Glick et al. also included a pretest–posttest design, measuring participants' attitudes toward astrology before and after they participated in the above conditions.

The researchers found that (1) skeptics accept positive personality descriptions as more accurate than negative ones, but believers accept a negative description as being equal in accuracy to a positive one; (2) believers and skeptics alike rated astrological descriptions as more accurate than nonastrological descriptions; and (3) skeptics, more so than believers, became more positive in their feelings toward astrology after receiving favorable horoscopes. Glick et al. proposed that skeptics are more open-minded, so they more easily change their opinion about astrology after receiving a positive description. Believers, however, seem to ignore the contradictions from a negative description, suggesting that believers and skeptics differ in terms of how they test these descriptions and evaluate the evidence that supports them.

What suggestions for additional research can you make?

First, you might examine how believers and skeptics test astrological predictions. For example, you might present them with a horoscope that is ultimately confirmed or disconfirmed by what "coincidentally" happens later in an experimental setting. Then, you could measure how the outcome of a prediction is evaluated by skeptics and believers, and how this evaluation influences their attitudes toward astrology.

Second, when believers are confronted with a negative statement that *disconfirms* their self-perceptions, they continue to maintain their original opinion. The implication is that believers in astrology do not apply the correct logic for testing hypotheses. Recall from Chapter 1 that we discussed using a deck of cards for testing a hypothesis about letters and numbers printed on the cards. Such procedures could be adapted to test for differences in logic and hypothesis testing between skeptics and believers.

Serial-Position Effects

A highly reliable finding in memory research is that when recalling a list of words, people tend to recall the first few and the last few items in the list best. Because recall changes as a function of an item's serial position in the list, this effect is called the *serial-position effect*. Usually, the list is presented auditorily and the words are single digits (e.g., four, seven, three, etc.). For reliability, participants perform *multiple trials*, recalling a number of different lists per condition. Then, we graph the recall for the words as a function of where in the list each word occurred. The graph produces a *serial-position curve*, as shown in Figure 12.2. Note that the higher recall of the first items in the list is called the "primacy effect" and the higher recall of the final items is called the "recency effect."

One explanation for the recency effect is that the final few items in a list have most recently entered into memory, so they are in some sense "fresher." Some researchers (e.g., Crowder, 1982) have proposed that these items are better recalled because there is an "echo" in memory of the most recently spoken words. The final word in the list, for example, is recalled best because no words come after it that might interfere with its echo.

How would you test this explanation?

FIGURE 12.2 Idealized Serial-Position Curve

Shown here is participants' recall of 8-item lists as a function of each item's position in the presented list.

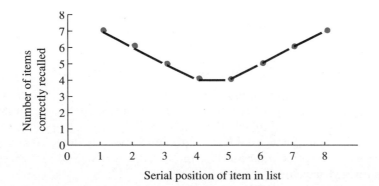

Researchers have tested this proposal by speaking an additional word at the end of the list, called a "stimulus suffix." When the lists consist of digits, the suffix for every list is usually the digit *zero*. Participants are told not to remember the zero; it is merely the signal to recall the list, and they are to "ignore" it. In control conditions, a tone is the recall signal. Because the tone is so different from the list of words, it should not interfere with the echo of previous words, so the control group should exhibit the typical high recency. Conversely, the zero should reduce the freshness of the final list items and fill the echo, so the experimental group should exhibit reduced recency. In fact, the zero does this, and the lowered recency is called the "suffix effect." (See Turner et al. [1987] for a review.)

The reason that the suffix disrupts recency is not known. Originally, its effect was thought to be limited to spoken words only. Yet, suffix effects have also been found when the zero is silently mouthed by the experimenter or by participants, and when hearing impaired participants see the list and suffix presented in sign language. In addition, suffix effects have been shown to occur when spoken words in the list have different vowels but not when they have different consonants. Thus, the suffix effect is not restricted to auditory stimuli, yet it does not always work with auditory stimuli. This inconsistency makes the notion of an "echo" very suspect.

Although there have been many explanations for this effect, one that has received virtually no attention concerns the assumption that participants can in fact "ignore" the zero at the end of the list. But how do they know that the word zero is the one to ignore unless they first pay attention to it? You would think that they must first identify this word in order to recognize that it is *not* part of the list to be remembered. A tone, by contrast, can be ignored instantly, because it is so obviously different from the preceding words. Thus, you might investigate whether participants can (or do) ignore the zero. If not, is the zero at first treated as part of the list, thereby confusing participants? Or, does a list followed by a zero require greater attention than a list followed by a tone, and does this greater attention cause decreased recall of the list?

How would you study whether participants do ignore the suffix?

You might measure the reaction time of participants to determine whether there are differences in their ability to recognize the end of a list when it is signaled by a tone or zero. If the zero takes longer to recognize, then there is something about it, in terms of the attention it requires, that is different from the control condition. If so, then a confounding has occurred in previous research, because the tone and the zero are not equivalent signals for the end of the list.

Alternatively, you might first identify some words that are easy to recognize and some that are difficult to recognize. Then, using these words in place of the zero, you can see whether they alter the recency effect. Or, you might give participants a cue to forewarn them that the zero or tone is about to occur. For example, you might ring a bell just prior to the zero. If reading the list aloud, you could change your tone of voice and inflection, or make a movement, to signal that the zero is about to occur. If such cues eliminate the suffix effect, then you have evidence that the zero normally reduces the recency effect because of the attention it demands or the confusion it produces.

Attractiveness and Height

Shepard and Strathman (1989) investigated whether women prefer to date taller men and whether they consider taller men more attractive. They also investigated whether men prefer to date shorter women and whether they consider shorter women more attractive.

How would you study the relationship between height and attraction?

Shepard and Strathman conducted a *correlational study*, presenting males and females with a questionnaire that asked for the number and height of their recent dates as well as for a rating of each date's attractiveness. Participants were also asked whether they preferred to date a person who was shorter than, taller than, or the same height as themselves. The researchers found that females reported that they dated tall males more frequently than short or medium males. They also reported a preference for taller men, but they did not rate their taller dates as more attractive. Interestingly, short and medium-height males reported that they went on dates just as often as did tall males. Overall, the males preferred shorter female dates, rated them as more attractive, and dated them more frequently.

What problem do these self-reports present?

These self-reports may be unreliable for several reasons: (1) Participants might have inaccurately estimated a date's height, especially after the fact; (2) A date's personality and compatibility might have influenced participants' perception of the date's attractiveness; and (3) A "bad" date might have biased participants so that they remembered their dates as shorter or taller than they actually were. Further, the females reported fewer dates with short or medium-height men, but these males reported the *same* frequency of dates as tall men. Yet, the shorter males were dating *somebody*! Therefore, the self-reports of either the males or the females must have been in error.

What suggestions for additional research can you make?

Rather than relying solely on self-reports about participants' past dating experiences, Shepard and Strathman (1989) conducted an additional experiment in which they manipulated height and measured attractiveness. They presented a photograph of the upper bodies of a male and female facing each other. In the photograph, the male was either 5 inches taller, the same height, or 5 inches shorter than the female. Females rated the man as more attractive when he was taller. Males, however, did not rate a female differently depending on her relative height.

You might also determine why the females' reports of seldom dating short men do not correspond to the high frequency of dating reported by short men. Perhaps the males or females are erroneous in their reports because of pressure to give the socially desirable response. If so, the number of erroneous reports should increase when the researcher strongly implies such demand characteristics through instructions or the task. Also, you might investigate whether the contradictory results occur because of a definitional problem having to do with the term *taller*. Stereotypically, most people would agree that a man whose height is 7 feet is "tall," and that one who is 5 feet is "short." However, *taller* can be a relative personal term: For a woman whose height is 4 feet 6 inches, a man whose height is 5 feet is "taller." To what extent do males and females use the stereotypic or the personal definition when selecting or describing dates?

There is an ecological issue here as well: Women *are*, on average, shorter than men. The opportunities for dates are greater, then, if women accept taller men and men accept shorter women, so their "preferences" may simply reflect the facts of life. Does the fact that most men are taller than most women lead to a stereotype of the ideal date? As we saw when discussing Horner (1972), people tend to anticipate negative consequences when violating sex-role stereotypes. To what extent do the preceding studies measure stereotyped responses instead of actual attraction? And, finally, is it appropriate to conclude that being taller always makes a male more attractive to a woman? Is there a point at which taller is not better because it becomes "too tall"?

The Influence of Color

Research from environmental psychology suggests that the color of walls, furniture, or floors has an influence on various aspects of behavior. For example, "warm" colors (those close to red) are often believed to be arousing, to increase physical performance, and to improve mood. "Cool" colors (those close to blue) are believed to be soothing, to lower performance, and to have a dulling effect on mood.

How would you design a study to test these beliefs?

One obvious way to manipulate color in the environment is to test people in different rooms that are painted different colors. In each room, you can have participants perform a physical task or provide responses that indicate their mood. For example, Kwallek, Lewis, and Robbins (1988) asked people to type business forms for 20 minutes after placing them in either a red or blue "office," and then had them complete a questionnaire describing their anxiety, mood, and general arousal. After resting in another room, participants either returned to the same colored office or were switched to the different colored office and then performed additional typing and completed another questionnaire. Those who were moved to a different colored office made significantly more typing errors. And, the interaction showed that more errors occurred when participants moved from the blue to the red office than when they moved from the red to the blue. The mood data indicated that people remaining in the red office showed greater anxiety and stress, those remaining in the blue office showed greater depression, and those who were moved to different colored offices showed the greatest level of general arousal.

Because moving participants into a different colored room influences their behavior, a problem with this study is that initially placing them in the first office after they've entered the study from someplace else constitutes changing rooms in an uncontrolled manner. As an alternative approach, you might include a control condition that allows you to "reverse" the influence of any previous colored room.

How would you design this study?

Hamid and Newport (1989) studied how the color of a room influences behavior using an ABACAB *reversal design*. The control or *baseline*—condition A—was a gray room that presumably neutralized the influence of other colors. A pink room was condition B, and a blue room was condition C. The researchers measured hand strength and mood in six young children after they had experienced each colored room. Greater physical strength and more positive mood were found in the pink conditions.

What suggestions for additional research can you make?

If there is an influence of color on arousal and performance, then it might extend to many objects and situations. Would similar effects on typing errors occur depending on the color of the paper in a typewriter or the color of a computer display screen, or the color of the computer itself? In the previous chapter, we saw the influence of black uniforms on aggression, but the present research suggests that other colors of clothing might also affect behavior. We know, for example, that a person's clothing style influences how he or she is perceived in the workplace (e.g., Forsythe, 1990). Does wearing reddish or bluish clothes also influence perceptions? Also, in this chapter, we discussed how participants misattribute their arousal from fear as being due to sexual attraction: Is arousal from wall color or the color of clothing misattributed as sexual attraction? Or, as an *applied* topic, the colors in the environment might be important for maximizing worker productivity or for maximizing physical arousal in athletic events: Does wall color influence a salesperson's or a weight-trainer's success? And, finally, do certain colors play a role when we become overaroused, as discussed below?

Self-Consciousness and "Choking under Pressure"

An unusual behavior to study is the phenomenon of "choking under pressure." Baumeister (1984) proposed that inferior performance ("choking") occurs when we feel so pressured to perform well that we focus too much attention on the process of performing a task and not enough attention on the outcome of the task. Thus, in a self-fulfilling prophecy, the more we worry that things are going badly, the worse they go. Baumeister also proposed that personality characteristics play a role, such that, for example, a person who is more self-conscious should exhibit greater "choking."

How would you design a study to test these proposals?

In an experimental setting, you could create a task for participants in which you manipulate the amount of pressure they feel. The task should be a simple one in which errors are easily measured, such as having people quickly trace a pencil maze, solve simple math problems, or press one of several buttons to make a correct response. For example, Heaton and Sigall (1991) first classified participants along the quasi-independent variable of high or low self-consciousness. For experimental realism, they had participants in each condition form a "team." Then, they manipulated the pressure situation through the additional factors of (1) indicating that the participant's team was behind or ahead, and (2) having participants perform when alone, when watched by their team, or when watched by the opposing team. Choking was measured as the time it took each person to place variously shaped pegs in their corresponding holes. Participants who were low in self-consciousness choked depending on the audience characteristics, while those high in self-consciousness choked when their team was behind.

What suggestions for additional research can you make?

Apparently, people differing in self-consciousness perceive the source of pressure differently. The results for those with high self-consciousness suggest that they choked because of competitive pressure, so you might manipulate the situation for them in terms of the amount of competition involved. The results for those with low self-consciousness suggest that they choked because of their need for social approval, so for them you might manipulate the social setting. Also, consider the possibility of replicating this relationship between choking and pressure in a field setting. You might also extend this research to other personality traits, such as looking at whether being task or socially oriented plays a role in choking. Thus, for example, you might correlate participants' scores on these traits with how much they choke or, as above, examine how these traits interact with different conditions that promote choking. Alternatively, given that high pressure is a form of arousal, you might ask whether the color of the room in which someone is tested influences choking. Finally, you might ask whether a "lucky charm," such as a lucky shirt, is considered lucky because a person did *not* choke when wearing it. (And what color is it?)

PUTTING IT ALL TOGETHER

At this point, you *have* put it all together. By now, you understand the basic logic of the studies we've discussed, so you understand psychological research. Congratulations on mastering a complicated topic. If you still feel that you cannot evaluate and conduct the sophisticated research found in the psychological literature, remember that you are at a temporary disadvantage. The major difference between beginning student researchers and professional-level researchers is their knowledge of the psychological issues involved in any topic. You're probably not all that familiar with the existing theory and research on a particular behavior. If you read the literature, however, you'll learn the details of how a construct is conceptualized, along with the commonly used, successful methods of studying it. By filling in these gaps in your knowledge, you'll discover not only that you *can* evaluate and conduct real research but also that it's really a lot of fun.

REPORTING RESEARCH USING APA FORMAT

GETTING STARTED

To understand this appendix, recall the following:

- From Chapter 2, recall that research begins with broad constructs, is "whittled down" to precise operational definitions, and then is generalized back to the broad constructs.
- From Chapter 4, recall the requirements for designing the independent and dependent variable in an experiment.
- From Chapter 7, recall how to interpret the mean score in each condition, how to graph an experiment's results, and the independent samples *t*-test.

Your goals in this appendix are to learn:

- How to organize the needed information when reporting a study.
- The parts of an APA-style report and the purpose of each.
- What information should and should not be reported in a research report.
- The style and tone that a research report should have.

Recall that science is a community activity in which we try to correct one another's errors by skeptically evaluating each study. Also, recall that scientific facts are ultimately built through *replication* of findings. To allow critical evaluation and to build evidence through replication, researchers share the results of their studies by publishing them and thus contributing to the *research literature*. This appendix describes how to create a research article. By knowing the process an author uses in writing an article, you can read the literature more effectively. Also, as a psychology student, you'll probably be reporting your own study sooner or later. (To help you learn the material, this appendix is laid out like previous chapters, with study aids, end-of-chapter review questions, etc.)

In the following sections, we'll first design an experiment and then see what goes into a manuscript for reporting it in the literature. (The next appendix shows a completed report of the study.) Be forewarned that the study here is simple, so that you can understand it, even if you haven't read all of the chapters in this book. The idea is to show you the basics. However, follow these same rules even if you have a more elaborate experiment, as well as with other designs, whether descriptive, correlational, single-subject, and so on.

AN EXAMPLE STUDY

Here's a novel study: Bower, Karlin, and Dueck (1975) studied short-term memory by presenting participants with 28 simple cartoons called "droodles." Each droodle is a meaningless geometric shape, but it becomes meaningful when accompanied by a verbal interpretation. Two examples are shown in Figure A.1. Some participants were told that droodle A shows "a midget playing a trombone in a telephone booth" and that droodle B shows "an early bird that caught a very strong worm." Other participants were not given any interpretations. Bower et al. found that participants who were given interpretations could recall (sketch) more of the droodles than those who were not. The authors concluded that the interpretations made the droodles more "meaningful," allowing participants to integrate the droodles with their knowledge in memory. Then, when participants tried to recall the droodles, this knowledge provided useful "retrieval cues."

However, there is a potential flaw in this design: The interpretations not only make the droodles meaningful but do so in a humorous way. By using interpreta-

FIGURE A.1 Examples of "Droodles"

These droodles were accompanied by the following interpretations: (a) "A midget playing a trombone in a telephone booth" and (b) "An early bird that caught a very strong worm."

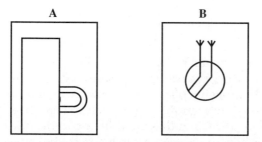

From G.H. Bower, M.B. Karlin, and A. Dueck (1975), Comprehension and memory for pictures, *Memory and Cognition*, 3(2), 216–220. Reprinted by permission of the Psychonomic Society, Inc. and the authors.

tions that are both humorous and meaningful, the study may have been confounded: On the one hand, the interpretations might make the droodles meaningful and thus more memorable, as the authors suggested. On the other hand, the interpretations might make the droodles humorous, and their humor might make the droodles more memorable. This second idea leads to a rival hypothesis: When the contexts in which stimuli occur differ in humor, differences in memory for the stimuli are produced.

The hypothesis suggests that greater humor *causes* improved memory, so a well-controlled, laboratory experiment is in order. In fact, the design of Bower et al. seems appropriate. They compared the effects on memory of an interpretation versus the absence of an interpretation. We could investigate our hypothesis by comparing humorous versus nonhumorous interpretations. The prediction is that droodles with humorous interpretations will be better recalled.

Let's say that we decide to test the above hypothesis. In the following discussion, we'll develop a very detailed design of the study. Not only will this provide you with practice applying design principles, but then you can see how much of the detail is later abbreviated or simply omitted in the report of the study.

We don't know very much about this topic, so the first step is . . . To the Literature!

Before proceeding, we need to be sure the study is rational, ethical, and practical. Rationally speaking, the idea that humor acts as a cue for recalling information seems to fit known memory processes (but we'll check), and understanding memory is a worthwhile psychological study. Ethically, asking participants to remember droodles doesn't appear to cause any harm (but we'll check). And practically speaking, such a study seems doable and does not require inordinate time, expense, or hard-to-find participants or equipment.

The Literature

A check of the *research literature* shows there are no studies that cause us to question the original procedure of presenting droodles as to-be-remembered stimuli. There are no ethical or practical concerns, and because this procedure produced informative and powerful results (they were significant), we can adopt it for our study.

The literature contains many studies that replicate the finding that the more meaningful a stimulus is, the better it is retained. For example, when learning a list of words, participants who use each word in a sentence will recall the words better than if they merely think of a rhyme for each word (see Lockhart & Craik, 1990).

Surprisingly, however, there is little research that directly studied how and why humor improves memory (but see McAninch, Austin & Derks, 1992, and Dixon, Willingham, Strano & Chandler, 1989). Numerous studies, however, do show that more *distinctive* stimuli are better retained than less distinctive stimuli (e.g., Schmidt, 1985). For example, in a list of words, a word printed in a different style of print is retained better than other words that are visually similar (Hunt & Elliott, 1980).

The literature will not always address an issue from exactly our perspective, so often we must generalize from previous findings and constructs to fit them to the hypothesis. Thus, in suggesting that humor influences memory, we can propose that a humorous interpretation makes a droodle more distinctive in memory, thereby making it more memorable. Essentially, then, we propose that humor is one component of the *construct* of distinctiveness—one way to make a stimulus distinctive.

Although the meaningfulness of a stimulus might seem to be the same thing as its distinctiveness, researchers do distinguish between the two concepts. Desrochers and Begg (1987), for example, suggest that distinctiveness is the extent to which unique cues are associated with the particular context in which the stimulus was encountered. Essentially, a distinctive event is notable and thus stands out in memory. Therefore, greater distinctiveness enhances access to the stimulus, allowing us to "find" it in memory. Meaningfulness, on the other hand, is the extent to which the components of the stimulus are organized and integrated. A meaningful event is tied together so that we know all of its "parts." Therefore, once we access a memory of a stimulus, greater meaningfulness enhances recall of the components of the stimulus (see also Einstein, McDaniel & Lackey, 1989).

Although the preceding discussion greatly simplifies the debate about the constructs of distinctiveness and meaningfulness, for our study it boils down to this: On the one hand, the importance of the interpretations in the original droodle study could be that they were humorous, and thus made the droodles more distinctive and in turn more memorable. On the other hand, the importance of the interpretations might have nothing to do with the humor involved. Instead, perhaps they made the droodles more meaningful and thus more memorable. Our task is to design a study that clearly shows the influence of humor, separate from the influence of meaningfulness.

By discussing the constructs of memory, humor, and meaningfulness, we have begun to create their *operational definitions*. Now we "whittle down" these constructs, completing the design by defining the specific variables and procedures.

Defining the Variables

Our independent variable involves changing the amount of humor given to the droodles by their interpretations. The challenge, however, is to manipulate the amount of humor while producing equally meaningful interpretations. If the droodles are not always equally meaningful, humor and meaningfulness will be confounded. Then we will be unable to tell whether more humor or more meaningfulness improves retention of a droodle.

What seems to make an interpretation in Bower et al. humorous is that it provides an unusual explanation involving unexpected objects, people, or animals. So, if we revise the original interpretations to provide common explanations involving predictable objects, people, and animals, they should be less humorous (and less distinctive) but just as meaningful as the originals. For example, from the humorous interpretation "This shows a midget playing a trombone in a telephone booth" we can derive the less humorous interpretation "This shows a telephone booth with a technician inside fixing the broken door handle." In both cases, the droodle features a telephone booth, so if a telephone booth is particularly meaningful and memorable, it is equally so in both the humorous and nonhumorous conditions. Also, both interpretations involve the meaningful integration of a person, a telephone booth, and an object (either a trombone or a door handle).

Thus, we will create two conditions of the independent variable: In one, we provide participants with nonhumorous interpretations, and in the other, we provide the corresponding humorous interpretations. If humor is an attribute that aids memory, then the humorous interpretations should produce better recall of the droodles. If humor is not psychologically important in this way, then there should be no difference in retention between the two conditions.

Now consider all of the details involved in devising a reliable and valid study. First, if there is only one droodle per condition, participants might forget or remember it because of some hidden peculiarity in it. Instead, the original Bower et al. study presented 28 droodles per condition, and we'll use the same number of droodles. The easiest way to obtain the droodles is to use the ones from Bower et al. If, instead, we decided to create stimuli, then we must control extraneous variables so that all stimuli are comparable. Thus, we would specify rules for creating the stimuli so that they all have equal complexity and memorability: All are of equal size, all are drawn in black ink, all contain only two basic geometric shapes, and so on. Although Bower et al. handed each drawing of a droodle to participants, for better control we can present the droodles using a slide projector with an electronic timer or have participants sit at a computer-controlled video monitor.

Also for consistency, all interpretations will contain roughly the same number and type of words, and all will begin with the phrase "This is a . . ." As in the original study, we will test participants one at a time, reading them the interpretation as they first view a droodle. We'll read all interpretations at the same speed and volume, with the same tone of voice and expressiveness. (To further ensure consistency, we might record the interpretations and time the playback to occur when participants view each droodle.) In addition, the humorous interpretations should all be consistently humorous for a wide range of participants, the nonhumorous interpretations should be consistently nonhumorous, and, as a group, the humorous interpretations should be consistently more humorous than the nonhumorous interpretations. (A *pilot study* would be useful for confirming this consistency.)

The dependent variable is recall of the droodles, but we must also decide how to define and measure it. As in Bower et al., the participants will study each droodle for 10 seconds, so that everyone has the same amount of study time and the same retention period. Immediately after all droodles have been presented, participants will sketch them on sheets of paper containing several, approximately 3-by-3-inch squares. They will place each droodle in a square, so that we can tell what shapes a participant believes go together to form one droodle.

Completing the Design

We could score the sketches as correct or incorrect ourselves, but our judgment might not be reliable. Instead, therefore, we'll enlist two other people as scorers who are "blind" to the purposes of the study. A response is correct if both scorers agree that it matches an original droodle.

We must also create clear and precise instructions for participants so that they know exactly what to do, and so that we can control their extraneous behaviors. The instructions should be worded identically for all conditions, consistently read or recorded, of the same duration, and so on. Further, the researcher must attempt to behave identically when testing all participants, and the environment should be constant for them all.

We must also decide on the specific participants that we'll test. Variables such as age, gender, and cultural background might influence the kind of material that people consider humorous. And we want them all to see the droodles clearly and to understand the interpretations. To keep such variables constant, say that we will randomly select as participants Introductory Psychology students who are similar in age and background, with good eyesight, hearing, and English abilities. To avoid practice effects from showing the same people the same droodles in both conditions, we'll test a separate, independent sample of participants in each condition, and we'll balance gender. To have a powerful N, we'll test 40 people per condition, selecting 20 males and 20 females for each.

Finally, we plan out the statistical analysis. Each person's score will be the total number of correctly recalled droodles. These are ratio scores that meet the requirements of *parametric* inferential statistics so we'll use the *independent samples* t-*test*. Because we predict that humor will *improve* recall scores, we have a *one-tailed test*. (Instead, we could perform the *one-way between-subjects ANOVA* on the factor of humorous/nonhumorous interpretations.)

Although there are other designs we might create, let's assume we conducted the above study and found that the average number of droodles recalled was 15.2 with nonhumorous interpretations and 20.5 with humorous interpretations. The *t*-test indicated a significant difference, so this is a "believable" relationship. Therefore, we interpret the results "psychologically," first inferring that humor does influence recall and then working back to the broader hypothetical constructs of how humor and distinctiveness operate on memory.

To share the results with other researchers, we'll prepare a written report of the study following *APA format*.

OVERVIEW OF A RESEARCH ARTICLE

Most reports of psychological research follow the rules set down in the ***Publication Manual of the American Psychological Association*** (2001). Now in its fifth edition, this is *the* reference source for answering *any* question regarding the organization, content, and style of a research report. It provides instructions about everything from the details of page layout and typing, to creating references and citations, to the broadest issues of overall organization and style.

Although "APA format" or "APA style" may appear to be a rigid, arbitrary set of rules, it is necessary. First, it minimizes publishing costs by defining precisely the space and effort that a report requires. It also specifies the information that a report should contain and how it should be reported. And, especially for beginning researchers, APA format is a useful organizational scheme. It tells you, as a reader, where to look in an article to find certain information and how to understand the shorthand codes used to present it. It tells you, as an author, how to organize a paper, what to say, and how to say it. And it provides you, as a researcher, with a framework for remembering the many aspects of a study that must be considered. Asking yourself the question "What will I say in each section of a report of this study?" is a cue for remembering the issues to deal with.

The sections of an article describe the various aspects of a study in the order in which they logically occur. We've seen that the flow of a study can be depicted using the diagram on the left in Figure A.2, in which we work from the general to the specific and then back to the general. Likewise, as on the right, an APA-style report is organized following these same steps, with four major sections:

FIGURE A.2 The Parallels Between Research Activity and APA Format

The flow of a study is from a general hypothesis to the specifics of the study, and then back to the general hypothesis. The APA format also follows this pattern.

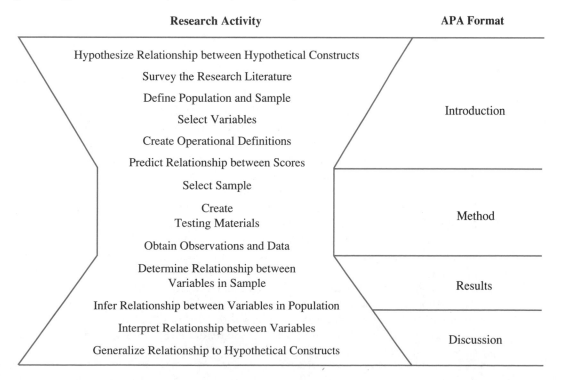

- The *Introduction* presents the hypothetical constructs as they are used in past research, develops your hypothesized relationship between the variables for the target population, and describes your predictions for the study.
- The *Method* section describes the specifics of your design and how the data were collected.
- The *Results* section reports the descriptive and inferential statistics performed and describes the statistical relationship found.
- The *Discussion* section interprets the results first in terms of the variables and then generalizes to the broader relationship between the hypothetical constructs with which you began.

REMEMBER The organization of a research report follows the logical order of the steps performed in conducting the research.

The ultimate goal of APA format is precision in communication. At the same time, you need to conserve space and avoid overstatements or redundancy. Thus, strive to state each idea clearly, to say it once, and to report only the necessary information. To meet the goal of precise yet concise communication, both the author and the reader make certain implicit assumptions.

The Assumptions of the Author and Reader

First, the reader assumes that the author understands statistics and research methods. (It is assumed that everyone has taken the college course that you are taking right now.) Also, we assume that the author has described any unusual or unexpected events, and that he or she is a reasonable, ethical, and competent researcher. Many things are left unsaid in a research article, because the reader can assume that commonly accepted procedures were used and that omitted details are unimportant. Thus, for example, do not say "I compared the obtained statistic to the critical value" because all researchers know this must be done. Stating it would be redundant.

The author also assumes that the reader is a competent psychologist. Therefore, a report does not give a detailed background of the topic under study, because the assumption is that the reader already knows something about it, or will read the references provided. The author also assumes that the reader understands statistics and research methods. *Do not teach statistics and design principles to the reader.* Do not say "Reliable data were important because . . ." or "A *t*-test was performed because . . ." The reader should already know why reliability is important and why a *t*-test is performed. Finally, always use the common technical terminology (such as reliable, valid, confounding) but without providing definitions. The author assumes that the reader either understands such terms or will find out what they mean.

As the author, you should focus on providing readers with the information they cannot get elsewhere—*your thoughts and actions as a researcher*. What conclusions did *you* draw from a previous article? What do *you* mean when using a particular hypothetical construct? What logic did *you* use in deriving a hypothesis or prediction? And what do *you* think a result indicates about the behavior under study? As the author, you are the expert, so give the reader the benefit of your wisdom. Your job is to describe clearly and concisely all of the important mental and physical activities that you performed in creating, conducting, and interpreting the study. The goal is to provide readers the information necessary to (1) understand the study, (2) evaluate the study, and (3) perform a literal replication of the study.

REMEMBER A good report allows the study to be fully understood, scientifically evaluated, and literally replicated.

Some Rules of Style

There are many specific rules for preparing a research article, so refer to the *Publication Manual* for complete instructions. Below are some general rules for preparing a research article that conforms to APA style:

1. A report describes a completed study, so it is written in the past tense ("I predic*ted* that . . ."). The exception is to state in the present tense any general conclusions that apply to present or future situations ("Humor influences recall by . . .").

2. Cite all sources from which you obtained information, using only the last names of the authors and the dates. You may use the reference as the subject of a sentence: "Smith and Jones (1998) defined distinctiveness as . . . ." Or, you may state an idea and provide the reference in parentheses: "Distinctiveness is defined as . . . (Smith & Jones, 1998)." (In a parenthetical citation, "&" is used instead of "and.") When citing an article with three to six authors, include all names the first time you cite it, but thereafter refer to it using only the last name of the first author and the Latin phrase *et al*. Thus, first we say "Bower, Karlin, and Dueck (1975)," but subsequently we say "Bower et al. (1975)." When citing an article with more than six authors, even the first time use only the first author and et al.

3. Refrain from directly quoting an article. Instead, paraphrase and summarize the idea, so that *you* tell the readers what they should understand about the idea. Also, talk about the study itself, not its authors. For example, the phrase "Bower et al." refers primarily to a reported experiment, not to the people who conducted it. Thus, we write "The results are reported *in* Bower et al. (1975)" instead of "The results are reported *by* Bower et al. (1975)."

4. To distinguish your study from other studies, refer to it as "this study" or "the present study." However, do not use these phrases in a way that attributes human actions to nonhuman sources, as in "This study attempted to demonstrate that . . . ."(A study or experiment is not alive, and so cannot *do* anything.) Instead use, "I" as the subject of these verbs. (Use "we" *only* if you have a co-author.)

5. Use accepted psychological terminology when possible. If you must use a nonstandard term or name a variable, define the word the first time it is used and then use *that* word consistently. In the droodle study, we'll define *humorous* and use only this term, rather than mixing in terms such as *funny* or *entertaining*. This prevents confusion about whether we mean something slightly different by *funny* or *entertaining*. In addition, avoid using contractions or slang. A reader from a different part of the country or another country may not understand such terms.

6. Avoid abbreviations. They are justified only if (a) a term consists of several words, (b) it appears *very* frequently throughout the report, and (c) you are not using many different abbreviations. If you must abbreviate, do so by creating an acronym, using the first letter of each word of the term. Define the complete term the first time it is used, with its acronym in parentheses. Thus, you might say "Short-term Memory (STM) is . . . ." Then use *only* the acronym, *except* as the first word of a sentence: There, always use the complete term.

7. Use words when describing numbers between zero and nine, and digits for numbers that are 10 and larger. However, use digits for any size number if (a) you are writing a series of numbers in which at least one is 10 or larger, or (b) the number contains a decimal or refers to a statistical result or to a precise measurement (such as a specific score or the number of participants). Thus, you would say "The three conditions, with 5 individuals per condition . . . ." But never begin a sentence with a number expressed in digits.

8. In research published before 1994, you'll see that the generic term *subjects* refers to the individuals that researchers study. A post-1994 change in APA style now requires the use of less impersonal and more precise terms. The generic term to use is *participants*, but where appropriate use more descriptive terms such as students, children, men, women, rats, and so on. In addition, APA rules stress that you avoid gender-biased language. Thus, refer to the gender of participants using the equivalent terms *male* and *female* and to individuals as *he* or *she*. When possible, use neutral terms such as *chairperson*.

9. Finally, use precise wording. In the droodle study, we won't say that participants "saw" or "looked at" a droodle, or that they "forgot" a droodle, because we don't *know* that these events occurred. We know only that participants were presented a droodle or failed to recall it.

THE COMPONENTS OF AN APA-STYLE RESEARCH ARTICLE

The rules presented here (and in the *Publication Manual*) describe how to prepare a *manuscript* that is ready for delivery to the journal publisher, who then prepares it to be printed. Therefore, your job is to follow the prescribed format, *not* to produce a pretty, final copy that looks like the journal article.

These are the major components of an APA-style manuscript in the order in which they occur:

> Title page
> Abstract page
> Introduction
> Method
>> Participants
>> Materials or Apparatus
>> Procedure
> Results
> Discussion
> References
> Tables and Figures

All parts are typed double-spaced, and without "justifying" the righthand margin. Use a 12 pt print font ("Times Roman" or "Courier" is preferred) and set one-inch margins for all sides. *Page numbers are placed in the upper right-hand corner of every page.* Everything in the manuscript is printed in black ink, and use a good-quality paper and printer. (It is also possible to submit the manuscript electronically to a journal.)

Note: A change in APA format is that now you virtually never underline words, including when referencing books or journals. Historically, underlining told the publisher to *italicize*. Now, if your word processor will do it, *you* italicize titles and symbols (as you'll see).

The following sections examine each component in detail, using examples from a manuscript of the droodle study. (The complete manuscript is presented in Appendix B.) Throughout this discussion, compare the previous steps we went through when designing the study—and all that was said—to what is actually reported. Translating and summarizing your thoughts and activities are the keys to creating a research report.

The Title

The **title** allows readers to determine whether they want to read the article. It should clearly communicate the variables and relationship being studied, but it should consist of no more than 12 words. Titles often contain the phrase "as a function of." For example, "Helping Behavior as a Function of Self-Esteem" indicates that the researcher examined the relationship between participants' helping behavior and different amounts of their self-esteem. A title such as "Decreased Errors in Depth Perception as a Function of Increased Illumination Levels" provides the added information that the observed relationship is negative, such that greater illumination is associated with fewer errors. Because illumination level can be manipulated easily, this title probably describes an experiment in which "illumination level" was the independent variable and "errors" was the dependent variable.

Titles also often begin with the phrase "Effect of," as in "Effect of Alcohol Consumption on Use of Sexist Language." The word *effect* means "influence." Such a title is a causal statement, implying that an experiment was conducted and that changes in the independent variable (amount of alcohol consumed) caused a change in the dependent variable (amount of sexist language used). Note the difference between effect (usually a noun) and affect (usually a verb). If *X affects Y*, then there is an *effect* of *X* on *Y*. (Here's a trick for remembering this distinction: *Effect* means *end result*, and both begin with *e*. *Affect* means *alter*, and both begin with *a*.)

The title should provide sufficient information for readers to determine whether the article is relevant to their literature search. Choose terms that are specific, and never use abbreviations or terms that need to be defined. Thus, for our study, we will not include "droodles" because most people won't know what they are. Instead, we might use the title "Effect of Humorous Interpretations on Immediate Recall of Nonsense Figures." This wording identifies the variables, specifying that we are studying short-term memory of drawings. Contrast this with such terrible titles as: "A Study of Humor and Memory" (of course it's a study!), or "When Does Memory Work Better?" (what does "work" mean?). Either of these would be useless for determining whether the article is relevant to a specific literature search.

In the manuscript, the title page is a separate page containing the title, your name, and the formal title of your college or university. A sample title page appears in Figure A.3. The title page is page number 1.

Notice that the title page also contains two other components. First, left of the page number is typed the **manuscript page header**, consisting of the first two or three words from *your* title. The header appears on all subsequent pages, so if any pages become separated, the publisher can identify them as belonging to your manuscript. (This is another reason for all researchers not to use titles beginning "A Study of.") Second, on the first line below the header is typed the words **Running head:** followed by a different, abbreviated title. This running head will be printed at the top of each page in the published article. (On this page of your textbook, the running head is "Reporting Research Using APA Format.")

The Abstract

Following the title page is the **abstract**, which is a brief summary of the study. The abstract describes the variables used, important participant characteristics, a brief description of the overall design, and the key relationship obtained. It also indicates the theoretical approach taken in interpreting the results, though often without giving the actual interpretation.

FIGURE A.3   Sample Title Page of a Research Manuscript

Notice the location and spacing of the various components.

```
                                            Effect of Humorous    1
           Running head: EFFECT OF HUMOROUS INTERPRETATIONS ON RECALL




                        Effect of Humorous Interpretations on
                         Immediate Recall of Nonsense Figures
                                  Gary W. Heiman
                                 Podunk University
```

Although the abstract accompanies the article, it is also reproduced in *Psychological Abstracts*, so it must be able to stand alone, containing no abbreviations or uncommon terms (no "droodles"). It should include only details that answer the reader's question: "Is this article relevant to my literature search?" Most authors write the abstract after they have written the report, so they can summarize the key points more easily. If you find it difficult to compress a lengthy paper into the required 100 to 120 words, think of the abstract as an elaboration of the title. Given the title, what else would you say to communicate the gist of the article? The abstract for the droodle study appears in Figure A.4. Notice that the centered heading reads "Abstract," that the abstract is *one* paragraph, and that the first line is *not* indented.

REMEMBER   The *title* describes the relationship under investigation. The *abstract* summarizes the report. Together, they allow readers to determine whether the article is relevant to their literature search.

The Introduction

The **Introduction** should reproduce the logic you used to derive the hypothesis and to design the study. The Introduction shows your "whittling down" process, beginning with broad descriptions of behaviors and hypothetical constructs and translating them into the specific variables of the study. It then describes the predicted relationship between scores that will be measured using the operational definitions.

Researchers read an introduction with two goals in mind. First, we want to understand the hypothesis and logic of the study. Thus, the author should introduce the psychological explanations being tested, the general design (e.g., whether correlational or experimental), the reasons that certain operational definitions are used, and why a particular result will support the predictions and hypothesis of the study. Both the purpose of the study and the population under study should be clear. (Unless stated otherwise, we assume that the study applies to the broadest population.) Readers also evaluate the hypothesis and its logic to be sure there are no circular *pseudo-explanations* and that *rival hypotheses* and *extraneous variables* have been considered.

The reader's second goal is to look for empirical evidence that supports the hypothesis. The Introduction is where virtually all references to past research occur, including those studies that do and do not support the hypothesis. Further, if the study is successful, the author will attempt to interpret and explain the findings "psychologically," so the Introduction also contains the conceptual and theoretical issues that will be discussed later in the paper.

The reader assumes that, unless otherwise noted, a study cited in support of a hypothesis is reasonably convincing. Previous studies are reported very briefly, usually with the author merely citing them by name and not explaining them in detail. If discussed at all, studies are described in terms of the specific information the author judged to be important when deriving his or her hypotheses. The details of a study are provided only when (1) they are necessary for the reader to

FIGURE A.4   Sample Abstract Page

The abstract page is page number 2.

                                        Effect of Humorous   2

                                Abstract

The effect of humor on the immediate recall of simple visual
stimuli was investigated. Eighty college students (20 men and 20
women per condition) viewed 28 nonsensical line drawings that
were each accompanied by either a humorous or nonhumorous verbal
interpretation. Although the interpretations were comparable in
the meaningfulness they conveyed, those participants presented
with humorous interpretations correctly recalled significantly
more drawings than those presented nonhumorous interpretations.
The results suggest that a meaningful and humorous context
provides additional retrieval cues beyond those cues provided by
a meaningful yet nonhumorous context. The effect of the cues
produced by humor is interpreted as creating a more distinctive
and thus more accessible memory trace.

understand the author's comments about that study, or (2) they are necessary for showing support for the author's position. Therefore, the Introduction does not usually contain such details as the number of participants, the statistics used, or other specifics of the design of the studies cited. (If readers want that kind of detail, they should go read the studies themselves!)

A portion of the Introduction for the droodle study appears in Figure A.5. (*Note*: The Introduction is not labeled as such, and the page begins by presenting the paper's title again.) Although we know how the study turns out, the Introduction is written as if we do not, describing the process we went through *before* collecting the data. Our Introduction begins with the hypothetical constructs of meaningfulness and its influence on memory. Then, we work from the broad ideas to the specific example of the droodle study. We immediately focus on the perspective we've taken to study the hypothetical constructs, and we tie in to the research literature by providing the major relevant conclusions from past research and their references. (We also identify when we are merely speculating.)

FIGURE A.5 Sample Portion of the Introduction

Note that the title is repeated and that we do not label this section as the Introduction.

```
                                    Effect of Humorous    3
              Effect of Humorous Interpretations
            on Immediate Recall of Nonsense Figures
       Researchers have consistently demonstrated that retention
  of to-be-learned material improves when the material is
  presented in a context that leads to meaningful processing
  (Lockhart & Craik, 1990). In particular, Bower, Karlin, and
  Dueck (1975) presented college students with a series of
  "droodles," which are each a meaningless line drawing that can
  be made meaningful by presentation of an accompanying verbal
  interpretation. Those individuals who were provided the
  interpretations correctly recalled (sketched) significantly more
  of the droodles immediately following their presentation than
  did those individuals given no interpretations. However, each
  interpretation in Bower et al. (1975) defined a droodle in a
  humorous fashion, using unexpected and incongruent actors and
  actions. Thus, differences in the meaningfulness attributed to
```

Notice: The purpose of the study is stated *early* in the Introduction—in this case, at the end of the first paragraph. In subsequent paragraphs, we retrace our logic, defining what we mean by the constructs of meaningfulness and distinctiveness and explaining how humor might influence memory. Then, we describe how we define and manipulate humor while keeping meaningfulness constant.

It is important to always make clear the connection between past research and the present study. Usually, after presenting previous findings, you can point out a question or flaw that has not been addressed. Once the background and important issues are discussed, you might say something like "However, this interpretation does not consider . . ." or "This variable, however, was not studied . . ." Then, address the problem you have raised.

Overall, the flow of the Introduction should lead up to a final paragraph that says something like "Therefore, in the present study . . ." Then, state the specific hypothesis and relationship to be studied, describe the general approach for measuring and manipulating the variables, and specify the prediction. The details of how the data were collected are provided in the next section.

> **REMEMBER** The *Introduction* presents all information that will be used to interpret the results: The conceptual and theoretical logic of the study, relevant past research, and the predictions of the study.

The Method

Next comes the **Method section**, which contains the information needed to understand, critique, and exactly replicate the data-collection procedures. To collect data, we need participants, testing materials and equipment, and a specific testing procedure and design. APA format requires that these topics be presented in three separate subsections, in this order: (1) Participants, (2) Materials or Apparatus, and (3) Procedure. Note: These three titles are italicized. See Figure A.6.

Participants   In the **Participants section**, you describe your participants so that other researchers can obtain comparable participants and look for uncontrolled participant variables. Thus, identify important characteristics (e.g., gender, age, school affiliation) and specify any criteria used when selecting them. If animals are tested, identify their species, genus, and strain and your supplier. Always report the number of individuals tested. Because their motivation is important, describe any form of reimbursement that was used. Also, in this section or in a letter sent to the journal editor, an author must certify that the participants were treated in accordance with the ethical principles of the APA.

Materials or Apparatus   The **Materials section**, sometimes called the **Apparatus section**, immediately follows the Participants section (see Figure A.6).

FIGURE A.6   Sample Portion of the Method Section

Notice the placement of the headings, as well as the use of capital letters and italics.

```
humorous interpretations should be more frequently recalled
than those accompanied by nonhumorous interpretations.
                              Method
Participants
       Forty female and 40 male undergraduate students from an
introductory psychology course at Podunk University each
received $3.00 for their voluntary participation. All were
between 20 and 22 years of age (mean age = 20.7 years), were
born in the United States, were raised in English speaking
families, and had normal or corrected eyesight and hearing.
Participants were randomly assigned to either the humorous or
nonhumorous condition, with 20 males and 20 females in each
condition.
Materials
       The 28 droodles from Bower et al. (1975) were reproduced,
each consisting of a black-ink line drawing involving two
```

Usually, it is called *Materials* because most studies involve mainly testing materials such as stimulus objects, tests and printed material, slides, drawings, and so on. Call it *Apparatus*, however, if testing mainly involves equipment such as computers, recording devices, and the like. (Don't be confused by the *Publication Manual* on this point: In Section 1.09, *Apparatus* appears to be preferred, but *Materials* is actually used throughout the examples of manuscripts shown in the "Sample Papers" that follow Section 5.29.) (If necessary, create two sections and use both titles.)

Regardless of its title, describe the relevant materials and apparatus, but without explaining *how* they are used. Again, organize the information according to the logical order in which the components occur: We'll present a droodle, give an interpretation, and then measure retention.

Describe equipment and material so that the reader can understand, evaluate, and reproduce them. If they are purchased, indicate the manufacturer and model, or the edition or version. If materials are borrowed from previous research, describe them and provide the citation. If you build equipment, describe it so it can be reproduced. If you create visual stimuli, describe their dimensions, their color, and so on. If you create verbal stimuli, describe the length of words or sentences, their meaning and content, their difficulty level, and so on. For questionnaires, describe the number of questions, their format, and the way in which participants indicate their responses. Also, report the reliability and validity of a procedure. For example, indicate the speed and error rates of equipment, because such rates affect reliability. With paper-and-pencil tests, either note their previously demonstrated validity and reliability or briefly report how you determined this.

Note that all physical dimensions are reported using the metric system, and that common units of measurement are abbreviated. Table A.1 provides the most common abbreviations used in psychological research. If you measure in non-metric units, report the measurement both in nonmetric and in converted metric units. (Only the abbreviation for inch—in.—has a period.)

Keep in mind that only *important* elements are reported. Readers know the necessary steps in designing a study, and generally understand why and how each component is chosen. (They've *taken* this course!) Therefore, do not specify such things as how participants were randomly selected or how you determined their age. Likewise, do not describe obvious equipment (e.g., whether participants used a pencil or a pen to complete a questionnaire, or what furniture was present in the room where testing took place). Note a detail only if it (1) would not be expected by a reasonable researcher or (2) would seriously influence the reliability or validity of the results.

Procedure   Next, the **Procedure section** describes how you brought the participants, materials, and apparatus together to actually perform the study. A portion of this section from the droodle study is presented in Figure A.7.

The best way to organize this section is to follow the temporal sequence that occurred in your study. The first thing we do is give participants their instructions, so first summarize the instructions. Then, describe the tasks in the order in which they were performed, as well as any controls you included, such as counterbalancing groups or randomizing trials. A useful strategy is to initially describe those aspects of the procedure that are common to all participants and then to distinguish one condition from another. Always work from the general to the specific. (*Note*: briefly report the outcome of any pilot study here, or in the above Materials section, wherever the study most directly applies.)

At this point, the various parts of the Method section should communicate the complete design of the study. If not, an optional *Design* section may be added.

TABLE A.1 Common Abbreviations Used in APA Format

Notice that these abbreviations do not take periods.

Unit	Symbol	Unit	Symbol
centimeters	cm	meters	m
grams	g	milliliters	mL
hours	hr	millimeters	mm
kilograms	kg	minutes	min
liters	L	seconds	s

FIGURE A.7   Sample Portion of the Procedure Section

```
with a loop attached to the lower right side. The humorous
interpretation was "This shows a midget playing a trombone in a
telephone booth." The nonhumorous interpretation was "This shows
a telephone booth with a repairman inside fixing the broken door
handle."
    Response forms for recalling the droodles consisted of a
grid of 3 by 3 in. (7.62 cm by 7.62 cm) squares printed on
standard sheets of paper.
Procedure
    Participants were tested individually and viewed all 28
droodles accompanied by either the humorous or nonhumorous
interpretations. Participants were instructed to study each
droodle during its presentation for later recall and were told
that the accompanying interpretation would be helpful in
remembering it. A timer in the slide projector presented each
```

This describes the layout of the study in terms of the conditions, participants, and variables used so that essentially a reader can diagram the study as we have in previous chapters. But, note that this section should be necessary only with a very complicated design, involving numerous groups or variables, or elaborate steps in testing.

In some instances, additional sections can be created—but, again, only if they are truly necessary. For example, if we took extensive steps to determine the reliability of a procedure and this element was central to the study, we might describe these steps in a *Reliability of Measures* section.

REMEMBER   The *Participants* section describes the important characteristics of the subjects, the *Materials* or *Apparatus* section describes the characteristics of the testing materials and equipment, and the *Procedure* section describes the testing situation and design.

The Results

The next section is the **Results section,** which reports the statistical procedures performed and the outcomes obtained. However, *do not* interpret the results here, only report them. A portion of the Results section for the droodle study is in Figure A.8.

Describe the results in the same order in which you perform the steps of the analysis. First, there must be some scores to analyze, so begin by describing the *scoring criteria* and tabulations used to produce each participant's score. (We described how each droodle was scored as correct or incorrect.) Also, describe any transformations performed, such as when converting number correct to a percentage. It is at this point that any information regarding the reliability of the data is noted (such as the *inter-rater reliability* of the scorers).

Next, any analysis then involves first computing the *descriptive statistics* that summarize the scores and relationship. At a minimum, report the mean and standard deviation for each condition. (In the next section, we'll discuss the symbols to use.) Next, we perform the appropriate inferential procedure, so next report the formal name for the procedure and describe how it was applied to the data. Be sure to use the technical terminology we've used (e.g., two-way, between-subjects, repeated measures, etc.). Then, report the results of the analysis. You must indicate the alpha level you used and report all significant *and* nonsignificant outcomes, and for each, the terms *significant* or *nonsignificant* must appear. (In a

FIGURE A.8   Sample Portion of the Results Section

Notice that the heading is centered and that statistical symbols are italicized.

```
          instructed to recall the droodles in any order, sketching each

          droodle within one grid on the response sheet.

                              Results

              Two assistants who were unaware of the purposes of the

          study scored the participants' sketches. A sketch was considered

          to indicate correct recall if both scorers agreed that it

          depicted a droodle. (On only 2% of the responses did the scorers

          disagree.) Each participant's score was then the total number of

          correctly recalled droodles.

              The mean number of droodles correctly recalled was 20.50 in

          the humorous interpretation condition (SD = 3.25) and 15.20 in

          the nonhumorous interpretation condition (SD = 4.19). With an

          alpha level of .05, a one-tailed independent samples t-test

          indicated a significant difference between the conditions,

          t(78) = 6.32, p <.05. The relationship between amount of humor
```

two-way ANOVA, report all significant and nonsignificant results, including the main-effect Fs, even if your interpretation will later focus on the interaction.)

If the results of the inferential procedure are significant, you have convincing evidence of a relationship, so next report any secondary analyses that describe the relationship. For example, with a correlation, we compute the regression line. Or, with a significant F, we perform post hoc comparisons. For each of these secondary analyses, again identify the procedure and then report the results. (The results from a *manipulation check* are usually reported here also.) In particular, remember that there are several ways to measure *effect size*, so indicate how you are computing it. For example, in the Droodle study, r^2_{pb} is appropriate for indicating the *proportion of variance accounted for*, and equals .34. We might have included the statement, "The effect size, as measured by r^2_{pb}, equaled .34."

Also, remember that when deciding whether any result is significant, we simply decide either "Yes, it is," or "No, it's not." One result cannot be "more significant" than another, nor can you have a "highly significant" result. (That's like saying "more yes," or "highly yes!") Also, do not attribute human actions to statistical procedures, saying such things as "according to the ANOVA . . ." or "the t-test gave significance." Instead, say "there were significant differences between the means" or "there was a significant effect of the independent variable."

Statistical Symbols   Type all statistical symbols in *italics* if you are using a word-processing program that allows it. Otherwise, underline each symbol and the publisher will convert them to italics.

There are two symbols in APA format that you are probably not expecting: The symbol for a mean is "M" and for a standard deviation is "SD." Otherwise, the symbols that we've used are the symbols used in APA format. Thus, the symbols r, r_s and r_{pb}, stand for the Pearson, Spearman, and point-biserial correlation coefficients, respectively. Likewise, we use F and t, (but, see the section in the manual for "Identifying Letters and Symbols").

Use symbols primarily in parenthetical statements or in tables, but not to replace words in a sentence: Saying "The mean was 4.15" or "The correlation coefficient equaled +.54" is correct. Saying "The M was . . ." or "The r equaled . . ." is not.

To report an inferential statistic, report the symbol for the statistic, the degrees of freedom in parentheses, the obtained value, and finally the probability of a Type I error. (With the *chi square* procedure, also report the total N.) In the Droodle study, we reported:

$$t(78) = 6.32, p < .05.$$

This indicates that we performed the t-test using 78 degrees of freedom, obtained an answer of 6.32, and that the probability (p) of a Type I error is less than .05. (Some computer programs give an exact probability, so for example, you might see $p = .034$.) Usually, we do not report critical values, the HSD values from post hoc comparisons, or other secondary values.

Figures   Because of cost and space considerations, include graphs, tables, or diagrams only when the information is so complicated that the reader will benefit from a visual presentation. Usually, graphs—called **Figures**—provide the clearest way to summarize the pattern in a relationship. However, you should also have something to say about each figure, telling readers what they should see in it. (For illustrative purposes, a figure is included in the droodle manuscript, although the relationship is so simple that it is really unnecessary.)

Every figure is numbered, even if there's only one. At the point in the narrative where readers should look at the figure, you should direct their attention to it, saying something like "As can be seen in Figure 1 . . . ." *Do not*, however, physically place the figure here (the publisher would do that). The graph is drawn on a separate page and placed at the *end* of the manuscript. For the Droodle manuscript, Figure A.9 shows how to refer to the figure, which is shown in Figure A.10. There are many rules for preparing a figure, so check the *Publication Manual*. Fully label each axis, using the names of the variables and their amounts. Use black ink, because color is expensive to publish (and a reader might be color blind!). If the figure contains more than one line, use different symbols for each (e.g., one solid line and one dashed). Then, provide a "legend" or "key" to the symbols at the side of the figure. (For an example, see Figure 8.1 or 8.2 in Chapter 8.)

Every figure has an explanatory title, called the **figure caption**, which briefly identifies the variables and relationship depicted. In Figure A.10 for the droodle study, the caption is "Mean number of droodles correctly recalled as a function of nonhumorous and humorous interpretations." *DO NOT*, however, actually place the figure caption on the figure—the publisher does that. Instead, create a list of figure captions for all of the figures in the report that is called the **Figure Caption page**. This is then another separate page at the end of the manuscript.

Tables   Create a **table** rather than a figure when it is important for the reader to see the precise numerical values of data. A table is called for when there are

FIGURE A.9   Sample Portion of the Results Section Showing Reference to a Figure

$t(78) = 6.32$, $p <.05$. The relationship between amount of humor and recall scores can be seen in Figure 1. Although a positive relationship was obtained, the slope of this curve indicates that the rate of change in recall scores as a function of increased humor was not large.

Discussion

The results of the present study indicate that humorous interpretations lead to greater retention of droodles than do

FIGURE A.10   Sample Figure

The figure caption reads: "Mean number of droodles correctly recalled as a function of nonhumorous and humorous interpretations."

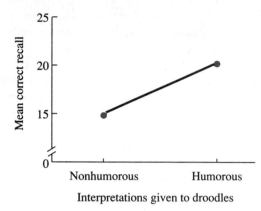

too many numbers to list in a sentence. For example, say that we had reason to compare male versus female participants, and we examined their recall of the individual droodles depending on whether the interpretation referred to humans, animals, plants, or objects. If we present this information in a sentence, it will be very dense and difficult to follow. Instead, a table is the way to go, as shown in Table A.2.

All tables are numbered consecutively, and, as with figures, the reader is directed to them by you at appropriate points in the Results section. The actual tables are placed at the end of the manuscript. Note that you *do* place the title for each table on the table itself. The title should clearly yet concisely summarize the table.

The layout should be such that the table can be easily understood. Type the table so it's against the left-hand margin, and limit using horizontal lines to only when they're really needed (vertical lines are almost never needed). All headings should be brief yet clear. Then, only digits are used to express quantities, and each is centered under its heading. (The *Publication Manual* provides detailed instructions for producing various tables.)

REMEMBER   The *Results* section summarizes the data and the relationship obtained, and reports the statistical procedures performed.

The Discussion

Next, in the **Discussion section**, you interpret the results and draw your conclusions. Here, the questions originally posed in the Introduction are answered.

TABLE A.2   Example APA-Style Table

Notice the table's title is italicized, and the table is double-spaced.

Recall of Droodle Types for Males and Females

	Gender			
	Males		Females	
Type	*M*	*SD*	*M*	*SD*
Human	2.33	0.68	3.55	1.01
Animal	2.14	0.46	4.21	0.98
Plant	5.70	1.86	3.23	2.79
Object	4.99	2.30	1.45	0.99

The Discussion section begins at the point where you have *already* reported a significant relationship (do not report any statistics here), so the question is "Do the results confirm (1) the predictions and thus (2) the hypothesis?" You can almost always answer this question by beginning the discussion with the phrase "The results of the present study . . ." (See Figure A.9 again.)

As the term *Discussion* implies, however, do not merely state the conclusions—*discuss* them. That is, after answering the original research question, explain what the answer tells us about the behavior. Recall from the diagram back in Figure A.2 that, in the Discussion section, we work backward from the specific to the general. Thus, beginning with the narrowly defined relationship in the study, generalize to the relationship between the variables that might be found with other individuals or situations. Then, generalize the findings based on the variables to the constructs you originally set out to study.

Begin by focusing on the descriptive statistics (inferential statistics are no help here). Throughout this book I've said that eventually we interpret a relationship "psychologically." Here is where you do that. So, become a psychologist again, translating the numbers into descriptions of behaviors and the variables that influence them. For example, the droodle study produced higher recall scores with humorous interpretations. Higher recall scores indicate better retention, a mental *behavior* that is different from what occurred when nonhumorous interpretations were given. Thus, based on the scores in each condition, the discussion proposes how manipulating humor influences the memory system. (See Figure A.11.) On the other hand, we cannot ignore that those droodles given nonhumorous interpretations were frequently recalled, so the addition of humor did not have a large effect. Thus, as here, researchers factor into their conclusions what the direction and rate of change in scores indicate, what the consistency or inconsistency in the relationship indicates, and what the proportion of variance accounted for indicates. Also, recall that in studies with more than two conditions, only some conditions might represent an actual relationship. In such cases, also consider why and how these results occur.

Remember that all explanations must rationally fit with previous findings and theoretical explanations. Thus, the goal is to provide an integrated and consistent explanation, answering the question "Given your findings and past findings, what is the present state of knowledge about the behavior or construct?" In the droodle study, for example, we relate our findings to current explanations of the role of distinctiveness and meaningfulness in memory. Notice, however, the use of such words as *presumably*, *probably*, and *apparently*. Do not say "prove" or provide explanations as if they are fact. And, although you may say *causes* or *influences*, the difficulty in identifying causal variables should lead you to use these words cautiously.

FIGURE A.11   Sample Portion of the Discussion Section

```
                                    Effect of Humorous    8
     nonhumorous interpretations. Because the meaningfulness of the
     droodles provided by the interpretations was presumably constant
     in both conditions, it appears that humor provides an additional
     source of retrieval cues. This conclusion is consistent with the
     proposal that humor increases the distinctiveness of a stimulus,
     thereby facilitating recall by increasing the accessibility of
     the stimulus in memory.
          The improvement in recall produced by humor, however, was
     relatively small. This result may be due to the fact that all
     droodles were made meaningful, although sometimes by a
     nonhumorous interpretation. As in other research (Lockhart &
```

At the same time, also consider any major flaws in the design that limit confidence in a conclusion. When looking for flaws, however, do not use the argument that the data may be unrepresentative or that a larger sample is needed. The significant inferential statistics have eliminated these arguments. Instead, raise questions based on these important design issues:

1. *Reliability*. Did changing the interpretations given to the droodles consistently manipulate the variable of humor? Did we consistently and only measure a person's recall of the droodles?

2. *Internal validity*. Were the humorous and nonhumorous interpretations equal in meaningfulness, or did the unusual humorous interpretation yield a broader meaning? If by manipulating humor, we also manipulated meaningfulness, then maybe greater meaningfulness produced the higher recall scores. If it is likely that this (or another) confounding occurred, then we have reduced internal validity for saying that amount of humor influenced recall.

3. *External validity*. Is it appropriate to generalize this relationship to other people and situations, or did our participants have an unusual sense of humor, so that the results are unique? Also, droodles are simple visual stimuli, so can we generalize the effect of humor to verbal material or to complex visual material?

4. *Content and construct validity*. Do the recall scores actually reflect "memory" for the droodles? Have we correctly defined "meaningfulness" and "humor" as they operate in nature? Also, we rather arbitrarily speculated that humor produces "distinctiveness," but we have no empirical evidence of this.

Do not try to hide or ignore any flaws that you find—we all know that it's impossible to conduct a perfect study. Instead, either provide counterarguments to explain why a flaw does not seriously reduce confidence in a conclusion, or qualify and limit your conclusions in light of the flaw.

Researchers often conclude the Discussion section by pointing out the next steps to be taken in the research area. Remember, as the author, you are the expert, so indicate what hypotheses should be tested next. (For example, we would note the lack of evidence that humor makes a stimulus more distinctive, and suggest that researchers attempt to confirm this hypothesis.)

REMEMBER The *Discussion section* answers the questions posed by the study, interpreting the results in terms of what is now known about the underlying behavior.

The Reference Page

The final section following the Discussion is the **Reference page**(s). This lists alphabetically the complete references for all sources cited in the article. *Each* *source should be one that you have read.* If, for example, you learn about Jones's article from reading Smith's report, you should read Jones, too (because Smith might be misleading). If you do not, then the reference to Jones should indicate that it is "as cited in" Smith.

As shown in Figure A.12, each reference is typed using the normal "hanging-indent" format. To reference a journal article, provide the last name and first initials of each author, listed in the same order as they appear in the article. Next, give the year of publication, the article's title, and the title of the journal, its volume number, and the page numbers of the article. Note: Journal and book titles and volume numbers are **NOT** underlined. They are in *italics*. The *Publication Manual* provides slightly different rules for referencing books, book chapters, magazines, material obtained from the Internet, and virtually any source you can imagine.

FIGURE A.12 Sample Portion of Reference Page

Notice the punctuation and italics.

```
                                        Effect of Humorous   10
                              References
         Bower, G. H., Karlin, M. B., & Dueck, A. (1975).
             Comprehension and memory for pictures. Memory and
             Cognition, 3, 216-220.
         Desrochers, A., & Begg, I. (1987). A theoretical account of
             encoding and retrieval processes in the use of imagery-
             based mnemonic techniques: The special case of the
             keyword method. In M. A. McDaniel & M. Pressley (Eds.),
             Imagery and related mnemonic processes: Theories,
             individual differences, and applications (pp. 56-57).
             New York: Springer-Verlag.
         Einstein, G. O., McDaniel, M. A., & Lackey, S. (1989).
             Bizarre imagery, interference, and distinctiveness.
             Journal of Experimental Psychology: Learning, Memory, and
             Cognition, 15. 137-146.
         Hunt, R. R., & Elliott, J. M. (1980). The role of
```

PUTTING IT ALL TOGETHER

Most research ideas come from the literature. Authors may suggest rival explanations for their results, or point out untested hypotheses. Also, no study is perfect, so you may find flaws that suggest a research hypothesis. Or, you may discover two published studies that contradict each other, so you can design a study to resolve the debate. You can also literally replicate a study, but it is more interesting and informative to also include a new condition or variable to the old design, so that you simultaneously expand our knowledge. For example, in replicating the droodle study, we might add a third, no-interpretation, control condition.

Developing a research idea will be easier if you recognize that any published article makes the study *sound like* it was a smooth-running, perfectly planned, well-organized process. In reality, it wasn't! An article will not mention the many people who volunteered for the study but never showed up. It will ignore the difficulty the researcher had in finding an artist who could draw droodles or the hours it took to invent their interpretations. And it will gloss over the several prior attempts, using different stimuli or procedures, that failed to produce interpretable results. Thus, although an article might give the impression that the researcher was omniscient and that the study ran like clockwork, don't be fooled. Research is much more challenging—and more fun—than that.

CHAPTER SUMMARY

1. A research report is organized based on the sequence in which the various aspects of the study occur.

2. Most psychological articles follow the rules in the *Publication Manual* of the *American Psychological Association*, so that they conform to "APA format."

3. A report should not present information that is redundant with a reader's knowledge or other reference sources. Rather, it should provide the necessary information for (a) understanding the study, (b) evaluating it, and (c) literally replicating it.

4. The *Title* should clearly communicate the variables and relationship being studied. The *Abstract* should summarize the report. Together, these elements allow readers to determine whether they want to read the article.

5. The *Introduction* presents all information that will be used to interpret the results. It reconstructs the logic and cites the literature the researcher used in working from the hypothetical constructs to the specific predicted relationship of the study.

6. The *Method* section provides the information needed to understand, critique, and literally replicate the data-collection procedures. It consists of three subsections: *Participants*, *Materials* or *Apparatus*, and *Procedure*.

7. The *Participants* section describes the subjects of a study in terms of their characteristics, their total number, and the reimbursement given.

8. The *Materials* or *Apparatus* section describes the characteristics of the stimuli, the response materials, and the equipment used to test participants. Information about the reliability and validity of the material and apparatus is also included here.

9. The *Procedure* section describes the situation(s) in which participants were tested. It should summarize the instructions given to participants and the task(s) performed by them, and complete the description of the design.

10. The *Results* section describes the statistical procedures performed and the outcomes obtained. In this order, it (a) describes the scores, (b) reports the descriptive statistics, (c) identifies each inferential procedure performed, and (d) reports the results of the procedure. Report primary analyses first, followed by secondary analyses.

11. In the *Discussion* section, the results are interpreted and the conclusions are drawn. The initial questions posed by the study are answered, and the findings are related to past findings, providing an integrated description of a behavior or construct. It is here that major potential flaws in the study are discussed.

12. In an APA-style manuscript, after the Discussion section comes the *References*, the *Tables*, the *Figure Caption page*, and the *Figures*.

KEY TERMS   (with page references)

abstract   412
apparatus section   417
discussion section   424
figures   423
figure caption   423
figure caption page   423
introduction   414
manuscript page header   412
materials section   417
method section   417
participants section   417

procedure section   419
Publication Manual of the American Psychological Association   406
reference page   427
research literature   403
results section   420
running head   402
table   423
title   411

REVIEW QUESTIONS

1. What are the three goals of a research report in terms of the information provided to the reader?

2. What is the source of the rules for creating a research report?

3. What are the six major sections in a report that occur prior to the references?

4. In a research report, (a) What does the author assume about the reader? (b) What does the reader assume about the author? (c) How does the author decide whether to include a piece of information?

5. (a) What are the two goals of the reader when reading the Introduction? (b) The information in the Method section should allow the reader to do what three things?

6. (a) When should you use abbreviations? (b) When do you use digits versus words for presenting numbers? (c) What is the rule regarding digits or abbreviations at the beginning of a sentence?

7. (a) What information should you include in the title of a research article? (b) What information should you include in the abstract of a research article?

8. From the reader's perspective, what is the purpose of reading your title and abstract?

9. (a) How do you create the page header that appears at the top of each page of a manuscript? (b) What is the running head, and how is it used?

10. (a) Summarize the information that is presented in the Introduction. (b) In general terms, what information about a study is not yet included here?

11. (a) What are the three standard components of the Method section? (b) What information is contained in each subsection? (c) In general terms, what information about a study is not yet reported in the Method section?

12. (a) How is the Results section organized? (b) In general terms, what information about a study is not yet reported here?

13. (a) When should you include a figure in a research report? (b) When should you include a table?

14. (a) How is the Discussion section related to the Introduction? (b) In addition to drawing a conclusion about your specific prediction, what other issues are addressed in the Discussion section?

APPLICATION QUESTIONS

15. For each of the following statements, indicate two reasons that its format is incorrect: (a) "40 students will hear the music and be tested." (b) "Because the critical value is 2.45 and the obtained value is 44.7, the results are very significant." (c) "The mean scores in the respective conditions for men were 1.4, 3.0, 2.7, 6.9, 11.8, 14.77, 22.31, 25.6, 33.7, and 41.2. For girls, the mean scores were . . ." (d) "To create the groups, the participants were split in half, with five individuals in each." (e) "The results were significant, indicating the null hypothesis should be rejected. Therefore, we conclude that the relationship demonstrates . . ." (f) Title: "Type of Interpretation as a Function of Remembering Funny Droodles."

16. (a) How do you organize the topics in the Introduction? (b) How do you organize the topics in the Procedure section? (c) How do you organize the topics in the Results section?

17. (a) What determines whether to have a Materials or an Apparatus section? (b) What determines whether to create additional sections in the *Method*?

18. Why would the interpretations given to the droodles in Figure A.1 not meet the APA *Publication Manual*'s present guidelines for acceptable language?

DISCUSSION QUESTIONS

19. In question 15, revise each statement so that it uses correct APA style.

20. Examine a published research article and discuss how it follows the diagram presented in Figure A.2.

21. (a) What practical application might the droodle study have, for example, in the preparation of lectures or textbooks? (b) Why might your confidence in such a generalization be limited? (c) How would you use the literature to increase your confidence?

22. A researcher obtains a correlation coefficient of $r = +.434$, which is not quite significant (the critical value is .44). Several participants, however, behaved contrary to the researcher's predictions. The study has potential life-saving applications, so to produce a significant r, the researcher eliminates the data from these "bad" participants and publishes the study. What is your reaction to this decision?

23. Perform an updated literature search about (a) distinctiveness versus meaningfulness and memory; (b) the original 1975 droodle study; (c) the influence of humor on memory.

SAMPLE APA-STYLE RESEARCH REPORT

Effect of Humorous   1

Running head: EFFECT OF HUMOROUS INTERPRETATIONS ON RECALL

Effect of Humorous Interpretations on

Immediate Recall of Nonsense Figures

Gary W. Heiman

Podunk University

Abstract

The effect of humor on the immediate recall of simple visual stimuli was investigated. Eighty college students (20 men and 20 women per condition) viewed 28 nonsensical line drawings that were each accompanied by either a humorous or nonhumorous verbal interpretation. Although the interpretations were comparable in the meaningfulness they conveyed, those participants presented with humorous interpretations correctly recalled significantly more drawings than those presented nonhumorous interpretations. The results suggest that a meaningful and humorous context provides additional retrieval cues beyond those cues provided by a meaningful yet nonhumorous context. The effect of the cues produced by humor is interpreted as creating a more distinctive and thus more accessible memory trace.

Effect of Humorous Interpretations

on Immediate Recall of Nonsense Figures

Researchers have consistently demonstrated that retention of to-be-learned material improves when the material is presented in a context that leads to meaningful processing (Lockhart & Craik, 1990). In particular, Bower, Karlin, and Dueck (1975) presented college students with a series of "droodles," which are each a meaningless line drawing that can be made meaningful by presentation of an accompanying verbal interpretation. Those individuals who were provided the interpretations correctly recalled (sketched) significantly more of the droodles immediately following their presentation than did those individuals given no interpretations. However, each interpretation in Bower et al. (1975) defined a droodle in a humorous fashion, using unexpected and incongruent actors and actions. Thus, differences in the meaningfulness attributed to the droodles may have been confounded by differences in the humor associated with the droodles. The purpose of the present study was to investigate the effect of humorous interpretations when the meaningfulness of the droodles is kept constant.

Few studies can be found that directly examine how the humor associated with a stimulus influences recall of the stimulus. However, it is reasonable to speculate that the relevant dimension of humor may be that it is simply one type of context that makes a stimulus meaningful. Desrochers and Begg (1987) defined the meaningfulness of a stimulus as the extent to

which the components of the stimulus are organized and
integrated. Therefore, meaningfulness provides retrieval cues
that enhance recall of the components of the stimulus, once the
stimulus has been accessed in memory. From this perspective,
either a humorous or a nonhumorous context should produce
equivalent recall of stimuli, as long as both contexts provide
an equivalent level of meaningful organization.

On the other hand, humor may play a different role than
that of only providing a meaningful context. Because it provides
an unusual and unexpected interpretation, humor may make a
stimulus more distinctive in memory. The distinctiveness of a
stimulus is defined as the number of novel attributes that it
can be assigned (Schmidt, 1985). Research has shown that greater
distinctiveness does improve retrieval (Hunt & Elliott, 1980).
Desrochers and Begg (1987) and Einstein, McDaniel, and Lackey
(1989) suggest that distinctiveness is created by unique cues
that are associated with the particular context in which the
stimulus was encountered. Therefore, distinctiveness enhances
access to the overall memory trace for a stimulus. From this
perspective, a humorous context should facilitate recall of a
stimulus to a greater extent than a nonhumorous context,
because, in addition to organizing the components of a stimulus
through its meaning, humor provides additional retrieval cues
that make the memory trace for the stimulus more distinctive and
thus more accessible.

In this study, I tested the above proposals by determining

whether droodles accompanied by humorous interpretations are better retained than when they are accompanied by nonhumorous interpretations. For each of the humorous interpretations of Bower et al. (1975), I produced a non-humorous version that would provide an equally meaningful interpretation of the droodle. If humor adds retrieval cues over and above those produced by meaningful processing, then droodles accompanied by humorous interpretations should be more frequently recalled than those accompanied by nonhumorous interpretations.

Method

Participants

Forty female and 40 male undergraduate students from an introductory psychology course at Podunk University each received $3.00 for their voluntary participation. All were between 20 and 22 years of age (mean age = 20.7 years), were born in the United States, were raised in English speaking families, and had normal or corrected eyesight and hearing. Participants were randomly assigned to either the humorous or nonhumorous condition, with 20 males and 20 females in each condition.

Materials

The 28 droodles from Bower et al. (1975) were reproduced, each consisting of a black-ink line drawing involving two interconnected geometric shapes. Droodles were copied to film slides for presentation by a standard Kodak carousel projector (model 28-b).

For each humorous interpretation in Bower et al. (1975), a
non-humorous version was created. Each interpretation consisted
of a 10 to 14 word sentence, beginning with the phrase "This
shows a. . . ." A humorous interpretation referred to an unusual
action by unexpected people or animals using incongruent
objects. A nonhumorous interpretation was derived by changing
the humorous interpretation so that it described common actions
by predictable actors using congruent objects. The meaning of
each droodle was altered as little as possible, with only the
humorous components being replaced with comparable, nonhumorous
components. For example, one droodle consisted of a rectangle
with a loop attached to the lower right side. The humorous
interpretation was "This shows a midget playing a trombone in a
telephone booth." The nonhumorous interpretation was "This shows
a telephone booth with a technician inside fixing the broken
door handle."

Response forms for recalling the droodles consisted of a
grid of 3 by 3 in. (7.62 cm by 7.62 cm) squares printed on
standard sheets of paper.

Procedure

Participants were tested individually and viewed all 28
droodles accompanied by either the humorous or nonhumorous
interpretations. Participants were instructed to study each
droodle during its presentation for later recall and were told
that the accompanying interpretation would be helpful in
remembering it. A timer in the slide projector presented each

Effect of Humorous   7

slide containing a droodle for 10 s, with approximately 2 s between slides. As each slide was presented, I recited the appropriate interpretation. The recall task began immediately after the final droodle was presented. Participants were instructed to recall the droodles in any order, sketching each droodle within one grid on the response sheet.

Results

Two assistants who were unaware of the purposes of the study scored the participants' sketches. A sketch was considered to indicate correct recall if both scorers agreed that it depicted a droodle. (On only 2% of the responses did the scorers disagree.) Each participant's score was then the total number of correctly recalled droodles.

The mean number of droodles correctly recalled was 20.50 in the humorous interpretation condition ($SD = 3.25$) and 15.20 in the nonhumorous interpretation condition ($SD = 4.19$). With an alpha level of .05, a one-tailed independent samples t-test indicated a significant difference between the conditions, $t(78) = 6.32$, $p < .05$. The relationship between amount of humor and recall scores can be seen in Figure 1. Although a positive relationship was obtained, the slope of this curve indicates that the rate of change in recall scores as a function of increased humor was not large.

Discussion

The results of the present study indicate that humorous interpretations lead to greater retention of droodles than do nonhumorous interpretations. Because the meaningfulness of the droodles provided by the interpretations was presumably constant in both conditions, it appears that humor provides an additional source of retrieval cues. This conclusion is consistent with the proposal that humor increases the distinctiveness of a stimulus, thereby facilitating recall by increasing the accessibility of the stimulus in memory.

The improvement in recall produced by humor, however, was relatively small. This result may be due to the fact that all droodles were made meaningful, although sometimes by a nonhumorous interpretation. As in other research (Lockhart & Craik, 1990), the meaningful processing produced by a nonhumorous interpretation may have provided relatively effective retrieval cues. Then the additional retrieval cues produced by the distinctiveness of a humorous interpretation would only moderately improve the retrievability of the droodles. In addition, these results may have occurred because a nonhumorous interpretation given to such a simple visual stimulus produced a reasonably distinctive trace. Additional unique cues provided by a humorous interpretation would then only moderately increase a droodle's distinctiveness, resulting in only a moderate improvement in recall.

It is possible, of course, that humor added to the meaningfulness of a droodle, instead of to its distinctiveness. Desrochers and Begg (1987) suggested that increased meaningfulness results in increased organization of a stimulus

Effect of Humorous   9

in memory. Humor may have added to the meaningfulness of a
droodle by providing additional ways to organize it, so that its
components were better retrieved. Further research is needed to
determine whether humor produces a more distinctive or a more
meaningful stimulus, especially when the stimulus is more
complex than a simple droodle.

Effect of Humorous   10

References

Bower, G. H., Karlin, M. B., & Dueck, A. (1975).
Comprehension and memory for pictures. *Memory and Cognition, 3,* 216-220.

Desrochers, A., & Begg, I. (1987). A theoretical account of encoding and retrieval processes in the use of imagery-based mnemonic techniques: The special case of the keyword method. In M. A. McDaniel & M. Pressley (Eds.), *Imagery and related mnemonic processes: Theories, individual differences, and applications* (pp. 56-77). New York: Springer-Verlag.

Einstein, G. O., McDaniel, M. A., & Lackey, S. (1989). Bizarre imagery, interference, and distinctiveness. *Journal of Experimental Psychology: Learning, Memory, and Cognition, 15,* 137-146.

Hunt, R. R., & Elliott, J. M. (1980). The role of nonsemantic information in memory: Orthographic distinctiveness effects on retention. *Journal of Experimental Psychology: General, 109,* 49-74.

Lockhart, R. S., & Craik, F. I. M. (1990). Levels of processing: A retrospective commentary on framework for memory research. *Canadian Journal of Psychology, 44,* 87-112.

Schmidt, S. R. (1985). Encoding and retrieval processes in the memory for conceptually distinctive events. *Journal of Experimental Psychology: Learning, Memory, and Cognition, 11,* 565-578.

Effect of Humorous   11

Figure Caption

Figure 1. Mean number of droodles correctly recalled as a

function of nonhumorous and humorous interpretations.

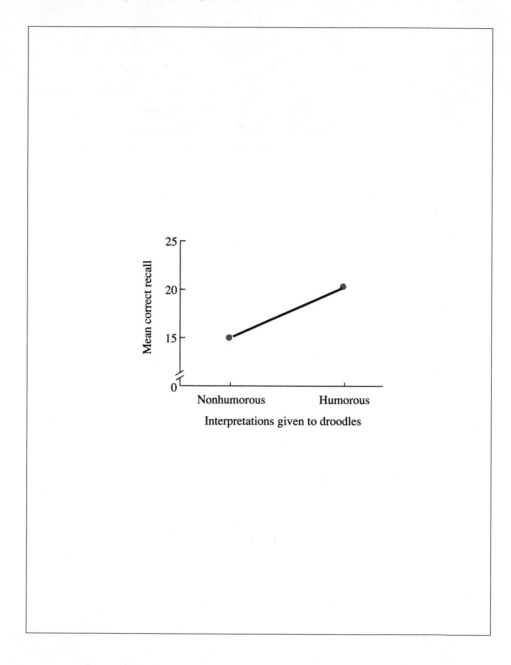

STATISTICAL PROCEDURES

C.1. MEASURES OF CENTRAL TENDENCY

These procedures are discussed in Chapter 7.

The Mean

The mean ($\overline{X}$) is found using the formula

$$\overline{X} = \frac{\Sigma X}{N}$$

where ΣX is the sum of the scores and N is the number of scores in the sample. For the scores 2, 1, 3, 7, 4, 5,

$$\overline{X} = \frac{\Sigma X}{N} = \frac{22}{6} = 3.667$$

The Median

The median is calculated by arranging all scores in the sample from lowest to highest. If N is an odd number, the median is the score that divides the distribution in two, with an equal number of scores below and above it. If N is an even number, the median is the average of the two middle scores. For the scores 7, 7, 9, 10, 12, 13, 13, 14, 18, the median score is 12.

The Mode

The mode is the most frequently occurring score or scores in the sample. For the scores 1, 2, 2, 2, 3, 3, 4, 4, 4, 4, 4, 5, 5, 6, the mode is 4. For the scores 1, 2, 2, 2, 2, 3, 3, 4, 4, 4, 4, 5, 5, 6, the modes are 2 and 4.

C.2. MEASURES OF VARIABILITY

Below are formulas for the sample and estimated population variance, the sample and estimated population standard deviation, and the range. Measures of variability are discussed in Chapter 7.

The Variance

There are two ways to calculate variance.

The Sample Variance   The sample variance (S_x^2) describes how far the sample scores are spread out around the sample mean. The formula is

$$S_x^2 = \frac{\Sigma X^2 - \frac{(\Sigma X)^2}{N}}{N}$$

where ΣX is the sum of the scores and $(\Sigma X)^2$ is the squared sum of the scores, ΣX^2 is the sum of squared scores, and N is the number of scores in the sample. For the scores 2, 3, 4, 5, 6, 7, 8,

$$S_x^2 = \frac{\Sigma X^2 - \frac{(\Sigma X)^2}{N}}{N} = \frac{203 - \frac{(35)^2}{7}}{7} = 4.0$$

The Estimated Population Variance   The estimated population variance (s_x^2) is computed using sample data, but it is an estimate of how far the scores in the population would be spread out around the population mean. The formula is

$$s_x^2 = \frac{\Sigma X^2 - \frac{(\Sigma X)^2}{N}}{N - 1}$$

where ΣX is the sum of the scores and $(\Sigma X)^2$ is the squared sum of the scores, ΣX^2 is the sum of the squared scores, and $N - 1$ is the number of scores in the sample minus 1. For the scores of 2, 3, 4, 5, 6, 7, 8,

$$s_x^2 = \frac{\Sigma X^2 - \frac{(\Sigma X)^2}{N}}{N-1} = \frac{203 - \frac{(35)^2}{7}}{6} = 4.67$$

The Standard Deviation

There are two ways to calculate the standard deviation.

The Sample Standard Deviation   The sample standard deviation (S_x) describes how far the sample scores are spread out around the sample mean. It is calculated as the square root of the sample variance. For the scores of 2, 3, 4, 5, 6, 7, 8,

$$S_x = \sqrt{\frac{\Sigma X^2 - \frac{(\Sigma X)^2}{N}}{N}} = \sqrt{\frac{203 - \frac{(35)^2}{7}}{7}} = 2.0$$

The Estimated Population Standard Deviation   The estimated population standard deviation (s_x) is computed using sample data, but it is an estimate of how far the scores in the population would be spread out around the population mean. It is calculated as the square root of the estimated population variance. For the scores of 2, 3, 4, 5, 6, 7, 8,

$$s_x = \sqrt{\frac{\Sigma X^2 - \frac{(\Sigma X)^2}{N}}{N-1}} = \sqrt{\frac{203 - \frac{(35)^2}{7}}{6}} = 2.16$$

The Range

The range is the distance between the two most extreme scores in a sample. The formula is:

range = highest score − lowest score

For the scores 2, 3, 4, 5, 6, 7, 8, the range equals 8 − 2, which is 6.

C.3. THE TWO-SAMPLE *t*-TEST

Below are the procedures for performing the independent samples (between-subjects) *t*-test and the dependent samples (within-subjects) *t*-test.

The Independent Samples *t*-test

This procedure is discussed in Chapter 7. Example data are shown in Table C.1.

Step 1   Determine the sum of scores (ΣX), the sum of squared scores (ΣX^2), the *n*, and the $\overline{X}$ in each condition.

Step 2   Calculate s_1^2, the estimated population variance based on the scores in the first condition, and s_2^2, the estimated population variance based on the scores of the second condition. Use the formula for the estimated population variance given in Section C.2.

Step 3   Calculate *t*:

$$t = \frac{(\overline{X}_1 - \overline{X}_2) - (\mu_1 - \mu_2)}{\sqrt{\left(\frac{(n_1-1)s_1^2+(n_2-1)s_2^2}{(n_1-1)+(n_2-1)}\right)\left(\frac{1}{n_1} + \frac{1}{n_2}\right)}}$$

where $\overline{X}_1$ and $\overline{X}_2$ are the means of the two conditions, $(\mu_1 - \mu_2)$ is the difference between the means predicted by the null hypothesis (usually this difference is zero), n_1 is the number of scores in the first condition, n_2 is the number of scores in the second condition, and s_1^2 and s_2^2 are from Step 2.

$$t = \frac{(11.5 - 14.1) - 0}{\sqrt{\left(\frac{(10-1)4.72+(10-1)5.88}{(10-1)+(10-1)}\right)\left(\frac{1}{10} + \frac{1}{10}\right)}}$$

$$t = \frac{-2.6}{\sqrt{(5.30)(.20)}} = \frac{-2.6}{1.030} = -2.524$$

Step 4   Find the critical value of *t* in Table D.1 of Appendix D. Degrees of freedom, *df*, equal $(n_1 - 1) + (n_2 - 1)$. For *df* = 18 and α = .05, the two-tailed critical value is ±2.101. If the computed value of *t* is *larger* than the critical value,

TABLE C.1   Data from a Two-Sample Between-Subjects Design

Condition 1	Condition 2
11	13
14	16
10	14
12	17
8	11
15	14
12	15
13	18
9	12
11	11
$\Sigma X = 115$	$\Sigma X = 141$
$\Sigma X^2 = 1365$	$\Sigma X^2 = 2041$
$\overline{X}_1 = 11.5$	$\overline{X}_2 = 14.1$
$n_1 = 10$	$n_1 = 10$
$s_1^2 = 4.72$	$s_2^2 = 5.88$

then the two means differ significantly. Here, the obtained t is beyond the critical value, so the results are significant. If t is *not* significant, do not perform Step 5.

Step 5   See Section C.6 for computing effect size and section C.7 for computing confidence intervals.

The Dependent Samples *t*-test

This procedure is discussed in Chapter 7. Example data are shown in Table C.2.

Step 1   Calculate the difference (D) between the two scores in each pair of scores formed by matching two participants or repeatedly measuring the same participant in both conditions.

Step 2   Calculate $\overline{D}$, the mean of the difference scores. Here, $\overline{D} = 18/5 = 3.6$.

Step 3   Calculate s_D^2, the estimated variance of the population of difference scores, found by entering the difference scores into the formula for s_x^2 in Section C.2. Here, $s_D^2 = 7.80$.

Step 4   Calculate t:

$$t_{\text{obt}} = \frac{\overline{D} - \mu_D}{\sqrt{(s_D^2)\frac{1}{N}}}$$

where μ_D is the average difference score between the conditions described by the null hypothesis (usually this is zero), N is the number of pairs of scores, and s_D^2 is from Step 3.

$$t = \frac{\overline{D} - \mu_D}{\sqrt{(s_D^2)\frac{1}{N}}} = \frac{+3.6 - 0}{\sqrt{(7.80)\left(\frac{1}{5}\right)}} = \frac{+3.6}{1.249} = 2.88$$

Step 5   Find the critical value of t in Table D.1 of Appendix D. Degrees of freedom, df, equal $N - 1$, where N is the number of difference scores. Above, for

TABLE C.2   Data from a Two-Sample Within-Subjects Design

Participants	Condition 1	−	Condition 2	=	Difference D		D^2
1	11	−	8	=	+3	=	9
2	16	−	11	=	+5	=	25
3	20	−	15	=	+5	=	25
4	17	−	11	=	+6	=	36
5	10	−	11	=	−1	=	1
	$\overline{X} = 14.80$		$\overline{X} = 11.20$		$\Sigma D = +18$		$\Sigma D^2 = 96$

$df = 4$ and $\alpha = .05$, the two-tailed critical value is ± 2.776. Again, if the obtained t is *larger* than the critical value, then the results are significant, and the mean scores in each condition (above, $\overline{X}_1 = 14.80$ and $\overline{X}_2 = 11.20$) differ significantly. If t is *not* significant, do not perform Step 6.

Step 6   See Section C.9 for computing effect size and Section C.7 for computing confidence intervals.

C.4. THE ONE-WAY ANALYSIS OF VARIANCE

Below are the procedures for performing a one-way between-subjects ANOVA and a one-way within-subjects ANOVA.

The One-Way Between-Subjects ANOVA

This procedure is discussed in Chapter 7. Example data for a one-way design having three levels (with five participants per level) are shown in Table C.3.

Step 1   Determine k, the number of levels in the factor; then determine the sum of scores (ΣX), the sum of squared scores (ΣX^2), the n, and the $\overline{X}$ in each level.

Step 2   Also, calculate the totals:

$$\Sigma X_{tot} = 40 + 30 + 15 = 85$$

$$\Sigma X_{tot}^2 = 354 + 220 + 55 = 629$$

$$N = 5 + 5 + 5 = 15$$

TABLE C.3   Data from a One-Way Between-Subjects Design

	Factor A		
Level A₁	*Level A₂*	*Level A₃*	
9	4	1	
12	6	3	
4	8	4	
8	2	5	
7	10	2	*Totals*
$\Sigma X = 40$	$\Sigma X = 30$	$\Sigma X = 15$	$\Sigma X_{tot} = 85$
$\Sigma X^2 = 354$	$\Sigma X^2 = 220$	$\Sigma X^2 = 55$	$\Sigma X_{tot}^2 = 629$
$n_1 = 5$	$n_2 = 5$	$n_3 = 5$	$N = 15$
$\overline{X}_1 = 8$	$\overline{X}_2 = 6$	$\overline{X}_3 = 3$	$k = 3$

Step 3   Compute the correction term (this is the name for a value used in subsequent calculations):

$$\text{Correction term} = \left(\frac{(\Sigma X_{tot})^2}{N} \right) = \frac{85^2}{15} = 481.67$$

Step 4   As you perform the following calculations, create the Analysis of Variance Summary Table shown in Table C.4.

Step 5   Compute the total sum of squares:

$$SS_{tot} = \Sigma X_{tot}^2 - \text{Step 3}$$
$$SS_{tot} = 629 - 481.67 = 147.33$$

Step 6   Compute the sum of squares between groups for factor A:

$$SS_A = \Sigma \left(\frac{(\text{sum of scores in each column})^2}{n \text{ of scores in the column}} \right) - \text{Step 3}$$

$$SS_A = \left(\frac{(40)^2}{5} + \frac{(30)^2}{5} + \frac{(15)^2}{5} \right) - 481.67 = 63.33$$

Step 7   Compute the sum of squares within groups:

$$SS_{wn} = SS_{tot} - SS_A = \text{Step 4} - \text{Step 5}$$
$$SS_{wn} = 147.33 - 63.33 = 84$$

Step 8   Compute the degrees of freedom:

a) For factor A: $df_A = k - 1$

$$df_A = 3 - 1 = 2$$

b) Within groups: $df_{wn} = N - k$

$$df_{wn} = 15 - 3 = 12$$

c) Total: $df_{tot} = N - 1$

$$df_{tot} = 15 - 1 = 14$$

Step 9   Compute the mean square for factor A:

$$MS_A = \frac{SS_A}{df_A} = \frac{\text{Step 6}}{\text{Step 8.a}}$$

$$MS_A = \frac{63.33}{2} = 31.67$$

TABLE C.4   Summary Table of One-Way Between-Subjects ANOVA

Source	Sum of Squares	df	Mean Square	F
Factor A	63.33	2	31.67	4.52
Within Groups	84.00	12	7.0	
Total	147.33	14		

Step 10   Compute the mean square within groups:

$$MS_{wn} = \frac{SS_{wn}}{df_{wn}} = \frac{\text{Step 7}}{\text{Step 8.b}}$$

$$MS_{wn} = \frac{84}{12} = 7.0$$

Step 11   Compute F:

$$F = \frac{MS_A}{MS_{wn}} = \frac{\text{Step 9}}{\text{Step 10}}$$

$$F = \frac{31.67}{7.0} = 4.52$$

Step 12   Find the critical value of F in Table D.2 of Appendix D, using df_A and df_{wn}. Above, for $df_A = 5\ 2$, $df_{wn} = 12$, and $\alpha = .05$, the critical value is 3.88. If the computed value of F is *larger* than the critical value, then somewhere among the means of the conditions at least two differ significantly. Here, the obtained F is beyond the critical value, so it is significant. When F is significant, perform Step 13.

Step 13   See Section C.5 for post hoc procedures, Section C.6 for computing effect size, and Section C.7 for computing confidence intervals.

The One-Way Within-Subjects ANOVA

This procedure is discussed in Chapter 7. Example data from a one-way repeated-measures design (with five participants) are shown in Table C.5.

Step 1   Determine k, the number of levels of the factor; then, determine the sum of scores (ΣX), the sum of squared scores (ΣX^2), the n, and the $\overline{X}$ in each level. Also, calculate the sum of the scores obtained by each subject, ΣX_{sub} (the sum of each row).

Step 2   Also, determine the totals:

$$\Sigma X_{tot} = 17 + 34 + 48 = 99$$
$$\Sigma X_{tot}^2 = 69 + 236 + 466 = 771$$
$$N = 5 + 5 + 5 = 15$$

Step 3   Compute the correction term:

$$\text{Correction term} = \frac{(\Sigma X_{tot})^2}{N} = \frac{99^2}{15} = 653.4$$

Step 4   As you perform the following calculations, create the Analysis of Variance Summary Table shown in Table C.6.

Step 5   Compute the total sum of squares:

$$SS_{tot} = \Sigma X_{tot}^2 - \text{Step 3}$$
$$SS_{tot} = 771 - 653.4 = 117.6$$

TABLE C.5   Data from a One-Way Repeated-Measures Design

Factor A

	Level A_1	*Level A_2*	*Level A_3*	ΣX_{sub}
Subject 1	2	7	9	18
Subject 2	6	8	11	25
Subject 3	3	5	8	16
Subject 4	2	7	10	19
Subject 5	4	7	10	21
				Totals
	$\Sigma X = 17$	$\Sigma X = 34$	$\Sigma X = 48$	$\Sigma X_{tot} = 99$
	$\Sigma X^2 = 69$	$\Sigma X^2 = 236$	$\Sigma X^2 = 466$	$\Sigma X_{tot}^2 = 771$
	$n_1 = 5$	$n_2 = 5$	$n_3 = 5$	$N = 15$
	$\bar{X}_1 = 3.4$	$\bar{X}_2 = 6.8$	$\bar{X}_3 = 9.6$	$k = 3$

Step 6 Compute the sum of squares for factor A:

$$SS_A = \sum \left(\frac{(\text{sum of scores in each column})^2}{n \text{ of scores in the column}} \right) - \text{Step 3}$$

$$SS_A = \left(\frac{(17)^2}{5} + \frac{(34)^2}{5} + \frac{(48)^2}{5} \right) - 653.4 = 96.4$$

Step 7 Compute the sum of squares for subjects:

$$SS_{subs} = \frac{(\Sigma X_{sub1})^2 + (\Sigma X_{sub2})^2 + \cdots (\Sigma X_{subn})^2}{k} - \text{Step 3}$$

$$SS_{subs} = \frac{(18)^2 + (25)^2 + (16)^2 + (19)^2 + (21)^2}{3} - 653.4$$

$$SS_{subs} = 15.6$$

Step 8 Compute the sum of squares for the interaction of A by subjects:

$$SS_{A \times subs} = SS_{tot} - SS_A - SS_{subs} = \text{Step 5} - \text{Step 6} - \text{Step 7}$$

$$SS_{A \times subs} = 117.6 - 96.4 - 15.6 = 5.6$$

Step 9 Compute the degrees of freedom:

(a) Factor A: $df_A = k - 1$

$$df_A = 3 - 1 = 2$$

(b) For A by subjects: $df_{A \times subs} = (k - 1)(\text{number of subjects} - 1)$

$$df_{A \times subs} = (3 - 1)(5 - 1) = 8$$

(c) Total: $df_{tot} = N - 1$

$$df_{tot} = 15 - 1 = 14$$

TABLE C.6 Summary Table of One-Way Within-Subjects ANOVA

Source	Sum of Squares	df	Mean Square	F
Factor A	96.40	2	48.20	68.86
Subjects	15.60			
A × Subjects	5.60	8	.70	
Total	117.60	14		

Step 10   Compute the mean square for factor A:

$$MS_A = \frac{SS_A}{df_A} = \frac{\text{Step 6}}{\text{Step 9.a}}$$

$$MS_A = \frac{96.4}{2} = 48.2$$

Step 11   Compute the mean square for A by subjects:

$$MS_{A \times subs} = \frac{SS_{A \times subs}}{df_{A \times subs}} = \frac{\text{Step 8}}{\text{Step 9.b}}$$

$$MS_{A \times subs} = \frac{5.6}{8} = .70$$

Step 12   Compute F:

$$F = \frac{MS_A}{MS_{A \times subs}} = \frac{\text{Step 10}}{\text{Step 11}}$$

$$F = \frac{48.2}{.70} = 68.86$$

Step 13   Find the critical value of F in Table D.2 of Appendix D, with df_A as the degrees of freedom between groups and $df_{A \times subs}$ as the degrees of freedom within groups. Above, for $\alpha = .05$, $df_A = 2$, and $df_{A \times subs} = 8$, the critical value is 4.46. The obtained F is larger than the critical value, so the obtained F is significant. When F is significant, perform Step 14.

Step 14   See Section C.5 for post hoc procedures, Section C.6 for computing effect size, and Section C.7 for computing confidence intervals.

C.5. TUKEY HSD POST HOC COMPARISONS

Below are two procedures for using the Tukey HSD Multiple Comparisons test, one for post hoc comparisons within significant main effects and the other for post hoc comparisons within significant interactions.

The Post Hoc Comparison for Main Effects

This procedure, discussed in Chapters 7 and 8, may be used with either a between-subjects or a within-subjects design in a one-way ANOVA, or to examine main-effect means in a multifactor ANOVA. It is appropriate *only* if the ns in all levels of the factor are equal.

Table C.7 presents the data in the one-way between-subjects ANOVA from Section C.4.

TABLE C.7   Data from a One-Way Between-Subjects Design

Factor A

Level A_1	Level A_2	Level A_3
9	4	1
12	6	3
4	8	4
8	2	5
7	10	2

$n_1 = 5$ $n_2 = 5$ $n_3 = 5$

$\overline{X}_1 = 8$ $\overline{X}_2 = 6$ $\overline{X}_3 = 3$ $k = 3$

Step 1   Find "q_k" in Table D.3 of Appendix D, using k (the number of levels in the factor) and the df used when calculating the denominator of the obtained F. Below, for $k = 3$, $df_{wn} = 12$; and $\alpha = .05$, $q_k = 3.77$.

Step 2   Compute HSD:

$$\text{HSD} = (q_k)\left(\sqrt{\frac{\text{denominator in } F \text{ ratio}}{n}}\right)$$

where "denominator in F ratio" is the MS used as the denominator when calculating the F, and n is the number of scores that each mean being compared is based upon. In the example data, $MS_{wn} = 7.0$ and $n = 5$.

$$\text{HSD} = (3.77)\left(\sqrt{\frac{7.0}{5}}\right) = 4.46$$

Step 3   Determine the differences between all means, by subtracting each mean from every other mean.

Step 4   Compare the absolute difference between any two means to the HSD value. If the difference is *greater* than the HSD, then these two means differ significantly. Above, the difference between $\overline{X}_1 = 8$ and $\overline{X}_3 = 3$ is 5, which is greater than 4.46, so these means differ significantly. However, $\overline{X}_2 = 6$ differs from these means by less than 4.46, so it does not differ significantly from the other means.

The Post Hoc Comparison for Interaction Effects

This procedure, discussed in Chapter 8, is used to compare the cell means of an interaction in either a between-subjects, a within-subjects, or a mixed design. It involves a correction developed by Cicchetti (1972) that reduces the probability of making Type II errors, based on adjusting k so that it reflects the actual number of unconfounded comparisons being performed.

Table C.8 presents some data from a two-way, between-subjects ANOVA showing the scores—and means—from a 3 × 2 interaction.

Step 1   Determine the "adjusted k" from Table C.9. In the left-hand column, locate the type of interaction being examined, regardless of the order of the numbers describing the factors (e.g., a 3 × 2 design is the same as a 2 × 3 design). In the right-hand column is the adjusted value of k. In the example, the design is a 2 × 3, so the adjusted $k = 5$.

Step 2   Find "q_k" in Table D.3 of Appendix D, using the adjusted value of k and the df used when calculating the denominator of the F. Above, for $k = 5$, $df_{wn} = 12$, and for $\alpha = .05$, $q_k = 4.51$.

Step 3   Compute HSD:

$$\text{HSD} = (q_k)\left(\sqrt{\frac{\text{denominator in } F \text{ ratio}}{n}}\right)$$

where "denominator in F ratio" is the MS used as the denominator when calculating the F. The n is the number of scores that each mean being compared is based upon. In a between-subjects ANOVA, the F for the interaction is called $F_{A \times B}$, and the denominator is MS_{wn}. The data in Table C.8 would produce a significant interaction, with an $MS_{wn} = 8.22$. Each cell contains three scores, so $n = 3$.

$$\text{HSD} = (4.51)\left(\sqrt{\frac{8.22}{3}}\right) = 7.47$$

TABLE C.8   Data from a Two-Way Between-Subjects Design

		Factor A	
	A_1	A_2	A_3
B_1	4 9 11	8 12 13	18 17 15
	$\overline{X} = 8$ $n = 3$	$\overline{X} = 11$ $n = 3$	$\overline{X} = 16.7$ $n = 3$
B_2	2 6 4	9 10 17	6 8 4
	$\overline{X} = 4$ $n = 3$	$\overline{X} = 12$ $n = 3$	$\overline{X} = 6$ $n = 3$

Factor B

TABLE C.9   Values of Adjusted k

Design of Study	Adjusted Value of k
2 × 2	3
2 × 3	5
2 × 4	6
3 × 3	7
3 × 4	8
4 × 4	10
4 × 5	12

Step 4   Determine the differences between all *unconfounded* means. In other words, compare only pairs of means that differ along only *one* variable. Thus, *within each row* of the diagram of the study (as in Table C.8), subtract each mean from every other mean. Then, *within each column*, subtract each mean from every other mean. However, do not compare any means that are located diagonally from each other in the diagram (because they come from cells that are confounded).

Step 5   Compare the absolute differences between any two means to the HSD value. If the difference is *greater* than the HSD, then these two means differ significantly. Thus, in the upper row of Table C.8, only the means of 8 and 16.7 differ by more than 7.47, so this difference is significant. In the lower row, the only significant difference is between the means of 4 versus 12. In the columns, the only significant difference is between the means of 16.7 versus 6.

C.6. MEASURES OF EFFECT SIZE IN *t*-TESTS AND ANOVA

These procedures are discussed in Chapter 8. Compute effect size in *t*-tests by computing r_{pb}^2, and compute effect size in ANOVA by computing η^2.

Effect Size in *t*-tests

This procedure can be used to compute r_{pb}^2 in an independent samples (between-subjects) *t*-test and in a dependent samples (within-subjects) *t*-test. Calculate r_{pb}^2 using the formula:

$$r_{pb}^2 = \frac{(t)^2}{(t)^2 + df}$$

where $(t)^2$ is the squared value of the obtained *t*, and *df* are the degrees of freedom, calculated in the *t*-test.

For example, in the independent samples *t*-test in Section C.3, $t = -2.524$ and $df = 18$. Thus:

$$r_{pb}^2 = \frac{(t)^2}{(t)^2 + df} = \frac{2.524^2}{2.524^2 + 8} = .44$$

(*Note*: The square root of r_{pb}^2 equals r_{pb}, which is the correlation coefficient between the independent and dependent variables.)

Effect Size in ANOVA

Eta squared (η^2) may be calculated for each between-subjects or within-subjects main effect or interaction in an ANOVA, using the formula

$$\eta^2 = \frac{\text{sum of squares for the effect}}{SS_{tot}}$$

where "sum of squares for the effect" is the sum of squares used in calculating the numerator of the *F*. The SS_{tot} is the total sum of squares in the ANOVA. For example, the one-way between-subjects ANOVA from Section C.4 produced Table C.10.

The effect size for factor A is:

$$\eta^2 = \frac{SS_A}{SS_{tot}} = \frac{63.33}{147.33} = .43$$

(The square root of η^2 equals η, the correlation coefficient between the independent and dependent variables.)

C.7. CONFIDENCE INTERVALS

This procedure is discussed in Chapter 7. Below are the formulas for computing a confidence interval from the results of a *t*-test and from an ANOVA.

Confidence Intervals in *t*-tests

The formula for a confidence interval for a population mean (μ) represented by a sample mean is

$$\left(\frac{s_x}{\sqrt{n}}\right)(-t_{crit}) + \overline{X} \leq \mu \leq \left(\frac{s_x}{\sqrt{n}}\right)(+t_{crit}) + \overline{X}$$

Step 1   Compute s_x from the scores in the group, using the formula for the estimated population standard deviation in Section C.2.

Step 2   Determine *n*, the number of scores in the group.

TABLE C.10 Summary Table of One-Way Between-Subjects ANOVA

Source	Sum of Squares	df	Mean Square	F
Factor A	63.33	2	31.67	4.52
Within Groups	84.00	12	7.0	
Total	147.33	14		

Step 3 Find t_{crit}, the two-tailed value in Table D.1 of Appendix D, for $df = n - 1$, where n is the number of scores in the group. Using $\alpha = .05$ creates a 95% confidence interval, and using $\alpha = .01$ creates a 99% confidence interval.

Step 4 Compute $\overline{X}$, the mean of the scores in the group.

As an example, say that a condition in a between-subjects t-test produces the following data: $n = 9$, $s_x = 2.25$, and $\overline{X} = 11.5$. The two-tailed t_{crit} for $df = 8$ and $\alpha = .05$ is ± 2.306. Thus:

$$\left(\frac{s_x}{\sqrt{n}}\right)(-t_{crit}) + \overline{X} \leq \mu \leq \left(\frac{s_x}{\sqrt{n}}\right)(+t_{crit}) + \overline{X}$$

$$\left(\frac{2.25}{\sqrt{9}}\right)(-2.306) + 11.5 \leq \mu \leq \left(\frac{2.25}{\sqrt{9}}\right)(+2.306) + 11.5$$

$$-1.73 + 11.5 \leq \mu \leq +1.73 + 11.5$$

$$9.77 \leq \mu \leq 13.23$$

The 95% confidence interval for the population mean represented by this sample mean is 9.77 to 13.23.

Confidence Intervals in ANOVA

To compute the confidence interval for the population mean, μ, represented by the mean of any level or cell in an ANOVA, use this formula:

$$\left(\sqrt{\frac{MS_{wn}}{n}}\right)(-t_{crit}) + \overline{X} \leq \mu \leq \left(\sqrt{\frac{MS_{wn}}{n}}\right)(+t_{crit}) + \overline{X}$$

Step 1 Determine MS_{wn}, the denominator used in computing F.

Step 2 Determine n, the number of scores that the mean is based on.

Step 3 Find t_{crit}, the two-tailed value in Table D.1 of Appendix D, for the df used in computing the denominator of the obtained F. Using $\alpha = .05$ creates a 95% confidence interval, and using $\alpha = .01$ creates a 99% confidence interval.

Step 4 Compute $\overline{X}$, the mean of the level or cell being described.

For example, say that a condition in a between-subjects ANOVA produced a $\overline{X} = 8.0$ with $n = 5$, and in computing the main effect F involving that condition, $MS_{wn} = 7.0$, and $df_{wn} = 12$. The two-tailed t_{crit} for $df = 12$ and $\alpha = .05$ is ± 2.179. Thus:

$$\left(\sqrt{\frac{7.0}{5}}\right)(-2.179) + 8.0 \leq \mu \leq \left(\sqrt{\frac{7.0}{5}}\right)(+2.179) + 8.0$$

$$-2.578 + 8.0 \leq \mu \leq +2.578 + 8.0$$

$$5.42 \leq \mu \leq 10.58$$

The 95% confidence interval for the population mean represented by this sample mean is 5.42 to 10.58.

C.8. PEARSON CORRELATION COEFFICIENT, LINEAR REGRESSION, AND STANDARD ERROR OF THE ESTIMATE

Below are procedures for computing the Pearson r, the linear regression equation, and the standard error of the estimate. These procedures are discussed in Chapter 9.

The Pearson Correlation Coefficient

Example data are shown in Table C.11.

Step 1   Calculate ΣX, the sum of the X scores, and $(\Sigma X)^2$, the squared sum of the X scores.

TABLE C.11   Data for Pearson Correlation Coefficient

Participant	X Score	Y Score	XY
1	1	2	2
2	1	4	4
3	2	4	8
4	2	6	12
5	2	2	4
6	3	4	12
7	3	7	21
8	3	8	24
9	4	6	24
10	4	8	32
11	4	7	28
$N = 11$	$\Sigma X = 29$	$\Sigma Y = 58$	$\Sigma XY = 171$
	$\Sigma X^2 = 89$	$\Sigma Y^2 = 354$	
	$(\Sigma X)^2 = 841$	$(\Sigma Y)^2 = 3364$	

Step 2   Calculate ΣY, the sum of the Y scores, and $(\Sigma Y)^2$, the squared sum of the Y scores.

Step 3   Calculate ΣX^2, the sum of the squared X scores, and ΣY^2, the sum of the squared Y scores.

Step 4   Calculate ΣXY, the sum after multiplying each X score in a pair times its corresponding Y score.

Step 5   Determine N, the number of pairs of scores in the sample.

Step 6   Calculate r:

$$r = \frac{N(\Sigma XY) - (\Sigma X)(\Sigma Y)}{\sqrt{[N(\Sigma X^2) - (\Sigma X)^2][N(\Sigma Y^2) - (\Sigma Y)^2]}}$$

$$r = \frac{11(171) - (29)(58)}{\sqrt{[11(89) - 841][11(354) - 3364]}}$$

$$r = \frac{199}{\sqrt{[138][530]}} = +.736$$

Step 7   Find the critical value of r in Table D.4 of Appendix D, using degrees of freedom (df) equal to $N - 2$, where N is the number of pairs of scores. Above, for $df = 9$ and $\alpha = .05$, the two-tailed critical value is $\pm.602$, so the obtained r is significant.

The Linear Regression Equation

Step 1   Compute b, the slope of the regression line:

$$b = \frac{N(\Sigma XY) - (\Sigma X)(\Sigma Y)}{N(\Sigma X)^2 - (\Sigma X)^2}$$

In the example in Table C.11, $\Sigma X = 29$, $\Sigma Y = 58$, $\Sigma XY = 171$, $\Sigma X^2 = 89$, $(\Sigma X)^2 = 841$, and $N = 11$:

$$b = \frac{11(171) - (29)(58)}{11(89) - 841} = +1.44$$

Step 2   Compute a, the Y intercept:

$$a = \overline{Y} - (b)(\overline{X})$$

Using the preceding data, $\overline{Y} = \frac{58}{11} = 5.27$, $b = 1.44$, and $\overline{X} = \frac{29}{11} = 2.64$:

$$a = \overline{Y} - (b)(\overline{X}) = 5.27 - (+1.44)(2.64) = +1.47$$

Step 3   Complete the linear regression equation:

$$Y' = b(X) + a$$

From above, $b = +1.44$ and $a = +1.47$, so:

$$Y' = +1.44(X) + 1.47$$

Step 4   To compute a participant's predicted score (Y') multiply the participant's X score times the slope and add the Y intercept. For example, using the preceding regression equation, the predicted score for someone scoring an $X = 2$ is

$$Y' = +1.44(2) + 1.47 = 4.35$$

The Standard Error of the Estimate

The standard error of the estimate $(S_{y'})$ is calculated as:

$$S_{y'} = (S_y)\left(\sqrt{1 - r^2}\right)$$

Step 1   Use the formula for the sample standard deviation in Section C.2 to find S_y, the sample standard deviation of the Y scores.

Step 2   Compute r^2, the squared value of the Pearson correlation coefficient.
For the preceding linear regression example, $N = 11$, $\Sigma Y = 58$, and $\Sigma Y^2 = 354$, so $S_y = 2.093$ and $r = +.736$:

$$S_{y'} = (S_y)\left(\sqrt{1 - r^2}\right) = (2.093)\left(\sqrt{1 - .736^2}\right) = 1.42$$

C.9. SPEARMAN CORRELATION COEFFICIENT

Below is the procedure for computing the Spearman correlation coefficient, as discussed in Chapter 9.

This procedure is used when participants are rank-ordered on each variable and no two participants receive the same rank within a variable. (Special procedures are needed with "tied ranks"—for example, if two subjects are ranked first on variable X. Consult a statistics text.)

Example data are shown in Table C.12.

Step 1   Compute each D, the difference between a participant's X and Y scores.

Step 2   Compute ΣD^2, the sum of the squared Ds.

Step 3   Determine N, the number of pairs of scores in the sample.

TABLE C.12 Data for Spearman Correlation Coefficient

Participant	Rank on X Variable		Rank on Y Variable		D	D^2
1	4	−	3	=	1	1
2	1	−	1	=	0	0
3	9	−	8	=	1	1
4	8	−	6	=	2	4
5	3	−	5	=	−2	4
6	5	−	4	=	1	1
7	6	−	7	=	−1	1
8	2	−	2	=	0	0
9	7	−	9	=	−2	4

$$N = 9 \qquad\qquad\qquad \Sigma D^2 = 16$$

Step 4   Compute r_s.

$$r_s = 1 - \frac{6(\Sigma D^2)}{N(N^2 - 1)}$$

$$r_s = 1 - \frac{6(16)}{9(81 - 1)} = 1 - .133 = +.867$$

Step 5   Find the critical value of r_s in Table D.5 of Appendix D, with degrees of freedom (df) equal to N, the number of pairs of scores. Above, for $df = 9$ and $\alpha = .05$, the two-tailed critical value is $\pm.683$, so the obtained r_s is significant.

C.10. CHI SQUARE PROCEDURES

Below are the one-way chi square, the two-way chi square, and the procedures for computing effect size (the phi coefficient and C coefficient).

The One-Way Chi Square

This procedure is discussed in Chapter 7. Example data from a one-way design with two categories are shown in Table C.13.

Step 1   Determine the observed frequency (f_o) in each category (i.e., count the number of subjects falling into each category).

Step 2   Determine the expected frequency (f_e) in each category. This is equal to the probability that a subject will fall into that category if the null hypothesis

is true, multiplied by the total N in the study. When we are testing for no difference, the expected frequency in each group equals $f_e = \frac{N}{k}$, where k is the number
of categories. Thus, above, for each category, $f_e = \frac{60}{2} = 30$.

Step 3   Compute χ^2:

$$\chi^2 = \Sigma\left(\frac{(f_o - f_e)^2}{f_e}\right)$$

$$\chi^2 = \frac{(20 - 30)^2}{30} + \frac{(40 - 30)^2}{30} = 3.33 + 3.33 = 6.66$$

Step 4   Find the critical value of χ^2 in Table D.6 of Appendix D, for $df = k -$
1, where k is the number of categories. For $\alpha = .05$ and $df = 1$, the critical value
is 3.84, so the obtained χ^2 above is significant.

The Two-way Chi Square

This procedure is discussed in Chapter 8. Example data from a two-way design
with two categories per variable are shown in Table C.14.

Step 1   Determine the observed frequency, (f_o), in each category (i.e., count
the number of participants falling in each category).

Step 2   Compute the total of the observed frequencies in each row and in each
column. Also, determine N, the total number of participants.

Step 3   Compute the expected frequency (f_e) for each cell:

$$\text{cell } f_e = \frac{(\text{cell's row total})(\text{cell's column total})}{N}$$

Thus, for the upper left-hand cell in Table C.14, $f_e = \frac{(35)(30)}{80} = 13.125$.

Step 4   Compute χ^2:

$$\chi^2 = \Sigma\left(\frac{(f_o - f_e)^2}{f_e}\right)$$

TABLE C.13   Data from a One-Way Chi Square Design

Variable A

Category 1	Category 2	
$f_o = 20$ $f_e = 30$	$f_o = 40$ $f_e = 30$	$k = 2$ $N = 60$

$$\chi^2 = \left(\frac{(25 - 13.125)^2}{13.125}\right) + \left(\frac{(10 - 21.875)^2}{21.875}\right) +$$

$$\left(\frac{(5 - 16.875)^2}{16.875}\right) + \left(\frac{(40 - 28.125)^2}{28.125}\right)$$

$$\chi^2 = 10.74 + 6.45 + 8.36 + 5.01 = 30.56$$

Step 5 Find the critical value of χ^2 in Table D.6 of Appendix D, for $df =$ (number of rows $- 1$)(number of columns $- 1$). For $\alpha = .05$ and $df = (2 - 1)(2 - 1) = 1$, the critical value $= 3.84$. If the obtained χ^2 is significant (as above), go to Step 6.

Step 6 Compute the effect size.

In a 2 × 2 chi square, compute the phi coefficient squared, ϕ^2:

$$\phi^2 = \frac{\chi^2}{N}$$

where χ^2 is the obtained value of chi square, and N is the total number of participants in the study. Above, $\chi^2 = 30.56$ and $N = 80$, so $\phi^2 = \frac{30.56}{80} = .38$. (The square root of ϕ^2 equals ϕ, the correlation coefficient between the two variables.)

In a two-way chi square that is not a 2 × 2 design, compute C^2, the contingency coefficient squared:

$$C^2 = \frac{\chi^2}{\chi^2 + N}$$

where χ^2 is the obtained value of chi square, and N is the total number of subjects in the study. (The square root of C^2 equals C, the correlation coefficient between the two variables.)

TABLE C.14 Data from a Two-Way Chi Square Design

Variable A

		Category 1	Category 2	
Variable B	Category 1	$f_o = 25$ $f_e = 13.125$ (35)(30)/80	$f_o = 10$ $f_e = 21.875$ (35)(30)/80	Row total = 35
	Category 2	$f_o = 5$ $f_e = 16.875$ (45)(30)/80	$f_o = 40$ $f_e = 28.125$ (45)(50)/80	Row total = 45
		Column total = 30	Column total = 50	N = 80

C.11. MANN–WHITNEY *U* AND WILCOXON *T* TESTS

Below are the procedures for performing the nonparametric versions of *t*-tests.

The Mann–Whitney *U* Test for Independent Samples

The Mann–Whitney test, discussed in Chapter 7, is analogous to the independent samples *t*-test for ranked data. It is appropriate when the *n* in each condition is *less* than 20. Table C.15 shows such data.

Step 1   Compute the sum of the ranks (ΣR) and the *n* for each group.

Step 2   Compute U_1 for group 1, using the formula

$$U_1 = (n_1)(n_2) + \frac{n_1(n_1 + 1)}{2} - \Sigma R_1$$

where n_1 is the *n* of group 1, n_2 is the *n* of group 2, and ΣR_1 is the sum of ranks from group 1. From above,

$$U_1 = (5)(5) + \frac{5(5 + 1)}{2} - 17 = 40 - 17 = 23.0$$

Step 3   Compute U_2 for group 2, using the formula

$$U_2 = (n_1)(n_2) + \frac{n_2(n_2 + 1)}{2} - \Sigma R_2$$

where n_1 is the *n* of group 1, n_2 is the *n* of group 2, and ΣR_2 is the sum of ranks from group 2. From above:

$$U_2 = (5)(5) + \frac{5(5 + 1)}{2} - 38 = 40 - 38 = 2.0$$

TABLE C.15   Ranked Data from a Two-Sample Between-Subjects Design

	Condition 1	Condition 2
Rank-order scores	2	7
	1	8
	5	10
	3	4
	6	9
	$\Sigma R = 17$	$\Sigma R = 38$
	$n = 5$	$n = 5$

Step 4 Determine the obtained value of *U*. In a two-tailed test, the *smaller* value of U_1 or U_2 is the obtained value of *U*. Above, the obtained *U* is $U_2 = 2.0$. In a one-tailed test, one group will be predicted to have the higher ranks and thus the larger sum of ranks. The corresponding value of *U* from that group is the obtained value of *U*.

Step 5 Find the critical value of *U* in Table D.7 of Appendix D, using n_1 and n_2. Above, for a two-tailed test with $n_1 = 5$ and $n_2 = 5$, the critical value is 2.0. The obtained value of *U* is significant (and the two groups differ significantly) if *U* is *equal to or less than* the critical value, so the above obtained value is significant. (No procedure is available for directly calculating effect size.)

The Wilcoxon *T* Test for Dependent Samples

The Wilcoxon test, discussed in Chapter 8, is analogous to the dependent samples *t*-test for ranked data. It is used to transform interval or ratio scores to ranked scores. Table C.16 shows such data.

Step 1 Determine the difference score (*D*) in each pair of the raw interval or ratio scores. It makes no difference which score is subtracted from which, but subtract the scores the same way in all pairs.

Step 2 Determine *N*, the number of *nonzero* difference scores. Above, disregard subject 10 because there is zero difference, so $N = 9$.

Step 3 Assign ranks to the nonzero difference scores. Ignoring the sign of each difference, assign the rank of "1" to the smallest difference, the rank of "2" to the second smallest difference, and so on.

TABLE C.16 Data from a Two-Sample Within-Subjects Design

Participant	Condition 1		Condition 2		Difference (D)	Ranked Scores	R−	R+
1	54	−	76	=	−22	6	6	
2	58	−	71	=	−13	4	4	
3	60	−	110	=	−50	9	9	
4	68	−	88	=	−20	5	5	
5	43	−	50	=	−7	3	3	
6	74	−	99	=	−25	7	7	
7	60	−	105	=	−45	8	8	
8	69	−	64	=	+5	2		2
9	60	−	59	=	+1	1		1
10	52	−	52	=	0	...		...

$$N = 9 \quad \Sigma R = 42 \quad \Sigma R = 3$$

Step 4   Separate the ranks so that the $R-$ column contains the ranks assigned to negative differences in Step 3. The $R+$ column contains the ranks assigned to positive differences.

Step 5   Compute the sum of ranks (ΣR) for the column labeled $R+$, and compute ΣR for the column labeled $R-$.

Step 6   Determine the obtained value of T. In a two-tailed test, T equals the *smaller* ΣR found in Step 5. Here, the smaller $\Sigma R = 3$, so the obtained $T = 3$. In a one-tailed test, whether most differences are positive or negative will be predicted, and the ΣR that is predicted to be smaller is the obtained value of T.

Step 7   Find the critical value of T in Table D.8 of Appendix D, using N, the number of nonzero difference scores. Above, for $N = 9$ and $\alpha = .05$, the critical value is 5.0. The obtained T is significant (and the two groups differ significantly) when T is *equal to or less than* the critical value, so the above T is significant. (No procedure for computing effect size is available.)

C.12. KRUSKAL–WALLIS H AND FRIEDMAN χ^2 TESTS

Below are the procedures for performing the nonparametric versions of the one-way ANOVA and the corresponding post hoc tests.

The Kruskal–Wallis H Test

The Kruskal–Wallis H test, discussed in Chapter 7, is analogous to a between-subjects one-way ANOVA for ranks. It requires three or more levels of the factor, with at least five participants per level. Table C.17 shows such data.

TABLE C.17   Ranked Data from a One-Way Between-Subjects Design

Factor A

Level 1	Level 2	Level 3
2	3	14
6	5	15
4	7	10
8	9	12
1	11	13

$\Sigma R_1 = 21$	$\Sigma R_2 = 35$	$\Sigma R_3 = 64$	$k = 3$
$n_1 = 5$	$n_2 = 5$	$n_3 = 5$	$N = 15$

Step 1   Compute the sum of the ranks (ΣR) in each condition (i.e., each column). Also, note the n in each condition, as well as k, the number of levels.

Step 2   Compute the sum of squares between groups:

$$SS_{bn} = \Sigma\left(\frac{(\Sigma R)^2}{n}\right)$$

where $(\Sigma R)^2$ is the squared sum of ranks for each level, and n is the n of the level:

$$SS_{bn} = \left(\frac{(21)^2}{5} + \frac{(35)^2}{5} + \frac{(64)^2}{5}\right) = 88.2 + 245 + 819.2 + 1152.4$$

Step 3   Compute H:

$$H = \left(\frac{12}{N(N+1)}\right)(SS_{bn}) - 3(N+1)$$

where N is the total N of the study, and SS_{bn} is from Step 2:

$$H = \left(\frac{12}{15(15+1)}\right)(1152.4) - 3(15+1) = (.05)(1152.4) - 48 = 9.62$$

Step 4   The critical values of H are χ^2 values; find these in Table D.6 of Appendix D, using $df = k - 1$, where k is the number of levels in the factor. Above, for $df = 2$ and $\alpha = .05$, the critical value is 5.99. If the obtained value of H is *larger* than the critical value of χ^2, then the H is significant (and there is at least one significant difference between the groups). When H is significant, go to Step 5.

Step 5   Perform post hoc comparisons by comparing each pair of conditions using the Mann–Whitney procedure in Section C.11. Treat each pair of conditions as if they constituted the entire study and re-rank the scores. Then, compute the obtained U and determine whether it is significant.

Step 6   Compute η^2, the effect size:

$$\eta^2 = \frac{H}{N-1}$$

where H is the value computed in the Kruskal–Wallis test (Step 3), and N is the total number of subjects.

The Friedman χ^2 Test

The Friedman χ^2 test, discussed in Chapter 7, is analogous to a repeated-measures one-way ANOVA for ranks. It requires three or more levels of the factor. If there are only three levels of the factor, there must be at least 10 subjects in the study. If there are only four levels of the factor, there must be at least five subjects. Table C.18 shows such data.

TABLE C.18 Ranked Scores from a One-Way Repeated-Measures Design

Factor A

	Condition 1	Condition 2	Condition 3	
Subject 1	1	2	3	
Subject 2	1	3	2	
Subject 3	1	2	3	
Subject 4	1	3	2	
Subject 5	2	1	3	
Subject 6	1	3	2	
Subject·7	1	2	3	
Subject 8	1	3	2	
Subject 9	1	3	2	
Subject 10	2	1	3	
	$\Sigma R_1 = 12$	$\Sigma R_2 = 23$	$\Sigma R_3 = 25$	$N = 10$
	$\overline{X} = 1.2$	$\overline{X} = 2.3$	$\overline{X} = 2.5$	

Step 1   If not already ranked, then rank-order the scores *within* each participant. That is, assign "1" to the lowest score received by subject 1, "2" to the second lowest score received by subject 1, and so on. Repeat the process for each subject.

Step 2   Compute the sum of the ranks (ΣR) in each condition (i.e., each column).

Step 3   Compute the mean rank in each condition, by dividing the sum of ranks (ΣR) by the number of subjects.

Step 4   Compute the sum of squares between groups:

$$SS_{bn} = (\Sigma R_1)^2 + (\Sigma R_2)^2 + \cdots (\Sigma R_k)^2$$

$$SS_{bn} = (12)^2 + (23)^2 + (25)^2 = 1298$$

Step 5   Compute the Friedman χ^2:

$$\chi^2 = \left(\frac{12}{(k)(N)(k + 1)}\right)(SS_{bn}) - 3(N)(k + 1)$$

where N is the total number of subjects, k is the number of levels of the factor, and SS_{bn} is from Step 4:

$$\chi^2 = \left(\frac{12}{(3)(10)(3 + 1)}\right)(1298) - 3(10)(3 + 1) = (.10)(1298) - 120 = 9.80.$$

Step 6   Find the critical value of χ^2 in Table D.6 of Appendix D, for $df = k - 1$, where k is the number of levels in the factor. Above, for $df = 2$ and $\alpha = .05$, the critical value is 5.99. The obtained χ^2 is larger than the critical value, so the results are significant (and there is at least one significant difference between the levels). When χ^2 is significant, perform Steps 7 and 8.

Step 7   Perform post hoc comparisons using Nemenyi's procedure.[1]

(a) Compute the critical difference:

$$\text{Critical difference} = \sqrt{\left(\frac{k(k+1)}{6(N)}\right)(\text{critical value of } \chi^2)}$$

where k is the number of levels of the factor, N is the total number of subjects, and the critical value of χ^2 is the critical value used to test the Friedman χ^2 (Step 6).

$$\text{Critical difference} = \sqrt{\left(\frac{3(3+1)}{6(10)}\right)(5.99)} = \sqrt{(.2)(5.99)} = \sqrt{1.198} = 1.09$$

(b) Subtract each mean rank from the other mean ranks. Any absolute difference between two means that is greater than the critical difference is a significant difference. In Table C.18 the differences between the mean rank of 1.2 in condition 1 and the other mean ranks are 1.10 and 1.30, respectively, so they are significant differences. The difference between the means of conditions 2 and 3 is .20, which is not a significant difference.

Step 8   Compute η^2, the effect size:

$$\eta^2 = \frac{\chi^2}{(N)(k) - 1}$$

where χ^2 was computed in the Friedman χ^2 test (Step 6), N is the number of subjects, and k is the number of levels of the factor. Thus:

$$\eta^2 = \frac{\chi^2}{(N)(k) - 1} = \frac{9.80}{(10)(3) - 1} = \frac{9.80}{30 - 1} = .34$$

---

[1]As reported in Linton & Gallo, 1975.

STATISTICAL PROCEDURES

STATISTICAL TABLES

TABLE D.1   Critical Values of t

	Two-tailed test			One-tailed test	
	Level of significance			Level of significance	
df	$\alpha = .05$	$\alpha = .01$	df	$\alpha = .05$	$\alpha = .01$
1	12.706	63.657	1	6.314	31.821
2	4.303	9.925	2	2.920	6.965
3	3.182	5.841	3	2.353	4.541
4	2.776	4.604	4	2.132	3.747
5	2.571	4.032	5	2.015	3.365
6	2.447	3.707	6	1.943	3.143
7	2.365	3.499	7	1.895	2.998
8	2.306	3.355	8	1.860	2.896
9	2.262	3.250	9	1.833	2.821
10	2.228	3.169	10	1.812	2.764
11	2.201	3.106	11	1.796	2.718
12	2.179	3.055	12	1.782	2.681
13	2.160	3.012	13	1.771	2.650
14	2.145	2.977	14	1.761	2.624
15	2.131	2.947	15	1.753	2.602
16	2.120	2.921	16	1.746	2.583
17	2.110	2.898	17	1.740	2.567
18	2.101	2.878	18	1.734	2.552
19	2.093	2.861	19	1.729	2.539
20	2.086	2.845	20	1.725	2.528
21	2.080	2.831	21	1.721	2.518
22	2.074	2.819	22	1.717	2.508
23	2.069	2.807	23	1.714	2.500
24	2.064	2.797	24	1.711	2.492
25	2.060	2.787	25	1.708	2.485
26	2.056	2.779	26	1.706	2.479
27	2.052	2.771	27	1.703	2.473
28	2.048	2.763	28	1.701	2.467
29	2.045	2.756	29	1.699	2.462
30	2.042	2.750	30	1.697	2.457
40	2.021	2.704	40	1.684	2.423
60	2.000	2.660	60	1.671	2.390
120	1.980	2.617	120	1.658	2.358
∞	1.960	2.576	∞	1.645	2.326

TABLE D.2   Critical Values of *F*

Critical values for α = .05 are in **dark numbers.**
Critical values for α = .01 are in light numbers.

Degrees of freedom within groups (degrees of freedom in denominator of F ratio)	α	\multicolumn{10}{c}{Degrees of freedom between groups (degrees of freedom in numerator of F ratio)}
		1	2	3	4	5	6	7	8	9	10
1	.05	**161**	**200**	**216**	**225**	**230**	**234**	**237**	**239**	**241**	**242**
	.01	4,052	4,999	5,403	5,625	5,764	5,859	5,928	5,981	6,022	6,056
2	.05	**18.51**	**19.00**	**19.16**	**19.25**	**19.30**	**19.33**	**19.36**	**19.37**	**19.38**	**19.39**
	.01	98.49	99.00	99.17	99.25	99.30	99.33	99.34	99.36	99.38	99.40
3	.05	**10.13**	**9.55**	**9.28**	**9.12**	**9.01**	**8.94**	**8.88**	**8.84**	**8.81**	**8.78**
	.01	34.12	30.82	29.46	28.71	28.24	27.91	27.67	27.49	27.34	27.23
4	.05	**7.71**	**6.94**	**6.59**	**6.39**	**6.26**	**6.16**	**6.09**	**6.04**	**6.00**	**5.96**
	.01	21.20	18.00	16.69	15.98	15.52	15.21	14.98	14.80	14.66	14.54
5	.05	**6.61**	**5.79**	**5.41**	**5.19**	**5.05**	**4.95**	**4.88**	**4.82**	**4.78**	**4.74**
	.01	16.26	13.27	12.06	11.39	10.97	10.67	10.45	10.27	10.15	10.05
6	.05	**5.99**	**5.14**	**4.76**	**4.53**	**4.39**	**4.28**	**4.21**	**4.15**	**4.10**	**4.06**
	.01	13.74	10.92	9.78	9.15	8.75	8.47	8.26	8.10	7.98	7.87
7	.05	**5.59**	**4.47**	**4.35**	**4.12**	**3.97**	**3.87**	**3.79**	**3.73**	**3.68**	**3.63**
	.01	12.25	9.55	8.45	7.85	7.46	7.19	7.00	6.84	6.71	6.62
8	.05	**5.32**	**4.46**	**4.07**	**3.84**	**3.69**	**3.58**	**3.50**	**3.44**	**3.39**	**3.34**
	.01	11.26	8.65	7.59	7.01	6.63	6.37	6.19	6.03	5.91	5.82
9	.05	**5.12**	**4.26**	**3.86**	**3.63**	**3.48**	**3.37**	**3.29**	**3.23**	**3.18**	**3.13**
	.01	10.56	8.02	6.99	6.42	6.06	5.80	5.62	5.47	5.35	5.26
10	.05	**4.96**	**4.10**	**3.71**	**3.48**	**3.33**	**3.22**	**3.14**	**3.07**	**3.02**	**2.97**
	.01	10.04	7.56	6.55	5.99	5.64	5.39	5.21	5.06	4.95	4.85
11	.05	**4.84**	**3.98**	**3.59**	**3.36**	**3.20**	**3.09**	**3.01**	**2.95**	**2.90**	**2.86**
	.01	9.65	7.20	6.22	5.67	5.32	5.07	4.88	4.74	4.63	4.54
12	.05	**4.75**	**3.88**	**3.49**	**3.26**	**3.11**	**3.00**	**2.92**	**2.85**	**2.80**	**2.76**
	.01	9.33	6.93	5.95	5.41	5.06	4.82	4.65	4.50	4.39	4.30
13	.05	**4.67**	**3.80**	**3.41**	**3.18**	**3.02**	**2.92**	**2.84**	**2.77**	**2.72**	**2.67**
	.01	9.07	6.70	5.74	5.20	4.86	4.62	4.44	4.30	4.19	4.10
14	.05	**4.60**	**3.74**	**3.34**	**3.11**	**2.96**	**2.85**	**2.77**	**2.70**	**2.65**	**2.60**
	.01	8.86	6.51	5.56	5.03	4.69	4.46	4.28	4.14	4.03	3.94
15	.05	**4.54**	**3.68**	**3.29**	**3.06**	**2.90**	**2.79**	**2.70**	**2.64**	**2.59**	**2.55**
	.01	8.68	6.36	5.42	4.89	4.56	4.32	4.14	4.00	3.89	3.80

TABLE D.2   (cont.) Critical Values of *F*

Degrees of freedom within groups (degrees of freedom in denominator of F ratio)	α	Degrees of freedom between groups (degrees of freedom in numerator of F ratio)									
		1	2	3	4	5	6	7	8	9	10
16	.05	4.49	3.63	3.24	3.01	2.85	2.74	2.66	2.59	2.54	2.49
	.01	8.53	6.23	5.29	4.77	4.44	4.20	4.03	3.89	3.78	3.69
17	.05	4.45	3.59	3.20	2.96	2.81	2.70	2.62	2.55	2.50	2.45
	.01	8.40	6.11	5.18	4.67	4.34	4.10	3.93	3.79	3.68	3.59
18	.05	4.41	3.55	3.16	2.93	2.77	2.66	2.58	2.51	2.46	2.41
	.01	8.28	6.01	5.09	4.58	4.25	4.01	3.85	3.71	3.60	3.51
19	.05	4.38	3.52	3.13	2.90	2.74	2.63	2.55	2.48	2.43	2.38
	.01	8.18	5.93	5.01	4.50	4.17	3.94	3.77	3.63	3.52	3.43
20	.05	4.35	3.49	3.10	2.87	2.71	2.60	2.52	2.45	2.40	2.35
	.01	8.10	5.85	4.94	4.43	4.10	3.87	3.71	3.56	3.45	3.37
21	.05	4.32	3.47	3.07	2.84	2.68	2.57	2.49	2.42	2.37	2.32
	.01	8.02	5.78	4.87	4.37	4.04	3.81	3.65	3.51	3.40	3.31
22	.05	4.30	3.44	3.05	2.82	2.66	2.55	2.47	2.40	2.35	2.30
	.01	7.94	5.72	4.82	4.31	3.99	3.76	3.59	3.45	3.35	3.26
23	.05	4.28	3.42	3.03	2.80	2.64	2.53	2.45	2.38	2.32	2.28
	.01	7.88	5.66	4.76	4.26	3.94	3.71	3.54	3.41	3.30	3.21
24	.05	4.26	3.40	3.01	2.78	2.62	2.51	2.43	2.36	2.30	2.26
	.01	7.82	5.61	4.72	4.22	3.90	3.67	3.50	3.36	3.25	3.17
25	.05	4.24	3.38	2.99	2.76	2.60	2.49	2.41	2.34	2.28	2.24
	.01	7.77	5.57	4.68	4.18	3.86	3.63	3.46	3.32	3.21	3.13
26	.05	4.22	3.37	2.98	2.74	2.59	2.47	2.39	2.32	2.27	2.22
	.01	7.72	5.53	4.64	4.14	3.82	3.59	3.42	3.29	3.17	3.09
27	.05	4.21	3.35	2.96	2.73	2.57	2.46	2.37	2.30	2.25	2.20
	.01	7.68	5.49	4.60	4.11	3.79	3.56	3.39	3.26	3.14	3.06
28	.05	4.20	3.34	2.95	2.71	2.56	2.44	2.36	2.29	2.24	2.19
	.01	7.64	5.45	4.57	4.07	3.76	3.53	3.36	3.23	3.11	3.03
29	.05	4.18	3.33	2.93	2.70	2.54	2.43	2.35	2.28	2.22	2.18
	.01	7.60	5.42	4.54	4.04	3.73	3.50	3.33	3.20	3.08	3.00
30	.05	4.18	3.33	2.93	2.70	2.54	2.43	2.35	2.28	2.22	2.18
	.01	7.60	5.42	4.54	4.04	3.73	3.50	3.33	3.20	3.08	3.00
31	.05	4.17	3.32	2.92	2.69	2.53	2.42	2.34	2.27	2.21	2.16
	.01	7.56	5.39	4.51	4.02	3.70	3.47	3.30	3.17	3.06	2.98

TABLE D.2 (cont.) Critical Values of *F*

Degrees of freedom within groups (degrees of freedom in denominator of F ratio)	α	Degrees of freedom between groups (degrees of freedom in numerator of F ratio)									
		1	2	3	4	5	6	7	8	9	10
32	.05	4.15	3.30	2.90	2.67	2.51	2.40	2.32	2.25	2.19	2.14
	.01	7.50	5.34	4.46	3.97	3.66	3.42	3.25	3.12	3.01	2.94
34	.05	4.13	3.28	2.88	2.65	2.49	2.38	2.30	2.23	2.17	2.12
	.01	7.44	5.29	4.42	3.93	3.61	3.38	3.21	3.08	2.97	2.89
36	.05	4.11	3.26	2.86	2.63	2.48	2.36	2.28	2.21	2.15	2.10
	.01	7.39	5.25	4.38	3.89	3.58	3.35	3.18	3.04	2.94	2.86
38	.05	4.10	3.25	2.85	2.62	2.46	2.35	2.26	2.19	2.14	2.09
	.01	7.35	5.21	4.34	3.86	3.54	3.32	3.15	3.02	2.91	2.82
40	.05	4.08	3.23	2.84	2.61	2.45	2.34	2.25	2.18	2.12	2.07
	.01	7.31	5.18	4.31	3.83	3.51	3.29	3.12	2.99	2.88	2.80
42	.05	4.07	3.22	2.83	2.59	2.44	2.32	2.24	2.17	2.11	2.06
	.01	7.27	5.15	4.29	3.80	3.49	3.26	3.10	2.96	2.86	2.77
44	.05	4.06	3.21	2.82	2.58	2.43	2.31	2.23	2.16	2.10	2.05
	.01	7.24	5.12	4.26	3.78	3.46	3.24	3.07	2.94	2.84	2.75
46	.05	4.05	3.20	2.81	2.57	2.42	2.30	2.22	2.14	2.09	2.04
	.01	7.21	5.10	4.24	3.76	3.44	3.22	3.05	2.92	2.82	2.73
48	.05	4.04	3.19	2.80	2.56	2.41	2.30	2.21	2.14	2.08	2.03
	.01	7.19	5.08	4.22	3.74	3.42	3.20	3.04	2.90	2.80	2.71
50	.05	4.03	3.18	2.79	2.56	2.40	2.29	2.20	2.13	2.07	2.02
	.01	7.17	5.06	4.20	3.72	3.41	3.18	3.02	2.88	2.78	2.70
55	.05	4.02	3.17	2.78	2.54	2.38	2.27	2.18	2.11	2.05	2.00
	.01	7.12	5.01	4.16	3.68	3.37	3.15	2.98	2.85	2.75	2.66
60	.05	4.00	3.15	2.76	2.52	2.37	2.25	2.17	2.10	2.04	1.99
	.01	7.08	4.98	4.13	3.65	3.34	3.12	2.95	2.82	2.72	2.63
65	.05	3.99	3.14	2.75	2.51	2.36	2.24	2.15	2.08	2.02	1.98
	.01	7.04	4.95	4.10	3.62	3.31	3.09	2.93	2.79	2.70	2.61
70	.05	3.98	3.13	2.74	2.50	2.35	2.23	2.14	2.07	2.01	1.97
	.01	7.01	4.92	4.08	3.60	3.29	3.07	2.91	2.77	2.67	2.59
80	.05	3.96	3.11	2.72	2.48	2.33	2.21	2.12	2.05	1.99	1.95
	.01	6.96	4.88	4.04	3.56	3.25	3.04	2.87	2.74	2.64	2.55
100	.05	3.94	3.09	2.70	2.46	2.30	2.19	2.10	2.03	1.97	1.92
	.01	6.90	4.82	3.98	3.51	3.20	2.99	2.82	2.69	2.59	2.51

TABLE D.2   (cont.) Critical Values of F

Degrees of freedom within groups (degrees of freedom in denominator of F ratio)	α	Degrees of freedom between groups (degrees of freedom in numerator of F ratio)									
		1	2	3	4	5	6	7	8	9	10
125	.05	3.92	3.07	2.68	2.44	2.29	2.17	2.08	2.01	1.95	1.90
	.01	6.84	4.78	3.94	3.47	3.17	2.95	2.79	2.65	2.56	2.47
150	.05	3.91	3.06	2.67	2.43	2.27	2.16	2.07	2.00	1.94	1.89
	.01	6.81	4.75	3.91	3.44	3.14	2.92	2.76	2.62	2.53	2.44
200	.05	3.89	3.04	2.65	2.41	2.26	2.14	2.05	1.98	1.92	1.87
	.01	6.76	4.71	3.88	3.41	3.11	2.90	2.73	2.60	2.50	2.41
400	.05	3.86	3.02	2.62	2.39	2.23	2.12	2.03	1.96	1.90	1.85
	.01	6.70	4.66	3.83	3.36	3.06	2.85	2.69	2.55	2.46	2.37
1000	.05	3.85	3.00	2.61	2.38	2.22	2.10	2.02	1.95	1.89	1.84
	.01	6.66	4.62	3.80	3.34	3.04	2.82	2.66	2.53	2.43	2.34
∞	.05	3.84	2.99	2.60	2.37	2.21	2.09	2.01	1.94	1.88	1.83
	.01	6.64	4.60	3.78	3.32	3.02	2.80	2.64	2.51	2.41	2.32

TABLE D.3 Values of the Studentized Range Statistic (q_k)

Values of q_k *for* $\alpha = .05$ *are* **dark numbers** *and for* $\alpha = .01$ *are* light numbers.

Degrees of freedom within groups (degrees of freedom in denominator of F ratio)	α	\multicolumn{9}{c}{k = number of means being compared}
		2	3	4	5	6	7	8	9	10
1	.05	18.0	27.0	32.8	37.1	40.4	43.1	45.4	47.4	49.1
	.01	90.0	135	164	186	202	216	227	237	246
2	.05	6.09	8.3	9.8	10.9	11.7	12.4	13.0	13.5	14.0
	.01	14.0	19.0	22.3	24.7	26.6	28.2	29.5	30.7	31.7
3	.05	4.50	5.91	6.82	7.50	8.04	8.48	8.85	9.18	9.46
	.01	8.26	10.6	12.2	13.3	14.2	15.0	15.6	16.2	16.7
4	.05	3.93	5.04	5.76	6.29	6.71	7.05	7.35	7.60	7.83
	.01	6.51	8.12	9.17	9.96	10.6	11.1	11.5	11.9	12.3
5	.05	3.64	4.60	5.22	5.67	6.03	6.33	6.58	6.80	6.99
	.01	5.70	6.97	7.80	8.42	8.91	9.32	9.67	9.97	10.2
6	.05	3.46	4.34	4.90	5.31	5.63	5.89	6.12	6.32	6.49
	.01	5.24	6.33	7.03	7.56	7.97	8.32	8.61	8.87	9.10
7	.05	3.34	4.16	4.69	5.06	5.36	5.61	5.82	6.00	6.16
	.01	4.95	5.92	6.54	7.01	7.37	7.68	7.94	8.17	8.37
8	.05	3.26	4.04	4.53	4.89	5.17	5.40	5.60	5.77	5.92
	.01	4.74	5.63	6.20	6.63	6.96	7.24	7.47	7.68	7.87
9	.05	3.20	3.95	4.42	4.76	5.02	5.24	5.43	5.60	5.74
	.01	4.60	5.43	5.96	6.35	6.66	6.91	7.13	7.32	7.49
10	.05	3.15	3.88	4.33	4.65	4.91	5.12	5.30	5.46	5.60
	.01	4.48	5.27	5.77	6.14	6.43	6.67	6.87	7.05	7.21
11	.05	3.11	3.82	4.26	4.57	4.82	5.03	5.20	5.35	5.49
	.01	4.39	5.14	5.62	5.97	6.25	6.48	6.67	6.84	6.99
12	.05	3.08	3.77	4.20	4.51	4.75	4.95	5.12	5.27	5.40
	.01	4.32	5.04	5.50	5.84	6.10	6.32	6.51	6.67	6.81
13	.05	3.06	3.73	4.15	4.45	4.69	4.88	5.05	5.19	5.32
	.01	4.26	4.96	5.40	5.73	5.98	6.19	6.37	6.53	6.67
14	.05	3.03	3.70	4.11	4.41	4.64	4.83	4.99	5.13	5.25
	.01	4.21	4.89	5.32	5.63	5.88	6.08	6.26	6.41	6.54
16	.05	3.00	3.65	4.05	4.33	4.56	4.74	4.90	5.03	5.15
	.01	4.13	4.78	5.19	5.49	5.72	5.92	6.08	6.22	6.35

TABLE D.3   (cont.) Values of the Studentized Range Statistic (q_k)

Values of q_k *for* $\alpha = .05$ *are* **dark numbers** *and for* $\alpha = .01$ *are* light numbers.

Degrees of freedom within groups (degrees of freedom in denominator of F ratio)	α	\multicolumn{9}{c}{k = number of means being compared}
		2	3	4	5	6	7	8	9	10
18	.05	2.97	3.61	4.00	4.28	4.49	4.67	4.82	4.96	5.07
	.01	4.07	4.70	5.09	5.38	5.60	5.79	5.94	6.08	6.20
20	.05	2.95	3.58	3.96	4.23	4.45	4.62	4.77	4.90	5.01
	.01	4.02	4.64	5.02	5.29	5.51	5.69	5.84	5.97	6.09
24	.05	2.92	3.53	3.90	4.17	4.37	4.54	4.68	4.81	4.92
	.01	3.96	4.54	4.91	5.17	5.37	5.54	5.69	5.81	5.92
30	.05	2.89	3.49	3.84	4.10	4.30	4.46	4.60	4.72	4.83
	.01	3.89	4.45	4.80	5.05	5.24	5.40	5.54	5.56	5.76
40	.05	2.86	3.44	3.79	4.04	4.23	4.39	4.52	4.63	4.74
	.01	3.82	4.37	4.70	4.93	5.11	5.27	5.39	5.50	5.60
60	.05	2.83	3.40	3.74	3.98	4.16	4.31	4.44	4.55	4.65
	.01	3.76	4.28	4.60	4.82	4.99	5.13	5.25	5.36	5.45
120	.05	2.80	3.36	3.69	3.92	4.10	4.24	4.36	4.48	4.56
	.01	3.70	4.20	4.50	4.71	4.87	5.01	5.12	5.21	5.30
∞	.05	2.77	3.31	3.63	3.86	4.03	4.17	4.29	4.39	4.47
	.01	3.64	4.12	4.40	4.60	4.76	4.88	4.99	5.08	5.16

From B. J. Winer, *Statistical Principles in Experimental Design,* McGraw-Hill, 1962; abridged from H. L. Harter, D. S. Clemm, and E. H. Guthrie, The Probability Integrals of the Range and of the Studentized Range, WADC Tech. Rep. 58–484, Vol. 2, 1959, Wright Air Development Center, Table II.2, pp. 243–281. Reproduced with permission of McGraw-Hill, Inc.

TABLE D.4   Critical Values of the Pearson Correlation Coefficient (r)

	Two-tailed test			*One-tailed test*	
	Level of significance			*Level of significance*	
df (no. of pairs − 2)	*α = .05*	*α = .01*	*df (no. of pairs − 2)*	*α = .05*	*α = .01*
1	.997	.9999	1	.988	.9995
2	.950	.990	2	.900	.980
3	.878	.959	3	.805	.934
4	.811	.917	4	.729	.882
5	.754	.874	5	.669	.833
6	.707	.834	6	.622	.789
7	.666	.798	7	.582	.750
8	.632	.765	8	.549	.716
9	.602	.735	9	.521	.685
10	.576	.708	10	.497	.658
11	.553	.684	11	.476	.634
12	.532	.661	12	.458	.612
13	.514	.641	13	.441	.592
14	.497	.623	14	.426	.574
15	.482	.606	15	.412	.558
16	.468	.590	16	.400	.542
17	.456	.575	17	.389	.528
18	.444	.561	18	.378	.516
19	.433	.549	19	.369	.503
20	.423	.537	20	.360	.492
21	.413	.526	21	.352	.482
22	.404	.515	22	.344	.472
23	.396	.505	23	.337	.462
24	.388	.496	24	.330	.453
25	.381	.487	25	.323	.445
26	.374	.479	26	.317	.437
27	.367	.471	27	.311	.430
28	.361	.463	28	.306	.423
29	.355	.456	29	.301	.416
30	.349	.449	30	.296	.409
35	.325	.418	35	.275	.381
40	.304	.393	40	.257	.358
45	.288	.372	45	.243	.338
50	.273	.354	50	.231	.322
60	.250	.325	60	.211	.295
70	.232	.302	70	.195	.274
80	.217	.283	80	.183	.256
90	.205	.267	90	.173	.242
100	.195	.254	100	.164	.230

From Table VI of R. A. Fisher and F. Yates, *Statistical for Biological, Agricultural and Medical Research*, 6th ed. London: Longman Group Ltd., 1974. Reprinted by permission of Addison Wesley Longman, Ltd.

STATISTICAL TABLES

TABLE D.5   Critical Values of the Spearman Correlation Coefficient (r_s)

Note: *To find the critical value for an N not given, find the critical values for the N above and below your N, add them together, and then divide the sum by 2.*

	Two-tailed test			One-tailed test	
	Level of significance			Level of significance	
N (no. of pairs)	$\alpha = .05$	$\alpha = .01$	N (no. of pairs)	$\alpha = .05$	$\alpha = .01$
5	1.000	—	5	.900	1.000
6	.886	1.000	6	.829	.943
7	.786	.929	7	.714	.893
8	.738	.881	8	.643	.833
9	.683	.833	9	.600	.783
10	.648	.794	10	.564	.746
12	.591	.777	12	.506	.712
14	.544	.715	14	.456	.645
16	.506	.665	16	.425	.601
18	.475	.625	18	.399	.564
20	.450	.591	20	.377	.534
22	.428	.562	22	.359	.508
24	.409	.537	24	.343	.485
26	.392	.515	26	.329	.465
28	.377	.496	28	.317	.448
30	.364	.478	30	.306	.432

Table, "Critical Values of the Spearman Correlation Coefficient, r_s." From E. G. Olds (1949), The 5 Percent Significance Levels of Sums of Squares of Rank Differences and a Correction, *Ann. Math. Statist.*, **20**, 117–118, and E. G. Olds (1938), Distribution of Sums of Squares of Rank Differences for Small Numbers of Individuals, *Ann. Math. Statist.*, **9**, 133–148. Reprinted with permission of the Institute of Mathematical Statistics.

TABLE D.6 Critical Values of Chi Square (χ^2)

df	Level of significance	
	$\alpha = .05$	$\alpha = .01$
1	3.84	6.64
2	5.99	9.21
3	7.81	11.34
4	9.49	13.28
5	11.07	15.09
6	12.59	16.81
7	14.07	18.48
8	15.51	20.09
9	16.92	21.67
10	18.31	23.21
11	19.68	24.72
12	21.03	26.22
13	22.36	27.69
14	23.68	29.14
15	25.00	30.58
16	26.30	32.00
17	27.59	33.41
18	28.87	34.80
19	30.14	36.19
20	31.41	37.47
21	32.67	38.93
22	33.92	40.29
23	35.17	41.64
24	36.42	42.98
25	37.65	44.31
26	38.88	45.64
27	40.11	46.96
28	41.34	48.28
29	42.56	49.59
30	43.77	50.89
40	55.76	63.69
50	67.50	76.15
60	79.08	88.38
70	90.53	100.42

From Table IV of R. A. Fisher and F. Yates, *Statistical Tables for Biological, Agricultural and Medical Research*, 6th ed. London: Longman Group Ltd., 1974. Reprinted by permission of Addison Wesley Longman Ltd.

STATISTICAL TABLES

TABLE D.7   Critical Values of the Mann–Whitney U

To be significant, the U must be equal to or be *less than the critical value. (Dashes in the table indicate that no decision is possible.) Critical values for α = .05 are* **dark numbers** *and for α = .01 are* light numbers.

Two-tailed test

n_2 (no. of scores in Group 2)	α	n_1 (no. of scores in Group 1)								
		1	2	3	4	5	6	7	8	9
1	.05	—	—	—	—	—	—	—	—	—
	.01	—	—	—	—	—	—	—	—	—
2	.05	—	—	—	—	—	—	—	0	0
	.01	—	—	—	—	—	—	—	—	—
3	.05	—	—	—	—	0	1	1	2	2
	.01	—	—	—	—	—	—	—	—	0
4	.05	—	—	—	0	1	2	3	4	4
	.01	—	—	—	—	—	0	0	1	1
5	.05	—	—	0	1	2	3	5	6	7
	.01	—	—	—	—	0	1	1	2	3
6	.05	—	—	1	2	3	5	6	8	10
	.01	—	—	—	0	1	2	3	4	5
7	.05	—	—	1	3	5	6	8	10	12
	.01	—	—	—	0	1	3	4	6	7
8	.05	—	0	2	4	6	8	10	13	15
	.01	—	—	—	1	2	4	6	7	9
9	.05	—	0	2	4	7	10	12	15	17
	.01	—	—	0	1	3	5	7	9	11
10	.05	—	0	3	5	8	11	14	17	20
	.01	—	—	0	2	4	6	9	11	13
11	.05	—	0	3	6	9	13	16	19	23
	.01	—	—	0	2	5	7	10	13	16
12	.05	—	1	4	7	11	14	18	22	26
	.01	—	—	1	3	6	9	12	15	18
13	.05	—	1	4	8	12	16	20	24	28
	.01	—	—	1	3	7	10	13	17	20
14	.05	—	1	5	9	13	17	22	26	31
	.01	—	—	1	4	7	11	15	18	22
15	.05	—	1	5	10	14	19	24	29	34
	.01	—	—	2	5	8	12	16	20	24
16	.05	—	1	6	11	15	21	26	31	37
	.01	—	—	2	5	9	13	18	22	27
17	.05	—	2	6	11	17	22	28	34	39
	.01	—	—	2	6	10	15	19	24	29
18	.05	—	2	7	12	18	24	30	36	42
	.01	—	—	2	6	11	16	21	26	31
19	.05	—	2	7	13	19	25	32	38	45
	.01	—	0	3	7	12	17	22	28	33
20	.05	—	2	8	13	20	27	34	41	48
	.01	—	0	3	8	13	18	24	30	36

TABLE D.7 (cont.) Critical Values of the Mann–Whitney U

Two-tailed test

				n_1 (no. of scores in Group 1)						
10	11	12	13	14	15	16	17	18	19	20
—	—	—	—	—	—	—	—	—	—	—
—	—	—	—	—	—	—	—	—	—	—
0	0	1	1	1	1	1	2	2	2	2
—	—	—	—	—	—	—	—	—	0	0
3	3	4	4	5	5	6	6	7	7	8
0	0	1	1	1	2	2	2	2	3	3
5	6	7	8	9	10	11	11	12	13	13
2	2	3	3	4	5	5	6	6	7	8
8	9	11	12	13	14	15	17	18	19	20
4	5	6	7	7	8	9	10	11	12	13
11	13	14	16	17	19	21	22	24	25	27
6	7	9	10	11	12	13	15	16	17	18
14	16	18	20	22	24	26	28	30	32	34
9	10	12	13	15	16	18	19	21	22	24
17	19	22	24	26	29	31	34	36	38	41
11	13	15	17	18	20	22	24	26	28	30
20	23	26	28	31	34	37	39	42	45	48
13	16	18	20	22	24	27	29	31	33	36
23	26	29	33	36	39	42	45	48	52	55
16	18	21	24	26	29	31	34	37	39	42
26	30	33	37	40	44	47	51	55	58	62
18	21	24	27	30	33	36	39	42	45	48
29	33	37	41	45	49	53	57	61	65	69
21	24	27	31	34	37	41	44	47	51	54
33	37	41	45	50	54	59	63	67	72	76
24	27	31	34	38	42	45	49	53	56	60
36	40	45	50	55	59	64	67	74	78	83
26	30	34	38	42	46	50	54	58	63	67
39	44	49	54	59	64	70	75	80	85	90
29	33	37	42	46	51	55	60	64	69	73
42	47	53	59	64	70	75	81	86	92	98
31	36	41	45	50	55	60	65	70	74	79
45	51	57	63	67	75	81	87	93	99	105
34	39	44	49	54	60	65	70	75	81	86
48	55	61	67	74	80	86	93	99	106	112
37	42	47	53	58	64	70	75	81	87	92
52	58	65	72	78	85	92	99	106	113	119
39	45	51	56	63	69	74	81	87	93	99
55	62	69	76	83	90	98	105	112	119	127
42	48	54	60	67	73	79	86	92	99	105

TABLE D.7   (cont.) Critical Values of the Mann–Whitney U

One-tailed test

n_2 (no. of scores in Group 2)	α	n_1 (no. of scores in Group 1)								
		1	2	3	4	5	6	7	8	9
1	.05	—	—	—	—	—	—	—	—	—
	.01	—	—	—	—	—	—	—	—	—
2	.05	—	—	—	—	0	0	0	1	1
	.01	—	—	—	—	—	—	—	—	—
3	.05	—	—	0	0	1	2	2	3	3
	.01	—	—	—	—	—	—	0	0	1
4	.05	—	—	0	1	2	3	4	5	6
	.01	—	—	—	—	0	1	1	2	3
5	.05	—	0	1	2	4	5	6	8	9
	.01	—	—	—	0	1	2	3	4	5
6	.05	—	0	2	3	5	7	8	10	12
	.01	—	—	—	1	2	3	4	6	7
7	.05	—	0	2	4	6	8	11	13	15
	.01	—	—	0	1	3	4	6	7	9
8	.05	—	1	3	5	8	10	13	15	18
	.01	—	—	0	2	4	6	7	9	11
9	.05	—	1	3	6	9	12	15	18	21
	.01	—	—	1	3	5	7	9	11	14
10	.05	—	1	4	7	11	14	17	20	24
	.01	—	—	1	3	6	8	11	13	16
11	.05	—	1	5	8	12	16	19	23	27
	.01	—	—	1	4	7	9	12	15	18
12	.05	—	2	5	9	13	17	21	26	30
	.01	—	—	2	5	8	11	14	17	21
13	.05	—	2	6	10	15	19	24	28	33
	.01	—	0	2	5	9	12	16	20	23
14	.05	—	2	7	11	16	21	26	31	36
	.01	—	0	2	6	10	13	17	22	26
15	.05	—	3	7	12	18	23	28	33	39
	.01	—	0	3	7	11	15	19	24	28
16	.05	—	3	8	14	19	25	30	36	42
	.01	—	0	3	7	12	16	21	26	31
17	.05	—	3	9	15	20	26	33	39	45
	.01	—	0	4	8	13	18	23	28	33
18	.05	—	4	9	16	22	28	35	41	48
	.01	—	0	4	9	14	19	24	30	36
19	.05	0	4	10	17	23	30	37	44	51
	.01	—	1	4	9	15	20	26	32	38
20	.05	0	4	11	18	25	32	39	47	54
	.01	—	1	5	10	16	22	28	34	40

TABLE D.7 (cont.) Critical Values of the Mann–Whitney U

One-tailed test

				n_1 (no. of scores in Group 1)						
10	11	12	13	14	15	16	17	18	19	20
—	—	—	—	—	—	—	—	—	0	0
—	—	—	—	—	—	—	—	—	—	—
1	1	2	2	2	3	3	3	4	4	4
—	—	—	0	0	0	0	0	0	1	1
4	5	5	6	7	7	8	9	9	10	11
1	1	2	2	2	3	3	4	4	4	5
7	8	9	10	11	12	14	15	16	17	18
3	4	5	5	6	7	7	8	9	9	10
11	12	13	15	16	18	19	20	22	23	25
6	7	8	9	10	11	12	13	14	15	16
14	16	17	19	21	23	25	26	28	30	32
8	9	11	12	13	15	16	18	19	20	22
17	19	21	24	26	28	30	33	35	37	39
11	12	14	16	17	19	21	23	24	26	28
20	23	26	28	31	33	36	39	41	44	47
13	15	17	20	22	24	26	28	30	32	34
24	27	30	33	36	39	42	45	48	51	54
16	18	21	23	26	28	31	33	36	38	40
27	31	34	37	41	44	48	51	55	58	62
19	22	24	27	30	33	36	38	41	44	47
31	34	38	42	46	50	54	57	61	65	69
22	25	28	31	34	37	41	44	47	50	53
34	38	42	47	51	55	60	64	68	72	77
24	28	31	35	38	42	46	49	53	56	60
37	42	47	51	56	61	65	70	75	80	84
27	31	35	39	43	47	51	55	59	63	67
41	46	51	56	61	66	71	77	82	87	92
30	34	38	43	47	51	56	60	65	69	73
44	50	55	61	66	72	77	83	88	94	100
33	37	42	47	51	56	61	66	70	75	80
48	54	60	65	71	77	83	89	95	101	107
36	41	46	51	56	61	66	71	76	82	87
51	57	64	70	77	83	89	96	102	109	115
38	44	49	55	60	66	71	77	82	88	93
55	61	68	75	82	88	95	102	109	116	123
41	47	53	59	65	70	76	82	88	94	100
58	65	72	80	87	94	101	109	116	123	130
44	50	56	63	69	75	82	88	94	101	107
62	69	77	84	92	100	107	115	123	130	138
47	53	60	67	73	80	87	93	100	107	114

From the *Bulletin of the Institute of Educational Research,* 1, No. 2, Indiana University, with permission of the publishers.

STATISTICAL TABLES

TABLE D.8   Critical Values of the Wilcoxon T

Two-tailed test

N	$\alpha = .05$	$\alpha = .01$	N	$\alpha = .05$	$\alpha = .01$
5	—	—	28	116	91
6	0	—	29	126	100
7	2	—	30	137	109
8	3	0	31	147	118
9	5	1	32	159	128
10	8	3	33	170	138
11	10	5	34	182	148
12	13	7	35	195	159
13	17	9	36	208	171
14	21	12	37	221	182
15	25	15	38	235	194
16	29	19	39	249	207
17	34	23	40	264	220
18	40	27	41	279	233
19	46	32	42	294	247
20	52	37	43	310	261
21	58	42	44	327	276
22	65	48	45	343	291
23	73	54	46	361	307
24	81	61	47	378	322
25	89	68	48	396	339
26	98	75	49	415	355
27	107	83	50	434	373

TABLE D.8 (cont.) Critical Values of the Wilcoxon *T*

One-tailed test

N	α = .05	α = .01	N	α = .05	α = .01
5	0	—	28	130	101
6	2	—	29	140	110
7	3	0	30	151	120
8	5	1	31	163	130
9	8	3	32	175	140
10	10	5	33	187	151
11	13	7	34	200	162
12	17	9	35	213	173
13	21	12	36	227	185
14	25	15	37	241	198
15	30	19	38	256	211
16	35	23	39	271	224
17	41	27	40	286	238
18	47	32	41	302	252
19	53	37	42	319	266
20	60	43	43	336	281
21	67	49	44	353	296
22	75	55	45	371	312
23	83	62	46	389	328
24	91	69	47	407	345
25	100	76	48	426	362
26	110	84	49	446	379
27	119	92	50	466	397

From F. Wilcoxon and R. A Wilcox, *Some Rapid Approximate Statistical Procedures.* New York: Lederle Laboratories, 1964. Reproduced with the permission of the American Cyanamid Company.

GLOSSARY

Abstract   In an APA-style research report, the brief summary of the study (up to 120 words) that immediately follows the title page

Alpha   The Greek letter α, which symbolizes the criterion for rejecting the null hypothesis

Alternate forms   Different versions of the same questionnaire

Alternative hypothesis   The statistical hypothesis describing the population parameters that the sample data represent if the predicted relationship does exist. See also *Null hypothesis*

Analysis of variance   The parametric procedure for determining whether significant differences exist in an experiment involving two or more sample means

ANOVA   See *Analysis of variance*

APA's Ethical Principles   The code of conduct adopted by the American Psychological Association in 1992 to govern the care of human and nonhuman research participants

Apparatus section   The section in an APA-style research report in which materials and apparatus used in the study are described; the section is called Apparatus if testing mainly involves equipment such as computers, recording devices, etc. See also *Materials section*

Applied research   Research conducted for the purpose of solving an existing, real-life problem

Archival research   Research for which written records constitute the source of data on one or more variables

As a function of   The way to describe a relationship in a scientific study

Automation   The practice of using electronic or mechanical devices to present stimuli and to measure and record responses

Bar graph   A graph in which a free-standing vertical bar is centered over each score on the *X* axis; used when the independent variable is a normal or ordinal variable

Barnum statements   Questions or statements that are so global and vague that everyone would agree with them or select the same response for them

Baseline   The level of performance on the dependent variable when the independent variable is not present, used as a comparison to the level of performance when the independent variable is present

Baseline design   A single-subject design in which performance when the independent variable is not present is compared to performance when the variable is present

Basic research   Research conducted simply to produce knowledge about nature

Between-subjects ANOVA   The type of ANOVA that is performed when a study involves no matching or repeated measures

Between-subjects design   An experimental design in which participants are randomly assigned to each condition or are matched across conditions

Carry-over effects   The influence that a subject's experience of a trial has on his or her performance of subsequent trials

Case study   An in-depth description of one subject, organization, or event

Causal hypothesis   A hypothesis that tentatively explains a particular influence on, or cause of, a behavior

Ceiling effects   A restriction of range problem that occurs when a task is too easy, causing most or all scores to approximate the highest possible score

GLOSSARY

493

Cell   In a multifactor ANOVA, the combination of one level of one factor with a level of the other factor(s)

Closed-ended question   In a questionnaire or interview, a question accompanied by several alternative answers from which the subject must select

Cluster sampling   A sampling technique in which certain groups are randomly selected and all individuals in each group are observed

Coefficient of determination   The proportion of variance accounted for by a relationship; computed by squaring the correlation coefficient

Cohort design   A factorial design consisting of a longitudinal study of several groups, each from a different generation

Cohort effects   A situation that occurs when age differences are confounded by differences in participant history

Collapsing across a variable   To combine scores from the different amounts or categories of that variable

Complete counterbalancing   Testing different participants with different orders so that all possible orders of conditions or trials occur in a study

Complete factorial design   A research design in which all levels of each factor are combined with all levels of the other factor(s)

Conceptual replication   The repeated test or confirmation of a hypothesis using a design different from that of the original study

Concurrent validity   The extent to which a procedure correlates with the present behavior of participants

Condition   An amount or category of the independent variable that creates the specific situation under which participants' scores on the dependent variable are measured

Confederates   People enlisted by a researcher to act as other participants or "accidental" passers-by, thus creating a social situation to which "real" participants can then respond

Confidence interval   A statistically defined range of values of the population parameter, any one of which the sample statistic is likely to represent

Confounding   A situation that occurs when an extraneous variable systematically changes along with the variable we hypothesize is a causal variable

Confounding variable   See *Confounding*

Construct validity   The extent to which a measurement reflects the hypothetical construct of interest

Content analysis   A scoring procedure for open-ended questions in which the researcher counts specific words or themes in a response

Content validity   The extent to which a measurement reflects the variable or behavior of interest

Contingency coefficient   The statistic that describes the strength of the relationship in a two-way chi square when there are more than two categories for either variable; symbolized as C

Control   The elimination of unintended, extraneous factors that might influence the behavior being studied

Control group   Participants who are measured on the dependent variable but receive zero amount of the independent variable, thus providing a baseline for determining the effect of the treatment on the experimental group

Convenience sampling   A sampling technique in which the researcher studies participants who are conveniently available

Convergent validity   The extent to which scores from one procedure are positively correlated with scores obtained from another procedure that is already accepted as valid

Converging operations   Two or more procedures that together eliminate rival hypotheses and bolster conclusions about a particular behavior

Correlation coefficient   See *Pearson correlation coefficient; Point-biserial correlation coefficient; Spearman correlation coefficient*

Correlational design   A research design which measures participants' scores on two or more variables to determine whether the scores form the predicted relationship

Counterbalancing   The process of systematically changing the order of trials for different participants in a balanced way, so as to counter the biasing influence of any one order

Criterion validity   The extent to which the scores from a procedure correlate with an observable behavior, such that the procedure is capable of distinguishing between subjects on the basis of that behavior

Cross-sectional design A quasi-experimental between-subjects design in which participants are observed at different ages or at different points in a temporal sequence

Data The scores of participants in psychological research that reflect a behavior

Debriefing The procedure by which researchers inform participants about all aspects of a study after they have participated in it, in order to remove any negative consequences of the procedure

Deception The creation of an artificial situation or a "cover story" that disguises a study

Demand characteristics Cues within the research context that guide or bias a participant's behavior

Dependent samples *t*-test The statistical procedure that is appropriate when the scores meet the requirements of a parametric test, the research design involves matched groups or repeated measures, and there are only two conditions of the independent variable

Dependent variable In an experiment, the variable that is measured under each condition of the independent variable

Descriptive hypothesis A hypothesis that tentatively describes a behavior in terms of its characteristics or the situation in which it occurs

Descriptive design See *Descriptive research*

Descriptive research The observation and description of a behavior, the situation it occurs in, or the individuals exhibiting it

Descriptive statistics Mathematical procedures for summarizing and describing the important characteristics of a sample of data

Design The specific manner in which a research study will be conducted

Determinism The idea that behavior is solely influenced by natural causes and does not depend on choice or "free will"

Diffusion of treatment A threat to internal validity that arises when participants in one condition are aware of the treatment given in other conditions

Discriminant analysis A procedure by which participants are categorized along a qualitative *Y* variable using several quantitative predictor (*X*) variables

Discriminant validity The extent to which the scores obtained from one procedure are not correlated with the scores obtained from another procedure that measures other variables or constructs

Discussion section The section in an APA-style research report in which results are interpreted and conclusions drawn

Distractor task A task designed to distract participants away from demand characteristics

Double-barreled questions Questions that have more than one component

Double-blind procedure A research procedure in which both the researcher who interacts with the participants and the participants themselves are unaware of the treatment being presented

Ecological validity The extent to which an experimental situation can be generalized to natural settings and behaviors

Effect size An indication of how dramatically an independent variable influences a dependent variable

Empirical knowledge Knowledge obtained through observation of events

Error in prediction The amount of error that occurs in predicting unknown scores

Error variance The variability in *Y* scores at each *X* score

Eta squared The proportion of variance in the dependent variable that is accounted for by changing the levels of a factor, thus describing the measurement of effect size in a sample; symbolized as η^2

Environmental variable An aspect of the environment in a study that can influence a participant's behavior

Experiment A design in which one variable is actively changed or manipulated and scores on another variable are measured to determine whether there is a relationship

Experimental group(s) Those participants who receive a nonzero amount of the independent variable (i.e., who experience the treatment) and are then measured on the dependent variable

Experimental methods The research methods used to test causal hypotheses

Experimental realism The extent to which the experimental task engages participants psychologically, such that they become less concerned with demand characteristics

Experimenter expectancies Subtle cues provided by the experimenter about the responses that participants should give in a particular condition

Ex post facto research Research conducted after a phenomenon has occurred

External validity The extent to which our results generalize to other participants and other situations

Extraneous variables Variables that may potentially influence the results of a study but are not the variables of interest (e.g., participant, researcher, environmental, or measurement variables)

Face validity The extent to which a measurement procedure appears to measure what it is intended to measure

Factor See *Independent variable*

Factor analysis A procedure in which correlations between responses to questionnaire or interview questions are used to discover common underlying factor

Factorial design See *Complete factorial design*

Falsifiable The requirement that the test of a scientific hypothesis can possibly show that the hypothesis is incorrect

Field experiment An experiment conducted in a natural setting

Field survey A procedure in which participants complete a questionnaire or interview in a natural setting

Figure caption An explanatory title provided with a figure in an APA-style research report

Figure caption page A separate page at the end of an APA-style research report that contains all captions for figures in the paper

Figures In an APA-style research report, graphs that summarize the pattern in a relationship in a visual presentation

Filter question General question asked in an interview or questionnaire that determines whether participants should answer additional, detailed questions

Floor effects A restriction of range problem that occurs when a task is too difficult, causing most or all scores to approximate the lowest possible score

Forced-choice procedure A measure in which participants must select from a limited set of choices, such as a multiple-choice test

Friedman test The one-way within-subjects ANOVA for ordinal scores, performed when there are more than two levels of one factor

Funnel question General question asked in an interview or questionnaire that leads to more specific questions

Generalize To apply the conclusions of a study to other individuals or situations

Habituation The process by which participants are familiarized with a procedure before actual data collection begins, in order to reduce reactivity

Hawthorne effect A bias in participants' behavior—usually an improvement in performance—that results from the special treatment and interest shown by a researcher

Human Subjects Review Committee A committee at colleges and research institutions charged with the responsibility of reviewing all prospective research procedures to ensure the ethical and safe treatment of participants

Hypothesis A formally stated expectation about a behavior that defines the purpose and goals of a research study

Hypothetical construct An abstract concept used in a particular theoretical manner to relate different behaviors according to their underlying features or causes

Independent samples *t*-test The statistical procedure that is appropriate when the scores meet the requirements of a parametric test, the research design involves a between-subjects design, and there are two conditions of the independent variable

Independent variable In an experiment, the variable that is systematically changed or manipulated by the researcher; also called a factor

Individual differences The characteristics that make individuals different from one another and that produce different responses to the same situation

Inferential statistics Mathematical procedures for deciding whether a sample relationship represents a relationship that actually exists in the population

Informed consent The procedure by which researchers inform participants about a laboratory experiment prior to their participation in it, out of respect for participants' rights to control what happens to them

Instructions What the researcher tells the participants at the beginning of a study. Instructions describe the sequence of events, identify the stimuli participants should attend to, and explain how participants should indicate responses

Instrumentation effects Changes in measurement procedures that occur through use of equipment over time, making the measurements less reliable

Interaction effect The influence that the combination of levels from the factors has on dependent scores

Internal validity The extent to which the observed relationship reflects the relationship between the variables in a study

Inter-rater reliability The extent to which raters agree on the scores they assign to a participant's behavior

Interrupted time-series design A quasi-experimental repeated-measures design in which observations are made at several spaced times before and after a treatment

Interval scale A measurement scale in which each score indicates an actual amount, an equal unit of measurement separates consecutive scores, zero is not a true zero value, and negative scores are possible

Intervening variable An internal participant characteristic that is influenced by the independent variable and, in turn, influences the dependent variable

Introduction The section of an APA-style research report that presents the hypothetical constructs as they are used in past research, develops the hypothesized relationship between the variables for the target population, and provides the specific predictions of the study

Kruskal–Wallis test The nonparametric version of the one-way between-subjects ANOVA for ranked scores

Lawfulness The assumption that events can be understood as a sequence of natural causes and effects

Leading questions Questions that are so loaded with social desirability or experimenter expectancies that there is one obvious response

Level Another name for a condition of the independent variable

Likert-type questions A measure in which participants rate statements, such as when using a scale of 1 to 5 where 1 indicates "strongly agree" and 5 indicates "strongly disagree"

Linear regression The procedure for predicting participants' scores on one variable based on the linear relationship with participants' scores on another variable

Linear regression equation The equation that defines the straight line summarizing a linear relationship by describing the value of Y' at each X

Linear regression line The straight line that summarizes the scatterplot of a linear relationship by, on average, passing through the center of all Y scores

Linear relationship A relationship between the X and Y scores in a set of data in which the Y scores tend to change in only one direction as the X scores increase, forming a slanted straight regression line on a scatterplot

Line graph A graph on which adjacent data points are connected with straight lines; used when the independent variable implies a continuous, ordered amount

Literal replication The precise duplication of the specific design and results of a previous study

Longitudinal design A quasi-experimental design in which a researcher repeatedly measures a group of participants in order to observe the effect of the passage of time

Main effect In a multifactor ANOVA, the influence on the dependent scores of changing the levels of one factor, ignoring all other factors in the study

Manipulation check A measurement, in addition to the dependent variable, that determines whether each condition of the independent variable had its intended effect

Mann–Whitney test   The nonparametric version of the independent samples *t*-test for ranked scores

Manuscript page header   In an APA-style research manuscript, the first two or three words of the title typed to the left of the page number on all pages

Margin of error   The confidence interval that is computed when estimating the population's responses to a field survey

Matched-groups design   A research design in which each participant in one condition is matched with a participant in every other condition along an extraneous participant variable

Materials section   The section in an APA-style research report in which materials and apparatus in the study are described; the section is called Materials if testing mainly involves stimulus objects, tests and printed material, slides, drawings, etc. See also *Apparatus section*

Mean   The average of a group of scores, interpreted as the score around which the scores in a distribution tend to be clustered

Measure of central tendency   A score that summarizes the location of a distribution on a variable by indicating where the center of the distribution tends to be located

Measurement variable   An aspect of the stimuli or the measurement procedure in a study that can influence a participant's score

Measures of variability   Numbers that summarize the extent to which the scores in a distribution differ from one another

Median   The score located at the 50th percentile

Meta-analysis   Statistical procedures for combining, testing, and describing the results from different studies

Method section   The section in an APA-style research report that describes the specifics of the design and how the data were collected; it includes the Participants, Apparatus/Materials, and Procedure subsections

Mode   The most frequently occurring score in a set of data

Model   A generalized, hypothetical description that, by analogy, explains the process underlying a set of common behaviors

Multifactor experiment   An experiment in which the researcher examines multiple independent variables and their interactions

Multiple baselines across behaviors   The practice of measuring a baseline for several behaviors from one participant and applying the treatment to each behavior at a different time

Multiple baselines across participants   The practice of measuring a baseline for several individuals on the same behavior, but introducing the treatment for each at a different time

Multiple baselines across situations   The practice of establishing a baseline for one behavior on the same participant in different situations

Multiple-baseline design   A research design in which a baseline is established for one behavior from several participants, for several behaviors from one participant, or for one behavior from one participant in several situations

Multiple correlation and regression   Statistical procedures performed when multiple predictor (X) variables are being used to predict one criterion (Y) variable

Multiple raters   The practice of having more than one rater judge each participant's behavior in a study

Multiple time-series design   A quasi-experimental repeated-measures design in which an experimental group and a nonequivalent control group are observed at several spaced times before and then after a treatment

Multiple trials   The procedure of observing each participant several times in a condition to avoid bias from one unique trial

Multivariate statistics   The inferential statistical procedures used when a study involves multiple dependent variables

Naturalistic observation   The unobtrusive observation of a wide variety of participants' behaviors in an unstructured fashion

Negative linear relationship   A linear relationship in which the Y scores tend to decrease as the X scores increase

Nominal scale   A measurement scale in which each score identifies a quality or category and does not indicate an amount

Nonequivalent control group   In a quasi-experiment, a control group whose participant characteristics and experiences are different from those of the experimental group

Nonexperimental methods See *Descriptive methods*

Nonlinear relationship A relationship between the *X* and *Y* scores in a set of data in which the *Y* scores change their direction of change as the *X* scores change

Nonparametric inferential statistics Inferential procedures employed to analyze interval or ratio scores that are not normally distributed, or to analyze nominal or ordinal scores

Nonprobability sampling Collectively, the sampling techniques in which every potential participant in the population does not have an equal likelihood of being selected for participation in a study

Nonsignificant Describes results that are considered likely to result from sampling error when the predicted relationship does not exist; it indicates failure to reject the null hypothesis

Nonsymmetrical carry-over effects The result when the carry-over effects from one order of conditions do not balance out those of another order

Normal distribution A frequency distribution for a set of data, usually represented by a bell-shaped curve that is symmetrical about the mean

Null hypothesis The statistical hypothesis describing the population parameters that the sample data represent if the predicted relationship does not exist. See also *Alternative hypothesis*

Objectivity The requirement that a researcher's personal biases, attitudes, or subjective impressions do not influence the study's observations or conclusions

Observational research Research wherein participants are observed in an unobtrusive manner

One-group pretest–posttest design A quasi-experimental pretest–posttest design for which there is no control group

One-tailed test The test used to evaluate a statistical hypothesis that predicts that scores will only increase or only decrease

One-way ANOVA The analysis of variance performed when an experiment has only one independent variable

One-way chi square The chi square procedure performed when a study examines category membership along one variable

One-way design A research design involving the manipulation of just one independent variable

Open-ended question In a questionnaire or interview, a question for which the subject determines both the alternatives to choose from and the response

Operational definition The definition of a construct or variable in terms of the operations used to measure it

Order effects The influence on a particular trial that arises from its position in a sequence of trials

Ordinal scale A measurement scale in which scores indicate rank order or a relative amount

Parametric inferential statistics Inferential procedures employed to analyze normally distributed interval or ratio scores

Parsimonious The requirement that a scientific hypothesis must be as simple as possible

Partial correlation A procedure in which the correlation between two variables is determined while keeping the influence of other variables constant

Partial counterbalancing Balancing order effects by testing different participants using only some of the possible orders

Participant observation The observation of a group in which the researcher is an active member

Participants The individuals in a sample

Participant variable The personal characteristics and experiences of participants that may influence their responses

Participants section The section in an APA-style research report that describes important characteristics of participants

Pearson correlation coefficient The correlation coefficient that describes the strength and type of a linear relationship; symbolized as *r*

Peer review The practice of having a research report manuscript reviewed by several psychologists knowledgeable about the research topic to prevent scientific fraud and to ensure quality research

Phi coefficient The statistic that describes the strength of the relationship in a two-way chi square when there are only two categories for each variable; symbolized as ϕ

Physical risk The potential for something in a study (equipment, presenting stimuli, etc.) to physically endanger participants

Pilot study A miniature version of a study used by researchers to test a procedure prior to the actual study

Placebo An inactive substance that provides the demand characteristics of a manipulation while presenting zero amount of the independent variable, thus serving as a control in an experiment

Planned comparisons In ANOVA, statistical procedures for comparing only some conditions in an experiment

Point-biserial correlation coefficient A statistic that describes the strength of the relationship between two conditions of the independent variable and an interval or ratio dependent variable; symbolized as r_{pb}.

Population The infinitely large group of all possible individuals of interest in a specific, defined situation

Positive linear relationship A linear relationship in which the Y scores tend to increase as the X scores increase

Post hoc comparisons In ANOVA, statistical procedures for comparing all possible pairs of conditions, to determine which ones differ significantly from each other

Power The probability that a statistical test will detect a true relationship and allow the rejection of a false null hypothesis

Powerful design An experimental design that is more likely to produce a clear, convincing, and strong sample relationship

Practice effects The influence on performance that arises from practicing a task

Practice trials The testing of participants as in the real study, but the data from these trials are not included when analyzing the results

Precise The requirement that a scientific hypothesis should contain terms that are clearly defined

Prediction A specific statement as to how we will see a behavior manifested in a research situation, describing the specific results that we expect will be found

Predictive validity The extent to which a procedure allows for accurate predictions about a subject's future behavior

Pretest A measure used to identify and select potential participants, prior to conducting a study

Pretest–posttest design A research design in which participants are measured before and after a treatment

Probability sampling Collectively, the sampling techniques in which every potential participant in the population has an equal likelihood of being selected for participation in a study

Procedure section The section in an APA-style research report that describes how the participants, materials, and apparatus are brought together to perform the study

Program evaluation The procedures undertaken to evaluate the goals, activities, and outcomes of social programs

Projective test A psychological test in which participants are asked to create a description or interpretation of an ambiguous stimulus, onto which they project their hidden feelings or attributes

Proportion of variance accounted for The proportion of the error in predicting scores that is eliminated when, instead of using the mean of Y, we use the relationship with the X variable to predict Y scores; the proportional improvement in predicting Y scores thus achieved

Pseudo-explanation A circular statement that explains an event simply by renaming it

Psychological Abstracts A monthly publication that describes studies recently published in psychology journals

Psychological risk The potential for something in a study (manipulation, deception, etc.) to cause participants psychological distress

Publication Manual of the American Psychological Association The definitive reference source for answering any question regarding the organization, content, and style of a research manuscript

Quasi-experiment A study in which subjects cannot be randomly assigned to any condition but, instead, are assigned to a particular condition on the basis of some inherent characteristic

Quasi-independent variable The independent variable in a quasi-experiment

Quota sampling A sampling technique in which, using convenience sampling, the sample has the same percentage of each subgroup as that found in the population

Random assignment A method of selecting a sample for an experiment such that the condition each participant experiences is determined in a random and unbiased manner

Randomization The creation of different random orders of trials or conditions under which different participants are tested

Raters People enlisted by the researcher to judge participants' behavior. Raters are usually kept blind to the hypothesis and specific conditions and are trained to use the researcher's scoring criteria

Ratio scale A measurement scale in which each score indicates an actual amount, an equal unit of measurement separates consecutive scores, zero means zero amount, and negative scores are not possible

Rational The requirement that a scientific hypothesis should logically fit what is already known about the laws of behavior

Reaction time The amount of time a participant takes to respond to a stimulus

Reactivity The bias in responses that occurs when participants know they are being observed

Reference page The final section in an APA-style research report in which complete references for all sources cited in the article are listed alphabetically

Regression toward the mean A change in extreme scores toward less extreme scores that occurs because random influences are not consistently present

Relationship A pattern in which a change in one variable is accompanied by a consistent change in the other

Reliability The extent to which a measurement is consistent, can be reproduced, and avoids error

Repeated-measures design A research design in which each participant is measured under all conditions of an independent variable

Replication The process of repeatedly conducting studies that test and confirm a hypothesis so that confidence in its truth can be developed

Representative sample A sample whose characteristics and behaviors accurately reflect those of the population from which it is drawn

Research ethics The concern for balancing a researcher's right to study a behavior with the right of participants to be protected from abuse

Research literature Research studies published in professional books and psychological journals

Researcher variables The behaviors and characteristics of the researcher that may influence a participant's response

Response scale The number and type of choices provided for each question in a questionnaire or interview

Response set A bias toward responding in a particular way because of previous responses made

Restriction of range Improper limitation of the range of scores obtained on one or both variables, leading to an underestimation of the strength of the relationship between the variables

Results section The section in an APA-style research report that describes the statistical procedures performed and statistical outcomes obtained

Reversal design A research design in which the researcher alternates between the baseline condition and the treatment condition

Review article A report that summarizes a large body of published theoretical and empirical literature dealing with a particular topic

Role playing The practice of having participants pretend they are in a particular situation and observing their behavior or having them describe how they would behave; used to reduce physical or psychological risk

Running head The abbreviated title printed at the top of each page in a published research article

GLOSSARY

Sample A relatively small subset of a population that is selected to represent or stand in for the population

Sample standard deviation The square root of the sample variance

Sample variance The average of the squared deviations of the scores around the mean

Sampling error The difference, due to random chance, between a sample statistic and the population parameter it represents

Scales of measurement Ways to measure scores in a scientific study; the scales are nominal, ordinal, interval, and ratio

Scientific fraud The practice of faking results by reporting data from a study inaccurately, publishing data when no research was conducted, or plagiarizing the work of others

Scientific method The totality of assumptions, attitudes, goals, and procedures for creating and answering questions about nature in a scientific manner

Scoring criteria The system for assigning different scores to different participant responses in a study

Selection criteria The definition of participants in terms of the characteristics required for allowing them to participate in the study

Selection test A test, such as a college entrance exam, that selects people based on scores and can predict future performance

Self-report A measure in which participants describe their feelings or thoughts

Sensitive dependent measure A precise measurement of subtle differences in behavior

Significant Describes results that are considered too unlikely to result from chance sampling error if the predicted relationship does not exist; it indicates rejection of the null hypothesis

Simple main effect The effect of one factor at one level of a second factor

Simple random sampling The selection of participants in an unbiased manner so that all members of the population have an equal chance of being selected

Single-blind procedure A research procedure in which participants are unaware of the treatment they are receiving

Single-subject design A repeated-measures experiment conducted on one participant

Small N research A single-subject design (with an N of 1) replicated on a small number of other participants

Snowball sampling A sampling technique in which the researcher contacts potential participants who have been identified by previously tested participants

Social desirability The demand characteristic that causes participants to provide what they consider to be the socially acceptable response

Social Science Citation Index A reference source that identifies a given research article by authors and date, and then lists subsequent articles that have cited it

Sorting task A measure in which participants sort stimuli into different groups

Spearman correlation coefficient The correlation coefficient that describes the linear relationship between pairs of ranked scores; symbolized as r_s

Split-half reliability The consistency with which participants' scores on some trials match their scores on other trials

Squared correlation coefficient The proportion of total variance in Y scores that is systematically associated with changing X scores

Standard deviation See *Sample standard deviation*

Standard error of the estimate A standard deviation indicating the amount that the actual Y scores in a sample differ from, or are spread out around, their corresponding Y' scores; symbolized as $S_{Y'}$

State characteristic A temporary, changeable attribute that is influenced by situational factors

Stratified random sampling A sampling technique involving the identification of important subgroups in the population, followed by the proportionate random selection of participants from each subgroup

Strength of the relationship The extent to which one value of Y within a relationship is consistently associated with one and only one value of X; also called the degree of association

Strong manipulation Manipulation of the independent variable in such a way that participants' behavior is greatly differentiated, thus producing large differences in dependent scores between the conditions

Structured interview   An interview in which participants are asked a specific set of predetermined questions in a controlled manner

Subject history   The bias that arises due to participants' experiences that influence repeated measures

Subject maturation   The bias that arises due to the changes that occur as an individual grows older and more mature that influence repeated measures

Subject mortality   The loss of participants because their participation dies out before the study is completed

Subject sophistication   The bias in our results that arises when participants are knowledgeable about research, such that their responses are not generalizable to the population

Subjects   See *Participants*

Systematic   The idea that research observations are obtained in a methodical, step-by-step fashion

Systematic naturalistic observation   The unobtrusive observation of a particular behavior or situation in a structured fashion

Systematic random sampling   A sampling technique in which every nth subject is selected from a list of the members of the population

Systematic variable   is a variable that changes consistently

Systematic variance   The differences in Y scores that occur with, or are associated with, changes in the X variable

Table   A display of results in an APA-style research report that lists precise numerical values of means, percentages, etc.

Temporal validity   The extent to which our experimental results can be generalized to other time frames

Testable   The requirement that it must be possible to devise a test of a scientific hypothesis

Test–retest reliability   The consistency with which participants obtain the same overall score when tested at different times

Theory   A logically organized set of proposals that defines, explains, organizes, and interrelates our knowledge about many behaviors

Three-way design   A research design involving the manipulation of three independent variables

Three-way interaction effect   The interaction of three factors such that the two-way interaction between two factors changes as the levels of the third factor change

Time-series design   A quasi-experimental repeated-measures design in which participants' behavior is sampled before and after the occurrence of an event

Title   The name given to a research article; no more than 12 words that clearly communicate the variables and relationships being studied

Trait characteristic   An attribute that is stable over time and not easily influenced by situational factors

Treatment   Another name for a condition of an independent variable

True experiment   A study in which the researcher actively changes or manipulates a variable that participants are exposed to by the researcher

True independent variable   An independent variable in which participants can be randomly assigned to conditions

Two-sample t-test   See *Dependent samples t-test; Independent samples t-test*

Two-tailed test   The test used to evaluate a statistical hypothesis that predicts a relationship, but not whether scores will increase or decrease

Two-way between-subjects ANOVA   The parametric analysis performed when there is no matching or repeated measures of participants in a two-factor design

Two-way between-subjects design   A research design in which a different group of participants is tested under each condition of two independent variables

Two-way chi square   The chi square procedure performed in testing whether, in the population, frequency of category membership on one variable is independent of frequency of category membership on the other variable

Two-way design   A research design involving the manipulation of two independent variables

Two-way interaction effect   The interaction of two factors such that the relationship between one factor and the dependent scores is different for and depends on each level of the other factor

Two-way mixed design   A research design involving one within-subjects factor and one between-subjects factor

Two-way within-subjects ANOVA   The analysis performed when matched groups or the same repeatedly measured participants are tested in all conditions of two independent variables

Type I error   A statistical decision-making error in which the null hypothesis is rejected even though it is true

Type II error   A statistical decision-making error in which the null hypothesis is retained even though it is false

Type of relationship   The form of the pattern between the X scores and the Y scores in a set of data, determined by the overall direction in which the Y scores change as the X scores change

Unconfounded comparisons   Comparisons of cell means that differ along only one factor

Univariate statistics   Statistics that involve one dependent variable

Unobtrusive measures   Procedures by which participants' behavior is measured without their being aware that measurements are being made

Unstructured interview   An interview in which the questions are not rigidly predetermined, thus allowing for substantial discussion and interaction between participant and interviewer

Unsystematic variable   is one that changes with no consistent pattern

Validity   The extent to which a procedure measures what it is intended to measure

Variability   Showing inconsistency in scores within a condition

Variable   Any measurable aspect of a behavior or influence on behavior that may change

Variance   See *Sample variance; Error variance; Systematic variance*

Volunteer bias   The bias that arises from the fact that a given sample contains only those participants who are willing to participate in the study

Wilcoxon test   The nonparametric version of the dependent samples *t*-test for ranked scores

Within-subjects ANOVA   The ANOVA performed when all factors involve matching or repeated measures

Within-subjects design   An experimental design in which the same participants are repeatedly measured in all conditions of the factors

Yes–no task   The simplest forced-choice procedure, in which participants are asked questions with "yes" or "no" answers

Y prime   The value of Y that falls on the regression line above any X; symbolized as Y'

REFERENCES

Allen, J. B., Kendrick, D. T., Linder, D. E., & McCall, M. A. (1989). Arousal and attraction: A response-facilitation alternative to misattribution and negative-reinforcement models. *Journal of Personality and Social Psychology, 57,* 261–270.

American Psychological Association. (1992). Ethical principles of psychologists and code of conduct. *American Psychologist, 47,* 1597–1611.

American Psychological Association. (2001). *Publication manual of the American Psychological Association* (5th ed.). Washington, DC: Author.

Anderson, P. (1983). Decision making by objection and the Cuban missile crisis. *Administrative Science Quarterly, 28,* 201–222.

Baumeister, R. F. (1984). Choking under pressure: Self-consciousness and paradoxical effects of incentives on skillful performance. *Journal of Personality and Social Psychology, 46,* 610–620.

Bell, P. A. (1980). Effects of heat, noise, and provocation on retaliatory evaluative behavior. *Journal of Social Psychology, 110,* 97–100.

Bell, P. A., & Baron, R. A. (1976). Aggression and heat: The mediating role of negative affect. *Journal of Applied Social Psychology, 6,* 18–30.

Bergin, A. (1966). Some implications of psychotherapy research for therapeutic practice. *Journal of Abnormal Psychology, 71,* 235–246.

Berkowitz, L. (1987). Mood, self-awareness, and willingness to help. *Journal of Personality and Social Psychology, 52,* 721–729.

Boesch-Acherman, H., & Boesch, C. (1993). Tool use in wild chimpanzees: New light from dark forests. *Current Directions in Psychological Science, 2,* 18–21.

Bower, G. H., Karlin, M. B., & Dueck, A. (1975). Comprehension and memory for pictures. *Memory and Cognition, 3*(2), 216–220.

Bramel, D., & Friend, R. (1981). Hawthorne, the myth of the docile worker, and class bias in psychology. *American Psychologist, 36,* 867–878.

Brown, S. W. (1985). Time perception and attention: The effect of prospective versus retrospective paradigms and task demands on perceived duration. *Perception and Psychophysics, 38,* 115–124.

Cahoon, D., & Edmonds, E. M. (1980). The watched pot still won't boil: Expectancy as a variable in estimating the passage of time. *Bulletin of the Psychonomic Society, 16,* 115–116.

Campbell, D. T. (1969). Reforms as experiments. *American Psychologist, 24,* 409–429.

Campbell, D. T., & Stanley, J. C. (1963). *Experimental and quasi-experimental designs for research.* Boston: Houghton Mifflin.

Carlson, M., Marcus-Newhall, A., & Miller, N. (1990). Effects of situational aggression cues: A quantitative review. *Journal of Personality and Social Psychology, 58,* 622–633.

Cherry, F., & Deaux, K. (1978). Fear of success versus fear of gender-inappropriate behavior. *Sex Roles, 4,* 97–100.

Christensen, L. (1988). Deception in psychological research: When is it justified? *Personality and Social Psychology Bulletin, 14,* 664–675.

Cicchetti, D.V. (1972). Extension of multiple range tests to interaction tables in the analysis of variance. *Psychological Bulletin, 77,* 405–408.

Cohen, B., Waugh, G., & Place, K. (1989). At the movies: An unobtrusive study of arousal-attraction. *The Journal of Social Psychology, 129,* 691–693.

Cohen, B.H. (2001). *Explaining psychological statistics* (2nd ed.). New York: John Wiley & Co.

Cohen, J. (1988). *Statistical power analysis for the behavioral sciences.* Hillsdale, NJ: Lawrence Erlbaum Associates.

Connors, J. G., & Alpher, V. S. (1989). Alcohol themes within country-western songs. *International Journal of the Addictions, 24,* 445–451.

Cook, T. D., & Campbell, D. T. (1979). *Quasi-experimentation: Design and analysis issues for field settings.* Chicago: Rand McNally.

Crowder, R. G. (1982). A common basis for auditory sensory storage in perception and immediate memory. *Perception & Psychophysics, 31,* 477–483.

Cunningham, M. R. (1989). Reactions to heterosexual opening gambits: Female selectivity and male responsiveness. *Personality and Social Psychology Bulletin, 15,* 27–41.

Desrochers, A., & Begg, I. (1987). A theoretical account of encoding and retrieval processes in the use of imagery-based mnemonic techniques: The special case of the keyword method. In M. A. McDaniel & M. Pressley (Eds.), *Imagery and related mnemonic processes: Theories, individual differences, and applications* (pp. 56–77). New York: Springer-Verlag.

Dixon, P. N., Willingham, W., Strano, D. A., & Chandler, C. K. (1989). Sense of humor as a mediator during incidental learning of humor-related material. *Psychological Reports, 64,* 851–855.

Dorfman, D. D. (1978). The Cyril Burt question: New findings. *Science, 201,* 1177–1186.

Duclos, S. E., Laird, J. D., Schneider, E., Sexter, M., Stern, L., & Van Lighten, O. (1989). Emotion-specific effects of facial expressions and postures on emotional experience. *Journal of Personality and Social Psychology, 57,* 100–108.

Dutton, D. G., & Aron, A. P. (1974). Some evidence for heightened sexual attraction under conditions of high anxiety. *Journal of Personality and Social Psychology, 30,* 510–517

Eagly, A. H., Ashmore, R. D., MaKijani, M. G., & Longo, L. C. (1991). What is beautiful is good but . . . : A meta-analytic review of research on the physical attractiveness stereotype. *Psychological Bulletin, 110,* 109–128.

Einstein, G. O., McDaniel, M. A., & Lackey, S. (1989). Bizarre imagery, interference, and distinctiveness. *Journal of Experimental Psychology: Learning, Memory, and Cognition, 15,* 137–146.

Erdley, C. A., & D'Agostino, P. R. (1988). Cognitive and affective components of automatic priming effects. *Journal of Personality and Social Psychology, 54,* 741–747.

Flowers, J. H., Warner, J. L., & Polansky, M. L. (1979). Response and encoding factors in "ignoring" irrelevant information. *Memory and Cognition, 7,* 86–94.

Forsythe, S. M. (1990). Effect of applicant's clothing on interviewer's decision to hire. *Journal of Applied Social Psychology, 20,* 1579–1595.

Frank, M. G., & Gilovich, T. (1988). The dark side of self- and social perception: Black uniforms and aggression in professional sports. *Journal of Personality and Social Psychology, 54,* 74–85.

George, J. M., Reed, T. F., Ballard, K. A., Colin, J., & Fielding, J. (1993). Contact with AIDS patients as a source of work-related distress: Effects of organizational and social support. *Academy of Management Journal, 36,* 157–171.

Gladue, B. A., & Delaney, H. J. (1990). Gender differences in perception of attractiveness of men and women in bars. *Personality and Social Psychology Bulletin, 16,* 378–391.

Glick, P., Gottesman, D., & Jolton, J. (1989). The fault is not in the stars: Susceptibility of skeptics and believers in astrology to the Barnum effect. *Personality and Social Psychology Bulletin, 15,* 572–583.

Goodall, J. (1986). *The chimpanzees of Gombe: Patterns of behavior.* Cambridge, MA: Belknap Press.

Goodall, J. (1990). *Through a window: My thirty years with the chimpanzees of Gombe.* Boston: Houghton Mifflin.

Hamid, P. N., & Newport, A. G. (1989). Effect of colour on physical strength and mood in children. *Perceptual and Motor Skills, 69,* 179–185.

Haney, C., Banks, W. C., & Zimbardo, P. G. (1973). Interpersonal dynamics in a simulated prison. *International Journal of Criminology and Penology, 1,* 69–97.

Hanssel, C. E. M. (1980). *ESP and parapsychology: A critical reevaluation.* Buffalo, NY: Prometheus Books.

Harrison, L., & Gfroerer, J. (1992). The intersection of drug use and criminal behavior: Results from the national household survey on drug abuse. *Crime and Delinquency, 38,* 422–443.

Hayduk, L. A. (1983). Personal space: Where we now stand. *Psychological Bulletin, 94,* 293–335.

Heaton, A. W., & Sigall, H. (1991). Self-consciousness, self-presentation, and performance under pressure: Who chokes and when. *Journal of Applied Social Psychology, 21,* 175–188.

Heslin, R., & Boss, D. (1980). Nonverbal intimacy in airport arrival and departure. *Personality and Social Psychology Bulletin, 6,* 248–252.

Hicks, R. E., Miller, G. W., & Kinsbourne, M. (1976). Prospective and retrospective judgments of time as a function of amount of information processed. *American Journal of Psychology, 89,* 719–730.

Hinkle, P. E., Wiersma, W., & Jurs, S. G. (1998). *Applied statistics for the behavioral sciences* (4th ed.). Boston: Houghton Mifflin.

Holmes, D.S. (1976a). Debriefing after psychological experiments I: Effectiveness of post-deception dehoaxing. *American Psychologist, 31,* 858–867.

Holmes, D.S. (1976b). Debriefing after psychological experiments II: Effectiveness of post-deception desensitizing. *American Psychologist, 31,* 868–875.

Horner, M. S. (1972). Toward an understanding of achievement-related conflicts in women. *Journal of Social Issues, 28,* 157–175.

Hunt, R. R., & Elliott, J. M. (1980). The role of nonsemantic information in memory: Orthographic distinctiveness effects on retention. *Journal of Experimental Psychology: General, 109,* 49–74.

Isen, A. M., Daubman, K. A., & Nowicki, G. P. (1987). Positive affect facilitates creative problem solving. *Journal of Personality and Social Psychology, 52,* 1122–1131.

Joynson, R. B. (1989). *The Burt Affair.* London: Routledge.

Kanuk, L., & Berenson, C. (1975). Mail surveys and response rates: A literature review. *Journal of Marketing Research, 12,* 440–453.

Kendrick, D. T., Cialdini, R., & Linder, D. (1979). Misattribution under fear-producing circumstances: Four failures to replicate. *Personality and Social Psychology Bulletin, 5,* 329–334.

Koocher, G. P. (1977). Bathroom behavior and human dignity. *Journal of Personality and Social Psychology, 35,* 120–121.

Krippendorf, K. (1980). *Content analysis: An introduction to its methodology.* Beverly Hills, CA: Sage.

Kwallek, N., Lewis, C. M., & Robbins, A. S. (1988). Effects of office interior color on workers' mood and productivity. *Perceptual and Motor Skills, 66,* 123–128.

Lavrakas, P. J. (1993). *Telephone survey methods* (2nd ed.). Thousand Oaks, CA: Sage.

Linton, M., & Gallo, P. S. (1975). *The practical statistician: Simplified handbook of statistics.* Monterey, CA: Brooks/Cole.

Lockhart, R. S., & Craik, F. I. M. (1990). Levels of processing: A retrospective commentary on the framework for memory research. *Canadian Journal of Psychology, 44,* 87–112.

Mastrofski, S., & Parks, R. B. (1990). Improving observational studies of police. *Criminology, 28,* 475–496.

Mathews, K. E., Jr., & Cannon, L. K. (1975). Environmental noise level as a determinant of helping behavior. *Journal of Personality and Social Psychology, 32,* 571–577.

May, J. L., & Hamilton, P. A. (1980). Effects of musically evoked affect on women's interpersonal attraction toward and perceptual judgments of physical attractiveness in men. *Motivation and Emotion, 4*(3), 217–228.

McAninch, C. B., Austin, J. L., & Derks, P. L. (1992). Effect of caption meaning on memory for nonsense figures. *Current Psychology: Research and Reviews, 11,* 315–323.

McCarty, D., Diamond, W., & Kaye, M. (1982). Alcohol, sexual arousal, and the transfer of excitation. *Journal of Personality and Social Psychology, 42,* 977–988.

McConnell, J. V., Cutler, R. L., & McNeil, E. B. (1958). Subliminal stimulation: An overview. *American Psychologist, 13,* 229–242.

Mednick, M. T., Mednick, S. A., & Mednick, E. V. (1964). Incubation of creative performance and specific associative priming. *Journal of Abnormal and Social Psychology, 69,* 84–88.

Middlemist, R. D., Knowles, E. S., & Matter, C. F. (1976). Personal space invasions in the lavatory: Suggestive evidence for arousal. *Journal of Personality and Social Psychology, 33,* 541–546.

Middlemist, R. D., Knowles, E. S., & Matter, C. F. (1977). What to do and what to report: A reply to Koocher. *Journal of Personality and Social Psychology, 35,* 122–124.

Milgram, S. (1963). Behavioral study of obedience. *Journal of Abnormal and Social Psychology, 67,* 371–378.

Monahan, L., Kuhn, D., & Shaver, P. (1974). Intrapsychic versus cultural explanations of the "fear of success" motive. *Journal of Personality and Social Psychology, 29,* 60–64.

Mulligan, R. M., & Schiffman, H. R. (1979). Temporal experience as a function of organization in memory. *Bulletin of the Psychonomic Society, 14,* 417–420.

Nelson, D. L., & Sutton, C. (1990). Chronic work stress and coping: A longitudinal study and suggested new directions. *Academy of Management Journal, 33,* 859–869.

Nolen-Hoeksema, S., & Morrow, J. (1991). A prospective study of depression and posttraumatic stress symptoms after a natural disaster: The 1989 Loma Prieta earthquake. *Journal of Personality and Social Psychology, 61,* 115–121.

Orne, M. T. (1962). On the social psychology of the psychological experiment: With particular reference to demand characteristics and their implications. *American Psychologist, 17,* 776–783.

Ornstein, R. E. (1969). *On the experience of time.* Baltimore: Penguin Books.

Pfungst, O. (1911). *Clever Hans (the horse of Mr. von Osten): A contribution to experimental animal and human psychology.* New York: Holt, Rinehart & Winston.

Posavac, E. J., & Carey, R. G. (1989). *Program evaluation* (3rd ed.). Englewood Cliffs, NJ: Prentice Hall.

Robinson, J. P., Shaver, P. R., & Wrightsman, L. S. (1991). *Measures of personality and social psychological attitudes* (Vol. 1). San Diego, CA: Academic Press.

Roethlisberger, F. J., & Dickson, W. J. (1939). *Management and the worker.* Cambridge, MA: Harvard University Press.

Roper Organization. (1992). *Unusual personal experiences: An analysis of the data from three national surveys.* Las Vegas, NV: Bigelow Holding.

Rosenhan, D. L. (1973). On being sane in insane places. *Science, 179,* 250–258.

Rosenthal, R., & Jacobson, L. (1966). Teachers' expectancies: Determinants of pupils' I.Q. gains. *Psychological Reports, 19,* 115–118.

Rosenthal, R., & Rosnow, R. L. (1975). *The volunteer subject.* New York: Wiley.

Schacter, S., Goldman, R., & Gordon, A. (1968). Effects of fear, food deprivation and obesity on eating. *Journal of Personality and Social Psychology, 10,* 91–97.

Schmidt, S. R. (1985). Encoding and retrieval processes in the memory for conceptually distinctive events. *Journal of Experimental Psychology: Learning, Memory, and Cognition, 11,* 565–578.

Shadish, W.R., Cook, T.D., & Campbell, D.T. (2002). *Experimental and quasi-experimental* designs for generalized causal inference. Boston: Houghton Mifflin Co.

Shah, I. (1970). *Tales of the Dervishes*. New York: Dutton.

Shepard, J. A., & Strathman, A. J. (1989). Attractiveness and height: The role of stature in dating preference, frequency of dating, and perceptions of attractiveness. *Personality and Social Psychology Bulletin, 15,* 617–627.

Sidman, M. (1960). *Tactics of scientific research.* New York: Basic Books.

Silverman, L. H., Ross, D. L., Adler, J. M., & Lustig, D. A. (1978). Simple research paradigm for demonstrating subliminal psychodynamic activation: Effects of Oedipal stimuli on dart-throwing accuracy in college males. *Journal of Abnormal Psychology, 87,* 341–357.

Silverman, L. H., & Weinberger, J. (1985). Mommy and I are one: Implications for psychotherapy. *American Psychologist, 40,* 1296–1308.

Smith, P. C., Kendall, L. M., & Hulin, C. L. (1969). *The measurement of satisfaction in work and retirement.* Chicago: Rand McNally.

Strack, F., Martin, L. L., & Stepper, S. (1988). Inhibiting and facilitating conditions of the human smile: A nonobtrusive test of the facial feedback hypothesis. *Journal of Personality and Social Psychology, 5,* 768–777.

Stroop, J. R. (1935). Studies of interference in serial verbal reactions. *Journal of Experimental Psychology, 18,* 643–662.

Turner, M. L., LaPointe, L. B., Cantor, J., Reeves, C. H., Griffeth, R. H., & Engle, R. W. (1987). Recency and suffix effects found with auditory presentation and with mouthed visual presentation: They're not the same thing. *Journal of Memory and Language, 26,* 138–164.

Wason, P. C. (1968). Reasoning about a rule. *Quarterly Journal of Experimental Psychology, 20,* 273–281.

White, G. L., & Knight, T. D. (1984). Misattribution of arousal and attraction: Effects of salience of explanations for arousal. *Journal of Experimental Social Psychology, 20,* 55–64.

NAME INDEX

SUBJECT INDEX

Questions to consider when drawing inferences from a study

Research Term	Inferences Made
▪ Reliability	Do the scores reflect error?
▪ Content Validity	Do the scores reflect the variable?
▪ Construct Validity	Do the scores reflect the hypothetical construct?
▪ Internal Validity	Does the relationship reflect the variables in the study?
▪ External Validity	Does the relationship generalize beyond the study?
▪ Ecological Validity	Do the results generalize to natural behaviors and situations?
▪ Temporal Validity	Do the results generalize to other time frames?